EUROPEAN COMMUNITY LAW OF STATE AID

EUROPEAN COMMUNITY LAW OF STATE AID

KELYN BACON
Barrister, Brick Court Chambers

OXFORD
UNIVERSITY PRESS

OXFORD
UNIVERSITY PRESS

Great Clarendon Street, Oxford OX2 6DP

Oxford University Press is a department of the University of Oxford.
It furthers the University's objective of excellence in research, scholarship,
and education by publishing worldwide in

Oxford New York

Auckland Cape Town Dar es Salaam Hong Kong Karachi
Kuala Lumpur Madrid Melbourne Mexico City Nairobi
New Delhi Shanghai Taipei Toronto

With offices in

Argentina Austria Brazil Chile Czech Republic France Greece
Guatemala Hungary Italy Japan Poland Portugal Singapore
South Korea Switzerland Thailand Turkey Ukraine Vietnam

Oxford is a registered trade mark of Oxford University Press
in the UK and in certain other countries

Published in the United States
by Oxford University Press Inc., New York

First published 2009

British Library Cataloguing in Publication Data
Data available

Library of Congress Cataloging in Publication Data
Data available

Typeset by Cepha Imaging Private Ltd, Bangalore, India
Printed by the MPG
Books Group in the UK

ISBN 978–0–19–954301–4

1 3 5 7 9 10 8 6 4 2

THE AUTHORS

Kelyn Bacon (author and general editor) is a barrister at Brick Court Chambers, where she specializes in EU and competition law. She has appeared in a number of high profile competition and State aid cases in the English and European courts, and has lectured and published widely in the fields of State aid and competition law. She is a co-author and the general editor of the State aid section in the *Law of the European Union* looseleaf encyclopaedia (OUP).

Rachel Bickler is a solicitor and managing associate at the Brussels office of Nabarro LLP. She has experience in a wide range of European law matters, including competition law, procurement, State aid, consumer and trade law. She was a contributing author of *Local Government Contracts and Procurement* (Butterworths, 2002) and *Energy Law and Regulation of the European Union* looseleaf (Sweet & Maxwell). She also sits on, and is the former chair of, the Law Society's EU Committee.

Michael Cardwell is Professor of Agricultural Law at the University of Leeds, and was previously a solicitor at Burges Salmon, Bristol. His research interests focus on the Common Agricultural Policy and agriculture in world trade, and his publications include *The European Model of Agriculture* (OUP, 2004).

Lesley Davey is a solicitor in the competition group at Reed Smith (which merged with Richards Butler LLP in 2007). She advises on all aspects of EU and UK competition law, including State aid and public procurement legislation. She is also co-editor of *A Practical Guide to National Competition Rules Across Europe* (Kluwer, 2007).

James Flynn QC is a barrister at Brick Court Chambers from where he practises principally in EU and competition law. As well as advising and appearing in leading State aid cases in the English and European courts, he has published several articles and co-edited *The Law of State Aid in the European Union* (OUP, 2004). Before returning to the Bar in 1996, he practised for several years as a solicitor at Linklaters in London and Brussels, and spent three years as a Legal Secretary at the European Court of Justice in Luxembourg.

Katherine Holmes is a solicitor in the competition group and a partner of Reed Smith, having previously been a senior in-house competition counsel. She advises clients in all areas of UK and EU competition law, including State aids, and on competition related litigation/arbitration. She is a past chairman of the Joint Working Party on Competition Law of the Bars and Law Societies of the UK.

Fred Houwen is a solicitor in the competition group at Reed Smith. He advises on all aspects of EU and UK competition and regulatory law including distribution and licensing arrangements, mergers, joint ventures, State aids, and competition-related litigation. He previously worked as a legal adviser at the Office of Fair Trading dealing with competition law enforcement, market investigations, appeals, and mergers.

Damir Kaufman is a Director at the Ministry of Finance in Zagreb, Croatia. He drafted both the first and the current State Aid Acts and Regulations in Croatia, and is a member of the State aid Committee responsible for publishing EC State aid rules in Croatian. Prior to taking up his current position he did a Masters degree at University College London, and predoctoral research in subsidies at Fordham University.

Cyrus Mehta is a partner in Nabarro LLP, where he heads the EU/competition group. He is a specialist in competition law, related areas of regulation, and public law, and also has extensive experience in acting for central government, local authorities and other public bodies in the area of competition law, State aid and procurement law. His practice includes cases before the UK and EU competition authorities as well as the English and European courts. He is a past chairman of the Law Society's European Group.

Alison Oldale is a director at LECG, an economic consulting firm. She has provided economic advice on a wide range of competition cases in the EU, including various State aid matters, and covering a wide range of industries. She has a PhD in Industrial Organization from the London School of Economics.

Henri Piffaut is a director at LECG, an economic consulting firm, and heads its Brussels office. He specializes in providing economic advice on EU competition cases and, in particular, State aid issues. Before joining LECG in 2006 he spent 12 years at DG Competition of the European Commission dealing with a wide range of cases, and previously worked in corporate finance in Paris and London.

Ilan Sherr is a solicitor and associate in Nabarro LLP in London. He is a specialist in UK and EU competition law, having advised on a range of competition enquiries and investigations, notably in the newspaper publishing, healthcare, sports broadcasting and groceries sectors, as well as competition litigation in the High Court.

Richard Waite is a solicitor in the competition group at Reed Smith. He advises on all aspects of competition and regulatory issues under both UK and EU law, including investigations into alleged anti-competitive behaviour, handling multi-jurisdictional mergers, and advising on State aids.

Noel Watson-Doig is a solicitor at the BBC specializing in EU, competition and public procurement law. He previously worked as a research fellow at the British Institute of International and Comparative Law and as a stagiaire at the Court of First Instance in Luxembourg.

Fiona Wishlade is Associate Director of the European Policies Research Centre at the University of Strathclyde in Glasgow. She has led a number of projects in the field of regional development policies and State aid control for the European Commission, the OECD, most EU15 governments and other organizations. She has also advised on State aid in many of the new Member States, and is the author of *Regional State Aid and Competition Policy* (Kluwer, 2003) as well as a number of articles and book chapters.

FOREWORD

There has never been a better time to produce a practitioner's textbook on State aid. The current global financial debacle and government rescues of threatened banking institutions, followed by recession in a good many European countries, brings the EU State aid regime into focus more than ever before. Not only do the recent banking bail-outs themselves raise State aid questions, but we are entering a period, which may be prolonged, during which the governments of Member States will be faced with many calls to extend aid to industries hit by the downturn and the credit famine.

'Cometh the hour, cometh the man'—or in this case the woman. I can think of no-one better qualified for the task of producing the definitive practitioner's handbook on this complex subject than Kelyn Bacon. Not only has she already written articles and lectured regularly on aspects of State aid, but she has also been instructed as counsel in many of the most important aid cases both in national courts and in the European Court of Justice in Luxembourg.

Until the seminal case of *R v Attorney General ex p ICI* the general perception was that the State aid regime amounted to little more than a debate between Member States and the EC Commission, with the possibility of infraction proceedings in the Court of Justice as a last resort. *ICI* demonstrated for the first time, at least in the United Kingdom, that Articles 87 and 88 of the EC Treaty have real teeth. Competitors of a company which is the recipient of aid can go to a national court to stop the grant of that aid unless and until it has been notified to, and approved by, the Commission. Any aid unlawfully paid must be repaid and if the government granting it is held to have flouted the rules, then damages may be claimed by disadvantaged businesses in accordance with the principles in Case C-48/93 *R v Secretary of State for Transport ex p Factortame Ltd.* With enhanced awareness of the significance of the 'standstill' requirement in the last sentence of Article 88(3) the number of challenges based on it mushroomed in the English courts. (See for example *R v Commrs of Customs & Excise ex p Lunn Poly*, *R v Secretary of State for Trade and Industry ex p BT3G*, *R v Commrs of Inland Revenue ex p Professional Contractors' Group* and *R (British Aggregates Association) v HM Treasury*, in most of which Kelyn Bacon appeared as counsel.) Even so, compared with the detailed treatment afforded to the other competition provisions of the EC Treaty, State aid has tended to be regarded by textbook editors and commentators as something of a Cinderella subject. So a text of this quality, written by Kelyn Bacon and other acknowledged specialists, is particularly welcome.

The book's structure and layout are designed to satisfy both the practitioner's need to find the answer to a particular question quickly and the more relaxed reader's desire for a comprehensive account of the subject. After an introductory chapter outlining the political and economic bases for the rules, the following three chapters describe in detail the concept of aid, the general principles governing the compatibility of aid with Community law, and relevant international agreements. Each of the next eleven chapters covers a specific type of aid, identifying and analysing relevant secondary legislation, Commission decisions and guidelines, and Court of Justice case-law. The last three chapters are concerned with procedures, dealing in detail with the Commission's supervisory role and with the enforcement of State aid rules at both European Court and national court levels. Each chapter is helpfully split into individually titled paragraphs, making the book both easy to find one's way around and visually attractive. Most important of all, it is written in a clear, economical and thoroughly readable style, which is a credit to the general editor and the distinguished group of co-authors assembled by her.

In short, *European Community Law of State Aid* is a thoroughly researched, well-presented, bang up-to-date and user-friendly treatise on a difficult subject. Quite simply, it contains everything one needs to know about the law and practice relating to State aid. No practitioner advising in this area and no-one else who is interested in the subject-matter can afford not to have a copy.

Sir Gerald Barling
President of the Competition Appeal Tribunal
November 2008

PREFACE

During the decade in which this book has been in contemplation, the Community law of State aid has changed beyond recognition. From being, in the early 1990s, a very under-developed subject, the last ten years have seen a surge in State aid policy-making, with the most recent legislative reform initiatives being set out in the 2005 State Aid Action Plan. This has led among other things to the adoption of the General Block Exemption Regulation this summer, consolidating a number of separate earlier block exemptions and bringing together the assessment of horizontal and regional aid, for the first time, under a single set of common provisions. Reflecting the increasing importance of State aid enforcement in the priorities of the Commission and the Member States, the European Court has had to deal with a large number of State aid cases in recent years, many of which have raised complex issues of law and policy. In addition, as in other fields of competition law, the Commission has increasingly emphasized the important role of national courts, thereby encouraging the enforcement of State aid law through private litigation as a complement to regulatory intervention.

In the wake of these far-reaching changes, the aim of this book is to provide a comprehensive description of both the jurisprudence of the European Court on State aid and the Commission's decisional practice, as well as the legislation and guidelines that have been adopted in this area. The size of this task is demonstrated by the fact that, in the course of writing this book, the number of authors has grown from two to 15. Without the considerable expertise, time and effort of my co-authors this book would not have been possible. It goes without saying that the views expressed in all of the chapters are purely personal, and should not be taken as representing the views of any organisation or institution to which the authors belong; nor should anything in this book be taken as constituting legal advice.

Several other individuals deserve particular mention. Professor Claus-Dieter Ehlermann introduced me to the subject of State aid in 1996 at the European University Institute in Florence, and encouraged me in my first academic forays into this field. Subsequently, since arriving at Brick Court, I have been fortunate to be involved in a number of domestic and European State aid cases, most often with Sir Gerald Barling who has been my colleague and friend for the last ten years. The arguments developed in those cases formed the basis of much of the structure and content of Chapter 2. Carsten Zatschler contributed substantial material to early drafts of Chapters 3 and 17, and has provided valuable insights into numerous aspects of substantive State aid law and European Court procedure; Urs Haegler assisted with the research for Chapter 1; and Luca Rubini provided many helpful comments on Chapter 4. I am also extremely grateful to my successive research assistants Thomas Karalis, Paul Stuart, Katy Everett and Rowena Moffatt, whose enthusiasm and diligence enabled this book to be completed far faster than it would otherwise have been. Finally, Luke Adams and his team at OUP have given us tremendous support through all stages of the writing and production process.

We have generally attempted to describe the law as it stood at 1 September 2008, although we have been able to take account of a number of developments since that date. In particular, we have endeavoured to incorporate in Chapter 7 the main changes in the Commission's policy on rescue and restructuring aid for (in particular) financial institutions, precipitated by the 2008 'credit crisis', as well as some of the recent cases approving aid on the new basis. Chapter 7 also refers briefly to the Commission's 'Temporary framework for State aid measures to support access to finance in the current financial and economic crisis' adopted on 17 December 2008, although this came too late for us to include any significant discussion of the Framework's contents.

In addition to these very recent developments, a large number of consultations on other State aid guidelines and policy documents are ongoing at the time of writing and are expected to conclude by the time this book is published (or shortly thereafter). As regards *substantive* policy, these include consultations on new guidelines on training aid, aid to disadvantaged and disabled workers and regional aid to large investment projects; and revised rules for State funding of public service broadcasting. In terms of *procedure*, the Commission is consulting on a new Commission notice on State aid enforcement by national courts (to replace the 1995 notice on cooperation between national courts and the Commission in the State aid field), and a 'Best Practice Code' which is intended to provide guidance on the day-to-day conduct of the Commission's State aid proceedings. These all highlight the fact that the field of State aid law is currently one of the most dynamic and fast-moving in the area of Community law, presenting a constant challenge for both practitioners and the authors of State aid textbooks.

Kelyn Bacon
December 2008

NOTE ON CITATION

This text uses the post-Amsterdam Treaty numbering of articles of the EC Treaty. As is by now conventional, when the text includes a direct quotation from a judgment that precedes the Amsterdam renumbering, the new article number is substituted, in square brackets, for the original number.

Most judgments of the European Court referred to in the text have been reported in the official European Court Reports (ECR), and for these the relevant ECR reference is given. An increasing number of judgments and orders of the European Court are not, however, reported in the ECR series; and in some cases the judgment is too recent to have been reported there. In those cases the date of the judgment is given instead of an ECR reference.

Commission decisions taken following a formal investigation procedure are published in full in the Official Journal (OJ), as are the authentic language versions of decisions to initiate the formal investigation procedure (together with a 'meaningful summary' in the language of the OJ in question). In those cases the OJ reference is given where available. If the decision has not yet been published the case number and date of the decision are given. Where the Commission closes a case following a preliminary examination of the notification or complaint, only a summary of the decision is published in the OJ, with the full text in the authentic language (now, increasingly, accompanied by an English or French translation) available on the Commission's website. In such cases the case number and date of the decision are given rather than the OJ reference.

For State aids that are covered by a block exemption and are therefore non-notifiable, no decision arises, but Member States are still required to provide summaries of the aids that have been granted. These summaries are published in the OJ as well as the Commission's website; in the few instances where the text cites such aids, the OJ reference is given.

CONTENTS—SUMMARY

CONTENTS

TABLE OF CASES AND DECISIONS

ALPHABETICAL TABLE OF EUROPEAN COURT CASES

AceaElectrabel v Commission (Case T-303/05) (pending) . . . 16.59
ADBHU (Case 240/83) [1985] ECR 531 . . . 2.60, 2.70
Administración del Estado v Juntas Generales de Guipúzcoa (Cases C-400–402/97) [2000] ECR I-1073 . . . 2.124
Administración del Estado v Xunta de Galicia (Case C-71/04) [2005] ECR I-7419 . . . 2.146
Adria-Wien Pipeline (Case C-143/99) [2001] ECR I-8365 . . . 2.02, 2.05, 2.13, 2.86, 2.111, 2.113, 2.121, 2.127, 2.129, 2.130, 5.13, 14.12, 16.02, 18.02
AEM v Autorità per l'energia elettrica e per gas (Case C-128–129/03) [2005] ECR I-2861 . . . 2.80
Agrana Zucker und Stärke v Commission (Case T-187/99) [2001] ECR II-1587 . . . 3.28, 3.31, 3.44, 3.45
Ahmed Saeed Flugreisen and Silver Line Reisebüro (Case 66/86) [1989] ECR 803 . . . 3.69, 3.84
Air Bourbon v Commission (Case T-321/04) [2005] ECR II-3469 . . . 17.51
Air France v Commission (Case T-358/94) [1996] ECR II-2109 . . . 2.02, 2.04, 2.33, 2.35, 2.98, 2.104, 2.106
Air Liquide Industries Belgium (Cases C-393/04 and C-41/05) [2006] ECR I-5293 . . . 2.80, 2.87, 2.118, 2.134, 2.143, 18.20
Air One v Commission (Case T-395/04) [2006] ECR II-1343 . . . 16.74, 16.75, 17.41, 17.42, 17.77, 17.79
AITEC v Commission (Cases T-447–449/93) [1995] ECR II-1971 . . . 2.136, 2.137, 2.144, 3.54
Albako Margarinefabrik Maria von der Linde (Case 249/85) [1987] ECR 2345 . . . 16.90
Albany (Case C-67/96) [1999] ECR I-5751 . . . 3.70, 3.84, 3.87
Alitalia v Commission ('Alitalia I') (Case T-296/97) [2000] ECR II-3871 . . . 2.33, 2.35, 2.36, 2.37, 2.39, 17.51, 17.62, 17.63, 17.72
Alitalia v Commission ('Alitalia II') (Case T-301/01) (judgment of 9 July 2008) . . . 2.39, 7.02, 7.08, 12.38, 16.68, 17.33, 17.38, 17.63, 17.72, 17.74
Almelo (Case C-393/92) [1994] ECR I-1477 . . . 3.69, 3.84, 3.86

NUMERICAL TABLE OF EUROPEAN COURT OF JUSTICE CASES

NUMERICAL TABLE OF COURT OF FIRST INSTANCE CASES

ALPHABETICAL TABLE OF COMMISSION STATE AID DECISIONS

NUMERICAL TABLE OF COMMISSION STATE AID DECISIONS

By decision number

By case number

TABLE OF NATIONAL CASES

United Kingdom

France

United States

TABLES OF TREATIES AND LEGISLATION

TABLE OF EU/EC TREATIES AND AGREEMENTS

TABLE OF EC REGULATIONS

TABLE OF EC DIRECTIVES

TABLE OF ECSCC/EC/EFTA DECISIONS

ECSC decisions

EC decisions

EFTA Surveillance Authority decisions

TABLE OF NOTICES, GUIDELINES AND OTHER INFORMAL TEXTS

EC Commission

EFTA Surveillance Authority

OECD

TABLE OF INTERNATIONAL TREATIES, CONVENTIONS AND AGREEMENTS

TABLE OF NATIONAL LEGISLATION

Croatia

Part I

GENERAL RULES

1

INTRODUCTION TO STATE AID LAW AND POLICY

A. Overview

Introduction. The purpose of this book is to set out the detailed rules for the application of the European Community State aid rules (both substantive and procedural) by the Commission, European Court and national courts. These detailed rules are addressed in Chapters 2 to 18 below. Practitioners seeking an immediate answer to a practical problem should turn to those chapters. The aim of this chapter, by contrast, is to provide an introduction to the political and economic themes that have shaped the development of State aid law and practice within the Community over the last decades. **1.01**

The Treaty provision. The basic legal framework governing State aid control is set out in Articles 87 and 88 of the EC Treaty, of which the substantive rules are contained in Article 87. That provision is split into three parts. **1.02**

(a) The first part, Article 87(1), sets out a general prohibition. It defines aid that is *prima facie* prohibited and unlawful, ie aid provided through State resources that 'distorts, or threatens to distort, competition by favouring certain undertakings or the production of certain goods'.

(b) The second part, Article 87(2), lists the type of aid deemed to be compatible with the common market: that is aids that have a social character granted to individual consumers, aids to make good the damage caused by national disasters or exceptional occurrences, and aid granted to certain areas of Germany affected by the division of that country.

(c) The third part, Article 87(3), allows the Commission to permit a number of categories of aid for which any anti-competitive effects are outweighed by other benefits.

1.03 **Comparison with other competition provisions.** The structure of Article 87(1) described above means that, like other pillars of competition policy (merger control and the control of anti-competitive business practices), State aid control instructs the Commission to prohibit activities that could harm competition unless there are sufficiently good grounds to allow these activities to go ahead. Consistent with this, the European Court has insisted on 'the broad unity of purpose between the competition provisions of the Treaty.'[1] Yet the practice of State aid control is rather different. In reality, little analysis has hitherto gone into screening out activities that have no real impact on competition when imposing the initial prohibition. The result is a largely formalistic notion of harm to competition, and consequently a prohibition that catches a wide range of measures.[2] Far more attention is paid to balancing any harm against the potential benefits of the aid, when assessing whether a State measure should benefit from a derogation from the prohibition (ie whether it is to be regarded as compatible with the common market). The range of benefits that the Commission can consider in this context is very broad, including not only improvements to economic efficiency, but also issues of equity such as social cohesion. In principle this gives the Commission a very wide discretion in deciding whether the benefits of an aid outweigh the harm to competition.

1.04 **The role of secondary legislation and soft law.** In practice the Commission has limited its discretion to approve State aid through a mixture of secondary legislation and soft law in the form of detailed guidelines. This reflects at least two factors. First, using soft law makes it easier for the Commission to resist political pressure in individual cases by committing itself to particular tests and standards. This strengthens the hand of the Commission in imposing its view of 'good' aid on Member States. Some have claimed that this gives the Commission a tool for directing the aid policies of Member States.[3] Secondly, using soft law and secondary legislation

[1] Case 6/72 *Europemballage v Commission* [1973] ECR 215.

[2] See eg the list at para 2.06 below.

[3] M Blauberger, 'From Negative to Positive Integration? European State Aid Control through Soft and Hard Law' *Max Planck Institute for the Study of Societies*, Discussion Paper 04/04 (2008).

allows the Commission to handle an increasing workload more effectively, and provides greater certainty to Member States when planning their actions.

State Aid Action Plan. In March 2000 members of the EU met at the Lisbon summit to discuss methods of encouraging growth and development in the EU. Their conclusions became known as the 'Lisbon Strategy'. The Lisbon Strategy was re-launched in 2005, with an agenda to develop growth and jobs in the Community. This sparked a period of modernization and reform across all areas of the Community, including State aids. The proposed implementation of the State aid reforms was outlined by the Commission in June 2005 in a 'State Aid Action Plan'.[4] The Commission did not propose any limitation to the current wide scope of the prohibition in Article 87(1). Instead, it proposed wide-ranging changes to the secondary legislation and guidelines governing the analysis of whether an aid falls under the derogations in Article 87(3). This package of proposed measures had the objective of achieving less and better targeted State aid, a more refined economic approach, more effective and transparent procedures and a shared responsibility between the Commission and Member States.[5] It is also noticeable that the State Aid Action Plan is very specific about the Commission's priorities when granting a derogation: it will be more likely to approve aids that promote the objectives of the Lisbon Agenda for growth and jobs. Many of the reforms proposed in the State Aid Action Plan have now been implemented, with the most significant being the adoption in 2008 of the new General Block Exemption Regulation ('GBER') covering both horizontal and regional aid. **1.05**

Implications of the reforms. The reform of State aid is likely to have at least two effects. First, since its guidelines are increasingly grounded in firmer analytical foundations, in support of a more explicit agenda, the Commission's ability to resist political pressure in individual cases may be enhanced. We can expect that notifying States will increasingly design aid to make sure that it falls within either one of the block exemptions, or failing that within the relevant guidelines. Secondly, it is clear that the new policy approach is based on wider and more rigorous economic and financial principles, and recent decisions show that Member States are supplying more economic and financial analysis to support their notifications. Nevertheless, the Commission is still hampered by weak investigative powers, and the quality of its analysis is often still well below that seen in other areas of competition policy. **1.06**

[4] State Aid Action Plan: Less and better targeted state aid: a roadmap for state aid reform 2005–2009, COM(2005) 107 final.

[5] ibid, para 18.

B. Why governments grant State aid

1. Government and markets

1.07 **Markets and economic efficiency.** Modern European economies rely heavily on markets and private undertakings to decide what goods to make and sell, what capital projects to fund, what R&D to undertake, and where all these activities should take place. There are many reasons for this, from the belief that competitive markets are an important protector of liberty,[6] to more economic concerns with efficiency. Economists are fond of quoting the first and second welfare theorems, which state that (under certain conditions) market allocations will achieve static efficiency: no one can be made better off without someone being worse off as a result.[7] But perhaps more important in supporting the view of the current Competition Commissioner, Neelie Kroes, that markets and competition are a key source of benefit for European citizens[8] is the impressive body of research and experience showing that competition between free undertakings spurs investment, productive efficiency, and innovation.[9]

1.08 **Government and markets.** Modern European economies do not, however, rely on markets and private undertakings for everything, and do not leave markets and undertakings completely free from interference and regulation. This is not surprising. Markets, after all, do not *always* deliver efficient outcomes. In any case governments often pursue goals that have nothing to do with economic efficiency, and spend large amounts on a wide variety of policies. For example:

(a) Governments are often directly involved in the provision of public services such as health services, education, social welfare, national defence, law and order and environmental protection.

---

[6] Yergin and Stanislaw note that according to the ordoliberal view competition was the best way to prevent excessive private or public concentrations of power, and was the best guarantee of political liberty, as well as providing a superior economic mechanism: see D Yergin, and J Stanislaw, *Commanding Heights: The Battle for the World Economy* (Simon and Schuster 2002), pp 16–17.

[7] HW Friederiszick, L-H Röller and V Verouden, 'European State Aid Control: An Economic Framework' in P Buccirossi (ed), *Handbook of Antitrust Economics*, (MIT Press, 2008), p 632.

[8] 'The bitter experience of history has demonstrated that engineering the creation or protection of national "champions"—yielding to the temptation for governments to "pick winners"—is not the way to succeed in the global economy': Commissioner Neelie Kroes, 'Industrial Policy and Competition Law & Policy', Speech at the Fordham University School of Law, New York, 14 September 2006, press release SPEECH/06/499.

[9] For example, empirical work on the European and US banking markets show that deregulation leads to cost efficiencies: J Gual and D Neven, 'Market Services and European Integration: issues and challenges', in *European Economy – Social Europe (Reports and Studies) No. 3* (European Commission 1993), 151–82; and J Jayaratne and P Strahan, 'Entry Restrictions, Industry Evolution, and Dynamic Efficiency: Evidence from Commercial Banking' (1993) *Journal of Law and Economics*, Vol 41(1), 239–73. Alesina et al also show that for OECD countries deregulation has tended to increase investment, especially in the utilities, transport and communications sectors: A Alesina *et al*, 'Regulation and Investment' (2005) *Journal of the European Economic Association*, Vol 3(4), 791–825.

(b) Governments also play an active role in managing important sectors of the economy, often where the sector is dominated by a former state monopoly, such as in telecoms or energy.[10]

(c) States are active in many aspects of consumer protection. In the UK for example the OFT has a mandate to conduct market studies to identify and address 'all aspects of market failure, from competition issues to consumer detriment and the effect of government regulations.'[11]

(d) Governments may also regulate markets for a variety of other reasons, such as the need to manage systemic risks in the financial sector.

State aid is thus just one of many channels through which governments have an impact on the functioning of markets and economies. It is, however (as will become apparent from the rest of this book), probably the channel that is most tightly regulated under Community law.

2. The pattern of spending on State aid

The magnitude of government spending on State aid. The value of total State aid in 2006 for the EU 25 was €66.7 billion,[12] which corresponds to an average of 0.58% of GDP for those countries. Comparing State aid to other forms of government spending confirms that, across the EU, State aid remains a minor aspect of government activity. EU-wide government spending in 2006 was €5,400 billion, implying that State aid accounted for 1.24% of total government spending. These figures, however, mask significant regional variations. Total UK State aid amounted to €4.2 billion in 2006, representing 0.22% of UK GDP or 0.6% of total UK central government spending during that period. On the other hand in Malta, which grants the highest percentage of State aid of any EU Member State, the figures for the same year were 1.77% of GDP and 4.00% of total government spending.[13] **1.09**

Horizontal versus sectoral aid. The Commission distinguishes between horizontal and sectoral State aid. Horizontal aid concerns schemes potentially benefiting all companies, regardless of their industry. Sectoral aid is targeted at specific industries or sectors (or companies within those sectors). In 1992 sectoral aid accounted for 48% of EU State aid, and by 2006 that figure had fallen to 15%.[14] This trend is in line with the clear preference on the part of the Commission for **1.10**

---

[10] Where sectoral regulation provides specific rights to some undertakings, this may be equivalent to providing funding to them.

[11] Office of Fair Trading, 'Market Studies – Guidance on the OFT Approach', November 2004.

[12] Data obtained from the Commission website; figures exclude aid to railways.

[13] Figures exclude aid for agriculture, fisheries and transport.

[14] Figures exclude aid for agriculture, fisheries and transport.

horizontal aid, which is considered to distort markets less than sectoral aid does.[15]

1.11 **The distribution of horizontal aid.** Horizontal aid tends to be focused on areas where it is believed that markets alone will not deliver outcomes that are socially or politically optimal. For example, companies may be reluctant to spend enough on basic R&D if they fear that their rivals stand to benefit from any results; SMEs may be unable to raise sufficient capital because they do not have a sufficiently long track record; and governments may wish to support depressed regions for reasons of social cohesion. In 2006, 85.2% of EU 25 State aid went to horizontal schemes, with varying aims such as the environment (31.2% of all horizontal State aid), regional aid (22.0%), R&D&I (16.4%), SMEs (12.8%), employment (7.9%), energy (2.9%), culture and heritage conservation (2.8%), training (1.7%), commerce, export and internationalisation aid (1.5%), and risk capital (0.7%). As for the UK, 89.8% of its State aid was granted for horizontal schemes, with a greater emphasis on environment and risk capital and less weight on employment.[16]

1.12 **The distribution of sectoral aid.** The reasons why some sectors benefit from sectoral aid are varied and sometimes reflect historical accident. Broadcasting benefits from sectoral aid because it is felt that access to information is a basic requirement in a functioning democracy, and there are concerns that coverage in rural areas may not be provided by unregulated markets. Shipbuilding also gets special treatment because of perceived structural features that have led to cyclical over-capacity. More historically, coal has been an important focus of Community policy since the Communities' foundation, motivated in large part by a desire that Europe be self-sufficient in energy. In 2006, sector-specific State aid accounted for 14.8% (€7.1 billion) of EU 25 State aid, and for the UK this figure is 10.2% (€315 million).[17]

---

15 In 2005, Commissioner Neelie Kroes said: 'I welcome the shift in all Member States away from supporting individual companies or particular sectors towards tackling horizontal objectives such as R&D, the environment and cohesion': press release IP/05/457. See also Friederiszick, Röller and Verouden, 'European State Aid Control: An Economic Framework' in P Buccirossi (ed), *Handbook of Antitrust Economics* (MIT Press 2008) p 652.

16 Figures exclude aid for agriculture, fisheries and transport.

17 Figures exclude aid for agriculture, fisheries and transport. Recent high-profile cases of ad hoc rescue and restructuring aid include Bankgesellschaft Berlin in Germany (Case N 49/2006 *Amendment of the BGB decision* (26 April 2006)), Alstom and Bull in France (Decision 2005/418/EC *Alstom* [2005] OJ L150/24 and Decision 2005/941/EC *Bull* [2005] OJ L342/81), British Energy in the UK (Decision 2005/407/EC *British Energy* [2005] OJ L142/26), and Alitalia in Italy (Decision 2006/176/EC *Alitalia* [2006] OJ L69/1).

C. The aims of Community State aid control

1. Role of Community oversight of State aid

Justification for State aid control. State aid has the capacity to distort competition by interfering with the level playing field on which companies compete, with the potential consequence that less efficient companies can account for a larger share of output. State aid control gives the Commission a role in preventing such distortions, unless there is a good enough reason why the aid should be granted. This point is nicely captured in a speech by Lowri Evans, where she said: **1.13**

> There are strong reasons for State aid control in the EU. State aid is a tool that can be put to good and bad uses. State aid can be abused to protect national players, keeping inefficient firms afloat, distorting competition and artificially maintaining costly, fragmented markets. But State aid can also be used positively to embrace globalization by better targeting public funds towards growth and jobs in open and competitive markets—supporting economic reform to deliver long-term competitiveness. The Commission, in that context, is a referee making sure that when State aid is given, it is overall for the benefit of the Union, because the positive side in terms of growth, jobs, social cohesion, or the environment say, outweigh the negative side in terms of distortions to competition and trade.[18]

As the following paragraphs explain, such distortions may be both intended and unintended.

Preventing intended distortions. Perhaps the most important reason for imposing Community oversight on State aid is in order to prevent countries from deliberately using State aid to benefit their own enterprises at the expense, among others, of rivals located in other Member States. Governments can favour their own enterprises in many ways, for example by subsidizing their exports, paying for their R&D, imposing import tariffs, and offering attractive terms to overseas investors. This can create benefits for the national economy. A larger share of industry profits will be earned domestically, and other sectors of the economy may also benefit by supplying inputs, sharing the benefits of a more skilled workforce, and so on. Community control of this type of government activity can help avoid two inefficiencies. **1.14**

(a) First and most important, government aid to a 'national champion' can distort the international level playing field on which companies compete, and may mean that less efficient companies end up accounting for higher levels of output.

(b) Second, Community control can limit wasteful spending on State aid by preventing a 'prisoners' dilemma'. Aid by one country could trigger retaliation

[18] Lowri Evans (currently Deputy Director-General – Operations, DG COMP), 'State Aid Reform: Where Do We Stand? Status of the State Aid Action Plan', Speech at the IBC Global Conference, Brussels, 7 November 2006.

from another. These two acts may partially cancel each other out, thus limiting their impact on market outcomes. But the two governments will be worse off because they have both spent resources to no benefit. By limiting the discretion of national governments to grant aid, Community control can help avoid this waste.[19]

1.15 **Preventing unintended distortions.** Even if a government does not intend to favour its domestic enterprises at the expense of others, State aid may still distort the level playing field as an unintended side effect of a measure whose purpose is purely domestic.[20] It is well established that State aid is an objective concept and that aid is defined in relation to its effects rather than its purpose.[21] Community oversight provides a mechanism by which these spillovers are taken into account.

1.16 **Examples.** Several recent cases involving formal investigations by the Commission illustrate the nature of Community oversight and the Commission's concerns.

- *Volkswerft Stralsund.*[22] In August 2005, Germany notified to the Commission its intention to grant regional investment aid in favour of Volkswerft Stralsund, a shipbuilding company located in Mecklenburg Vorpommern. Concerned by the fact that this regional investment aid could not only be used to increase the productivity of the firm, as assessed by Germany, but also to increase its production capacity, the Commission decided to open a formal investigation procedure. It subsequently found that the aid was not aimed at helping this firm to increase its production capacity and that, according to the competitors, it would not distort competition in the EU. The Commission accordingly approved the aid.
- *French R&D aid to Peugeot-Citroën for hybrid diesel car.*[23] In November 2007 the Commission decided to open a formal investigation into a proposed €96 million State aid for Peugeot-Citroen and its partners, to support the development of a hybrid diesel car. Whilst the aid appeared to meet two horizontal objectives covered by Community guidelines (environment and R&D), the Commission questioned whether the aid really addressed a market failure, as Peugeot-Citroen's competitors had also started to develop such a car without similar

---

[19] See eg Friederiszick, Röller and Verouden, 'European State Aid Control: An Economic Framework' in P Buccirossi (ed), *Handbook of Antitrust Economics* (MIT Press 2008), pp 638–9. However, some authors have noted that under certain circumstances competition between countries can enhance overall efficiency; see eg T Besley and P Seabright, 'The Effects and Policy Implications of State Aids to Industry: An Economic Analysis' (2001) *Economic Policy*, Vol 14(28) 13–53.

[20] Friederiszick, Röller and Verouden, 'European State Aid Control: An Economic Framework' in P Buccirossi (ed), *Handbook of Antitrust Economics* (MIT Press 2008), pp 638–9.

[21] See para 2.03 below.

[22] Decision 2007/402/EC *Volkswerft Stralsund* [2006] OJ L151/33.

[23] Decision in Case C 51/2007 *VHD programme* (13 November 2007) and press release IP/07/1679.

State support. The case was closed in January 2008 after the State aid proposal was withdrawn by France.

- *Vauxhall car training.*[24] In February 2007, the UK notified to the Commission a plan to provide aid to the Vauxhall plant at Ellesmere Port, which its owner General Motors had selected to produce its new compact car. In order to be able to produce this car, training for the employees was necessary. The proposed State subsidies were targeted at this training programme. In July 2007 the Commission decided to open a formal investigation into the necessity and specificity of the proposed aid. The aid was ultimately approved on the grounds that the costs of the usual training and the training specific for the introduction of this new car was not included in the proposed aid. Instead, the aid was targeted at a training programme that would enable the employees to acquire 'skills which are transferable to other firms or industries'.
- *Pickman.*[25] The Commission decided to open a formal investigation into aid granted to the Spanish firm Pickman, which produces dishes and chinaware. Following a complaint by a competitor, the Commission found that Pickman had received support from the regional and national authorities in Spain in the form of loans and debt rearrangements. The Commission has raised concerns that this support is firm-specific and aimed at artificially keeping an inefficient firm in business,[26] resulting in a distortion of competition. This investigation is ongoing at the time of writing.
- *French State guarantee for Finnish nuclear power plant operator TVO.*[27] In September 2007, the Commission closed its formal investigation into a guarantee by the French government covering a loan granted to the Finnish electricity producer TVO. With this loan, TVO purchased part of a nuclear plant from the French company Areva. The investigation showed that TVO would have had sufficient access to the financial markets to finance the project without the French Government's action, and that the guarantee premium paid by TVO to the French Government was not below the market price. The guarantee did not therefore confer an advantage on TVO, and hence did not constitute State aid.
- *Sicilian regional aid scheme.*[28] In 2005, Italy notified to the Commission a proposed regional aid scheme 'designed to promote the setting up of new companies and to narrow the gap between companies in Sicily and companies located

[24] Decision in Case C 23/2007 *Vauxhall Motors* (16 April 2008).

[25] Decision in Case C 20/2007 *Pickman* [2007] OJ C239/12.

[26] According to Commissioner Neelie Kroes, 'We must ensure that companies in difficulties do not benefit from illegal and repeated public support without undergoing the necessary restructuring to return to viability': press release IP/07/897; and see further generally Chapter 7 below.

[27] Decision 2008/281/EC *TVO guarantee* [2008] OJ L89/15.

[28] Decision 2007/493/EC *Sicilian regional aid scheme* [2007] OJ L183/41.

in other regions of Italy.'[29] The scheme provided for a reduction in the rate of the Italian regional tax on productive activity, for cooperatives and private security firms. The Commission considered that the aid would distort competition without promoting growth, with no demonstrated link between the design of the aid and the objectives that it purported to serve. The aid was therefore prohibited.[30]

2. The Article 87(1) prohibition

1.17 **The goal of preventing distortions to competition.** In the State Aid Action Plan the Commission sets out its current view about the role of State aid control. It starts by insisting on the importance of competition as a means of promoting consumer welfare and promoting the efficient allocation of resources: '[c]ompetition is furthermore essential to enhance the competitiveness of the European economy, by creating an environment in which efficient and innovative companies are rewarded properly'.[31] The State Aid Action Plan goes on to describe the particular role of State aid control in protecting competition as being to maintain a level playing field. It sets out two reasons why this is important. First, it ensures that market forces reward the most competitive companies, to the benefit of European competitiveness. Second, it prevents companies accumulating market power, which could lead to higher prices and lower quality.[32]

1.18 **Absence of consumer welfare as a goal in approach to Article 87(1).** The statements in the State Aid Action Plan in support of a goal of consumer welfare, and expressing a concern about market power, are notable as rare references to the concepts in the practice of State aid control. Writing before the State Aid Action Plan was published, Martin and Strasse said that in practice State aid control has often placed relatively little weight on consumer welfare.[33] This is certainly true of Article 87(1), which contains no explicit or implicit requirement to show the creation of a harmful degree of market power, or harm to consumers in any other way.

1.19 **The standard of proof for showing a distortion of competition.** Not only is there no requirement to show that State aid will lead to consumer harm, but there is not even, in practice, any need for extensive analysis showing a material distortion to the level playing field in the first place. The basic test for a distortion of competition is whether the recipient of the aid was strengthened (for example

[29] ibid, para 9.

[30] ibid, paras 18–31 and 46, and press release IP/07/159.

[31] State Aid Action Plan: Less and better targeted state aid: a roadmap for State aid reform 2005–2009, COM(2005) 107 final, paras 5 and 6.

[32] ibid, para 7.

[33] See eg S Martin and C Strasse, 'La Politique Communautaire des Aides d'État Est-elle une Politique de Concurrence?' *Concurrences*, 2005 Vol 3: 52–9.

because its costs were reduced) compared to others competing in intra-Community trade. However it is not necessary to define the relevant market, or confirm that there are competitors at all (a measure benefiting a whole sector can be aid); there is no need to show that the impact is substantial; and indeed the goods and services for which competition is distorted need not be the ones affected by the aid.[34]

Selectivity and distortion of competition. On its face, there is another element of the definition of an aid in Article 87(1) that could screen out measures that are unlikely to have a material effect on competition. This is the criterion that an aid must 'favour certain undertakings or the production of certain goods', or in other words, an aid must be selective.[35] In practice, however, the selectivity test plays a limited role in screening out measures from further scrutiny. In one sense the test is rather strict: the fact that a measure benefits undertakings in just one Member State is irrelevant to an assessment of whether it is selective. What matters is a comparison between the undertakings affected by the measure and others *in the same Member State*. This can mean there is no causal link between the selective nature of an aid and any distortion of competition.[36] On the other hand the comparison between the affected undertaking and others in the same Member State brings a wide range of potential measures within the ambit of the prohibition. Almost all State measures affect different undertakings and sectors to different degrees, so that almost all measures are potentially caught by this condition. While there are some limits to the concept of selectivity, the principles underlying these are often ambiguous and hard to apply. **1.20**

The problem of 'over-inclusiveness'. All of this has led some commentators to refer to a problem of 'vast over-inclusion'[37] and to call for reforms that would require a more robust analysis of the potential for a State measure to distort competition in order to limit the scope of the prohibition.[38] **1.21**

Commission's approach. The Commission's package of State aid reforms ignores the calls to limit the application of Article 87(1) by strengthening the analysis of **1.22**

[34] See generally paras 2.134–2.140 below.

[35] See para 2.02 below and discussion of selectivity criterion at paras 2.109–2.132.

[36] C Ahlborn and C Berg, 'Can State Aid Learn from Antitrust? The Need for a Greater Role for Competition Analysis under the State Aid Rules' in Biondi, Eeckhout and Flynn (eds), *The Law of State Aid in the European Union* (OUP 2004) p 54, noting that in Case 203/82 *Commission v Italy* [1983] ECR 2525 the discrimination was between sectors in Italy employing many women, and others in Italy employing fewer. However the impact on competition occurred between the favoured Italian companies and their foreign counterparts.

[37] Ahlborn and Berg, ibid, p 51.

[38] Ahlborn and Berg, ibid, p 54; Papandropoulus et al, 'Selectivity, Economic Advantage, Distorition of Competition and Effect on Trade' in J Derenne and M Merola, *Economic Analysis of State Aid Rules-Contributions and Limits* (Berlin 2006), p 123; and Friederiszick, Röller and Verouden 'European State Aid Control: An Economic Framework' in P Buccirossi (ed), *Handbook of Antitrust Economics* (MIT Press 2008) pp 656–60.

distortion of competition, or through any other means. Instead, as noted at para 1.05 above, the Commission has concentrated on reforms to the assessment of compatibility under Article 87(3). There are a number of possible reasons why the Commission has not sought to limit the scope of Article 87(1).

(a) The Commission bears the burden of proof for showing that a measure is aid, but lacks strong investigative powers. A high standard of proof of, for example, a distortion of competition might make it impossible for the Commission to sustain a prohibition decision in some cases.

(b) The low threshold for a distortion of competition may reflect the fact that there is no need to show that an aid has had actual effects; it is enough to show that it is liable to distort competition. But this is not a very satisfactory explanation. Merger control also involves an ex ante analysis of the potential, rather than actual, effects of a change to the market. Yet the Commission must provide extensive factual analysis in order to support a finding that a proposed transaction would harm competition.[39]

(c) Some commentators point to the role of history and politics. On that view, the wide scope of the prohibition has arisen as the European Court has sought to empower the Commission against the resistance of Member States.[40] The Commission is now reluctant to limit the application of Article 87(1) because the status quo, combined with the discretion the Commission enjoys in applying the derogation in Article 87(3), gives it a unique role in harmonizing the goals that Member States pursue in their aid policies. It is suggested that the Commission is anxious to extend, rather than limit, this role.[41]

Whatever the Commission's reasoning, the result is a wide prohibition of aid, which has only been limited by the Court on a fairly piecemeal basis,[42] without any coherent economic rationale.

3. The derogations in Article 87(2) and (3)

1.23 **Distinction between Article 87(2) and (3).** If a government measure is found to be a State aid under Article 87(1), it can still be approved if it satisfies the conditions

[39] See eg Guidelines on the assessment of horizontal mergers under the Council Regulation on the control of concentrations between undertakings [2004] OJ C31/5.

[40] M Blauberger, 'From Negative to Positive Integration? European State Aid Control through Soft and Hard Law', *Max Planck Institute for the Study of Societies*, Discussion Paper 04/04 (2008), p 8 and references therein.

[41] ibid.

[42] See eg the Court's attempts to demarcate non-aid elements of public service compensation in Case C-53/00 *Ferring v ACOSS* [2001] ECR I-9067 and Case C-280/00 *Altmark* [2003] ECR I-7747, the adherence to a formal State resources criterion in Case C-379/98 *PreussenElektra* [2001] ECR I-2099, and the finding of lack of selectivity in Case C-308/00 *GIL Insurance* [2004] ECR I-4777 and Case T-233/04 *Netherlands v Commission* (judgment of 10 April 2008).

of Article 87(2) or (3). The exemptions in Article 87(2) are mandatory—if the aid falls within one of the categories specified therein, the Commission is required to approve it and has no discretion. The purpose of these exemptions is to declare lawful three specific categories of aid: social aids to individual consumers, disaster aid and aid compensating for the cold war division of Germany. The vast majority of cases, however, are assessed not under Article 87(2) but under Article 87(3), for which the Commission has a wide discretion. While Article 87(3) specifies a number of categories of aid that may be approved, covering regional, horizontal and sectoral aids, the underlying principle is that measures falling under that provision should help achieve an objective of common interest.

The objectives of common interest. The range of potential objectives of a common interest is very broad. Sometimes they aim to support consumer welfare and the efficient allocation of resources (as when they are targeted at market failures). But the State Aid Action Plan also notes that they may also promote a wider set of social and political objectives such as 'sustainable growth, competitiveness, social and regional cohesion and environmental protection'.[43] Thus one commentator has observed that 'the common interest comprises both an economic efficiency dimension (efficient functioning of markets) and an equity dimension.'[44] The Commission's role in deciding whether a State aid is justified by an objective of common interest gives the Commission a tool for what has been called 'positive integration': rather than merely preventing actions that harm competition, the discretion the Commission has in interpreting the derogation in Article 87(3) gives it the ability to influence the aid policy of Member States.[45] In the State Aid Action Plan the Commission announces its proposed intention to use this tool in order to further the goals of the re-launched Lisbon Strategy for growth and jobs. **1.24**

The Commission's priorities. The Commission is more likely to grant a derogation under Article 87(3) if it addresses a market failure, such as a suboptimal level of R&D&I, insufficient risk capital available or insufficient investment in human capital.[46] The Commission also places emphasis on the achievement of 'social and economic cohesion and sustainable development',[47] and its specific objectives in **1.25**

[43] State Aid Action Plan: Less and better targeted state aid: a roadmap for state aid reform 2005–2009, COM(2005) 107 final, para 10.

[44] L Evans, 'Delivering the State Aid Reform' (2006) *Concurrences*, Vol 4, 7–9. Note that many economists would dispute the claim that social welfare has an equity dimension.

[45] M Blauberger, 'From Negative to Positive Integration? European State Aid Control through Soft and Hard Law' *Max Planck Institute for the Study of Societies*, Discussion Paper 04/04 (2008), p 7.

[46] State Aid Action Plan: Less and better targeted state aid: a roadmap for state aid reform 2005–2009, COM(2005) 107 final, paras 24–32.

[47] ibid, p 8.

this respect include the provision of high quality services of general economic interest, the reduction of disparities between the regions of Europe, environmental protection, and greater investment in modern transport, energy and information and communication technology infrastructures.[48]

1.26 **Shaping Community State aid policy.** It is apparent from the discussion above that it is Article 87(3), rather than any other provision in the Community State aid rules, that has been used by the Commission to shape the policy and direction of State aid control within the Community. The way in which this has been achieved in practice, in particular through secondary legislation and soft law, is discussed in the next section.

D. Implementing State aid policy

1.27 **Implementing Article 87(3).** As well as the specific provisions in the Treaty, State aid control is subject to a significant body of secondary legislation and soft law comprising block exemptions and other regulations, guidelines, frameworks, communications, consultation documents and notices. Almost all relate to the practical application of Article 87(3). They embody three policy choices on the part of the Commission. First, their content encourages particular policy choices by Member States when directing their State aid spending. Secondly, the volume and detail of the soft law embodies a choice about the relative importance of rules versus discretion. Thirdly, the content of the soft law embodies choices about the extent to which exemptions will be based on effects as opposed to form. These points are discussed in turn in sections 1 to 3 below. Finally, section 4 discusses the more refined economic approach to State aid policy that has been adopted by the Commission in recent years.

1. Guiding the aid policies of Member States

1.28 **Resisting political pressure.** One function of secondary legislation and soft law is to enable the Commission to resist political pressure from Member States. Absent the various block exemptions and guidelines, the wide discretion of the Commission in applying Article 87(3), and the controversies both within and without the Commission about what constitutes 'good' aid, could leave it exposed to lobbying by particular Member States based on their specific political situations. Of course, this is still bound to occur on occasion.[49] But by limiting its discretion through the

[48] ibid, paras 33–4 and 39–47.

[49] Particularly in the highly sensitive context of rescue and restructuring aid: see Chapter 7 below.

use of legislation and soft law, the Commission has effectively limited the scope for such pressure.[50]

Guiding the aid policies of Member States. The Commission's success in using secondary legislation and soft law as a means of strengthening its position with respect to the Member States has allowed it to pursue an increasingly positive agenda for determining the aid policies of Member States. As noted above, this is sometimes referred to as 'positive integration'.[51] This has been demonstrated, most clearly, in the new approach to State aid policy set out in, and pursued since, the State Aid Action Plan. **1.29**

2. Rules versus discretion

The debate about rules versus discretion. The most striking feature of the secondary legislation and soft law surrounding the application of Article 87(3) is just how much of it there is, and how much concrete detail it provides about when the Commission is likely to grant a derogation. This volume and detail embody a clear choice on the part of the Commission to favour rules over discretion when assessing compatibility. The degree of discretion that competition agencies and courts should have when balancing pro-competitive and anti-competitive effects is the subject of a long standing debate in the context of assessing unilateral conduct.[52] But the arguments wielded on either side are relevant when assessing the proper legal framework for State aid control as well. **1.30**

In favour of discretion. On one side of the debate, there are those that consider that there is no reason why courts and competition regulators should not be 'free to ramble through the wilds of economic theory in order to administer a flexible approach'—using the language of *US v Topco*.[53] This view gives rise to the application of an unstructured rule of reason approach which involves the complex **1.31**

---

[50] M Blauberger, 'From Negative to Positive Integration? European State Aid Control through Soft and Hard Law' *Max Planck Institute for the Study of Societies*, Discussion Paper 04/04 (2008). See also N Pesaresi and M Van Hoof, 'State aid control : an introduction' in Mederer, Pesaresi and Van Hoof (eds), *EU Competition law* Vol IV, State Aid, (Claeys & Casteels 2008), para 1.34.

[51] M Blauberger,'From Negative to Positive Integration? European State Aid Control through Soft and Hard Law' *Max Planck Institute for the Study of Societies*, Discussion Paper 04/04 (2008).

[52] See eg the *Sony/BMG* saga illustrating different approaches to the question of the Commission's discretion. In 2004 the Commission approved the merger of Sony and Bertelsman Music Group (BMG): Decision 2005/188/EC *Sony/BMG* [2005] OJ L62/30. Following a complaint from a third party, Impala, the CFI remitted the decision to the Commission on the grounds that it was vitiated by manifest errors of assessment and was inadequately reasoned: Case T-464/04 *Impala v Commission* [2006] ECR II-2289. Bertelsmann and Sony then appealed that judgment to the ECJ, which found that the CFI had committed a number of errors of law in its judgment, and acknowledged the Commission's discretion when carrying out complex economic assessments. The ECJ therefore, annulled the CFI's judgment: Case C-413/06 P *Bertelsmann and Sony v Impala* (judgment of 10 July 2008).

[53] *US v Topco Associates* [1972] 405 US 596.

balancing of effects that are either beneficial or detrimental to overall welfare. The report by the Economic Advisory Group on Competition Policy for DG Competition advocated this approach in the context of Article 82 reform.[54] The obvious benefit of this approach is that it is very flexible, allows all relevant factors to be taken into account, and does not prejudge the importance of those factors in any particular case.

1.32 **In favour of rules.** On the other side of the debate, those that favour rules, or some type of structured rule of reason, over unfettered discretion[55] point to important costs associated with a rule of reason. Rules increase transparency. In the State aid context, this means that Member States are better able to predict whether or not their aid is likely to benefit from a derogation under Article 87(3). This in turn makes it easier for countries to give aid in such a way as to limit (or entirely eliminate, in cases falling within one of the block exemptions) the burden of a State aid investigation. The policy choice to limit discretion and provide extensive guidance about how the Commission will perform compatibility assessments perhaps reflects the view that the benefits to governments of speedy and certain confirmations of their own policy choices to award State aid outweigh the costs of the inevitable errors and inconsistencies.

1.33 **The extent of errors and inconsistencies.** Needless to say the extent of the costs of errors and inconsistencies itself depends on the content of the secondary legislation and soft law, and an important aspect of this is the extent to which the rules set out therein reflect an effects-based analysis of State aid.

3. Effects-based versus form-based analysis

1.34 **Form-based approach in State aid control.** The proliferation of block exemptions and guidelines has been criticized for leading to 'analysis by pigeon-holing', whereby the assessment of State aid comprises little more than fitting the aid into the right guideline 'box' based only on its form. Since each box is governed by its own idiosyncratic rules and thresholds, errors and inconsistencies are unavoidable.[56] The rigid way in which the guidelines have typically been applied has also come in for criticism as reflecting an approach which is too form based:

> [T]he various 'soft law' provisions have typically been applied in a rather strict, formalistic way. There is little scope for approving State aid measures which do not

---

[54] See also Gaul et al, 'An Economic Approach to Article 82' (2005) Report for the European Commission.

[55] See C Ahlborn and J Padilla, 'From Fairness To Welfare: Implications for the Assessment of Unilateral Conduct Under EC Competition Law' in Claus-Dieter Ehlermann and Mel Marquis (eds), *European Competition Law Annual 2007: A Reformed Approach to Article 82 EC* (Hart Publishing, 2008).

[56] See C Ahlborn and C Berg, 'Can State Aid Learn from Antitrust? The Need for a Greater Role for Competition Analysis under the State Aid Rules' in Biondi, Eeckhout and Flynn (eds), *The Law of State Aid in the European Union* (Oxford University Press 2004), pp 47–8.

meet the conditions set out in the provisions but which would very likely be benign. Alternatively, disallowing State aid measures which meet the conditions, but which are likely to be ineffective or distort competition is not envisaged.[57]

Potential compatibility of guidelines with an effects-based approach. However the use of secondary legislation and guidelines does not in itself preclude a commitment to a largely effects-based analysis of whether an aid is compatible with the Treaty. What matters is whether the rules set out within the legislation and guidelines are based on an economic analysis of the probable effects of particular classes of aid on welfare and efficiency, or whether instead the rules reflect judgments that particular types of aid are undesirable for other reasons (for example because they limit the economic freedom of some market participants) or indeed reflect uninformed prejudice about what aids should be allowed. Reflecting a growing commitment to effects-based analysis, the Commission in its State Aid Action Plan announced its intention to adopt a more 'refined economic approach' to evaluating State aid,[58] which will focus on an *effects-based* analysis of both sides of the balance in Article 87(3): the costly distortions that State aid can generate on the one hand,[59] and the necessity for aid, and the reasons why markets are unable to deliver the desired benefit, on the other.[60] The Commission accepts that perhaps the proliferation of different guidelines, and the inevitable inconsistencies, has gone too far.[61] However it remains committed to providing governments with extensive guidance about how Article 87(3) will be applied. The reformed approach is discussed in more detail in the next section. **1.35**

4. A more refined economic approach?

Market failure as a reason for State aid. The more refined economic approach to assessing the compatibility of a State aid under Article 87(3) set out in the State Aid Action Plan puts market failures at the heart of its approach. According to this, a State aid can be compatible with the Treaty if it corrects a market failure 'thereby improving the functioning of markets and enhancing European competitiveness.' The only other justifications are for aids that are targeted at social and equity goals, rather than improved economic performance.[62] The claim that government intervention in economic activities can be justified by the existence **1.36**

---

[57] Friederiszick, Röller and Verouden, 'European State Aid Control: An Economic Framework' in P Buccirossi (ed), *Handbook of Antitrust Economics*, (MIT Press 2008) p 630.

[58] State Aid Action Plan: Less and better targeted State aid: a roadmap for State aid reform 2005–2009, COM(2005) 107 final, p 18.

[59] ibid, para 22.

[60] ibid, para 23.

[61] ibid, para 17.

[62] ibid, para 10.

of market failures is a common one.[63] The logic for this position is as follows. Good outcomes are the ones that properly functioning competitive markets deliver. However in practice markets can be subject to failures which mean that market outcomes are not efficient. In such circumstances, State intervention to correct the market failure is legitimate. For example companies may not invest enough in training because spillovers (or 'externalities') mean their rivals will get some of the benefits if staff often move employer. In this example government provision of, or support for, vocational training projects could help the economy achieve closer to optimal levels.

1.37 **Cost-benefit analysis and the balancing test.** The existence of a market failure is not itself a sufficient justification for providing State aid.[64] Governments have many policy tools at their disposal and aid may not be the most appropriate response. Moreover State aid is costly, involving public funds that could have been used elsewhere, and finally it may distort the market by disturbing the level playing field on which firms compete for funding and for customers.[65] These considerations are reflected in the Commission's 'balancing test' in the evaluation of whether to approve aids, as now applied to all cases assessed under Article 87(3).[66] In a paper on the reform of State aid control originally written while still Chief Economist at DG Comp, Lars Hendrik Röller, together with his co-authors, claimed that the balancing test essentially uses cost-benefit analysis as a means of identifying which State aids fall under the derogation in 87(3).[67] Cost-benefit analysis is the standard tool for assessing whether public sector projects should be funded and is, for example, explicitly required by the EU Regulations for Structural Funds and the Cohesion Fund.[68]

1.38 **Theory versus practice.** By stating that it wants to base the analysis of compatibility of an aid on a review of its costs and benefits, the Commission has taken

---

[63] See eg Friederiszick, Röller and Verouden, 'European State Aid Control: An Economic Framework' in P Buccirossi (ed), *Handbook of Antitrust Economics* (MIT Press 2008), pp 632–3; J Vickers 'State aid and distortions of competition', Speech to the UK Presidency seminar on State aid, 14 July 2005 where he states that subsidies are often defended with the claim that they correct a market failure; and JE Stiglitz, *Principles of Microeconomics* (WW Norton & Company 1997), p 153, where the author claims that government may be able to enhance efficiency in the economy by correcting an existing market failure.

[64] See also J Vickers, 'State aid and distortions of competition', Speech to the UK Presidency seminar on State aid, 14 July 2005, p 4.

[65] Friederiszick, Röller and Verouden, 'European State Aid Control: An Economic Framework' in P Buccirossi (ed), *Handbook of Antitrust Economics* (MIT Press 2008), p 637.

[66] See further paras 3.28 below.

[67] Friederiszick HW, L-H Röller and V Verouden, 'European State Aid Control: An Economic Framework' in P Buccirossi (ed), *Handbook of Antitrust Economics* (MIT Press 2008), p 648.

[68] Council Regulation (EC) 1083/2006 laying down general provisions on the European Regional Development Fund, the European Social Fund and the Cohesion Fund [2006] OJ L210/25, Article 40(e).

a clear step in the direction of an effects-based approach to State aid control. In practice the analysis is likely to fall short of this for a number of reasons. Some of the main difficulties are discussed in the following paragraphs.

Continued role for guidelines. The more refined economic approach is being implemented in particular through guidelines: since the adoption of the State Aid Action Plan, the Commission has issued several new regulatory frameworks and guidelines, and others are currently under review.[69] While these new guidelines may well take into account the more coherent effects-based approach of the balancing test, it is also likely that they will continue to embody a number of simplifications and presumptions. This is because the development of these guidelines will inevitably reflect some of the same pressures that have shaped the existing approach: a desire to resist political pressure through pre-commitment, a desire to provide certainty to notifying Member State and the reality that the Commission still lacks the investigative powers needed to conduct its own analysis, so that precise guidelines become a tool for eliciting relevant information from notifying states. **1.39**

Investigative powers. The Commission's ability to conduct sophisticated effects-based analysis continues to be limited by the fact that the Commission lacks the ability to gather the necessary data, a problem that is not addressed in the State Aid Action Plan. As noted in a recent paper by the current Chief Economist at DG Comp: **1.40**

> [T]he implementation of a rigorous economic assessment is hampered by limited powers of investigation: obtaining much of the necessary information hinges on a sufficient level of cooperation by member States and the provision of information by third parties. It seems to us that further improvements in the investigative powers of the Commission are hard to dispense with.[70]

Analysis of benefits. A further casualty of the translation of the more refined economic approach into practice is the analysis of the benefits of an aid. The Commission has opted to put clear guidance about the priorities States should pursue when designing aid ahead of a thorough analysis of the merits of individual schemes. The State Aid Action Plan highlights a number of general areas where market failures lead to underinvestment. It then raises a strong presumption that any aid that increases spending in this general area is beneficial. It is very likely that these presumptions will carry over into the guidelines. In the new R&D&I **1.41**

[69] The Commission aims at largely completing the process by 2009 (see European Commission, 'Vademecum Community Rules on State Aid', February 2007). An important example of guidelines still under revision are those that deal with rescue and restructuring aid.

[70] D Neven and V Verouden, 'Towards a more refined economic approach in State aid control' in Mederer, Pesaresi and Van Hoof (eds), *EU Competition law*, Vol IV, State Aid (Claeys & Casteels 2008), para 1.373.

framework, for example, the Commission states that the main evidence it will consider when assessing whether an aid confers a benefit is whether it leads to higher R&D spending. However analysing the sources of market failure in itself cannot identify which projects should be funded. It may be the case that market failures lead to under-investment in basic R&D, because companies know that their rivals are likely to learn of their results and get some of the benefits. Even so, that does not mean that every basic R&D project would or indeed should have been funded by markets in the absence of the market failure. The point that not all R&D spending is beneficial has been forcefully made by the Economic Advisory Group on Competition Policy.[71]

1.42 **Analysis of effect of competition and trade.** The analysis of aid for R&D also illustrates the area in which the Commission's assessment of the economic effects of a State aid remains the most disappointing, namely the assessment of the impact of an aid on competition and trade. The Commission's current R&D&I Framework, which came into force in January 2007,[72] usefully lists a number of ways that an aid could be harmful: it could deter rivals from making their own investments; it could increase the market power of the recipient; and it could maintain an inefficient company. However there is no suggestion that the required analysis of these potential effects should draw on the experience and standards that have been developed in other areas of competition law. Notably, for example, there is no requirement to define the market within which the impact on competition is to be assessed, let alone a requirement to do so to the standard that is required for merger control. Not surprisingly the result is that the analysis of the harm to competition in recent decisions remains rather loose.[73]

1.43 **Conclusion.** Even if, in practice, the Commission's more refined economic approach falls short of an entirely rigorous case-by-case cost-benefit analysis of proposed aids, it still has the potential to lead to decisions that are significantly more grounded in the economic and financial analysis of effects than before. There is now a clearly articulated conceptual framework that identifies a number of substantive points that need to be established, and where economic and financial analysis can provide the most credible evidence. This is an encouraging start, which will doubtless continue to be developed over the next years.

[71] Commentary by the Economic Advisory Group on Competition Policy (EAGCP) on the draft Community Framework for State Aid for Research, Development and Innovation, July 2006.

[72] Community Framework for State aid for Research and Development and Innovation [2006] OJ C323/1, discussed in detail in Chapter 8 below.

[73] See eg Decision in Case N 195/2007 *Rolls-Royce Deutschland* (11 March 2008), Decision in Case N 435/2007 *'MINimage' programme* (30 January 2008), Decision in Case N 887/2006 *Projet Bernin 2010* (10 July 2007), Decision in Case N 854/2006 *TVMSL programme* (10 May 2007).

2

THE DEFINITION OF STATE AID

Main legislation and guidelines

Commission Regulation (EC) 1998/2006 on the application of Articles 87 and 88 of the Treaty to *de minimis* aid [2006] OJ L379/5

Communication on State aid elements in sales of land and buildings by public authorities ('Communication on land sales') [1997] OJ C209/3

Notice on the application of the State aid rules to measures relating to direct business taxation ('Notice on direct business taxation') [1998] OJ C384/3

Commission Notice on the application of Articles 87 and 88 of the EC Treaty to State aid in the form of guarantees ('Notice on State guarantees') [2008] OJ C155/10, as corrected [2008] OJ C244/32

A. Introduction

2.01 **Article 87(1) EC.** The basic prohibition on the grant of State aid is contained in Article 87(1). That Article also defines the concept of aid. It provides:

> Save as otherwise provided in this Treaty, any aid granted by a Member State or through State resources in any form whatsoever which distorts or threatens to distort competition by favouring certain undertakings or the production of certain goods shall, in so far as it affects trade between Member States, be incompatible with the common market.

State aid as defined in Article 87(1) is thus prohibited, save to the extent that the aid is permitted by other Treaty provisions. The main derogations from the prohibition on aid are set out in Article 87(2) and (3), and Article 86(2). These are discussed in detail in Chapter 3. This chapter will address the concept, or definition, of aid as set out in Article 87(1).

2.02 **Elements of definition.** The jurisprudence of the European Court has not yet provided a consistent and comprehensive interpretation of the conditions for State aid under Article 87(1). While the Court's definition of aid is often still based on the actual wording of Article 87(1),[1] in practice the Court has not adhered rigidly to that formulation. In particular, it is by now well established that the criteria of 'granted by a Member State or through State resources' are not alternative; rather, it is necessary to show *both* that the measure is a 'State measure', *and* that it has been granted through State resources. The Court has also consistently held that no actual effect on either competition or trade is required. The condition of 'aid . . . in any form whatsoever' and the criterion of 'favouring' have equally been elaborated by an extensive body of case-law. The cumulative result of the Court's interpretation of Article 87(1), therefore, is that in order to fall within that Article a measure must satisfy the following four criteria:

(a) there must be aid in the sense of a benefit or advantage;[2]
(b) which is granted by the State[3] and through State resources;[4]

[1] For recent examples see Case C-172/03 *Heiser* [2005] ECR I-1627, para 27; Case C-237/04 *Enirisorse v Sotacarbo* [2006] ECR I-2843, para 39; Case T-34/02 *EURL Le Levant 001 v Commission* [2006] ECR II-267, para 110.

[2] AG Jacobs in Case C-256/97 *DMT* [1999] ECR I-3913, para 29.

[3] ie is imputable to the State: Case T-358/94 *Air France v Commission* [1996] ECR II-2109, para 55; Case C-482/99 *France v Commission ('Stardust Marine')* [2002] ECR I-4397, para 51; Case C-345/02 *Pearle* [2004] ECR I-7139, para 35; Cases T-228 and 233/99 *Westdeutsche Landesbank v Commission* [2003] ECR II-435, para 179; Case T-351/02 *Deutsche Bahn v Commission* [2006] ECR II-1047, para 101.

[4] Case C-379/98 *PreussenElektra* [2001] ECR I-2099, para 58; Case C-345/02 *Pearle* [2004] ECR I-7139, para 35.

(c) which favours certain undertakings or the production of certain goods ('selectivity');[5] and
(d) which is liable to distort competition and affect trade between Member States.[6]

These criteria are considered in detail in sections B to E below. This section sets out some general considerations which apply to the analysis of aid, whichever criterion is being considered, and gives examples of the types of measure which have hitherto been found to constitute aid.

Objective definition. The concept of aid within Article 87(1) is a legal concept **2.03** which is to be interpreted on the basis of objective factors,[7] without any room for discretion.[8] The provision does not distinguish between measures of State intervention by reference to their causes or aims, but defines them in relation to their effects.[9] Accordingly, a State may not avoid characterization of a measure as aid on the grounds that it is a fiscal measure, or pursues economic or social aims[10] or pursues public interest goals such as environmental objectives,[11] or is motivated by the desire to maintain the prestige and credibility of the State.[12] In broad terms, therefore, the general interest objective of a measure cannot *per se* exclude the application of Article 87(1): there is no 'rule of reason' or concept of 'objective justification' in the interpretation of Article 87(1).[13] The obverse is also true: the fact that a measure, which confers a benefit on certain undertakings,

[5] Case C-200/97 *Ecotrade* [1998] ECR I-7907, para 40; Case C-143/99 *Adria-Wien Pipeline* [2001] ECR I-8365, para 41; Cases T-127, 129 and 148/99 *Diputación Foral de Álava v Commission* [2002] ECR II-1275 para 144; Case C-172/03 *Heiser* [2005] ECR I-1627, para 40.

[6] Case C-372/97 *Italy v Commission* [2004] ECR I-3679, para 44; Case C-148/04 *Unicredito Italiano* [2005] ECR I-11137, para 55.

[7] Case C-83/98P *France v Ladbroke Racing and Commission* [2000] ECR I-3271, para 25; Case T-98/00 *Linde v Commission* [2002] ECR II-3961, para 40; Case T-152/99 *Hijos de Andrés Molina v Commission* [2002] ECR II-3049, para 159.

[8] Case T-67/94 *Ladbroke Racing v Commission* [1998] ECR II-1, para 52.

[9] Case 173/73 *Italy v Commission* [1974] ECR 709, para 13; a statement which has been repeated in numerous judgments since including Case C-56/93 *Belgium v Commission* [1996] ECR I-723, para 79; Case C-75/97 *Belgium v Commission ('Maribel bis/ter')* [1999] ECR I-3671, para 25; and Case C-172/03 *Heiser* [2005] ECR I-1627, para 46.

[10] Case 173/73 *Italy v Commission* [1974] ECR 709, para 13 (reduction of social charges); Case 310/85 *Deufil v Commission* [1987] ECR 901, paras 7–8 (conjunctural policy); Case 57/87 *Greece v Commission* [1988] ECR 2855, para 9 (monetary policy); Case C-75/97 *Belgium v Commission ('Maribel bis/ter')* [1999] ECR I-3671, para 25 (creation of jobs); Case C-5/01 *Belgium v Commission ('Cockerill Sambre')* [2002] ECR I-11991, paras 45–7 (creation of jobs); Cases T-269, 271 and 272/99 *Diputación Foral de Guipúzcoa* [2002] ECR II-4217, para 63; and Cases T-346-348/99 *Diputación Foral de Alava v Commission* [2002] ECR II-4259, paras 54 and 63 (encouraging economic development and investment in Basque region of Spain).

[11] Case T-109/01 *Fleuren Compost v Commission* [2004] ECR II-127, para 54.

[12] Cases T-204 and 270/97 *EPAC v Commission* [2000] ECR II-2267, paras 75–6.

[13] This should not be confused with the principle that a measure which is justified by the nature or general scheme of the system falls outside the selectivity or favouring criterion, and is therefore not aid: see para 2.127 *et seq* below.

pursues a patently political aim does not render it a State aid where the conditions of Article 87(1) are not satisfied.[14] The objective nature of the concept of aid also means that the Commission (if it is deciding the matter) cannot be bound by a different assessment in a previous decision.[15]

2.04 **Definition of State.** The concept of State within Article 87(1) is not limited to the federal or central authorities of a Member State, but includes regional and local bodies, whatever their status.[16] State aids may therefore emanate from any body within the public sector.[17]

2.05 **Form of aid not material.** Article 87(1) applies to aids 'in any form whatsoever'. Thus, while the paradigm form of aid is a straightforward subsidy, the ECJ has consistently held that the concept of aid is wider than that of a subsidy. Its seminal statement was given in the *Steenkolenmijnen* case:[18]

> A subsidy is normally defined as a payment in cash or in kind made in support of an undertaking other than the payment by the purchaser or consumer for the goods or services which it produces. An aid is a very similar concept which, however, places emphasis on its purpose and seems especially devised for a particular object which cannot normally be achieved without outside help. The concept of aid is nevertheless wider than that of a subsidy because it embraces not only positive benefits, such as subsidies themselves, but also interventions which, in various forms, mitigate the charges which are normally included in the budget of an undertaking and which, without, therefore, being subsidies in the strict meaning of the word, are similar in character and have the same effect.[19]

2.06 **Examples of aid.** It follows from both the wide definition of State bodies which may grant aid, as well as the broad concept of aid, that Article 87(1) embraces a variety of financial transfers by public authorities. These include capital investments and injections,[20] interest free loans,[21] loans on preferential interest terms

---

14 Case C-56/93 *Belgium v Commission* [1996] ECR I-723, para 79.

15 Cases C-341-342/06 P *Chronopost v Ufex* (judgment of 1 July 2008), para 95.

16 Case 248/84 *Germany v Commission* [1987] ECR 4013, para 17; Cases T-127, 129 and 148/99 *Diputación Foral de Álava v Commission* [2002] ECR II-1275 para 142; Cases T-346-348/99 *Diputación Foral de Álava v Commission* [2002] ECR II-4259, para 62; Case C-88/03 *Portugal v Commission ('Azores')* [2006] ECR I-7115, para 55.

17 See Case T-358/94 *Air France v Commission* [1996] ECR II-2109, para 56.

18 Case 30/59 *Steenkolenmijnen v High Authority* [1961] ECR 1, p 19, in relation to Article 4(c) ECSC.

19 See also Case C-387/92 *Banco Exterior de España* [1994] ECR I-877, para 13; Case C-143/99 *Adria-Wien Pipeline* [2001] ECR I-8365, para 38; Case C-237/04 *Enirisorse v Sotacarbo* [2006] ECR I-2843, para 42.

20 Case 323/82 *Intermills v Commission* [1984] ECR 3809; Case 318/82 *Netherlands and Leeuwarder Paperienfabriek v Commission* [1985] ECR 809; Case C-142/87 *Belgium v Commission* [1990] ECR I-959; Case C-303/88 *Italy v Commission* [1991] ECR I-1433; Case C-305/89 *Italy v Commission ('Alfa Romeo')* [1991] ECR I-1603.

21 Case T-214/95 *Vlaams Gewest v Commission* [1998] ECR II-717.

(so-called 'soft loans')[22] or without sufficient security,[23] interest rate subsidies[24] and contributions to a social plan implemented by an undertaking making a large number of redundancies.[25] *Indirect financial measures* are also included, such as the waiver of public debts,[26] exemption from obligations to pay fines or other pecuniary penalties,[27] late payment facilities,[28] and the informal tolerance of persistent non-payment of taxes, charges and other debts.[29] *State guarantees* or securities for loans may also be aid, where they enable the undertaking to obtain a more favourable rate of interest than would otherwise have been charged,[30] or where the loan could not have been obtained at all without the State guarantee.[31] *Tax exemptions* or reduced rates of tax[32] are frequently found to be aid, as are tax credits,[33] reductions in an undertaking's tax base,[34] reductions in employers' social security contributions,[35] and the deferral of tax,[36] including by means of special depreciation allowances which have the effect of a tax deferral.[37] A system which assesses taxable profits of certain undertakings only on a cost-plus basis may also constitute aid.[38] The *provision of goods or services at an undervalue* or on preferential

---

22 Case 57/86 *Greece v Commission* [1988] ECR 2855; Case 63/87 *Greece v Commission* [1988] ECR 2875; Case 102/87 *France v Commission* [1988] ECR 4067; Cases C-15/98 and C-105/99 *Italian Republic and Sardegna Lines v Commission* [2000] ECR I-8855.

23 Case C-457/00 *Belgium v Commission ('Verlipack')* [2003] ECR I-6931.

24 Case 57/86 *Greece v Commission* [1988] ECR 2855; Case T-55/99 *CETM v Commission* [2000] ECR II-3207; Case C-114/00 *Spain v Commission* [2002] ECR I-7657.

25 Case C-241/94 *France v Commission ('Kimberly Clark')* [1996] ECR I-4551.

26 Case C-200/97 *Ecotrade* [1998] ECR I-7907, para 43; Case C-295/97 *Rinaldo Piaggio* [1999] ECR I-3735, para 42.

27 *Ecotrade* and *Rinaldo Piaggio,* ibid.

28 Case T-46/97 *SIC v Commission* [2000] ECR II-2125.

29 Case C-480/98 *Spain v Commission ('Magefesa')* [2000] ECR I-8717; Case C-415/03 *Commission v Greece* [2005] ECR I-3875; Case T-36/99 *Lenzing* [2004] ECR II-3597.

30 Case C-404/97 *Commission v Portugal* [2000] ECR I-4897, per AG Ruiz-Jarabo Colomer at paras 47–8.

31 Case C-288/96 *Germany v Commission* [2000] ECR I-8237; Cases T-204 and 270/97 *EPAC v Commission* [2000] ECR II-2267, paras 68–71.

32 Case C-387/92 *Banco Exterior de España* [1994] ECR I-877; Case C-200/97 *Ecotrade* [1998] ECR I-7907; Case C-172/03 *Heiser* [2005] ECR I-1627. A system which from its inception taxes some operators but not others may also equate to a tax exemption: Case C-53/00 *Ferring v ACOSS* [2001] ECR I-9067, para 20.

33 Case C-6/97 *Italy v Commission* [1999] ECR I-2981, Cases T-269, 271 and 272/99 *Diputación Foral de Guipúzcoa v Commission* [2002] ECR II-4217.

34 Cases T-346-348/99 *Diputación Foral de Alava v Commission* [2002] ECR II-4259.

35 Case 173/73 *Commission v Italy* [1974] ECR 709; Case C-251/97 *France v Commission* [1999] ECR I-6639.

36 Case C-256/97 *DMT* [1999] ECR I-3913; Case C-156/98 *Germany v Commission* [2000] ECR I-6857, para 24.

37 Case T-308/00 *Salzgitter v Germany* [2004] ECR II-1933 and appeal in Case C-408/04 P *Commission v Salzgitter* (judgment of 22 April 2008).

38 Cases C-182 and 217/03 *Belgium and Forum 187 v Commission* [2006] ECR I-5479, paras 90–102.

terms may be aid, including for example the sale of land,[39] provision of energy at a preferential tariff to certain undertakings,[40] the provision of logistical and commercial assistance without normal consideration,[41] the supply of an intangible asset such as a client list,[42] or reciprocal supply agreements between a public and private undertaking on terms giving an economic advantage to the private undertaking.[43] *Payments for public services* may also fall within Article 87(1) in certain circumstances,[44] as may purchases of services which are not in fact required.[45] The Commission has also found that a mere *loan announcement* constituted State aid,[46] even though the loan was never actually implemented.

2.07 **Measures having equivalent effect to State aid.** The ECJ has rejected several attempts by the Commission to expand the control of State aid still further by the introduction of the concept of a measure equivalent to State aid which could be challenged under Article 10 EC. On both occasions the Commission relied upon the argument to avoid the requirement that the aid be granted through State resources. In the *Poor farmers* case, the Court stated trenchantly that Articles 87 and 88 left no scope for a parallel concept of 'measures equivalent to aid' subject to different rules from those which apply to aid properly so-called.[47] It found, however, that on the facts Article 87(1) did cover the measure, which was decided and financed by a public body. The Commission put forward a slightly different argument in *PreussenElektra*, which concerned German legislation supporting suppliers of electricity from renewable sources, by requiring purchases of electricity by private electricity distribution undertakings at State-fixed minimum prices.[48] In the alternative to its arguments that the benefits were financed through State resources (which were also rejected),[49] the Commission argued that the

[39] See Commission Communication on State aid elements in sales of land and buildings by public authorities [1997] OJ C209/3; Cases T-127, 129 and 148/99 *Diputación Foral de Álava v Commission* [2002] ECR II-1275 para 72; and Case T-274/01 *Valmont v Commission* [2004] ECR II-3145.

[40] Cases 67, 68 and 70/85 *Van der Kooy v Commission* [1988] ECR 219; Case C-56/93 *Belgium v Commission* [1996] ECR I-723, para 10.

[41] Case C-39/94 *SFEI v La Poste* [1996] ECR I-3547, para 57; and Cases C-341-342/06 P *Chronopost v Ufex* (judgment of 1 July 2008) (though finding on the facts that there was no State aid).

[42] Second judgment in Case T-613/97 *Ufex v Commission* [2006] ECR II-1531, paras 164–71 (though on appeal ECJ held no aid on facts of case: *Chronopost v Ufex*, ibid).

[43] Case T-158/99 *Thermenhotel Stoiser Franz v Commission* [2004] ECR II-1, para 107 (though no aid found on facts of case).

[44] Case C-53/00 *Ferring v ACOSS* [2001] ECR I-9067, para 27; Case C-280/00 *Altmark* [2003] ECR I-7747, paras 87-95; Cases C-34-38/01 *Enirisorse v Ministero delle Finanze* [2003] ECR I-14243, paras 22-40. See further below at paras 2.63–2.75.

[45] Case T-14/96 *Bretagne Angleterre Irlande (BAI) v Commission* [1999] ECR II-139; Cases C-442 and 471/03 P *P&O European Ferries (Vizcaya) v Commission* [2006] ECR I-4845.

[46] Decision 2006/621/EC *France Télécom* [2006] OJ L257/11 (under appeal in Cases T-425 and 444/04 *France and France Télécom v Commission*).

[47] Case 290/83 *Commission v France ('Poor farmers')* [1985] ECR 439, para 18.

[48] Case C-379/98 *PreussenElektra* [2001] ECR I-2099.

[49] See para 2.93 below.

measure infringed Article 10, and that it should therefore be dealt with by a teleological extension of the notion of State aid in Article 87(1).[50] The ECJ held, however, that Article 10 could not be used to extend the scope of Article 87(1) in this way.[51]

B. Benefit or advantage

Introduction. The question of whether a measure which, on its face, benefits an undertaking is in fact to be regarded as a benefit or advantage within Article 87(1) has given rise to considerable case-law. In the paradigm case of a direct grant to an ailing undertaking, the advantage will not be difficult to identify. In other cases, however, the question may be less straightforward. Section 1 below sets out general principles which have been developed by the Court in the context of identifying the relevant advantage. The following sections then address a number of specific issues which have given rise to problems in the application of this criterion. **2.08**

1. General principles

Normal market conditions. The test for the type of benefit or advantage which falls within Article 87(1) has been expressed in a variety of slightly different ways, including the tests of whether the undertaking receives a benefit which it would not have received 'in the normal course of events on the private market',[52] whether the State has granted 'certain unmarketlike advantages . . . which are liable to improve the economic situation of the undertaking which benefits from them in comparison with that of other undertakings',[53] and whether the conduct of the State is 'economically rational'.[54] The classic test applied by the ECJ, however, is whether an undertaking obtains an economic advantage which it would not have received under 'normal market conditions'.[55] **2.09**

Role of the State. The application of the 'normal market conditions' criterion requires a distinction to be drawn between cases where the State (or public authority) **2.10**

[50] By analogy with the line of cases including Case C-2/91 *Meng* [1993] ECR I-5751, concerning the application of Article 10 together with Article 81 EC to measures introduced by Member States which render the competition laws ineffective.

[51] Case C-379/98 *PreussenElektra* [2001] ECR I-2099, paras 63–5 and see also opinion of AG Jacobs at paras 180–5.

[52] Case C-256/97 *DMT* [1999] ECR I-3913, opinion of AG Jacobs at para 31; see also Case C-39/94 *SFEI v La Poste* [1996] ECR I-3547, opinion of AG Jacobs at para 60.

[53] Case C-44/93 *Namur-Les Assurances v OND* [1994] ECR I-3829, per AG Lenz at para 66.

[54] Case T-98/00 *Linde v Commission* [2002] ECR II-3961, paras 45 and 49.

[55] Case C-39/94 *SFEI v La Poste* [1996] ECR I-3547, para 60; Case C-256/97 *DMT* [1999] ECR I-3913, para 22; Case T-46/97 *SIC v Commission* [2000] ECR II-2125, para 78.

acts in the exercise of its sovereign or public functions, and cases where it acts as a market participant.[56] Where the State exercises its sovereign functions to enact legislation in (for example) the field of taxation or social security, there is no extraneous 'normal market' comparator. Whether the legislation produces a benefit to some undertakings will therefore simply turn on the effects of the legislation itself. However, where the State acts as a market participant, there is a relevant comparator: a private commercial actor on the market. The existence of an advantage may therefore be determined by considering what the beneficiary undertaking would have received from a hypothetical commercial actor.

2.11 **State performing mixed functions.** In some cases the State may be performing both the role of a regulator and the role of a market participant. In such a case, its regulatory functions have to be taken into account in determining whether there is an advantage within the meaning of Article 87(1). This problem has arisen in relation to the grant of third generation (3G) mobile telephony licences. In *Bouygues v Commission*, the Court upheld the Commission's decision that the reduction in the fees payable for the 3G licences granted by France to SFR and Orange was not State aid. While the assets in question (the public airwaves) had an economic value and constituted State resources, it was necessary to take into account that the Member States are both managers of those public assets and telecommunications regulators.[57] Under the Community telecommunications rules, Member States are free to choose the procedure for the award of 3G licences provided, and are not required to use a public auction. Even an award of licences free of charge would not, therefore, constitute State aid provided that the same terms were applied to all operators without distinction.[58]

2.12 **Comparator in same Member State.** In order to identify what constitutes an advantage, it is necessary to determine the reference point against which the advantage is to be compared.[59] As the Commission observed in a recent decision, 'the determination of the reference framework is of particular importance because

[56] See extensive discussion of this distinction by AG Fennelly in Case C-390/98 *Banks v Coal Authority* [2001] ECR I-6117, opinion paras 19-20, and AG Léger in Case C-280/00 *Altmark* [2003] ECR I-7747, second opinion paras 20–3.

[57] Case T-475/04 *Bouygues v Commission* [2007] ECR II-2097, para 104. See similar comments by the Court of Appeal in the UK judicial review proceedings following the 3G licence auction: *R v Secretary of State for Trade and Industry, ex p BT3G and One2One* [2001] 3 CMLR 61 (Court of Appeal), paras 47–53. Note however that the mixed roles of the State in such a case may also indicate that a decision was not motivated purely by objective economic considerations, but was also influenced by political concerns: Case C-200/97 *Ecotrade* [1998] ECR I-7907 para 39 and opinion of AG Fennelly at para 28.

[58] *Bouygues v Commission,* ibid, paras 108–10.

[59] Case T-308/00 *Salzgitter v Commission* [2004] ECR II-1933, para 81; this part of the judgment approved on appeal in Case C-408/04 P *Commission v Salzgitter* (judgment of 22 April 2008), para 109. In many cases this question will overlap with the question of whether the measure is selective, and similar considerations will therefore arise in both respects: see para 2.111 below.

the very existence of an economic advantage can only be established in comparison to one system of financial charges known as "normal" in the geographical area of reference.'[60] The relevant comparator is the situation in the Member State in question. Given the significant disparities between the legislative and regulatory regimes in different Member States, a comparison between the economic situation of the beneficiary and the situation of comparable or competing undertakings in other Member States would be meaningless, since it would be a comparison of different factual and legal situations.[61] For that reason, the Court has consistently held that a measure may be an advantage even where its purpose is to compensate for a disadvantage affecting undertakings in one Member State compared with their competitors in other Member States, or to achieve parity with the competitive situation prevailing in other Member States.[62] By contrast, in certain circumstances a measure which removes a structural disadvantage by comparison with competitors in the *same* Member State might not be aid.[63]

Contemporaneous comparison. The proper comparison is between the situation of the beneficiary and that of other undertakings at the time of the grant of aid. It is irrelevant that the position of the undertaking is better or worse in comparison with the situation under the law as it previously stood, or has not altered over time.[64] For that reason a measure may be regarded as aid even where it is the continuation or prolongation of a previous system of support, and therefore does not produce any 'new' advantage for the undertakings in question. In *Greece v Commission* the ECJ ruled that an interest repayment on loans for certain exports constituted aid. It rejected the Greek government's argument that the system **2.13**

---

60 Decision in Case N 597/2006 *Greek pension reform* (10 October 2007), para 67.

61 Case T-308/00 *Salzgitter v Commission* [2004] ECR II-1933, para 81; this part of the judgment approved on appeal in Case C-408/04 P *Commission v Salzgitter* (judgment of 22 April 2008), para 109.

62 Cases 6 and 11/69 *Commission v France* [1969] ECR 523, para 21; Case 173/73 *Italy v Commission* [1974] ECR 709, paras 12, 17; Case C-6/97 *Italy v Commission* [1999] ECR I-2981, para 21; Case C-172/03 *Heiser* [2005] ECR I-1627, paras 52–4. This point is also made in relation to the existence of a distortion of competition: see para 2.140 below.

63 See Case T-157/01 *Danske Busvognmænd v Commission* [2004] ECR II-917, para 57, where the Court commented that a measure compensating employees of the State-owned company Combus for the transfer of their status from State employee (official) to employees under a private contract was not State aid, because (inter alia) its purpose was 'to replace the privileged and costly status of the officials employed by Combus with the status of employees on a contract basis comparable to that of employees of other bus transport undertakings competing with Combus. The intention was thus to free Combus from a structural disadvantage it had in relation to its private-sector competitors.'

The Commission, however, has doubted whether this is good law: Decision 2008/722/EC *OTE voluntary retirement scheme* [2008] OJ L243/7, para 92. Note also that a Member State cannot defend a tax exemption granted to one group of undertakings on the grounds that a different exemption from the same tax is granted to other groups of undertakings: Cases C-182/03 and C-217/03 *Belgium and Forum 187 v Commission* [2006] ECR I-5479, para 112.

64 Case C-143/99 *Adria-Wien Pipeline* [2001] ECR I-8365, para 41; Case C-172/03 *Heiser* [2005] ECR I-1627, opinion of AG Tizzano at para 51.

simply replaced an earlier system of preferential interest rates on loans for exports, which had not been examined by the Commission. The Court held that it was irrelevant that, by comparison with the previous export credit system, the repayment of interest was economically neutral in its effect on the competitiveness of Greek exports: the question was simply whether the present system, viewed independently from its predecessor, favoured certain undertakings.[65]

2.14 **Consideration of transaction as a whole.** In assessing the existence of aid in a State intervention, it is necessary to consider the transaction as a whole, rather than looking at individual elements of the transaction in isolation. Thus a transaction such as a capital investment which, taken alone, might fall outside Article 87(1), may be regarded as aid when combined with other types of financial intervention.[66] It may also be necessary to consider the method of financing the aid, as for example where a subsidy is funded by parafiscal levies imposed on an industry.[67] On the other hand a subsidy which would appear to amount to aid may not do so when the commercial context is taken into consideration.[68] For similar reasons, when the circumstances as a whole are looked at, a payment by the State to one or more undertakings will not constitute aid where it constitutes the repayment of sums unduly levied,[69] or where it represents compensation for damages which the public authorities have caused.[70]

2.15 **Ascertainability of advantage.** It has been suggested that, in order for a measure to constitute aid, the amount of aid must be capable of being determined. An uncertain and unquantifiable advantage would on that view not fall within Article 87(1).[71] That suggestion was firmly rejected in the *Ecotrade* case, which concerned special insolvency rules which applied to particular large undertakings. Advocate General Fennelly commented that it was in the nature of insolvency

---

[65] Case 57/86 *Greece v Commission* [1988] ECR 2855, para 10. See also Case C-126/91 *GEMO* [2003] ECR I-13769, opinion of AG Jacobs at para 77. See also generally on export credit arrangements Communication of the Commission to the Member States pursuant to Article 93(1) of the EC Treaty applying Articles 92 and 93 of the Treaty to short-term export-credit insurance [1997] OJ C281/4 as amended [2005] OJ C325/22.

[66] See Commission Notice on public authorities' holdings in company capital, *Bulletin of the European Communities* 9/84, p 93, section 3.4 and Case C-457/00 *Belgium v Commission ('Verlipack')* [2003] ECR I-6931, paras 77–80.

[67] See further paras 2.76–2.81 below.

[68] See eg Case T-98/00 *Linde v Commission* [2002] ECR II-3961, paras 51–4, where a Commission decision finding an investment subsidy to be aid was annulled for failure to examine whether it reflected the terms which would have been agreed between commercial operators, or to establish whether the subsidy exceeded the cost of the beneficiary's contractual obligations.

[69] Case 61/79 *Denkavit* [1980] ECR 1205, para 31; Case 811/79 *Ariete* [1980] ECR I-2545, paras 14–16; Case 826/79 *Mireco* [1980] ECR 2559, para 15.

[70] Cases 106–120/87 *Asteris v Greece* [1988] ECR 5515, para 23.

[71] Case C-21/88 *Du Pont de Nemours* [1990] ECR I-889, opinion of AG Lenz at para 58; Cases C-52–54/97 *Epifanio Viscido* [1998] ECR I-2629, opinion of AG Jacobs at para 15.

proceedings that it could not be predicted, with absolute certainty, that one procedure or another would invariably lead to greater or lesser losses for the creditors. It was sufficient, in his view, that there was a 'considerable likelihood' that the application of the special procedure would result in greater losses to the State *qua* creditor.[72] The Court concurred, ruling that the legislation did place the undertakings to which it applied in a more favourable situation than others, 'inasmuch as it allows them to continue trading in circumstances in which that would not be allowed if the usual insolvency rules were applied'.[73]

Contingent advantage. A measure may also constitute a benefit or advantage even where the substantive assistance granted by the State is not immediate, but is subject to a contingency.[74] That is the case in particular for State guarantees. In such a case the immediate advantage caught by the State aid rules is not the payment by the State under the guarantee (which may or may not ultimately be called upon) but the fact that this contingent promise of payment enables the undertaking to obtain credit on more favourable terms than it would otherwise have offered, or where no credit would have been offered at all absent the State guarantee.[75] **2.16**

Contingent advantage and general aid schemes. A distinction must be drawn, however, between a case where the measure is implemented in favour of a certain undertaking but where (as in the case of a guarantee) the advantage is contingent, and a case where the measure has not yet in fact been applied. This issue arises in the case of general aid schemes. In examining a general aid scheme, it is not necessary to show that any undertakings have actually benefited from the application of the scheme.[76] However, if it is alleged that the scheme has been implemented in favour of a certain undertaking, then this is an assertion of individual aid, and it is necessary to show an actual advantage to the undertaking concerned. In that respect it is not sufficient that the undertaking has applied for aid, where the aid has not yet been authorized.[77] **2.17**

Indirect advantages. In some cases the aid may procure advantages for entities other than the direct beneficiary. This may occur where the direct beneficiary of an aid is an individual, but where the measure indirectly benefits a related **2.18**

[72] Case C-200/97 *Ecotrade* [1998] ECR I-7907, opinion para 31.

[73] ibid, judgment para 41. See also C-295/97 *Rinaldo Piaggio* [1999] ECR I-3735, para 40.

[74] See AG Fennelly in Case C-200/97 *Ecotrade* [1998] ECR I-7907, opinion para 31, making clear that a contingent advantage would fall within Article 87(1).

[75] See further para 2.42 below.

[76] *A fortiori* it is no answer to say that only a small percentage of eligible undertakings have actually benefited in practice: see Cases C-182 and 217/03 *Belgium and Forum 187 v Commission* [2006] ECR I-5479, para 105.

[77] Cases T-127, 129 and 148/99 *Diputación Foral de Álava v Commission* [2002] ECR II-1275, paras 178–97.

undertaking. There may also be cases where a measure benefiting one undertaking also entails an indirect benefit to another undertaking. These cases are addressed below at paras 2.27–2.32.

2.19 **Exemption from unlawful charge.** An exemption from a charge may be regarded as an advantage to the beneficiary undertaking even if the charge itself is unlawful. The *Heiser* case concerned an Austrian VAT provision which exempted medical practitioners from an adjustment normally required where input tax had been deducted in respect of VAT-exempt transactions. Mr Heiser, a dentist, had argued that the provision was not an advantage, since the adjustment was itself contrary to Community law. The ECJ held that, even if the adjustment was unlawful (a matter on which it did not rule) the legislation was liable to have an impact as long as it was not repealed, or at least as long as its unlawfulness was not established. It therefore created a charge which was normally in the budget of dentists such as Mr Heiser. The exemption from the adjustment therefore constituted an advantage within Article 87(1).[78]

2.20 **Avoiding a charge not normally borne by other undertakings.** A measure which exempts an undertaking from what would otherwise be an exceptional charge may not be regarded as an advantage. In *Enirisorse*,[79] an Italian law allowed, by way of derogation, shareholders to withdraw at any time from the capital of a specific public limited company (Sotacarbo), subject to relinquishing all claims over its assets. That right did not exist for shareholders of other public limited companies. However the ECJ agreed with the Commission that this was not an advantage, either for the shareholders (who would not be reimbursed for the value of their shares) or for the undertaking (since shareholders had the right but were under no obligation to withdraw). Nor did the fact that the shareholders were precluded from reimbursement constitute an advantage to the undertaking, since in the normal case no right of withdrawal and hence no right of reimbursement would have arisen. The legislation therefore did not seek to reduce a charge which the company would 'normally have had to bear'.[80] As Advocate General Poiares Maduro noted, the position would have been different if, under the general law, the shareholders were entitled to withdraw and redeem their shares: in that case, the loss of the right to reimbursement would plainly have conferred an economic advantage on Sotacarbo.[81]

2.21 **Imposition of special charges.** Unlike Article 4(c) ECSC, which prohibited not only aids granted by States, but also special charges imposed by States, the State aid provisions of the EC Treaty do not contain any concept of 'negative aid', in the

[78] Case C-172/03 *Heiser* [2005] ECR I-1627, paras 37–8.
[79] Case C-237/04 *Enirisorse v Sotacarbo* [2006] ECR I-2843.
[80] ibid, para 48.
[81] ibid, opinion para 33.

sense of the imposition of a selective charge on a group of undertakings. The Court has consistently rejected attempts to elide the concepts of aid and special charges,[82] and has emphasized that there is a clear distinction between the regime for State aids in Articles 87–89 EC, and the rules in Articles 96–97 EC concerning distortions of competition arising from differences between the laws, regulations and administrative provisions of the Member States, including in particular their tax provisions.[83] In certain cases, however, the identification and assessment of aid may require consideration of charges imposed on undertakings. That arises in particular in considering parafiscal charges and differential taxation, addressed at sections 8 and 9 below. The scope of Articles 87 and 88 in this context is of particular significance for the remedies which may be granted in national courts: if a charge constitutes State aid itself, or a measure giving effect to that aid, and has not been notified to and approved by the Commission, it will fall within the prohibition on the implementation in Article 88(3), and the taxpayer will be able to claim reimbursement.[84]

2. The beneficiary of aid

The concept of 'undertaking'. Article 87(1) by its terms applies only to benefits or advantages granted to undertakings. It is well established that, in the context of competition law, the concept of an undertaking encompasses every entity engaged in an economic activity, regardless of whether the body is established under public or private law,[85] or the way in which it is financed.[86] Any activity consisting in offering goods or services on a given market is regarded as an economic activity.[87] Those principles apply as much to the State aid rules as they does to Articles 81 and 82.[88] The reference to 'undertakings' in Article 87(1) thus includes self-employed professionals who carry on an economic activity such as dentists,[89] **2.22**

---

[82] See, in relation to Article 4(c) European Coal and Steel Community Treaty 1951 (ECSC), Case C-390/98 *Banks v Coal Authority* [2001] ECR I-6117, para 34: 'a single measure cannot at the same time constitute both an aid and a special charge within the meaning of Article 4(c) of the ECSC Treaty.'

[83] AG Geelhoed in Case C-308/01 *GIL Insurance* [2004] ECR I-4777, opinion paras 58–67; Case C-174/02 *Streekgewest* [2005] ECR I-85, para 24 and opinion of AG Geelhoed at paras 28–9.

[84] See Chapter 18 below.

[85] See Case 118/85 *Commission v Italy* [1987] ECR 2599, para 11; and for an example of a private company carrying out non-economic activity see Decision in Case NN 76/2002 *Technology Transfer Institutes* (19 February 2003).

[86] Case C-41/90 *Höfner and Elser* [1991] ECR I-1979, para 21; Cases C-180–184/98 *Pavlov* [2000] ECR I-6451, para 74; and Cases C-159–160/91 *Poucet and Pistre* [1993] ECR I-637, para 17.

[87] Case C-35/96 *Commission v Italy* [1998] ECR I-3851, para 36; Cases C-180-184/98 *Pavlov* [2000] ECR I-6451, para 75; Case C-309/99 *Wouters* [2002] ECR I-3851, para 47.

[88] See eg Case C-237/04 *Enirisorse v Sotacarbo* [2006] ECR I-2843, paras 28–9.

[89] Case C-172/03 *Heiser* [2005] ECR I-1627, para 26.

as well as non-profit making undertakings provided that they are offering goods or services on the market.[90] The fact that goods or services are provided in the course of activities in public interest or social assistance fields such as scientific research, education, art or health does not prevent this from constituting an economic activity.[91] Vocational training is therefore an economic activity where it constitutes a market training activity, addressed to undertakings and their employees as well as individuals, paying a market price.[92]

2.23 **Non-economic activities.** Matters which are intrinsically prerogatives of the State (such as ensuring internal and external security, the administration of justice, the conduct of foreign relations and other exercises of official authority) are excluded from the application of the competition rules. The same applies for the provision of public sector services such as the public administration, heritage conservation and environmental protection,[93] along with certain air traffic control[94] and anti-pollution surveillance[95] activities. For this reason a transfer of assets between different levels of government (for example a transfer of land from central to regional governmental bodies) falls outside the State aid rules.[96] Services such as national education are also excluded from the application of the competition rules, on the basis that the State, in establishing and maintaining an education system, is not seeking to engage in gainful activity but is fulfilling its duty towards its own population in the social, cultural and educational fields.[97] Other examples of non-economic activities include the provision of a social security scheme founded on a solidarity mechanism,[98] support to establishments providing training and rehabilitation of seriously disabled people,[99] the payment of

[90] Case C-222/04 *Ministero dell'Economia e delle Finanze v Cassa di Risparmio di Firenze* [2006] ECR I-289, para 123. cf Decision in Case N 558/2005 *Support to establishments of professional activity for seriously disabled people* (27 June 2007), paras 52–61: no genuine economic activity where the sale of goods and services was ancillary to the rehabilitation purpose of the establishments, and where all revenues were reinvested in the establishments.

[91] *Cassa di Risparmio di Firenze*, ibid, paras 122–3.

[92] Decision 2006/225/EC *Italian training institutions* [2006] OJ L81/25, paras 48 and 58.

[93] Decision in Case N 46/2007 *Welsh public sector network scheme* (30 May 2007), para 17.

[94] Case C-364/92 *SAT Fluggesellschaft v Eurocontrol* [1994] ECR I-43.

[95] Case C-343/95 *Diego Calí* [1997] ECR I-1547.

[96] Decision in Case N 277/2003 *Transfer of nature protection areas in the new German Länder* (26 April 2006). See also Decision in Case NN 86/2001 *Aer Rianta* (5 October 2001), para 4, indicating that the same applies where assets are transferred from a part of the public administration to a State-owned firm whose activity is functionally the same.

[97] Case 263/86 *Humbel* [1988] ECR 5365; and Decision 2006/225/EC *Italian training institutions* [2006] OJ L81/25, paras 44–9.

[98] Cases C-159-160/91 *Poucet and Pistre* [1993] ECR I-637; Cases C-266/04 etc *Distribution Casino France* [2005] ECR I-9481, para 54.

[99] Decision in Case N 558/2005 *Support to establishments of professional activity for seriously disabled people* (27 June 2007).

contributions to non-profit making organizations,[100] and the construction of railway infrastructure.[101]

Shareholders as undertakings. In the *Cassa di Risparmio di Firenze* case, the question arose whether an Italian banking foundation was to be considered as an undertaking by virtue of its controlling shareholding in a banking company.[102] The Court held that the mere fact of holding shares, even a controlling shareholding, is insufficient to characterize the shareholder as an 'undertaking' carrying on an economic activity, if it gives rise simply to the normal rights of a shareholder such as the right to receive dividends. On the other hand a controlling shareholder which is involved directly or indirectly in the management of the company must be regarded as participating in the economic activity carried on by the controlled undertaking, and must therefore itself also be regarded as an undertaking within Article 87(1).[103] **2.24**

Public undertakings. Provided that the undertaking carries on an economic activity, it makes no difference whether it is privately or publicly owned. Article 87(1) thus applies equally to aid granted to a public undertaking,[104] or to a private undertaking funded through State resources.[105] The Court has emphasized that, in accordance with Article 86(1), the competition rules apply without distinction to public and private undertakings.[106] That does not prevent the particular characteristics of the beneficiary from being taken into account in determining whether the transaction would have occurred under normal market conditions.[107] In addition, where the undertaking performs tasks of general interest, compensation for those tasks may fall outside Article 87(1),[108] or the provisions of Article 86(2) may apply.[109] **2.25**

Benefits to individuals. Article 87(1) does not apply to benefits to individuals or private households. Thus a grant to a private consumer is not *per se* aid.[110] But an undertaking may still benefit from such a grant even where the direct recipient is **2.26**

[100] Case C-222/04 *Ministero dell'Economia e delle Finanze v Cassa di Risparmio di Firenze* [2006] ECR I-289, paras 120–1.

[101] Decision in Case N 478/2004 *Coras Iompair Eireann* (7 June 2006), paras 24–34.

[102] Case C-222/04 *Ministero dell'Economia e delle Finanze v Cassa di Risparmio di Firenze* [2006] ECR I-289.

[103] ibid, paras 111–13.

[104] See eg Cases C-34–38/01 *Enirisorse v Ministero delle Finanze* [2003] ECR I-14243.

[105] See eg Case C-237/04 *Enirisorse v Sotacarbo* [2006] ECR I-2843, paras 32–3.

[106] Cases T-228 and 233/99 *Westdeutsche Landesbank v Commission* [2003] ECR II-435, paras 193 and 266.

[107] ibid, para 270.

[108] See paras 2.63–2.75 below.

[109] Cases T-228 and 233/99 *Westdeutsche Landesbank v Commission* [2003] ECR II-435, para 273 and see Chapter 3 below.

[110] See eg Decision in Case N 142/2005 *Low Carbon Car Grant Programme* (26 April 2006), section 3.1.

an individual. As the Court has noted, that is implicit in Article 87(2)(a), from which it follows that aid having a social character granted to individual consumers is capable of coming within the scope of Article 87(1).[111] It follows that benefits to individuals may be considered State aids where the measure procures an indirect advantage to specific undertakings. The following paragraphs address specific examples of this principle.

2.27 **Employees.** Benefits to workers provided under general employment legislation, such as general social security schemes for redundancy benefits and early retirement pensions, are not to be regarded as State aid within the meaning of Article 87(1) insofar as the benefit is provided directly to the employee without involving the undertakings concerned. In the *Danish bus* case, the Court applied the same principle to bonus payments to State employees seconded to Combus, to compensate them for the transfer of their status to contractual employees of Combus as part of its privatization. Accordingly, the payments were not State aid.[112] However a payment to employees which relieves an undertaking of costs which it would otherwise have had to bear will constitute an advantage within the meaning of Article 87(1). This will normally be the case for any wage subsidy, since in principle the wages and allowances payable to an undertaking's employees are regarded as part of the undertaking's normal operating costs.[113] Thus in *Steenkolenmijnen* the Court scrutinized a German proposal to grant mine-workers a tax-free shift bonus, to be paid by the undertakings by deduction from tax paid on wages. While the measure proposed did not involve any direct financial advantage for the undertakings, it was clear from the circumstances that the bonus would make it possible to avoid an increase in miners' wages, which would have otherwise been necessary in order to prevent the threatened departures of mine-workers to other industries. Therefore, the Court held, the bonus amounted to an indirect wage subsidy, reducing costs which the undertakings would otherwise have had to bear.[114] The same result was reached in *Cockerill Sambre* in relation to transitional supplements paid to employees as compensation for a reduction in their working hours resulting from a collective agreement. The Court held that the measure was State aid, even though such compensation was not required either by law or under the terms of the collective agreement.[115]

[111] Case T-93/02 *Confédération nationale du Crédit Mutuel v Commission ('Livret bleu')* [2005] ECR II-143, para 95.

[112] Case T-157/01 *Danske Busvognmænd v Commission* [2004] ECR II-917, paras 55–7. The measure did not reduce the costs which an undertaking would normally have had to bear: the transfer of employment status was precisely in order to put the company on the same footing as its competitors.

[113] Case T-36/99 *Lenzing* [2004] ECR II-3597, para 146.

[114] Case 30/59 *Steenkolenmijnen v High Authority* [1961] ECR 1, p 29.

[115] Case C-5/01 *Belgium v Commission ('Cockerill Sambre')* [2002] ECR I-11991, paras 37–9. See also Case C-241/94 *France v Commission ('Kimberly Clark')* [1996] ECR I-4551, opinion of AG

Education and training. Traditionally, the view has been taken that assistance provided by the public authorities for education, including vocational training programmes, is not State aid, since the financing of vocational training and retraining is one of the Member States' responsibilities towards the work force.[116] A training programme may also not benefit specific undertakings.[117] But the financing of vocational training programmes might exceptionally amount to State aid where specific training is involved, corresponding to the needs of a particular undertaking, which would otherwise have to be provided at the expense of the employer.[118] A French scheme assisting young students and trainees with air travel costs from the French overseas departments to the French mainland also constituted aid. Although the grants were made directly to the individuals concerned, they favoured air services operating between the French mainland and the overseas departments, and generated additional demand for those services.[119] 2.28

Consumers of specific products. A tax incentive to an individual may constitute State aid where it is conditional on the purchase of a particular product. This was the case for UK grants to support the purchase of low CO_2 cars. Although most of the recipients would be private consumers, the Commission could not exclude the existence of aid at the level of car manufacturers, since it would benefit that sector by comparison with other sectors, and within that sector would benefit manufacturers who produced environmentally friendly cars.[120] Similarly, grants to consumers to subsidize the purchase or rental of digital television equipment have also been considered to be State aid, on the grounds that such grants provide an indirect advantage to the television platform operators and broadcasters, by allowing them to develop their digital audiences.[121] 2.29

Tax incentives for investors. A tax concession conditional on investment in a limited category of undertakings may constitute aid to those undertakings. A German tax concession to taxpayers investing in new companies situated in the 2.30

Jacobs, paras 48–64 (aid for social plan following large-scale redundancies); Case T-36/99 *Lenzing* [2004] ECR II-3597, para 146 (State aid existing in allowing undertaking not to honour instalments repaying wage costs which had been met by the Spanish State fund Fogasa). But cf 24th Report on Competition Policy (1994), p 501: no State aid where payments to employees of a bankrupt company are the result of general scheme which is automatically applicable and has no sectoral effect.

[116] 9th Report on Competition Policy (1979), para 194 and Decision 93/193/EEC *Industrial enterprises in Modane* [1993] OJ L85/22, 23.

[117] See Case C-225/91 *Matra v Commission* [1993] ECR I-3203, paras 29–30.

[118] Decision 91/390/EEC *Saint-Gobain* [1991] OJ L215/11, 12.

[119] Decision in Case NN 25/2005 *Mobility passport* (20 April 2005), para 25; see also similar scheme for Réunion approved in Decision in Case N 656/2006 *Réunion social aid scheme* (4 December 2006), para 17.

[120] Decision in Case N 142/2005 *Low Carbon Car Grant Programme* (26 April 2006).

[121] Decision in Case N 546/2006 *French digital television* (6 December 2006); Decision 2007/374/EC *Digital decoders – Italy* [2007] OJ L147/1 (under appeal in Case T-96/07 *Telecom Italia Media v Commission*).

new German *Länder* or in Berlin, and with no more than 250 employees, was thus held to be aid to those undertakings despite the fact that the investors took independent decisions as to whether to invest.[122] An exemption from a withholding tax on distributions will, likewise, constitute an advantage to the company making the distribution in terms of easier access to risk/debt capital, due to the higher return to investors resulting from the exemption.[123]

2.31 **Indirect aid to second undertaking.** Where aid is granted directly to one undertaking, but also indirectly benefits a second undertaking, both may be brought within the scope of the State aid rules. One example is where the direct aid recipient is granted the aid on condition that it provides an advantage (in the form of finance, services, premises, etc) to another undertaking or defined group of undertakings.[124] In the *Verlipack* case the Belgian public authorities had granted a loan to a German company, Heye-Glas, to enable that company to make substantial investments in Verlipack, including the recapitalization of two of Verlipack's plants. The CFI upheld the Commission's decision that, given the strict financial allocation clauses of the loan, Heye was obliged to pass on the funds to Verlipack, and Verlipack was therefore the true recipient of the aid.[125] Another example of indirect aid is *Netherlands v Commission*[126] and *Kuwait Petroleum v Commission*,[127] where the ECJ and CFI respectively upheld a decision of the Commission concerning a Dutch subsidy to petrol stations situated within a certain radius from the German border to compensate them for the loss of market share due to the lower excise duty levied in Germany. Although the subsidy to individual petrol station dealers was covered by the *de minimis* notice, the Commission had found that it also constituted indirect State aid in favour of those oil companies that had agreed (in their contracts with dealers) to reimburse the dealers any discount they offered to prevent loss of market share. In such cases, the cumulative effect of the advantage that each oil company drew from the petrol stations linked to it risked exceeding the *de minimis* threshold; that indirect aid therefore fell within Article 87(1). The ECJ in the *Netherlands* case (whose judgment was followed by the CFI

[122] C-156/98 *Germany v Commission* [2000] ECR I-6857. See also Case T-308/00 *Salzgitter v Commission* [2004] ECR II-1933, paras 38–41; this part of the judgment approved on appeal in Case C-408/04 P *Commission v Salzgitter* (judgment of 22 April 2008), para 109. Note, however, that cases of this nature must be carefully reasoned: see Case T-34/02 *EURL Le Levant 001 v Commission* [2006] ECR II-267, paras 118–20, regarding the absence of explanation concerning an aid to investors in a cruise vessel which was said to confer a competitive advantage on the undertaking managing that vessel.

[123] Decision 2006/940/EC *1929 holding companies* [2006] OJ L366/47.

[124] Decision 2000/625/EC *Sea transport of Irish livestock* [2000] OJ L263/17, para 71.

[125] Case C-457/00 *Belgium v Commission ('Verlipack')* [2003] ECR I-6931, paras 52–61. See also Decision 2000/625/EC *Sea transport of Irish livestock* [2000] OJ L263/17, paras 71–3 (aid provided directly to Gaelic Ferries, but beneficiaries held to be the Irish livestock operators).

[126] Case C-382/99 *Netherlands v Commission* [2002] ECR I-5163.

[127] Case T-354/99 *Kuwait Petroleum v Commission* [2006] ECR II-1475.

in *Kuwait Petroleum*) agreed: the subsidy mitigated the burden of those obligations, where they existed. It was immaterial that the Member State was not party to the contracts and did not even know the extent to which they existed.[128]

Transfer of assets of undertaking affected by aid. An undertaking may also be an indirect aid beneficiary where it acquires assets from the recipient of aid.[129] The same applies in relation to the acquisition of the beneficiary undertaking itself. The question in both cases is whether the purchaser receives an advantage that it would not have obtained under normal market conditions.[130] Thus where an aid beneficiary has been sold following an open tender under non-discriminatory competitive conditions and at a market price, the purchaser cannot be regarded as having benefited from an advantage in relation to other operators. In such a case, the purchase price reflects the consequences of the previous aid, and the benefit of the aid is retained by the seller.[131] **2.32**

3. Private investor and private creditor tests

Origins of principle. One of the earliest statements of the principle behind the private investor test was made by Advocate General Slynn in the *Van der Kooy* case, where he commented that: **2.33**

> It is of the essence of a State aid that it is non-commercial in the sense that the State steps in where the market would not. The State may have its reasons for doing so but they are not commercial in the ordinary sense of the word. Thus the State may subscribe for shares in a company or lend money, but when it does so to an extent or on terms which would not be acceptable to the commercial investor, it is granting aid which falls within Article [87] if the tests of that provision are satisfied.[132]

It follows from that principle that where the State *does* act on terms which would be acceptable to a commercial actor, Article 87(1) is not engaged. This is also required by the principle of equal treatment as between private and public undertakings.[133]

---

128 Case C-382/99 *Netherlands v Commission* [2002] ECR I-5163, paras 55–68.

129 For an unusual fact situation see Decision in Case NN 8/2007 *Financing of workforce reduction measures of RTVE* (7 March 2007), where the State public broadcaster RTVE was restructured, with the result that aid directly received by the old RTVE ultimately favoured the new RTVE.

130 Cases T-127, 129 and 148/99 *Diputación Foral de Álava v Commission* [2002] ECR II-1275, paras 134–8 (sale of assets); Case C-390/98 *Banks v Coal Authority* [2001] ECR I-6117, para 77 (sale of undertaking).

131 *Banks*, ibid, paras 77–8; Case C-277/00 *Germany v Commission* [2004] ECR I-3925, para 80; Cases C-328/99 and C-399/00 *Italy v Commission* [2003] ECR I-4035, para 83. The consequence is that the aid must be recovered from the seller: see paras 16.98–16.101 below for a discussion of this and related problems of recovery.

132 Cases 67, 68 and 70/85 *Van der Kooy v Commission* [1988] ECR 219, p 251.

133 Case C-303/88 *Italy v Commission* [1991] ECR I-1433, paras 19–20; Case C-261/89 *Italy v Commission* [1991] ECR I-4437, para 15; Case C-358/94 *Air France v Commission* [1996] ECR II-2109, 70; Case T-296/97 *Alitalia v Commission ('Alitalia I')* [2000] ECR II-3871, para 80; Cases T-127, 129 and 148/99 *Diputación Foral de Álava v Commission* [2002] ECR II-1275, para 100.

2.34 **Basic principle.** The reasoning above has developed into a principle which is used to determine whether a benefit or advantage has been conferred through State intervention in the market. In broad terms, the question is whether the apparent advantage is one which would or could have been obtained from a commercial actor, or market economy operator, acting with a view to obtaining a normal return. The early use by the Court of the principle concerned capital investments.[134] In such cases, the Court has held that it is necessary to compare the conduct of the State with a private investor (or 'market economy investor' hence the frequent reference to this test as the 'market economy investor principle' or 'MEIP'). In other situations, however, where the State acts not as an investor but as a creditor, a private investor comparison will not be appropriate; rather, the correct comparison is with a 'private creditor'. That analysis has neither the same meaning nor the same function as the private investor test,[135] and requires quite different considerations to be taken into account.[136] The discussion below therefore considers separately the private investor and private creditor tests. Sections 4 to 6 below address the application of the broad principle to other examples of commercial action by the State.

(a) Private investor test (or 'MEIP')

2.35 **Private investor test.** A capital injection by the State or public authorities cannot be regarded as State aid where a private investor operating under normal market conditions would have made the investment.[137] In considering that question, it is necessary to consider whether, in similar circumstances, a private investor of a size

[134] See for example Case 234/84 *Belgium v Commission* 1986 ECR 2263, paras 9–18; Case C-301/87 *France v Commission ('Boussac')* [1990] ECR I-307, paras 38–9; Case C-142/87 *Belgium v Commission ('Tubemeuse')* [1990] ECR I-959, paras 22–9; Case C-305/89 *Italy v Commission ('Alfa Romeo')* [1991] ECR I-1603, paras 17–24.

[135] See comments of AG Poiares Maduro in Case C-276/02 *Spain v Commission* [2004] ECR I-8091, opinion para 25.

[136] C-342/96 *Spain v Commission* ('*Tubacex*') [1999] ECR I-2459, para 46; Case C-256/97 *DMT* [1999] ECR I-3913, opinion of AG Jacobs, para 35 ('both the private investor and a private creditor test are essentially a private market test. It is, in my view, useful to draw the closest comparison possible, which in this case would be with a private creditor and the terms that creditor might offer to a customer-debtor finding itself in financial difficulties'). Drawing a clear line is difficult in some cases where the State acts both as an investor and as a creditor: Case T-152/99 *Hijos de Andrés Molina v Commission* [2002] ECR II-3049. In that case capitalization of the undertaking's debt to the State was assessed under the private investor test, but the Court pointed out at para 167 that the correct comparator in relation to the remission of debt was a private creditor seeking to obtain repayment.

[137] Case C-142/87 *Belgium v Commission* [1990] ECR I-959, paras 22–9; Case C-303/88 *Italy v Commission ('ENI-Lanerossi')* [1991] ECR I-1433, paras 20–4; Case C-305/89 *Italy v Commission ('Alfa Romeo')* [1991] ECR I-1603, paras 19–20; Case T-358/94 *Air France v Commission* [1996] ECR II-2109, para 70; Case T-11/95 *BP Chemicals v Commission* [1998] ECR II-3235, para 116; Cases C-328/99 and C-399/00 *Italy and SIM 2 Multimedia v Commission* [2003] ECR I-4035, para 38.

comparable to the public body in question would have provided capital of such an amount.[138] Another way of putting the same question is to ask whether a private investor would have entered the transaction on the same terms and, if not, on what conditions he might have done so.[139] In making that analysis, it has to be assumed that the private investor has the same information on the financial situation of the undertaking as that available to the public authorities.[140] The foreseeable developments in the market must also be taken into account.[141] A measure may not be regarded as State aid simply because, with the benefit of hindsight, the investment was not a prudent one. Rather, the economic rationality of the State's conduct must be determined in the context of the period during which the measures were actually taken.[142]

Long-term profitability.[143] A private investor would normally seek to achieve the maximum return possible on the investment.[144] But that does not mean that the behaviour of the State must necessarily be compared with that of a private investor seeking to realize a profit in the short term. Where the State is already a shareholder in the undertaking, it is appropriate to compare its investment to that of a private holding company or private group of undertakings pursuing a structural policy, and guided by prospects of profitability in the longer term.[145] Thus just as a private shareholder might reasonably subscribe capital necessary to secure the survival of an undertaking which is experiencing temporary difficulties but is capable of becoming profitable again, possibly after a reorganization, a State-owned parent or holding company may also temporarily bear the losses of a subsidiary in order to **2.36**

[138] Case C-305/89 *Italy v Commission ('Alfa Romeo')* [1991] ECR I-1603, para 19; Case T-234/95 *DSG v Commission* [2000] ECR II-2603, para 119; Case T-296/97 *Alitalia v Commission ('Alitalia I')* [2000] ECR II-3871, para 96; Cases T-228 and 233/99 *Westdeutsche Landesbank v Commission* [2003] ECR II-435, para 245.

[139] Case T-16/96 *Cityflyer Express v Commission* [1998] ECR II-757, para 51; *Westdeutsche Landesbank v Commission*, ibid, para 245.

[140] Case C-482/99 *France v Commission ('Stardust Marine')* [2002] ECR I-4397, para 70; Case C-457/00 *Belgium v Commission ('Verlipack')* [2003] ECR I-6931, para 47.

[141] *Stardust Marine*, ibid, para 70; Cases T-228 and 233/99 *Westdeutsche Landesbank v Commission* [2003] ECR II-435, para 246; Cases C-328/99 and C-399/00 *Italy v Commission* [2003] ECR I-4035, paras 38 and 40.

[142] *Stardust Marine*, ibid, para 71. The Court went on to find that the Commission had incorrectly taken as its point of reference a period later than the period during which the aid was actually granted: paras 72–81.

[143] Many cases concern the restructuring of an unprofitable undertaking. However it should be noted that the private investor principle applies equally to investments in profitable undertakings: Cases T-228 and 233/99 *Westdeutsche Landesbank v Commission* [2003] ECR II-435, paras 208–14.

[144] *Westdeutsche Landesbank v Commission*, ibid, para 314.

[145] Case C-305/89 *Italy v Commission ('Alfa Romeo')* [1991] ECR I-1603, para 20; Case C-42/93 *Spain v Commission* [1994] ECR I-4175, para 14; Case C-256/97 *DMT* [1999] ECR I-3913, para 24; Case T-234/95 *DSG v Commission* [2000] ECR II-2603, para 120; Case T-296/97 *Alitalia v Commission ('Alitalia I')* [2000] ECR II-3871, paras 84 and 96.

enable the subsidiary to close down under the best possible conditions.[146] In such circumstances the decisions of the State holding company may also legitimately take into account considerations such as a desire to protect the group's image or to redirect its activities.[147] However if an injection of capital by a public investor disregards any prospect of profitability, even in the long term, it is liable to be regarded as aid.[148] The Court has thus held that the Commission was entitled to find a capitalization operation to be aid where the beneficiary's financial situation, particularly its volume of debt, was such that a normal return on the investment could not be expected within a reasonable period of time, and where there was no reliable restructuring plan which would enable the undertaking to regain viability.[149]

2.37 **Evidence of actual private investor.** It is not necessary to show that an actual private investor has in fact participated in the capital of the undertaking in question. But where, at the same time as the public investment, a significant capital contribution is made by an independent private investor in comparable circumstances, that is good evidence that the private investor test is satisfied.[150] This 'concomitance test' does not apply, however, to investments made by employees of the beneficiary undertaking. In *Alitalia* it was argued that a recapitalization of the airline by the Italian State financing company IRI was not State aid on the grounds, *inter alia*, that the company's employees had agreed to take shares in Alitalia in exchange for wage freezes. The Court held that the Commission had been right to reject that argument. The employees' participation was motivated by the desire to keep their jobs and ensure the survival of Alitalia. That was not comparable to the conduct of a private investor, which would be guided by the prospects of profitability of the investment.[151] The concomitance test is also inapplicable where private investments have been influenced by State declarations of support for the company in question.[152]

2.38 **Assessment of series of investments.** Where a public undertaking has made capital injections into a subsidiary which are classified as aid, that does not automatically mean that a later capital injection will also be aid. It is necessary to consider, in particular, the chronology of the investments and whether the later

---

[146] Case C-303/88 *Italy v Commission ('ENI-Lanerossi')* [1991] ECR I-1433, para 21; Cases T-126-127/96 *BFM and EFIM v Commission* [1998] ECR II-3437, para 80.

[147] *Italy v Commission ('ENI-Lanerossi')*, ibid, para 21.

[148] ibid, para 22; Cases T-126-127/96 *BFM and EFIM v Commission* [1998] ECR II-3437, para 80; Case T-234/95 *DSG v Commission* [2000] ECR II-2603, para 121.

[149] Case T-152/99 *Hisjos de Andrés Molina v Commission* [2002] ECR II-3049, paras 130–2.

[150] Case T-296/97 *Alitalia v Commission ('Alitalia I')* [2000] ECR II-3871, para 81.

[151] ibid, paras 82–4.

[152] Decision 2006/621/EC *France Télécom* [2006] OJ L257/11, para 227 (under appeal in Cases T-425 and 444/04 *France and France Télécom v Commission*): see further para 2.44 below.

investment can reasonably be severed from the earlier injections,[153] as well as any other relevant factors as outlined in the next paragraph.

Other factors to take into account. The other relevant factors to be taken into account in determining whether a private investor would have entered the transaction on the same terms will vary from case to case. A mechanical or formal assessment of the facts is not appropriate;[154] rather, if the Commission is examining such a case it is required to make a complete analysis of all factors that are relevant to the transaction at issue and its context. These may include: **2.39**

(a) the situation of the beneficiary undertaking and the relevant market, at the time of the decision to make the specific investment;[155]
(b) the liquidity of the capital which is being contributed;[156]
(c) a comparison may be made between the internal rate of return on the investment and the minimum rate which a private investor would require.[157] In an appropriate case that minimum rate could be based on the average rate of return in the sector concerned.[158] The level of risk of an investment might in some cases, however, require a higher rate of return in other cases; equally an informed private investor might accept a lower rate of return on the basis of economic considerations other than the optimization of his return.[159] Which is the case for a specific transaction will depend upon its individual features.

Distinction between State as investor and State as public authority. Only the obligations that the State would have to assume as owner of the share capital of a company may be taken into account in considering whether a private investor would have chosen to make an investment rather than allowing the liquidation of an undertaking. Thus the State may not rely on social costs such as the cost of redundancies and payment of unemployment benefits, which do not devolve on the State as a shareholder but are incurred by the State as a public authority.[160] **2.40**

---

[153] Case T-11/95 *BP Chemicals v Commission* [1998] ECR II-3235, paras 170–1.

[154] cf Cases C-329/93, C-62/95 and C-63/95 *Germany v Commission* [1996] ECR I-5151, para 36 in the context of a State guarantee.

[155] Case T-11/95 *BP Chemicals v Commission* [1998] ECR II-3235, para 171; Cases T-228 and 233/99 *Westdeutsche Landesbank v Commission* [2003] ECR II-435, para 251.

[156] Cases T-228 and 233/99 *Westdeutsche Landesbank v Commission* [2003] ECR II-435, paras 328–9, holding that a private investor could not expect the same return on non-liquid funds as it would for liquid capital.

[157] Case T-296/97 *Alitalia v Commission ('Alitalia I')* [2000] ECR II-3871, paras 98–100. However the Court went on to annul the Commission's decision on the basis that it had made errors of assessment and reasoning in fixing the minimum and internal rates, on the basis of which the assessment under the private investor test was made. The new decision was subsequently upheld by the Court: Case T-301/01 *Alitalia v Commission ('Alitalia II')* (judgment of 9 July 2008).

[158] Cases T-228 and 233/99 *Westdeutsche Landesbank v Commission* [2003] ECR II-435, para 254.

[159] ibid, para 270.

[160] Case C-278/92 *Spain v Commission* [1994] ECR I-4103, para 22; Decision 2008/722/EC *OTE voluntary retirement scheme* [2008] OJ L243/7, paras 85–6.

(b) Applications of the private investor test

2.41 **Loans.** While the paradigm application of the private investor test still remains that of a capital investment by the State, the test has also been applied to loans by public authorities.[161] In most cases where a 'soft loan' is granted on preferential terms, for example as to interest, the aid element of a loan is the difference between the interest rate which the undertaking should have paid[162] and the rate actually paid. In such a case it will only be necessary to repay the interest differential.[163] But in an extreme case, where an unsecured loan is given to a company which under normal circumstances would have been entirely unable to obtain finance (for example because its prospects of repaying the loan are very poor) then the Commission has stated that the loan effectively equates to a grant payment. Repayment may therefore be ordered in respect of the entirety of the loan.[164]

2.42 **Guarantees: existence of advantage.** The private investor test also applies to the grant of a State guarantee where the State does not receive an appropriate premium for that guarantee. Even if no payments are ever made by the State under the guarantee, the guarantee enables the borrower to obtain better financial terms for a loan than those normally available on the financial markets.[165] In some circumstances, the guarantee may also amount to aid to the lender, for example where a guarantee is given *ex post* in respect of a loan, without the terms of the loan being adjusted.[166] As with any application of the private investor principle, the assessment of whether an individual case satisfies the test may be complex and require consideration of a number of factual and economic issues.[167] In order to simplify this exercise, the Commission's Notice on State guarantees states that the

[161] Where the issue is the initial grant of a loan and the terms on which it is made. Where the question concerns the later rescheduling or waiver of the debt, the comparator is with a private creditor: see below at paras 2.45–2.49.

[162] Which will be dependent on its financial position and the security which it can offer.

[163] See eg Case T-16/96 *Cityflyer v Commission* [1998] ECR II-757, paras 53–6.

[164] See eg Case T-234/95 *DSG* [2000] ECR II-2603, para 184; Case C-457/00 *Belgium v Commission ('Verlipack')* [2003] ECR I-6931.

[165] Commission Notice on the application of Articles 87 and 88 of the EC Treaty to State aid in the form of guarantees ('Notice on State guarantees') [2008] OJ C155/10, as corrected [2008] OJ C244/32, sections 2.1–2.2. There may also be aid where the State does not act as a rational creditor in securing repayment of any amount it has to settle under the guarantee agreement. That question is separate from the issue of whether the guarantee itself is aid (Case T-318/00 *Freistaat Thüringen v Commission* [2005] ECR II-4179, para 126), and the comparator is a private creditor.

[166] Notice on State guarantees, section 2.3; and see Decision 2001/89/EC *Crédit Foncier* [2001] OJ L34/36, para 50.

[167] See eg Cases C-329/93, C-62/95 and C-63/95 *Germany v Commission* [1996] ECR I-5151, where the central issue was the difference between the stock market price of shares purchased with the assistance of a guarantee, and the (higher) actual purchase price paid. The Court held at para 33 that the stock market price of the shares could not be decisive, and other relevant factors included the past movement of that price, the intrinsic worth of the undertaking, the additional value which may have been contributed by the block of shares, the inside information the parties to the agreement had on the market in question and on the situation of the competing undertakings, and the

Commission will not consider a State guarantee to be an aid if the borrower is not in financial difficulty, a 'market-oriented' price for the guarantee is paid, and the guarantee is linked to a specific financial transaction, is for a fixed maximum amount and limited in time, and does not cover more than 80% of the outstanding loan.[168] Where the borrower is a small or medium-sized enterprise (SME), the strict condition of a 'market-oriented' price for the guarantee is not applied; instead the Commission will consider whether the guarantee involves aid or not by reference to the annual premium charged by the State, based on the rating of the borrower.[169] The Notice on State guarantees also sets out the conditions under which the Commission rules out the presence of aid in guarantee schemes (as opposed to ad hoc guarantees).[170]

Guarantees: valuation of advantage. Where a guarantee does not comply with the private investor principle it will entail State aid, if the other conditions of Article 87(1) are satisfied (which will normally be the case). However it may be difficult to establish the extent of the 'advantage' conferred by a guarantee, and hence the amount of aid repayable. For individual guarantees, the amount of aid is normally calculated as the difference between the market price of the guarantee and the price actually paid. Where the market does not provide guarantees for the type of transaction concerned, the aid element is calculated in the same way as the grant equivalent of a 'soft loan', ie the difference between the market interest rate for the loan without a guarantee, and the interest rate obtained by the borrowing company with the benefit of the guarantee.[171] **2.43**

France Télécom. The *France Télécom* case[172] illustrates the difficult questions that may arise in the field of guarantees and loans. Following France Télécom's financial crisis in 2002, the French government made several undertakings to support the company. Subsequently, a recovery plan was adopted which included the announcement by the government of a shareholder loan in the form of a €9 billion **2.44**

forecasts of how the share price would develop, having regard in particular to the situation of the market on which the undertaking operated.

168 Notice on State guarantees, section 3.2. The similar criteria in the earlier (2000) version of this Notice were applied in Decision in Case N 131/2006 *Netherlands 'Growth Facility' guarantee scheme* (12 October 2006), and Decision 2008/281/EC *TVO guarantee* [2008] OJ L89/15.

169 See Notice on State guarantees, section 3.3. The other conditions referred to in section 3.2 of the Notice must, however, still be satisfied.

170 ibid, sections 3.4–3.5.

171 ibid, section 4.2; and see section 4.3 on the calculation for SMEs, and sections 4.4–4.5 on guarantee schemes. Some case-law suggests that where the State guarantee enables a borrower to obtain a loan which it could not otherwise have obtained at all, the entire amount of the loan may be regarded as aid, regardless of whether the interest rate charged for the loan was normal on the capital market: Case C-288/96 *Germany v Commission* [2000] ECR I-8237, paras 30–1 and 40–1.

172 Decision 2006/621/EC *France Télécom* [2006] OJ L257/11 (under appeal in Cases T-425 and 444/04 *France and France Télécom v Commission*).

credit line. Although the loan agreement was ultimately never signed or implemented, the Commission considered that it constituted State aid, since a private investor would not have made a similar announcement of credit at that time without a thorough audit of the company's financial situation. Nor could reliance be placed on the subsequent successful (private) recapitalization, since the market was by then 'contaminated' by the State declarations of support.[173] However, recovery was not ordered in view of the novelty of the Commission's analysis, and because quantification of the aid was too difficult.[174]

(c) Private creditor test

2.45 **Private creditor test.** Where the State's relationship to the undertaking is that of a creditor, rather than an investor, the decisive test is whether the advantage to the undertaking is more favourable than that which would be granted, under similar conditions, by a private creditor to a debtor undertaking.[175] There is an advantage within Article 87(1) if the undertaking would manifestly have been unable to obtain comparable facilities from a private creditor in the same situation as the public body in question.[176] As with the private investor, the comparator private creditor must be assumed to be in the same situation as the public body in question.[177] If the public body enjoys special rights or guarantees, or its debts are preferential debts, these are factors to be taken into account.[178] In particular, in such a case, it is not appropriate to draw a comparison with private creditors who do not enjoy such advantages and who may therefore agree to less favourable repayment terms.[179]

2.46 **Long-term minimization of losses.** It must be assumed that a private creditor is an efficient economic operator[180] who would aim to recover the sum due or minimize his losses rather than passively allowing debt to build up. If the most effective way of recovering the debt is to allow an undertaking to go into liquidation, it must be assumed that the private creditor would not seek to prevent that outcome.[181] But the public authorities are entitled to take a long-term view and are not expected to demand that a company be declared insolvent as soon as it fails. It is quite conceivable that a private creditor, with significant resources at its

---

173 ibid, para 227.

174 See further para 16.107 below.

175 Case C-256/97 *DMT* [1999] ECR I-3913, para 25; Case C-276/02 *Spain v Commission* [2004] ECR II-8091, opinion of AG Poiares Maduro at para 24.

176 Case T-46/97 *SIC v Commission* [2000] ECR II-2125, para 95.

177 Case C-256/97 *DMT* [1999] ECR I-3913, opinion of AG Jacobs at para 36.

178 Case T-152/99 *Hijos de Andrés Molina v Commission* [2002] ECR II-3049, para 135.

179 Case T-36/99 *Lenzing* [2004] ECR II-3597, paras 155–6.

180 See Case C-276/02 *Spain v Commission* [2004] ECR II-8091, opinion of AG Poiares Maduro at para 36.

181 Case C-256/97 *DMT* [1999] ECR I-3913, opinion of AG Jacobs at para 36.

disposal, might have an interest in maintaining the activity of a debtor undertaking for a certain period, if the cost of immediate liquidation would be higher than the cost of granting aid.[182] Conversely, however, it is not acceptable for public authorities to allow debts to be run up over long periods without the slightest prospect of improvement.[183]

Other factors to take into account. As with the private investor test, the factors to be taken into account in applying the private creditor test will vary from case to case. Without setting out an exhaustive list, the cases suggest that the following considerations are relevant, in addition to those set out in the foregoing two paragraphs: **2.47**

(a) whether the arrangements were negotiated at arm's length;[184]
(b) the nature and extent of any security held by the creditor;[185]
(c) whether the measure will contribute to making the undertaking economically viable and improving its long-term financial position;[186]
(d) whether the State can rely on the recovery of the debts owed to it within a reasonable period;[187]
(e) whether the settlement enables the State to avoid the uncertainty of litigation;[188] and
(f) the amount the creditor would receive in the event of liquidation.[189]

(d) Applications of the private creditor test

Arrangements to repay debts. The private creditor test is typically applied in the case of late payment facilities granted by the State. In such a case, the fact that the State has charged interest or imposed penalties in respect of the payments does not automatically undo the advantage gained by the undertaking. The litmus test remains whether, taking all the circumstances into account, the facilities would have been granted by a private creditor.[190] The private creditor test was also applied **2.48**

[182] Case C-480/98 *Spain v Commission ('Magefesa')* [2000] ECR I-8717, opinion of AG Mischo at paras 35–6; Case C-276/02 *Spain v Commission* [2004] ECR II-8091, opinion of AG Poiares Maduro, para 39. See also generally Decision 2005/407/EC *British Energy* [2005] OJ L142/26.

[183] *Spain v Commission ('Magefesa')*, ibid, opinion of AG Mischo at para 37.

[184] Decision 2005/407/EC *British Energy* [2005] OJ L142/26, para 258.

[185] Case T-152/99 *Hijos de Andrés Molina v Commission* [2002] ECR II-3049, para 168.

[186] ibid, para 168; Case C-276/02 *Spain v Commission* [2004] ECR II-8091, opinion of AG Poiares Maduro, para 40.

[187] *Spain v Commission*, ibid, opinion of AG Poires Maduro, para 40.

[188] Case T-46/97 *SIC v Commission* [2000] ECR II-2125, para 99.

[189] Case T-152/99 *Hijos de Andrés Molina v Commission* [2002] ECR II-3049, para 168, noting that if it transpired that, in the event of liquidation, the undertaking's assets would be sufficient only to cover mortgage and preferential claims, ordinary claims would have no value, so that acceptance by an ordinary creditor of the cancellation of a major part of its claim would not really be a sacrifice.

[190] Case C-256/97 *DMT* [1999] ECR I-3913, paras 20–5; Case T-46/97 *SIC v Commission* [2000] ECR II-2125, para 95; Case T-36/99 *Lenzing* [2004] ECR II-3597, para 139.

in the *Tubacex* case where a public body, Fogasa, gave workers unpaid salary in the event of the insolvency of their employer, and then concluded repayment agreements with the relevant undertakings. The Commission had used the comparator of a private investor granting a loan. The Court held, however, that the correct comparator was that of a private creditor which seeks to recover sums due to it, and to that end concludes agreements with the debtor to reschedule the debts or to arrange repayment by instalments.[191] Equally, when assessing a price reduction granted on the sale of assets, which had the effect of reducing the buyer's debts to the public seller, the appropriate comparator is a private creditor seeking to obtain payment, rather than a private investor seeking long-term profit from the transaction.[192]

2.49 **Waiver of debts.** In an extreme case, where the indebtedness of an undertaking means that a debt (such as that arising from a loan or the calling of a guarantee) cannot be repaid at all, it may be reasonable for the State as creditor to extinguish the debt, or convert it to equity.[193] If the circumstances are such that the measure produces no real advantage to the undertaking, there is no aid. On the other hand there might be aid if there is evidence that the State never genuinely intended the debt to be repaid, or has not conducted itself like a rational economic operator in taking all possible steps to obtain repayment.[194]

4. Land sales

2.50 **Requirement for market price.** The sale of land by a public authority at an undervalue constitutes aid in the sense of a benefit or advantage, and will fall within Article 87(1) if the other conditions of that Article are satisfied. In order to determine whether there is aid, it is therefore necessary to determine whether the price is lower than the price which would have been paid under normal market conditions.[195] If a market price is paid, no element of aid will exist. If a lower price is paid, there will be aid equal to the difference between what the purchaser in fact paid, and what it would have had to pay in an arm's length transaction on the open market to buy an equivalent property from a private vendor, at the time of the transaction.[196]

---

[191] Case C-342/96 *Spain v Commission* ('*Tubacex*') [1999] ECR I-2459, para 46.

[192] Case T-198/01 *Technische Glaswerke Ilmenau v Commission* [2004] ECR II-2717, para 99 (upheld on appeal in Case C-404/04 P *Technische Glaswerke Ilmenau v Commission*).

[193] Case T-110/97 *Kneissl Dachstein Sportartikel v Commission* [1999] ECR II-2881, paras 119–20; Case T-123/97 *Salomon v Commission* [1999] ECR II-2925, paras 63–4 and Decision in Case N 472/2007 *Restructuring aid to Compel Rail* (2 April 2008).

[194] Case T-318/00 *Freistaat Thüringen v Commission* [2005] ECR II-4179, para 126.

[195] Case T-274/01 *Valmont v Commission* [2004] ECR II-3145, para 45; second judgment in Case T-366/00 *Scott v Commission* [2007] ECR II-797, para 93.

[196] *Scott v Commission*, ibid, para 105.

'Safe harbour' conditions. The Commission's 1997 Communication on land sales[197] sets out a procedure allowing Member States to handle such sales in a way that ensures that the normal market price is paid, and thus precludes the existence of aid. For that 'safe harbour' to apply, either the sale must follow an unconditional bidding procedure, or the sale must be at a market value established by independent valuers. 2.51

Unconditional bidding procedure. No aid will exist if the sale of land and buildings follows a sufficiently well publicized, open and unconditional bidding procedure, comparable to an auction, accepting the best or only bid. In such a case the sale is by definition at market value, even if a prior valuation suggested a different price.[198] An offer is regarded as sufficiently well publicized where it is repeatedly advertised over period of two months or more in the national press, estate gazettes or other appropriate publications, and through estate agents addressing a broad range of potential buyers. Sales of land and buildings which may attract international investors should be advertised in publications with a regular international circulation, and through estate agents with international clients.[199] In order for the sale to be unconditional, the buyer must be free to use the land for his own purposes. That does not, however, exclude planning restrictions, or restrictions imposed for the prevention of public nuisance, environmental protection, or to avoid purely speculative bids.[200] If any other special conditions are imposed on the sale, it is only regarded as unconditional if all potential buyers would have to and would be able to meet those obligations.[201] 2.52

Independent valuation. If such an unconditional bidding procedure is not used, then an independent valuation should be carried out by one or more independent asset valuers[202] prior to the sale negotiations, in order to establish the market value[203] on the basis of generally accepted market indicators and valuation standards. The market price thus established is the minimum purchase price that can be agreed without granting State aid.[204] If that market value cannot be obtained 2.53

[197] Communication on State aid elements in sales of land and buildings by public authorities (Communication on land sales) [1997] OJ C209/3.

[198] ibid, point II.1.

[199] ibid, point II.1(a).

[200] ibid, point II.1(b).

[201] ibid, point II.1(c).

[202] An asset valuer must be a person of good repute who has obtained an appropriate degree or equivalent qualification, and must have suitable experience and be competent in valuing land and buildings in the location and of the category of the asset in question: Communication on land sales, point II.2(a).

[203] Defined as the price at which the land and buildings could be sold under private contract between a willing seller and an arm's length buyer on the date of valuation, assuming that the property is publicly exposed to the market, that market conditions permit orderly disposal, and that a normal period is available for the negotiation of the sale: ibid, point II.2(a).

[204] ibid, point II.2(a).

after reasonable efforts to sell the land, the price may be reduced by up to 5%. If this still does not allow a sale, a new valuation may be carried out to take account of the offers received.[205] Special obligations relating to the land may be attached to the sale provided that every potential buyer is required and able to fulfil them; these may be taken into account in determining the market value of the land.[206]

2.54 **Subsequent valuations.** Failure to satisfy the above conditions will not automatically render the transaction State aid. The key question is still whether the sale price paid was a market price.[207] That must be established by the most reliable method possible: failure to carry out a sufficiently careful valuation may render a State aid decision liable to annulment.[208] If an expert valuation report is relied upon, it must be based on objective evidence rather than on unsubstantiated assertions.[209] The fact that a subsequent valuation report suggests a price higher than the sale price does not automatically mean that the transaction involved State aid, particularly given the uncertain and retrospective nature of such a valuation.[210] Rather, it is necessary to determine whether the sale price deviates sufficiently from the valuation to justify a finding that there was a benefit to the purchaser.[211] Where a number of subsequent reports are available, it is necessary to consider the range of prices given in the reports. In *Diputación Foral de Álava* the CFI annulled part of a Commission decision concerning aid elements in the sale of a plot of land, on the basis that it arbitrarily took as a definitive market price the valuation in only one of the four available reports, which it verified by reference to the average value of the ranges given in the other three report. The correct approach was to look at the four reports as a whole, three of which confirmed the sale price to be a market price, or within the range of reasonable prices for the plot.[212]

2.55 **Payment conditions.** Independent of the sale price of land sold by a public undertaking, the circumstances of payment by the private purchaser may amount to aid where the payment conditions do not correspond to those which would be imposed by a private vendor. A proper analysis of this question must be carried out in each case: the Court held, for example, that the mere fact that a public undertaking allows the purchaser to occupy land for a number of months without

---

205 ibid, point II.2(b).

206 ibid, point II.2(c).

207 Cases T-127, 129 and 148/99 *Diputación Foral de Álava v Commission* [2002] ECR II-1275, para 85.

208 Second judgment in Case T-366/00 *Scott v Commission* [2007] ECR II-797, in particular paras 108 and 158–9.

209 Case T-274/01 *Valmont v Commission* [2004] ECR II-3145, para 71.

210 See *Valmont v Commission*, ibid, para 45; and second judgment in Case T-366/00 *Scott v Commission* [2007] ECR II-797, para 93.

211 *Valmont v Commission*, ibid, para 45.

212 Cases T-127, 129 and 148/99 *Diputación Foral de Álava v Commission* [2002] ECR II-1275, paras 63–92.

payment does not automatically give rise to State aid, in circumstances where this is justified by legal and practical considerations.[213]

5. Provision of assets or services

Sale or supply of public assets. As with land sales, the sale or provision of other public assets is not regarded as aid where the sale takes place under normal market conditions, but may constitute aid where the assets are supplied or sold at an undervalue or on preferential terms.[214] This principle extends to intangible assets, such as goodwill.[215] In *Van der Kooy* natural gas had been sold to glasshouse growers at a preferential tariff by the company Gasunie, which was controlled by the Netherlands State. The Court held that there was not aid if it were demonstrated that the preferential tariff was, in the context of that market, objectively justified by economic reasons such as the need to withstand competition on the same market from other sources of energy, the price of which was competitive.[216] That statement does not imply, however, a general principle of 'objective justification' on economic grounds where an advantage is conferred on particular operators, whether by sale of assets or otherwise. Rather, as was explained later in *Mauro Alzetta*, the Court was simply applying the established test that, in classifying a measure as State aid, it is necessary to determine whether a private operator would have entered the transaction on the same terms.[217] **2.56**

Provision of services. The provision of services by a public undertaking may constitute State aid if the services in question are provided for free in circumstances where the cost would normally be borne by the undertakings,[218] or where **2.57**

[213] Cases T-127, 129 and 148/99 *Diputación Foral de Álava v Commission* [2002] ECR II-1275, paras 93–108.

[214] Cases C-341-342/06 P *Chronopost v Ufex* (judgment of 1 July 2008), para 123; and see Case T-198/01 *Technische Glaswerke Ilmenau v Commission* [2004] ECR II-2717 (upheld on appeal in Case C-404/04 P *Technische Glaswerke Ilmenau v Commission*). In most cases, the reference point will be the market value of the asset; but in exceptional cases it may be necessary simply to look at the terms offered to other operators: see para 2.11 above.

[215] In Case T-613/97 *Ufex v Commission* [2006] ECR II-1531 the CFI considered that the transfer to Chronopost of the client base of one of La Poste's products was State aid. Its judgment was overruled by the ECJ in Cases C-341-342/06 P *Chronopost v Ufex* (judgment of 1 July 2008), paras 121–32, on the grounds that it had not been demonstrated that the asset had been transferred free of charge, as alleged, and that there was no distortion of competition in any event (see further para 2.58 below). The ECJ did not dispute, however, that the supply of an intangible asset could, in principle, amount to State aid.

[216] Cases 67, 68 and 70/85 *Van der Kooy v Commission* [1988] ECR 219, para 30; see also Case C-56/93 *Belgium v Commission* [1996] ECR I-723, para 10 concerning Gasunie's preferential tariff for nitrate fertilizer producers.

[217] Cases T-298/97 etc *Mauro Alzetta v Commission* [2000] ECR II-2319, para 99.

[218] Case C-126/91 *GEMO* [2003] ECR I-13769, paras 30–3 (free collection of animal carcasses and slaughterhouse waste held to be aid on basis that waste disposal a normal cost of an undertaking).

services are provided at a price lower than would be charged in normal market conditions or otherwise on preferential terms.[219] However, in assessing the 'normal market' price of services provided by a public undertaking it will often not be possible to find an appropriate private comparator: a public undertaking will frequently have resources of a scale which necessarily would not be available to a private undertaking, particularly where it is entrusted with services of general economic interest.

2.58 ***Chronopost*** **cases.** The problem of assessing the market price of services provided by a public undertaking arose in the cases concerning the provision of logistical and commercial assistance by the French monopoly postal service La Poste to its subsidiary Chronopost, which operated on the competitive market for express delivery services. Following a complaint by SFEI, the Commission decided that the services provided by La Poste were supplied under normal business conditions and did not constitute State aid. That decision was partially annulled by the CFI on the grounds that the Commission should have verified whether the payment received by La Poste was comparable to that demanded by a private undertaking or group of undertakings *not* operating in a reserved sector.[220] The ECJ disagreed. Since La Poste was entrusted with the provision of a universal postal service, it required substantial infrastructure and resources (ie the postal network) enabling it to provide that service to all users, even in sparsely populated areas. Such a network was not a market network and would not have been created by a private undertaking. The situation of La Poste was therefore not comparable with that of a private undertaking not operating in a reserved sector. Instead, it was necessary to determine the normal market price on the basis of the available 'objective and verifiable' data.[221] On that basis the Court held that:

> there is no question of State aid to SFMI-Chronopost if, first, it is established that the price charged properly covers all the additional, variable costs incurred in providing the logistical and commercial assistance, an appropriate contribution to the fixed costs arising from use of the postal network and an adequate return on the capital investment in so far as it is used for SFMI-Chronopost's competitive activity and if, second, there is nothing to suggest that those elements have been underestimated or fixed in an arbitrary fashion.[222]

The case was therefore remitted to the CFI, which again partially annulled the Commission's decision, on the basis of insufficient reasoning regarding the costs of the logistical and commercial assistance provided, as well as the Commission's

---

[219] Cases C-341-342/06 P *Chronopost v Ufex* (judgment of 1 July 2008), para 123.

[220] Case T-613/97 *Ufex v Commission* [2000] ECR II-4055, paras 74–5.

[221] Cases C-83, 93 and 94/01 P *Chronopost v Ufex* [2003] ECR I-6993, paras 31–8, and opinion of AG Tizzano, paras 38–62.

[222] ibid, judgment para 40.

erroneous determination that the supply of a client list was not aid.[223] Yet again, the ECJ on appeal disagreed, categorically rejecting the suggestion that the Commission's reasoning was insufficient,[224] ruling that it had not been established that the client list had been supplied free of charge, as alleged, and commenting that the transfer of the client list had not in any event had any apparent effect on the conditions of competition on the relevant market.[225] This second time round, the Court felt able to rule on the merits of the application for annulment itself, and gave final judgment dismissing that application.[226] The Commission's decision that there was no State aid was therefore ultimately upheld.

Normal function of public authorities. No State aid will arise where the provision of the asset or service forms part of the normal functions of the public authority in question. An example was the provision by the UK Ministry of Agriculture, Fisheries and Food (as it was then) of standardized record books to cattle and sheep producers, with the aim of ensuring that they kept an accurate livestock record of the information required from them by the public authorities.[227] **2.59**

6. Purchase of commercial goods and services

General principle. The purchase by the State of goods and services from a commercial operator does not in principle amount to State aid. This principle was endorsed by the Court in *ADBHU*, concerning indemnities granted to undertakings collecting and/or disposing waste oils, where it ruled that the indemnities did not constitute aid but were rather consideration for the services performed by the undertakings.[228] The same may be true of a subsidy granted to an undertaking which is demonstrated to be an economically rational consideration for the provision of goods and services.[229] However, in line with the position now taken in relation to payments for public services (see paras 2.63–2.75 below), the purchase by the State of other goods and services may be subject to close scrutiny where this does not occur on the basis of objective and transparent criteria. It is not sufficient simply to show that the parties to a purchase agreement have undertaken reciprocal commitments.[230] Rather, in determining whether the transaction might **2.60**

---

223 Second judgment in Case T-613/97 *Ufex v Commission* [2006] ECR II-1531.

224 Cases C-341-342/06 P *Chronopost v Ufex* (judgment of 1 July 2008), paras 88–114.

225 ibid, paras 121–32.

226 ibid, paras 141–64.

227 Decision in Case N 599/1999 *Standardised record books for cattle and sheep farmers* (14 December 1999).

228 Case 240/83 *ADBHU* [1985] ECR 531, para 18.

229 See Case T-98/00 *Linde v Commission* [2002] ECR II-3961, the Commission's decision finding there to be State aid was annulled on the grounds that the impugned subsidy was a normal commercial transaction, representing consideration for the construction and operation of a carbon monoxide plant.

230 Case T-14/96 *Bretagne Angleterre Irlande (BAI) v Commission* [1999] ECR II-139, para 71.

involve aid, two questions arise: whether the transaction takes place on normal commercial terms, and whether there is a genuine requirement for the goods or services.

2.61 **Normal commercial transaction.** Where the purchase of goods and services has taken place following a sufficiently advertised open tender procedure, this normally rules out the possibility that the purchase is a disguised aid to a specific undertaking.[231] Where such a tender has not taken place, the Commission may consider carefully whether the terms of the purchase agreement are comparable with those of similar private commercial agreements. If the Commission applies by analogy the *Altmark* criteria for payments for public services, it will be necessary to consider whether the payment represents a strict *quid pro quo* for the goods or services provided, and whether the undertaking chosen is efficient.[232]

2.62 **Genuine requirement for goods or services.** Even if it is shown that the purchase agreement has been concluded on normal commercial terms, and that the agreed goods or services have been supplied to the State, it is also necessary to demonstrate that the State actually requires those goods or services. This issue arose in the cases concerning the Basque authorities' purchase of travel vouchers for the P&O ferry service between Bilbao and Portsmouth, to be used to subsidize travel by (among others) school groups, students and the elderly.[233] The Commission initially indicated that it considered the agreement, concluded in 1992, to be State aid on the basis of a number of considerations, including that the agreed price for the 26,000 vouchers was higher than the commercial rate. Following discussions with the Commission, a new agreement was proposed, under which 46,500 vouchers would be purchased, but at a price which was below the advertised brochure price for the tickets in question. On that basis the Commission terminated the State aid procedure. That decision was annulled in *BAI v Commission*, where the Court noted that the overall payment to P&O under the 1995 agreement was even higher than under the 1992 agreement, and found that there was no evidence to support the conclusion that whereas only 26,000 vouchers were required in 1992, 46,500 such vouchers were required in 1995.[234] The Court plainly considered that the increase in the number of vouchers was simply a device to maintain the level of the payment to P&O, and did not reflect the actual needs of the

---

231 See Cases T-116 and 118/01 *P&O European Ferries (Vizcaya) v Commission* [2003] ECR II-2957, para 118; Decision in Case N 46/2007 *Welsh public sector network scheme* (30 May 2007), para 18; Decision in Case NN 24/2007 *Prague municipal wireless project* (30 May 2007), para 29.

232 See paras 2.72–2.73 below.

233 Case T-14/96 *Bretagne Angleterre Irlande (BAI) v Commission* [1999] ECR II-139; Cases T-116 and 118/01 *P&O European Ferries (Vizcaya) v Commission* [2003] ECR II-2957; and Cases C-442 and 471/03 P *P&O European Ferries (Vizcaya) v Commission* [2006] ECR I-4845.

234 *Bretagne Angleterre Irlande (BAI) v Commission*, ibid, paras 74–6.

Basque authorities.[235] Following the judgment, the Commission re-opened the State aid procedure, and found the agreement to constitute State aid on essentially the same grounds as relied upon by the Court in the *BAI* judgment.[236] The decision was upheld by both the CFI and the ECJ in *P&O European Ferries (Vizcaya) v Commission*.[237]

7. Payments for public services

Two competing analyses. The principle that aid represents an advantage that would not have been obtained under 'normal market conditions' implies that payments by the State for services at the normal market price should not be regarded as aid. That should apply, in particular, to payments for the performance of public service obligations. But the question of whether that is indeed the case has produced a long debate in the Commission and European Courts. The competing views have become known as the 'compensation approach', under which such measures are not regarded as State aid provided that they do not exceed the appropriate remuneration for the public service costs, and the 'State aid approach', under which such measures should constitute State aid, but may be justified under Article 86(2) if the conditions of that derogation are fulfilled.[238] **2.63**

Early use of compensation approach. Until the late 1990s, the established practice of the Commission was that payments representing a *quid pro quo* for the performance of public service obligations did not amount to an 'advantage' to the undertaking and therefore did not constitute State aid within Article 87(1).[239] This approach followed the line taken in the *ADBHU* case, considered at para 2.60 above. **2.64**

State aid approach in CFI. The Commission's policy was reconsidered by the CFI in *FFSA* where the Court held that, contrary to the arguments of the Commission, tax concessions granted by the French Government to La Poste did constitute State aid within the meaning of Article 87(1), even where those concessions were lower than La Poste's additional costs entailed by its public service constraints, such as the obligation to maintain post offices throughout the country.[240] **2.65**

---

[235] ibid, para 79.

[236] Decision 2001/247/EC *Ferries Golfo de Vizcaya* [2001] OJ L89/28. Notably, the Commission found that out of the 46,500 vouchers purchased, only 16,052 had been distributed by the Basque authorities: (Decision paras 50–1), and it further emerged that of those 16,052 only 9,000 had actually been used (Cases T-116 and 118/01 *P&O European Ferries (Vizcaya) v Commission* [2003] ECR II-2957, para 131).

[237] Cases T-116 and 118/01 [2003] ECR II-2957 (see in particular paras 113–37); and Cases C-442 and 471/03 P [2006] ECR I-4845 (see in particular paras 38–52).

[238] See opinion of AG Jacobs in Case C-126/91 *GEMO* [2003] ECR I-13769, paras 94–5.

[239] See comments of AG Tizzano in Case C-53/00 *Ferring v ACOSS* [2001] ECR I-9067, opinion para 56.

[240] Case T-106/95 *FFSA v Commission* [1997] ECR II-229, para 167.

However it held that the measures could be considered compatible with the common market on the basis of the derogation provided in Article 86(2), where the strict conditions of that Article were satisfied.[241] The same approach was taken by the CFI in *SIC*, regarding Portuguese measures in favour of the broadcaster RTP. The Commission had found that certain grants did not constitute aid, since they were intended to offset the cost of meeting RTP's public service obligations. The Court annulled the decision, stating that:

> the fact that a financial advantage is granted to an undertaking by the public authorities in order to offset the cost of public service obligations which that undertaking is claimed to have assumed has no bearing on the classification of that measure as aid within the meaning of Article [87(1)] of the Treaty, although that aspect may be taken into account when considering whether the aid in question is compatible with the common market under Article [86(2)] of the Treaty.[242]

2.66 **Return to compensation approach.** The approach of the CFI did not survive for long. A year after the ruling in *SIC*, the ECJ gave judgment in *Ferring*, a case concerning a French tax levied on the wholesale sales of medicinal products by pharmaceutical laboratories.[243] The tax, which was not imposed on (competing) sales of medicines by wholesale distributors, was intended to restore the balance of competition between the different wholesale distribution channels, and to compensate for the public service obligations imposed on wholesale distributors but not on pharmaceutical laboratories. Advocate General Tizzano argued that the ECJ should *not* adopt the *FFSA* and *SIC* approach.[244] The ECJ agreed, referring to the *ADBHU* case and stating that provided that the tax on direct sales imposed on pharmaceutical laboratories corresponded to the additional costs actually incurred by wholesale distributors in discharging their public service obligations, the advantage to the wholesale distributors could be regarded as compensation for the services they provide and not an 'advantage' for the purposes of Article 87(1).[245] Moreover, if the exemption *did* exceed the additional costs then Article 86(2) could not apply, since the surplus could not be regarded as necessary to enable the undertakings to carry out their public service tasks.[246]

---

[241] ibid, paras 170–8; approach to application and interpretation of Article 86(2) upheld by ECJ on appeal in Case C-174/97 P *FFSA v Commission* [1998] ECR I-1303.

[242] Case T-46/97 *SIC v Commission* [2000] ECR II-2125, para 84. In that case, unlike *FFSA*, the Commission had not applied the Article 86(2) derogation.

[243] Case C-53/00 *Ferring v ACOSS* [2001] ECR I-9067.

[244] ibid, in particular opinion para 61: 'if the State imposes certain public service obligations on an undertaking, then covering the additional costs arising from the performance of those obligations confers no advantage on the undertaking in question, but serves, if anything, to ensure that it is not unjustly disadvantaged *vis-à-vis* its competitors. . . . the measure taken by the public authorities ends up having an economically neutral effect on the undertaking concerned, which derives from it neither advantage nor disadvantage'.

[245] ibid, para 27.

[246] ibid, paras 32–3.

Altmark. The ECJ had the opportunity to review the position in its judgment in the *Altmark* case.[247] Among other issues, the case concerned the question of whether the grant of subsidies to Altmark Trans for the operation of a public bus service constituted State aid. Notwithstanding two trenchant opinions by Advocate General Léger[248] rejecting the reasoning in *Ferring* and proposing a return to the State aid approach, the Court upheld *Ferring*. It thus confirmed that a State measure is not caught by Article 87(1) where it compensates for public service obligations provided by an undertaking, such that the undertaking does not enjoy a real financial advantage.[249] However in order for that to be the case, four conditions must be satisfied.[250] Those conditions have now been considered in a number of subsequent cases. In most cases, they have been strictly applied. In the *BUPA* case, however, the CFI suggested that a more flexible approach could be taken to the conditions in certain circumstances. The following paragraphs first set out the *Altmark* conditions as normally applied. The specific circumstances of the *BUPA* case are then discussed. **2.67**

First condition: clearly defined public service obligations. The recipient undertaking must actually have public service obligations to discharge, and the obligations must be clearly defined.[251] The concept of a public service obligation for this purpose corresponds to that of a service of general economic interest (or 'SGEI') for the purposes of Article 86(2),[252] and as in respect of Article 86(2) the Member State concerned has a broad jurisdiction to define SGEIs within its territory.[253] It cannot however be assumed simply from the nature of the services that they constitute clearly defined public service duties.[254] The public service tasks in question must be external to the undertakings concerned, and thus do not **2.68**

---

[247] Case C-280/00 *Altmark* [2003] ECR I-7747.

[248] The *Ferring* judgment was delivered after the oral hearing but before the first opinion of AG Léger. Shortly after that opinion was given, AG Jacobs gave his opinion in Case C-126/01 *GEMO* [2003] ECR I-13769, proposing a quite different approach. The oral hearing was reopened in order to allow the parties to comment upon both the *Ferring* judgment and the opinion of AG Jacobs in *GEMO*. In his second opinion, AG Léger maintained his position that the measures should be regarded as aid. The Court, however, essentially adopted the approach suggested by AG Jacobs in its judgment which followed.

[249] Case C-280/00 *Altmark* [2003] ECR I-7747, para 87; confirmed in Case T-266/02 *Deutsche Post v Commission* (judgment of 1 July 2008), para 72.

[250] *Altmark*, ibid, paras 89–93 and 95. The burden of proof will depend on the context. In a national court, depending upon the national procedural rules, it may be for a competitor alleging an unlawful grant of aid to show that at least one of the *Altmark* conditions is not met: Case C-526/04 *Laboratoires Boiron* [2006] ECR I-7529, paras 50–7.

[251] Case C-280/00 *Altmark*, ibid, para 89, stating further that on the facts of the case, the obligations had to be clear from the national legislation and/or the licences at issue. Case T-289/03 *BUPA v Commission* (judgment of 12 February 2008), para 181 indicates that this also requires an act of 'entrustment' analogous to the requirement under Article 86(2).

[252] *BUPA*, ibid, para 162.

[253] See further para 3.82 below.

[254] Cases C-34-38/01 *Enirisorse v Ministero delle Finanze* [2003] ECR I-14243, paras 33–4.

include measures designed to support the interests of specific undertakings even if those measures have general social goals, such as the improvement of employee relations.[255]

2.69 **Market regulation.** The Court's case-law suggests that the obligation must be imposed over and above the duties normally incumbent upon an undertaking, as provided by relevant sectoral regulations or collective agreements.[256] To similar effect, legal obligations imposed on an undertaking or a number of undertakings do not in themselves lead to the conclusion that the undertaking is required to discharge public service obligations,[257] although the imposition of such obligations may form part of an SGEI mission.[258]

2.70 **Examples.** Reference should be made to examples of SGEIs set out in Chapter 3.[259] In addition, examples of obligations accepted by the Court as constituting public service obligations in the context of an Article 87(1) analysis include the provision of tax assistance services,[260] the provision of a stable electricity supply,[261] a requirement that wholesale pharmaceutical distributors have at their disposal a permanent range of medicinal products,[262] the provision of private medical insurance,[263] the collection or disposal of waste oil,[264] and the operation of urban, suburban or regional scheduled transport services.[265]

2.71 **Second condition: objective parameters.** The parameters on the basis of which the compensation is calculated must be established in advance in an objective and transparent manner. The purpose of this condition is to prevent the Member State conferring an economic advantage which may favour the recipient undertaking over competing undertakings,[266] in other words to preclude any abuse of the concept of an SGEI.[267] This condition is not satisfied where the information provided by the Member State does not show exactly what the purported public service

---

255 Case C-251/97 *France v Commission* [1999] ECR I-6639, AG Fennelly, opinion para 20.

256 ibid, judgment para 40. See also Case T-157/01 *Danske Busvognmænd v Commission* [2004] ECR II-917, paras 75–83 and 98, suggesting that the voluntary assumption of public service obligations, following a tender procedure which did not provide for subsidies, is not sufficient.

257 Case T-289/03 *BUPA v Commission* (judgment of 12 February 2008), para 178; Decision in Case C 34/2006 *North Rhine-Westphalia DTT* (23 October 2007), para 93.

258 *BUPA v Commission*, ibid, para 179.

259 See paras 3.84–3.85 below.

260 Case C-451/03 *Servizi Ausiliari Dottori Commercialisti* [2006] ECR I-2941.

261 Decision 2007/580/EC *Slovenian green electricity scheme* [2007] OJ L219/9, paras 102–3.

262 Case C-53/00 *Ferring v ACOSS* [2001] ECR I-9067, para 27.

263 Case T-289/03 *BUPA v Commission* (judgment of 12 February 2008).

264 Case 240/83 *ADBHU* [1985] ECR 531, para 18.

265 Case C-280/00 *Altmark* [2003] ECR I-7747, para 95.

266 ibid, para 90.

267 Case T-289/03 *BUPA v Commission* (judgment of 12 February 2008), para 214.

comprises, the details of the costs of the service, or how the compensation has been assessed.[268]

Third condition: requirement of strict *quid pro quo*. The compensation cannot exceed what is necessary to cover all or part of the costs incurred in the discharge of public service obligations, taking into account any relevant receipts and a reasonable profit.[269] An unsubstantiated claim that aid is designed to offset additional costs will therefore not suffice;[270] instead, it will almost certainly be necessary to produce detailed information relating to the costs of the undertaking in question.[271] In national court proceedings where a third party is alleging the grant of State aid, it is unlikely that they would have access to this information, and the court may need to order the beneficiary to produce relevant documents and data.[272] **2.72**

Fourth condition: efficient undertaking comparator. Where the undertaking which is to discharge the public service obligations is not chosen pursuant to a public procurement procedure, which would allow for the selection of the tenderer capable of providing those services at least cost,[273] the *Altmark* test provided that the level of compensation must be determined on the basis of an analysis of the costs which a typical and well-run undertaking would have incurred in discharging those obligations, taking into account the relevant receipts and a reasonable profit.[274] A strict application of this condition is likely to be difficult to satisfy[275]—indeed, in some cases it may not even be possible to identify such an 'average' undertaking in the State in question.[276] The condition was however held **2.73**

---

[268] Cases C-34-38/01 *Enirisorse v Ministero delle Finanze* [2003] ECR I-14243, para 37; and Case T-157/01 *Danske Busvognmænd v Commission* [2004] ECR II-917, para 98.

[269] Case C-280/00 *Altmark* [2003] ECR I-7747, para 92.

[270] See Case C-251/97 *France v Commission* [1999] ECR I-6639, paras 44–6, reaching the same conclusion.

[271] The Commission has rejected the suggestion that this criterion is only applicable in cases where the relevant costs, revenues and reasonable profits can be calculated: Decision in Case C 34/2006 *North Rhine-Westphalia DTT* (23 October 2007), paras 98–9. See Case C-280/00 *Altmark* [2003] ECR I-7747 for a case in which a negative Commission decision was annulled for failure to check the detailed information provided in this respect by the German government.

[272] Case C-526/04 *Laboratoires Boiron* [2006] ECR I-7529, paras 53–5.

[273] eg the procedure in Decision in Case N 475/2003 *New electricity generation capacity* (16 December 2003).

[274] Case C-280/00 *Altmark* [2003] ECR I-7747, para 93.

[275] It was not satisfied in the Decisions in Cases N 541 and 542/2004 *Dutch health insurance RES* (3 May 2005), section 3.4.1; or NN 8/2007 *Financing of workforce reduction measures of RTVE* (7 March 2007), where the Commission held that a well-run undertaking would not have built up an excessive workforce so would not have needed compensation for its corresponding reduction (para 29); or N 822/2006 *Post Office debt payment funding* (7 March 2007), where no information had been provided on the costs of a typical undertaking (para 23).

[276] See eg Decision 2006/237/EC *AVR* [2006] OJ L84/37, para 73.

to be satisfied in the case of support for a Slovenian lignite-fired electricity plant.[277] While it had not been chosen on the basis of the public procurement procedure, the Commission noted that Slovenia had demonstrated that the choice of the plant was the one that led to providing the service at the least cost to the community, and had therefore used the most economically efficient way to achieve the public service obligation of producing electricity with domestic fuel.[278]

2.74 **More flexible approach in *BUPA*.** By contrast with the strict approach adopted in *Altmark* and subsequent judgments, in its judgment in the *BUPA* case the CFI adopted a very different approach to the *Altmark* criteria, in particular the second to fourth criteria. In that case, 'risk equalization' payments were required to be made by providers of private medical insurance on the Irish market with a low risk profile. The payments then subsidized the provision of insurance by providers with a higher risk profile. It was clear that there was no direct relationship between the payments (on the one hand) and the costs incurred by the higher risk insurers (on the other), and that no comparison had been made between the costs of the potential recipients of risk equalization payments and those of an efficient operator. Indeed, the Commission had effectively accepted that the *Altmark* test was not satisfied.[279] The Court disagreed, however, holding that the *Altmark* test was satisfied and that the measure did not constitute State aid within Article 87(1).[280] While the Court accepted that the scheme could not strictly fulfil the third *Altmark* criterion, it held that the mechanism of the scheme was consistent with the spirit and purpose of that condition.[281] As regards the fourth condition, the Court said that in this case there was no need to draw a comparison with the costs of an efficient operator, it being sufficient for the Commission to satisfy itself that the payments under the scheme did not entail the possibility of offsetting costs that might result from inefficiency.[282] It remains to be seen whether this more flexible approach will be followed in future cases, particularly in the ECJ.[283]

2.75 **Recourse to Article 86(2).** If the *Altmark* conditions (possibly qualified as in the *BUPA* judgment) are not satisfied then the compensation granted to the undertaking will, in principle, fall within Article 87(1). In such cases the measure will have to be notified to and approved by the Commission before it may be implemented.

---

277 Decision 2007/580/EC *Slovenian green electricity scheme* [2007] OJ L219/9.

278 ibid, paras 111–22.

279 By defending its decision solely on the basis of Article 86(2). This was not surprising, since the decision under appeal (Decision in Case N 46/2003 *Irish health insurance RES* (13 May 2003)) had been adopted before the *Altmark* judgment was published.

280 Case T-289/03 *BUPA v Commission* (judgment of 12 February 2008), para 258.

281 ibid, paras 233–8.

282 ibid, paras 248–9.

283 The *BUPA* case itself was not, however, appealed to the ECJ.

In many cases involving public service compensation, where the measure is aid within Article 87(1), it may nevertheless be exempted under Article 86(2) where the conditions of that exemption are satisfied.[284] Those conditions are discussed in Chapter 3 below.

8. Parafiscal charges

Issues. Parafiscal charges (sometimes referred to as quasi-fiscal charges) are charges dedicated to a particular purpose.[285] Charges may often be levied on a particular industrial sector and used to finance activities benefiting the sector as a whole, such as promotional and marketing activities[286] or collective research.[287] In many cases the beneficiaries will be institutions not carrying on economic activities, and Article 87 will therefore not apply.[288] Where the beneficiaries are undertakings, however, two further issues may arise in determining the application of the State aid rules. The first is whether the funds constitute aid. The second is whether the charges themselves may be challenged under Articles 87 and 88. **2.76**

Benefits funded by parafiscal charges. The Court has not had any hesitation in categorizing the application of funds financed by parafiscal charges as State aid where the effect is to favour some undertakings over others. It is well established that an advantage may still exist even where the aid is funded wholly or partly through contributions imposed by the public authorities and levied on undertakings including the recipients of the aid.[289] **2.77**

Challenges to the charge itself. The more difficult question is the legality of the charge which finances the fund. Even though Article 87 does not, on its face, prohibit the imposition of a tax or charge, undertakings have sought to use it to obtain the reimbursement of parafiscal charges on the grounds that they are used to finance State aid, and are therefore also prohibited under Articles 87 and 88. The Court has always acknowledged the close relationship between an aid and a charge which finances the aid, emphasizing in *France v Commission* that in order **2.78**

---

284 And, of course, other exemptions may also apply: see Decision in Cases N 541 and 542/2004 *Dutch health insurance RES* (3 May 2005) where the measure was approved partly on the basis of Article 86(2) and partly on the basis of Article 87(3)(c).

285 Cases C-34-38/01 *Enirisorse v Ministero delle Finanze* [2003] ECR I-14243, opinion of AG Stix-Hackl para 167; Case C-526/04 *Laboratoires Boiron* [2006] ECR I-7529, opinion of AG Tizzano para 43.

286 See eg Case 78/76 *Steinike und Weinlig v Germany* [1977] ECR 595.

287 See eg Case 47/69 *France v Commission* [1970] ECR 487.

288 See eg Cases 266/04 etc *Distribution Casino France* [2005] ECR I-9481, para 54.

289 Case 78/76 *Steinike und Weinlig v Germany* [1977] ECR 595, para 22; Case 259/85 *France v Commission* [1987] ECR 4393, paras 23–4. This is of course subject to the other State aid conditions, in particular the criteria that the measure be imputable to the State and constitute a burden on State resources. That was the case in *Steinike* but will not be so for every aid financed by a parafiscal charge: see Case C-345/02 *Pearle* [2004] ECR I-7139, paras 35–9, discussed at para 2.107 below.

to apply Article 87(1) it is necessary to consider all the legal and factual circumstances surrounding the aid, including whether there is an imbalance between the charges imposed and the benefits derived from the aid. Consequently the aid cannot be considered separately from the effects of its method of financing.[290] But it has not always been clear whether, in cases where the aid is inextricably linked to the charge, Article 87(1) is regarded as attaching to both the aid and the charge, or whether the charge is simply part of the context which enables prohibition of the aid element of the measure.[291] Thus while the Court has emphasized that a single measure cannot constitute both an aid and a special charge,[292] and that Article 87(1) addresses the use to which the fund is put, rather than the levying of the charge itself,[293] its early case-law suggested that a parafiscal charge might itself constitute State aid incompatible with the common market.[294] This issue was clarified by the Court in the *Van Calster* and *Streekgewest* cases, which have been followed in subsequent judgments.

2.79 **Charge must be integral part of aid measure.** *Van Calster* was a reference for a preliminary ruling in proceedings brought by Mr Van Calster and Mr Cleeren for reimbursement of parafiscal charges levied by the public authorities on trade in cattle, which were used to fund measures to combat animal disease and improve animal health and hygiene. It was not disputed that the use of the fund constituted State aid; that aid had, however, been approved by the Commission. The question was whether the retroactive imposition of parafiscal charges under the scheme was prohibited under Articles 87 and 88. Applying *France v Commission*, the Court held that the State aid rules do cover the method of financing an aid where that method 'forms an integral part of the measure', in the sense that the charges are designed 'specifically and exclusively' to finance the aid.[295] In such a case, the notification of the aid under Article 88(3) must also cover the method of financing, so that the Commission may consider the measure on the basis of all the facts.[296] It follows that if a charge which is integral to an aid measure is

---

[290] Case 47/69 *France v Commission* [1970] ECR 487, paras 7–8; and see Cases C-261-262/01 *Van Calster* [2003] ECR I-12249, paras 46–9.

[291] See comments of AG Stix-Hackl in Cases C-34/01 to C-38/01 *Enirisorse v Ministero delle Finanze* [2003] ECR I-14243, opinion paras 167–71, and AG Jacobs in Cases C-261–262/01 *Van Calster* [2003] ECR I-12249, opinion paras 29–33.

[292] Case C-390/98 *Banks v Coal Authority* [2001] ECR I-6117, para 34.

[293] Cases C-78-83/90 *Compagnie Commerciale de l'Ouest* [1992] ECR I-1847, para 32, cited in Case C-17/91 *Lornoy* [1992] ECR I-6523, para 28 and Cases C-144-145/91 *Demoor Gilbert* [1992] ECR I-6613, para 24.

[294] *Compagnie Commerciale de l'Ouest*, ibid, para 35; *Lornoy*, ibid, para 32; *Demoor Gilbert*, ibid, para 28.

[295] Cases C-261-262/01 *Van Calster* [2003] ECR I-12249, paras 44–9. See also Cases C-34–38/01 *Enirisorse v Ministero delle Finanze* [2003] ECR I-14243, para 43; and Cases C-266/04 etc *Distribution Casino France* [2005] ECR I-9481, para 34.

[296] *Van Calster*, ibid, paras 50–1.

implemented in breach of the obligation to notify, the national courts must order reimbursement.[297] That was indeed the situation on the facts of *Van Calster*, where the parafiscal charges had been imposed retroactively in respect of a period predating the Commission decision approving the aid.

Charge must be hypothecated to aid. The Court's reasoning on the concept of a charge 'integral' to the aid measure was further refined in *Streekgewest*, where again reimbursement of a charge was sought, this time in relation to a Dutch waste levy. The Court ruled as follows: **2.80**

> the Treaty makes a clear distinction between, on the one hand, the regime in Articles [87, 88 and 89 EC], concerning State aid and, on the other, that in Articles [96 and 97 EC] concerning the distortions which arise from differences between the laws, regulations or administrative provisions of the Member States and, in particular, their tax provisions.
>
> Taxes do not fall within the scope of the provisions of the Treaty concerning State aid unless they constitute the method of financing an aid measure, so that they form an integral part of that measure.
>
> For a tax, or part of a tax, to be regarded as forming an integral part of an aid measure, it must be hypothecated to the aid measure under the relevant national rules, in the sense that the revenue from the tax is necessarily allocated for the financing of the aid. In the event of such hypothecation, the revenue from the tax has a direct impact on the amount of the aid and, consequently, on the assessment of the compatibility of the aid with the common market . . . where there is such a link between the aid measure and its financing, the notification of the aid provided for in Article [88(3)] of the Treaty must also cover the method of financing, so that the Commission may consider it on the basis of all the facts. If this requirement is not satisfied, it is possible that the Commission may declare that an aid measure is compatible when, if the Commission had been aware of its method of financing, it could not have been so declared . . .[298]

The decisive test is thus whether the charge is hypothecated to an aid measure in that the tax revenue is 'necessarily allocated for the financing of the aid'.[299]

Factors showing no hypothecation. Where the authorities have a genuine discretion in allocating the revenue from the levy to various purposes, not limited to the aid, the levy cannot be regarded as hypothecated to the aid, and it will therefore fall **2.81**

[297] *Van Calster*, ibid, paras 52–4. See also Cases C-34-38/01 *Enirisorse v Ministero delle Finanze* [2003] ECR I-14243, paras 45–6, noting that the unlawfulness only concerned the proportion of the charge which was used to fund the State aid. The remaining proportion of the charge paid into the Exchequer was not affected.

[298] Case C-174/02 *Streekgewest* [2005] ECR I-85, paras 24–6.

[299] See also Case C-175/02 *Pape* [2005] ECR I-127, para 15; Case C-128–129/03 *AEM v Autorità per l'energia elettrica e per gas* [2005] ECR I-2861, para 46; Cases C-393/04 and C-41/05 *Air Liquide Industries Belgium* [2006] ECR I-5293, para 46.

outside the scope of Articles 87 and 88.[300] Different principles also apply where the contested measure is differential taxation, such that the aid takes the form of an exemption from the disputed charge. This is discussed in the next section.

9. Differential taxation

2.82 **Issues.** The application of the State aid rules to differential taxation is closely related to the problem of parafiscal charges. Claims based on differential taxation may arise where a State taxes two groups of undertakings at different rates, or where it taxes one group of undertakings but does not impose the tax at all on another group. In both cases, it is often claimed that the lower or nil rate tax constitutes an aid; and proceedings are then brought for reimbursement of the additional tax burden on the non-aided undertakings. These claims raise two issues. First, it must be determined whether the differential rates of tax do amount to aid to the lower-taxed or non-taxed group of undertakings. If that is proven, then the second question is whether the higher-taxed undertakings may use Articles 87 and 88 to claim reimbursement of the higher tax burden.

2.83 **Existence of aid.** Where a State measure imposes differential rates of tax on two groups of undertakings, it may be difficult to determine whether it should be analysed as an exemption to the lower-taxed or non-taxed group, which might be aid, or conversely as a selective charge to the higher-taxed group, which cannot itself be aid. In some cases the reality may be that a selective charge or higher rate is a disguised tax exemption for the non-taxed or lower-taxed undertakings, such that the measure can properly be said to be an aid measure.[301] But that is not true of every case. Furthermore, as a matter of policy, to regard every instance of selective or differential taxation as an aid to the non-taxed or lower-taxed undertakings would have wide-reaching effects not contemplated by the Article 87(1) prohibition. This point was made by the Commission in the *Fediol* case concerning subsidies under the GATT Subsidies Code. The Commission had to consider whether differential rates of tax imposed by Argentina on exports of soya bean products amounted to a subsidy. It noted that a subsidy involved a charge on the public account, and that the concept of charge on the public account

> includes the waiving by the authorities of taxes or other dues owed. The Commission notes that the case in point, however, involves not the waiving of a tax but the non-creation of an additional tax burden. To regard such a non-creation generally as

[300] Case C-175/02 *Pape v Minister van Landbouw* [2005] ECR I-127, paras 14–17 (Dutch levy on manure). This principle might not apply if the legislation is drafted to include such a discretion as a matter of form, but where there is no genuine intention to exercise that discretion.

[301] See eg the comments of the Court in Case C-526/04 *Laboratoires Boiron* [2006] ECR I-7529, paras 33–5.

a subsidy would be to hold the very fact that a government levies tax on some people or products but not others as equivalent to a financial contribution to the latter.[302]

Ferring. The question is therefore how to distinguish between cases where a selective charge is in fact to be analysed as tax relief to the lower-taxed or non-taxed group, and cases where it is simply a charge that falls outside Article 87. That arose in *Ferring* where the claimants in the national proceedings sought reimbursement of a French tax levied on wholesale sales of medicinal products by pharmaceutical laboratories, on the grounds that the tax was not imposed on the same sales by competing wholesale distributors.[303] Advocate General Tizzano pointed out that *any* new tax imposed on one group of economic operators could be seen, in broad terms, as an advantage conferred on other operators who were not subject to the tax.[304] Such a broad interpretation of aid would not respect either the letter or the spirit of Article 87(1), and would risk unjustified interference in the fiscal policies of Member States. However an interpretation of Article 87(1) which excluded any finding of aid resulting from the non-imposition of a new tax on certain economic operators would allow Member States to circumvent the State aid rules. Thus whether the non-imposition of a tax amounted to the grant of a selective advantage had to be determined on a case-by-case basis having regard to the competitive relationship between the operators, the reason for the tax and its effects. In this case the legislation amounted, in his view, to the deliberate grant of a tax advantage to wholesale distributors. It therefore conferred a selective advantage within the meaning of Article 87(1).[305] The Court agreed with this analysis of the French legislation, and held that imposing the sales tax on wholesale distributors equated to granting them a tax exemption.[306] 2.84

The present position. The current position is therefore that differential taxation may be regarded as State aid to the lower-taxed or non-taxed group of undertakings where the purpose and effects of the scheme show that the intention is to grant a fiscal advantage to that group. On the other hand there will not be aid where the 'norm' is the absence of tax or lower tax, and the true purpose and effect 2.85

---

[302] Decision 85/239/EEC *Argentinian soya meal* [1985] OJ L108/28, at para 7.4. The Commission's position was upheld by the ECJ: Case 187/85 *Fediol v Commission* [1988] ECR 4155. cf also AG Römer in Case 9/70 *Grad v Finanzamt Traunstein* [1970] ECR 825, para 6, assuming that while the imposition of tax charges on a competitor might indirectly favour the undertaking not so charged, such measures did not fall within the scope of Article 87(1).

[303] See para 2.66 above.

[304] Case C-53/00 *Ferring v ACOSS* [2001] ECR I-9067, opinion para 36. See also AG Fennelly in Case C-390/98 *Banks v Coal Authority* [2001] ECR I-6117, para 19 of opinion: 'any distinction between undertakings or sectors to the benefit of certain among them may be construed as an aid to those treated more favourably'.

[305] *Ferring v ACOSS*, ibid, opinion paras 37–41.

[306] *Ferring v ACOSS*, ibid, judgment para 20. See also Case C-526/04 *Laboratoires Boiron* [2006] ECR I-7529.

of the scheme is to impose a special charge on the higher-taxed group. An example is an environmental levy which is imposed on specific products to deter their use.[307] The correct analysis thus turns on identifying the correct 'norm', which may not always be easy.

2.86 **Relationship with selectivity criterion.** For practical purposes, where sectoral differentiation is concerned, the Court may often avoid a precise identification of the relevant 'norm' by asking instead whether the different treatment is justified by the nature and general scheme of the system. If it is, the measure is in any event not State aid within Article 87(7), regardless of whether it should be regarded as producing an advantage to certain undertakings.[308] Obversely, if no justification can be found in the logic of the system for the different treatment of groups of undertakings, that is a strong indication that the measure should be regarded as a selective advantage and hence aid for the lower-taxed or non-taxed group.[309]

2.87 **Challenges to the tax itself: typical exemption cases.** From the perspective of a competitor of the aid beneficiary, the most important issue in a case of differential taxation is likely not to be the aid itself in the form of the tax exemption, but rather the tax burden to which other undertakings are subject.[310] The higher rate of tax is of course not itself a State aid. But, as set out in section 8 above, a charge financing aid may in some circumstances fall within the scope of the Articles 87 and 88. It is clear, and the Court has confirmed, that the hypothecation principle developed in relation to parafiscal charges will not apply to the normal case of differential taxation, where the aid is a straightforward exemption from a tax imposed on other undertakings. In that case the application and extent of the exemption will generally not depend on the tax revenue;[311] indeed, the tax revenue may not be earmarked for a specific purpose at all.[312] In such cases, where the tax and the exemption are discrete and independent measures, there is no reason to impugn both under the State aid rules, and the prohibition on aid will extend only to the exemption.[313]

---

307 Case T-210/02 *British Aggregates v Commission* [2006] ECR II-2789, para 116.

308 As the Court found in Case C-308/01 *GIL Insurance v Commrs of Customs & Excise* [2004] ECR I-4777, paras 73–8 (on which see further para 2.131 below). See also Case T-210/02 *British Aggregates Association v Commission* [2006] ECR II-2789, paras 122–39.

309 See approach of the Court in Case C-143/99 *Adria-Wien Pipeline* [2001] ECR I-8365.

310 The 2006 Study on the enforcement of State aid law at national level, commissioned by DG Competition, notes that in the vast majority of cases brought by private parties in the national courts, the claimant sought relief from a tax burden from which another party was exempted: see para 18.05 below.

311 Case C-174/02 *Streekgewest* [2005] ECR I-85, paras 28–9; Cases C-266/04 etc *Distribution Casino France* [2005] ECR I-9481, paras 41–3; Cases C-393/04 and C-41/05 *Air Liquide Industries Belgium* [2006] ECR I-5293, para 46.

312 *Air Liquide Industries Belgium*, ibid, opinion of AG Tizzano para 72.

313 ibid, opinion of AG Tizzano paras 73–4.

2.88 **Exception: deliberate asymmetric taxation.** In some exceptional cases, a State may choose from the outset to tax one group of undertakings while not imposing the tax on a competing group, with the objective of distorting competition in favour of the non-taxed group. In such a case, the asymmetric imposition of tax is not the *result* of the aid, but rather the *means* by which the aid is granted. In this situation the imposition of the tax, while not itself constituting State aid, is an act giving effect to an aid measure which will fall within Articles 87 and 88. This was the case in *Laboratoires Boiron*,[314] a preliminary reference concerning the legislation at issue in the *Ferring* case.[315] In an important and carefully reasoned judgment, the Court concluded that the aid measure was the tax itself, and not an exemption which was separable from the tax. The taxed undertakings were therefore entitled to plead that the charge was itself an unlawful aid measure, for the purposes of claiming reimbursement.[316] The peculiar facts of that case highlight, however, that this situation is likely to be rare by comparison with the large number of cases in which an exemption is granted from a generally applicable tax, and where no claim to reimbursement will lie.

C. State resources and imputability

2.89 **Introduction.** The reference in Article 87(1) to the involvement of State resources has provoked considerable controversy. On its face, Article 87(1) applies to aid 'granted by a Member State or through State resources'. The question has been whether this should be interpreted as setting out two alternative conditions, or whether an effect on State resources is in fact an essential condition of State aid. The matter was not settled until *PreussenElektra*,[317] where the Court finally determined that a measure was not State aid unless it was financed through public resources. Section 1 below sets out the development of the debate on this issue. The following two sections address the application of the State resources criterion in practice: section 2 considers the test for determining whether a fund constitutes a 'State resource', and section 3 addresses the types of measure that will constitute a direct or indirect grant through State resources. Finally, section 4 addresses the criterion of imputability to the State.

[314] Case C-526/04 *Laboratoires Boiron v ACOSS* [2006] ECR I-7529.
[315] See para 2.84 above.
[316] Case C-526/04 *Laboratoires Boiron* [2006] ECR I-7529, paras 30–40.
[317] Case C-379/98 *PreussenElektra* [2001] ECR I-2099.

1. The State resources debate

2.90 **Narrow view.** The narrow view, that financing through public resources is a constitutive element of the definition of State aid,[318] was first expressed in the *van Tiggele* case concerning the fixing of minimum retail prices for spirits. Advocate General Capotorti stated that a State aid must entail 'a burden on the public finances in the form either of expenditure or of reduced revenue.' The Court agreed, holding that the intervention by the State through price fixing did not amount to the grant of advantages through State resources, and therefore was not State aid.[319] The same approach was adopted by the Court in *Sloman Neptun*, concerning a German law allowing shipowners to employ Philippino seafarers on terms other than those in German collective agreements, by registering in an international register rather than the usual German register. This had the practical effect that the Philippino employees could be paid 20% less than their German colleagues. But it was held to fall outside Article 87(1), since the benefit to the shipowners flowed not from the State but from the employees, through the reduction in their potential salaries.[320] The Court reached the same conclusion in *Kirsammer-Hack*, where the exclusion of small businesses from the German system of protection of workers against unfair dismissal was held not to infringe Article 87(1), since the benefit to those businesses did not entail any direct or indirect transfer of State resources.[321] Five years later, in *Epifanio Viscido*, the Court stated trenchantly that the 'non-application of generally applicable legislation concerning fixed-term employment contracts to a single undertaking does not involve any direct or indirect transfer of State resources to that undertaking'. Article 87(1) therefore did not apply to rules allowing the Italian postal service to recruit on the basis of fixed-term contracts, by derogation for the normal requirement of contracts of indeterminate duration.[322]

2.91 **Wider view.** A wider view was adopted in many cases, particularly in the 1970s and 1980s. On that interpretation of Article 87(1), any measure which confers economic advantages on specific undertakings, and which is the result of conduct attributable to the State, should constitute State aid regardless of whether it involves any financial burden for the State.[323] The primary consideration is therefore the effect of the aid, rather than the financial burden on the institution which grants the aid. In *Norddeutsches Vieh- und Fleischkontor*,[324] a case which concerned

[318] See Case C-379/98 *PreussenElektra* [2001] ECR I-2099, opinion of AG Jacobs, para 116.

[319] Case 82/77 *Openbaar Ministerie of the Kingdom of the Netherlands v van Tiggele* [1978] ECR 25, p 52 (AG Capotorti) and para 25 of judgment.

[320] Cases C-72-73/91 *Sloman Neptun* [1993] ECR I-887, para 19.

[321] Case C-189/91 *Kirsammer-Hack* [1993] ECR I-6185, paras 16–18.

[322] Cases C-52-54/97 *Epifanio Viscido* [1998] ECR I-2629, paras 14–15.

[323] cf Case C-379/98 *PreussenElektra* [2001] ECR I-2099, opinion of AG Jacobs, para 115.

[324] Cases 213-215/81 [1982] ECR 3583.

the allocation of import quotas for beef and veal, Advocate General VerLoren van Themaat thought it possible to argue that the grant by Member States of pecuniary advantages which were not paid for by the Member States would be caught by Article 87. He mentioned the examples of reduced rates which Member States might require private electricity companies or haulage contractors to grant to certain undertakings or in respect of certain products.[325] Further support for this view came in the *Poor Farmers* case, where aid granted to poor farmers was financed through a fund operated not by the State, but by an autonomous (albeit public) body. The Commission took the view that the measure was not, therefore, State aid, although it thought that it could be regarded as a measure equivalent to State aid contrary to Article 10 of the Treaty. The Court rejected any notion of a 'measure equivalent to aid',[326] and ruled that the assistance was covered by Article 87. In that respect, it stated that '[a]s is clear from the actual wording of Article [87(1)], aid need not necessarily be financed from State resources to be classified as State aid.'[327] In two further cases, the Court indicated that it was not necessary to show financing through State resources, provided that it could be shown that the aid was granted as a result of the actions of a Member State.[328] The strongest attack on the State resources criterion was made, however, by Advocate General Darmon in the *Sloman Neptun* case. In that opinion, following an extensive survey of the previous case-law, as well as the position under United States law and the GATT, the Advocate General concluded that the 'public' nature of the aid required under Article 87(1) related more to the authority which adopted the measure, than to the origin of the funds.[329] Advocate General Darmon maintained this view in the subsequent case of *Kirsammer-Hack*.[330]

Arguments of principle. A number of arguments of principle support the wider view. On the basis of the consistent rule that the existence of aid is to be assessed by the effects, and not the form, of the measure, a State measure conferring advantages on specific undertakings but financed through private undertakings may have identical effects to a similar measure financed through public resources. Indeed, the measure may be *more* distortive of competition where its cost is borne by competitors of the aided undertakings (as in *PreussenElektra*), rather than being 2.92

[325] ibid, p 3617; cf judgment of Court, para 2.99 below.

[326] Case 290/83 *Commission v France ('Poor Farmers')* [1985] ECR 439, para 18; and see para 2.7 above.

[327] *Commission v France ('Poor Farmers')*, ibid, para 14.

[328] Cases 67, 68 and 70/85 *Van der Kooy v Commission* [1988] ECR 219, paras 32–9; Case 57/86 *Greece v Commission* [1988] ECR 2855, paras 11–13.

[329] Cases C-72–73/91 *Sloman Neptun* [1993] ECR I-887, opinion paras 12–46, and in particular paras 40–1.

[330] Case C-189/91 *Kirsammer-Hack* [1993] ECR I-6185, opinion paras 18–27. As discussed in para 2.90 above, in both the *Sloman Neptun* and *Kirsammer-Hack* cases the Court rejected this interpretation in favour of the narrow approach.

spread among the general public (as with a measure financed directly from State coffers). The formal requirement of a grant through State resources may also allow Member States to circumvent the State aid rules by adopting schemes which provide for a direct transfer from third parties to the aided undertakings.[331] On the other hand, the wider reading would bring a greater number of measures within the potential scope of the provision. It would also have the effect of focusing the inquiry in many cases on the selectivity requirement, which has been notoriously difficult to apply.[332]

2.93 **Clarification in *PreussenElektra*.** The opportunity to clarify the law came in the *PreussenElektra* case in 2001. At issue was the German *Stromeinspeisungsgesetz*, which required private electricity distribution undertakings to purchase a certain amount of electricity from renewable energy sources at State-fixed minimum prices, with the difference between those prices and the market electricity prices being payable partly by private conventional electricity suppliers. PreussenElektra was an operator of conventional and nuclear power stations in Germany. It claimed repayment of payments it had been required to make to the regional electricity supplier Schleswag, on the basis that the legislation was contrary to the Treaty provisions on State aid. The German court referred the matter to the ECJ which held, concurring with the opinion of Advocate General Jacobs, that the legislation was not granted through State resources and therefore did not amount to State aid.

> [T]he case-law of the Court of Justice shows that only advantages granted directly or indirectly through State resources are to be considered aid within the meaning of Article [87(1)]. The distinction made in that provision between aid granted by a Member State and aid granted through State resources does not signify that all advantages granted by a State, whether financed through State resources or not, constitute aid but is intended merely to bring within that definition both advantages which are granted directly by the State and those granted by a public or private body designated or established by the State . . .
>
> In this case, the obligation imposed on private electricity supply undertakings to purchase electricity produced from renewable energy sources at fixed minimum prices does not involve any direct or indirect transfer of State resources to undertakings which produce that type of electricity.
>
> Therefore, the allocation of the financial burden arising from that obligation for those private electricity supply undertakings as between them and other private undertakings cannot constitute a direct or indirect transfer of State resources either.

---

[331] See in particular comments of AG Jacobs in Case C-379/98 *PreussenElektra* [2001] ECR I-2099, opinion paras 137–45; and AG Darmon in Cases C-72-73/91 *Sloman Neptun* [1993] ECR I-887, opinion paras 40–2.

[332] See comments of AG Jacobs in Cases C-52-54/97 *Epifanio Viscido* [1998] ECR I-2629, opinion para 16; and *PreussenElektra*, ibid, opinion para 157.

> In those circumstances, the fact that the purchase obligation is imposed by statute and confers an undeniable advantage on certain undertakings is not capable of conferring upon it the character of State aid within the meaning of Article [87(1)] of the Treaty.
>
> That conclusion cannot be undermined by the fact . . . that the financial burden arising from the obligation to purchase at minimum prices is likely to have negative repercussions on the economic results of the undertakings subject to that obligation and therefore entail a diminution in tax receipts for the State. That consequence is an inherent feature of such a legislative provision and cannot be regarded as constituting a means of granting to producers of electricity from renewable energy sources a particular advantage at the expense of the State.[333]

Cumulative interpretation of Article 87(1). Following *PreussenElektra*, it is now clear that notwithstanding the wording of Article 87(1) the conditions of a grant by the State and a grant through State resources are to be interpreted as cumulative, rather than alternative.[334] It is therefore necessary to show *both* that aid is imputable to the State[335] *and* that it involves State resources. However that has not prevented both Courts from continuing, in many cases, to set out the State aid criteria by reference to a simple restatement of the wording of Article 87(1).[336] In view of the clarification delivered by the Court, that approach should probably now be avoided. **2.94**

2. Type of fund constituting a 'State resource'

Government funds and assets. The funds and assets of central government constitute State resources. The same applies for the funds and assets of regional or local government.[337] Where the aid derives from a measure of general or specific taxation, the purpose of the tax is irrelevant: the question of whether State resources are involved is an objective one. Thus the State resources criterion is satisfied where aid results from a levy system (for example an environmental tax) which is not intended to generate revenue for the State, but is rather designed to regulate the conduct of undertakings.[338] Nor is it relevant to inquire whether the State has used its resources in a manner which is economically prudent, or has acted as an entrepreneur. That issue goes to whether there is a benefit or advantage, but does not affect the question of whether the resources in question are public in nature.[339] **2.95**

333 Case C-379/98 *PreussenElektra* [2001] ECR I-2099, paras 58–62.

334 See also Case C-126/91 *GEMO* [2003] ECR I-13769, para 24.

335 See paras 2.104–2.108 below.

336 See eg Case C-280/00 *Altmark* [2003] ECR I-7747, para 75; Case C-172/03 *Heiser* [2005] ECR I-1627, para 27; Case T-93/02 *Confédération nationale du Crédit Mutuel ('Livret bleu')* [2005] ECR II-143, para 77.

337 See eg Cases T-228 and 233/99 *Westdeutsche Landesbank v Commission* [2003] ECR II-435.

338 Case C-159/01 *Netherlands v Commission* [2004] ECR I-4461, para 51.

339 Cases T-228 and 233/99 *Westdeutsche Landesbank v Commission* [2003] ECR II-435, para 181.

2.96 **Public and private undertakings.** State aid may also be financed through funds in the hands of a public or private undertaking. As the Court explained in *Steinike und Weinlig*, when applying Article 87 regard must be had to the effects of the aid, and not to the status of the institutions entrusted with the distribution and administration of the aid.[340] However, where aid is alleged to be granted through a public or private undertaking, it is necessary to show that the funds in question are under State control and thus available to the public authorities.[341] This will turn on the facts of each case, and will involve consideration of factors such as the extent of the State shareholding, and the State's involvement in appointment of the governing board of the undertaking.[342]

2.97 **Parafiscal charges and other compulsory contributions.** As with funds derived from general taxation, a fund may be regarded as 'State resources' where it is derived from parafiscal charges or other compulsory contributions, where the fund is under the control of the public authorities.[343] However the *Pearle* case indicates that where parafiscal levies are earmarked for a specific purpose, and are not made available to the public authorities, the fund may not constitute State resources.[344]

2.98 **Private deposits which are not permanent assets of State.** A fund made up of voluntary private deposits, which can be withdrawn by the private savers, may also constitute State resources where it represents assets which are at the disposal of the public authorities. In *Air France* the Court considered whether the relevant funds financing the aid constituted State resources. In that respect, it accepted that the funds which financed the aid were private funds which could be withdrawn by depositors, and were therefore not permanently at the disposal of the public sector. However the deposits produced a constant balance which the aid-granting public body was able to use as if the funds were permanently at its disposal. Accordingly, the Court held that the funds were State resources regardless of the

---

340 Case 78/76 *Steinike und Weinlig v Commission* [1977] ECR 595, para 21; see also Case T-136/05 *Salvat père & fils v Commission* [2007] ECR II-4063, para 139.

341 Case 173/73 *Commission v Italy* [1974] ECR 709, para 16; Case C-83/98 P *France v Ladbroke Racing and Commission* [2000] ECR I-3271, para 50; Case C-482/99 *France v Commission ('Stardust Marine')* [2002] ECR I-4397, para 37; Cases C-328/99 and C-399/00 *Italy v Commission* [2003] ECR I-4035, para 33; Case C-278/00 *Greece v Commission* [2004] ECR I-3997, para 52.

342 Case C-482/99 *France v Commission ('Stardust Marine')*, ibid, *Greece v Commission*, ibid; see also Case T-136/05 *Salvat père & fils v Commission* [2007] ECR II-4063, paras 140–65.

343 Case 173/73 *Commission v Italy* [1974] ECR 709, para 16; Decision 2007/580/EC *Slovenian green electricity scheme* [2007] OJ L219/9, paras 66–74. See also Case 78/76 *Steinike und Weinlig v Commission* [1977] ECR 595, paras 19–22 and para 2.77 above. The same applies to, for example, funds derived from television licence fees once they form part of the budget of the State or a public authority: Decision 2006/513/EC *Berlin-Brandenburg DTT* [2006] OJ L200/14, para 52.

344 Case C-345/02 *Pearle* [2004] ECR I-7139, para 36; see also para 2.107 below.

fact that they were repayable.[345] By contrast, voluntary contributions paid by private undertakings and which are not controlled by the State do not constitute State resources, even if they pass through the hands of the State en route to the ultimate beneficiary.[346]

Community resources. Resources of the European Community do not constitute State resources for the purpose of Article 87(1). Accordingly the incorrect allocation of a Community tariff quota was held not to constitute State aid, since the term 'State resources' presupposes that the resources from which the aid is granted emanate from a Member State, rather than the Community.[347] On the other hand, once Community resources come under the control of a Member State (as in the case of European structural funds) they are regarded as State resources.[348] **2.99**

3. Type of measure constituting a grant through State resources

Direct or indirect grant. The aid must be granted 'directly or indirectly' through State resources.[349] A subsidy or other positive transfer of State resources will constitute a direct grant. This category of measure includes, for example, capital investments, loans and payments for goods and services.[350] However it is well established that no actual transfer is required.[351] It is sufficient that the State foregoes revenue that it would otherwise have received.[352] **2.100**

Tax exemptions and other waivers of charges. It follows from the principle of 'foregoing revenue' that tax exemptions and other waivers of charges which would otherwise have fallen due to the State may, where the other aid conditions are satisfied, constitute State aid within Article 87(1). Thus State aid may be granted through the waiver of public debts or penalties, the exemption from or reduction of tax by various means, and the provision of goods and services at an undervalue.[353] **2.101**

[345] Case T-358/94 *Air France v Commission* [1996] ECR II-2109, paras 63–7. See also C-83/98 P *France v Ladbroke Racing and Commission* [2000] ECR I-3271, para 50.

[346] Decision in Case N 514/2001 *Universal Banking Services* (13 February 2002), para 23.

[347] Cases 213–215/81 *Norddeutsches Vieh- und Fleischkontor* [1982] ECR 3583, para 22.

[348] See eg Decision in Case N 157/2006 *South Yorkshire digital region broadband project* (22 November 2006), para 29. For further discussion of the complex application of the State aid rules to structural funds see P Nicolaides, 'Puzzles of State Aid: Structural Funds, Cumulation and De Minimis' (2005) 3 *European State Aid Law Quarterly* 433.

[349] Case 82/77 *Openbaar Ministerie of the Kingdom of the Netherlands v van Tiggele* [1978] ECR 25, para 25; Cases C-72–73/91 *Sloman Neptun* [1993] ECR I-887, para 19; Cases C-52–54/97 *Epifanio Viscido* [1998] ECR I-2629, para 13; Case C-379/98 *PreussenElektra* [2001] ECR I-2099, para 58.

[350] See cases cited at para 2.06 above.

[351] See eg Case C-387/92 *Banco Exterior de España* [1994] ECR I-877, para 14 (tax exemption); C-404/97 *Commission v Portugal* [2000] ECR I-4897, para 45 (State guarantee); and Cases T-204/97 and T-270/97 *EPAC v Commission* [2000] ECR II-2267, para 81 (State guarantee).

[352] Case C-172/03 *Heiser* [2005] ECR I-1627, opinion of AG Tizzano para 52.

[353] See cases cited at para 2.06 above. Where, however, the loss of tax revenue is an incidental effect of a general measure, this does not constitute aid: see para 2.126 below.

Moreover, a measure such as a tax exemption will be regarded as granted through State resources even if it has the net effect of increasing the revenues of a Member State, for example by encouraging the establishment of certain undertakings in that Member State. The material factor is not whether the measure ultimately does or does not result in a loss of State revenue, but rather whether the aid results in a shortfall compared to the application of the normal rules.[354] The Court has also held that the establishment of an emissions trading scheme involved State resources, since the tradable emissions allowances resulted from emissions standards set by the State free of charge, whereas they could have been sold or put up for auction.[355]

2.102 **Potential burdens on State resources.** State guarantees are also regarded as a grant through State resources.[356] While the guarantee might never be called upon, it nevertheless entails a contingent liability, and would constitute an additional burden for the State in the event of its implementation.[357] In similar vein, the announcement of a loan to France Télécom was regarded as a potential burden on State resources, even though the loan agreement was never signed: as long as it was not rescinded, France Télécom could have signed it and called upon the loan at any time, so that the State had to keep the corresponding resources at France Télécom's disposal.[358]

2.103 **Payments by third parties.** The outcome of the debate discussed above is that Article 87(1) does *not* cover aid measures that simply require payments from, or impose losses upon, private individuals, without the direct or indirect involvement of State resources. The classic example is a price fixing measure, such as those in issue in *Van Tiggele* and *PreussenElektra*.[359] A Belgian scheme similar to that in *PreussenElektra*, that required electricity supply companies to buy a certain amount of green electricity each year, was also held not to involve State resources.[360]

---

[354] Cases C-182 and 217/03 *Belgium and Forum 187 v Commission* [2006] ECR I-5479, paras 128–9 and opinion of AG Léger paras 307–9. If under the legal order of a Member State a charge is not normally imposed for a particular service or benefit, then the provision of that service or benefit cannot be regarded as involving State resources: see EFTA Surveillance Authority Decision 314/08/COL *Leifur Eiríksson Air Terminal* (4 June 2008).

[355] Case T-233/04 *Netherlands v Commission* (judgment of 10 April 2008), para 75.

[356] See cases cited at para 2.06 above.

[357] Cases T-204/97 and T-270/97 *EPAC v Commission* [2000] ECR II-2267, para 80.

[358] Decision 2006/621/EC *France Télécom* [2006] OJ L257/11, paras 195-196 (under appeal in Cases T-425 and 444/04 *France and France Télécom v Commission*).

[359] See paras 2.90 and 2.93 above; but cf Decision in Case N 6a/2001 *Irish electricity generated out of peat* (30 October 2001) where it was difficult to determine whether this was simply a mechanism for payments by third parties directly to the aid beneficiary.

[360] Decision in Case N 550/2000 *Green electricity certificates* (25 July 2001). cf however Case T-233/04 *Netherlands v Commission* (judgment of 10 April 2008), distinguishing a Dutch emissions trading scheme from the Belgian and German green electricity requirements; and Decision 2007/580/EC *Slovenian green electricity scheme* [2007] OJ L219/9, paras 66–74, concerning a scheme financed partly through parafiscal taxes which came under the control of the public authorities, which was held to constitute State aid.

Many employment measures will also fall within this category, as the *Sloman Neptun* line of cases demonstrates.[361] In this context, it is not sufficient that the losses for third parties may entail a corresponding reduction in tax revenue from the State from those affected third parties: this is considered too remote an effect on State resources to be relevant.[362]

4. The imputability criterion

Imputability criterion. It is well established in the case-law of the Court that a measure is only State aid if it is attributable[363] or imputable[364] to the State. Article 87(1) thus does not apply to acts of private undertakings which may have the same or similar economic effects as aids resulting from acts of the State. In many cases, the nature of the measure allows State imputability to be assumed. For example, since legislative power is one of the constitutional powers of a State, an aid resulting from legislative measures is necessarily imputable to the State.[365] But where an advantage is granted through the resources of a public or publicly owned undertaking, imputability to the State cannot be inferred. While the control exercised by the public authorities may in some cases imply that the measure should be imputed to the State, the day to day business decisions of a publicly owned undertaking taken without any interference by the public authorities should fall outside the scope of the State aid rules.[366] Hence in *Stardust Marine* the Court held that it was not sufficient that financial assistance measures were adopted by public undertakings under the control of the State; it was necessary to go further and examine whether the public authorities were actually involved in the adoption of the measures.[367] **2.104**

Indicators of imputability. Where aid is granted through the resources of a public undertaking, therefore, it will be necessary to consider the circumstances and context of the case in order to determine whether it may be imputed to the public authorities or whether, by contrast, the measure must be regarded as having been **2.105**

---

[361] See discussion at para 2.90 above.

[362] Cases C-72-73/91 *Sloman Neptun* [1993] ECR I-887, para 21; and Case C-200/97 *Ecotrade* [1998] ECR I-7907, para 36 and opinion of AG Fennelly at para 24.

[363] Cases 67, 68 and 70/85 *Van der Kooy v Commission* [1988] ECR 219, para 28; Case C-303/88 *Italy v Commission ('ENI-Lanerossi')* [1991] ECR I-1433, para 11; Case T-358/94 *Air France v Commission* [1996] ECR II-2109, para 61.

[364] Case T-358/94 *Air France v Commission* [1996] ECR II-2109, para 55; Case C-482/99 *France v Commission ('Stardust Marine')* [2002] ECR I-4397, para 24; Cases C-182 and 217/03 *Belgium and Forum 187 v Commission* [2006] ECR I-5479, para 127.

[365] Case T-358/94 *Air France v Commission* [1996] ECR II-2109, para 59. See also *Belgium and Forum 187 v Commission*, ibid, para 128.

[366] cf Case C-482/99 *France v Commission ('Stardust Marine')* [2002] ECR I-4397, opinion of AG Jacobs, para 55.

[367] ibid, judgment para 52; see also Case T-442/03 *SIC v Commission* (judgment of 26 June 2008), para 95.

adopted as a result of the autonomous actions of that undertaking. The following factors in particular are relevant in determining imputability:

(a) the way in which the undertaking was established;[368]
(b) the legal status of the undertaking (in the sense of its being subject to public law or ordinary company law);[369]
(c) the integration of the undertaking into the structures of the public administration;[370]
(d) the degree of supervision and management of the body by the public authorities. This may include consideration of the extent of the shareholding (if any) of the State, the extent to which the governing board of the undertaking is appointed by the State,[371] and any control over the budget of the undertaking;[372]
(e) the nature of the undertaking's activities and the exercise of those activities on the market in normal conditions of competition with private operators,[373] and the extent to which the undertaking performs regulatory functions;[374]
(f) the extent to which the contested decision was subject to the approval of, or requirements imposed by, the public authorities;[375]
(g) the way in which the measure is presented by the public authorities.[376]

2.106 **Formal independence or autonomy insufficient.** The above criteria show that, while the legal status and structure of the undertaking will be relevant, other factors must be taken into account. It follows that the formal independence of a public body from the State authorities will not suffice, in itself, to exclude State attributability. In the *Air France* case it was held that the conduct of a public sector body, the Caisse des Dépôts et Consignations ('the Caisse'), was attributable to the State even though it enjoyed legal autonomy from the political authorities of

368 See eg Decision 2006/513/EC *Berlin-Brandenburg DTT* [2006] OJ L200/14, para 53 (public authority established by a State Treaty of the Länder of Berlin and Brandenburg).

369 Case C-482/99 *France v Commission ('Stardust Marine')* [2002] ECR I-4397, para 56.

370 ibid.

371 Cases 67, 68 and 70/85 *Van der Kooy v Commission* [1988] ECR 219, para 36, finding that the undertaking Gasunie acted under the control of the public authorities since, *inter alia*, the State directly/indirectly held 50% of its shares and appointed half of the members of its supervisory board. See also Case C-305/89 *Italy v Commission ('Alfa Romeo')* [1991] ECR I-1603, paras 14–16; and Case C-482/99 *France v Commission ('Stardust Marine')* [2002] ECR I-4397, para 56.

372 Decision 2006/513/EC *Berlin-Brandenburg DTT* [2006] OJ L200/14, para 53.

373 Case C-482/99 *France v Commission ('Stardust Marine')* [2002] ECR I-4397, para 56.

374 Decision 2006/513/EC *Berlin-Brandenburg DTT* [2006] OJ L200/14, para 53.

375 Case C-482/99 *France v Commission ('Stardust Marine')* [2002] ECR I-4397, para 55; Cases 67, 68 and 70/85 *Van der Kooy v Commission* [1988] ECR 219, para 36; Case C-305/89 *Italy v Commission ('Alfa Romeo')* [1991] ECR I-1603, paras 14–16.

376 Case 290/83 *Commission v France ('Poor Farmers')* [1985] ECR 439, para 15, commenting that the measure in question was 'put forward by the Government as forming part of a body of measures in favour of farmers which were all notified to the Commission'.

the State. The Court observed that Community law could not permit the rules on State aid to be circumvented merely through the creation of autonomous institutions charged with allocating aid.[377] The Caisse had been established by legislation, and placed under the supervision of the legislature. Its tasks were governed by statutory and regulatory rules, and its directors were appointed by the State. These features were sufficient to show that the Caisse belonged to the public sector, and that its conduct was attributable to the State.[378]

Initiative of public authorities. To demonstrate imputability it is not necessary to show that the public authorities specifically incited the public undertaking to take the aid measures in question.[379] Where the organization of the measure does originate with the State, however, that is likely to show imputability to the State, even if the measure is actually carried out by private undertakings.[380] Conversely the fact that the initiative for a measure clearly comes from a private body will be a strong indicator that it is not imputable to the State. In *Pearle* the Court considered the lawfulness of levies which were paid to a central industry board, and earmarked to finance collective advertising for opticians' businesses. The levy and campaign were both adopted at the request of the Netherlands Opticians' Union (NUVO), a private association. The Court found that the measure was not State aid, noting that the industry board served merely as the vehicle for the levying and allocating of resources collected for a commercial purpose determined by the trade, which had nothing to do with a policy determined by the Netherlands authorities.[381] **2.107**

Implementation of European Directives. Where a State measure transposes Community provisions into national law, the provision at issue is not imputable to the State, but is rather regarded as emanating from an act of the Community legislature. Any resulting benefit for certain undertakings is therefore not State aid within Article 87(1). This is the case even where the Directive allows for alternative implementation which could avoid the distortion of competition.[382] **2.108**

---

[377] Case T-358/94 *Air France v Commission* [1996] ECR II-2109, para 62.

[378] ibid, paras 58–61.

[379] Case C-482/99 *France v Commission ('Stardust Marine')* [2002] ECR I-4397, paras 53–4; Case T-442/03 *SIC v Commission* (judgment of 26 June 2008), paras 96–7.

[380] Case C-126/91 *GEMO* [2003] ECR I-13769, para 26; and see AG Slynn in Cases 67, 68 and 70/85 *Van der Kooy v Commission* [1988] ECR 219, p 250 applying a criterion of whether the undertaking acted 'at the behest or under the dominant or effective influence of the State'.

[381] Case C-345/02 *Pearle* [2004] ECR I-7139, para 37. Although it is not entirely clear whether in this respect the Court specifically had in mind the criterion of imputability, or the requirement of a grant through State resources, its reasoning on this point appears to relate more to the imputability aspect of the problem: see also opinion of AG Ruiz-Jarabo Colomer, paras 74–6, to which the Court refers in para 37. See also Decision 2005/407/EC *British Energy* [2005] OJ L142/26, para 294 (no evidence that renegotiation of BNFL's supply contracts with BE took place at the instigation of the State).

[382] Case T-351/02 *Deutsche Bahn v Commission* [2006] ECR II-1047, paras 99–106.

D. Favouring certain undertakings (selectivity)

2.109 **Purpose of the condition.** The condition that the aid must favour specific undertakings or sectors is one of the defining features of State aid.[383] The purpose of the condition is to avoid an enquiry into the entire legislative regime in Member States by reference to rules applicable in other states. Advocate General Fennelly thus commented in *Ecotrade* that:

> The alternative would imply a generalised review of all State regulation in such fields, by reference to the yardstick, not of the normally applicable rules in that State (for these themselves would be the subject-matter of examination), but, presumably, of the regulations in the other Member States. This would be counter-productive, by penalising those States whose general economic organisation and regulation was the most competitive.[384]

2.110 **Problem areas.** While a key condition of State aid, the selectivity test is probably the most difficult of the State aid conditions to apply in practice, since not every measure that produces an advantage for one or more groups of undertakings over others will fall within the Article 87(1) prohibition. In that respect, two particular cases may be identified. First, the advantage to certain undertakings may be only an incidental effect of a measure which is in fact a 'general measure', applying to all undertakings. Secondly, the different treatment may be justified by the nature and scheme of the system, when the relevant overall system is identified. This section examines first the types of measures which may in principle be regarded as selective, before addressing the measures which are not regarded as selective, either because they are general measures, or because they are justified by the nature and scheme of the system.[385]

1. Selective measures

2.111 **The relevant comparison.** A measure is in principle selective if it produces advantages exclusively for certain undertakings or certain sectors of activity.[386] To determine whether that is the case, it is necessary first to define the point of

---

[383] Case C-200/97 *Ecotrade* [1998] ECR I-7907, para 40; C-295/97 *Rinaldo Piaggio* [1999] ECR I-3735, para 39; C-172/03 *Heiser* [2005] ECR I-1627, para 40; Case C-148/04 *Unicredito Italiano* [2005] ECR I-11137, para 44; Cases C-182 and 217/03 *Belgium and Forum 187 v Commission* [2006] ECR I-5479, para 119.

[384] *Ecotrade*, ibid, opinion para 25.

[385] For an early discussion of the problems of distinguishing between State aids and general measures see K Bacon, 'State Aids and General Measures' (1997) 17 *Yearbook of European Law* 269.

[386] Case T-55/99 *CETM v Commission* [2000] ECR II-3207, para 39; Case T-152/99 *Hijos de Andrés Molina v Commission* [2002] ECR II-3049, para 156; Case T-210/02 *British Aggregates v Commission* [2006] ECR II-2789, para 105.

reference for the comparison.[387] That is not always easy.[388] The Court has held that the comparison must be made with undertakings which are in a 'comparable legal and factual situation', in the light of the objective pursued by the measure in question.[389] As with the question of whether the aid produces a benefit or advantage, the comparison must also relate to undertakings in the same Member State. A measure is not selective simply because it produces an advantage for undertakings in one Member State which is not enjoyed by undertakings in a comparable position in other Member States. Equally, a selective aid may not be defended on the grounds that its aim is to produce parity with the situation in other Member States.[390]

Aids to specific undertakings. The paradigm State aid remains an aid granted to a specific undertaking, ie an individual aid. But most aids will not fall into that category. This section gives examples of the main types of selective aid that have been addressed in the case-law. **2.112**

Direct benefit to particular sectors. The reference in Article 87(1) to 'favouring ... the production of certain goods' makes clear that aid to specific sectors is to be regarded as selective, and the Court has confirmed that a measure may constitute State aid even when it concerns an entire economic sector.[391] Examples include tax measures favouring Italian road hauliers[392] or the banking sector,[393] a rebate on energy taxes for undertakings in the manufacturing sector,[394] a VAT measure **2.113**

---

387 See AG Cosmas in Case C-353/95 *Tiercé Ladbroke v Commission* [1997] ECR I-7007, opinion para 30; and C-88/03 *Portugal v Commission* [2006] ECR I-7115, para 56. This exercise has also been referred to as determining whether the measure constitutes a derogation from the 'legal norm': AG Darmon in Cases C-72–73/91 *Sloman Neptun* [1993] ECR I-887, opinion paras 50 and 53.

388 See the early discussion of this problem by AG Darmon in Case C-189/91 *Kirsammer-Hack* [1993] ECR I-6185, opinion paras 58–61.

389 Case C-143/99 *Adria-Wien Pipeline* [2001] ECR I-8365, para 41; Case C-409/00 *Spain v Commission* [2003] ECR I-1487, para 47; Case C-308/01 *GIL Insurance* [2004] ECR I-4777, para 68; Case C-172/03 *Heiser* [2005] ECR I-1627, para 40; C-88/03 *Portugal v Commission* [2006] ECR I-7115, paras 54 and 56. On this basis the Court annulled a decision which had found an emissions trading scheme to constitute State aid: the Court considered that the undertakings not subject to the scheme were not in a legal and factual situation comparable to those subject to the measures in question: Case T-233/04 *Netherlands v Commission* (judgment of 10 April 2008), paras 88–96.

390 See para 2.12 above, with further references.

391 Case C-148/04 *Unicredito Italiano* [2005] ECR I-11137, paras 44–8; Case C-66/02 *Italy v Commission* [2005] ECR I-10901, paras 94–8. See also opinion of AG Tizzano in Case C-172/03 *Heiser* [2005] ECR I-1627, para 43.

392 Case C-6/97 *Italy v Commission* [1999] ECR I-2981.

393 Case C-148/04 *Unicredito Italiano* [2005] ECR I-11137; Case C-66/02 *Italy v Commission* [2005] ECR I-10901.

394 Case C-143/99 *Adria-Wien Pipeline* [2001] ECR I-8365. cf opinion of AG Mischo in that case, taking the view that the measures did not constitute aid. cf also Case C-75/97 *Belgium v Commission ('Maribel bis/ter')* [1999] ECR I-3671, para 28, indicating that a tax reduction for employers employing manual workers would not in itself be selective.

affecting all medical practitioners in Austria,[395] and a reduction in Belgian social security contributions applicable to employers in sectors as diverse as the extraction of non-energy materials, the chemical industry, the metal-processing industry, the precision instrument and optical instrument industries, transport related activities, horticulture, forestry, and the exploitation of forests.[396] Provided that the aid measure favours specific undertakings or sectors, it does not matter that the aid is granted to a very large group of beneficiaries. The Court has thus repeatedly emphasized that State aid may exist notwithstanding the high number of eligible undertakings, and the diversity and size of the sectors to which those undertakings belong.[397] A measure may also be selective where the beneficiaries are indefinite in number and are not individually identified. In such a case, however, the measure is characterized as an aid scheme rather than an individual aid.[398]

2.114 **Indirect benefit to particular sectors.** A measure may also constitute selective aid where it indirectly benefits a particular sector. In *Commission v Italy* the Court enforced a Commission decision concerning an Italian measure granting greater reductions in employers' sickness insurance contributions for female employees than male employees. The measure was found to be State aid on the basis that it favoured industries employing large numbers of female workers, such as the textile, clothing, footwear and leather goods sectors.[399]

2.115 **Selection by size and resources.** Aid measures targeted at SMEs or self-employed persons, which are not available to larger undertakings, are normally selective.[400] However in many cases aid of this nature will be compatible with the common market on the basis of Commission rules applying to SMEs, discussed in detail in Chapter 10 below. Less frequently, a State may introduce measures benefiting large undertakings under specified conditions, such as the Italian special insolvency rules at issue in the *Ecotrade* case, which benefited large industrial undertakings in difficulties which owed particularly large debts to certain (mainly public)

[395] Case C-172/03 *Heiser* [2005] ECR I-1627.

[396] C-75/97 *Belgium v Commission ('Maribel bis/ter')* [1999] ECR I-3671.

[397] ibid, para 32; Case C-143/99 *Adria-Wien Pipeline* [2001] ECR I-8365, para 48.

[398] Case T-55/99 *CETM v Commission* [2000] ECR II-3207, para 40; Case C-409/00 *Spain v Commission ('Spanish trucks II')* [2003] ECR I-1487, paras 48–9; Case C-126/91 *GEMO* [2003] ECR I-13769, para 39; Case C-172/03 *Heiser* [2005] ECR I-1627, para 42.

[399] Case 203/82 *Commission v Italy* [1983] ECR 2525. See also Decision in Case N 142/2005 *Low Carbon Car Grant Programme* (26 April 2006) where a grant scheme for consumers purchasing low CO_2 cars potentially benefited car manufacturers producing environmentally friendly cars.

[400] Case T-55/99 *CETM v Commission* [2000] ECR II-3207; Case C-351/98 *Spain v Commission ('Spanish trucks')* [2002] ECR I-8031; Case C-409/00 *Spain v Commission ('Spanish trucks II')* [2003] ECR I-1487.

classes of creditors.[401] Such a measure is also liable to be regarded as selective in one or more respects. Similar considerations apply to measures which favour undertakings which make particularly large investments. In a series of cases the CFI considered a system of tax credits created by the legislation of the Basque provinces of Álava, Vizcaya and Guipúzcoa.[402] The credits were granted in respect of investments in new fixed assets, which exceeded ESP 2.5 billion. The Basque authorities, as well as several beneficiaries of the credits, claimed that the legislation was not selective, arguing that the threshold of ESP 2.5 billion was an objective quantitative criterion. The Court rejected these submissions, finding that the financial threshold meant that the credits were reserved only for undertakings with significant financial resources. The Commission had therefore been right to consider that the measures were selective within the meaning of Article 87(1).[403]

Particular geographic regions. Aid to a specific region within a Member State may fall within the scope of Article 87(1).[404] The Court has recently confirmed that a measure may be selective where it contains a 'criterion relating to geographic location in a defined part of the territory of a Member State'.[405] So, for example, a German tax incentive for investment was held to be State aid, on the basis that it only applied to investment in new companies situated in the new German Länder or in Berlin.[406] In some cases, however, the relevant reference framework for comparison may itself be a particular region, so that measures conferring an advantage in only that region will not be selective. This is considered below at paras 2.123–2.125. **2.116**

Public undertakings and public services. State measures which accord preferential treatment to public undertakings, or undertakings providing public services, are likely to be regarded as selective.[407] Insofar as the measures provide **2.117**

[401] Case C-200/97 *Ecotrade* [1998] ECR I-7907; and see C-295/97 *Rinaldo Piaggo* [1999] ECR I-3735.

[402] Cases T-127, 129 and 148/99 *Diputación Foral de Álava v Commission* [2002] ECR II-1275; Cases T-92 and 103/00 *Territorio Histórico de Álava v Commission* [2002] ECR II-1385; and T-269, 271 and 272/99 *Diputación Foral de Guipúzcoa v Commission* [2002] ECR II-4217.

[403] *Diputación Foral de Álava*, ibid, paras 155–61; *Territorio Histórico de Álava,* ibid, paras 37–41; *Diputación Foral de Guipúzcoa*, ibid, paras 53–7.

[404] Case 248/84 *Germany v Commission* [1987] ECR 4013.

[405] Case T-308/00 *Salzgitter v Commission* [2004] ECR II-1933, para 38; this part of the judgment approved on appeal in Case C-408/04 P *Commission v Salzgitter* (judgment of 22 April 2008), para 109.

[406] Case C-156/98 *Germany v Commission* [2000] ECR I-6857; and see para 2.29 above.

[407] See Notice on the application of the State aid rules to measures relating to direct business taxation ('Notice on direct business taxation') [1998] OJ C384/3, para 19; Case T-55/99 *CETM v Commission* [2000] ECR II-3207, where the groups benefiting from the subsidy included local and regional public bodies and bodies providing public services; and Case C-222/04 *Ministero dell'Economia e delle Finanze v Cassa di Risparmio di Firenze* [2006] ECR I-289, para 136 concerning tax advantages for legal persons governed by public law and certain foundations.

compensation for public services, however, consideration would need to be given to whether there is in fact an advantage (see paras 2.63–2.73 above), and whether the provisions of Article 86(2) might apply (see Chapter 3 below).

2.118 **Selection by other criteria.** The categories of selective aids are not closed. Other cases in which aid has been regarded as selective include measures which favour only national products which are exported,[408] a tax on the use of motors which exempted motors used in natural gas compression stations,[409] a highly specific tax concession which benefited only newly established firms with paid up capital of at least ESP 20 million, which carried out investment of at least ESP 80 million in fixed assets and which created at least 10 jobs,[410] Italian employment measures which were designed to benefit (and in fact only benefited) a specific undertaking,[411] Luxembourg's special tax regime for so-called '1929' holding companies,[412] and the Belgian tax regime for coordination centres.[413]

2.119 **Discretionary administrative practices.** A measure which itself is not selective may be regarded as selective where there is an element of discretion in its administration. The Commission has stated that every administrative decision which departs from the general tax rules to the benefit of individual undertakings leads to a presumption of State aid, and must be analysed in detail.[414] This issue first arose in the *Kimberly Clark* case concerning the participation of the French National Employment Fund ('FNE') in companies' redundancy arrangements. While the assistance given was not limited, by the terms of the scheme, to any category of undertakings, the scheme was held to be selective since the FNE could vary the terms of the assistance in a number of respects, including the choice of beneficiaries, the amount of the aid and the conditions under which it was provided.[415] The principle has consistently been endorsed by the Court in its

---

[408] Cases 6 and 11/69 *Commission v France* [1969] ECR 523 (preferential rediscount rate for exports, applicable to all national products exported); Case 57/86 *Greece v Commission* [1988] ECR 2855 (interest repayment on loans for exports for all products except petroleum products). cf Decision in Case NN 20/2006 *Belgian tax on collective investment undertakings* (26 April 2006)—the abolition of a tax on collective investment units marketed abroad was not export aid, since it flowed from the nature of the new taxation criteria, under which tax was only levied on units of collective investment undertakings that were sold on the Belgian market.

[409] Cases C-393/04 and C-41/05 *Air Liquide Industries Belgium* [2006] ECR I-5293, paras 31–2.

[410] Cases T-92 and 103/00 *Territorio Histórico de Álava v Commission* [2002] ECR II-1385, paras 49–50; Cases T-346-348/99 *Diputación Foral de Alava v Commission* [2002] ECR II-4259, para 53.

[411] Cases T-239 and 323/04 *Italy and Brandt v Commission* [2006] ECR II-3265, para 66.

[412] Decision 2006/940/EC *1929 holding companies* [2006] OJ L366/47.

[413] Cases C-182 and 217/03 *Belgium and Forum 187 v Commission* [2006] ECR I-5479.

[414] Notice on direct business taxation, para 22.

[415] Case C-241/94 *France v Commission ('Kimberly Clark')* [1996] ECR I-4551, paras 23–4.

subsequent case-law,[416] which has also emphasized that it is not necessary to show that the conduct of the State body in administering the aid is arbitrary: it is sufficient that the body has a discretion in determining whether to grant aid or the terms under which it is given.[417]

Favouring undertakings outside target group. The fact that the benefit from a measure may extend to an undertaking or undertakings which are not in the specific target group also does not undermine the specificity of measure, or allow the Member State to claim that the measure is a general one. Thus in *GEMO* the ECJ held that a free service for the collection and disposal of animal carcasses and slaughterhouse waste 'essentially benefits farmers and slaughterhouses', and was therefore a selective measure, even if others might also occasionally benefit, such as owners of domestic animals, zoos, and public authorities.[418] For the same reason, the specificity of a measure such as a tax exemption is not excluded by the existence of other exemptions for different undertakings.[419] **2.120**

2. General measures

Basic test. A State measure which benefits *all* undertakings in the national territory, without distinction, is a general measure and does not constitute State aid.[420] General measures include measures of social or economic policy which apply 'to persons in accordance with objective criteria without regard to the location, sector or undertaking in which the beneficiary may be employed'.[421] **2.121**

Examples of general measures. The standard example is a measure which applies uniformly to *all* companies, for example the uniform reduction of corporation tax within a given Member State. The fact that such a measure may favour all national undertakings over their competitors in other Member States, and may incidentally affect certain undertakings more than others (by virtue of the fact that some **2.122**

[416] See eg Case C-200/97 *Ecotrade* [1998] ECR I-7907, para 40; C-295/97 *Rinaldo Piaggio* [1999] ECR I-3735, para 39; Case C-256/97 *DMT* [1999] ECR I-3913, para 27; Case C-480/98 *Spain v Commission ('Magefesa')* [2000] ECR I-8717, para 19 and opinion of AG Mischo para 14; Case T-36/99 *Lenzing* [2004] ECR II-3597, paras 129–33.

[417] See Cases T-127, 129 and 148/99 *Diputación Foral de Álava v Commission* [2002] ECR II-1275, para 154; Cases T-92 and 103/00 *Territorio Histórico de Álava v Commission* [2002] ECR II-1385, para 35; and Case T-36/99 *Lenzing* [2004] ECR II-3597, para 132.

[418] Case C-126/91 *GEMO* [2003] ECR I-13769, paras 36–9. See also Case C-169/84 *CdF Chimie v Commission* [1990] ECR I-3083, para 22.

[419] Cases C-182 and 217/03 *Belgium and Forum 187 v Commission* [2006] ECR I-5479, para 120.

[420] Case C-143/99 *Adria-Wien Pipeline* [2001] ECR I-8365, para 35; and see AG Alber in Case C-409/00 *Spain v Commission ('Spanish trucks II')* [2003] ECR I-1487, opinion paras 60, 65; and see Notice on direct business taxation, para 13. cf the earlier contrary opinion of AG Capotorti in Case 249/81 *Commission v Ireland ('Buy Irish')* [1982] ECR 4005, p 4031.

[421] Commission notice on cooperation between national courts and the Commission in the State aid field [1995] OJ C312/8, para 7.

may have greater liabilities to corporation tax than others), does not make it selective.[422] Other examples include the following:

(a) A general reduction on tax on labour. This is not State aid even though it produces a greater advantage for labour-intensive undertakings than capital-intensive undertakings.[423]

(b) Tax incentives for investment. Tax incentives for environmental, R&D or training investment will not necessarily constitute State aid although they favour only the firms which undertake such investment.[424] The same may apply to other investment incentives, such as the German tax concession for investment in the new German Länder or Berlin. The measure was deemed selective inasmuch as it produced an *indirect* advantage for undertakings in those regions of Germany.[425] By contrast, it was accepted that the *direct* advantage to the investors was not State aid to those undertakings, since it was applicable without distinction to all economically active persons.[426]

(c) Tax benefits for budgetary reserves. A German law obliged nuclear power plants to establish budgetary reserves, to cover the cost of shutting the plants down. These reserves, spread over the life of the plant, had the effect of reducing their tax liability. The measure was, however, general in application as beneficial fiscal treatment of such reserves was available to all companies. The fact that nuclear power plant operators could establish larger reserves because of the greater cost of shutting down their plants did not render the measure a selective advantage.[427]

(d) Insolvency rules. Spanish legislation which provided that debts of undertakings which had been declared insolvent ceased to accrue interest from the date of the declaration of insolvency was not State aid, since it applied to all undertakings alike, and did not constitute favourable treatment for any undertaking or category of undertakings. By contrast, the non-payment by those undertakings of taxes and social security contributions was aid, since it

---

422 cf comments of AG Darmon in Cases C-72-73/91 *Sloman Neptun* [1993] ECR I-887, opinion para 62.

423 Notice on direct business taxation, para 14; Decision in Case N 184/2007 *Cuneo fiscal* (12 September 2007), para 27. See to analogous effect Decision in Case N 271/2006 *Tax relief for supply of surplus heating* (20 December 2006): no aid resulted from general reduction of tax on surplus heat.

424 Notice on direct business taxation, para 14.

425 Case C-156/98 *Germany v Commission* [2000] ECR I-6857, and see discussion at para 2.30 above.

426 ibid, para 23.

427 Decision in Case NN 137/2001 *Reserves for nuclear power station waste management and decommissioning* (11 December 2001); appeal dismissed in Case T-92/02 *Stadtwerke Schwäbisch Hall v Commission* (judgment of 26 January 2006), and on different grounds in Case C-176/06 P *Stadtwerke Schwäbisch Hall v Commission* (judgment of 29 November 2007).

resulted not from the application of general laws, but rather from the discretion exercised by the public authorities.[428]

(e) Indemnification rules. Dutch legislation provided for the indemnification of undertakings when authorities withdrew or imposed changes on environmental permits. The application of this to a car dismantling company which was required to relocate for environmental reasons was not a State aid, since a 'general system for indemnifications derives directly from constitutional rights of properly as recognised by the judicial system'.[429]

(f) Emissions ceiling and trading scheme. Dutch legislation set ceilings for the emission of nitrogen oxide by large industrial facilities, combined with a scheme for the trading of emissions allowances. While the tradability of the allowances constituted an advantage for the undertakings subject to the scheme, their legal and factual situation was not comparable to that of the undertakings to which the ceiling did not apply.[430]

Regional general measures. In certain circumstances a measure may also be a general measure, rather than a selective aid, where it applies to all undertakings within a specific region. The question of when this may occur has been addressed in the context of regional taxation. As with other aid measures targeted at specific regions, a regional tax exemption may in principle fall within Article 87(1).[431] Difficulties arise, however, in relation to measures which are implemented by devolved or autonomous regions. Where a regional authority has a degree of fiscal autonomy, the fact that it chooses to set a lower tax rate than another regional authority in the same Member State should not automatically imply that State aid is being granted. This question was addressed in two recent cases: *Portugal v Commission* and *UGT-Rioja*. **2.123**

Portugal v Commission.[432] *Portugal v Commission* concerned a law adopted by the legislature of the Azores archipelago, which granted a reduction in both income and corporation tax to all natural and legal persons in that region. The Court noted that the key question was the relevant geographic reference framework, in order to establish whether the Azores measure was selective by comparison with the 'normal' rate of taxation.[433] The answer to this question depended on whether the measure was adopted by a regional authority with a sufficient **2.124**

---

428 Case C-480/98 *Spain v Commission ('Magefesa')* [2000] ECR I-8717, in particular opinion of AG Mischo.

429 Decision in Case N 575/2005 *Relocation of car dismantling company Steenbergen* (20 December 2006), para 25.

430 Case T-233/04 *Netherlands v Commission* (judgment of 10 April 2008) (under appeal on this point in Case C-279/08 P *Commission v Netherlands*).

431 See para 2.116 above.

432 C-88/03 *Portugal v Commission* [2006] ECR I-7115.

433 ibid, paras 54–6.

degree of autonomy in relation to central government. Three situations can be distinguished:

(a) Cases where the central government unilaterally decides that the applicable national tax rate should be reduced within a defined geographic area. Such a measure is likely to be regarded as selective, since it is taken by a single body applying to only part of the territory within its competence.[434]

(b) Cases where fiscal competence is distributed such that all local authorities at the same level (regions, districts or others) have the autonomous power to decide, within the limit of their powers, the tax rate applicable in their territory. In this scenario local differences cannot be regarded as selective since there is no single 'normal' rate of taxation against which the local variation could be compared.[435]

(c) Cases where a regional or local authority adopts a tax rate lower than the national rate, which is applicable only to undertakings in the territory within its competence. In this case, the measure escapes classification as selective where the relevant authority is institutionally, procedurally and economically autonomous.[436] The Court elaborated on the criterion of autonomy as follows, at paragraphs 66–8 of its judgment:

> In the [third] situation, the legal framework appropriate to determine the selectivity of a tax measure may be limited to the geographical area concerned where the infra-State body, in particular on account of its status and powers, occupies a fundamental role in the definition of the political and economic environment in which the undertakings present on the territory within its competence operate.
>
> . . . in order that a decision taken in such circumstances can be regarded as having been adopted in the exercise of sufficiently autonomous powers, that decision must, first of all, have been taken by a regional or local authority which has, from a constitutional point of view, a political and administrative status separate from that of the central government. Next, it must have been adopted without the central government being able to directly intervene as regards its content. Finally, the financial consequences of a reduction of the national tax rate for undertakings in the region must not be offset by aid or subsidies from other regions or central government.
>
> It follows that political and fiscal independence of central government which is sufficient as regards the application of Community rules on State aid presupposes . . . that the infra-State body not only has powers in the territory within its competence to adopt measures reducing the tax rate, regardless of any

[434] ibid, opinion of AG Geelhoed para 51; though note that the Court at para 64 of its judgment is silent as to whether this situation would be regarded as selective.

[435] ibid, judgment para 64 and opinion paras 52–3.

[436] ibid, opinion para 54 and judgment paras 65–7. cf earlier contrary opinion of AG Saggio in Cases C-400-402/97 *Administración del Estado v Juntas Generales de Guipúzcoa* [2000] ECR I-1073, paras 36–8 (case subsequently withdrawn before proceeding to judgment).

considerations related to the conduct of the central State, but that in addition it assumes the political and financial consequences of such a measure.

In the case of the Azores, the Court held that these conditions were not fulfilled, on the grounds that the measures were effectively subsidised by central government. The Commission was, accordingly, right to consider the tax reduction to be selective.[437]

UGT-Rioja.[438] Two years later, in the case of *UGT-Rioja*, the Court applied the test of institutional, procedural and economic autonomy to the adoption of a corporation taxation rate in the Basque Country which was lower than the rate normally prevailing in Spain.[439] While the Court ultimately left it to the national court to decide whether the three conditions were satisfied in relation to the Basque regional authorities, it was inclined to the view that at least the first two conditions *were* satisfied.[440] Moreover, as regards the third condition of economic and financial autonomy, the Court emphasized that the mere fact of financial transfers between the central State and the relevant regional bodies did not itself mean that the regional authorities were not financially autonomous in relation to their tax measures. The key question was rather whether the Spanish State compensated the Basque authorities for the consequences of their lower tax rates.[441] The Court's reasoning in this case and *Portugal v Commission* is likely to be of importance particularly to those Member States which devolve specific competences to some, but not all, regions (ie 'asymmetric' devolution) and which are therefore likely to fall within the third of the scenarios outlined by the Court in *Portugal v Commission*.[442] **2.125**

General measures resulting in a loss of tax revenue. A general measure will not fall within Article 87(1) simply because it results in a loss of tax revenue for the State. In *Sloman Neptun* the Court considered legislation which disapplied German employment law in the case of contracts between certain shipping undertakings and crew members who were neither nationals nor residents of an EU Member State. The practical result was that the crew members concerned were paid less, with a consequential loss of tax revenue to the German State. But the Court rejected the argument that this rendered the measure a State aid, stating that the potential loss of tax revenue was inherent in the system and not a means **2.126**

---

437 Case C-88/03 *Portugal v Commission* [2006] ECR I-7115, paras 71–9.

438 Cases C-428–434/06 *UGT-Rioja* (judgment of 11 September 2008).

439 ibid, para 51, and paras 53–60 confirming that these are the only conditions to be satisfied in order for the territory to be itself the relevant reference framework for the assessment of selectivity.

440 ibid, paras 86–7 (institutional autonomy) and 95–110 (procedural autonomy).

441 ibid, paras 123–40.

442 See for example the recent judgment concerning Gibraltar's corporation tax: Cases T-211 and 215/04 *Gibraltar v Commission* (judgment of 18 December 2008).

of granting a particular advantage to the undertakings concerned.[443] Similar statements have been made in subsequent cases concerning the application of insolvency rules which result in the loss of tax revenue for the State.[444]

3. Measures justified by the nature or scheme of the system

2.127 **The test.** Even where a measure is shown to be selective in principle, it will fall outside the terms of Article 87(1) where the advantage to an undertaking or group of undertakings arises from and is justified by 'the nature or general scheme' of the system in question. This principle was established in the early case-law of the Court, in the *Italy v Commission* case, and has been referred to and confirmed in numerous subsequent cases.[445] Other cases have referred, similarly, to justification on the basis of the 'nature or structure' of the system,[446] or on the basis of the 'logic' of the system.[447] The classic example of a measure justified by the logic of the system is a tax structure containing policy-driven differentials, such that taxpayers paying tax at the higher rate could not claim that those falling in lower tax bands benefited from State aid. Almost all of the cases discussed below where this type of justification has been accepted are tax measures of this nature.

2.128 **Burden and standard of proof.** A justification on the basis of the nature or scheme of the system takes the measure outside Article 87(1); it is not an exemption of the kind set out in Article 87(2) and (3). Nevertheless, such a justification has hitherto been regarded by the Court as an exception to the prohibition of State aid, for which the burden of proof rests on the Member State which has introduced the impugned measure.[448] Moreover, the concept of a justification in

---

443 Cases C-72-73/91 *Sloman Neptun* [1993] ECR I-887, para 21.

444 Case C-200/97 *Ecotrade* [1998] ECR I-7907, para 36 and C-480/98 *Spain v Commission ('Magefesa')* [2000] ECR I-8717, para 18.

445 Case 173/73 *Italy v Commission* [1974] ECR 709, para 15; C-75/97 *Belgium v Commission ('Maribel bis/ter')* [1999] ECR I-3671, para 39; Case C-251/97 *France v Commission* [1999] ECR I-6639, para 36; Case C-143/99 *Adria-Wien Pipeline* [2001] ECR I-8365, para 42; Case C-351/98 *Spain v Commission ('Spanish trucks')* [2002] ECR I-8031, para 42; Cases T-269, 271 and 272/99 *Diputación Foral de Guipúzcoa v Commission* [2002] ECR II-4217, para 60; Cases T-346–348/99 *Diputación Foral de Alava v Commission* [2002] ECR II-4259, para 58; C-159/01 *Netherlands v Commission* [2004] ECR I-4461, para 42, Case T-210/02 *British Aggregates v Commission* [2006] ECR II-2789, para 107.

446 Case T-55/99 *CETM v Commission* [2000] ECR II-3207, para 52; Cases T-127, 129 and 148/99 *Diputación Foral de Álava v Commission* [2002] ECR II-1275, para 163; Case C-409/00 *Spain v Commission ('Spanish trucks II')* [2003] ECR I-1487, para 52.

447 Case C-353/95 *Tiercé Ladbroke v Commission* [1997] ECR I-7007, para 35; Case C-6/97 *Italy v Commission* [1999] ECR I-2981, opinion of AG Ruiz-Jarabo, para 27; Case C-53/00 *Ferring v ACOSS* [2001] ECR I-9067, para 17; Case C-172/03 *Heiser* [2005] ECR I-1627, opinion of AG Tizzano, para 47; Case T-210/02 *British Aggregates v Commission* [2006] ECR II-2789, para 152; Case C-222/04 *Ministero dell'Economia e delle Finanze v Cassa di Risparmio di Firenze* [2006] ECR I-289, para 137.

448 Case C-6/97 *Italy v Commission* [1999] ECR I-2981, opinion of AG Ruiz-Jarabo, para 27; C-159/01 *Netherlands v Commission* [2004] ECR I-4461, paras 43–6; Case C-88/03 *Portugal v*

the nature or general scheme of the system has been interpreted strictly.[449] It is not sufficient simply to claim that a selective measure is justified by the nature and general scheme of a system; rather, such a claim must be supported by specific and detailed arguments on the facts.[450]

Conditions for justification. Until very recently, the case-law of the Court provided little guidance as to what would be regarded as a justification relating to the 'nature and general scheme of the system'. As Advocate General Fennelly has pointed out, although the term was coined by the Court in *Italy v Commission*, the Court did not go on to explain what might be included within the concept.[451] Some clarification was provided by the Commission in its 1998 Notice on direct business taxation.[452] Since then, the Court has addressed the question in a number of cases in which a 'nature and general scheme of the system' justification has been claimed. From the analysis of both the Court and the Commission, two key principles can be derived. First, it is insufficient simply to show that there is an external 'objective justification' or legitimate aim for the measure, such as a social, regional or environmental objective.[453] If that were the case, the Member State could avoid the application of Article 87(1) simply by invoking the legitimacy of its aim, which has never been permitted as a matter of principle.[454] Rather, the justification must be related to the 'internal logic' of the system of which the measure falls part.[455] In other words, the differential effects of the measure must derive 'directly from the basic or guiding principles' of the relevant system.[456] Secondly, there must be a direct causal link between that logic and the measure in question;[457] in **2.129**

Commission [2006] ECR I-7115, opinion of AG Geelhoed, para 75. See also Notice on direct business taxation, para 23.

449 Cases T-127, 129 and 148/99 *Diputación Foral de Álava v Commission* [2002] ECR II-1275, para 250.

450 AG Fennelly in Case C-83/98P *France v Ladbroke Racing and Commission* [2000] ECR I-3271, opinion para 26.

451 *France v Ladbroke Racing and Commission*, ibid, opinion para 19.

452 Notice on direct business taxation, paras 23–7.

453 ibid, para 26; Case T-55/99 *CETM v Commission* [2000] ECR II-3207, para 53; Case C-409/00 *Spain v Commission ('Spanish trucks II')* [2003] ECR I-1487, opinion of AG Alber para 65; Case C-143/99 *Adria-Wien Pipeline* [2001] ECR I-8365, paras 49–53. Case C-172/03 *Heiser* [2005] ECR I-1627, para 46; Case C-88/03 *Portugal v Commission* [2006] ECR I-7115, para 81.

454 Case T-55/99 *CETM v Commission* [2000] ECR II-3207, para 53; Case C-172/03 *Heiser* [2005] ECR I-1627, para 46 and AG Tizzano, opinion para 45; and see para 2.3 above.

455 Cases T-127, 129 and 148/99 *Diputación Foral de Alava v Commission* [2002] ECR II-1275, para 164; Cases T-92 and 103/00 *Territorio Histórico de Álava* v *Commission* [2002] ECR II-1385, para 60; Case T-233/04 *Netherlands v Commission* (judgment of 10 April 2008), para 88.

456 Notice on direct business taxation, para 16.

457 Case C-83/98P *France v Ladbroke Racing and Commission* [2000] ECR I-3271, opinion of AG Fennelly para 26; Case C-88/03 *Portugal v Commission* [2006] ECR I-7115, para 81.

other words, the differentiation between undertakings must be consistent with the justification that is put forward.[458]

2.130 **Identifying the 'system'.** In order to determine whether a measure is consistent with the logic of the system of which it forms part, a central question is the identification of the relevant system.[459] This is not always straightforward. A common error is to regard the 'general system' as the aid measure itself, and rely on policy justifications for that measure. If that were correct, then almost every aid measure would justify itself. Rather, it is necessary to refer to a broader benchmark applying to the generality of undertakings, against which the particular provisions alleged to be aid may be measured. That benchmark should be relatively easy to identify in cases where an exemption is created for a certain category of undertakings, derogating from a rule previously applicable to all undertakings. But where a system from its inception distinguishes between different groups of undertakings, for example by treating the manufacture of goods differently from the provision of services, the identification of the system may not be obvious.[460] In difficult cases of this nature, it may be necessary to consider carefully the purpose and effect of the provisions.

2.131 **Recent case-law examples.** Until recently, most cases that considered the 'nature or general scheme of the system' justification went on to reject the application of the principle on the facts. More recently, however, the principle has been applied in a number of cases resulting in findings that the measures in question were not selective and hence not aids within Article 87(1). An early judgment of the Court to this effect was *GIL Insurance*, where different rates of insurance premium tax (IPT) were held to be justified on the basis of deterring tax avoidance: the differential was introduced to counteract the practice of taking advantage of the difference between the standard rate of IPT and that of VAT, by manipulating the prices of rental or sale of appliances and of the associated insurance.[461] Subsequent judgments have included *British Aggregates Association*, finding exemptions in an aggregates levy to be consistent with its environmental objectives,[462] and *Netherlands v Commission*,

[458] A condition satisfied in Case T-233/04 *Netherlands v Commission* (judgment of 10 April 2008), paras 88 and 99; but not in Case T-55/99 *CETM v Commission* [2000] ECR II-3207, para 54; Case C-143/99 *Adria-Wien Pipeline* [2001] ECR I-8365, para 52; or Cases C-182 and 217/03 *Belgium and Forum 187 v Commission* [2006] ECR I-5479, paras 125–6.

[459] Case T-55/99 *CETM v Commission* [2000] ECR II-3207, para 53, commenting on the failure to do so in that case.

[460] See comments of AG Mischo in Case C-143/99 *Adria-Wien Pipeline* [2001] ECR I-8365, opinion paras 41–2.

[461] Case C-308/01 *GIL Insurance* [2004] ECR I-4777, paras 73–8; cf the earlier contrary judgment of the UK Court of Appeal in *R v Customs and Excise Commissioners, ex parte Lunn Poly* [1999] 1 CMLR 1357.

[462] Case T-210/02 *British Aggregates Association v Commission* [2006] ECR II-2789, in particular paras 122–38; consistent with the judgment of the UK High Court in *R (British Aggregates Association) v HM Treasury* [2002] 2 CMLR 51.

making a similar finding regarding an emissions trading scheme for nitrogen oxide which applied only to large industrial facilities.[463]

Other examples. A progressive rate of income or profit taxation may be justified on the basis of the redistributive aim pursued by the tax system.[464] Similarly it is common to impose lighter administrative and regulatory requirements on SMEs; such rules may fall outside the definition of aid altogether, where it can be shown that they are justified by the smaller size and lesser resources of those undertakings.[465] The Commission has also held that the German taxation of energy products used for heating and fuel purposes, but not those used for mineralogical and duel-use processes, was consistent with the nature and logic of the German energy tax system,[466] as was an Italian tax reduction scheme applying to all undertakings in all sectors, save for certain public utilities and public administrations,[467] and an Irish holding company scheme for share disposals, that excluded the disposal of shares deriving the greater part of their value from land or minerals.[468] **2.132**

E. Distortion of competition and effect on trade

1. General principles

Distinct conditions. The final requirement under Article 87(1) is that the measure should be liable to distort competition and affect trade between Member States. These conditions are closely related and are often considered together.[469] But the two conditions remain distinct and should not be conflated. A measure may distort competition, but relate to a wholly local situation. Equally, a measure may affect a market in which there is intra-Community trade, but the distortion or likely distortion of competition may not properly be demonstrated. **2.133**

Liable to distort competition and affect inter-State trade. In the early case-law of the Court, it was sometimes doubted whether the questions of distortion of **2.134**

463 Case T-233/04 *Netherlands v Commission* (judgment of 10 April 2008), paras 97–9 (under appeal on this point in Case C-279/08 P *Commission v Netherlands*); see also para 2.122(f) above.

464 Notice on direct business taxation, para 24; Cases T-127, 129 and 148/99 *Diputación Foral de Álava v Commission* [2002] ECR II-1275, para 164; Cases T-92 and 103/00 *Territorio Histórico de Álava* v *Commission* [2002] ECR II-1385, para 60.

465 See AG Fennelly in Case C-200/97 *Ecotrade* [1998] ECR I-7907, opinion para 26; and Notice on direct business taxation, para 27.

466 Decision in Case N 820/2006 *Tax exemptions for certain energy intensive processes* (7 February 2007). See also Decision in Cases NN 30b/2000 and N 678/2001 *Zero rate for green electricity* (28 November 2001); and Decision 2002/676/EC, ECSC *Dual-use exemption in UK Climate Change Levy* [2002] OJ L229/15.

467 Decision in Case N 184/2007 *Cuneo fiscal* (12 September 2007).

468 Decision in Case N 354/2004 *Company holding regime* (22 November 2004), para 14.

469 See Cases T-298/97 etc *Mauro Alzetta v Commission* [2000] ECR II-2319, para 81; Case T-288/97 *Regione Friuli Venezia Giulia v Commission* [2001] ECR II-1169, para 41.

competition and effects on inter-State trade properly formed part of the definition of State aid at all. In *Van de Kooy v Commission*, Advocate General Slynn opined that the obligation to notify under Article 88 was not limited to those aids which distorted competition and affected trade between Member States; rather, these were matters to be examined by the Commission during its review of the aid.[470] This view did not, however, gain widespread acceptance. The consensus which has now emerged is that it is necessary to show, for the purposes of Article 87(1), at least that the measure is liable to distort competition and affect trade between Member States.[471]

2.135 **No necessity to show actual effects.** No actual effects on competition and trade have to be demonstrated.[472] This is the case even if the measure has already been implemented so that, in theory, its actual effects could be evaluated. The Court's reasoning is that, for new aids which have not been implemented, the Commission cannot determine whether the proposed aid does affect competition and trade, but can only assess whether it might potentially do so.[473] It follows that, in the case of non-notified aid, if the Commission were required to demonstrate the actual effect of the aid on competition and trade, it would favour those Member States which granted aid in breach of the obligation to notify.[474]

2.136 ***Ex ante* evaluation.** The analysis of the effects of the aid measure must be made on the basis of the *ex ante* or *a priori* characteristics of the aid or aid scheme, even if the measure in issue is a non-notified aid which has already been implemented. Indeed, if a non-notified aid was likely to distort competition and affect trade at the time of its entry into force, the condition is satisfied even where the measure transpires to have had little competitive effect. Again, the reasoning is that a Member State which has failed to notify an aid scheme should not be placed in

---

470 Cases 67, 68 and 70/85 *Van der Kooy v Commission* [1988] ECR 219, p 255. See also the similar comments of AG Lenz in Case C-44/93 *Namur-Les Assurances v OND* [1994] ECR I-3829, para 66.

471 Case C-372/97 *Italy v Commission* [2004] ECR I-3679, para 44; Case C-148/04 *Unicredito Italiano* [2005] ECR I-11137, para 55; Cases C-393/04 and C-41/05 *Air Liquide Industries Belgium* [2006] ECR I-5293, para 34. See similar test of 'likely' to affect trade in Case T-34/02 *EURL Le Levant 001 v Commission* [2006] ECR II-267, para 110. Some earlier cases adopted a slightly broader formulation of whether the measure was 'capable' of affecting trade and distorting competition: Case C-387/92 *Banco Exterior de España* [1994] ECR I-877, para 15; Cases T-298/97 etc *Mauro Alzetta v Commission* [2000] ECR II-2319, para 80. The Court in Case C-172/03 *Heiser* [2005] ECR I-1627 appears to regard these as interchangeable: cf paras 27 and 33, but this approach is questionable.

472 Case C-374/97 *Italy v Commission*, ibid, para 44; Cases T-304 and 316/04 *Italy and Wam v Commission* (judgment of 6 September 2006), para 64.

473 Cases T-298/97 etc *Mauro Alzetta v Commission* [2000] ECR II-2319, para 77.

474 See eg Case C-301/87 *France v Commission ('Boussac')* [1990] ECR I-307, para 33; Case C-298/00 P *Italy v Commission* [2004] ECR I-4087, para 49; Cases C-346 and 529/03 *Atzeni v Regione autonoma della Sardegna* [2006] ECR I-1875, para 74.

a better position than a State which has complied with its obligation to notify.[475] The question is therefore whether, at the time of grant of the aid, effects on competition and inter-State trade could have been foreseen. This is a dynamic assessment, which must take account of the likely prospects and developments in the conditions of competition and trade.[476] This does not, however, prevent the Commission from strengthening its case by reference to evidence of actual effects, where these confirm the Commission's analysis of the situation at the time the aid was granted.[477]

Extent of reasoning required. It follows from the foregoing that the threshold for proof of an effect on competition and trade is a relatively low one, and no detailed evidence is required. It is thus not necessary to define the market in question or analyse its structure, or provide evidence of trade flows between Member States.[478] Nevertheless, these effects cannot simply be assumed from the circumstances. It is important for the Commission, in any decision finding State aid, to set out the relevant circumstances leading to the conclusion that the measure is liable to distort competition and affect inter-State trade.[479] A decision which carries out no examination at all of the likely effects of the aid is liable to be annulled.[480] The Court has also annulled a decision concerning aid supporting trade in non-EU countries, which did refer to principles alleged to establish an effect on inter-State trade (such as the international and Community activities of the aid beneficiary, and the fact that the aid improved the position of the beneficiary vis-à-vis firms from other Member States), but did not clearly establish the link between those principles and the facts of the case.[481] **2.137**

2. Distortion of competition

Improvement in financial position. The classic test for a distortion of competition is whether the aid strengthens the position of an undertaking in relation to **2.138**

[475] Case C-351/98 *Spain v Commission* [2002] ECR I-8031, paras 66–7.

[476] AG Fennelly in Case C-83/98 P *France v Ladbroke Racing and Commission* [2000] ECR I-3271, opinion para 31.

[477] See Case C-142/97 *Tubemeuse* [1990] ECR I-959, para 39; Cases T-447-449/93 *AITEC v Commission* [1995] ECR II-1971, para 141; Case C-415/96 *Spain v Commission* [1998] ECR I-6993, para 41.

[478] Cases T-298/97 etc *Mauro Alzetta v Commission* [2000] ECR II-2319, para 95; Case T-55/99 *CETM* [2000] ECR II-3207, para 102.

[479] See Cases 296 and 318/82 *Netherlands and Leeuwarder Papierwarenfabriek v Commission* [1985] ECR 809, para 24; Case 248/84 *Germany v Commission* [1987] ECR 4013, para 18; Cases T-447-449/93 *AITEC v Commission* [1995] ECR II-1971, para 141; Cases C-15/98 and 105/99 *Italy and Sardegna Lines v Commission* [2000] ECR I-8855, para 66.

[480] As was the case in, for example, *Italy and Sardegna Lines v Commission*, ibid; and Case T-34/02 *EURL Le Levant 001 v Commission* [2006] ECR II-267.

[481] Cases T-304 and 316/04 *Italy and Wam v Commission* (judgment of 6 September 2006), para 76.

its competitors.[482] However, this does not require an evaluation of the position of the undertaking's competitors. In fact, it is not necessary to establish the existence of actual competing undertakings at all:[483] that is clear from the fact that a measure may be regarded as aid even if it extends to a whole sector.[484] Rather, the strengthening of a competitive position is assessed simply by reference to the advantage given to the beneficiary, the crucial question being whether that undertaking's financial position as a whole is improved by the aid.[485] The Court has therefore held that aid which is intended to relieve an undertaking of the expenses which it would normally have had to bear in its day-to-day management or its usual activities in principle distorts competition.[486]

2.139 **Competitive conditions in relevant Member State.** As with the question of whether the measure constitutes a benefit or advantage, the relevant reference point is the competitive position in the Member State before the adoption of the measure.[487] If aid is granted in a sector characterized by intense competition, it will usually distort or at least risk distorting competition.[488] Similarly where an economic sector, such as the financial services sector, has been liberalized at Community level thus enhancing the competition which prevailed in that sector, this may indicate that the aid has an actual or potential effect on competition.[489]

2.140 **Competitive conditions in other Member States.** The fact that the measure does not extend to undertakings in other Member States is not relevant: a State authority cannot be criticized for not extending the benefit of the measure to undertakings not established in its territory; and such undertakings are in any event in a wholly different position to undertakings established within the territory.[490] For the same reason, a measure does not cease to distort competition simply because it seeks to offset a competitive disadvantage suffered by undertakings within that

---

[482] Case 730/79 *Philip Morris v Commission* [1980] ECR 2671, para 11; Case C-148/04 *Unicredito Italiano* [2005] ECR I-11137, para 56; Cases C-182 and 217/03 *Belgium and Forum 187 v Commission* [2006] ECR I-5479, para 131.

[483] AG Darmon in Cases C-72-73/91 *Sloman Neptun* [1993] ECR I-887, opinion para 61.

[484] See para 2.113 above.

[485] See Cases 62 and 72/87 *Exécutif Régional Wallon v Commission* [1988] ECR 1573, opinion of AG Lenz para 20, and judgment paras 14–15; and Case T-14/96 *Bretagne Angleterre Irlande (BAI) v Commission* [1999] ECR II-139, para 78.

[486] Case T-459/93 *Siemens* v *Commission* [1995] ECR II-1675, paras 48 and 77; Case T-214/95 *Vlaamse Gewest* v *Commission* [1998] ECR II-717, para 43; Case T-217/02 *Ter Lembeek v Commission* [2006] ECR II-4483, para 177.

[487] See para 2.12 above.

[488] Case T-214/95 *Vlaamse Gewest* v *Commission* [1998] ECR II-717, para 46; Case T-217/02 *Ter Lembeek v Commission* [2006] ECR II-4483, para 178.

[489] Case C-222/04 *Ministero dell'Economia e delle Finanze v Cassa di Risparmio di Firenze* [2006] ECR I-289, paras 142, 145.

[490] Case C-351/98 *Spain v Commission* [2002] ECR I-8031, para 57.

Member State, compared to those in other States.[491] Thus in a recent decision, the Commission ruled against a proposed change to the Swedish system of deductions from taxable income for fishermen. Sweden's argument that the aim of the change was to bring its tax regime into line with neighbouring states (Denmark and Norway) did not prevent the measure from constituting aid.[492] Even if other Member States grant illegal aid to similar undertakings this does not 'cancel out' the negative competitive effects of the aid; on the contrary, it increases the damage to the common market.[493]

Relationship with the selectivity condition. The existence of a distortion of competition is closely related to the question of whether an aid is selective. But it is not sufficient simply to recycle the findings on selectivity so as to conclude that a distortion of competition exists, or is likely to exist. Therefore, even if the circumstances of the aid show that there is plainly a distortion of competition, the Commission is required to refer in its decisions to the particular facts relied upon to support its conclusions on this condition.[494] **2.141**

3. Effect on inter-State trade

Jurisdictional threshold. The condition that the aid must be liable to affect inter-State trade is not a mere formality, but is an important requirement, since it marks the dividing line between the jurisdiction of the Community authorities and the area reserved to the independent action of the Member States.[495] It is therefore necessary to show that the aid strengthens the position of an undertaking compared with other undertakings competing in intra-Community trade.[496] **2.142**

Factors indicating inter-State trade. The condition is undoubtedly met where the beneficiary undertaking is carrying on a cross-border activity, or where the sector affected by the aid is characterized by a substantial level of trade between **2.143**

[491] Cases T-298/97 etc *Mauro Alzetta v Commission* [2000] ECR II-2319, paras 100–1; Case T-55/99 *CETM v Commission* [2000] ECR II-3207, para 85; Case C-298/00 P *Italy v Commission* [2004] ECR I-4087, paras 61–2.

[492] Decision 2006/269/EC *Tax deductions for professional fishermen (Sweden)* [2006] OJ L99/21, para 32.

[493] Case 78/76 *Steinike und Weinlig v Germany* [1977] ECR 595, para 24; Case T-214/95 *Vlaams Gewest v Commission* [1998] ECR II-717, para 54; and more recently Decision 2005/122/EC *Dutch shipyards* [2005] OJ L39/48, para 17.

[494] See Cases C-15/98 and 105/99 *Italian Republic and Sardegna Lines v Commission* [2000] ECR I-8877, paras 66–7.

[495] Case T-93/02 *Confédération nationale du Crédit Mutuel ('Livret bleu')* [2005] ECR II-143, para 82.

[496] Case 730/79 *Philip Morris v Commission* [1980] ECR 2671, para 11; Case C-53/00 *Ferring* [2001] ECR I-9067, para 21; Case C-148/04 *Unicredito Italiano* [2005] ECR I-11137, para 56; Cases C-393/04 and C-41/05 *Air Liquide Industries Belgium* [2006] ECR I-5293, para 35.

Member States.[497] But it is not necessary for the aid beneficiary to be involved in intra-Community trade itself.[498] Even where the beneficiary undertaking does not export its products, but operates only at a local level, the aid may still affect inter-State trade by increasing domestic production, with the effect that undertakings in other Member States have less chance of exporting their products to the market in that Member State.[499] The aid might also enable an undertaking to engage in cross-border activity where it has not done so previously.[500] An effect on inter-State trade is particularly likely to be found where aid is granted to a market with overcapacity,[501] where the beneficiaries are established close to the border between two Member States,[502] where the relevant markets contain a large number of multinational undertakings,[503] where the aid favours international groups,[504] or (as with the criterion of distortion of competition) where the sector has been liberalized at Community level.[505] The support for exports outside the Community may also have a secondary effect on intra-Community trade.[506]

2.144 **Foreseeable developments in trade.** It is also relevant to consider the foreseeable developments in Community trade, since the test relates to the likely effects of the measure. Even if there is no actual trade between Member States at the time when the aid is granted, the condition of a likely effect on inter-State trade may be satisfied where it is foreseeable that there will be a substantial growth in intra-Community

---

[497] See eg Case 173/74 *Commission v Italy* [1974] ECR 709, para 19; Case C-256/97 *DMT* [1999] ECR I-3913, para 29; Cases T-204/97 and T-270/97 *EPAC v Commission* [2000] ECR II-2267, para 85; Case C-113/00 *Spain v Commission* [2002] ECR I-7601, para 50, Case C-114/00 *Spain v Commission* [2002] ECR I-7657, para 65.

[498] Cases C-393/04 and C-41/05 *Air Liquide Industries Belgium* [2006] ECR I-5293, para 35.

[499] Case 102/87 *France v Commission* [1988] ECR 4067, para 19; Case C-303/88 *Italy v Commission* [1991] ECR I-1433, para 27; Case C-75/97 *Belgium v Commission ('Maribel bis/ter')* [1999] ECR I-3671, paras 47, 49; Cases T-298/97 etc *Mauro Alzetta v Commission* [2000] ECR II-2319, para 91; Case C-280/00 *Altmark* [2003] ECR I-7747, paras 77–8. The wide scope of this criterion is illustrated by the Decision in Case N 542/2005 *Individual aid for literary periodical* (21 December 2005), where the Commission found the criterion to be satisfied in the case of state support for a Slovakian literary magazine, notwithstanding the limited circle of readers and the language barrier.

[500] Case C-148/04 *Unicredito Italiano* [2005] ECR I-11137, para 58.

[501] See eg Case C-305/89 *Italy v Commission ('Alfa Romeo')* [1991] ECR I-1603, para 26; Case T-55/99 *CETM v Commission* [2000] ECR II-3207, paras 86-87; Case C-351/98 *Spain v Commission* [2002] ECR I-8031, para 64.

[502] Case C-310/99 *Italy v Commission* [2002] ECR I-2289, paras 84–5.

[503] Case C-53/00 *Ferring v ACOSS* [2001] ECR I-9067, para 21.

[504] Cases C-182 and 217/03 *Belgium and Forum 187 v Commission* [2006] ECR I-5479, para 134.

[505] Case C-148/04 *Unicredito Italiano* [2005] ECR I-11137, para 57; Case C-66/02 *Italy v Commission* [2005] ECR I-10901, para 116; Case C-222/04 *Ministero dell'Economia e delle Finanze v Cassa di Risparmio di Firenze* [2006] ECR I-289, para 142.

[506] See Communication of the Commission to the Member States pursuant to Article 93(1) of the EC Treaty applying Articles 92 and 93 of the Treaty to short-term export-credit insurance [1997] OJ C281/4 as amended [2005] OJ C325/22.

trade in the product.[507] In the *Tubemeuse* judgment, the ECJ accepted that the aid granted to Tubemeuse, whose exports outside the Community when the contested decision was adopted accounted for some 90% of its turnover, satisfied the condition of inter-State trade since the company's stated object was to concentrate on other markets. 'It was thus reasonably foreseeable that Tubemeuse would redirect its activities towards the internal Community market.'[508] On occasion, the Court has accepted an even lower standard. In *Heiser*, an effect on trade was found in respect of small amounts of aid to medical practitioners in Austria, on the grounds that it was 'not inconceivable' that practitioners in Austria might be in competition with those established in another Member State.[509]

Cases where no effect on inter-State trade. It may be seen from the above that the cases where no actual or potential effect on inter-State trade can be shown are likely to be rare. One exception, however, is where a market has not been liberalized at the time of the aid. In the *Sardegna Lines* case a 1997 decision concerning aid for Sardinian shipping companies was annulled on the grounds (among others) that the Commission had failed to take into account the fact that until 1 January 1999 island cabotage in the Mediterranean was excluded from the liberalization of maritime transport services within Member States. Although at the hearing the Commission had pointed to various factors showing that this did not preclude an effect on inter-State trade in maritime services, these had not been identified in its decision.[510] The Court has also doubted whether an effect on trade existed in the case of aid for a cruise vessel intended for operation in a French overseas territory, which was not part of the EU.[511] More generally, Advocate General Jacobs has commented that: **2.145**

> In economic sectors with little competition in intra-Community trade such as car repairs, taxi services, or sectors with prohibitive transport costs, aid of a relatively

[507] Cases T-447/93 to T-449/94 *AITEC v Commission* [1995] ECR II-1971, paras 139, 141; Cases T-298/97 etc *Mauro Alzetta v Commission* [2000] ECR II-2319, para 80.

[508] Case C-142/87 *Belgium v Commission ('Tubemeuse')* [1990] ECR I-959, paras 35–40. See also Cases T-304 and 316/04 *Italy and Wam v Commission* (judgment of 6 September 2006), para 63, ruling that it could not be excluded that aid to support trade in non-EU countries would have an effect on trade, but specific reasoning would be required to support such a finding.

[509] Case C-172/03 *Heiser* [2005] ECR I-1627, paras 33, 35, and see opinion of AG Tizzano, para 58.

[510] Cases C-15/98 and C-105/99 *Italian Republic and Sardegna Lines v Commission* [2000] ECR I-8855, paras 68–70; a new decision reaching substantially the same conclusion as the original decision was adopted by the Commission in 2007: see Decision 2008/92/EC *Aid to the Sardinian shipping sector* [2008] OJ L29/24. See also Cases T-298/97 etc *Mauro Alzetta v Commission* [2000] ECR II-2319, para 143.

[511] Case T-34/02 *EURL Le Levant 001 v Commission* [2006] ECR II-267, paras 115–17, though not coming to a definitive conclusion on this point, since raised in the context of a plea of lack of reasons.

> small amount granted to small undertakings operating on essentially local markets might not affect trade between member States.[512]

These cases only emphasize, however, the limited situations where an absence of inter-State trade may plausibly be claimed.

4. *De minimis* aids

2.146 **No jurisprudential *de minimis* rule.** The Court has consistently emphasized that even a very small amount of aid, granted to relatively small undertakings, may distort competition and affect trade between Member States. It has therefore rejected arguments that Article 87(1) should be read so as to exclude insignificant or *de minimis* amounts of aid.[513] As the Court has pointed out, where the benefit to an undertaking is limited, competition is distorted to a lesser extent, but is still distorted.[514] Accordingly, it is not necessary to show that the effects on competition and inter-State trade are significant or substantial:[515] there is no threshold or percentage below which it may be considered that competition and trade are not affected, within the meaning of Article 87(1).[516]

2.147 **Commission practice.** Even if Article 87(1) itself does not exclude *de minimis* aids, the Commission has taken the view that not all aid has a perceptible impact on trade and competition between Member States, in particular small amounts of aid to SMEs.[517] In 1992, in an effort to reduce the administrative burden on SMEs, as well as the Member States and the Commission itself, and allow the Commission to concentrate its resources on cases of real importance, the Commission introduced a *de minimis* rule in its guidelines on State aid for SMEs. This set a threshold figure below which Article 87(1) could be said not to apply. A measure falling below this threshold was exempt from the obligation to notify.[518] In 1996, this rule was amended and incorporated in a specific notice on the

---

512 Case C-126/91 *GEMO* [2003] ECR I-13769, opinion para 145; and similar statement in Case C-113/00 *Spain v Commission* [2002] ECR I-7601, opinion para 25. The principle was applied in Decision 2001/605/EC *Renove II* [2001] OJ L 212/34, para 29 (other parts of the decision annulled in Case C-409/00 *Spain v Commission ('Spanish trucks II')* [2003] ECR I-1487).

513 Case 57/86 *Greece v Commission* [1988] ECR 2855, paras 17–18; Case C-142/87 *Belgium v Commission* [1990] ECR I-959, para 43; Case C-310/99 *Italy v Commission* [2002] ECR I-2289, para 86; Case C-172/03 *Heiser* [2005] ECR I-1627, para 32.

514 Case T-214/95 *Vlaams Gewest v Commission* [1998] ECR II-717, para 46.

515 Case T-55/99 *CETM v Commission* [2000] ECR II-3207, para 94.

516 See Case C-71/04 *Administración del Estado v Xunta de Galicia* [2005] ECR I-7419, para 41.

517 See eg comment in Decision in Case N 599/1999 *Standardised record books for cattle and sheep farmers* (14 December 1999) that the measure budgeted at £150,00 in total, representing about €1 per recipient, would have a 'purely hypothetical' effect on trade between Member States.

518 Community guidelines on State aid for small and medium-sized enterprises (SMEs) [1992] OJ C213/2, para 3.2.

de minimis rule, which covered a broader range of measures.[519] This did not, however, resolve the tension between the Commission practice and that of the Court, which continued to reject any *de minimis* rule in the context of Article 87(1). To address this problem, and to increase transparency and legal certainty, the *de minimis* rule was ultimately incorporated in Regulation 69/2001.[520] This was replaced by Regulation 1998/2006, which applies from 1 January 2007 to 31 December 2013.[521]

***De minimis* Regulation.** Regulation 1998/2006 applies to aid to undertakings in all sectors, subject to the following exceptions: aid for the fishery and aquaculture sectors, aid for the primary production of agricultural products, certain aid to undertakings active in the processing and marketing of agricultural products, export aid, aid favouring domestic over imported goods, aid for undertakings active in the coal sector, aid for the acquisition of road freight transport vehicles and aid for undertakings in difficulty.[522] In all other cases, *de minimis* aid may be granted up to a ceiling of €200,000 per undertaking, over any period of three years, or €100,000 per undertaking in the road transport sector. The aid must also be 'transparent', such that it is possible to calculate precisely the gross grant equivalent of the aid ex ante without need to undertake a risk assessment. In such cases, the aid is deemed not to meet the criteria of Article 87(1) and does not need to be notified under Article 88(3).[523] Separate Regulations have been adopted setting out the *de minimis* rules applicable to the primary production of agricultural products, and the fisheries sector. These are considered in Chapter 11 below.[524] **2.148**

Aids falling outside the Regulation. On the basis of the Court's case-law above, the *de minimis* rule will not apply to any aid falling outside the scope of the relevant *de minimis* Regulation. In those cases, the prohibition in Article 87(1) and the notification requirement in Article 88(3) will continue to apply even to very small grants of State aid. This is consistent with the practice of the Court in relation to earlier *de minimis* legislation.[525] Furthermore, even in a sector covered **2.149**

---

[519] Commission notice on the de minimis rule for State aid [1996] OJ C68/9.

[520] Commission Regulation (EC) 69/2001 on the application of Articles 87 and 88 of the EC Treaty to *de minimis* aid [2001] OJ L10/30.

[521] Commission Regulation (EC) 1998/2006 on the application of Articles 87 and 88 of the Treaty to *de minimis* aid [2006] OJ L379/5.

[522] ibid, Article 1.

[523] ibid, Article 2; and see in this connection Communication from the Commission on the revision of the method for setting the reference and discount rates [2008] OJ C14/6.

[524] See paras 11.18–11.20 (agriculture) and 11.63 (fisheries) below.

[525] See regarding the transport sector Cases T-298/97 etc *Mauro Alzetta v Commission* [2000] ECR II-2319, para 86; Case C-351/98 *Spain v Commission* [2002] ECR I-8031, paras 61–5; Case C-409/00 *Spain v Commission* [2003] ECR I-1487, paras 76–7; Case C-372/97 *Italy v Commission* [2004] ECR I-3679, paras 58–9; and regarding the agriculture and fisheries sectors Case C-113/00

by the Regulations, it appears that they will not apply to a measure which does not limit the amount of aid which may be received by an individual undertaking to the specified ceilings.[526]

Spain v Commission [2002] ECR I-7601, para 35; Case C-114/00 *Spain v Commission* [2002] ECR I-7657, para 51; Case C-278/00 *Greece v Commission* [2004] ECR I-3997, paras 69–75.

526 See Case C-156/98 *Germany v Commission* [2000] ECR I-6857, paras 39–40; Case C-172/03 *Heiser* [2005] ECR I-1627, para 34; and the two petrol station cases Case C-382/99 *Netherlands v Commission* [2002] ECR I-5163 and Case T-354/99 *Kuwait Petroleum v Commission* [2006] ECR II-1475, discussed at para 2.31 above.

3

COMPATIBILITY OF AID—GENERAL PRINCIPLES

Main legislation and guidelines

Council Regulation (EC) 994/98 on the application of Articles 92 and 93 of the Treaty establishing the European Community to certain categories of horizontal State aid ('Enabling Regulation') [1998] OJ L142/1

Commission Regulation (EC) 800/2008 on the application of Articles 87 and 88 of the Treaty declaring certain categories of aid compatible with the common market (General Block Exemption Regulation) ('GBER') [2008] OJ L214/3

Decision 2005/842/EC on the application of Article 86(2) of the EC Treaty to State aid in the form of public service compensation granted to certain undertakings entrusted with the operation of services of general economic interest ('Article 86(2) Decision') [2005] OJ L312/67

Community framework for State aid in the form of public service compensation ('Article 86(2) Framework') [2005] OJ C297/4

A. Introduction

3.01 **Overview of derogations.** Article 87(1) EC establishes a presumption that the State aid measures satisfying the criteria laid down in that provision are unlawful and prohibited. The wide interpretation given to the concept of aid[1] means that a large swathe of national economic policy measures are in principle caught by this prohibition. But the introductory words of Article 87(1) ('Save as otherwise provided in this Treaty . . .') themselves make clear that this prohibition is neither absolute nor unconditional,[2] and the Treaty provides for a number of derogations. First and foremost, Article 87(2) and (3) establishes wide exceptions to the prohibition in Article 87(1). Article 86(2) has also been of increasing significance in allowing undertakings delivering services of general economic interest to receive State aid. In addition, the Council has the power under Article 87(3)(e) and the third subparagraph of Article 88(2) to create new derogations for measures not covered by any of the existing ones. Particular exceptions also apply to the agriculture, fisheries and transport sectors. It is this range of derogations from the general prohibition of State aids which forms the subject of the present chapter, which addresses the interpretation and application of the derogations in general terms, as well as the relevant block exemptions and guidelines. Chapters 5 to 15 contain more detailed discussion of the application of the derogations in the cases of horizontal aids, aids to specific sectors and regional aid.

3.02 **Articles 87(2) and (3).** Article 87(2) and (3) provide as follows:

> (2) The following shall be compatible with the common market:
> (a) aid having a social character, granted to individual consumers, provided that such aid is granted without discrimination related to the origin of the products concerned;
> (b) aid to make good the damage caused by natural disasters or exceptional occurrences;
> (c) aid granted to the economy of certain areas of the Federal Republic of Germany affected by the division of Germany, in so far as such aid is required in order to compensate for the economic disadvantages caused by that division.

[1] See Chapter 2 above.

[2] Case 78/76 *Steinike & Weinlig* [1977] ECR 595, para 8.

(3) The following may be considered to be compatible with the common market:
  (a) aid to promote the economic development of areas where the standard of living is abnormally low or where there is serious underemployment;
  (b) aid to promote the execution of an important project of common European interest or to remedy a serious disturbance in the economy of a Member State;
  (c) aid to facilitate the development of certain economic activities or of certain economic areas, where such aid does not adversely affect trading conditions to an extent contrary to the common interest;
  (d) aid to promote culture and heritage conservation where such aid does not affect trading conditions and competition in the Community to an extent that is contrary to the common interest;
  (e) such other categories of aid as may be specified by decision of the Council acting by a qualified majority on a proposal from the Commission.

It will be apparent that the exceptions in these two paragraphs of Article 87 are quite distinct in nature. Article 87(2) enumerates types of aid which are *automatically* lawful and which the Commission must therefore declare compatible if the relevant conditions are satisfied. In practice, however, this provision is now only of minor importance due to the very limited categories of aid to which it applies. Article 87(2)(c) in particular, providing for 'cold war' aids to Germany, has fallen almost completely into disuse. A far more important role is played by Article 87(3), which contains a list of types of aid which the Commission has the *power* to authorize. This confers upon the Commission a wide discretion, which the Commission has used to direct aid according to Community policy objectives. Notwithstanding that discretion, however, both Article 87(2) and Article 87(3) alike are subject to the principle that, as derogations from the general prohibition of aid in Article 87(1), they should be interpreted narrowly.[3]

Article 86(2). Article 86(2) provides that: 3.03

> Undertakings entrusted with the operation of services of general economic interest or having the character of a revenue-producing monopoly shall be subject to the rules contained in this Treaty, in particular to the rules on competition, in so far as the application of such rules does not obstruct the performance, in law or in fact, of the particular tasks assigned to them. The development of trade must not be affected to such an extent as would be contrary to the interests of the Community.

This provision thus removes undertakings engaged in the delivery of services in the public interest from the application of the Treaty if certain conditions are met. Its application to the Treaty's rules on competition and free movement of goods and services is well established. But the interaction between Article 86(2) and the

[3] Case C-156/98 *Germany v Commission* [2000] ECR I-6857, para 49; Case 730/79 *Philip Morris v Commission* [1980] ECR 2671, opinion of AG Caportorti at p 2701; Case C-301/87 *France v Commission ('Boussac')* [1990] ECR I-307, opinion of AG Jacobs para 70; Case T-171/02 *Regione autonoma della Sardegna v Commission* [2005] ECR II-2123, para 165.

State aid rules is not straightforward. In terms of substance, the scope of the provision has been reduced to some extent in the wake of the *Ferring* and *Altmark* judgments, and the relationship between Article 87(1) and Article 86(2) has still to be clarified. From a procedural perspective, there is an unresolved debate about the direct effect of the provision, although it is now clear that a State aid falling with Article 86(2) must still be notified to and approved by the Commission prior to implementation.

3.04 **Derogations created by the Council.** The Treaty provides for Council intervention in State aid cases in two respects. Article 87(3)(e) allows the Council, following a proposal by the Commission, to establish further categories of aid which may be declared compatible by the Commission, in addition to the existing categories set out in Article 87(3)(a) to (d). In relation to any further categories so established, the Commission's supervisory role remains intact. By contrast, the third subparagraph of Article 88(2) allows the Council in exceptional circumstances to clear individual aid measures itself. This enables the Council effectively to bypass (though not overrule) the Commission.

3.05 **Burden of proof.** A consequence of the narrow interpretation of derogations is that it is for the person invoking them—usually the aid beneficiary or the Member State wanting to pay the aid—to establish that the conditions for the application of the derogation are satisfied.[4] According to the ECJ, 'a Member State which seeks to be allowed to grant aid by way of derogation from the Treaty rules has a duty to collaborate with the Commission. In pursuance of that duty, it must in particular provide all the information to enable the Commission to verify that the conditions for the derogation sought are fulfilled.'[5]

B. Article 87(2)—automatic compatibility

3.06 **Mandatory exemptions.** The types of aid enumerated in Article 87(2) are always exempted from the general prohibition of aids under Article 87(1). These aids still need to be notified to the Commission under Article 88(3) and are subject to the standstill clause contained in the third sentence of that provision. But the Commission has no discretion as to whether or not to authorize the aid.[6] Its procedure is merely aimed at ascertaining that the conditions set out in Article 87(2)

4 See Case 730/79 *Philip Morris v Commission* [1980] ECR 2671, opinion of AG Caportorti at p 2702; Case 248/84 *Germany v Commission* [1987] ECR 4013, opinion of AG Darmon at para 8; Case C-277/00 *Germany v Commission* [2004] ECR I-3925, para 55 (specifically in relation to Article 87(2)(c)).

5 Case C-364/90 *Italy v Commission* [1993] ECR I-2097 at para 20.

6 See eg Case T-268/06 *Olympiaki Aeroporia Ypiresies ('Olympic Airways') v Commission* (judgment of 25 June 2008), para 53 in relation to Article 87(2)(b).

are in fact fulfilled. The following sections consider in more detail the interpretation and application of each of the three exemptions in Article 87(2).

1. Article 87(2)(a)—social aids

Scope. Aids having a social character directly granted to individual consumers are exempted from the general prohibition of aid under Article 87(1), provided that they are granted without discrimination related to the origin of the products concerned. The way in which the aids are granted (eg through vouchers, distribution in kind or discounts) is irrelevant in this context as long as it can be ensured that the aid in fact benefits individual consumers. **3.07**

Social character. The aid should be limited to certain categories of consumers whose situation justifies social intervention. This has included various aid schemes for categories of individuals travelling between outlying islands and mainland Europe, for example between the French overseas departments and mainland France,[7] aid supporting high-risk public sector workers subscribing to sickness and incapacity insurance contracts,[8] and aids to low-income groups purchasing digital television equipment.[9] **3.08**

Individual consumers. The meaning of the term 'consumer' under Article 87(2)(a) is necessarily limited to that of final consumers only, as the social character of the aids in question could otherwise not be achieved. The requirement that aid be directly granted to 'individual' consumers has substantially limited its scope of application. But it seems likely that it is not necessary to verify that each and every beneficiary is in need of aid for social reasons. This may allow Member States to grant aid under Article 87(2)(a) to some more general categories of its population. For example, in the air transport field, in order to have a social character aid should, in principle, only cover specific categories of passengers travelling on a route—eg children, disabled people and people on low incomes). However, the Commission has expressed the view that if a particular route links an underprivileged region, or mainly islands (making its population more dependent on air transport), social aid could cover the entire population of the region.[10] **3.09**

---

[7] See eg Decision in Case NN 25/2005 *Mobility passport* (20 April 2005); Decision in Case N 656/2006 *Réunion social aid scheme* (4 December 2006) and cases referred to in n 11 thereof.

[8] Decision in Case N 911/2006 *Protection social complémentaire des agents de l'État* (30 May 2007).

[9] Decisions in Cases N 546/2006 *French digital television* (6 December 2006); and N 622/2003 *Austrian fund for digitalization* (16 March 2005). But cf Decision 2007/374/EC *Digital decoders – Italy* [2007] OJ L147/1: subsidy to entire population not within Article 87(2)(a) simply because it inevitably assisted certain consumers in need of aid.

[10] Commission guidelines on the Application of Articles 92 and 93 of the EC Treaty and Article 61 of the EEA agreement to State aids in the aviation sector [1994] OJ C350/5, para 24.

3.10 **Without discrimination.** The requirement that aid must be granted without discrimination related to the origin of the products is designed to prevent disguised benefits to certain undertakings or sectors. In order to determine whether this condition is satisfied, it must be ascertained whether consumers benefit from the aid in question irrespective of the economic operator supplying the product or service.[11] It will be difficult to prove that this criterion is met where only one operator is actually operating on a particular market, as for example where a flight or shipping route is subsidized out of public funds. In such a case, the very fact that subsidies are necessary to make a service viable will often act as a sufficient barrier to market entry to keep a local monopoly in place, and thus entail all aid being paid (in practice) to one and the same undertaking. The burden is therefore on the Member State and the intended aid beneficiary to establish that the ultimate consumers could also benefit from the aid at issue by using the services of other companies capable of fulfilling the social objective pursued.[12] The non-discrimination test was not satisfied in the *P&O European Ferries (Vizcaya)* case, where travel vouchers were only purchased from one particular ferry line which had not been 'selected in a transparent manner', and where the authorities 'might have achieved identical social goals with a diversified travel offer', benefiting a range of ferry operators.[13]

3.11 **Relationship with Article 87(1).** Many if not most social aids granted to individual consumers will lack the degree of specificity or selectivity required to satisfy the criteria of Article 87(1). As a consequence, Article 87(2)(a) is likely to become relevant only where the aid to individual consumers does involve indirect benefits to particular producers. An example would be national authorities purchasing foodstuffs from particular producers to pass the products on for free to individual consumers who would not otherwise have purchased those goods, or at least not from the same producer.[14] In those cases, it will usually be all the more important for the Member State to be able to show that the particular producers were chosen by transparent means.

---

[11] Cases T-116 and 118/01 *P&O European Ferries (Vizcaya) v Commission* [2003] ECR II-2957, para 163 (upheld on appeal in Case C-442/03 P *P&O European Ferries (Vizcaya) v Commission* [2006] ECR I-4845).

[12] Cases T-116/01 and T-118/01 *P&O European Ferries (Vizcaya) v Commission*, ibid, para 167 (upheld on appeal in Case C-442/03 P *P&O European Ferries (Vizcaya) v Commission*, ibid).

[13] Case C-442/03 P *P&O European Ferries (Vizcaya) v Commission* [2006] ECR I-4845, paras 123–7.

[14] Case T-93/02 *Confédération nationale du Crédit mutuel v Commission ('Livret bleu')* [2005] ECR II-143, paras 94–5.

2. Article 87(2)(b)—disaster aids

Scope. Aids necessary to make good the damage caused by natural disasters or exceptional occurrences are exempted from the general prohibition of aids under Article 87(1).[15] As with other derogations from Article 87(1), however, the provision is interpreted narrowly.[16] The Commission has interpreted Article 87(2)(b) to include national aids compensating for material damage of all kinds caused by earthquakes, floods,[17] avalanches and landslides. Exceptional circumstances such as wars, internal disturbances or strikes and, with certain reservations, nuclear disasters[18] and fires (depending on their extent) are to be treated in the same way.[19] In order to facilitate rapid crisis management, the Commission will authorize aid schemes in the agricultural sector to compensate for the damages of natural disasters, provided that a sufficiently precise description can be established.[20] **3.12**

Strict interpretation. As an exception from the general principle of incompatibility of State aid, the notions of 'natural disaster' and 'exceptional occurrence' are to be interpreted strictly.[21] The Commission also takes the view that an exceptional occurrence is something which is, by its nature, unforeseeable, and that the exemption therefore cannot be applied to aid having a preventive character.[22] **3.13**

No overcompensation. In order to be compatible under Article 87(2)(b), the aid must be proportional to the damage caused by the exceptional occurrence, and must not result in overcompensation.[23] A direct causal link[24] is therefore required between the damage caused and the natural disaster and a precise determination of the damage suffered by the affected producers is necessary.[25] A Member State **3.14**

---

[15] Case T-171/02 *Regione autonoma della Sardegna v Commission* [2005] ECR II-2123, para 165.

[16] Case C-278/00 *Greece v Commission* [2004] ECR I-3997, para 81; Cases C-346 and 529/03 *Atzeni v Regione Autonoma della Sardegna* [2006] ECR I-1875, para 79; and Case T-268/06 *Olympiaki Aeroporia Ypiresies ('Olympic Airways') v Commission* (judgment of 25 June 2008), para 52.

[17] See specifically Decision in Case N 463a/2006 *Reconstruction loan to make good the damage caused by the 2006 flood* (11 December 2006).

[18] Consequences of the Chernobyl nuclear disaster were raised by the Greek government in Case C-278/00 *Greece v Commission* [2004] ECR I-3997, paras 78–89, without being as such criticized by the ECJ.

[19] Decision 2001/259/EC *Greek fruit and vegetable growers* [2001] OJ L93/48, para 30.

[20] Community guidelines for State aid in the agriculture and forestry sector 2007–2013 ('Agriculture Guidelines') [2006] OJ C319/1, para 121; see further Chapter 11 below.

[21] Decision 2000/625/EC *Sea transport of Irish livestock* [2000] OJ L263/17, para 83.

[22] ibid, para 92.

[23] Decision in Case N 463a/2006 *Reconstruction loan to make good the damage caused by the 2006 flood* (11 December 2006), para 28.

[24] Case C-156/98 *Germany v Commission* [2000] ECR I-6857, para 54; Case C-301/96 *Germany v Commission* [2003] ECR I-9919, para 72; Case C-278/00 *Greece v Commission* [2004] ECR I-3997, para 82; and Cases C-346 and 529/03 *Atzeni v Regione Autonoma della Sardegna* [2006] ECR I-1875, para 79.

[25] Case C-73/03 *Spain v Commission* (judgment of 11 November 2004), para 37; Case T-268/06 *Olympiaki Aeroporia Ypiresies ('Olympic Airways') v Commission* (judgment of 25 June 2008), para 52.

should demonstrate that the aid will be calculated as precisely as possible so as to compensate each affected producer exactly for the disadvantage suffered by him. Recourse to average figures for an industry will not, generally, suffice.[26] On the other hand, the Commission does not require Member States to undertake the individual processing of potentially thousands of applications, each involving relatively small sums of money, to exclude overcompensation altogether.[27]

3.15 **Bad weather.** Bad weather conditions such as frost, hail, ice, rain and drought are not regarded as natural disasters. However in the agricultural sector, where the damage suffered by the aid recipient represents at least 30% of normal production, compensation for farmers may be authorized under Article 87(3)(c).[28]

3.16 **Plant and animal disease.** As a general rule, outbreaks of animal or plant diseases are not considered to constitute natural disasters or exceptional occurrences.[29] Thus, an invasion of field mice in Greek melon and watermelon crops was not considered capable of being covered by Article 87(2)(b), the Commission noting that this was a recurring phenomenon in Greece.[30] Exceptionally, however, Article 87(2)(b) has been applied to aid compensating for damage caused by the BSE crisis.[31] Such aids may, however, be approved under Article 87(3)(c), where they are part of a programme for the prevention, control or eradication of the disease concerned.[32]

3.17 **11 September 2001.** Following the terrorist attacks of 11 September 2001, and the effect of those attacks on the aviation industry, the Commission considered that aid could be approved under Article 87(2)(b) to compensate for the extra cost of insurance, and to cover the losses incurred as a result of American airspace being closed for four days.[33] The Commission subsequently approved aid for airlines granted by a number of Member States on this basis.[34] In the *Olympic Airways* case, however, the CFI held that approval could not be limited to compensation

---

[26] *Spain v Commission*, ibid, paras 39–41.

[27] Decision 2000/760/EC *Irish livestock farmers* [2000] OJ L305/11, para 82.

[28] Agriculture Guidelines para 125, departing from the Commission's former practice of approving such aids on the basis of Article 87(2)(b). For an example of an aid scheme adopted on this principle see Decision in Case NN 54a/2004 *National solidarity fund for natural disasters* (7 June 2005) and decisions taken under that scheme.

[29] Agriculture Guidelines para 122.

[30] Decision 2001/259/EC *Greek fruit and vegetable growers* [2001] OJ L93/48, paras 32–4.

[31] See eg Decision in Case NN 46/2001 *Aid to stock farmers hit by the BSE crisis* (25 July 2001); Decision in Case N 164/2001 *Support following price decreases in the beef sector* (25 July 2001); Decision in Case N 170/2001 *Programme to assure survival of agricultural undertakings* (25 July 2001); Decision in Case N 193/2001 *Support for voluntary feed tests and liquidity aid for cattle farms* (25 July 2001).

[32] Agriculture Guidelines para 132.

[33] Communication on the repercussions of the terrorist attacks in the United States on the air transport industry, COM(2001) 574.

[34] See further para 12.40 below.

for the losses incurred from 11 to 14 September. Aid compensating later losses was thus compatible with the common market, provided that there was a direct causal connection with the exceptional occurrence, and that the loss could accurately be evaluated.[35]

Normal commercial conduct. Article 87(2)(b) does not cover aid to remedy a situation arising out of the normal commercial decisions of one or more undertakings. The Commission thus rejected its application in the case of aid to subsidize a sea transport service for Irish livestock, following P&O's decision to discontinue the carriage of livestock on its ferry service between Ireland and France.[36] **3.18**

Industrial action. It is unclear as to whether industrial action can be brought within the notion of 'exceptional circumstances'. While the Commission has accepted that 'public disorder and strikes' may be covered by Article 87(2)(b),[37] strikes on their own can probably not be regarded as truly exceptional, and the degree of public disorder associated with them would in any event be likely to be the relevant criterion for bringing them within the exception. **3.19**

3. Article 87(2)(c)—cold war aids to Germany

Scope. Under this provision, aid granted to the economy of certain areas of Germany affected by the cold war division of Germany is exempted from the general prohibition of aids under Article 87(1) insofar as such aid is required in order to compensate for the economic disadvantages caused by that division. **3.20**

Disadvantages covered. The ECJ has held that the expression 'division of Germany' refers historically to the establishment of the dividing line between the zone occupied by the Soviet forces and those occupied by France, the United Kingdom and the United States in 1948. The economic disadvantages caused by that division therefore mean the economic disadvantages caused in certain areas of Germany by the geographical isolation which the establishment and maintenance of that physical frontier entailed, such as the breaking of communication links or the loss of markets as a result of the severance of commercial relations between the two parts of German territory.[38] **3.21**

---

[35] Case T-268/06 *Olympiaki Aeroporia Ypiresies ('Olympic Airways') v Commission* (judgment of 25 June 2008), para 53.

[36] Decision 2000/625/EC *Sea transport of Irish livestock* [2000] OJ L263/17, para 86. It also noted that it was not relevant that this decision might have constituted an abuse of a dominant position contrary to Article 82 EC: paras 94–5.

[37] Decision 2002/597/EC *Italian agricultural credit operations* [2002] OJ L194/37.

[38] Case C-156/98 *Germany v Commission* [2000] ECR I-6857, para 52; Case C-334/99 *Germany v Commission* [2003] ECR I-1139, para 120; Cases C-57 and 61/00 P *Freistaat Sachsen v Commission* [2003] ECR I-9975, paras 21–2.

3.22 **Historic application.** Article 87(2)(c) has in the past been used to cover special aid in favour of expellees, refugees and victims of the war or of the dismantling of plants, as well as aid for the regions adjoining the Soviet zone and West Berlin.

3.23 **Consequences of German reunification.** The provision remains in force unaffected by the Treaty on European Union or by the Treaty of Amsterdam, both of which were adopted after the reunification of Germany. The ECJ has assumed that this was the consequence of a conscious choice on the part of the Member States and has concluded from this that the provision is not deprived of its purpose by German reunification.[39] But the practical importance of this provision is for obvious reasons much diminished nowadays, although a flurry of cases was sparked off by reunification itself as the German government tested to what extent Article 87(2)(c) might be relied upon after reunification.[40]

3.24 **Application to the new Länder.** Although, following the reunification of Germany, Article 87(2)(c) may be applied to the new Länder, such application can only be on the same conditions as those applicable in the old Länder during the period preceding the date of reunification.[41] It follows that the exemption does not cover aid to regions of eastern Germany after reunification, to compensate for the backwardness in their economic development which could be attributed to the politico-economic system established there during the division of Germany.[42] This is because only disadvantages resulting from the geographical split caused by the division of Germany are covered, and the socio-economic differences are not the consequence of that split.[43] The fact that they were the cause of the split and thus closely related to it has not impressed the ECJ, which has repeatedly relied on the principle that exceptions must be construed narrowly in this context.[44]

C. Article 87(3)—discretionary compatibility

3.25 **Application of Article 87(3) in practice.** Article 87(3) gives the Commission a power to exempt particular types of aid from the general prohibition contained in Article 87(1). But it is under no obligation to do so. In consequence, the

[39] Case C-156/98 *Germany v Commission* [2000] ECR I-6857, paras 47–8, and Case C-334/99 *Germany v Commission* [2003] ECR I-1139, para 116.

[40] See eg Case C-156/98 *Germany v Commission*, ibid; Case C-334/99 *Germany v Commission*, ibid; Case C-301/96 *Germany v Commission* [2003] ECR I-9919.

[41] Case C-156/98 *Germany v Commission*, ibid, para 51; Case C-277/00 *Germany v Commission* [2004] ECR I-3925, para 49.

[42] Case C-334/99 *Germany v Commission* [2003] ECR I-1139, para 121, and Case C-301/96 *Germany v Commission* [2003] ECR I-9919, para 70.

[43] Case C-301/96 *Germany v Commission*, ibid, paras 75–6.

[44] ibid, para 66.

Commission enjoys a wide discretion in its application of Article 87(3).[45] In recent years, block exemptions have been adopted covering many categories of aid falling under Article 87(3). Most important of these is the new General Block Exemption Regulation ('GBER').[46] Where an aid is not covered by one of the block exemptions, the Commission will often apply one of its sets of guidelines to assess whether it may still be approved on an individual basis. Finally, where an aid falls outside the relevant guidelines or where no guidelines exist for a certain type of aid measure, the Commission will apply Article 87(3) directly.

Structure of this section. The framework for analysis set out in the preceding paragraph is discussed in sections 1 to 7 below. Section 1 examines the general framework within which the Commission will assess the compatibility of an aid, and the general limitations on the exercise of the Commission's discretion in that respect. Sections 2 and 3 address the Commission's use of block exemptions and guidelines in clarifying the circumstances in which aid may be approved either automatically (block exemptions) or following notification (guidelines). Sections 4 to 7 then address specific principles applicable to the interpretation of each of the four categories of aid listed in Article 87(3)(a) to (d). **3.26**

1. General principles

Case by case analysis. The exercise of the Commission's discretion in the application of Article 87(3) involves assessments of an economic and social nature which must be made within a Community rather than a merely national context.[47] When the Commission examines the compatibility of a State aid with the common market it must take all the relevant factors into account, including, where appropriate, the circumstances already considered in a prior decision and the obligations which that decision may have imposed on a Member State.[48] What particular factors are relevant in any given case will depend primarily on the objectives pursued by the exception that is relied upon. **3.27**

Balancing test. While the relevant factors may differ according to the particular case in hand and the particular provision of Article 87(3) under which approval is sought, every decision by the Commission on the compatibility of an aid must balance the positive impact of the aid measure (reaching an objective of **3.28**

---

45 Case C-225/91 *Matra v Commission* [1993] ECR I-3203, paras 23–5; and Case 310/85 *Deufil v Commission* [1987] ECR 901, para 18.

46 Commission Regulation (EC) 800/2008 on the application of Articles 87 and 88 of the Treaty declaring certain categories of aid compatible with the common market (General Block Exemption Regulation) ('GBER') [2008] OJ L214/3.

47 Case 730/79 *Philip Morris v Commission* [1980] ECR 2671, paras 24–6; Case C-301/87 *France v Commission* [1990] ECR I-307, para 49.

48 Case C-261/89 *Italy v Commission* [1991] ECR I-4437, para 20.

common interest) against its potentially negative side effects (distortions of trade and competition). This balancing test was set out in the State Aid Action Plan[49] and has been developed subsequently in the Commission's guidelines and decisional practice regarding specific cases or types of cases. In general terms, the balancing test requires the following questions to be asked.[50]

(a) Is the aid measure aimed at a well-defined objective of common interest?
(b) Is the aid well designed to deliver the objective of common interest (ie does the proposed aid address a market failure or other valid objective)? In particular:
   (i) is the aid measure an appropriate instrument?
   (ii) is there an incentive effect, ie does the aid change the behaviour of firms?
   (iii) is the aid measure proportional, ie could the same change in behaviour be obtained with less aid?
(c) Are the distortions of competition and effect on trade limited, so that the overall balance is positive?

The second part of this balancing exercise includes considerations of both necessity[51] and proportionality. In other words, the aid measure must not go beyond what is necessary to achieve the intended objective.

3.29 **Operating aid.** In principle, Article 87(3) does not apply to operating aid, ie aid intended to relieve an undertaking of the expenses which it would itself normally have had to bear in its day-to-day management or its usual activities. The reason is that the effect of such aid is by its nature to distort competition in the sectors in which it is granted, without achieving the Article 87(3) objectives.[52] The Commission has, however, indicated that operating aid for certain exceptional horizontal purposes will be permitted.[53]

3.30 **Other Treaty provisions.** In principle, an aid measure which contravenes other Treaty provisions, such as Article 90 EC concerning internal taxation, cannot be authorized by the Commission.[54] The Commission also has to take into account the overarching aim of the Treaty, set out in Article 3(1)(g) EC, of ensuring that

---

[49] State Aid Action Plan: Less and better targeted state aid: a roadmap for state aid reform 2005–2009, COM(2005) 107 final, para 19: see further para 3.36 below.

[50] See eg Decision in Case C 34/2006 *North Rhine-Westphalia DTT* (23 October 2007), para 141.

[51] Which is an established requirement under Article 87(3): see Case T-187/99 *Agrana Zucker und Stärke v Commission* [2001] ECR I-1587, para 74.

[52] Case C-301/87 *France v Commission ('Boussac')* [1990] ECR I-307, para 50; Case C-86/89 *Italy v Commission* [1990] ECR I-3891, para 18; Case T-348/04 *SIDE v Commission* (judgment of 15 April 2008), para 99.

[53] eg operating aid for energy saving measures (para 5.46 below) and renewable energy production (para 14.17 below).

[54] Case 73/79 *Commission v Italy* [1980] ECR 1533, para 11.

competition in the internal market is not distorted,[55] as well as—where relevant—other Treaty provisions such as Article 152(1) EC, according to which a high level of human health protection is to be ensured in the definition and implementation of Community policies and activities, and Article 153(2) EC referring to consumer protection requirements. The Commission may further be limited by provisions of secondary legislation.[56] This does not, however, mean that the Commission is required in an aid investigation to apply the rules laid down for review of the application of other provisions of the Treaty. Rather, the Commission must make an assessment by reference to other Treaty provisions only where the failure to comply with those provisions 'would necessarily affect the compatibility of the aid with the common market'.[57]

Global decisions concerning aid schemes. Rather than examining aid measures on an individual basis, the Commission may, by means of a positive or conditional decision, declare an aid scheme planned by a Member State compatible as a whole with the common market. The Member State concerned can then dispense with notifying the Commission of individual aid measures taken pursuant to that scheme, subject, where appropriate, to the conditions imposed by the Commission in that respect.[58] When it assesses the description of such a project and its compatibility with the common market, the Commission is entitled to confine itself to examining its general characteristics, as they appear from the complete notification, without being required to examine each particular case in which it applies.[59] But this system cannot lead to individual aid measures being granted which, although consistent with one of the objectives of Article 87(3)(a) to (d) EC, would not be necessary in order for that objective to be met.[60] The Commission must therefore check that planned aid schemes submitted for its examination are set up in such a way as to ensure that the individual aid measures to be granted according to their provisions will be limited to firms which are actually eligible for them.[61] **3.31**

[55] Case T-214/95 *Vlaamse Gewest v Commission* [1998] ECR II-717, para 89.

[56] Case C-113/00 *Spain v Commission ('Extremadura')* [2002] ECR I-7601, paras 73–7; Case C-456/00 *France v Commission* [2002] ECR I-11949, paras 32–3; also see Evans, 'Law, Policy and Equality in the European Union: The Example of State Aid Control' [1998] 23 ELR 434, 438.

[57] Case T-289/03 *BUPA v Commission* (judgment of 12 February 2008), para 314.

[58] Case C-47/91 *Italy v Commission* [1994] ECR I-4635, para 21, and Case C-321/99 P *ARAP v Commission* [2002] ECR I-4287, para 72.

[59] Case 248/84 *Germany v Commission* [1987] ECR 4013, para 18; Case C-75/97 *Belgium v Commission* [1999] ECR I-3671, para 48; Cases C-15/98 and C-105/99 *Italy and Sardegna Lines v Commission* [2000] ECR I-8855, para 51; Case C-351/98 *Spain v Commission* [2002] ECR I-8031, para 67; and Case C-278/00 *Greece v Commission* [2004] ECR I-3997, para 24.

[60] Case 730/79 *Philip Morris v Commission* [1980] ECR 2671, para 17; Case T-187/99 *Agrana Zucker und Stärke v Commission* [2001] ECR II-1587, para 74; Case T-126/99 *Graphischer Maschinenbau v Commission* [2002] ECR II-2427, para 34.

[61] Case T-171/02 *Regione autonoma della Sardegna v Commission* [2005] ECR II-2123, para 104.

3.32 **Scrutiny by the European Courts.** Judicial review of the manner in which the Commission's discretion is exercised is confined to establishing that the rules of procedure and the rules relating to the duty to give reasons have been complied with, verifying the accuracy of the facts relied on, and considering whether there has been an error of law, manifest error of assessment in regard to the facts or misuse of powers.[62] In order to establish a manifest error of fact, the evidence adduced must show that the factual assessments in the Commission's decision were implausible.[63] As the question of whether or not a particular aid measure meets the criteria laid down in any of the subparagraphs of Article 87(3) is not a pure question of law, the European Courts cannot decide whether a specific aid measure is compatible with the common market, or even give guidance to that effect. A preliminary reference inviting the ECJ to do so would therefore be inadmissible.[64]

2. Block exemptions

3.33 **Objectives.** The introduction of block exemptions in the State aid field followed positive experiences gained from the use of similar regulations in the antitrust field. In addition to providing legal certainty regarding certain types of aid, block exemptions reduce the administrative burden and workload of the Commission, allowing it to concentrate its resources on the more problematic cases. At the same time, block exemptions also remove the administrative burden on public authorities of the Member States in applying for the approval of aid, and allow the grant of qualifying aid to be significantly expedited without the need for prior notification to and authorization by the Commission. The block exemption system has proved extremely successful, with 1,100 block exempted measures introduced by the Member States in 2007 alone.[65]

3.34 **Article 89 and Enabling Regulation.** Article 89 of the EC Treaty empowers the Council, acting on a proposal from the Commission, to 'make appropriate regulations for the application of Articles 87 and 88'. On the basis of that provision, the Council adopted the so-called 'Enabling Regulation'[66] in 1998, empowering the Commission to adopt block exemption regulations declaring whole categories of horizontal aids to be compatible with the common market and exempt from the

---

[62] Case C-351/98 *Spain v Commission* [2002] ECR I-8031, para 74; C-456/00 *France v Commission* [2002] ECR I-11949, para 41; Case C-148/04 *Unicredito Italiano* [2005] ECR I-11137, para 71; and see further Chapter 17 below.

[63] Case T-348/04 *SIDE v Commission* (judgment of 15 April 2008), para 97.

[64] Case C-297/01 *Sicilcassa* [2003] ECR I-7840, para 47.

[65] State Aid Scoreboard, Spring 2008 update, COM(2008) 304 final, p 39.

[66] Council Regulation (EC) 994/98 on the application of Articles 92 and 93 of the Treaty establishing the European Community to certain categories of horizontal State aid ('Enabling Regulation') [1998] OJ L142/1.

notification requirement in Article 88(3). The Enabling Regulation allows the Commission to adopt block exemptions concerning four specific horizontal objectives, namely aid for small and medium-sized enterprises (SMEs), research and development, environmental protection and employment and training, as well as regional aid.[67] Where a block exemption of this nature is adopted, its effect is to exempt aid from prior notification and approval where certain conditions are met and specific information formalities complied with. The Enabling Regulation also empowers the Commission to adopt a *de minimis* block exemption, declaring that, provided that aid granted to the same undertaking over a given period of time does not exceed a certain fixed amount, certain aids do not meet the criteria in Article 87(1) and are therefore exempt from the notification procedure.[68]

First wave of block exemptions. Pursuant to the Enabling Regulation, block exemption regulations were initially adopted covering aids to training,[69] SMEs[70] and employment.[71] These areas were selected on the basis that the Commission had sufficient experience in them through its decisional practice to identify the circumstances in which aid was largely innocuous. In 2006, the Commission added to these a block exemption to cover certain types of regional aid.[72] The Commission has also adopted a general *de minimis* block exemption,[73] and specific *de minimis* block exemptions for agriculture and fisheries respectively.[74] **3.35**

State Aid Action Plan. In June 2005 the Commission adopted a 'State Aid Action Plan', proposing extensive reforms to State aid policy and procedure.[75] This set out proposals for a package of measures with the objective of achieving less and better targeted State aid, a more refined economic approach, more effective and transparent procedures and a shared responsibility between the Commission and **3.36**

67 ibid, Article 1.

68 ibid, Article 2(1).

69 Commission Regulation (EC) 68/2001 on the application of Articles 87 and 88 of the EC Treaty to training aid [2001] OJ L10/20, as amended [2004] OJ L63/20.

70 Commission Regulation (EC) 70/2001 on the application of Articles 87 and 88 of the EC Treaty to State aid to small and medium-sized enterprises [2001] OJ L10/33, as amended [2004] OJ L63/22.

71 Commission Regulation (EC) 2204/2002 on the application of Articles 87 and 88 of the EC Treaty to State aid for employment [2002] OJ L337/3, as corrected [2002] OJ L349/126.

72 Commission Regulation (EC) 1628/2006 on the application of Articles 87 and 88 of the Treaty to national regional investment aid [2006] OJ L302/29.

73 Commission Regulation (EC) 1998/2006 on the application of Articles 87 and 88 of the Treaty to *de minimis* aid [2006] OJ L379/5.

74 Commission Regulation (EC) 1535/2007 on the application of Articles 87 and 88 of the Treaty to *de minimis* aid in the sector of agricultural production [2007] OJ L337/35; and Commission Regulation (EC) 875/2007 on the application of Articles 87 and 88 of the EC Treaty to *de minimis* aid in the fisheries sector and amending Regulation No 1860/2004 [2007] OJ L193/6.

75 State Aid Action Plan: Less and better targeted state aid: a roadmap for state aid reform 2005–2009, COM(2005) 107 final; see para 1.05 above for the background to this reform initiative.

Member States.[76] A key reform proposed in this respect was the simplification and consolidation of the existing separate horizontal aid block exemptions into a single general block exemption. After extensive consultation, the GBER was adopted on 7 July 2008.[77]

3.37 **The GBER.** The GBER came into force on 29 August 2008 and is due to expire on 31 December 2013.[78] It repeals the previous block exemptions on regional aid and aid for training, SMEs and employment, and replaces them with a single block exemption covering all four categories of aid. In addition, the GBER applies to a number of further categories of aid not previously block exempted, namely aid for female entrepreneurship, environmental aid, aid in the form of risk capital, aid for R&D&I and aid for disadvantaged and disabled workers. The GBER's common and procedural provisions are set out in detail in Chapter 5 below. Chapters 5 to 6, 8 to 12 and 14 to 15 then address the specific provisions of the GBER that are relevant to those chapters, respectively.

3.38 **Legal status.** As regulations in the sense of Article 249(2) EC, block exemption regulations (including the GBER) are directly applicable in the Member States. National authorities can therefore rely on them in granting aids, and competitors can require compliance with them by instigating proceedings in the national courts. They are also binding on the Commission, which can only depart from the principles set out in them by amending the regulations themselves.[79]

3.39 **Temporal application: general rules.** Block exemptions, like other substantive provisions of Community law, have no retroactive effect unless, exceptionally, it clearly follows from their terms or general scheme that such was the intention of the legislature, that the purpose to be achieved so demands and that the legitimate expectations of those concerned are duly respected.[80] That is so irrespective of whether the rules might produce favourable or unfavourable effects for the person concerned.[81] It has been held that the application of criteria laid down by compatibility rules which entered into force after the notification of the aid in question is tantamount to giving those rules retroactive effect.[82] Accordingly, block exemptions should in principle only be applied to aid measures implemented after their publication.

[76] ibid, para 18.

[77] Press release IP/08/1110.

[78] GBER Article 45.

[79] Pursuant to the procedure in Article 4 of the Enabling Regulation.

[80] Cases 212-217/80 *Salumi* [1981] ECR 2735, para 9; Case 21/81 *Bout* [1982] ECR 381, para 13; Case C-34/92 *GruSa Fleisch* [1993] ECR I-4147, para 22; Cases C-74-75/00 P *Falck and Acciaierie di Bolzano v Commission* [2002] ECR I-7869, para 119; and Case T-357/02 *Freistaat Sachsen v Commission* [2007] ECR II-1261, para 98.

[81] Case T-348/04 *SIDE v Commission* (judgment of 15 April 2008), para 54.

[82] Case T-357/02 *Freistaat Sachsen v Commission* [2007] ECR II-1261, para 102.

Temporal application: GBER. The GBER contains specific transitional provisions which permit the application of the block exemption to individual aid granted before its entry into force, if it fulfils the conditions in the GBER. In addition, any aid granted before 31 December 2008, which does not satisfy the conditions of the GBER but does fulfil the conditions of one or more of the previous block exemptions for regional aid and aid for training, SMEs and employment, is still deemed compatible with the common market and exempt from notification.[83] **3.40**

Aid falling outside a block exemption. Aid which does not meet all the criteria laid down by a block exemption will often still be capable of authorization, particularly on the basis of the guidelines that have been adopted for many types of aid (see next section). However it must be notified to and authorized by the Commission in the usual way before it may be granted. It is also advisable to notify aid which is thought to fall within a block exemption, but where doubts remain. In such a case, the onus will in practice be on the Member State to show that the envisaged aid is indeed compatible with the common market. **3.41**

3. Guidelines

Adoption of guidelines. In order to make its decisional practice more transparent and predictable in cases which are not covered by one or other of the block exemptions, the Commission has published a wide variety of guidance documents setting out its policies on individual categories of aid falling under Article 87(3). Individually, these are referred to variously as Guidelines, Frameworks and Notices; collectively they are referred to in this book as, simply, 'guidelines'. The guidelines currently applied by the Commission include the 2008 Environmental Aid Guidelines, the 2004 Rescue and Restructuring Guidelines, the R&D&I Framework, the 2006 Risk Capital Guidelines, the 2007–2013 Regional Aid Guidelines, and a number of specific guidelines applicable in the agriculture, fisheries, transport, media and communications sectors.[84] **3.42**

Practical effect. Where such guidelines exist, the Commission's practice has been to apply the rules laid down therein rather as it would apply criteria set out in secondary legislation. A refusal to authorize aid will in most cases be justified by reference to the applicable guidelines, identifying in which respect the criteria laid down therein are not satisfied. The Court has expressly endorsed the right of the Commission to use guidelines, holding that the Commission's adoption and use of such documents does not exceed the limits of its discretion, or waive that discretion.[85] **3.43**

[83] GBER Article 44(1) and (2).

[84] Discussed in Chapters 5, 7–9 and 11–15 below.

[85] Case T-214/95 *Vlaamse Gewest v Commission* [1998] ECR II-717, para 89; Case T-349/03 *Corsica Ferries France v Commission* [2005] ECR II-2197, para 140.

3.44 **Subordinate nature.** Guidelines cannot affect the scope of secondary legislation,[86] and may not depart from the rules of the Treaty.[87] Thus in as far as guidelines seek to interpret the substantive scope of the individual categories under Article 87(3), they are amenable to judicial review by the European Court.[88]

3.45 **Temporal application.** As guidelines in many cases merely codify the Commission's existing practice in the light of its experience gained through individual decisions in a particular field,[89] rather than setting out completely new policies, there is in many cases no objection to guidelines being applied to aid measures notified before their publication.[90] This practice is followed by the European Court, which refers to guidelines even where they would not normally have been temporally applicable.[91] Where, by contrast, the Commission changes its policy and adopts guidelines reflecting its new approach, it will only be able to apply those guidelines to cases notified after their adoption,[92] unless they are clearly intended to apply with retroactive effect,[93] for which there must normally be good reasons.[94] For example, new Community guidelines on environmental protection published in 2001, replacing previous guidelines published in 1994, expressly provided that the Commission was to apply the guidelines to all aid projects in respect of which it would be called upon to take a decision after the guidelines had been published in the Official Journal, even where the projects had been notified prior to that date.[95] The CFI held that the Commission was entitled to apply the new guidelines and not the guidelines in force at the time of the notification.[96] On the other hand, in the case of the Commission's Communication on operating loans, where there was no provision regarding retroactivity in the new rules, the CFI found that the Commission rightly examined an aid scheme in the light of the rules deriving from its previous practice and not on the basis of the new rules.[97]

[86] Case 310/85 *Deufil v Commission* [1987] ECR 901, para 22; Case C-382/99 *Netherlands v Commission* [2002] ECR I-5163, para 24; Case T-187/99 *Agrana Zucker und Stärke v Commission* [2001] ECR II-1587, para 56.

[87] *Deufil v Commission*, ibid, para 22; Case C-288/96 *Germany v Commission* [2000] ECR I-8237, para 62; and Case C-382/99 *Netherlands v Commission*, ibid, para 24.

[88] See recently Case T-268/06 *Olympiaki Aeroporia Ypiresies ('Olympic Airways') v Commission* (judgment of 25 June 2008), para 53, discussed at para 3.17 above.

[89] Case T-214/95 *Vlaamse Gewest v Commission* [1998] ECR II-717, para 79.

[90] Case T-187/99 *Agrana Zucker und Stärke v Commission* [2001] ECR II-1587, para 56.

[91] Case C-113/00 *Spain v Commission ('Extremadura')* [2002] ECR I-7601, para 71.

[92] Cases 212-217/80 *Salumi* [1981] ECR 2735, para 9; Case 21/81 *Bout* [1982] ECR 381, para 13; Case C-34/92 *GruSa Fleisch* [1993] ECR I-4147, para 22; Cases C-74-75/00 P *Falck and Acciaierie di Bolzano v Commission* [2002] ECR I-7869, para 119.

[93] Case T-357/02 *Freistaat Sachsen v Commission* [2007] ECR II-1261, para 98.

[94] Case 98/78 *Racke* [1979] ECR 69, para 20; and Cases 212-217/80 *Salumi* [1981] ECR 2735, para 10.

[95] Community guidelines on State aid for environmental protection [2001] OJ C37/3, point 82.

[96] Case T-176/01 *Ferriere Nord v Commission* [2004] ECR II-3931, para 137.

[97] Case T-190/00 *Regione Siciliana v Commission* [2003] ECR II-5015, paras 94–6.

Binding nature of guidelines. The Commission is bound by the guidelines and notices that it issues in the area of supervision of State aid, provided that they do not depart from the rules in the Treaty and (in the case of guidelines adopted under Article 88(1)) are accepted by the Member States.[98] This principle is based, in particular, on the protection of legitimate expectations and legal certainty,[99] which have consistently been held by the ECJ to form part of the legal order of the Community.[100] Therefore where the Commission has set out its policy in published guidelines, beneficiaries of aid will in principle be justified in expecting that that policy will be adhered to. Failure to do so may result in the annulment of a Commission decision.[101] As a consequence, the European Court will, on a challenge to the validity of a Commission decision, verify carefully whether the criteria set out in the relevant guidelines have been correctly interpreted and applied by the Commission.[102] **3.46**

4. Article 87(3)(a)—cohesion aid

Scope. Article 87(3)(a) permits the Commission to authorize aids to promote the economic development of areas where the standard of living is abnormally low or where there is serious underemployment. This provision applies to territories where the economic situation is extremely unfavourable in relation to the Community as a whole[103] (per capita GDP not exceeding 75% of the Community average)[104] and is thereby intended to further cohesion in the Community. **3.47**

Relationship with Article 87(3)(c). Regions covered by Article 87(3)(a) are less developed than the ones to which Article 87(3)(c) applies, the latter provision permitting the development of certain areas in a Member State which are disadvantaged merely in relation to the national average.[105] These provisions taken **3.48**

---

98 Case C-409/00 *Spain v Commission* [2003] ECR I-1487, para 95; Case T-198/01 *Technische Glaswerke Ilmenau v Commission* [2004] ECR II-2717, para 149; Case T-176/01 *Ferriere Nord v Commission* [2004] ECR II-3931, para 134; Case T-349/03 *Corsica Ferries France v Commission* [2005] ECR II-2197, para 139.

99 Case 310/85 *Deufil v Commission* [1987] ECR 901, para 22; Case C-313/90 *CIRFS v Commission* [1993] ECR I-1125, paras 34 and 36; Case C-311/94 *IJssel-Vliet Combinatie v Minister van Economische Zaken* [1996] ECR I-5023, para 42. The principle of equal treatment may also apply in this context: Case T-214/95 *Vlaamse Gewest v Commission* [1998] ECR II-717, para 89.

100 Cases 205-215/82 *Deutsche Milchkontor v Germany* [1983] ECR 2633, para 30; Cases C-31-44/91 *Alois Lageder v Amministrazione delle Finanze dello Stato* [1993] ECR I-1761, para 3; Cases C-80-82/99 *Flemmer* [2001] ECR I-7211, para 60.

101 Case T-73/98 *Prayon Rupel v Commission* [2001] ECR II-867.

102 Case C-303/88 *Italy v Commission ('ENI-Lanerossi')* [1991] ECR I-1433, paras 36–7; Case C-382/99 *Netherlands v Commission* [2002] ECR I-5163, paras 24–7; Case T-73/98 *Prayon Rupel v Commission* [2001] ECR II-867, para 71; Case T-35/99 *Keller and Keller Meccanica v Commission* [2002] ECR II-261, para 77; Case T-171/02 *Regione autonoma della Sardegna v Commission* [2005] ECR II-2123, paras 28–35 and 113–25.

103 Case C-113/00 *Spain v Commission ('Extremadura')* [2002] ECR I-7601, para 65.

104 Guidelines on National Regional Aid for 2007-2013 [2006] OJ C54/13, para 16.

105 ibid.

together are routinely relied upon for the grant of regional aid, which constitutes the single largest heading under which aid is paid in the Community and which is addressed in detail in Chapter 15 below.

3.49 **Importance of Community interest.** A notable difference in the wording of Article 87(3)(a) and (c) is the absence in the former provision of the condition that the aid should not 'adversely affect trading conditions to an extent contrary to the common interest'. This implies greater latitude in granting aid to undertakings in regions which do not meet the criteria laid down in that exemption.[106] But the ECJ has held that the difference in wording cannot lead to the conclusion that the Commission should take *no* account of the Community interest when applying Article 87(3)(a), or that it must confine itself to verifying the specifically regional impact of the measures involved, without assessing their impact on the relevant market or markets in the Community as a whole. The Commission is as always bound not only to verify that the measures are such as to contribute effectively to the economic development of the regions concerned, but also to evaluate the impact of the aid on trade between Member States, and in particular to assess the sectoral repercussions the aid may have at Community level.[107]

5. Article 87(3)(b)—aids to important projects and to remedy serious disturbances

3.50 **Scope.** Under Article 87(3)(b), two types of aid may be authorized by the Commission. The first is aid to promote the execution of an important project of common European interest. The second is aid to remedy a serious disturbance in the economy of a Member State.

3.51 **Important projects of common European interest.** The Commission's standard practice has developed four criteria which must be met for aid to be capable of authorization under this limb:[108]

(a) the aid must promote a project, 'promote' being taken to mean action which contributes to implementation of the project,
(b) it must be a specific, precise and clearly defined project,
(c) the project must be important both quantitatively and qualitatively, but especially qualitatively,
(d) the project must be 'of common European interest' and, as such, be of benefit to the whole of the Community.

[106] Case C-169/95 *Spain v Commission* [1997] ECR I-135, para 16.
[107] Case C-113/00 *Spain v Commission ('Extremadura')* [2002] ECR I-7601, para 67.
[108] See in particular Decision 96/369/EC *German airlines* [1996] OJ L146/42 and Decision 2001/780/EC *Iveco* [2001] OJ L292/58.

Meaning of 'common European interest'. The last of the above criteria is in practice likely to be the most difficult one to overcome as, in a Community of 27 Member States, it is unlikely that the actions of any one single Member State, confined almost necessarily to its own territory, will meet the threshold of being of benefit to the whole of the Community. Moreover, it is not sufficient that the overall *objective* is in the common European interest. Rather, it is the specific *project* implemented by the measure which has to be of common European interest and of European scale, forming part of a transnational European programme supported jointly by a number of governments of the Member States, or arising from concerted action by a number of new Member States.[109] This means that even major national initiatives pursuing policies encouraged by the Commission will not usually suffice. It has thus been held that privatization undertaken by a Member State cannot in itself be regarded as amounting to a project of common European interest,[110] nor does a project of common European interest arise simply because the investments envisaged enable a new technology to be used.[111] 3.52

Examples. Projects covered by Article 87(3)(b) will by their nature be likely to have a high research and development content. Examples are the approval of aid in favour of the channel tunnel rail link project,[112] and an investment plan for financing the Belgian TGV.[113] 3.53

Serious disturbances in the economy of a Member State. The disturbance in issue must affect the economy of a Member State as a whole, rather than merely the economy of one of the Member State's regions or areas.[114] Both the Commission and the European Court have taken a narrow view of the scope of this exemption, only accepting its application in exceptional circumstances. The provision has been applied to two cases of aid in Greece, one for a large-scale privatization programme,[115] and the other for the Greek cement manufacturer Heracles, part of which was approved as an individual application of an economic stabilization and recovery programme.[116] The Commission has stated several times, however, that it does not consider that aid benefiting only one operator or sector will fall within this provision. Its application was thus rejected in relation to restructuring aid to 3.54

109 Decision in Case C 34/2006 *North Rhine-Westphalia DTT* (23 October 2007), para 191.

110 Case C-148/04 *Unicredito Italiano* [2005] ECR I-11137, para 76.

111 Cases C-62 and 72/87 *Exécutif régional wallon and Glaverbel v Commission* [1998] ECR I-1573, paras 20–6.

112 Decision in Case N 706/2001 *Channel tunnel rail link* (24 April 2002).

113 Decision in Case N 800/1996 *Belgian TGV* (18 December 1996).

114 Case C-301/96 *Germany v Commission* [2003] ECR I-9919, para 106. Where only particular regions of a Member State are disadvantaged, Article 87(3)(a) and (c) will apply.

115 Decision in Case NN 11/91 *Greek privatisation aid* (31 July 1991).

116 Decision 2000/199/EC *Heracles* [2000] OJ L66/1, following the annulment of the Commission's earlier decision in that case, in Cases T-447–449/93 *AITEC v Commission* [1995] ECR I-1971.

Crédit Lyonnais in 1998,[117] and more recently in relation to rescue aid granted to Northern Rock.[118] The derogation was also held to be inapplicable to disturbances caused in certain parts of Germany as a consequence of reunification. While German unification did have negative effects on the German economy, these alone were not deemed sufficient to apply Article 87(3)(b).[119] In 2008, however, the Commission decided that Article 87(3)(b) could be applied to certain types of State support for financial institutions, necessitated by the global financial crisis.[120]

6. Article 87(3)(c)—aid to promote the development of certain economic activities or of certain economic areas

3.55 **Development of economic activities or areas.** Article 87(3)(c) is the widest and most often relied upon basis for authorizing aid. It applies expressly both to sectoral aids (targeted at certain economic activities) and to regional aids (targeted at certain economic areas). The Commission in addition relies on the provision for clearing horizontal aids tailored to benefit particular activities or areas. All three basic aid categories thus in one way or another find their basis in Article 87(3)(c).

3.56 **Common interest limitation.** Article 87(3)(c) (along with Article 87(3)(d)) contains the specific condition that the aid must not adversely affect trading conditions to an extent contrary to the common interest. This qualification itself includes the principle of proportionality, ie that the aid must be limited to the minimum necessary.[121] The common interest condition is now likely to be assessed as part of the balancing exercise which the Commission carries out in respect of all decisions taken under Article 87(3).[122] In the specific context of Article 87(3)(c), however, the common interest requirement may be interpreted quite broadly. In a recent decision, the Commission considered that the common interest criterion was satisfied by Greek aid to the ex-monopoly telecommunications provider OTE to compensate it for extra costs deriving from a period when the company operated under a monopoly regime. In particular, the Commission held that the aid contributed to the ongoing transformation of OTE from an ex-monopolist to a company subject to the same legal framework as other private operators, and the envisaged relinquishment by the Greek State of its control over

117 Decision 98/490/EC *Crédit Lyonnais* [1998] OJ L221/28, p 64.

118 Decision in Case NN 70/2007 *Northern Rock* (5 December 2007), para 38.

119 Case C-301/96 *Germany v Commission* [2003] ECR I-9919, paras 103–10.

120 Communication on the application of State aid rules to measures taken in relation to financial institutions in the context of the current global financial crisis, 13 October 2008, discussed further at para 7.16 below.

121 Case T-349/03 *Corsica Ferries France v Commission* [2005] ECR II-2197, para 317.

122 See eg Decision in Case C 34/2006 *North Rhine-Westphalia DTT* (23 October 2007), paras 139–50.

the company, and enabled the company to adjust to the liberalized electronic communications market.[123]

National reference point. In contrast to aids falling under Article 87(3)(a), Article 87(3)(c) relies on a comparison not with the Community average but measures disadvantage by reference with the national average. This standard is more easily satisfied in the more prosperous Member States, with the consequence that much of the aid authorized under Article 87(3)(c) benefits the poorer regions of the wealthier parts of the Community. However, the Commission's assessment also encompasses economic and social evaluations based on Community standards, with the result that Member States are not quite as free to aid their poorer regions as might be imagined. **3.57**

Relationship with common market organization. Much of the aid granted under Article 87(3)(c) is agricultural aid, where conflicts may arise with the regulation on the common organization of the market. Where that is the case, Member States are under an obligation to refrain from taking any measures which might undermine or create exceptions to that common organization.[124] It follows that the Commission's assessment of State aid in a sector where a common organization of the market has been established involves examining the effect which such aid may have on the operation of that common organization. In other words, recourse by a Member State to the provisions of Articles 87, 88 and 89 cannot receive priority over the provisions of the regulation on the common organization of the market concerned.[125] Furthermore, it is clear that Article 36 of the EC Treaty recognizes the priority of the common agricultural policy over the objectives of the Treaty in the field of competition.[126] Where there is a common organization of a market, the Commission's decisions must therefore be compatible with the market organization before the State aid provisions of the Treaty even come into play. **3.58**

Examples. A very large number of aid measures are approved each year on the basis of Article 87(3)(c). This is not surprising given its scope as the primary exemption for most forms of horizontal aid, as well as many sectoral and regional aids. The diversity of its scope is illustrated by the fact that in 2007 alone, the measures approved under Article 87(3)(c) ranged from a scheme aimed at encouraging the construction of special housing for elderly people,[127] to a project designed **3.59**

[123] Decision 2008/722/EC *OTE voluntary retirement scheme* [2008] OJ L243/7, paras 106–9.

[124] Case C-1/96 *R v Minister of Agriculture, Fisheries and Food, ex p Compassion in World Farming* [1998] ECR I-1251, para 41; Case C-507/99 *Denkavit* [2002] ECR I-169, para 32.

[125] Case 177/78 *McCarren* [1979] ECR 2161, para 11; Case C-456/00 *France v Commission* [2002] ECR I-11949, para 32; and see further Chapter 11 below.

[126] Case C-280/93 *Germany v Council* [1994] ECR I-4973, para 61.

[127] Decision in Case N 798/2006 *Support for construction of special housing for elderly people* (7 March 2007).

to facilitate broadband access in rural North Yorkshire,[128] and a scheme designed to preserve biodiversity in the Peak District National Park.[129]

7. Article 87(3)(d)—aid to promote culture and heritage conservation

3.60 **Origin and temporal application.** The power to exempt aid to promote culture and heritage conservation from the general prohibition laid down in Article 87(1) was introduced into the EC Treaty by the Treaty on European Union, which entered into force on 1 November 1993. As a general principle, the substantive rules of Community law are not retroactive unless expressly stipulated, and no transitional provisions existed for the application of Article 87(3)(d). As a result, the derogation cannot lawfully be applied by the Commission to approve aid that was implemented (without notification) prior to 1 November 1993.[130]

3.61 **Scope.** The provision has been used to approve aid to the film industry,[131] as well as aid for theatre, dance and music.[132] Article 87(3)(d) will also in principle apply to the publishing and media sectors, as well as the traditional artistic forms such as art galleries and photography. The Commission has not adopted any general guidelines covering this exemption, but the Broadcasting and Cinema Communications[133] are both of relevance.

3.62 **Identifiable culture product.** Despite the relatively wide interpretation of the notion of 'culture', it is not sufficient that the aid should promote culture in a broad sense. Rather, the Commission considers that the 'culture' derogation must be applied only in cases where the culture product is clearly identified or identifiable.[134] It also takes the view that the notion of culture must be applied to the content and nature of the product in question, and not to the medium or its distribution *per se*.[135] The Commission has thus refused to apply the derogation to aid to broadcasters of digital terrestrial television, on the basis that the aid was not related to any particular cultural content that would otherwise not be broadcast, nor was it targeted at certain types of broadcaster that would otherwise not be present on the

[128] Decision in Case N 746/2006 *North Yorkshire NYNET Project* (21 February 2007).

[129] Decision in Case N 295/2007 *Peak District National Park Authority, Environmental Quality Mark* (25 July 2007).

[130] Case T-348/04 *SIDE v Commission* (judgment of 15 April 2008), paras 54–61.

[131] See paras 13.68 *et seq* below.

[132] Decision in Case N 340/2007 *Aid for theatre, dance, music and audiovisual activities in the Basque country* (18 July 2007).

[133] Communication on the application of State aid rules to public service broadcasting [2001] OJ C320/5 and Communication on certain legal aspects relating to cinematographic and other audiovisual works [2002] OJ C43/6; see further Chapter 13 below.

[134] Decision 2006/513/EC *Berlin-Brandenburg DTT* [2006] OJ L200/14, para 122; and Decision in Case C 34/2006 *North Rhine-Westphalia DTT* (23 October 2007), para 195.

[135] Decision in Case N 458/2004 *Editorial Andaluza Holding* (14 December 2004), para 11; Decision in Case C 34/2006 *North Rhine-Westphalia DTT* (23 October 2007), para 195.

terrestrial platform.[136] It has also said that the argument that 'promoting the economic activities that constitute the lifeblood of Venice contributes to conservation of the city, which Unesco has designated as belonging to the world cultural heritage' was too superficial and vague in relation to this exemption.[137]

Sports. Of particular interest is the question whether sporting activities are potentially covered by the notion of 'culture'. This is important in view of the increasingly commercial nature of professional sporting activities. It is also of relevance in considering State support to school sports and local sports clubs. Aids granted in that context will, however, under the Commission's current practice often constitute training aids under Regulation 68/2001.[138] That has been relied upon by the Commission, for example, in approving payments to French professional sports clubs to further their educational programmes.[139] **3.63**

Problems resulting from exclusion of sports. The omission of an explicit reference to sporting activities in Article 87(3)(d) was probably unintentional, and may be remedied by a wide interpretation of the concept of culture. The rationale for including culture in Article 87(3)(d) applies with equal force to most sporting activities: both culture and sports are primarily pursued not as economic activities but as leisure activities, where the economic interests of the organisers have in principle only a second-ranking importance. In many circumstances, it will be extremely difficult to draw a meaningful distinction between sports and culture—examples are figure skating, ballet, chess, and all manner of 'traditional' sporting activities closely linked to national cultures, such as caber tossing or wild boar hunting. **3.64**

Non-commercial nature. The commercial nature of an activity will clearly be a relevant factor in the assessment of whether it qualifies as cultural. In its second[140] *CELF* decision, the Commission authorized aid to the Coopérative d'exportation du livre français for the handling of small book orders from customers abroad, but noted that this excluded text books for schools, which were ordered in large quantities for each school year.[141] What degree of commercial input is permissible **3.65**

---

[136] Decision 2006/513/EC *Berlin-Brandenburg DTT* [2006] OJ L200/14, para 122; and Decision in Case C 34/2006 *North Rhine-Westphalia DTT* (23 October 2007), para 196.

[137] Decision 2000/394/EC *Venice and Chioggia* [2000] OJ L150/50, para 82 (under appeal in a number of pending cases including Case T-218/00 *Cooperativa Mare Azzurro* and Case T-264/00 *Compagnia Generale delle Acque*).

[138] Commission Regulation (EC) 68/2001 on the application of Articles 87 and 88 of the EC Treaty to training aid [2001] OJ L10/20.

[139] Decision in Case N 118/2000 *Public Grants to Professional Sports Clubs* (25 April 2001).

[140] The first having been annulled by the CFI in Case T-49/93 *SIDE v Commission* [1995] ECR II-2501.

[141] Decision 1999/133/EC *CELF* [1999] OJ L44/37, p 52. The fact that the commercial nature of an activity is taken into account in assessing whether aid qualifies as cultural should also meet the main objection to extending Article 87(3)(d) to sporting activities, namely that these are often

is an open question and will probably depend on the particular cultural sector concerned. In the film industry, for example, commercial interests will usually play a significant role. Nevertheless it is well established that the industry may receive aid under Article 87(3)(d).[142] This is clearly the right result, as the commercial elements of a project will often contribute to the propagation of the cultural values. Considering the large sums necessary to create cultural works such as films, it is unrealistic and unsustainable for such undertakings concerned to be funded solely by the State or, for example, by charitable donations.

3.66 **Heritage conservation.** Article 87(3)(d) also covers aids to heritage conservation. However, that concept must be interpreted strictly. The ECJ has rejected the suggestion that the growing of crops in glasshouses might be undertaken in the furtherance of natural heritage conservation in the Netherlands.[143] On the other had, the derogation has been applied to aid to sustain traditional Cypriot handicraft manufacturing,[144] and aid to promote heritage conservation in the United Kingdom.[145]

D. Article 86(2) and services of general economic interest

1. Introduction

3.67 **Objective.** Article 86(2) forms an integral part of the Community policy on services of general economic interest ('SGEIs').[146] It is concerned with reconciling the Community objectives (including competition) with the effective provision of public service tasks. Many Member States have strong public service traditions which would be undermined if the Treaty rules, in particular as regards the free movement of goods and the freedom to provide services as well as competition, were to be applied to them. Examples are universal coverage obligations imposed on postal and telecommunications operators. In this context, a State aid measure

more commercialized. Properly applied to sporting activities, the same standard would result in the exclusion of the few truly commercialized sports, leaving only the ones practised by amateurs or semi-professionals.

142 See para 3.61 above.

143 Case C-159/01 *Netherlands v Commission* [2004] ECR I-4461. See also Decision 2000/394/EC *Venice and Chioggia* [2000] OJ L150/50, para 81 rejecting the application of Article 87(3)(d) to relief from social security contributions in Venice (under appeal in a number of pending cases including Case T-218/00 *Cooperativa Mare Azzurro* and Case T-264/00 *Compagnia Generale delle Acque*).

144 Decision in Case N 536/2006 *Development of Cyprus handicraft* (21 February 2007).

145 Decision in Case N 356/2006 *Historic Environment Regeneration Scheme* (19 October 2006).

146 For an overview of the current Community policy in this area see Communication on Services of general interest, including social services of general interest: a new European commitment, COM(2007) 724 final.

in favour of an SGEI is compatible with the common market where the conditions of Article 86(2) are satisfied. Increasing liberalization of more and more industry sectors is likely to result in frequent reliance on Article 86(2), as a need for a basic level of public services remains.[147]

Notification requirement. The application of Article 86(2) does not prevent a measure from being classified as State aid.[148] That being the case, a controversial question has been whether an aid falling under Article 86(2) must be notified to the Commission under Article 88(3). In that respect, the Court has repeatedly confirmed that a measure which constitutes State aid within the meaning of Article 87(1) must be notified to and approved by the Commission before implementation, even if it is compatible with the common market by virtue of Article 86(2).[149] That approach must be regarded as correct as a matter of principle: where Article 86(2) applies, as appears from its wording, it removes the measures which it covers from the application of the other Treaty rules only *to the extent* that the application of those Treaty rules would obstruct the performance of the public service obligations in issue. As compliance with the notification requirement and concomitant standstill obligation contained in Article 88(3) could not of themselves obstruct the performance of public service obligations, a State aid should remain subject to the rules in Article 88(3) even if it falls within Article 86(2). A Member State must therefore notify a State aid to the Commission even where it considers that the Article 86(2) conditions are satisfied. The only exception is for cases falling within the Article 86(2) Decision, discussed in section 2 below. **3.68**

Direct effect of Article 86(2). Article 86(2) has been held to be directly effective in the field of competition and the provision of services.[150] In principle, there is no reason why it should not be directly effective in relation to the State aid rules. The Court has not yet, however, ruled on the issue.[151] That is perhaps because its approach to the notification of aids falling within Article 86(2) renders the question of direct effect irrelevant: since such aids must still be notified to and approved by the Commission, there is no scope for a national court itself to give a ruling on the application of Article 86(2). **3.69**

[147] For example, public voice telephony is today provided throughout the Community under universal service obligations defined in Community legislation, notwithstanding the complete liberalization of the telecoms sector in 1998.

[148] Case C-172/03 *Heiser* [2005] ECR I-1627, para 51.

[149] Case C-332/98 *France v Commission* [2000] ECR I-4833, paras 31–3, Cases C-261/01 and C-262/01 *van Calster* [2003] ECR I-12249, para 61; *Heiser*, ibid, para 51.

[150] Case 66/86 *Ahmed Saeed Flugreisen* [1989] ECR 803, paras 55–7; Case C-260/89 *ERT* [1991] ECR I-2925, para 34; Case C-320/91 *Corbeau* [1993] ECR I-2533, para 20; Case C-393/92 *Almelo* [1994] ECR I-1477, paras 50–1.

[151] Although differing views have been expressed by its Advocates General: cf Case C-53/00 *Ferring v ACOSS* [2001] ECR I-9067, opinion of AG Tizzano paras 78–81 (direct effect); and Case C-280/00 *Altmark* [2003] ECR I-7747, second opinion of AG Léger paras 56–8 (no direct effect).

3.70 **Relationship with Article 87(1).** Although Article 86(2) has been described on a number of occasions as 'the central provision' of the EC Treaty for determining the position of undertakings performing public service tasks in the context of the State aid rules,[152] its importance has been diminished following the ECJ's *Ferring*[153] and *Altmark*[154] judgments on the definition of aid, discussed in Chapter 2. The result of that case-law is that if the compensation paid for discharging public service obligations does not exceed the costs incurred in the performance of those obligations, according to the conditions specified in *Altmark*, the advantage does not constitute State aid and there is no need to rely on Article 86(2).[155] Equally if the compensation *does* exceed the costs associated with the public service obligations, it will be difficult to show that it is proportionate for the purposes of Article 86(2).[156] Many cases will therefore either be regarded as not aid under *Altmark*, or fall outside Article 86(2) altogether. Article 86(2) remains of importance, however, for cases where the compensation is commensurate with the costs of the public service obligations, but where the *Altmark* conditions are not satisfied, for example where an efficient undertaking comparator is lacking,[157] or where the parameters of the compensation have not been defined in advance in a sufficiently transparent manner.

3.71 **Article 86(2) Decision and Framework.** In the light of the judgments of the European Court in cases such as *Altmark*, as well as the increasing reliance on Article 86(2) in the State aid context, the Commission adopted in 2005 a Decision[158] and Framework[159] on the application of Article 86(2) to State aids. The Article 86(2) Decision provides a 'safe harbour' for certain kinds of aids for SGEIs. Where the specific conditions of that Decision are satisfied, the measure is regarded as compatible with the common market and does not have to be notified

---

152 Case C-202/88 *France v Commission* [1991] ECR I-1223, para 12; Case C-67/96 *Albany* [1999] ECR I-5751, para 103; AG Léger in his first Opinion in Case C-280/00 *Altmark Trans* [2003] ECR I-7747, para 80; and see Commission Communication on Services of general interest in Europe [2001] OJ C17/4, para 19.

153 Case C-53/00 *Ferring v ACOSS* [2001] ECR I-9067.

154 Case C-280/00 *Altmark* [2003] ECR I-7747.

155 Case C-53/00 *Ferring v ACOSS* [2001] ECR I-9067, para 27.

156 *Ferring v ACOSS*, ibid, para 32; and see eg Decision 2008/136/EC *Dutch public broadcasters* [2008] OJ L49/1 where the overcompensation which led to the non-fulfilment of the *Altmark* criteria also meant that Article 86(2) could not apply.

157 See eg Decision in Cases N 541 and 542/2004 *Dutch health insurance RES* (3 May 2005); but cf Case T-289/03 *BUPA v Commission* (judgment of 12 February 2008), para 246, suggesting that on the very similar facts of that case a strict application of this requirement was not necessary, such that the *Altmark* test was indeed satisfied.

158 Decision 2005/842/EC on the application of Article 86(2) of the EC Treaty to State aid in the form of public service compensation granted to certain undertakings entrusted with the operation of services of general economic interest ('Article 86(2) Decision') [2005] OJ L312/67.

159 Community framework for State aid in the form of public service compensation ('Article 86(2) Framework') [2005] OJ C297/4.

to the Commission. This is addressed in section 2 below. Where the aid does not fall within the terms of the Article 86(2) Decision, it will fall to be assessed under the terms of the Article 86(2) Framework and the case-law of the Court. This is addressed in section 3.

2. Article 86(2) Decision

Status. The Article 86(2) Decision was adopted under Article 86(3) EC, which gives the Commission the power of adopting directives or decisions for the application of Article 86(2). Where the Decision applies, and subject to any stricter provisions contained in sectoral legislation, aid measures are exempt from the obligation of notification in Article 88(3) of the Treaty.[160] Accordingly, while the Decision is not formally a block exemption, it fulfils much the same purpose. **3.72**

Exempt categories of aid. The Decision applies to four categories of aid:[161] **3.73**

(a) Public service compensation granted to undertakings with an average annual turnover before tax of less than €100 million (or €800 million balance sheet turnover, in the case of credit institutions) during the two financial years preceding that in which the SGEI was assigned. The compensation in question must amount to less than €30 million, taking an annual average during the contract period or over a period of five years.

(b) Public service compensation granted to hospitals and social housing undertakings carrying out activities designated by the Member State concerned as SGEIs.

(c) Public service compensation for air or maritime links to islands on which average annual traffic does not exceed 300,000 passengers during the two financial years preceding the assignment of the SGEI.

(d) Public service compensation for airports and ports for which average annual traffic during the two financial years preceding the assignment of the SGEI does not exceed one million passengers in the case of airports, and 300,000 passengers in the case of ports.

Transport sector. The Decision does not apply to aid granted to undertakings in the inland transport sector. It does cover aid in the fields of air and maritime transport, but only insofar as the aid also complies with Regulations 2408/92 and 3577/92, where applicable.[162] **3.74**

Entrustment. The Decision only applies where responsibility for operation of the SGEI is entrusted to the undertaking concerned by way of one or more **3.75**

---

160 Article 86(2) Decision, Articles 1 and 3.
161 ibid, Article 2(1).
162 ibid, Article 2(2); see further Chapter 12 below.

official acts. The act must specify the nature and duration of the public service obligation, the undertaking and territory concerned, the nature of any special or exclusive rights assigned to the undertaking, the parameters for calculating, controlling and reviewing the compensation, and the arrangements for avoiding and repaying any overcompensation.[163]

3.76 **Permitted compensation.** The amount of compensation granted must not exceed what is necessary to cover the costs incurred in discharging the public service obligations, taking into account the relevant receipts and a reasonable profit on any own capital necessary for discharging those obligations.[164] The allowable costs comprise all the costs incurred in the operation of the SGEI. Where the undertaking carries out both SGEI and other activities, the costs allocated to the SGEI should follow a standard fully distributed cost methodology: ie they may cover all the variable costs incurred in providing the service, a proportionate contribution to fixed costs common to both the SGEI and non-SGEI activities, and a reasonable profit.[165] The revenue calculation must include at least the entire revenue earned from the SGEI, though the Member State is also permitted to assign profits accruing from other activities to the financing of the SGEI.[166] Finally, 'reasonable profit' is defined as a rate of return on own capital that takes account of the risk, or absence of risk, incurred by the undertaking by virtue of the intervention by the Member State, particularly if the State grants special or exclusive rights. That rate should not normally exceed the average rate for the sector concerned in recent years. Where there is no comparable undertaking in the sector concerned, a comparison may be made with undertakings in other Member States or other sectors, provided that due account is taken of the particular characteristics of each sector.[167]

3.77 **Control of overcompensation.** Procedures must be in place to verify that no overcompensation takes place and that any overcompensation found to have been paid is repaid. Where overcompensation does not exceed 10% of the amount of the annual compensation (or 20% in the case of an undertaking in the social housing sector that only operates SGEIs), it may be carried forward to the next annual period and deducted from the amount of compensation payable in respect of that period.[168]

---

163 ibid, Article 4.

164 ibid, Article 5(1).

165 ibid, Article 5(2). In such cases, the undertaking's internal amounts must show separately the costs associated with the SGEI and those of other services, as well as the parameters for allocating costs and revenues: ibid, Article 5(5).

166 ibid, Article 5(3).

167 ibid, Article 5(4).

168 ibid, Article 6.

3. Article 86(2) cases falling outside the Decision

Commission discretion and scope of judicial review. Aids which are outside the terms of the Article 86(2) Decision must be notified to and approved by the Commission in the normal way. As with aids falling under Article 87(2), if the conditions of Article 86(2) are satisfied then the aid must be held to be compatible with the common market. The Commission thus does not have a 'discretion' as such in approving aids under Article 86(2), as it does in relation to measures relying on Article 87(3). On the other hand, the Commission is required to evaluate whether the conditions are satisfied on the facts of a given case, which may involve complex determinations of fact. In practice that means that while the European Court can exercise strict control over whether the relevant criteria have been considered by the Commission, it will allow the Commission considerable latitude in its factual assessment of matters such as the calculation of costs of the public service, for the purposes of establishing the proportionality of the subsidy.[169] The Court has recently characterized this as an exercise of reviewing whether the Commission's assessment is 'sufficiently plausible' to support its findings.[170] 3.78

Burden of proof. Consistent with the position under Article 87(2) and (3), it is incumbent on a Member State which invokes Article 86(2) EC to show that the conditions for application of that provision are fulfilled.[171] The Member State must therefore indicate the reasons why it considers that the service in question, because of its specific nature, deserves to be characterized as an SGEI and to be distinguished from other economic activities.[172] Nevertheless, as set out below, Member States have a wide discretion both to define SGEIs and to provide proportionate compensation for the performance of those services.[173] 3.79

Outline of conditions. As a provision which derogates from the rules of the Treaty, Article 86(2) EC must, like the derogations in Article 87(2) and (3), be interpreted strictly.[174] The case-law and the Commission's decisional practice, read together with the Article 86(2) Framework, indicate that five conditions must be satisfied for the application of Article 86(2). First, there must be a genuine SGEI. Secondly, the undertaking must be 'entrusted' with the operation of that service. Thirdly, the measure must be necessary. Fourthly, the measure must be proportionate, which includes a test of whether there is overcompensation. Finally, the 3.80

[169] Case T-17/02 *Olsen v Commission* [2005] ECR II-2031, paras 266–7; and Case T-289/03 *BUPA v Commission* (judgment of 12 February 2008), para 269.

[170] *BUPA v Commission*, ibid, para 266.

[171] Case C-159/94 *Commission v France* [1997] ECR I-5815, para 94.

[172] Case T-289/03 *BUPA v Commission* (judgment of 12 February 2008), para 172.

[173] See also specifically comments in *BUPA v Commission*, ibid, paras 214 and 268.

[174] Case 127/73 *BRT and SABAM* [1974] ECR 313, para 19; Case C-242/95 *GT-Link* [1997] ECR I-4449, para 50; Case C-157/94 *Commission v Netherlands* [1997] ECR I-5699, para 37.

derogation from the Treaty provisions must not affect the development of trade to an extent contrary to the interests of the Community.

3.81 **First condition: existence of SGEI.** There is no clear and precise regulatory definition of the concept of an SGEI, and no established legal concept fixing the conditions that must be satisfied before a Member State can properly invoke the existence of an SGEI mission.[175] While the classical type of SGEI is a 'universal service' responding to a need common to the whole population, or supplied throughout the whole territory, the Court has confirmed that the concept of an SGEI it is not restricted to a universal service in the strict sense. Hence the fact that SGEI obligations have only a limited territorial or material application, or that the services concerned are enjoyed by a limited group of users, does not necessarily prevent the services being classified as SGEIs within the meaning of Article 86(2).[176]

3.82 **Jurisdiction to define.** Member States are primarily responsible for defining what they regard as services of general economic interest on the basis of the specific features of the activities. They enjoy a wide discretion in the matter unless the area is specifically covered by Community legislation,[177] as are postal services, for example.[178] A Member State's definition of an SGEI can therefore only be subject to control for manifest error.[179] However in order to enable the Commission to carry out this limited scrutiny, the public service mission needs to be clearly defined.[180] In particular, the definition must be sufficiently precise to leave no doubt as to whether a certain activity performed by the operator is intended to be included in the public service remit or not.[181] The Commission also encourages Member States to consult widely when defining the public service obligations to be entrusted to undertakings.[182] It is also accepted that the Member State's power to define an SGEI is not unlimited and cannot be exercised arbitrarily for the sole purpose of removing a particular sector from the competition rules of the Treaty.[183]

175 Case T-289/03 *BUPA v Commission* (judgment of 12 February 2008), para 165.

176 ibid, paras 186–7.

177 Article 86(2) Framework, para 9; Case T-17/02 *Olsen v Commission* [2005] ECR II-2031, para 216.

178 Directive 97/67/EC of the European Parliament and of the Council of 15 December 1997 on common rules for the development of the internal market of Community postal services and the improvement of quality of service [1998] OJ L15/14.

179 Case T-17/02 *Olsen v Commission* [2005] ECR II-917, para 216; Case T-289/03 *BUPA v Commission* (judgment of 12 February 2008), paras 166 and 169; Case T-442/03 *SIC v Commission* (judgment of 26 June 2008), para 195; Article 86(2) Framework, para 9.

180 Case C-280/00 *Altmark* [2003] ECR I-7747, para 89; Case C-320/05 P *Olsen v Commission* (order of 4 October 2007), para 141.

181 Decision 2008/136/EC *Dutch public broadcasters* [2008] OJ L49/1, para 118, currently under appeal in Case T-231/06 *Netherlands v Commission* (pending).

182 Article 86(2) Framework, para 10.

183 Case T-289/03 *BUPA v Commission* (judgment of 12 February 2008), para 168.

Market regulation. The attribution of an SGEI mission may consist in an obligation imposed on a large number of, or indeed all, the operators active in a particular market. But the mere fact that a national legislature imposes rules of authorization, functioning or control on all the operators in a particular sector does not by itself mean that there is an SGEI mission.[184] **3.83**

Examples of SGEIs. Examples of SGEIs given by the Commission in a recent Communication on Services of general interest are energy, telecommunications, transport, audiovisual broadcasting, postal services, education, water supply, waste management, health and social services.[185] The European Court has recognized as SGEIs the obligation to supply electricity in a specified territory, such that all consumers receive uninterrupted supplies in sufficient quantities to meet demand at any time, at uniform tariff rates and on non-discriminatory, objective terms has been held to be covered,[186] as well as the obligation to provide 'at any time and to any user a universal mooring service, for reasons of safety in port waters'.[187] It has also applied SGEI rules to television undertakings entrusted with a public-service task,[188] air carriers obliged to operate routes which are not commercially viable,[189] a fund entrusted with managing a supplementary pension scheme which fulfilled an essential social function in a State's pensions system,[190] the provision of private medical insurance,[191] making a public telephone network available to users,[192] the distribution of post throughout the national territory at uniform tariffs,[193] and the management of certain waste with a view to dealing with an environmental problem.[194] **3.84**

Activities not accepted as SGEIs. On the other hand, the ECJ has held that the concept of SGEI does not include dock work,[195] the operation of a commercial port,[196] funds transfers between Member States by banks,[197] or certain services dissociable from the universal postal service.[198] It has also refused to apply **3.85**

---

184 Case T-289/03 *BUPA v Commission* (judgment of 12 February 2008), paras 178–9 and 183.

185 Communication on Services of general interest, including social services of general interest: a new European commitment, COM(2007) 724 final, para 2.

186 Case C-393/92 *Almelo* [1994] ECR I-1477, para 48.

187 Case C-266/96 *Corsica Ferries France* [1998] ECR I-3949, para 45.

188 Case 155/73 *Sacchi* [1974] ECR 409, paras 13–15.

189 Case 66/86 *Ahmed Saeed Flugreisen and Silver Line Reisebüro* [1989] ECR 803, para 66.

190 Case C-67/96 *Albany* [1999] ECR I-5751, para 105.

191 Case T-289/03 *BUPA v Commission* (judgment of 12 February 2008), paras 174–6.

192 Case C-18/88 *GB-Inno-BM* [1991] ECR I-5941, para 16.

193 Case C-320/91 *Corbeau* [1993] ECR I-2533, para 15; and see recently Decision in Case N 822/2006 *Post Office debt payment funding* (7 March 2007).

194 Case C-209/98 *Sydhavnens Sten & Grus* [2000] ECR I-3743, para 75.

195 Case C-179/90 *Merci convenzionali porto di Genova* [1991] ECR I-5889, para 27.

196 Case C-242/95 *GT-Link* [1997] ECR I-4449.

197 Case 172/80 *Züchner* [1981] ECR 2021, para 7.

198 Case C-320/91 *Corbeau* [1993] ECR I-2533, para 19.

Article 86(2) to a competitive bus service for which the operator was chosen by an open tender, on the basis that this was 'not a sector reserved to a single undertaking whose specific costs resulting from the provision of a public service had to be compensated in order to eliminate the financial burden on the undertaking'.[199]

3.86 **Second condition: entrustment.** The second condition is that the undertaking must have been 'entrusted' with the operation of the SGEI by an act of a public authority,[200] such that the provision of the service in question is compulsory.[201] However, that does not mean that a legislative measure or regulation is required. An undertaking may be entrusted with the operation of an SGEI by way of a ministerial instruction.[202] Entrustment may also occur through the grant of a concession,[203] particularly where concessions have been granted in order to give effect to SGEI obligations entrusted to undertakings by statute.[204] The CFI has also held that the entrustment of SGEI tasks is not vitiated by the fact that the undertaking has subsequently unilaterally withdrawn from part of the service entrusted to it.[205]

3.87 **Content of entrusting act.** Consistent with the Article 86(2) Decision, the Article 86(2) Framework indicates that the official act entrusting the undertaking with the SGEI should specify the nature and duration of the public service obligation, the undertaking and territory concerned, the nature of any special or exclusive rights assigned to the undertaking, the parameters for calculating, controlling and reviewing the compensation, and the arrangements for avoiding and repaying any overcompensation.[206] While it is clearly preferable for these details to be set out in a concise manner in the relevant entrusting act, it is doubtful whether the Commission could refuse to approve State aid under Article 86(2) just because one or more of these transparency conditions was not fulfilled, especially since the European Court has not ever applied such strict criteria in the interpretation of Article 86(2). Indeed in *Albany*, the ECJ indicated that the mere fact of creating a sectoral pension fund, and of requesting the public authorities to make affiliation to that fund compulsory, was enough to support the conclusion that the fund

199 Case T-157/01 *Danske Busvognmænd v Commission* [2004] ECR II-917, para 92.

200 Cases T-204/97 and T-270/97 *EPAC v Commission* [2000] ECR II-2267, para 126; Case T-17/02 *Olsen v Commission* [2005] ECR II-2031, para 186; Case T-289/03 *BUPA v Commission* (judgment of 12 February 2008), para 181.

201 *BUPA v Commission*, ibid, paras 188–90.

202 Decision in Case N 822/2006 *Post Office debt payment funding* (7 March 2007), paras 37–8.

203 Case C-393/92 *Almelo* [1994] ECR I-1477, para 47; Case T-17/02 *Olsen v Commission* [2005] ECR II-917, paras 187–8.

204 Case C-159/94 *Commission v France* [1997] ECR I-5815, para 66.

205 Case T-17/02 *Olsen v Commission* [2005] ECR II-2031, paras 189–90.

206 Article 86(2) Framework, para 12; and see Case T-289/03 *BUPA v Commission* (judgment of 12 February 2008), para 181, confirming that the official act must 'clearly define' the SGI obligations.

constituted an undertaking entrusted with the operation of an SGEI within the meaning of Article 86(2).[207]

Third condition: necessity. Article 86(2) derogates from the State aid rules only to the extent that these would obstruct the performance of the entrusted SGEI. It must therefore be shown that the contested measure is necessary to enable the entrusted undertaking to perform the SGEI under economically acceptable conditions.[208] Earlier judgments and decisions indicated a strict interpretation of this principle, with the objective of Article 86(2) being to ensure not the survival of the entrusted undertaking, but the economic viability of the particular SGEI task. So while it has never been necessary for the Member State to prove that the economic viability of the undertaking entrusted with the SGEI would be threatened in the absence of the aid,[209] the Commission and Court took the view that the purpose of the Article 86(2) exception is 'to protect the fulfilment of a task of general economic interest and not to shelter specific undertakings'.[210] Thus in the *Danish bus* case the Court held that the necessity condition was not satisfied, since even if the aid beneficiary were to go bankrupt in the absence of State support, its transport contracts could easily be taken over by other operators.[211] More recently, however, a more flexible approach has been adopted. The Court has indicated that the Commission's review of the necessity of a system is 'necessarily limited to ascertaining whether, first, the system is founded on economic and factual premises which are manifestly erroneous and whether, second, the system is manifestly inappropriate for achieving the objectives pursued'.[212] **3.88**

Fourth condition: proportionality. In addition to the test of necessity, the Commission will consider more generally whether the measures are proportionate, by assessing whether other means less restrictive of competition could have **3.89**

[207] Case C-67/96 *Albany* [1999] ECR I-5751.

[208] Cases C-147–148/97 *Deutsche Post* [2000] ECR I-825, para 49; Case T-157/01 *Danske Busvognmænd v Commission* [2004] ECR II-917, para 96.

[209] Case C-159/94 *Commission v France* [1997] ECR I-5815, para 94.

[210] Decision 97/310/EC *Portuguese telecommunications markets* [1997] OJ L133/19, para 10. See also Case 258/78 *Nungesser* [1982] ECR 2015, paras 8–9.

[211] Case T-157/01 *Danske Busvognmænd v Commission* [2004] ECR II-917, para 94.

[212] Case T-289/03 *BUPA v Commission* (judgment of 12 February 2008), para 266. See also Case T-17/02 *Olsen v Commission* [2005] ECR II-2031, para 280, where the Court appeared to regard it as sufficient that the decision indicated that the subsidy was strictly proportional to the additional cost associated with the performance of the public service obligations in question, without stating explicitly that the aid was necessary to ensure the provision of the SGEI. The judgment was upheld on appeal in Case C-320/05 P *Olsen v Commission* (order of 4 October 2007) without this specific point being addressed. In a similar vein see Decision in Case NN 8/2007 *Financing of workforce reduction measures of RTVE* (7 March 2007) where Article 86(2) was applied to aid to compensate the public broadcaster RTVE for workforce reduction measures.

been adopted.[213] In general terms, the Commission is permitted to be flexible and allow Member States a wide discretion in this respect.[214] However one aspect of the proportionality test is a requirement to demonstrate that the compensation does not exceed the amount necessary to offset the losses incurred in the operation of the SGEI in question,[215] and it seems likely that stricter control will be exercised by the Commission in this respect.

3.90 **Existence of overcompensation.** To determine whether there is overcompensation, account must be taken of not only the costs of the SGEI following a fully distributed cost methodology, but also any direct or indirect revenues derived from it.[216] It may also be necessary to consider whether those revenues have been artificially depressed by the undertaking concerned.[217] The undertaking is also permitted to enjoy a reasonable profit for discharging the SGEI obligations. Consistent with the Article 86(2) Decision, the Article 86(2) Framework defines a reasonable profit as a rate of return on own capital that takes account of the risk, or absence of risk, incurred by the undertaking by virtue of the intervention by the Member State, particularly if the State grants special or exclusive rights. That rate should not normally exceed the average rate for the sector concerned in recent years. Where there is no comparable undertaking in the sector concerned, a comparison may be made with undertakings in other Member States or other sectors, provided that due account is taken of the particular characteristics of each sector.[218] The test for compensation under Article 86(2) thus appears to be almost identical to the test of a strict *quid pro quo* in the *Altmark* judgment, the main difference being that the level of compensation permissible under Article 86(2) is apparently not limited to the costs of an efficient operator,[219] nor is there any requirement for a competitive tendering procedure.[220]

---

[213] Decision 2006/237/EC *AVR* [2006] OJ L84/37, paras 97–8, and see para 108 regarding a specific aid measure regarded as disproportionate.

[214] Case T-289/03 *BUPA v Commission* (judgment of 12 February 2008), para 299.

[215] C-340/99 *TNT Traco v Poste Italiane* [2001] ECR I-4109, paras 57–8; Article 86(2) Framework, para 14. cf Case T-289/03 *BUPA v Commission*, ibid, para 237, where the Court considered that even though the equivalent *Altmark* condition could not strictly be satisfied since the legislation in question did not determine the costs of the SGEI obligation, the legislation was nevertheless 'consistent with the spirit and purpose' of the condition; this reasoning was then applied to the Article 86(2) test at para 297.

[216] Decision in Case N 822/2006 *Post Office debt payment funding* (7 March 2007), para 42; Article 86(2) Framework, paras 14 and 17.

[217] Decision 2008/136/EC *Dutch public broadcasters* [2008] OJ L49/1, paras 125–6, currently under appeal in Case T-231/06 *Netherlands v Commission* (pending).

[218] Article 86(2) Framework, paras 14 and 18.

[219] Decision in Cases N 541 and 542/2004 *Dutch health insurance RES* (3 May 2005): Article 86(2) applied even though *Altmark* efficient operator condition not satisfied; and Decision in Case NN 8/2007 *Financing of workforce reduction measures of RTVE* (7 March 2007), para 46.

[220] Case T-442/03 *SIC v Commission* (judgment of 26 June 2008), para 145.

Control of overcompensation. Commission policy is to exclude overcompensation not only *ex ante* but also *ex post*, by requiring the State in question to verify the actual costs of the SGEI and adjust the aid level if necessary.[221] Overcompensation may be carried forward to the next year provided that it does not exceed 10% of the amount of annual compensation. Exceptionally, overcompensation in excess of 10% may be approved where this is necessary for the operation of the SGEI, for example where the SGEI incurs costs that vary significantly from year to year, as in the case of specific investments.[222] **3.91**

Fifth condition: effect on development of trade not contrary to the Community interest. The ECJ has not yet ruled on the content and scope of the final requirement in Article 86(2).[223] Certain Advocates General have, however, taken up a position on this issue. In their view, an effect on the development of intra-Community trade within the meaning of Article 86(2), unlike the classic definition of the concept of measures having an effect equivalent to a quantitative restriction, calls for proof that the measure in issue has in fact had a substantial effect on intra-Community trade.[224] In its Article 86(2) Decision, the Commission considers that small amounts of compensation granted to undertakings providing services of general economic interest whose turnover is limited do not affect the development of trade and competition to such an extent as would be contrary to the interests of the Community.[225] It has likewise recognized that the intensity of distortion of competition in certain sectors where there is less cross-border competition in any event, such as healthcare and social housing, is not necessarily proportionate to the level of turnover and compensation.[226] **3.92**

E. Authorization of State aid by the Council

Article 87(3)(e). Article 87(3)(e) provides: **3.93**

> The following may be considered to be compatible with the common market:
>
> [. . .]
>
> (e) such other categories of aid as may be specified by decision of the Council acting by a qualified majority on a proposal from the Commission.

---

[221] Decision 2006/237/EC *AVR* [2006] OJ L84/37, para 92.

[222] Article 86(2) Framework, para 20.

[223] Although the CFI's judgment in Case T-289/03 *BUPA v Commission* (judgment of 12 February 2008), paras 306–9 implicitly accepts that this fifth condition is relevant in the application of Article 86(2).

[224] AG Rozès in Case 78/82 *Commission v Italy* [1983] ECR 1955, para VI-C; AG Cosmas in Case C-157/94 *Commission v Netherlands*, [1997] ECR I-5699, para 126; and AG Léger in Case C-309/99 *Wouters* [2002] ECR I-1577, para 166.

[225] Decision on the application of Article 86(2) [2005] OJ L312/67, recital (15).

[226] ibid, recital (16).

3.94 **Article 88(2).** The third and fourth sub-paragraphs of Article 88(2) provide:

> On application by a Member State, the Council may, acting unanimously, decide that aid which that State is granting or intends to grant shall be considered to be compatible with the common market, in derogation from the provisions of Article 87 or from the regulations provided for in Article 89, if such a decision is justified by exceptional circumstances. If, as regards the aid in question, the Commission has already initiated the procedure provided for in the first subparagraph of this paragraph, the fact that the State concerned has made its application to the Council shall have the effect of suspending that procedure until the Council has made its attitude known.
>
> If, however, the Council has not made its attitude known within three months of the said application being made, the Commission shall give its decision on the case.

3.95 **Purpose.** In order for the Commission to be able to authorize aid, the aid measure in question must be capable of being brought within one of the specific grounds in Article 87(3)(a) to (d). If that is not possible, but authorization is nevertheless desirable, resort must be had either to the procedure under Article 87(3)(e), which allows the Council to add further categories in which the Commission may authorize aid measures, or to the third subparagraph of Article 88(2), which allows the Council in exceptional circumstances to clear individual aid measures, thus bypassing the Commission. Article 87(3)(e) and the third sub-paragraph of Article 88(2) in this way provide a useful safety-valve in case the main State aid provisions prove too rigid.

1. Council action on a proposal from the Commission

3.96 **Scope.** The Council, acting by a qualified majority on a proposal from the Commission, has the power to add further categories of aid to those contained in Article 87(3). The Council's discretion in choosing what categories of aid to list is very wide in this context.[227] The voting rights for the purposes of obtaining a qualified majority are laid down in Article 205(2) EC. The Council can amend the Commission's proposal, but in that case has to act unanimously, pursuant to Article 250(1) EC.

3.97 **Limitations.** This provision is subject to the qualification contained in the first line of Article 87(3) that aid merely 'may be considered to be compatible with the common market' if it falls into one of the listed categories. As a consequence, the Council cannot use Article 87(3)(e) to enable the grant of aid which is not compatible with the common market and the Commission is under the same obligation as in respect of the other categories of aid listed in Article 87(3) to ascertain

---

[227] Case 74/76 *Iannelli & Volpi* [1977] ECR 557, para 11.

that this condition is met.[228] The Commission thus retains a measure of discretion as to what particular aids to authorize.[229]

Application of measures adopted under Article 87(3)(e). If a particular aid measure is compatible with the common market because the conditions laid down in Article 87(1) are not met, a derogation adopted on the basis of Article 87(3)(e) cannot apply, because such derogations necessarily presuppose that the aid in question is incompatible with the common market under Article 87(1) taken on its own.[230] As a consequence, the CFI has annulled a Commission decision which applied the so-called 'Seventh Directive' on aid to shipbuilding without first examining how the aid in question met three of the four conditions laid down in Article 87(1).[231] **3.98**

Aid falling outside a measure adopted under Article 87(3)(e). Where State aid is covered by derogating rules adopted under Article 87(3)(e), that aid is, as a matter of principle, at the outset incompatible with the common market and is considered to be compatible with the common market only on condition that it complies with the criteria for derogation contained in the decision approving that system.[232] Accordingly, where the Commission finds that aid authorized under that scheme is no longer covered by it, it is not required to reassess its compatibility in relation to the criteria set out in Article 87(1) or to determine whether it affects trade between Member States and distorts competition.[233] **3.99**

Examples. The only area in which Article 87(3)(e) had been used for a long time had been to authorize aids to shipbuilding. Council Directive 90/684/EEC of 21 December 1990 on aid to shipbuilding[234] ('the Seventh Directive') was adopted on the basis of Article 87(3)(e) and lays down specific rules applicable to aid to that sector. The application of the relevant provisions of the Seventh Directive was extended by two subsequent Council regulations.[235] This area is now covered by a Framework.[236] Article 87(3)(e) has also been used in the field of coal. The ECSC **3.100**

---

228 Case C-311/94 *IJssel-Vliet Combinatie v Minister van Economische Zaken* [1996] ECR I-5023, paras 36–7; and Case C-288/96 *Germany v Commission* [2000] ECR I-8237, paras 62–5.

229 Case C-400/92 *Germany v Commission* [1994] ECR I-4701, paras 20–1.

230 Case T-34/02 *EURL Le Levant 001 v Commission* [2006] ECR II-267, para 114.

231 ibid, para 125.

232 Cases C-356/90 and C-180/91 *Belgium v Commission* [1993] ECR I-2323, paras 30 and 33; Case C-36/00 *Spain v Commission* [2002] ECR I-3243, para 47.

233 *Spain v Commission*, ibid, para 48.

234 [1990] OJ L380/27.

235 Council Regulation (EC) No 3094/95 [1995] OJ L332/1 and Council Regulation (EC) No 1904/96 [1996] OJ L251/5. See also Council Regulation (EC) No 1177/2002 concerning a temporary defensive mechanism to shipbuilding [2002] OJ L172/1, as amended [2004] OJ L81/6.

236 Framework on State aid to shipbuilding [2003] OJ C317/11.

Treaty and the rules adopted for its application[237] expired on 23 July 2002. The Council used a regulation adopted under Article 87(3)(e) and Article 89 to fill the legislative gap created as regards the continued need of the coal industry of subsidies over and above that of other industries.[238]

2. Council action on application of a Member State

3.101 **Scope.** Article 88(2), third subparagraph, gives the Council the power to decide that aid granted or intended to be granted is to be considered compatible with the common market. In this respect, it must act on the application of a Member State only, and must reach a unanimous decision. Unlike Council action under Article 87(3)(e), which enables the Council to decide that *categories of aid* are to be considered compatible with the common market, decisions under the third subparagraph of Article 88(2) concern specific aid measures.

3.102 **Exceptional circumstances.** As is clear from its very wording, the third subparagraph of Article 88(2) EC can only be invoked in exceptional circumstances.[239] While no definition of that expression exists, Advocate General Cosmas has expressed the view that it 'involves the idea of something extraordinary and unforeseen or at least something not permanent or continuous and of course something other than normal'.[240] It has been held that when deciding whether exceptional circumstances exist, the Council is called upon to carry out an assessment of a complex economic situation and accordingly enjoys a wide discretion.[241] The European Courts must thus confine themselves to examining whether its decision contains a manifest error or constitutes a misuse of power or whether it clearly exceeded the bounds of its discretion.[242]

3.103 **No power to overrule Commission.** The Council does not have the power to rule on the compatibility with the common market of an aid in relation to which the Commission has already definitively ruled.[243] Therefore, where the Commission has adopted a decision finding an aid incompatible with the common market, the Council cannot declare the aid compatible with the common market on the basis

---

237 In particular Commission Decision 3632/93/ECSC establishing Community rules for State aid to the coal industry [1993] OJ L329/12.

238 Council Regulation (EC) No 1407/2002 on State aid to the coal industry [2002] OJ L205/1.

239 Case 156/77 *Commission v Belgium* [1978] ECR 1881, para 16; Case C-110/02 *Commission v Council* [2004] ECR I-6333, paras 30–1; Case C-399/03 *Commission v Council* [2006] ECR I-5629, para 24.

240 Case C-122/94 *Commission v Council* [1996] ECR I-881, opinion para 83.

241 ibid, judgment paras 18–19.

242 See Case 138/79 *Roquette Frères v Council* [1980] ECR 3333, para 25.

243 Case C-110/02 *Commission v Council* [2004] ECR I-6333, paras 32–3.

of the third subparagraph of Article 88(2).[244] This approach avoids the same State aid being the subject of contrary decisions taken successively by the Commission and the Council and thus contributes to legal certainty.[245] It is also consistent with the ECJ's case law according to which the definitive nature of an administrative decision which is acquired on the expiry of reasonable time-limits for bringing an action or by the exhaustion of remedies.[246]

No power to circumvent Commission recovery decision. The Council also lacks the power to thwart the effectiveness of a Commission decision declaring aid incompatible with the common market, by declaring compatible an aid measure whose aim is to allocate to beneficiaries of the illegal aid declared incompatible an amount designed to compensate them for the repayments which they are obliged to make pursuant to that decision.[247] **3.104**

Procedural requirements. It follows from the requirement for the Council to adopt its decision (if any) prior to the Commission decision, that the Member State must make its application to the Council before the Commission declares the aid incompatible with the common market.[248] If the Commission has already initiated the formal investigation procedure by that time, the application to the Council has the effect of suspending the procedure until the Council 'makes its attitude known'.[249] If the Council does not reach a decision within three months of the Member State's application, the Commission alone retains the competence to rule on the aid concerned.[250] **3.105**

Examples of application. The Council has made use of its powers under the third subparagraph of Article 88(2) in a wide variety of circumstances. One example involved Italy attempting to attenuate the consequences of Italian milk producers becoming liable to significant additional levies (over €1.3 billion) as a consequence of producing milk in excess of their reference quantities during the period from 1995 to 2002. This amount had to a large extent not been recovered by the Italian authorities following suspensions of payment obtained by the producers in issue in a vast number of actions then pending in the Italian Administrative Courts. Italy thus obtained the Council's approval to settle this pending litigation and to remove the social tensions that existed by allowing these milk producers to **3.106**

[244] Case C-110/02 *Commission v Council*, ibid, para 44; Case C-399/03 *Commission v Council* [2006] ECR I-5629, para 28.

[245] Case C-399/03 *Commission v Council*, ibid, para 25.

[246] Case C-453/00 *Kühne & Heitz* [2004] ECR I-837, para 24.

[247] Case C-110/02 *Commission v Council* [2004] ECR I-6333, paras 45 and 47; Case C-399/03 *Commission v Council* [2006] ECR I-5629, para 28.

[248] Case C-399/03 *Commission v Council*, ibid, para 24.

[249] Article 88(2), third subparagraph.

[250] Article 88(2), fourth subparagraph; Case C-110/02 *Commission v Council* [2004] ECR I-6333, para 33.

settle their outstanding debt by means of deferred payment without interest over a number of years.[251] A more recent example is an approval of aid to Cypriot farmers for the purpose of repaying agricultural debts created long before the accession of Cyprus to the European Union. Those debts were said to have arisen out of a succession of events starting with many tens of thousands of farmers and rural people being forced to abandon their farms and households after the Turkish invasion in 1974, and involving an unprecedented and severe drought which lasted for seven years in the 1990s.[252]

F. Other exceptions

3.107 **Agricultural products.** Article 36(1) EC provides that the competition rules apply to the production of and trade in agricultural products only to the extent determined by the Council by way of secondary legislation adopted under Article 37 EC. In contrast to other sectors, therefore, the Commission's authority to control and supervise State aids in the agricultural sector does not derive directly from the Treaty, but from secondary legislation and is subject to any restrictions which may have been laid down in that legislation. In practice, all the regulations establishing the common organisation of the market provide for the application of the State aid rules of Articles 87, 88 and 89 to the products covered by them, which means that they apply to the bulk of the agricultural sector, though subordinate to the specific provisions established by the regulations concerned. Thus the Commission cannot approve aid which is incompatible with the provisions governing a common organization of the market or which would interfere with the proper functioning of the common organization. Products not covered by any common organization of the market (such as potatoes, other than starch potatoes) are subject only to the provisions of Article 88(1) and the first sentence of Article 88(3). The Member States are therefore required to inform the Commission, in sufficient time to enable it to submit its comments, of any plans to grant or alter aid, but the Commission, although it may submit its comments, cannot oppose the granting of such aids.[253]

3.108 **Transport.** While the transport sector is in principle subject to Community competition rules, Article 73 EC declares aids to transport services compatible with the Treaty if they meet the needs of 'coordination of transport' or if they represent reimbursement for the discharge of certain obligations inherent in the concept of a public service. In addition, Article 76 EC prohibits Member States from granting

[251] Council Decision 2003/530/EC *Italian aid to milk producers* [2003] OJ L184/15.

[252] Council Decision 2006/39/EC *Cypriot farmers* [2006] OJ L23/78.

[253] See further Chapter 11 below.

support or protection to undertakings through favourable transport rates or conditions, unless authorized by the Commission. These provisions are applicable to transport by rail, road and inland waterways, alongside the general provisions of Articles 86 to 88 EC, whereas in the aviation and maritime transport sectors only the general rules of Articles 86 to 88 EC apply. The result is a complex interaction between the general State aid rules of the Treaty and specific prohibitions and exemptions applicable to certain forms of transport only. This is addressed in detail in Chapter 12 below.

Coal and steel. On a more historical note, a contrast can be drawn between the EC Treaty provisions and the equivalent provisions of the ECSC Treaty, applicable to State aids in the coal and steel sectors until 23 July 2002, when the EC Treaty provisions became applicable to those industry sectors as well on the expiry of the ECSC Treaty. The ECSC Treaty, Article 4(c) of which prohibited all types of State aids, did not itself contain any basis for authorizing State aids,[254] and even less so categories akin to those listed in Article 87(2) which are lawful *per se*. State aids in that context could only be authorized by means of specific secondary legislation adopted in the form of various State Aid Codes[255] under Article 95 ECSC. Both the coal and steel sectors are now subject to the general State aid rules of the Treaty, although the characteristics of these sectors mean that they are still governed by some specific sectoral rules.[256] **3.109**

254 But see Article 67 ECSC.
255 See Case C-441/97 P *Wirtschaftsvereinigung Stahl v Commission* [2000] ECR I-10293.
256 See further Chapter 14 below.

4

INTERNATIONAL AGREEMENTS

Main legislation and guidelines

EEA Agreement

Agreement between the EFTA States on the Establishment of a Surveillance Authority and a Court of Justice ('Surveillance and Court Agreement')

EFTA Surveillance Authority State Aid Guidelines

Interim Agreement on trade and trade-related matters between the European Community, of the one part, and the Republic of Croatia, of the other part – Final Act [2001] L330/3

Stabilization and Association Agreement between the European Communities and their Member States, of the one part, and the Republic of Croatia, of the other part ('Croatian SAA') [2005] OJ L26/3

Uruguay Round of Multilateral Trade Negotiations (1986–1994) – Agreement of Subsidies and Countervailing Measures ('SCM Agreement') [1994] OJ L336/156

A. Introduction

4.01 **Overview.** This book is, as its title makes clear, a text about Community State aid law. It is therefore not intended to contain a detailed treatment of the State aid rules applicable to third countries outside the Community. Nevertheless, it is appropriate to set out in outline the main international agreements concerning State aid which affect the Community, and which provide the international context within which the EC State aid rules are developed and implemented. These are summarized in the following paragraphs, and addressed in more detail in sections B to D below.

4.02 **EEA Agreement and accession countries.** Section B below addresses the application of the EC State aid rules to the EFTA Member States under the EEA Agreement. Section C then sets out the current state of play of State aid law in the countries currently in the process of negotiating EU membership. This covers (by way of background) the accession issues under the Europe Agreements that preceded the last two accession waves in 2004 and 2007, the current Stabilisation and Association Process, and the position in Croatia and Turkey, the candidate countries for accession to the EU which, at this point in time, have already started the negotiation process.[1]

4.03 **WTO system.** State subsidies have also been addressed on a global level, within the framework of the World Trade Organization (WTO). Section D below provides an overview of that framework, including the differences between the notions of WTO subsidies and EC State aid, and the relationship between the WTO and Community law. The WTO rules are, however, complex and reference should be made to more specialized texts where necessary.[2]

B. EEA Agreement

4.04 **EFTA and EEA.** The European Free Trade Association (EFTA) was established in 1960 as an alternative trading bloc to the then-EEC (now EU). The original members were the UK, Denmark, Norway, Sweden, Austria, Switzerland and Portugal. Iceland joined in 1970, Finland in 1986 and Liechtenstein in 1991.

---

[1] Croatia started the negotiation process in November 2005 and Turkey in October 2005.

[2] See eg Matsushita, Schoenbaum and Mavroidis, *The World Trade Organization: Law, Practice, and Policy* (2nd edn, Oxford University Press 2006); P Van den Bossche, *The Law and Policy of the World Trade Organization: Text, Cases and Materials* (2nd edn, Cambridge University Press 2008); L Rubini, *The Definition of Subsidy and State Aid – WTO and EC Law in Comparative Perspective* (Oxford University Press 2009); L Rubini, 'The International Context of EC State Aid Law and Policy: The Regulation of Subsidies in the WTO' and M Sánchez Rydelski, 'The EEA State Aid Regime', both in Biondi, Eeckhout and Flynn (eds), *The Law of State Aid in the European Union* (Oxford University Press 2004).

In May 1992 the EEA Agreement was concluded between the EFTA States (with the exception of Switzerland), the Community and all the EC Member States. It entered into force on 1 January 1994.[3] Following the accession of most of the EFTA States to the EU, the remaining non-EC members of the EEA are Norway, Iceland and Liechtenstein.

Substantive State aid rules. Article 61 of the EEA Agreement contains a provision virtually identical to that of Article 87 EC. Secondary EC State aid legislation (including in particular the various block exemptions) applies equally to the EFTA members of the EEA, subject to the adaptations specified in Annex XV to the EEA Agreement.[4] **4.05**

Enforcement jurisdiction. Article 62 of the EEA Agreement sets out the procedure for the enforcement of Article 61, and provides as follows: **4.06**

> 1. All existing systems of State aid in the territory of the Contracting Parties, as well as any plans to grant or alter State aid, shall be subject to constant review as to their compatibility with Article 61. This review shall be carried out:
>   (a) as regards the EC Member States, by the EC Commission according to the rules laid down in Article [88] of the Treaty establishing the European [. . .] Community;
>   (b) as regards the EFTA States, by the EFTA Surveillance Authority according to the rules set out in an agreement between the EFTA States establishing the EFTA Surveillance Authority which is entrusted with the powers and functions laid down in Protocol 26.
> 2. With a view to ensuring a uniform surveillance in the field of State aid throughout the territory covered by this Agreement, the EC Commission and the EFTA Surveillance Authority shall cooperate in accordance with the provisions set out in Protocol 27.

Thus within the Community, the Commission is responsible for the enforcement of the State aid rules following the normal procedures under Article 88 EC,[5] while the EFTA Surveillance Authority is responsible for enforcing Article 61 EEA in Norway, Iceland and Liechtenstein.

EFTA Surveillance Authority procedure. Procedural rules applicable to the EFTA Surveillance Authority are set out in Protocol 3 to the Agreement between the EFTA States on the Establishment of a Surveillance Authority and a Court of Justice, commonly known as the 'Surveillance and Court Agreement'. This was signed together with the EEA Agreement and entered into force with that Agreement on 1 January 1994. It was subsequently amended in 2001, to give effect to the developments in Commission State aid procedures following Regulation **4.07**

---

[3] By way of exception, in Liechtenstein the EEA Agreement entered into force on 1 January 1995.

[4] See also Article 7 of the EEA Agreement on the effect of EC Directives and Regulations.

[5] As to which see generally Chapter 16 below.

659/1999 (the 'Procedural Regulation'). Thus Article 1 of Part I of the Protocol contains identical provisions to those of Article 88 EC, and Part II of the Protocol essentially replicates the provisions of the Procedural Regulation.[6] Parts III and IV of the Protocol contain specific rules for the transport, coal and steel sectors. The Surveillance and Court Agreement also provides that the EEA State aid rules (both substantive and procedural) are to be interpreted in the same way as the EC State aid rules.[7]

4.08 **State aid guidelines.** The EFTA Surveillance Authority has adopted a set of State aid guidelines,[8] which aim to consolidate the Commission's procedural and substantive guidelines in the field of State aid into a single document. This is amended from time to time to take account of developments in Community State aid policy. At the time of writing, a new consolidated version of the guidelines is expected imminently, which should incorporate the most recent Community guidelines such as the 2008 Environmental Aid Guidelines.

C. Accession to the European Union

1. General framework and the Europe Agreements

4.09 **Europe and Association Agreements.** With the last two accession waves in 2004[9] and 2007,[10] the EU was enlarged with Member States which had mostly attained market economies in the very recent past, and whose track record of State intervention in the market was unusually[11] dense due to their previous political ideologies.[12] In order to prepare the candidate countries for their transition to the EU, bilateral agreements were concluded between those countries and the Community. These were Association Agreements in the case of Cyprus and Malta, concluded in the 1970s,[13] and Europe Agreements in the case of the other

[6] The detailed implementing rules for Article 27 of Part II of the Protocol have been specified in EFTA Surveillance Authority Decision 195/04/COL of 14 July 2004, which replicates the provisions of Regulation 794/2004 (the 'Implementing Regulation').

[7] Article 3 of the Surveillance and Court Agreement; and see Articles 6, 7 and 105–107 of the EEA Agreement.

[8] EFTA Surveillance Authority State Aid Guidelines, available on the website of the EFTA Surveillance Authority.

[9] Czech Republic, Cyprus, Estonia, Latvia, Lithuania, Hungary, Malta, Poland, Slovenia and Slovakia.

[10] Bulgaria and Romania.

[11] By comparison with the EU average.

[12] See eg comments of A Fornalczyck, 'State Aid Regulation in Candidate Countries: The Case of Poland' in Biondi, Eeckhout and Flynn (eds), *The Law of State Aid in the European Union* (Oxford University Press 2004), pp 133–4 and 143–4.

[13] Cyprus [1973] OJ L133/1 and Malta [1971] OJ L61.

accession candidates, concluded in the 1990s.[14] The Europe and Association Agreements provided a trade and trade-related framework, with a set of rules to prepare the candidate countries for accession. The level of implementation of these rules then presented a good guide as to the state of readiness of a candidate country to start the negotiation process and to accept the obligations of EU membership. The negotiation process itself was divided into thirty-one chapters, with separate negotiations on each of the chapters encompassing the whole *acquis*. Only after the negotiation process was finished was the Accession Treaty prepared and concluded for each new Member State.

State aid provisions in Europe Agreements. The State aid provisions in the Europe Agreements were based on the economic criteria set by the Copenhagen European Council in June 1993.[15] Thus, the candidate country was regarded as ready for accession only when it could demonstrate that all stakeholders therein, including public institutions and economic operators, applied the same State aid rules as if the country was already within the internal market, well before the actual date of accession. As with the other negotiation chapters, the negotiation chapter on competition, which included the State aid *acquis*, could only be closed if (1) there existed the necessary black-letter legislation in line with the current *acquis*, (2) there existed well positioned implementing institutional framework with adequate administrative capacities, and (3) there existed an enforcement record showing resolve in implementing and promoting State aid policy in line with the *acquis*. The legal basis for the implementation of these conditions was set up within specific clauses of the Europe Agreements providing a general prohibition of State aid similar to Article 87 EC, and stipulating that any practices contrary to that general prohibition were to be assessed on the basis of criteria arising from the application of the rules of Articles 87 EC.[16] **4.10**

Association Agreements. The Association Agreements, concluded several decades before the Europe Agreements, were more limited in their treatment of the State aid *acquis*. Neither of the original Association Agreements with Cyprus or Malta addressed the issue of State aid. In 1987, however, a Protocol laying down a second stage of the Cyprus Association Agreement was adopted. Among other things, this provided that the principles laid down in Article 87 EC would be applied in **4.11**

14 Bulgaria [1994] OJ L358, the Czech Republic [1994] OJ L360, Estonia [1998] OJ L68, Hungary [1993] OJ L347, Latvia [1998] OJ L26, Lithuania [1998] OJ L51, Poland [1993] OJ L348, Romania [1994] OJ L357, Slovakia [1994] OJ L359 and Slovenia [1999] OJ L51.

15 ie the existence of a functioning market economy and the capacity to cope with competitive pressure and market forces within the EU.

16 These provisions in the Europe Agreements were similar to those in the subsequent Stabilisation and Association Agreements: see further para 4.17 below.

the relations within the Association.[17] No such Protocol was adopted in the case of Malta, whose compliance with the State aid *acquis* was therefore simply a matter for the accession negotiation process.

4.12 **Accession Treaties.** When the State aid policy implementation conditions were met for each candidate country, that part of the negotiation chapter was provisionally closed pending the closure of all other chapters. After the closure of all of the negotiation chapters, an Accession Treaty containing the results of the negotiation process was prepared and concluded for the country in question. In terms of State aid the candidate country would by that stage have abolished or aligned incompatible aid measures, and would possibly have negotiated transitional periods for a number of very specific non-aligned aid measures. Each negotiated Accession Treaty therefore held a list of existing aid encompassing all aid measures granted before accession and continuing beyond that date, including those which (1) were deemed *per se* existing aid[18] and those that (2) had passed the relevant procedures under domestic legislation and were given the green light after being submitted to and examined by the Commission. Aid measures not included in the Accession Treaty list (including those submitted after the conclusion of the Treaty and the actual accession date) could qualify as existing aid after accession only if they passed the interim procedure set out in the Accession Treaty. This consisted of a two-step approval by the national State aid authority and the Commission. All other aid measures were deemed new aid in accordance with Article 88(3) EC.

2. Stabilization and Association Process

4.13 **Stabilization and Association Agreements.** In 1999 the EU consolidated its policy towards the countries of the former Yugoslavia (less Slovenia, which became a Member State in 2004 and had an accession agreement with the EU at that time, plus Albania), by offering the countries of the region an opportunity to move closer to the membership of the EU following the framework of a stabilization and association process. The basic instrument for the implementation of this Stabilization and Association Process (SAP) is a Stabilization and Association Agreement (SAA). This is a new class of agreement concluded between the European Communities and its Member States, on the one hand, and third countries, on the other hand, by which these countries may obtain status as potential

---

[17] Protocol laying down the conditions and procedures for the implementation of the second stage of the Agreement establishing an Association between the European Economic Community and the Republic of Cyprus and adapting certain provisions of the Agreement [1987] OJ L393/2, Article 27.

[18] Since these aid measures were granted before the dates were set for the 2004 and 2007 accession waves, the relevant date was set as 10 December 1994, the day following the Essen European Council where EU State aid expectations were clarified.

candidates for membership of the EU. SAAs have currently been concluded with Croatia, Macedonia, Albania, Montenegro, Serbia, and Bosnia & Herzegovina.

Entry into force of SAAs. Since the SAAs represent mixed agreements, ie agreements regulating both issues within the exclusive jurisdiction of the Community, and issues within the jurisdiction of the Member States, each SAA can only enter into force upon ratification by all of the parties to the agreement: ie the associating state, the Community itself and all of the EU Member States. Thus far this has only occurred in the case of Croatia (considered in section 3 below) and Macedonia. **4.14**

Aim of Stabilization and Association Process. While the SAAs represent instruments similar to the Europe Agreements, the status of a potential candidate for accession under an SAP is significantly different to that of candidates under the Europe Agreements. The Europe Agreements specifically stated that their final goal was to help the candidate country attain EU membership.[19] By contrast, the SAAs do not specifically state that the association thus created leads to EU membership. Rather, the aims of each SAA are to provide an appropriate framework for political dialogue, allowing the development of close political relations between the SAA country and the Community, to support the efforts of the SAA country to develop its economic and international cooperation, also through the approximation of its legislation to that of the Community, to support the efforts of the SAA country to complete the transition into a market economy, to promote harmonious economic relations and develop gradually a free trade area between the Community and the SAA country, and to foster regional cooperation in all the fields covered by the relevant SAA.[20] Thus, the final aim of the process is only indirectly and potentially EU membership. It is, however, based on its status as a potential candidate under an SAA that a country is subsequently called by the European Council (1) to become a candidate country and (2) to start the negotiation process. So far these have only occurred in the case of Croatia, which is considered in more detail below.[21] **4.15**

3. Croatia

Croatian SAA and Interim Agreement. The Croatian SAA was signed on 29 October 2001 and entered into force on 1 February 2005. It provides that the association between Croatia and the Community is to be implemented gradually, **4.16**

[19] See eg Europe Agreement establishing an association between the European Communities and their Member States, acting within the framework of the European Union, of the one part, and the Republic of Slovenia, of the other part [1999] OJ L51, recital (21) and Article 1(2), point 5.

[20] Croatian SAA [2005] OJ L26/3, Article 1(2).

[21] Macedonia became a candidate country on 16 December 2005, but has not yet started the negotiation process.

with full implementation to be achieved within six years of the agreement entering into force.[22] Pending the lengthy ratification procedure necessary for entry into force of the SAA,[23] an Interim Agreement on trade and trade-related matters was signed between Croatia and the European Community,[24] whose implementation did not require ratification by the Member States as it regulated only the issues within the exclusive jurisdiction of the Community. The Croatian Interim Agreement entered into force on 1 March 2002 and was applicable until 1 February 2005.

4.17 **State aid rules.** Although the SAA indicates a number of harmonization areas, the harmonization of competition and State aid law is uniquely regulated. According to Article 70(1) of the Croatian SAA any State aid which distorts or threatens to distort competition by favouring certain undertakings or certain products, in so far as it may affect trade between the Community and Croatia, is incompatible with the proper functioning of the SAA. In addition, Article 70(2) sets out that any practices contrary to that Article are to be assessed on the basis of criteria arising from the application of the competition rules applicable in the Community, in particular from Articles 81, 82, 86 and 87 of the EC Treaty and interpretative instruments adopted by the Community institutions. The full text of Article 70 is as follows:

> Article 70
>
> COMPETITION AND OTHER ECONOMIC PROVISIONS
>
> 1. The following are incompatible with the proper functioning of the Agreement, in so far as they may affect trade between the Community and Croatia:
>   (i) all agreements between undertakings, decisions by associations of undertakings and concerted practices between undertakings which have as their object or effect the prevention, restriction or distortion of competition;
>   (ii) abuse by one or more undertakings of a dominant position in the territories of the Community or of Croatia as a whole or in a substantial part thereof;
>   (iii) any State aid which distorts or threatens to distort competition by favouring certain undertakings or certain products.
> 2. Any practices contrary to this Article shall be assessed on the basis of criteria arising from the application of the competition rules applicable in the Community, in particular from Articles 81, 82, 86 and 87 of the Treaty establishing the European Community and interpretative instruments adopted by the Community institutions.
> 3. The Parties shall ensure that an operationally independent public body is entrusted with the powers necessary for the full application of paragraph 1 (i) and (ii) of this

[22] Croatian SAA[2005] OJ L26/3, Article 5(1). This clause is different for each SAA: eg a 10-year period is envisaged in the Macedonian and Albanian SAAs.

[23] See para 4.14 above.

[24] Interim Agreement on trade and trade-related matters between the European Community, of the one part, and the Republic of Croatia, of the other part—Final Act [2001] OJ L330/3.

Article, regarding private and public undertakings and undertakings to which special rights have been granted.

4. Croatia shall establish an operationally independent authority which is entrusted with the powers necessary for the full application of paragraph 1 (iii) of this Article within one year from the date of entry into force of this Agreement. This authority shall have, inter alia, the powers to authorise State aid schemes and individual aid grants in conformity with paragraph 2 of this Article, as well as the powers to order the recovery of State aid that has been unlawfully granted.
5. Each Party shall ensure transparency in the area of State aid, inter alia by providing to the other Party a regular annual report, or equivalent, following the methodology and the presentation of the Community survey on State aid. Upon request by one Party, the other Party shall provide information on particular individual cases of public aid.
6. Croatia shall establish a comprehensive inventory of aid schemes instituted before the establishment of the authority referred to in paragraph 4 and shall align such aid schemes with the criteria referred to in paragraph 2 within a period of no more than four years from the entry into force of this Agreement.
7. (a) For the purposes of applying the provisions of paragraph 1 (iii), the Parties recognise that during the first four years after the entry into force of this Agreement, any public aid granted by Croatia shall be assessed taking into account the fact that Croatia shall be regarded as an area identical to those areas of the Community described in Article 87(3)(a) of the Treaty establishing the European Community.
   (b) Within three years form the entry into force of this Agreement, Croatia shall submit to the Commission of the European Communities its GDP per capita figures harmonised at NUTS II level. The authority referred to in paragraph 4 and the Commission of the European Communities shall then jointly evaluate the eligibility of the regions of Croatia as well as the maximum aid intensities in relation thereto in order to draw up the regional aid map on the basis of the relevant Community guidelines.
8. With regard to products referred to in Chapters II of Title IV:
   —paragraph 1 (iii) shall not apply;
   —any practices contrary to paragraph 1 (i) shall be assessed according to the criteria established by the Community on the basis of Articles 36 and 37 of the Treaty establishing the European Community and specific Community instruments adopted on this basis.
9. If one of the Parties considers that a particular practice is incompatible with the terms of paragraph 1 of this Article, it may take appropriate measures after consultation within the Stabilisation and Association Council or after thirty working days following referral for such consultation.

Nothing in this Article shall prejudice or affect in any the taking, by either Party, of antidumping or countervailing measures in accordance with the relevant Articles of GATT 1994 and WTO Agreement on Subsidies and Countervailing Measures or related internal legislation.

Requirement for domestic prohibition of State aid. The effect of Article 70 of the Croatian SAA is that even during the pre-accession period for Croatia, the substantive Community competition and State aid rules are introduced in the **4.18**

Croatian legal order via the SAA itself,[25] qualified only by the requirement that the aid must affect trade between the Community and Croatia. This is the only area where the SAA takes effect directly in the Croatian domestic legal order, as opposed to providing the framework for harmonization on the basis of Croatian implementing legislation. In addition, Article 70 requires that Croatia must establish an operationally independent authority with powers to authorize State aid schemes and individual aid grants, and with powers to order the recovery of State aid that has been unlawfully granted (paragraph 4). Croatia must also ensure transparency in the area of State aid by regular annual reporting following the methodology and the presentation of the Community survey on State aid (paragraph 5). It must also establish a comprehensive inventory of aid schemes instituted before the establishment of the operationally independent authority and align such schemes with the Community State aid rules within a period of no more than four years from the entry into force of the SAA (paragraph 6). Aid in the agriculture and fisheries sector is, however, excluded from this regime (paragraph 8).

4.19 **Regional aid.** Article 70(7) provides that during the first four years after the entry into force of the SAA, any State aid granted by Croatia shall be assessed on the basis that Croatia is regarded as an area identical to those areas of the Community described in Article 87(3)(a) EC. As further specified in that provision, a regional aid map on the basis of the relevant Community guidelines was drawn up and submitted to the Commission; this entered into force on 7 May 2008.[26]

4.20 **Implementation of Article 70.** As noted above, Article 70 has the effect of introducing the Community State aid rules in the Croatian domestic legal order. However Article 70 only sets out the basic substantive prohibition and central procedural rules, with the Community secondary legislation and case-law incorporated by reference. The detailed implementation of these rules was left to domestic legislation. To this end, Croatia introduced its first Act on State Aids in 2003, amended that Act in 2004,[27] and finally enacted a second Act on State Aids in 2005 for the purpose of full harmonization of its domestic law with Community law.[28] The institutional framework introduced by the first Act on State Aids identified the Croatian Competition Agency, created in 1995 by the Competition

[25] ie in addition to the separate general provision in the SAA requiring harmonization of Croatian legislation with the Community *acquis*: Croatian SAA [2005] OJ L26/3, Article 69. cf the much less stringent provisions in the Europe Agreements, for example Article 65(3) of the Slovenian Europe Agreement, [1999] OJ L51; and see also Böhnel, 'Die Auswirkungen der Europa-Abkommen auf das Wettbewersbrecht in Mittel- und Osteuropa' (1998) 4 *Europäische Zeitschrift für Wirtschaftsrecht* 111–16.

[26] Decision on the Regional Aid Map (*Odluka o karti regionalnih potpora*), Official Gazette, no 52/2008.

[27] Act on State Aids (*Zakon o državnim potporama*), Official Gazette, no 47/2003, and amended by Amendments to the Act on State Aids, Official Gazette, no 60/2004.

[28] Act on State Aids (*Zakon o državnim potporama*), Official Gazette, no 140/2005.

Act,[29] as the authority to govern State aid control in addition to the competition law provisions that had already been introduced. On the basis of the same Act, the Croatian government enacted the first Regulation on State Aids[30] encompassing the majority of the State aid criteria set out in Article 70 of the SAA. In the second Regulation adopted under the second Act on State Aids,[31] the government was empowered to publish in the Croatian Official Gazette (1) a list of and (2) the original texts of the Community State aid rules translated in Croatian, with only minimal procedural requirements necessary to implement these into the Croatian domestic legal order.

4. Turkey

Ankara Agreement. Turkey concluded an association agreement with the Community in 1963. The Ankara Agreement entered into force in December 1964 and had for its aims a possible introduction of a customs union (after a transitional period of up to 23 years), introduction of the free movement of workers, services, capital and establishment, and the strengthening of Turkey for accession to the Community.[32] However, the accession process continued to stall until the conclusion of an additional Protocol in 1970 widening the existing agreement to include, among other things, provisions on harmonization of economic policy and legislation, and the gradual alignment of the Turkish agricultural policy with the Community Common Agricultural Policy. On the basis of this Protocol, the Community abolished customs and quantitative restrictions for almost all Turkish industrial products and provided Turkey with a number of agricultural concessions. In return, Turkey agreed to gradually lower its barriers on industrial products coming from the Community and to introduce the Common Customs Tariff. **4.21**

Current position. After the introduction of countervailing measures on both sides in the mid-1970s, a standstill ensued. This situation lasted until 1987 when Turkey formally applied for EU membership.[33] In 1990 the Community offered to conclude a customs union with Turkey instead, and in 1995 the Customs Union between the Community and Turkey was established with Decision 1/95 of the Accession Council. This Decision included provisions regarding the introduction of substantive and procedural State aid rules, including the requirement **4.22**

[29] Competition Act (*Zakon o zaštiti tržišnog natjecanja*), Official Gazette, no 48/1995.

[30] Regulation on State Aids (*Uredba o državnim potporama*) Official Gazette, no 121/2003.

[31] Regulation on State Aids (*Uredba o državnim potporama*) Official Gazette, no 50/2006.

[32] Article 28 of the Ankara Agreement stipulates that as soon as the operation of that Agreement has advanced far enough to justify envisaging full acceptance by Turkey of the obligations arising out of the Treaty establishing the European Economic Community, the Contracting Parties shall examine the possibility of the accession of Turkey to the Community.

[33] S Peers, 'Living in Sin: Legal Integration under the EC-Turkey Customs Union' (1996) 7 *European Journal of International Law* 411, 413.

(similar to that imposed on Croatia) to establish an independent State aid monitoring authority.[34] However by the time of its 2007 report on Turkey's accession progress, the Commission stated that no progress had yet been made on adopting State aid legislation or establishing an operationally independent State aid monitoring authority in Turkey.[35] At this point of time, Turkey has no State aid inventory and has not reported any State aid schemes to the Commission, although it seems that it has adopted a number of new aid schemes during the reporting period. The introduction of a proper State aid control system in Turkey therefore remains something for the future.

D. World Trade Organization

1. Background to GATT/WTO Subsidies Framework

4.23 GATT 1947. State aid, or subsidies in the language of the WTO, is not merely a concern of the EU and EEA, but is also one of the major stumbling blocks for international trade. The controversial task of determining which sorts of government activity create such an unacceptable advantage, and how to deal with that, has preoccupied the agenda of the WTO/GATT (General Agreement on Tariffs and Trade) system since its very beginning.[36] The original GATT of 1947 contained several provisions on subsidies and countervailing measures within Articles XVI, II, VI and III, applicable only to trade in goods but not to trade in services. Article XVI contained a single paragraph with a simple reporting requirement in respect of subsidies operating to reduce imports or increase exports. This was counterbalanced by Article II(2)(b) of GATT, which accepted the usage of

[34] See also the obligations set out in Council Decision 2006/35/EC on the principles, priorities and conditions contained in the Accession Partnership with Turkey [2006] OJ L22/34.

[35] Turkey 2007 Progress Report, SEC(2007) 1436, para 4.7.

[36] After initial steps at Bretton Woods in 1944, and the resolution of the Economic and Social Council in the United Nations in 1946 on setting up an International Trade Organization (ITO), negotiations were held at Lake Success (New York), Geneva and Havana during 1947–1948 where, *inter alia*, preparation of a multilateral treaty containing general principles of trade was agreed upon. By the end of 1947 this multilateral treaty in form of the General Agreement on Tariffs and Trade (GATT) was drafted and entered into force on 1 January 1948. Since the work on ITO stalled and finally ended in 1950, GATT gradually evolved into an international organization without legal personality based in Geneva. GATT served as the focal point of eight rounds of multilateral trade negotiations with the purpose of reducing tariffs and other barriers to international trade (Geneva 1947, Annecy 1949, Torquay 1950, Geneva 1956, Dillon 1960–61, Kennedy 1962–67, Tokyo 1973–79 and Uruguay 1986–1994). The Final Act of the Uruguay Round transformed the GATT into a new international organization with legal personality: the World Trade Organization (WTO). This came into being on 1 January 1995 on the basis of the package of agreements (WTO agreements) annexed to a single document, the Marrakesh Agreement Establishing the World Trade Organization (WTO Agreement). On the GATT/WTO history and institutional framework, see further Matsushita, Schoenbaum and Mavroidis, *The World Trade Organization: Law, Practice, and Policy*, pp 1–19.

countervailing and antidumping duties, even if that resulted in tariffs exceeding negotiated tariff commitments, as long as the duties were imposed in accordance with Article VI. Article VI set out three benchmarks for the use of countervailing duties: (1) any such duty could not exceed the estimated amount of the 'bounty or subsidy' granted on a product; (2) duties could not be imposed unless the effect of subsidization was such as to cause or threaten to cause material injury to an established domestic industry, or was such as to retard materially the establishment of a domestic industry; and (3) no product could be subjected to both antidumping and countervailing duties to compensate for the same situation, to the extent that subsidies might result in lower prices for exportation that could be treated as dumping. Subsidies were also considered in Article III(8)(b) where rules requiring member nations to treat domestic and imported products alike for the purposes of domestic tax and regulatory policies were subject to an exception allowing the payment of subsidies exclusively to domestic producers.

1954–55 Review. During the 1954–55 Review Session, Article XVI of the GATT **4.24** was amended to include commitments reducing the use of export subsidies. With respect to subsidies on primary products (defined as any product of farm, forest or fishery, or a mineral, in its natural form or else processed to the point customarily required for it to be marketed in substantial quantities in international trade) the commitment was to avoid the subsidies resulting in a trading nation obtaining a more than equitable share of world export trade. For other products the commitment was to avoid subsidies resulting in an export price of a product below the domestic price charged for the same product. The amended Article was thus something close to a prohibition of export subsidies on products other than primary products. In 1960 the GATT members approved an illustrative list of practices likely to result from the differential pricing of non-primary products in breach of Article XVI.

Tokyo Round. During the Tokyo Round, in 1973–1979, an agreement known as **4.25** the Subsidies Code was negotiated. The Subsidies Code included more stringent restrictions on export subsidies, more detailed procedures to be followed in investigations potentially leading to countervailing duties, and identification of a number of criteria for determining if a subsidised import was a cause or threat to material injury. An illustrative list of export subsidies was annexed to the Subsidies Code.

Uruguay Round. The Uruguay Round of GATT negotiations, in 1986–1994, **4.26** proposed separate rules for agricultural subsidies within the framework of the WTO Agreement on Agriculture,[37] and tackled subsidies in services, to a limited

---

37 Uruguay Round of Multilateral Trade Negotiations (1986–94), Annex 1, Annex 1A – Agreement on Agriculture [1994] OJ L336/22.

extent, within the framework of the General Agreement on Trade in Services (GATS).[38] Most importantly, however, the Uruguay Round established a new legal instrument for combating these government activities in form of the WTO Agreement on Subsidies and Countervailing Measures (generally referred to as the 'SCM Agreement').[39] This is described in more detail in the next section.

2. General Framework of the SCM Agreement

4.27 **Scope.** The SCM Agreement applies to trade in goods. It also took effect subject to the specific provisions in the Agreement on Agriculture during the (now expired) implementation period of that Agreement.[40]

4.28 **Definition of subsidies.** By contrast with the other GATT agreements, the SCM Agreement establishes for the first time a general definition of subsidies. The definition, in Article 1 of the SCM Agreement, stipulates that a subsidy entails a financial contribution by a government, in the form of a direct transfer of funds, a decision to forego revenue that is otherwise due, the provision of goods and services, or an income or price support scheme, but only if the financial contribution or an income or price support scheme confers a benefit. This requirement for a benefit (as with the similar requirement for a benefit or advantage under Article 87(1) EC)[41] indicates that not all government schemes, programmes and projects are subsidies; if for example a government delivers goods at market prices, no benefit arises and hence no subsidies exist. Article 1 SCM reads as follows:

> Definition of a Subsidy
>
> 1.1 For the purpose of this Agreement, a subsidy shall be deemed to exist if:
>
> (a)(1) there is a financial contribution by a government or any public body within the territory of a Member (referred to in this Agreement as 'government'), i.e. where:
>
> (i) a government practice involves a direct transfer of funds (e.g. grants, loans, and equity infusion), potential direct transfers of funds or liabilities (e.g. loan guarantees);
>
> (ii) government revenue that is otherwise due is foregone or not collected (e.g. fiscal incentives such as tax credits);
>
> (iii) a government provides goods or services other than general infrastructure, or purchases goods;
>
> (iv) a government makes payments to a funding mechanism, or entrusts or directs a private body to carry out one or more of the type of

---

38 Uruguay Round of Multilateral Trade Negotiations (1986-1994), Annex 1, Annex 1B – General Agreement on Trade in Services [1994] OJ L336/191. The relevant provision, Article XV of GATS, simply provides for negotiations on multilateral rules on subsidies, and for consultations between a Member aggrieved by a subsidy and the relevant subsidizing Member.

39 Uruguay Round of Multilateral Trade Negotiations (1986–1994), Annex 1, Annex 1A – Agreement on Subsidies and Countervailing Measures [1994] OJ L336/156.

40 See Agreement on Agriculture [1994] OJ L336/22, Article 21(1).

41 See para 2.02 above.

functions illustrated in (i) to (iii) above which would normally be vested in the government and the practice, in no real sense, differs from practices normally followed by governments;

or

(a)(2) there is any form of income or price support in the sense of Article XVI of GATT 1994;

and

(b) a benefit is thereby conferred.

1.2 A subsidy as defined in paragraph 1 shall be subject to the provisions of Part II or shall be subject to the provisions of Part III or V only if such a subsidy is specific in accordance with the provisions of Article 2.

Requirement of specificity. As the above definition demonstrates, the sole fact that a scheme or measure is a subsidy as defined in Article 1.1 is not enough to raise WTO constraints. Rather, only subsidies that are specific in nature may be condemned by the WTO rules, or may legitimately be subject to countervailing duties by the WTO members. This concept of specificity is analogous to the selectivity requirement under Article 87(1) EC,[42] and relates to the degree of targeting within the government scheme at hand. The concept is elaborated in Article 2 SCM as follows: **4.29**

Specificity

2.1 In order to determine whether a subsidy, as defined in paragraph 1 of Article 1, is specific to an enterprise or industry or group of enterprises or industries (referred to in this Agreement as 'certain enterprises') within the jurisdiction of the granting authority, the following principles shall apply:

(a) Where the granting authority, or the legislation pursuant to which the granting authority operates, explicitly limits access to a subsidy to certain enterprises, such subsidy shall be specific.

(b) Where the granting authority, or the legislation pursuant to which the granting authority operates, establishes objective criteria or conditions governing the eligibility for, and the amount of, a subsidy, specificity shall not exist, provided that the eligibility is automatic and that such criteria and conditions are strictly adhered to. The criteria or conditions must be clearly spelled out in law, regulation, or other official document, so as to be capable of verification.

(c) If, notwithstanding any appearance of non-specificity resulting from the application of the principles laid down in subparagraphs (a) and (b), there are reasons to believe that the subsidy may in fact be specific, other factors may be considered. Such factors are: use of a subsidy programme by a limited number of certain enterprises, predominant use by certain enterprises, the granting of disproportionately large amounts of subsidy to certain enterprises, and the manner in which discretion has been exercised by the granting authority in the decision to grant a subsidy. In applying this subparagraph, account shall be taken of the extent of diversification of

42 See para 2.02 above.

economic activities within the jurisdiction of the granting authority, as well as of the length of time during which the subsidy programme has been in operation.

2.2 A subsidy which is limited to certain enterprises located within a designated geographical region within the jurisdiction of the granting authority shall be specific. It is understood that the setting or change of generally applicable tax rates by all levels of government entitled to do so shall not be deemed to be a specific subsidy for the purposes of this Agreement.

2.3 Any subsidy falling under the provisions of Article 3 shall be deemed to be specific.

2.4 Any determination of specificity under the provisions of this Article shall be clearly substantiated on the basis of positive evidence.

Subsidies expressly limited to certain enterprises are therefore specific; conversely a scheme not favouring certain enterprises over others, and available on the basis of objective criteria or conditions to all eligible enterprises, is not specific. However, a subsidy that is designed in an apparently non-specific form may still be specific if it is *de facto* applied to certain undertakings but not others. Furthermore, regional schemes limited to a specific geographical region or regions within a State or within the jurisdiction of an administering authority, are specific unless they amount to the setting of generally applicable tax rates in specific regions by regional authorities competent to do so.[43]

4.30 **'Traffic lights' system.** A major innovation in the Agreement was the classification of subsidies into three categories, often referred to as 'red light', 'yellow light' and 'green light' categories. These are described in the following paragraphs.

4.31 **'Red light' prohibited subsidies.** Red light subsidies are entirely prohibited, and comprise two categories of subsidies: export subsidies, including, but not limited to, all subsidies listed in the illustrative list in Annex I to the SCM Agreement, and subsidies contingent on the use of domestic over imported goods. These two types of subsidies are defined as specific regardless of their structure (Article 2.3 and Article 3). Article 3 SCM reads as follows:

Prohibition

3.1 Except as provided in the Agreement on Agriculture, the following subsidies, within the meaning of Article 1, shall be prohibited:
   (a) subsidies contingent, in law or in fact, whether solely or as one of several other conditions, upon export performance, including those illustrated in Annex I;
   (b) subsidies contingent, whether solely or as one of several other conditions, upon the use of domestic over imported goods.

3.2 A Member shall neither grant nor maintain subsidies referred to in paragraph 1.

[43] See the similar approach to regional taxation under Article 87(1) EC, discussed at paras 2.123–2.125 above.

'Yellow light' actionable subsidies. The yellow light or actionable subsidies are not totally prohibited, but may be challenged where they are specific in nature and if they (1) cause an injury to a domestic industry of another Member, or (2) cause an impairment of the benefits of a tariff concession, or (3) represent a serious prejudice to the interests of another Member.[44] The first two notions derive from the GATT, where an injury was necessary in relation to the usage of countervailing duties, and new subsidies were recognized as having potential to impair the benefits of tariff concessions. The third notion of serious prejudice did not previously exist in the GATT, but was included in the Tokyo Round Subsidies Code. 'Serious prejudice' is defined in the SCM Agreement as a loss of exports by the complaining Member to the domestic market of the subsidizing Member, a loss of exports by the complaining Member to exporters from the subsidizing Member in the domestic market(s) of third countries, significant price undercutting by the subsidized product, or significant price suppression, price depression or lost sales in the same market, or an increase in the world market share of the subsidizing Member in a particular subsidized primary product or commodity as compared to the average share it had during the previous period of three years.[45] The burden of proof in demonstrating serious prejudice rests with the complaining Member. For a five-year period expiring in 2000, certain subsidies were deemed to result in serious prejudice.[46] That provision has now lapsed and has not been revived. **4.32**

'Green light' permitted subsidies. The final element of the SCM lights system was the green light subsidy category. As with the provision on deemed subsidies (see foregoing paragraph), this was introduced experimentally for a five-year period expiring in 2000, but has not been reintroduced since then. During the period while the green light system was in effect, selected types of subsidies were non-actionable even if they were specific and caused one of the harms listed in the foregoing paragraph. The three categories of subsidies protected from challenge were certain research and development subsidies, certain regional subsidies, and certain environmental subsidies.[47] Members complying with the restrictions within each category were allowed to grant subsidies that were shielded from challenges and countervailing measures, a system analogous (in the WTO context) to the block exemptions introduced in EC State aid law in recent years. **4.33**

WTO dispute resolution. A WTO Member may respond to subsidization by another Member by either multilateral or unilateral action. Multilateral action rests on the adjudication by a WTO dispute settlement panel of a challenge to the subsidy in question. In the case of a prohibited subsidy, the action calls for **4.34**

44 Article 5 SCM.
45 Article 6.3 SCM.
46 Article 6.1 SCM.
47 Article 8.2 SCM.

immediate withdrawal, and in the absence thereof the authorization of appropriate countermeasures. In the case of an actionable subsidy resulting in an adverse effect,[48] the offending Member may be requested to remove the effects or the scheme or to withdraw the subsidy in question. If the offending State does neither, the injured Member might be authorized to impose countermeasures commensurate with the degree and the effects of the subsidy. Appeals lie to the WTO Appellate Body.[49]

4.35 **Countervailing duties.** As an alternative to the multilateral action procedure, a WTO Member may take unilateral action against either a prohibited or an actionable subsidy, by imposing countervailing duties, where it can prove material injury to its domestic industry on its domestic market. The SCM Agreement contains a number of provisions regulating the imposition of countervailing duties, and sets out an array of substantive and procedural restrictions thereon. These rules by and large originate from the Tokyo Round Subsidies Code. Overall, the SCM Agreement makes clear that market related benchmarks must be the basis for valuing subsidies,[50] and requires that all relevant factors must be evaluated in determining whether an injury exists.[51]

3. WTO subsidies and the EC State aid rules

4.36 **The concept of aid.** The European Court has consistently rejected attempts to define the concept of a State aid under Article 87(1) by reference to the SCM definition of a subsidy.[52] The definition of a State aid is nevertheless very similar to that of a subsidy under the SCM Agreement. There are, however, several important differences.[53] One of the most significant differences is the absence, under the SCM definition, of a requirement that there should be a 'cost to government'—or, in the terminology of Community State aid law, a grant of aid 'through State resources'. While the European Commission had taken the view that a subsidy under the GATT Subsidies Code involved a charge on the public account,[54] the

48 See para 4.32 above.

49 See further Matsushita, Schoenbaum and Mavroidis, *The World Trade Organization: Law, Practice, and Policy*, pp 364–94.

50 Article 14 SCM.

51 Articles 15 and 16 SCM.

52 Case T-55/99 *CETM v Commission* [2000] ECR II-3207, para 50; Case C-351/98 *Spain v Commission ('Spanish Trucks')* [2002] ECR I-8031, para 44; Case C-409/00 *Spain v Commission ('Spanish Trucks II')* [2003] ECR I-1487, para 56.

53 See generally L Rubini, *The Definition of Subsidy and State Aid – WTO and EC Law in Comparative Perspective* (Oxford University Press 2009); and L Rubini, 'The International Context of EC State Aid Law and Policy: The Regulation of Subsidies in the WTO' in Biondi, Eeckhout and Flynn (eds), *The Law of State Aid in the European Union* (Oxford University Press 2004), pp 149–88.

54 Decision 85/239/EEC *Argentinian soya meal* [1985] OJ L108/28, at para 7.4, and see para 2.83 above.

same does not appear to be true under the SCM Agreement. As the Appellate Body pointed out in the *Canada Aircraft* case, the concept of 'financial contribution' by the government in Article 1.1(a)(1) of the SCM Agreement specifically extends, in subparagraph (iv), to a direction by the government to a private person to provide a subsidy. This may be compared with the case-law of the European Court which not only requires that a State aid be attributable to the Member State concerned, but also that it must be financed, directly or indirectly, through State resources, even where this excludes State measures that have exactly the same effect as grants through State resources.[55] It should also be noted that there are no provider-oriented restrictions in the definition of a subsidy under the SCM Agreement, by comparison with the definition of a State aid in Community law. Thus while State aid is, by definition, aid provided at the level of a Member State, and excludes aid provided by the Community, Community aid may be considered to be a subsidy under the SCM Agreement.

Enforcement. The more flexible interpretation of an aid under the SCM Agreement should nevertheless be seen in perspective: the decisional practice under the SCM Agreement is considerably less developed than the vast number of cases and Commission decisions that have been generated by Articles 87 and 88 EC. This in turn reflects the far more limited *ex ante* enforcement procedures under the WTO rules (as set out above), by comparison with the rigorous enforcement procedures for State aid in the EU including, in particular, the requirement for prior notification and scrutiny of proposed aids (as set out in Chapters 16 to 18 below). **4.37**

4. The WTO and Community law

Competence to conclude international agreements. Article 300 EC sets out the procedure whereby the European Community itself may negotiate and conclude international agreements. Its powers in this respect are limited to those areas where the EC Treaty provides for the conclusion of agreements between the European Community and one or more states or international organizations. Article 133 EC specifies the area of common commercial policy as being one of these areas. On this basis, the ECJ has upheld the exclusive competence of the European Community with respect to all issues connected with trade in goods, as these fall under the scope of Article 133 EC.[56] By contrast, regarding matters connected with trade in services and intellectual property rights, the Court considers that competence is shared between the Community and the Member States, since these matters (with a few exceptions) fall outside the scope of Article 133 EC, and **4.38**

[55] See paras 2.90–2.94 above.

[56] Opinion 1/94 regarding the Agreement Establishing the World Trade Organization [1994] ECR I-5267, para 34.

exclusive competence of the Community is not to be implied from the other Treaty provisions.[57]

4.39 **Direct effect.** Direct effect has not been extended to either the GATT[58] or the WTO agreements.[59] The ECJ has thus held that it can review the legality of a Community measure for compliance with the WTO rules only if the Community intends to implement a specific WTO obligation (the *Nakajima* test),[60] or if the Community act in question directly refers to a specific provision of a WTO agreement (the *Fediol* test).[61] The ECJ has also avoided providing direct effect to WTO panel and Appellate Body reports.[62] It follows that the Community takes a purely dualistic approach to the WTO agreements. While the WTO provides binding obligations for the Community, the implementation of these obligations is solely through their transposition into the domestic legal order of the Community and its Member States.

4.40 **Implementation of the SCM Agreement.** The SCM Agreement has been implemented in the Community by Regulation 2026/97 on subsidized imports.[63] In order to apply countervailing duties against a subsidy measure, the measure in question must be specific and must cause material injury to the Community industry. The countervailing measures may only be undertaken if (1) they are not contrary to the overall interests of the Community, and (2) the imposed countervailing measure is lower than the subsidy margin if such lower duty rate is sufficient to remove the injury suffered. The Commission has published guidelines on the methodology applicable to calculating the subsidy amounts, the investigation periods and the array of elements deductible from the subsidy.[64]

---

[57] ibid, paras 98 and 105.

[58] Cases 21–24/72 *International Fruit Co v Produktschap voor Groenten en Fruit* [1972] ECR 1219, 1228.

[59] Case C-149/96 *Portugal v Council* [1998] ECR I-7379.

[60] Case C-69/89 *Nakajima All Precision Co v Council* [1991] ECR I-2069, para 31.

[61] Case 70/87 *Fediol v Commission* [1989] ECR 1781, paras 19–22.

[62] eg Case T-254/97 *Fruchthandelsgesellschaft Chemnitz v Commission* [1999] ECR II-2743.

[63] Council Regulation (EC) 2026/97 on protection against subsidized imports from countries not members of the European Community [1997] OJ L228/1, as amended [2002] OJ L305/4 and [2004] OJ L77/12.

[64] Guidelines for the calculation of the amount of subsidy in countervailing duty investigations [1998] OJ C394/6.

Part II

SPECIFIC TYPES OF AID

5

ENVIRONMENTAL AID

Main legislation and guidelines

Commission Regulation (EC) 800/2008 on the application of Articles 87 and 88 of the Treaty declaring certain categories of aid compatible with the common market (General Block Exemption Regulation) ('GBER') [2008] OJ L214/3

Community guidelines on State aid for environmental protection ('2008 Environmental Aid Guidelines') [2008] OJ C82/1

A. Introduction

Environmental protection under the EC Treaty. The Community's environmental policy has a long history. It first found expression with the introduction of Article 3(1)(l) EC requiring that activities of the Community include 'a policy in the sphere of the environment'. On that basis, the First Environmental Action Programme was adopted in 1972. Subsequently, the Amsterdam Treaty in 1999 strengthened the Community's commitment to environmental policy by making the achievement of balanced and sustainable development one of the Treaty's principal objectives. To attain this goal, Article 6 EC requires that environmental **5.01**

policy objectives be integrated into all the Community's policies and activities. Article 174 EC then lays down the guiding principles and objectives of environmental policy. This includes the obligation to aim for a high level of 'environmental protection' and the principles that where possible preventative action be taken, that damage should as a priority be 'rectified at source' and that the polluter should pay.

5.02 **Environmental Action Programmes.** Since 1972, the Community has set out its environmental strategy in a series of Environmental Action Programmes.[1] The most recent of these is the Sixth Environmental Action Programme adopted on 22 July 2002, which sets out a ten-year framework for environmental policy until 2012.[2] This strategy identified four priority areas for action: (1) combating Climate Change; (2) reducing adverse environmental impact on health; (3) halting biodiversity loss and protecting nature; and (4) natural resource management and managing waste. In 2006, the Commission carried out a mid-term review of the Action Programme and an impact assessment to assess the level of progress made and the direction for the future.[3] That review particularly highlighted the enhanced political commitment to tackling climate change and meeting the Community's commitments under the 1992 UN Framework Convention on Climate and the Kyoto Protocol agreed in 1997.

5.03 **Environmental protection and energy policy.** The protection of the environment cannot be considered in isolation from the Community's energy policy. In March 2007 the European Council adopted an energy action plan for the period 2007–2009 ('the Energy Plan for Europe').[4] The core objectives of the policy are threefold: (1) increasing security of supply; (2) ensuring the competitiveness of European economies and the availability of affordable energy; and (3) promoting environmental sustainability and combating climate change. The Community also set itself ambitious targets for the reduction of greenhouse gas emissions, improving energy efficiency, increasing the share of renewable energy in terms of overall consumption and increasing the share of biofuels by 2020.[5] The importance attached to the reduction of emissions and the promotion of renewable and

[1] First EC Environmental Action Programme (1973–1976) [1973] OJ C112/1; Second EC Environmental Action Programme (1977–1981) [1977] OJ C139/1; Third EC Environmental Action Programme (1982–1986) [1983] OJ C46/1; Fourth EC Environmental Action Programme (1987–1992) [1987] OJ C328/1; Fifth Environmental Action Programme (1993–2000) [1993] OJ C138/1; and Sixth Environmental Action Programme (2001–2012) [2002] OJ L242/1.

[2] Sixth Environmental Action Programme (2001–2012) [2002] OJ L242/1.

[3] 2006 Environment Policy Review, COM(2007) 195 final.

[4] Presidency Conclusions, Brussels European Council 8/9 March 2007 (7224/1/07 REV 1 CONCL 1), Annex 1; see also Commission proposal package for climate change 2020, Europe's climate change opportunity, COM(2008) 30 final.

[5] An Energy Policy for Europe, COM(2007) 1 final; and Limiting Global Climate Change to 2 degrees Celsius – The way ahead for 2020 and beyond, COM(2007) 2 final.

sustainable energy is apparent from the emphasis given to these objectives in the 2008 Environmental Aid Guidelines, and the environmental protection measures in the new General Block Exemption Regulation ('GBER'), discussed below.

State aid policy. The result of the initiatives described above is that environmental protection is now one of the main factors taken into account in the definition and implementation of EC State aid policy. However, this does not mean that all environmental aid schemes will be automatically exempt. Whilst some forms of aid are considered as contributing to the general aims of sustainable development, aid which conflicts with the principle of internalizing costs or had adverse affects on either competition or trade is unlikely to be authorized. Proper scrutiny of State aids is particularly important given the rapid increase in expenditure by Member States for environmental purposes. That is apparent from the Commission's Spring 2008 State aid Scoreboard, which indicates that total expenditure doubled between 2001 and 2006 from €7 to €14 billion.[6] **5.04**

Early guidelines on environmental aid. The Commission issued its first memorandum on State aid in environmental matters in November 1974.[7] This was concerned with assisting businesses to meet minimum mandatory environmental standards. Revised guidelines in the 1980s broadly followed the same approach. In the 1990s however, the introduction of the polluter pays principle, under which economic agents are required to bear the full cost of the damage caused by polluting activities and internalize the cost to the environment of their activities, required a change in direction in the treatment of State aid. In 1994, the Commission adopted Environmental Aid Guidelines[8] that were intended to take account of the broader range of financial instruments available for promoting environmental objectives whilst at the same time ensuring that aid did not detract from the polluter pays principle or lead to competitive distortion. The application of the 1994 Guidelines was extended twice[9] and remained in place until the end of 2000 when the 2001 Environmental Aid Guidelines were adopted. **5.05**

2001 Environmental Aid Guidelines. The 2001 Guidelines revised the earlier rules to take into account, among other things, the increased action in the field of the environment motivated by the adoption of the Kyoto Protocol on Climate Change. They also took into account the use of the new forms or increased use of existing forms of operating aid and fiscal measures. In the seven years during **5.06**

[6] State Aid Scoreboard – Spring 2008 Update, COM(2008) 304 final. Note however that 53% of that expenditure related to environmental tax reductions or exemptions.

[7] Commission memorandum on State aid in environmental matters, SEC(74) 4264.

[8] Community guidelines on State aid for environmental protection [1994] OJ C72/3.

[9] Extension of the validity of the Community guidelines on State aid for environmental protection [2000] OJ C14/8; Extension of the validity of the Community guidelines on State aid for environmental protection [2000] OJ C184/25.

which the 2001 Guidelines were in force, the Commission took around 350 decisions. In the vast majority of cases (98%) the Commission found the measure not to constitute State aid at all, or to be compatible, either in the form in which the measures were notified or following agreed modification.[10] The 2001 Guidelines were due to expire at the end of 2007, but were briefly extended[11] to cover the period until the new Guidelines came into effect.

5.07 **2008 Environmental Aid Guidelines.** The 2008 Guidelines were eventually published on 1 April 2008 and took effect from the following day.[12] Prior to their adoption there was extensive consultation over how to refine the economic approach so that approved aid would provide incentives coherent with the Community's current environmental and energy policy objectives. The basic aims are that State aid for environmental purposes will result in a higher level of environmental protection than would occur without the aid, and that the positive effects of proposed measures should outweigh any negative effects on competition while taking into account the polluter pays principle. This is achieved through the application of the 'balancing test'. The 2008 Guidelines also include for the first time aid for early adaptation to standards, aid for environmental studies, aid for district heating, aid for waste management and aid related to tradable permit schemes. Another significant innovation is the introduction of a detailed assessment method for cases involving large amounts of aid to individual beneficiaries. The 2008 Guidelines have also generally increased the permissible aid intensity, which in certain cases extends to 100% of the eligible costs. However, there is no longer a bonus for aid-assisted areas or for renewable energy installations serving all the needs of a community.

5.08 **The GBER.** Aid falling within the scope of a block exemption is deemed to be automatically compatible with the common market, and does not require formal notification provided that certain conditions and procedural formalities are met. The Enabling Regulation in 1998 empowered the Commission to block exempt specific categories of aid, including aid for environmental protection.[13] Nevertheless, environmental aid was not among the first wave of Commission block exemptions. However, with the introduction of the GBER[14] the Commission decided to expand the scope of automatic exemption to certain types

10 State Aid Scoreboard – Spring 2008 Update, COM(2008) 304 final, p 3.

11 Commission communication concerning the extension of the validity of Community guidelines on State aid for environmental protection [2007] OJ C316/58.

12 Community guidelines on State aid for environmental protection ('Environmental Aid Guidelines') [2008] OJ C82/1.

13 Council Regulation (EC) 994/98 on the application of Articles 92 and 93 of the Treaty establishing the European Community to certain categories of horizontal State aid [1998] OJ L142/1, Article 1(1)(a)(iii). See further para 3.34 above.

14 Commission Regulation (EC) 800/2008 on the application of Articles 87 and 88 of the Treaty declaring certain categories of aid compatible with the common market (General Block Exemption Regulation) ('GBER') [2008] OJ L214/3.

of environmental investment aid and environmental aid in the form of tax reductions. This decision was taken based on experience gained through the practical application of the 2001 Guidelines. Consultations over the provisions were carried out in parallel to those for the introduction the 2008 Environmental Aid Guidelines. Consequently, the provisions on environmental aid in the GBER are complementary to, and should be interpreted in line with, the provisions of the Guidelines. Prior to the adoption of the GBER, all environmental aid measures eligible for approval had to be notified to the Commission. Now, many of those measures will benefit from automatic exemption. The GBER came into force on 29 August 2008 and is intended to apply until 31 December 2013.[15]

Methodology for the assessment of environmental aid. The GBER, together with the 2008 Environmental Aid Guidelines, establishes the following methodology for the assessment of environmental aid. **5.09**

(a) A number of environmental aid measures do not constitute State aid. This is considered in section B below.

(b) Where there is aid, the GBER enables environmental aid that complies with certain substantive and procedural requirements to be implemented without prior notification and approval. The scope of the GBER is discussed in detail in section C below.

(c) Environmental aid measures not eligible under the GBER may still be individually approved by the Commission under the conditions set out in the 2008 Guidelines. These conditions are discussed in detail in section D below.

Further discussion of energy-related environmental aid measures is contained in Chapter 14, to which reference should also be made.

B. Existence of aid

Article 87(1) issues. For State aid to arise, all of the criteria under Article 87(1) must be met. These are discussed in detail in Chapter 2 above. Many of the measures introduced by Member States to promote environmental objectives will not constitute State aid within Article 87(1). In some cases, this will be because the measure does not produce an actual advantage to any undertaking. More often, the measure will not involve State resources or will amount to a general measure. The aid will also not fall within Article 87(1) if it is *de minimis*. These issues are discussed in the next paragraphs. **5.10**

[15] ibid, Article 40.

5.11 **Absence of advantage.** A measure will only constitute State aid where it relieves undertakings of charges which they would normally have to bear. This will not be the case where the effect of an environmental measure is to require undertakings to internalize the environmental costs associated with their activities.[16] This was the case for a Dutch system for the waste disposal of car wrecks, financed by a levy on cars registered in the Netherlands. The Commission decided that the arrangement was to oblige car manufacturers and importers to internalize the environmental costs of their activities, and consequently it did not amount to State aid either to those undertakings, or to the undertakings involved in packaging, collecting, recycling and dismantling the car wrecks.[17] There will also not be aid to 'undertakings' within Article 87(1) where the beneficiaries of aid are individual consumers.[18]

5.12 **State resources.** A measure that does not involve any direct or indirect transfer of State resources does not amount to State aid. This will be the case where a Member State requires private electricity suppliers to purchase electricity from renewable resources at fixed minimum prices, a mechanism that has been adopted in several Member States, including Belgium and Germany[19] and is currently being considered in the UK.[20] By contrast, the Court considered that a Dutch scheme allowing undertakings to trade allowances for the emission of nitrogen oxide did involve State resources, since the allowances resulted from emissions standards set by the State free of charge, whereas they could have been sold or put up for auction.[21]

5.13 **Selective and general measures.** Environmental aid measures will often be selective, whether directly[22] or indirectly.[23] In such cases, the environmental aim of the measure will not automatically take it outside the scope of Article 87(1).[24] But where differential treatment of undertakings is consistent with the nature and logic of an environmental measure, that differential treatment will be regarded

[16] See Case C-126/01 *GEMO* [2003] ECR I-13769, AG opinion paras 68–9.

[17] Decision 2002/204/EC *Waste disposal system for car wrecks* [2002] OJ L68/18. (See also Decision 2004/317/EC *WRAP environmental grant funding* [2004] OJ L102/59, para 48, although not accepted on the facts.)

[18] eg Decision in Case N 142/2005 *Low Carbon Car Grant Programme* (26 April 2006).

[19] The seminal case is Case C-379/98 *PreussenElektra* [2001] ECR I-2099, discussed at paras 2.93–2.94 above. For similar cases raising this issue see paras 14.11 below.

[20] UK Renewable Energy Strategy: Consultation (26 June 2008), Department for Business Enterprise and Regulatory Reform.

[21] Case T-233/04 *Netherlands v Commission* (judgment of 10 April 2008), para 75.

[22] eg Case C-143/99 *Adria-Wien Pipeline* [2001] ECR I-8365.

[23] See eg Case C-126/01 *GEMO* [2003] ECR I-13769; Decision in Case N 142/2005 *Low Carbon Car Grant Programme* (26 April 2006).

[24] Case T-55/99 *CETM v Commission* [2000] ECR II-3207, paras 53–4; Case C-143/99 *Adria-Wien Pipeline* [2001] ECR I-8365, para 52.

as justified by the nature or scheme of the system and hence not a selective aid within Article 87(1).[25] There are also other circumstances where aid is not selective at all. For example, the Commission takes the view that indemnification of a company designed merely to compensate that company for damage resulting from an official act will not normally constitute a selective aid.[26]

***De minimis* aids.** Environmental aids may well also fall within the scope of the *de minimis* block exemptions. In such cases the aid is deemed not to meet the criteria of Article 87(1). The general *de minimis* Regulation is discussed in Chapter 2.[27] The separate *de minimis* Regulations applicable in the agriculture and fisheries sectors are addressed in Chapter 11.[28] **5.14**

C. General Block Exemption Regulation ('GBER')

Structure. The GBER is divided into three Chapters. Chapter I is largely procedural in nature and applies to all types of aid covered by the GBER. It provides common definitions of standard concepts, scope and exclusions, notification thresholds, conditions for exemption including transparency and the incentive effect, cumulation of aid, transparency and monitoring. Chapter II of the GBER then sets out the specific conditions applicable to different types of aid. Chapter III contains general provisions. These include transitional measures for aid adopted under the earlier block exemptions and provisions governing the entry into force and application of the GBER. Consistent with that structure, section 1 below will address the provisions of Chapter I relevant to environmental aid. It will also, more generally, set out the common conditions applicable to all types of aid covered by the GBER. Section 2 will then address the specific environmental aid exemptions in the GBER. **5.15**

1. Common and procedural provisions

Sectoral scope of environmental aid exemptions. The environmental aid provisions of the GBER apply to almost all sectors of the economy, including the **5.16**

[25] Case T-210/02 *British Aggregates Association v Commission* [2006] ECR II-2789, paras 122–38; Case T-233/04 *Netherlands v Commission* (judgment of 10 April 2008), paras 97–9 (see also paras 88–96 rejecting in any event the suggestion that the measure favoured undertakings that were in a comparable situation to those outside the scheme); and Decision in Case N 574/2004 *Waste tax for dredging sludge* (2 February 2005).

[26] Decision in Case N 575/2005 *Relocation of car dismantling company Steenbergen* (20 December 2006); Decision in Case N 304/2003 *Aid in favour of Akzo Nobel to stop chlorine transport* (16 June 2004).

[27] See para 2.148 above.

[28] See paras 11.18–11.20 (agriculture) and 11.63 (fisheries) below.

primary production of agricultural products,[29] the processing and marketing of agricultural products,[30] and the coal, steel, shipbuilding and synthetic fibres sectors.[31] The GBER does not, however, apply to environmental aid in the fishery and aquaculture sectors.[32]

5.17 **Common exclusions.** Six types of aid are excluded altogether from the GBER. These are:

(a) aid to export-related activities;[33]

(b) aid contingent upon the use of domestic over imported goods;[34]

(c) aid favouring activities in the processing and marketing of agricultural products, where the amount of the aid is fixed on the basis of the price or quantity of such products purchased from primary producers or put on the market by the undertakings concerned, or when the aid is conditional on being passed on to primary producers;[35]

(d) ad hoc aid granted to large enterprises, with the sole exception of ad hoc aid used to supplement aid granted on the basis of regional investment and employment aid schemes, in accordance with the terms of Article 13(1) of the GBER;[36]

(e) pursuant to the *Deggendorf* principle,[37] aid schemes which do not explicitly exclude from their scope aid to undertakings subject to an unpaid recovery order, and ad hoc aid in favour of undertakings subject to an outstanding recovery order;[38] and

(f) aid to undertakings in financial difficulties.[39] Such aid must be assessed on the basis of the 2004 Rescue and Restructuring Guidelines alone.[40] To reduce the administrative burden on Member States, however, the definition of an 'undertaking in difficulty' is simplified in the case of SMEs, compared to the definition used in those Guidelines.[41]

5.18 **General conditions for exemption.** Any aid granted on the basis of the GBER must, to be exempt from notification under Article 88(3), contain an express reference to the relevant provisions of the GBER by citing those provisions, the

[29] Save where covered by Regulation 1857/2006: see further Chapter 11 below.

[30] Subject to the common exclusion: see para 5.17(c) below.

[31] These sectors remain subject to exclusions for certain other kinds of aid.

[32] GBER, Article 1(3).

[33] ibid, Article 1(2)(a).

[34] ibid, Article 1(2)(b).

[35] ibid, Article 1(3)(c).

[36] ibid, Article 1(5).

[37] See para 16.59 below.

[38] GBER, Article 1(6)(a) and (b).

[39] ibid, Article 1(6)(c), and recital (15).

[40] Community guidelines on State aid for rescuing and restructuring firms in difficulty [2004] OJ C244/2: see further Chapter 7 below.

[41] GBER, recital (15) and Article 1(7).

title and the publication reference of the GBER in the Official Journal. In the case of aid schemes, this requirement applies both to the scheme itself and any individual aid granted under such a scheme. In the case of ad hoc aid the citation requirement only applies (obviously) to the individual aid itself.[42]

Aid intensities. For the purposes of calculating the aid intensity, as set out in the specific exemptions in the GBER, pre-tax figures are used. Aid payable in several instalments must be discounted to its value at the moment of granting, using as the relevant interest rate the reference rate applicable at the time of the grant. Where aid is awarded by means of tax exemptions or reductions on future taxes due, the discounting of aid tranches takes place on the basis of the reference rates applicable at the various times the tax advantages become effective.[43] **5.19**

Documentary evidence. Any eligible costs for which aid is claimed must be supported by clear and itemized documentary evidence.[44] **5.20**

Transparency. The GBER only applies to aid that is 'transparent'. This requires any aid measure benefiting from exemption to take one of a number of specified forms. Grants and interest rate subsidies are considered to be transparent, as are loans where the gross grant equivalent is calculated on the basis of the reference rate prevailing at the time of the grant. Only certain forms of guarantee schemes are considered to be transparent, however, and aid in the form of fiscal measures is only transparent where the measure contains an explicit cap ensuring that the applicable threshold is not exceeded. Capital injections and any other risk capital measures are not considered transparent, unless they meet the substantive criteria for risk capital exemption in Article 29 of the GBER. Aid in the form of repayable advances is only considered transparent if the total amount of the advance does not exceed the applicable thresholds in the GBER. If that threshold is expressed in terms of an aid intensity, the total amount of the advance expressed as a percentage of the eligible costs must not exceed the applicable intensity.[45] **5.21**

Individual notification thresholds. Under the GBER certain aids are excluded where the value of the financial assistance exceeds specified thresholds. This varies according to the type of aid in question. For investment aid for environmental protection the threshold is €7.5 million per undertaking per investment project.[46] **5.22**

---

42 ibid, Article 3.

43 ibid, Article 4(1) and (2). For the relevant reference rates see Communication from the Commission on the revision of the method for setting the reference and discount rates [2008] OJ C14/6 and the table of reference rates on the DG Comp website at <http://ec.europa.eu/comm/competition/state_aid/legislation/referencerates.html>.

44 GBER, Article 4(3).

45 ibid, Article 5.

46 ibid, Article 6. Such aid is then subject to a detailed assessment by the Commission: see paras 5.60 *et seq* below.

5.23 **Cumulation.** Aid that is exempted under the GBER can be cumulated with other aid exempted under the GBER, provided that the other aid measures concern different eligible costs. Where the eligible costs are overlapping (fully or in part), aid may not be cumulated either with other GBER-exempted aid, or with aid exempted under the general *de minimis* Regulation or other Community funding, if the cumulation would result in exceeding the highest aid intensity or aid ceiling applicable under the GBER. The exception to that is aid in favour of disabled workers, which can be cumulated in relation to the same costs above the highest applicable thresholds in the GBER, provided that the cumulation does not result in an aid intensity of over 100% of the relevant costs. Detailed provisions set out the conditions under which aid for identifiable eligible costs may be cumulated with aid for non-identifiable eligible costs.[47]

5.24 **Incentive effect: basic conditions.** The GBER only applies to aid deemed to have an incentive effect. It should thus not apply to aid for activities in which the beneficiary would already engage under market conditions.[48] For SMEs, the necessary incentive effect is considered to exist if the beneficiary has submitted an application for aid to the Member State before work on the project or activity has started. For large enterprises, however, the conditions are more stringent. In addition to the requirement to submit an application for aid before work on the project or activity has started, the Member State is required to verify before granting the individual aid in question that the beneficiary has established and documented a material increase in the size or scope of the project/activity due to the aid, or a material increase in the total amount spent on the project/activity due to the aid, or a material increase in the speed of completion of the project/activity, or (in the case of regional investment aid) that the project would not have been carried out in the assisted region concerned in the absence of the aid. Special provisions apply, however to fiscal measures. In such cases the detailed rules for the establishment of an incentive effect do not apply provided that the measure is objective and non-discretionary, and has been adopted before work on the aided project or activity has started.[49]

5.25 **Incentive effect: deeming provisions.** In the case of certain types of aid covered by the GBER, the requirement of an incentive effect is deemed to be satisfied by the nature of the aid itself. In relation to environmental aid, this is the case for tax reductions that satisfy the conditions of Article 25 of the GBER.[50]

---

47 ibid, Article 7.

48 ibid, recital (28).

49 ibid, Article 8(1)–(4).

50 ibid, Article 8(5); see further para 5.35 below.

Reporting and monitoring. The final set of common conditions concerns the reporting and monitoring provisions for aid granted under the GBER. Member States adopting an aid scheme or granting ad hoc aid pursuant to the GBER must notify a summary of the measure concerned to the Commission within 20 working days of its entry into force. The summaries are then published by the Commission on the DG Comp website and in the Official Journal. In addition, the Member State concerned must make available the full text of the measure on the internet, and include within its summary to the Commission a link to that text. In addition to these general requirements, specific reporting rules apply to the grant of individual aid under the GBER.[51] The Commission is required to monitor regularly the aid measures of which it has been informed, under these provisions. If necessary the Commission may ask the Member State for further information. If the Member State does not comply with that request, the Commission may ultimately require the Member State to notify under Article 88(3) all or part of its aid measures that would otherwise be covered by the GBER.[52] 5.26

2. Specific environmental aid exemptions

Categories of environmental aid exemptions. The environmental aid exemptions are set out in Section 4 of Chapter II of the GBER. They encompass both investment measures and fiscal instruments, and exempt eight categories of aid: (1) investment aid for environmental protection improving on Community standards;[53] (2) aid for the acquisition of transport vehicles which go beyond Community standards; (3) aid for early adaptation to future Community standards for SMEs; (4) aid for investment in energy saving measures; (5) aid for investment in high efficiency cogeneration; (6) aid for investments to exploit renewable energy sources; (7) aid for environmental studies; and (8) aid in the form of tax reductions. The conditions for exemption in each case are described below. In all cases, aid is only exempted where it contributes to increasing the level of environmental protection.[54] 5.27

Aid for environmental protection beyond Community standards. Investment aid may be granted to undertakings to cover the extra costs involved in increasing 5.28

[51] ibid, Article 9; see also Article 11 for annual reporting requirements.

[52] ibid, Article 10.

[53] Defined in Article 17(3) as (a) a mandatory Community standard setting the levels to be attained in environmental terms by individual undertakings; or (b) the obligation to use the best available techniques as set out in the most recent relevant information published by the Commission pursuant to Article 17(2) of Council Directive 96/61/EC concerning integrated pollution prevention and control [1996] OJ L257/26.

[54] Defined in Article 17(1) as any action designed to remedy or prevent damage to physical surroundings or natural resources by the undertaking's own activities, or to reduce risk of such damage, or to lead to a more efficient use of natural resources including energy-saving measures and the use of renewable sources of energy.

the level of environmental protection either (a) by going beyond the relevant Community standard for environmental protection (even where the national standards are more stringent) or (b) by increasing the level of environmental protection in circumstances where no relevant Community standard exists.[55] However, aid may not be granted to bring companies into line with Community standards that have been adopted, but are not yet in force;[56] nor does the GBER cover aid for investments relating to the management of waste of other undertakings.[57] The maximum aid intensities are 35% for large enterprises, 45% for medium-sized enterprises and 55% for small enterprises.[58] There are detailed provisions in Article 18(5)–(7) defining the calculation of eligible costs, to ensure that the only costs covered are those related to the extra investment needed to achieve a higher standard of protection than that required without taking into account operating costs or benefits. These costs must be identified by reference to the counterfactual situation, in other words the level of investment made in the absence of aid.

5.29 **Aid for transport vehicles.** The GBER exempts aid for the acquisition of transport vehicles enabling undertakings active in the transport sector to go beyond Community standards for environmental protection or increase the level of environmental protection in the absence of Community standards. The exemption also applies to vehicles for road, railway, inland waterway and maritime transport that comply with Community standards already adopted, where they are acquired before the Community standards enter into force, and where the standards will not apply retroactively to already purchased vehicles. The maximum aid intensities are 35% for large enterprises, 45% for medium-sized enterprises and 55% for small enterprises. Eligible costs are the extra investment costs necessary to achieve a higher level of environmental protection, as calculated under Article 18(5).[59]

5.30 **Aid for early adaptation to future Community standards.** Generally speaking, aid to assist undertakings to meet their legal obligation to comply with Community environmental standards is not exempted. However, the GBER does permit measures designed to encourage SMEs to meet the additional costs to achieve the level of environmental protection under Community environmental standards well in advance of its legal obligation to do so. To benefit from exemption the investment must be implemented at least a year before the mandatory date for transposition of the standards in question. The aid intensity is set at 15% for small enterprises

[55] GBER, Article 18.

[56] Save in the case of aid for transport vehicles, discussed in para 5.29 below, and aid to assist SMEs to adopt to future Community standards, discussed in para 5.30 below.

[57] GBER, Article 18(9). This is covered in the 2008 Environmental Aid Guidelines: see para 5.51 below.

[58] GBER, Article 18(4).

[59] ibid, Article 19.

and 10% for medium-sized enterprises if the investment is implemented more than three years before the mandatory date of transposition. If the investment is implemented between one and three years before that date, only small enterprises are eligible for aid, and then only up to a maximum intensity of 10%. The eligible costs are the extra investment costs necessary to achieve the level of environmental protection required by the Community standard, as calculated under Article 18(5).[60] There is no equivalent exemption in the case of large enterprises.

Aid for energy saving measures. Energy saving measures are actions that enable undertakings to reduce the amount of energy used in their production cycle.[61] Aid for such measures is permitted up to a maximum intensity of 20% of eligible costs, but may be increased to 30% for medium-sized enterprises and 40% for small enterprises. The eligible costs are calculated on the basis set out in Article 18(6) and (7) of the GBER, without taking into account operating benefits and costs.[62] Where aid is designed to achieve energy savings beyond the level required by Community standards, it is permitted up to a maximum intensity of 60% for large enterprises, 70% for medium-sized enterprises and 80% for small enterprises. The eligible costs are the extra investments necessary to achieve energy savings beyond the level required by Community standards. These costs must also be calculated on the basis set out in Article 18(6) and (7) and must be calculated net of any operating benefits and costs resulting from energy savings in the first few years of the investment: three years in the case of SMEs, four years in the case of large undertakings outside the EU CO_2 Emission Trading System and five years in the case of large undertakings participating in the EU CO_2 Emission Trading System.[63] **5.31**

Aid for high-efficiency cogeneration. Environmental aid towards the extra investment costs necessary for an undertaking to build a high efficiency cogeneration[64] plant will be eligible for exemption. The maximum aid intensity is 45% for large enterprises, 55% for medium-sized enterprises and 65% for small enterprises. The eligible costs are the extra investment costs necessary to construct a high efficiency cogeneration plant, as calculated under Article 18(6) and (7).[65] **5.32**

---

[60] ibid, Article 20.

[61] ibid, Article 17(2).

[62] ibid, Article 21(4)–(5).

[63] ibid, Article 21(2)–(3). The period for large undertakings can be reduced to the first three years of the life of the investment where the depreciation level for investment is no more than three years.

[64] Defined in Article 17(9) as cogeneration meeting the criteria of Annex III to Directive 2004/8/EC on the promotion of cogeneration based on a useful heat demand in the internal energy market [2004] OJ L52/50 and satisfying the harmonised efficiency reference values established by Commission Decision 2007/74/EC establishing harmonised efficiency reference values for separate production of electricity and heat [2007] OJ L32/183.

[65] GBER, Article 22.

5.33 **Aid for renewable energy sources.** Aid may be granted to assist undertakings investing in the production of energy from renewable energy sources.[66] The costs that are eligible for exemption are the additional costs borne by the beneficiary compared with production from a conventional power plant or conventional heating system with the equivalent capacity, as calculated under Article 18(6) and (7). The maximum aid intensity is 45% for large enterprises, 55% for medium-sized enterprises and 65% for small enterprises.[67]

5.34 **Aid for environmental studies.** Environmental studies directly related to investment for the purpose of achieving environmental standards, achieving energy savings, or producing renewable energy[68] are eligible for aid. The maximum aid intensity is 50% of the costs of the study if carried out for large enterprises, 60% for studies carried out for medium-sized enterprises and 70% for studies carried out for small enterprises.[69]

5.35 **Aid in the form of tax reductions.** A framework for the Community's policy regarding the taxation of energy products and electricity is set out in Directive 2003/96/EC.[70] Environmental aids in the form of tax reductions on schemes fulfilling the conditions of that Directive are exempted under the GBER provided that the beneficiaries pay at least the Community minimum tax level set by Annex I to Directive 2003/96/EC. Tax reductions may be granted for no more than ten years. After this period such measures should be re-evaluated to assess whether they are still appropriate. The Commission has indicated that following such an assessment the measures or similar measures may be re-adopted.[71]

D. Authorization under Article 87(3)

1. General

5.36 **2008 Environmental Aid Guidelines.** The 2008 Environmental Aid Guidelines set out the circumstances in which the Commission will approve environmental aid that does not fall within the ambit of the GBER. The Guidelines apply to environmental aid in all sectors governed by the EC Treaty, including sectors subject to specific rules such as shipbuilding, motor vehicles, synthetic fibres, coal and steel. They do not, however, apply to the financing of environmental protection

---

66 Defined in GBER, Article 17(4) as wind, solar, geothermal, wave, tidal, hydropower installations, biomass, landfill gas, sewage treatment plant, gas and biogases.

67 GBER, Article 23.

68 As defined in GBER Articles 18, 21 and 23 respectively.

69 ibid, Article 24.

70 Council Directive 2003/96/EC restructuring the Community framework for the taxation of energy products and electricity [2003] OJ L283/51.

71 GBER, Article 25 and recital (47).

measures relating to air, road, railway, inland waterway and maritime transport infrastructure. In the agriculture and fisheries sectors, they only apply to the extent that the measures are not covered by the provisions governing those particular sectors.[72]

Balancing test. The principal basis of assessment of aid under the Guidelines is the 'balancing test' established in the Commission's State Aid Action Plan.[73] This test is designed to weigh the negative effects of the aid on competition and trade against the positive objectives in the common interest.[74] The first limb of the test examines whether the objective of the aid is in the common interest (which in the context of the Guidelines is the protection of the environment). The second limb involves assessment of how the aid is designed to deliver that objective, having regard to the appropriateness of the State aid, its incentive effect and the proportionality of the measure. Finally, the third limb examines whether the distortions of competition and trade are limited so that the overall balance is positive.[75] **5.37**

Applying the balancing test to environmental aid. In respect of certain environmental aid measures, where those measures meet certain conditions and parameters (such as aid intensities), there is a presumption that the balancing test leads to a positive result. The aid is therefore regarded as being compatible under Article 87(3) EC.[76] These measures are set out in Chapter 3 of the Guidelines, and addressed in sections 2, 3 and 4 below. Aid that falls outside those parameters, and which therefore carries a greater risk of distortion, must undergo a more detailed assessment to ascertain compliance with the balancing test.[77] This is described in Chapter 5 of the Guidelines and addressed at section 5 below. **5.38**

Cumulation. The aid ceilings under the Guidelines apply whether the aid provided comes purely from State resources or is partially Community funded. Environmental aid authorized under the Guidelines cannot be cumulated with other forms of financing if it results in a level of intensity higher than that permitted under the Guidelines. However, where costs eligible for environmental protection aid are also eligible (in whole or part) for aid for other purposes then the highest available ceiling will apply to the common portion of those costs. As with the GBER, aid for environmental protection cannot be cumulated with **5.39**

[72] 2008 Environmental Aid Guidelines, section 2.1; and see Chapter 11 below for detailed discussion of the State aid rules in the agriculture and fisheries sectors.

[73] State Aid Action Plan – Less and better targeted State aid: a roadmap for State aid reform 2005–2009, COM(2005) 107 final.

[74] 2008 Environmental Aid Guidelines, para 16; and see further para 3.28 above.

[75] See ibid, section 1.3 for more detail of these principles in the environmental aid sphere.

[76] ibid, para 39.

[77] ibid, para 40.

de minimis aid for the same eligible costs if this would result in an aid intensity higher than that fixed under the Guidelines.[78]

5.40 **Authorization outside the Guidelines.** There have also been instances in the past where the Commission has authorized environmental aid schemes based directly upon the application of Article 87(3)(c), although outside the scope of the Guidelines, on the basis that the measure is proportionate to the environmental objective sought and does not lead to an undue distortion of competition.[79] In the future, however, it is expected that such cases will be assessed under the general provisions of the Guidelines.

2. Compatible aid under Article 87(3)(c)

5.41 **Aid for environmental protection beyond Community standards.** Investment aid enabling an undertaking to either (a) increase the level of environmental protection resulting from its activities beyond the requirements imposed by an existing Community environmental standard[80] or (b) increase the level of environmental protection in the absence of Community standards, may be authorized. The objective is to assist enterprises to go beyond what is required under Community law and to support eco-innovation. Aid cannot be authorized under this heading to meet a standard that is already adopted but not yet in force. The aid must be limited to the extra investment costs necessary to achieve a higher level of environmental protection than required by the Community standards. The eligible costs in that respect are calculated in two steps: (1) identifying the cost related to achieving the higher level environmental protection compared to the counterfactual situation; and (2) deducting the operating benefits and adding the operating costs related to the extra investment over the first five years. The basic permitted aid intensity in relation to those eligible costs is 50%. However, that may be increased where aid is granted to SMEs or where the investment relates to the acquisition of an eco-innovation asset or project[81] up to the levels set out in the table below. Where aid is granted in a genuinely competitive bidding process on the basis of clear, transparent and non-discriminatory criteria, the aid intensity may amount to up to 100% of the eligible investment costs.[82]

---

[78] ibid, section 6.

[79] eg Decision in Case N 443/2003 *Second circuit water* (2 June 2004).

[80] Defined as (i) a mandatory Community standard setting the levels to be attained in environmental terms by individual undertakings; or (ii) the obligation under Council Directive 96/61/EC concerning integrated pollution and control [1996] OJ L257/26 to use the best available techniques as set out in the most relevant information published by the Commission pursuant to Article 17(2) of the Directive: 2008 Environmental Aid Guidelines, para 70(3).

[81] Defined as innovation activities resulting in or aimed at improving environmental protection. This includes new production processes, new products or services, and new business methods aimed at reducing risks for the environment: 2008 Environmental Aid Guidelines, para 70(4).

[82] ibid, section 3.1.1.

	Aid unrelated to eco-innovation	Aid in the field of eco-innovation
Large enterprises	50%	60%
Medium-sized enterprises	60%	70%
Small enterprises	70%	80%

Aid for transport vehicles. The provisions for aid for environmental protection going beyond Community standards apply in the transport sector. In addition, in relation to the acquisition of new transport vehicles for road, railway, inland waterway and maritime transport, aid for vehicles complying with adopted Community standards is permissible, when they are acquired before the entry into force of the standards and where the standards will not apply retroactively to already purchased vehicles.[83] 5.42

Aid for early adaptation to future Community standards. Aid to assist businesses to adapt to new Community standards with a higher level of environmental protection ahead of the mandatory application date may be approved where the investment is implemented and finalized at least one year before the new standard comes into force. The eligible costs are those relating to the extra investment required to achieve the higher level of environmental protection required under the new standard, relative to the cost of meeting the existing mandatory obligations. The costs must be calculated net of any operating benefits and costs related to the extra investment and arising in the first five years of the investment. The permitted aid intensities for large, medium-sized and small enterprises are as set out in the table below.[84] 5.43

	Implementation more than three years before standard enters into force	Implementation one to three years before standard enters into force
Large enterprises	15%	10%
Medium-sized enterprises	20%	15%
Small enterprises	25%	20%

Aid for environmental studies. One of the market failures associated with under-investment in environmental protection relates to lack of information concerning the potential benefits and cost savings that can accrue. Under the Guidelines, aid may be authorized to help cover the cost of environmental studies into (1) achieving a level of protection exceeding existing environmental standards or where no standards exist; or (2) achieving energy savings; or (3) producing renewable energy. 5.44

83 ibid, section 3.1.2.
84 ibid, section 3.1.3.

The maximum aid intensities are 50% for large enterprises, 60% for medium-sized enterprises and 70% for small enterprises.[85]

5.45 **Investment aid for energy saving measures.** Community and national targets have been set for achieving energy savings and the reduction of greenhouse gas emissions. There is pressure to try to ensure that these targets are met both in the private and public sector. In many cases measures taken to reduce energy use result in cost savings and that provides sufficient commercial incentive in itself to warrant introduction. However, where associated costs are higher than related benefits (for example where a project involves high up-front capital investment in plant or equipment) there may be insufficient short-to-medium term economic incentive for enterprises to invest. Support in the form of aid can therefore be authorized to meet the extra investment costs to achieve energy savings beyond the level required by Community standards. Such costs must be calculated net of any operating benefit and costs related to the extra investment for energy savings arising during the first few years of the investment: three years in the case of SMEs, four years in the case of large undertakings outside the EU CO_2 Emission Trading System and five years in the case of large undertakings participating in the EU CO_2 Emission Trading System.[86] The maximum aid intensities are 60% for large enterprises, 70% for medium-sized enterprises, 80% for small enterprises and 100% for aid provided following a competitive bidding process on non-discriminatory criteria.[87]

5.46 **Operating aid for energy saving measures.** Operating aid for energy saving may also be granted for a period of up to five years provided that it is limited to compensating for the net extra production cost once the benefit from energy saving has been deducted. Investment aid for new plans must similarly be deducted from the production costs. Aid which is gradually reduced may amount to up to 100% of extra costs in the first year but must be gradually reduced year-on-year to zero by the end of the fifth year. Aid that is not gradually reduced may not exceed 50% of eligible costs per annum.[88]

5.47 **Investment aid for renewable energy sources.** The Community is promoting increased use of energy from renewable sources[89] as part of its strategy to reduce

---

[85] ibid, section 3.1.4.

[86] The period for large undertakings can be reduced to the first three years of the life of the investment where the depreciation level for investment is no more than three years.

[87] 2008 Environmental Aid Guidelines, section 3.1.5.1; and see eg Decision in Case N 728/2006 *Energy savings and efficiency programme in Catalonia* (4 April 2007).

[88] 2008 Environmental Aid Guidelines, section 3.1.5.2; and see eg Decision in Case N 524/2004 *Investment aid for energy efficiency* (16 March 2005): the notified measures were designed to stimulate owners of public premises to invest in energy efficiency and energy savings. These were slightly modified and approved by the Commission in its Decision in Case N 312/2006 (26 June 2006).

[89] Defined as wind, solar, geothermal, wave, tidal, hydropower installations, biomass, landfill gas, sewage treatment plant gas and biogases: 2008 Environmental Aid Guidelines, para 70(5).

greenhouse gas emissions. It is recognized however that the cost of production from renewable energy may in some instances exceed that derived from fossil fuels. State aid may therefore be justified to bridge that gap. In the case of investment aid, eligible costs are those representing the extra costs borne by the beneficiary compared with a conventional power plant of the same capacity. These must be calculated net of operating benefits and costs related to the extra investment arising in the first five years. The maximum aid intensities are 60% for large enterprises, 70% for medium-sized enterprises, 80% for small enterprises and 100% for aid provided following a competitive bidding process on non-discriminatory criteria.[90]

Operating aid for renewable energy production. Operating aid for the production of renewable energy may be justified to cover the difference in cost between producing renewable energy and the market price of the form of energy concerned, whether the energy produced is for sale to the market or for own-consumption. The Guidelines provide a number of different options for the form in which aid may be granted. These are considered in detail in Chapter 14.[91] **5.48**

Aid for cogeneration. Other than the promotion of renewable energy, the EU's energy efficiency strategy also includes the promotion of cogeneration of heat and electricity. Investment aid for high-efficiency cogeneration[92] is available for both new plants and the improvement of existing plants, where the investment results in overall primary energy savings. Operating aid may be given for high-efficiency cogeneration on a similar basis as for renewable energy. In the case of investment aid, the eligible costs are deemed to be those necessary to realize a high-efficiency cogeneration plant compared with the reference investment and calculated net of benefit and costs related to the extra investment and arising in the first five years. The maximum aid intensities are 60% for large enterprises, 70% for medium-sized enterprises, 80% for small enterprises and 100% for aid provided following a competitive bidding process on non-discriminatory criteria.[93] **5.49**

Aid for energy-efficient district heating. Investment aid for energy-efficient district heating installations[94] (other than infrastructure) may be approved where it **5.50**

---

[90] 2008 Environmental Aid Guidelines, section 3.1.6.1. For examples of decisions approving schemes supporting investment in renewable energy see paras 14.18–14.20 below.

[91] See para 14.17 below.

[92] Defined as cogeneration meeting the criteria of Annex III to Directive 2004/8/EC on the promotion of cogeneration based on a useful heat demand in the internal energy market [2004] OJ L52/50 and satisfying the harmonised efficiency reference values established by Commission Decision 2007/74/EC establishing harmonised efficiency reference values for separate production of electricity and heat [2007] OJ L32/183: 2008 Environmental Aid Guidelines, para 70(11).

[93] 2008 Environmental Aid Guidelines, section 3.1.7.1.

[94] Defined as the supply of heat, either in the form of steam or hot water, from a central source of production through a transmission and distribution system to multiple buildings, for the purpose of heating: ibid, para 70(12).

leads to primary energy savings. Eligible costs are those that relate to the extra investment leading to energy-efficient district heating compared to the reference investment and must be calculated net of any operating benefits and costs related to the extra investment over the first five years. The maximum aid intensities are 50% for large enterprises, 60% for medium-sized enterprises, 70% for small enterprises and 100% for aid provided following a competitive bidding process on non-discriminatory criteria.[95]

5.51 **Aid for waste management.** Waste management is becoming an increasingly high profile concern in the Community. Consequently, State aid may be granted either to the producer of aid (as investment aid for environmental protection beyond Community standards)[96] or to enterprises involved in the management and recycling, re-utilization and recovery of waste generated by others.[97] In the latter case, investment aid is permitted where: (1) the investment is aimed at reducing pollution generated by third parties; (2) the aid does not relieve the normal costs of pollution that companies are required to bear under EU law; (3) the investment goes beyond the current state-of-the-art technologies or uses conventional technologies in an innovative manner; (4) but for the investment the pollutant materials would be disposed of or treated in a less environmentally friendly manner; and (5) the investment does not simply increase demand for the materials for recycling without increasing the collection of those materials. The eligible costs are limited to the extra costs borne by the beneficiary compared with conventional production and must be calculated net of any operating benefits and costs arising during the first five years. The maximum aid intensities are 50% for large enterprises, 60% for medium-sized enterprises and 70% for small enterprises.[98]

5.52 **Aid for the remediation of contaminated sites.** Under the polluter pays principle, the cost of environmental damage should be borne by the polluter. Thus State aid may not be granted to finance remediation of contaminated sites where the polluter can be identified.[99] However where environmental damage has been caused to a site affecting the quality of soil, surface or ground water and the polluter cannot be identified or cannot be made to bear the costs, the person

[95] ibid, section 3.1.8; and see eg Decision in Case N 455/2006 *Promotion of district heating – Lombardy* (8 May 2007).

[96] See para 5.41 above.

[97] Under the 2001 Environmental Aid Guidelines, aid was not authorized for the management of waste of other undertakings, although there were instances of the Commission approving such aid under the general provisions of Article 87(3)(c), eg Decision 2004/317/EC *WRAP lease guarantee fund* [2004] OJ L102/59; and Decision in Case N 196e/2005 *Programme for support of utilisation of waste* (21 December 2005).

[98] 2008 Environmental Aid Guidelines, section 3.1.9.

[99] ibid, para 132; Decision in Case N 385/2002 *Support for land remediation* (11 June 2003); Decision in Case N 85/2005 *Rehabilitation of polluted industrial sites* (27 July 2005); and Decision in Case N 117/2007 *Decontamination of the site Neue Maxhütte Stahlwerke* (3 September 2007).

responsible for remediation work may be eligible to receive State aid. The eligible costs are those related to the remediation work less the increase in the value of the land. The permitted aid intensity is up to 100% of those costs.[100]

Aid for the relocation of undertakings. Aid may be granted to undertakings to relocate to new sites for grounds relating to environmental protection or prevention of damage. The relocation must be required by a competent public authority or is a result of judicial or administrative proceedings, and the beneficiary must comply with the strictest environmental standards applicable in the new site location. To be eligible for relocation aid, the undertakings must be either (1) established in a Natura 2000 designated area[101] and carrying out activities creating major pollution, or (2) an establishment or installation falling within the scope of the Seveso II Directive.[102] In calculating eligible costs, the Commission will take into account the benefits such as the sale price or rent of the land abandoned (or compensation for such land) and other gains connected with the transfer or relating to a capacity increase. These will be set against the costs associated with the purchase of land or construction or purchase of new plant and any penalties imposed for leaving the original site. The maximum aid intensities are 50% for large enterprises, 60% for medium-sized enterprises and 70% for small enterprises.[103] **5.53**

Aid involved in tradable permit schemes. Since the adoption of the Kyoto Protocol and the adoption of legislation establishing a greenhouse gas emissions allowance trading scheme,[104] Member States have increasingly adopted trading schemes as way of achieving environmental protection targets. The Community has actively encouraged the use of such market-based instruments.[105] Their basic underlying principle is that where pollution bears a real economic cost, companies will tend to maximize their profits by reducing this cost component, thereby reducing pollution at the same time. Such schemes may result in State aid where there is an advantage provided to certain undertakings. In 2001, when the last **5.54**

[100] 2008 Environmental Aid Guidelines, section 3.1.10.

[101] Council Directive 92/43/EEC on the conservation of natural habitats and of wild fauna and flora [1992] OJ L206/7.

[102] Council Directive 96/82/EC on the control of major accident hazards involving dangerous substances [1997] OJ L10/13.

[103] 2008 Environmental Aid Guidelines, section 3.1.11; and see Decision in Case N 385/2002 *Support for land remediation* (11 June 2003) – a scheme by the UK Government to bring contaminated land, brownfield land and derelict land back into productive use; Decision in Case N 575/2005 *Relocation of car dismantling company Steenbergen* (20 December 2006); and Decisions in Cases N 601/2006 *Aid to waste managers moving for environmental reasons* (28 March 2007) and N 42/2000 *Local entrepreneurship (Trento)* (28 April 2000).

[104] Under Directive 2003/87/EC establishing a scheme for greenhouse gas emission allowance trading within the Community [2003] OJ L275/32.

[105] Market-based instruments for environment and related policy purposes, COM(2007) 140 final and European Environment Agency Report, No 1/2006 – Using the market for cost-effective environmental policy – Market based instruments in Europe.

Guidelines were adopted, the Commission considered that it lacked sufficient experience with such schemes to be in a position to lay down general conditions for authorization.[106] However, over the past few years, a number of such schemes were notified.[107] The Commission therefore decided to include provisions for authorizing State aid for emissions trading schemes in the 2008 Guidelines. The Commission considers that tradable schemes may involve State aid where for instance, a Member State grants, permits or allowances below market value.[108] Such aid may however be exempted where certain conditions are fulfilled. Specifically: (1) the permit scheme must be established in order to achieve environmental objectives that go beyond those achieved by mandatory Community standards; (2) the allocation must be carried out in a transparent manner based on objective criteria and the total amount of permit or allowances granted to an individual undertaking for a price below market value must not exceed its expected requirements; (3) the allocation method must be non-discriminatory unless favouring certain undertakings is justified by the environmental logic of the scheme itself or is consistent with other environmental policies; and (4) new entrants should not receive permits or allowances on more favourable conditions than existing undertakings in the same market. The Commission will also assess the necessity and the proportionality of State aid for any scheme (other than schemes established in accordance with Directive 2003/87/EC),[109] by considering whether beneficiaries are chosen on the basis of objective and transparent criteria, the effect of auctioning on production costs, the extent to which costs can be passed on to customers and the extent to which individual undertakings are able to reduce emission levels to make the price of certificates bearable.[110]

3. Compatible aid under Article 87(3)(b)

5.55 **Conditions.** The focus of the 2008 Environmental Aid Guidelines is on approval under Article 87(3)(c). Nevertheless, the Guidelines confirm that measures designed to promote the execution of important environmental projects of common European interest may be approved under Article 87(3)(b). For a project (or group of projects) to gain approval under this provision it must not be limited to one Member State or even the Member States involved in implementing it,[111] but must extend to the Community as a whole and must present a 'substantive

---

[106] Commission Guidelines on State aid for environmental protection [2001] OJ C37/3, para 71.

[107] eg Decision in Case N 47/2006 *Dispersed oil in produced water trading scheme* (19 July 2006).

[108] 2008 Environmental Aid Guidelines, paras 55 and 139.

[109] The Commission has already assessed the State aid involved in the NAPs under the EU emissions trading scheme: ibid, n 51.

[110] ibid, section 3.1.12.

[111] Although the Commission will consider more favourably projects involving undertakings from a significant number of Member States: ibid, para 149.

contribution to the Community objectives' in the field of environmental protection. It will also be necessary to demonstrate that the aid is necessary and that it provides an incentive for a high-risk project to be carried out. The level of importance of the project will be measured in terms of its size and the magnitude of its positive environmental impact.[112]

Aid level. Where an aid meets the requirements to be authorized under Article 87(3)(b), the Commission can exercise its discretion to authorize aid at a level higher than would be otherwise permitted under the Guidelines.[113] **5.56**

4. Reduction of or exemption from environmental taxes

Policy. An exemption from environmental taxes does not of itself aim at reaching higher environmental standards. Nevertheless, it is recognized that a temporary reduction or an exemption for certain undertakings or sectors from environmental taxes may be justified in order to make it feasible to adopt higher taxes for other undertakings.[114] The 2008 Guidelines maintain the principle that such measures, where they constitute aid,[115] may be approved provided that they contribute at least indirectly to an improvement of the level of environmental protection, and where the tax reductions or exemptions do not undermine the general objective pursued.[116] However, the Commission has introduced new criteria and rules to assess whether the measures are necessary and proportionate. In this respect, the 2008 Guidelines distinguish between taxes that are harmonized and those that are not. **5.57**

Harmonized taxes. In relation to environmental taxes harmonized at the Community level, a reduction or exemption is considered compatible under Article 87(3)(c), for a period of up to ten years, provided that the firms concerned pay at least the minimum Community tax level set by the applicable Directive.[117] **5.58**

Other cases. Where the reduction or exemption is from taxes not covered by Community legislation, or which are below the Community minimum tax level, tax reductions or exemptions may be approved for a period of up to ten years, where they are necessary and proportionate. They will be considered necessary **5.59**

---

112 ibid, para 147.

113 ibid, para 150.

114 Decision in Case N 866/2006 *Tax exemption: certain renewables in heat generation* (22 June 2007).

115 As to which see para 5.13 above and Chapter 2 generally.

116 2008 Environmental Aid Guidelines, Section 4.

117 For energy products and electricity, the Community minimum level is that which is laid down in Annex I to Council Directive 2003/96/EC of 27 October 2003 restructuring the Community framework for the taxation of energy products and electricity [2003] L283/51 (as amended).

where: (1) the choice of beneficiaries is based on objective, transparent and non-discriminatory criteria; (2) the environmental tax without deduction leads to a substantial increase in production costs for each sector or category of beneficiaries; and (3) the increase in production costs cannot be passed onto customers without leading to important sales reductions. Aid is considered proportionate where: (1) each individual beneficiary pays a proportion of the national tax that is broadly equivalent to the environmental performance of each beneficiary compared to the performance related to the best performing technique in the EEA; or (2) beneficiaries pay at least 20% of the national tax, unless a lower rate can be justified on the grounds of limited distortion of competition; or (3) the reductions or exemptions are conditional upon the conclusion of agreements between Member States and the recipients requiring them to meet certain requirements.

5. Detailed assessment

5.60 **Overview.** An important innovation under the 2008 Environmental Aid Guidelines is the introduction of a detailed assessment procedure for cases where high amounts of aid are granted, as well as in certain specified cases. In such cases, the Commission will carry out the balancing test on a case-by-case basis, by looking at the specific positive and negative effects of the aid.

5.61 **Measures subject to detailed assessment.** A detailed assessment must always be carried out for cases notified to the Commission pursuant to the requirement of individual notification in the GBER.[118] In addition, the detailed assessment procedure applies to individual measures covered by the 2008 Guidelines in six specific cases: (1) investment aid, where the aid amount exceeds €7.5 million per undertaking (even if part of an approved scheme); (2) operating aid for energy saving, where the aid amount exceeds €5 million per undertaking for five years; (3) operating aid for the production of renewable electricity and/or combined production of renewable heat, when the aid is granted to renewable electricity installations in sites where the resulting renewable electricity generation capacity exceeds 125 MW; (4) operating aid for the production of biofuels, when the aid is granted to biofuel production installations in sites where the resulting production exceeds 150,000 tonnes per year; (5) operating aid for cogeneration, where aid is granted to a cogeneration installation with the resulting cogeneration capacity exceeding 200 MW; and (6) operating aid to new plants producing renewable energy on the basis of a calculation of the external costs avoided.[119]

5.62 **Positive effects of aid.** When considering the positive effects of aid, the Commission will take into account the existence of a market failure, the

[118] 2008 Environmental Aid Guidelines, para 160(a), and see para 5.22 above.
[119] ibid, paras 160(b) and 161.

appropriateness of the aid measure, the incentive effect and necessity of the aid, and the proportionality of the aid.

Market failure. With regard to market failure in relation to environmental protection, the Commission is concerned not so much with considering whether certain conduct or goods are harmful (as this is usually evident) but rather the quantifiable extent to which proposed measures will improve environmental protection (for instance compared with existing Community or national standards). In considering aid to support adaptation to national standards that go beyond Community standards, the Commission will compare the costs experienced by the aid beneficiary with those of its principal competitors.[120] **5.63**

Appropriateness of the aid. Consideration will be given as to whether the measure proposed is the appropriate instrument to meet the desired environmental objective, or whether a less distortive instrument could have the same impact. This could, for instance, be demonstrated by producing an impact assessment that includes considerations of using policy options other than State aid. The Commission will also take account of evidence that the polluter pays principle will be respected.[121] **5.64**

Incentive effect and necessity. The Commission will closely examine the extent to which the proposed measure causes the beneficiary to increase the level of environmental protection. Evidence will need to be provided to demonstrate that, but for the aid, the particular investment or more environmental friendly processes or products would not have been adopted. The measure must either lead to an increase in the level of protection or enable it to be introduced more quickly. In considering how much of an incentive relates to the aid measure rather than to other factors, the Commission will examine features such as the extent to which production advantages from the project outweigh the cost of investment in environmental production; the impact of prevalent market conditions; the expectation concerning future mandatory standards; the level of risk associated with the investment and the level of likely profitability.[122] **5.65**

Proportionality. To establish proportionality the Member State must provide an accurate calculation of eligible costs, to demonstrate that these are limited to the extra costs necessary to achieve the level of environmental protection. Other factors that the Commission will examine are the extent to which the selection process is conducted in a transparent, fair and non-discriminatory manner, and evidence that the aid is limited to the minimum. The aid may, however, include **5.66**

120 ibid, paras 167–8.
121 ibid, paras 169–70.
122 ibid, paras 171–3.

a normal return on investment over the time period for which the investment is fully depreciated.[123]

5.67 **Negative effects of aid: distortion of competition and trade.** The second half of the balancing test is consideration of the negative effects of the aid. In this regard the Commission will assess any foreseeable distortion on competition in the markets affected by the aid (potentially not only the market in which the beneficiary is active but also those upstream, downstream or complementary to it). The first element to consider is the impact the aid has on a beneficiary's ability to increase or maintain sales.[124] The Commission will then consider whether the aid has a 'crowding out' effect, whether it supports inefficient firms, whether it strengthens market power, and the effects on trade and location.

5.68 **'Crowding out'.** State aid may have a 'crowding out' effect by giving domestic producers an advantage that reduces the incentive of competitors in other Member States from investing. The factors which will be relevant in assessing this include the amount, frequency and duration of aid, whether it is gradually decreased, the readiness of undertakings to meet future standards, the level of regulatory standards, the risk of cross-subsidization, technological neutrality and the existence of competing innovation.[125]

5.69 **Maintaining inefficient firms.** It is recognized that aid may be justified as a transitional measure to assist firms in moving towards a full allocation of negative externalities provided that it is not being used simply to maintain the operation of inefficient firms. In this respect the Commission will consider the nature and type of beneficiaries, the existence of overcapacity in the sector, normal behaviour in the sector, the relative importance of the aid in relation to variable production costs, the selection process and the selectivity of the aid.[126]

5.70 **Market power.** A further factor to consider is the extent to which the aid is likely to strengthen or maintain market power and lead to exclusionary behaviour. The Commission will therefore analyse the market power of the aid beneficiary and the structure of the relevant market, the impact on new entry, and any impact on product differentiation and price discrimination and buyer power. It is, however, unlikely to identify serious competition concerns where each aid beneficiary has a market share of below 25% and in markets where the Herfindahl-Hirschman Index[127] of market concentration is below 2000.[128]

---

[123] ibid, para 174.
[124] ibid, paras 175–7.
[125] ibid, paras 178–9.
[126] ibid, para 180.
[127] The HHI is a method of identifying concentration in a market by looking at the sum of the individual market shares of the leading competitors in a market.
[128] 2008 Environmental Aid Guidelines, paras 181–2.

Effects on trade and location. Aid for environmental protection can favour certain territories, by for instance reducing production, thereby attracting companies to relocate. The Commission has indicated that it considers evidence that a beneficiary has considered other locations for its investment as an indication that it is more likely that aid will distort competition.[129] **5.71**

Overall balance. The Commission will balance the effects of the environmental aid measure in the light of the considerations outlined above, to determine whether any distortions adversely affect trading conditions to an extent contrary to the common interest. In general, the higher the environmental benefit and the more clearly it is established that the aid amount is limited to the minimum necessary, the more likely a positive appraisal. The Commission may also satisfy the balancing test by adopting a conditional decision specifying, for example, lower aid intensities or additional requirements to improve the environmental effect of the measure.[130] **5.72**

[129] ibid, paras 183–5.
[130] ibid, paras 186–8.

6

EMPLOYMENT AND TRAINING AID

Main legislation and guidelines

Commission Regulation (EC) 800/2008 on the application of Articles 87 and 88 of the Treaty declaring certain categories of aid compatible with the common market (General Block Exemption Regulation) ('GBER') [2008] OJ L214/3

A. Introduction

EU objectives. Social and economic advancement is one of the main objectives of the common market, and employment and training are seen as fundamental to attaining these aims. The first objective set out in Article 2 of the Treaty of European Union (TEU) specifically states that it is an objective of the EU 'to promote economic and social progress and a high level of employment'.[1] Consistent with this aim, the 2005 re-launch of the Lisbon Strategy marked 'growth and jobs' as the cornerstone for the policy of reform and the method for stimulating greater economic development in the EU.[2] **6.01**

State aid policy. Many forms of State intervention to support employment and training will not constitute State aid, particularly where assistance is granted to **6.02**

1 TEU Article 2.

2 Working together for growth and jobs - A new start for the Lisbon Strategy, COM(2005) 24.

individuals, rather than undertakings, or where support is provided through general measures. The provision of educational and general vocational training to individuals (directly, or through educational institutions) is seen as a responsibility that a Member State owes to its subjects, and such measures are not generally considered to constitute State aid.[3] In some circumstances, however, the promotion of employment and the funding of training programmes may trigger State aid, for example where the State provides or supports training for specific sectors or undertakings. The Commission has, in the past, approved various forms of aid for employment and training as compatible with the common market. In the *Ford Genk* case, the Commission commented that 'training usually has positive external effects for society as a whole, since it increases the pool of skilled workers from which other firms may draw and improves the competitiveness of Community industry.'[4] Similarly, in the recitals to the new General Block Exemption Regulation ('GBER'), the Commission notes that 'The promotion of training and the recruitment of disadvantaged and disabled workers and compensation of additional costs for the employment of disabled workers constitute a central objective of the economic and social policies of the Community and of its Member States.'[5]

6.03 **Early guidelines and notices.** In 1995 the Commission published guidelines on aid to employment, which set out the Commission's policy in this area.[6] A number of subsequent guidelines were issued by the Commission providing further insight into the policy behind its State aid decisions regarding employment and training. These included a notice on the monitoring of State aid and reduction of labour costs,[7] a Community framework on training aid,[8] and (in 2000) a second set of guidelines on employment aid.[9]

6.04 **Block exemptions.** In 2001, pursuant to the Enabling Regulation,[10] the Commission adopted a block exemption for training aid, sometimes referred to as the 'TABER'.[11] The following year the Commission adopted a block exemption

---

3 See para 2.28 above.

4 Decision 2006/938/EC *Ford Genk* [2006] OJ L366/32, para 30.

5 Commission Regulation (EC) 800/2008 on the application of Articles 87 and 88 of the Treaty declaring certain categories of aid compatible with the common market (General Block Exemption Regulation) [2008] OJ L214/3, recital (61).

6 Guidelines on aid to employment [1995] OJ C334/4.

7 [1997] OJ C1/10.

8 [1998] OJ C343/10.

9 [2000] OJ C371/12.

10 Council Regulation (EC) 994/98 on the application of Articles 92 and 93 of the Treaty establishing the European Community to certain categories of horizontal State aid [1998] OJ L142/1; see further paras 3.34–3.35 above.

11 Commission Regulation (EC) 68/2001 on the application of Articles 87 and 88 of the EC Treaty to training aid [2001] OJ L10/20, as amended [2006] OJ L368/85, and extended by Commission Decision 2008/484/EC *Prolongation of certain State aid decisions* [2008] OJ L164/43.

for certain types of aid for employment, in particular schemes to encourage the creation of employment in deprived areas of the EU, and schemes promoting the employment of disabled or disadvantaged workers.[12] The block exemptions replaced the Commission's framework on training aid and guidelines on employment aid respectively, and allowed Member States to award certain types of training and employment aid without the need for approval or prior notification to the Commission.

The GBER. The employment and training aid block exemptions have now in turn been replaced by the provisions of the GBER. This came into force on 29 August 2008 and is due to expire on 31 December 2013. The GBER contains a number of provisions mirroring those in the old block exemptions, including an exemption for training aid[13] and a set of exemptions for aid for disadvantaged and disabled workers.[14] The aid intensities are, however, generally higher than under the old block exemptions. The GBER also provides for other types of employment aid to SMEs, and for the creation of new employment in deprived regions. By way of transitional provisions, any aid granted before 31 December 2008, which did not satisfy the conditions of the GBER but did fulfil the conditions of the old training or employment aid block exemptions, was still deemed compatible with the common market and exempt from notification.[15] **6.05**

Methodology for the assessment of employment and training aid. The GBER, together with the Commission's general rules for the approval of aid measures, establishes the following methodology for the assessment of aid for employment and training. **6.06**

(a) A number of employment and training measures do not constitute State aid within Article 87(1). These are considered in section B below.
(b) Where there is aid, the GBER enables employment and training aid that complies with certain substantive and transparency requirements to be implemented without prior notification and approval. The scope of the GBER in this respect is discussed in detail in section C below.
(c) Aid measures not eligible under the GBER may still be individually approved by the Commission under Article 87(2) and (3). This is discussed in section D below.

[12] Commission Regulation (EC) 2204/2002 on the application of Articles 87 and 88 of the EC Treaty to State aid for employment [2002] OJ L337/3, as amended [2006] OJ L368/85, and extended by Commission Decision 2008/484/EC *Prolongation of certain State aid decisions* [2008] OJ L164/43.

[13] GBER, Articles 38–39.

[14] ibid, Articles 40–42.

[15] ibid, Article 44(2).

B. Existence of aid

6.07 **Training measures.** The majority of funding for training will fall outside the scope of the competition rules where it is granted directly by the State to individuals,[16] or educational institutions.[17] These can be seen as social measures taken by the State for the direct benefit of its subjects.[18] Training measures may also not satisfy the condition of selectivity which constitutes an essential element of a State aid within the meaning of Article 87(1). In this respect, the Commission's old framework on training aid provides a number of examples of measures that are general measures rather than selective aids:

— schooling and initial training (such as apprenticeships and day release schemes),
— the training or re-training of unemployed people, including traineeships in enterprises,
— measures directly targeted at workers or even at certain categories of worker, affording them the opportunity of receiving training unconnected with the firm or industry in which they work (e.g. the 'learning account' system),
— general tax incentive schemes (e.g. tax credits) which are open to all firms investing in employee training and apply automatically.[19]

Some training measures will, however, benefit specific employers. Thus in the *Ford Genk* case, the aid was considered to be a specific measure caught by Article 87(1) as the training it funded was limited to Ford in Belgium.[20] Aid granted to Sabena under a scheme to provide employees with vocational training was also considered to be specific, as the Belgian authorities had the ability to exercise discretion over the recipients of the aid.[21] In contrast, aid measures that apply generally and are available automatically are likely to be considered to be general measures.[22]

6.08 **Employment measures.** Many employment measures do not involve State resources, so do not constitute State aid even though they may favour some undertakings over others.[23] Other measures may engage State resources, but fall

[16] See Reg 994/98 [1998] OJ L142/1, recital (6) and GBER recital (62). Similarly aid to socially vulnerable individuals, who were long term beneficiaries of State support, to relieve debt was not considered to constitute aid under Article 87(1) as it was conferred on individuals: Decision in Case N 314/2006 *Remission of debt to socially vulnerable groups* (6 December 2006), paras 16–17.

[17] Funding granted by the Czech Republic to Přerov Logistics College was not considered aid as national education establishments are not considered to be engaged in an economic activity: Decision in Case NN 54/2006 *Přerov Logistics College* (8 November 2006).

[18] See further para 2.28 above.

[19] Framework on training aid [1998] OJ C343/10, para 14.

[20] Decision 2006/938/EC *Ford Genk* [2006] OJ L366/32, para 15. See also Decision in Case 2007/612/EC *General Motors Antwerp* [2007] OJ L243/71, para 18.

[21] Decision 2001/698/EC *Sabena* [2001] OJ L249/21, applying the judgment of the ECJ in Case C-241/94 *France v Commission ('Kimberly Clark')* [1996] ECR I-4551.

[22] See further paras 2.109–2.132 above on the distinction between general and selective measures.

[23] As was the case in Cases C-72-73/91 *Sloman Neptun* [1993] ECR I-887 and Case C-189/01 *Kirsammer-Hack* [1993] ECR I-6185, discussed at para 2.90 above.

outside Article 87(1) on the grounds that they do not favour specific undertakings or the production of certain goods.[24] Thus financial support offered in the *Second German Social Security Code* to employers who recruited permanently unemployed individuals (to compensate for their reduced performance) was open to everyone, and the Commission considered that its automatic and indiscriminate nature rendered it a general measure that fell outside the scope of Article 87(1).[25] Historically, however, many employment aid measures have both been granted through State resources and have favoured specific undertakings or industries. This has been the case for a number of measures involving reductions in social contributions for specific (even if diverse) sectors.[26] Schemes that appear to be general may also be regarded as selective State aid where they confer a discretion that would allow for a distortion of competition.[27]

***De minimis* aids.** Aids for employment and training may well also fall within the scope of the *de minimis* block exemptions. In such cases the aid is deemed not to meet the criteria of Article 87(1). The general *de minimis* Regulation is discussed in Chapter 2.[28] The separate *de minimis* Regulations applicable in the agriculture and fisheries sectors are addressed in Chapter 11.[29] **6.09**

C. General Block Exemption Regulation ('GBER')

Structure. As described in more detail in Chapter 5 above, Chapter I of the GBER contains a set of common conditions and procedural provisions applicable to the various types of aid covered by the GBER. The relevant provisions of Chapter I are addressed in section 1 below. Sections 2–4 will then address the exemptions for specific and general training aid, and aid for disadvantaged and disabled workers, as set out in Chapter II of the GBER. In addition, it should be noted that the GBER provides for the exemption of SME and regional employment aid, where the employment is directly created by an investment project.[30] These exemptions are considered in Chapters 10 and 15 respectively. **6.10**

[24] See eg para 8 of the 1995 Guidelines on aid to employment [1995] OJ C344/4, and Reg 2204/2002 [2002] OJ L337/3, recital (6).

[25] Decision in Case N 594/2007 *Second German Social Security Code* (18 March 2008), paras 26–8. This was despite the fact that it was unlikely that such aid would be suitable for every sector.

[26] See eg Case 203/82 *Commission v Italy* [1983] ECR 2525 and Case C-75/97 *Belgium v Commission ('Maribel bis/ter')* [1999] ECR I-3671, discussed at paras 2.113–2.114 above.

[27] Case C-241/94 *France v Commission ('Kimberly Clark')* [1996] ECR I-4551, paras 23–4, and subsequent cases discussed at para 2.119 above.

[28] See para 2.148 above.

[29] See paras 11.18–11.20 (agriculture) and 11.63 (fisheries) below.

[30] GBER, Articles 13 (regional investment and employment aid) and 15 (SME investment and employment aid).

1. Common and procedural provisions

6.11 **Sectoral scope of exemptions.** The GBER's provisions on training aid and aid for disadvantaged and disabled workers apply to almost all sectors of the economy including the primary production, processing and marketing of agricultural products, the fishery and aquaculture sectors, and the steel, shipbuilding and synthetic fibres sectors.[31] In addition, the training aid exemption (but *not* the exemption for aid for disadvantaged and disable workers) applies in the coal sector.[32]

6.12 **Individual notification thresholds.** Under the GBER certain aids are excluded where the value of the financial assistance exceeds specified thresholds. This varies according to the type of aid in question. For training aid, the threshold is €2 million per training project. For aid for the recruitment of disadvantaged workers, the threshold is €5 million per undertaking per year. The threshold is €10 million per undertaking per year for aid for the employment of disabled workers in the form of wage costs, and aid compensating for the additional costs of employing disabled workers.[33]

6.13 **Common conditions.** In addition to the specific provisions referred to above on the scope of the exemptions for training aid and aid for disadvantaged and disabled workers, the GBER contains a number of general conditions common to all types of aid within its ambit. These are set out in detail in paras 5.17–5.26 above, to which reference should be made. In summary, these provisions concern:

(a) the exclusion of all forms of aid to certain undertakings and certain sectors;
(b) the general conditions for exemption of aid schemes and individual aid granted under such schemes, as well as for ad hoc individual aid;
(c) the basis of calculation of aid intensities;
(d) the requirement to provide documentary evidence of eligible costs;
(e) the requirement for exempted aid to be transparent;
(f) the conditions under which aid can be cumulated with other aid exempted under the GBER;
(g) the requirement for aid to have an incentive effect;[34] and
(h) the reporting and monitoring requirements applicable to all aid exempted under the GBER.

---

[31] ibid, Article 1(3). These sectors remain subject to exclusions for certain other kinds of aid.

[32] ibid, Article 1(3)(d).

[33] ibid, Article 6. The Commission is currently consulting on guidelines setting out its policy on the assessment of training aid and aid for the employment of disabled and disadvantaged workers, that is subject to individual notification pursuant to this condition.

[34] Deemed to be satisfied in the case of aid compensating for the additional costs of employing disabled workers if the conditions in Article 42(3) are met; and in the case wage subsidies for the recruitment of disadvantaged workers or the employment of disabled workers, if the aid leads to a net increase in the number of such workers employed: ibid, Article 8(5), paras 1 and 2.

2. Training aid

Specific and general training. The GBER draws a distinction between two types of training for which aid may be approved. *Specific training* is training that is 'directly and principally applicable to the employee's present or future position in the undertaking and providing qualifications which are not or only to a limited extent transferable to other undertakings or fields of work'.[35] By contrast, *general training* is not directly applicable to the employee's position in the undertaking, but rather provides more general qualifications that are transferable to other undertakings or fields. This would include, for example, training organized jointly by several undertakings, and training that is recognized, certified or validated by public authorities or bodies, or similar institutions.[36] **6.14**

Costs eligible for aid. Training aid may be granted for the following eligible costs of a training project: trainers' personnel costs, travel and accommodation expenses for the trainer and trainees, other current expenses directly related to the project, such as materials and supplies, depreciation of any tools and equipment used exclusively for the training project, the cost of guidance and counselling services relating to the training project, and trainees' personnel costs and general indirect costs (administrative costs, rent, overheads) up to the amount of the total of the other eligible costs.[37] **6.15**

Aid intensities. In general, the aid intensity must not exceed 25% of the eligible costs for specific training, and 60% for general training. Higher levels of aid can be given, up to a maximum intensity of 80%, in the following three circumstances: (1) a further 10% can be awarded if the training is to be given to disabled or disadvantaged workers; (2) a further 10% may be awarded if the training is to be given to medium-sized enterprises; and (3) a further 20% may be awarded if the training is to be given to small enterprises.[38] Where the aid constitutes elements of both general and specific training that cannot be separated, or it is not possible to establish the specific or general character of the training aid project, the lower intensities applicable to specific training apply.[39] **6.16**

3. Aid for disadvantaged workers

Definition. The category of 'disadvantaged workers' under the GBER includes anyone who has not been in regular employment for the previous six months or more, anyone who has not obtained an upper-secondary educational or vocational **6.17**

35 ibid, Article 38(1).
36 ibid, Article 38(2).
37 ibid, Article 39(4).
38 ibid, Article 39(2).
39 ibid, Article 39(3).

qualification (ISCED 3),[40] anyone over the age of 50, any single adult with one or more dependents, women in sectors or professions that have a gender imbalance that is 25% or more than the national average gender imbalance, and anyone from an ethnic minority.[41] The GBER has also created a new category of aid that can be awarded to a 'severely disadvantaged worker'. This is defined as a person who has been unemployed for 24 months or more.[42]

6.18 **Form of exempted aid.** The GBER exempts aid *schemes* for the recruitment of disadvantaged workers, in the form of wage subsidies.[43] The exemption does not cover ad hoc wage subsidies to an individual enterprise.

6.19 **Aid intensity.** Wage subsidies can be granted up to a maximum of 50% of the wage costs, for a period of no more than 12 months following recruitment, or 24 months following recruitment if the aid is for a severely disadvantaged worker.[44]

6.20 **Other conditions.** Where the recruitment of the disadvantaged worker does not represent a net increase in the number of employees in the undertaking concerned, the position must have become vacant in the ordinary course of business, for example voluntary departure, retirement, or lawful dismissal. It must not have become vacant as a result of redundancy. As a default, the employer must offer the job for a minimum period of 12 months (or 24 months for severely disadvantaged workers), though will still be able to dismiss workers through lawful dismissal or for misconduct. That 12- (or 24-) month period may, however, be reduced in accordance with national employment laws in each Member State. In such cases, the permissible amount of aid is also reduced pro rata.[45]

4. Aid for disabled workers

6.21 **Definition.** Anyone who is recognized as disabled under national law will qualify as a 'disabled worker' under the GBER. In addition, the GBER includes as a 'disabled worker' any person with 'a recognised limitation which results from physical, mental or psychological impairment'.[46]

---

[40] ISCED 3 refers to the United Nations Educational, Scientific and Cultural Organization (UNESCO) categorization of education or vocational qualifications. It is an acronym for the International Standard Classification of Education (ISCED 1997). ISCED 3 refers to educational or vocational qualifications obtained after the completion of compulsory secondary education. It usually begins at age 15 or 16.

[41] GBER, Article 2(18).

[42] ibid, Article 2(19).

[43] ibid, Article 40(1), and see Article 2(2) for definition of an 'aid scheme'.

[44] ibid, Article 40(2) and (3).

[45] ibid, Article 31(4) and (5).

[46] ibid, Article 2(20).

Forms of exempted aid. The GBER exempts two types of aid for disabled workers. The first is aid in the form of subsidies of up to 75% of wages for the employment of disabled workers, for the duration of the worker's employment.[47] The second is aid compensating the employer for the additional costs of employing disabled workers. Compensation is permitted for up to 100% of the additional costs (ie costs other than wage costs) incurred by an employer in employing a disabled worker, that are solely incurred as a result of the worker being disabled.[48] The eligible expenses for this purpose are the costs of adapting the premises, the employment cost of staff assisting disabled workers, the costs of adapting additional equipment or software required for the worker, the cost of installing or expanding a sheltered employment establishment,[49] as well as any administration and transport costs resulting directly from employing the disabled worker.[50] **6.22**

Additional requirements. As with disadvantaged workers, where the recruitment of the disabled worker does not represent a net increase in the number of employees in the undertaking concerned, the position must have become vacant in the ordinary course of business, for example voluntary departure, retirement, or lawful dismissal. It must not have become vacant as a result of redundancy. As a default, the employer must offer the job for a minimum period of 12 months, though will still be able to dismiss workers through lawful dismissal or for misconduct. That 12-month period may, however, be reduced in accordance with national employment laws in each Member State. In such cases, the permissible amount of aid is also reduced pro rata.[51] **6.23**

D. Authorization under Article 87(2) and (3)

General. Employment and training aid falling outside the GBER[52] may still be notified to the Commission for approval under the provisions of Article 87(2) and (3). At the time of writing, the Commission was consulting on guidelines setting out its policy on the approval of training aid and aid for disabled and disadvantaged workers, that is subject to individual notification under the GBER. Reference should be made to those guidelines when finalized. For cases falling outside the guidelines, the general principles in Article 87(2) and (3) (set out in **6.24**

47 ibid, Article 41(1) and (2), an increase from 60% under the old training aid block exemption.

48 ibid, Article 42.

49 ie an establishment where at least 50% of workers are disabled: ibid, Article 2(21).

50 ibid, Article 42(3)(a)–(d).

51 ibid, Article 41(5).

52 eg aid exceeding the thresholds of aid amounts or aid intensities set out in the GBER.

Chapter 3 above) will continue to apply. The application of these principles to employment and training aid is discussed below.[53]

6.25 **Basis for approval.** In practice, the conditions of Article 87(2) will only apply to employment or training aid in very limited or extreme circumstances.[54] The more general conditions under Article 87(3) are more likely to apply, and of these reliance is most likely to be placed on Article 87(3)(c). This point was made in the old framework for training aid, where the Commission said that:

> The main ground for exemption is that provided for in Article [87(3)(c)], by virtue of which the Commission may authorise aid to facilitate the development of certain activities where it does not adversely affect trading conditions to an extent contrary to the common interest. Measures to improve the skills of a firm's workforce help to increase that firm's competitiveness and in so doing facilitate the development of certain activities. Training plays an essential part in introducing new technologies and stimulating innovation and investment. It may also help to create and maintain jobs. Training aid may thus fall within the exemption provided for in Article [87(3)(c)].[55]

Similarly aid for employment that is likely to result in 'net job creation' (ie is designed to increase the number of jobs available) may satisfy the Article 87(3)(c) criteria.[56] Article 87(3)(a) may also be applicable if the training or employment aid is specifically targeted to developing areas where the standard of living is abnormally low or there is serious underemployment.

6.26 **Balancing exercise.** In deciding whether or not the aid may be approved, the Commission will carry out the balancing exercise described in Chapter 3.[57] This enables the Commission to determine whether the aid measure strikes the right balance between positive developments allowed by a given measure and its negative effects on competition.[58] One of the factors in that balancing exercise is whether the aid produces an incentive effect. The importance of this element was underscored in the *Ford Genk* case, where the Commission refused training aid to cover the costs of training employees who would occupy a new function following a restructuring, commenting that:

> The company has no choice but to incur such training expenditure for the remaining work-force in order to replace the expertise that will be laid off. Consequently, the

---

53 Note also Decision 2006/938/EC *Ford Genk* [2006] OJ L366/32, para 19 indicating that even where the GBER does not apply, the Commission is likely to assess aid in accordance with the GBER's guiding principles.

54 The most likely being aid granted under Article 87(2)(b) for areas affected by natural disasters or exceptional occurrences.

55 Framework on training aid [1998] OJ C343/10, para 23.

56 See eg Decision in Case N 198/2005 *Fiscal aid for job creation in assisted areas* (7 December 2005), para 59 *et seq*.

57 See para 3.28 above; and for an example in relation to employment aid see Decision in Case N 581/2007 *Swedish employment aid scheme* (11 December 2007), para 40.

58 *Swedish employment aid scheme*, ibid, para 67.

aid in question would simply subsidise the company's normal and indispensable restructuring costs, which would have been incurred anyway, even without aid. So this aid does not seem necessary and, in any event, it will not result in additional training.[59]

Assessment of training aid. Specifically with regard to training, the Commission will assess whether the financial incentives are to be awarded for specific training,[60] which an undertaking is more likely to have needed to have financed itself anyway, or for general training, which involves transferable skills that are not applicable only or mainly to the employee's current position.[61] The Commission will view general training as more likely to comply with the requirements for exemption set out in Article 87(3)(c). 6.27

Examples. The Commission has recently approved the following types of training aid under Article 87(3)(c): 6.28

(a) training designed to help a firm's workforce to adapt to structural or technological changes;[62]
(b) training for workers on a new production platform, provided that market forces alone would not have provided an incentive for the undertaking to fund the training;[63]
(c) training aid for the mentoring of foreign workers;[64]
(d) general training on skills which increase the employability of the workforce.[65]

Conversely, the Commission has blocked aid for training in cases where the undertaking would have been required to provide the training itself, or involved non-transferable specific skills. It thus rejected certain types of training aid from Belgium to General Motors, as it related to skills that were necessary for the production of General Motors' new car models, which were likely to have been funded by General Motors without the aid.[66]

Assessment of employment aid. When assessing aid for employment under Article 87(3)(c), the Commission will specifically assess whether the aid will result 6.29

---

[59] Decision 2006/938/EC *Ford Genk* [2006] OJ L366/32, para 29.

[60] As defined in GBER Article 38(1); and see para 6.14 above.

[61] As defined in GBER Article 38(2); and see para 6.14 above.

[62] Decision 2001/698/EC *Sabena* [2001] OJ L249/21. The training covered a number of areas, including adapting to a new fleet of aircraft, the performance of more complex duties and other general training such as computer, language, communication and social training.

[63] Decision in Case C 35/2007 *Training aid to Volvo Cars in Gent* (11 March 2008), paras 25–9.

[64] Decision in Case N 383/2007 *Danish training aid for foreign workers* (10 September 2007).

[65] Decision in Case N 541/2006 *Italian training aid for Fiat Auto* (13 June 2007).

[66] Commission Decision in 2007/612/EC *General Motors Antwerp* [2007] OJ L243/71. In that case even general vocational skills, such as welding were seen to distort competition. However 'technical training' that required a lengthy training period, and involved skills and qualifications that were lacking in the Belgium labour market, was approved.

in net job creation. Aid that will increase the number of employed people and create new jobs (or new jobs for disabled or disadvantaged workers, as opposed to other workers) will therefore be likely to be regarded more favourably by the Commission than aid designed to protect existing jobs. Indeed, maintaining existing jobs, without any promotion of disadvantaged categories of workers, would essentially be a subsidy of labour costs and would need to be assessed as operating aid,[67] which is rarely approved under Article 87(3).[68]

6.30 **Examples.** The Commission has recently approved the following types of employment aid under Article 87(3)(c):

(a) reductions in social security contributions for certain service sectors, provided that it promotes net job creation;[69]
(b) wage subsidies granted for foreign workers in Denmark;[70]
(c) aid, in the form of grants; loans; tax reductions; etc, for firms employing persons held in detention in Poland;[71]
(d) aid in the form of grants, loans and tax reductions for firms to fund increased employment in assisted regions of Italy.[72]

---

67 See 23rd Report on Competition Policy (1993), para 439.

68 See para 3.29 above.

69 Decision in Case N 581/2007 *Swedish employment aid scheme* (11 December 2007); cf Decision 97/239/EC *Maribel bis/ter* [1997] OJ L95/25, where the aid did not promote the creation of new jobs but indeed benefited firms that had decided to decrease their workforce. (Decision confirmed by the ECJ in Case C-75/97 *Belgium v Commission ('Maribel bis/ter')* [1999] ECR I-3671).

70 Decision in Case N 383/2007 *Danish training aid for foreign workers* (10 September 2007). The aid exceeded the thresholds for the block exemption, and required notification.

71 Decision in Case N 519/2007 *Polish scheme for firms employing persons held in detention* (11 March 2008).

72 Decision in Case 198/2005 *Fiscal aid for job creation in assisted areas* (7 December 2005).

7

RESCUE AND RESTRUCTURING AID

Main legislation and guidelines

Community Guidelines on State aid for rescuing and restructuring firms in difficulty ('2004 Guidelines') [2004] OJ C244/2

Communication on the application of State aid rules to measures taken in relation to financial institutions in the context of the current global financial crisis ('Communication on the global financial crisis'), [2008] OJ C270/8

Communication on the recapitalization of financial institutions in the current financial crisis, [2009] OJ C10/2

Communication on a temporary framework for State aid measures to support access to finance in the current financial economic crisis, 17 December 2008, as amended on 25 February 2009

A. Introduction

Background. State aid for rescue and restructuring remains one of the most politi- **7.01**
cally controversial areas of State aid policy. In recent years, there has been a series of high profile and hotly contested cases in which the Commission has investigated and approved aid packages to major businesses in financial distress.[1] The grant of subsidies to support firms which run into financial difficulty can have a significant

[1] See for instance Decision 2005/418/EC *Alstom* [2005] OJ L150/24; Decision 2003/599/EC *Bull* [2003] OJ L209/1; Decision 2005/941/EC *Bull* [2005] OJ L342/81; Decision 2005/407/EC *British Energy* [2005] OJ L142/26; Decision in Case NN 42/2005 *Rover* (7 June 2005); and Decision in Case NN 70/2007 *Northern Rock* (5 December 2007).

distortive effect by protecting firms from normal market forces and maintaining inefficient businesses which, in the absence of State intervention, would be forced to exit from the market or to go through a fundamental restructuring such as the closure of loss-making activities. However, the loss of a business may have profound social effects as well as significant consequences for the local economy. The failure of one firm can also trigger the failure of other firms in a given region or sector, and have wider economic ramifications. A further conundrum for competition policy is that while State support to maintain a firm may have anticompetitive effects, there are also some circumstances in which the exit of a failing firm from the marketplace could reduce competition and lead to a monopoly or oligopoly situation. State aid policy recognizes and seeks to balance these political, economic and social considerations.

7.02 **Existence of aid.** In some cases State investment in an undertaking in difficulty will satisfy the private investor test and thus will not amount to aid.[2] Similarly, the write-off of debt may fall outside Article 87(1) on the grounds that it satisfies the private creditor test.[3] More often, however, the grant of State support for rescue and restructuring purposes will constitute a selective economic advantage to the undertaking which actually or potentially distorts competition within the meaning of Article 87(1). This type of aid will generally have effects on inter-State trade (save in domestic markets which are not susceptible to EU trade) by shifting the burden of structural change to other firms operating within the single market. It is unlikely that there will be many circumstances in which rescue and restructuring aid would constitute compensation for services of general economic interest (SGEIs) falling within the *Altmark* test.[4] However, there may be cases where the aid is provided to undertakings performing public interest tasks, for example credit institutions which are engaged in separate, ring-fenced, non-commercial activities such as the provision of social housing loans, in which case Article 86(2) may apply.[5] The restructuring of a business may also be assisted by general State measures providing social support to employees. These will fall outside the Article 87(1) where they are transparent and available to all undertakings in all sectors, without distinction.[6]

7.03 **Distinction between rescue and restructuring aid.** Rescue and restructuring aid encompasses State assistance granted to firms in difficulty, ie firms in a position of

---

[2] A claim recently rejected on the facts in Case T-301/01 *Alitalia* (judgment of 9 July 2008). See paras 2.33–2.44 above on the private investor test generally.

[3] See eg Decision in Case N 472/2007 *Restructuring aid to Compel Rail* (2 April 2008); and see paras 2.45–2.49 above on the private creditor test generally.

[4] See paras 2.67–2.73 above.

[5] See Case T-93/02 *Crédit Mutuel v Commission ('Livret bleu')* [2005] ECR II-143; and Case T-349/03 *Corsica Ferries France v Commission* [2005] ECR II-2197. See also the Commission's approval of a rescue loan for the Danish broadcaster TV2 Danmark, which distinguishes between aid for the broadcaster's public service mission and aid for its commercial activities: Decision in Case N 287/2008 *TV2/Danmark* (4 August 2008).

[6] See para 7.30 below and discussion of general measures at paras 2.121–2.126 above.

financial weakness or distress which are faced with the prospect of going out of business in the short, medium or long term. In acute cases, the firms may be on the brink of insolvency or liquidation. A clear distinction is generally drawn between rescue and restructuring aid. *Rescue aid* is a temporary short-term measure which is designed to provide immediate support to a firm, while a longer-term restructuring or liquidation plan is developed. *Restructuring aid* is all aid granted to support the reorganization and rationalization of the firm to restore long-term viability. An aid package may well cover both rescue and restructuring elements in order to fund the structural changes required to put the company on a profitable footing, but both elements are required to be assessed separately. The Commission's 2004 Guidelines on rescue and restructuring aid discussed below set out strict definitions of the concepts of 'rescue' and 'restructuring' aids as well as of a 'firm in difficulty'.

Community policy. The Commission first set out its policy on aid for rescue and restructuring in its 8th Report on Competition Policy in 1978,[7] and this approach was reflected in a number of Commission decisions during the 1980s and 1990s.[8] These, broadly speaking, adumbrated the formal policy framework which was later developed, balancing on the one hand the need for aid to minimize economic and social disruption with, on the other hand, the need to put in place a longer-term restructuring of the business to ensure its continued viability. In the light of the creation of the single market, and in the context of the recessionary years of the early 1990s, the Commission subsequently identified the need to create a more detailed framework of rules to control government grants towards failing firms and to facilitate structural changes to the economy.[9] **7.04**

1994 and 1999 Guidelines. In 1994 the Commission adopted its first Guidelines on State aid for rescue and restructuring firms in difficulty, noting that '[w]hile structural change is easier in an expanding economy, even in a recession it is undesirable that Member States should frustrate or unduly retard the process of the structural adjustments through subsidies to firms which would shift the burden of structural change on to other more efficient firms and encourage a subsidy race'.[10] The Commission subsequently supplemented the 1994 Guidelines **7.05**

---

[7] 8th Report on Competition Policy (1978), in particular paras 177, 227 and 228.

[8] eg Decision in Case C 25/89 *Quimigal* [1990] OJ C188/3; Decision 96/545/EC *Leuna-Werke* [1996] OJ L239/1; Decision in Case C 74/97 *Kali und Salz* [1998] OJ C197/7. See also a number of the early cases in the European Court, eg Case 323/82 *Intermills* [1984] ECR 3809; Case 318/82 *Leeuwarder Papierwarenfabriek* [1985] ECR 809; Case C-301/87 *France v Commission ('Boussac')* [1990] ECR 307; Case C-142/87 *Belgium v Commission ('Tubemeuse')* [1990] ECR 959; Case C-305/89 *Italy v Commission ('Alfa Romeo')* [1991] ECR 1603.

[9] See 24th Report on Competition Policy (1994), para 357: 'The main aim of [the Commission's] efforts to keep aid of this kind under tight control is to prevent Member States artificially propping up businesses which ought to disappear or restructure.'

[10] Community Guidelines on State aid for rescuing and restructuring firms in difficulty ('1994 Guidelines') [1994] OJ C368/12, para 1.1.

with special rules in the agricultural sector,[11] and extended the Guidelines until 1999.[12] In 1999, the Commission adopted revised Guidelines.[13] The Sixth and Seventh Surveys on State aid[14] had revealed an increase in ad hoc aid granted to firms in difficulty (even excluding the impact of grants to firms in the new German Länder following German reunification). The 1999 Guidelines thus sought to tighten the assessment of rescue and restructuring aid, while at the same time ensuring that sufficient account was taken of social and regional considerations in the various parts of the EU. To this end, the Guidelines created a new definition of 'a firm in difficulty', and further emphasized the differences between rescue aid (temporary assistance to keep an ailing firm afloat pending a long-term restructuring) and restructuring aid (the funding of measures to restructure a firm to restore it to long-term viability).

7.06 **2004 Guidelines.** The 1999 Guidelines were replaced with a third set of Guidelines in 2004, which apply until 9 October 2009.[15] The economic downturn in 2001/2002 had created an increase in the ad hoc aid paid to ailing firms, and the Commission wished to tighten further the conditions for approval of aid to firms in difficulty.[16] Following the conclusions of the European Council in 2001 and 2002, requiring further reductions in State aid as a percentage of gross domestic product,[17] rescue and restructuring aid continues to warrant close scrutiny. The Commission has commenced a consultation exercise with regard to its review of the 2004 Guidelines and is seeking views on the effects of the current rules. Rescue and restructuring aid continues to be a key area of concern for the Commission. It was recently noted that over half of the ad hoc rescue and restructuring decisions taken in the period 2000–2005 concerned unlawful aid, and that these make up an even higher proportion of the larger, more significant State aid cases.[18] Moreover, the overall volume of rescue and restructuring aid is accounted for by a relatively small number of larger cases, which tend to be concentrated in a limited number of Member States. The Commission's State Aid Action Plan

[11] Community Guidelines on State aid for rescuing and restructuring firms in difficulty [1997] OJ C283/2.

[12] Commission communication concerning the extension of the Guidelines on State aid for rescuing and restructuring firms in difficulty [1999] OJ C67/11.

[13] Community Guidelines on State aid for rescuing and restructuring firms in difficulty ('1999 Guidelines') [1999] OJ C288/2.

[14] COM (1998) 417 final; COM (1999) 148 final.

[15] Community Guidelines on State aid for rescuing and restructuring firms in difficulty ('2004 Guidelines') [2004] OJ C244/2.

[16] See Commission's Autumn 2004 State Aid Scoreboard for a review of the issues which had arisen under the 1999 Guidelines.

[17] Presidency Conclusions of Stockholm European Council, 23 and 24 March 2001, para 31; and Presidency Conclusions of Barcelona European Council, 15 and 16 March 2002, para 18.

[18] State aid scoreboard, Autumn 2006 update, COM (2006) 761 final.

singles out restructuring aid to large companies as having particularly significant distortive effects in the market.[19]

Assessment under the 2004 Guidelines. The 2004 Guidelines set out the circumstances in which rescue and restructuring aid is compatible with the common market, and may be authorized by the Commission in the exercise of its discretion under Article 87(3). The Commission's Guidelines on rescue and restructuring aid have been followed and applied by the Court in numerous cases.[20] The General Block Exemption Regulation ('GBER') does not cover rescue and restructuring aid; and indeed Article 1(6) of the GBER expressly excludes aid granted to undertakings in difficulty.[21] **7.07**

B. 2004 Guidelines

1. Basic concepts

Scope. The 2004 Guidelines are generally applicable to all sectors, with the exception of coal and steel.[22] They operate without prejudice to any specific sectoral rules relating to firms in difficulty. In addition, the 2004 Guidelines may not be used in a way which circumvents the principles laid down in other horizontal or sectoral frameworks or guidelines.[23] For example, while the 2004 Guidelines apply to rescue aid in the aviation sector, restructuring aid is also covered specifically by the 1994 Aviation Guidelines.[24] The Commission's 2007–2013 Regional Aid Guidelines also apply special rules in relation to large investment projects.[25] **7.08**

Form of aid. As the case-law of the European Court indicates, a wide range of State measures may constitute rescue and restructuring aid to firms in difficulty, including **7.09**

[19] For an economic assessment of the impact of rescue and restructuring aid, see 'Ex-post Evaluation of the Impact of Rescue and Restructuring Aid', London Economics, June 2004, prepared for the Commission. The report found that there was a high mortality rate of aid-receiving companies, particularly in the case of rescue aid. A key conclusion was that the recovery of an aid beneficiary is at the expense of EU competitors, confirming the Commission's view about the potentially distortive effect of this type of aid.

[20] See eg Case T-17/03 *Schmitz-Gotha v Commission* [2006] ECR II-1139.

[21] Commission Regulation (EC) 800/2008 on the application of Articles 87 and 88 of the Treaty declaring certain categories of aid compatible with the common market (General Block Exemption Regulation) ('GBER') [2008] OJ L214/3. The definition of an undertaking in difficulty is as set out in the 2004 Rescue and Restructuring Guidelines (see para 7.12 below). For SMEs, however, the GBER provides a simplified definition: see GBER recital (15) and Article 1(7).

[22] 2004 Guidelines, para 18.

[23] ibid, para 21.

[24] Commission guidelines on the application of Articles 92 and 93 of the EC Treaty and Article 61 of the EEA agreement to State aids in the aviation sector [1994] OJ C350/5, recently applied in Case T-301/01 *Alitalia* (judgment of 9 July 2008); see further para 12.38 below.

[25] Guidelines on National Regional Aid for 2007-13 [2006] OJ C54/13; see further paras 15.68–15.73 below.

capital injections, soft loans, waivers of debt or other obligations, and loan guarantees and indemnities.[26] Other types of aid are considered in the Commission's decisional practice, such as debt for equity swaps. In some circumstances, the State's indication that it would be prepared to provide financial support to a business in difficulty might itself constitute rescue or restructuring aid.[27] A State body which disposes of public assets at an undervalue as part of a restructuring programme (such as in the context of privatization) may also be granting State aid.[28] The extent to which the State's participation in the company itself involves State aid is assessed by reference to the private investor or private creditor principle. A further injection of capital by the State as shareholder will constitute State aid in circumstances where the undertaking would not have obtained the funds on the capital market.[29] The State is unlikely to be conforming to normal market disciplines where its participation (for example, through a further round of equity financing) is aimed at supporting a firm which does not have a long term viability.[30] Generally speaking, all of these types of aid measures which meet the definition of rescue or restructuring aid would fall to be considered under the 2004 Guidelines.

7.10 **Rescue aid.** Rescue aid is a temporary and short-term measure, the primary objective of which 'is to make it possible to keep an ailing firm afloat for the time needed to work out a restructuring or liquidation plan'.[31] It typically provides short-term liquidity support. The aid should provide no more than a short breathing space to make an assessment of the company's financial position and development plan to restore viability. Under the 2004 Guidelines, rescue aid must be limited to the minimum necessary and should not exceed six months, while a longer-term solution is worked out. It will typically cover the firm's day-to-day capital requirements such as staff costs, although the 2004 Guidelines (unlike earlier Guidelines)

---

[26] See para 2.06 above for a non-exhaustive list of case-law examples of State aid measures.

[27] Decision 2006/621/EC *France Télécom* [2006] OJ L257/11, concerning the Minister's announcement that the State 'would take appropriate steps' if France Telecom were to have financial problems (under appeal in Cases T-425 and 444/04 *France and France Télécom v Commission*).

[28] See paras 2.56–2.59 above.

[29] See generally paras 2.33 *et seq* above on the application of the private investor/creditor principles. In its Decision in Case NN 70/2007 *Northern Rock* (5 December 2007) the Commission found that the Bank of England had not provided aid insofar as it had provided temporary liquidity support to Northern Rock secured against high quality collateral and at a penal interest rate.

[30] Case C-301/87 *France v Commission ('Boussac')* [1990] ECR I-307, para 40; Case C-303/88 *Italy v Commission ('ENI-Lanerossi')* [1991] ECR I-1433, para 3; Case C-305/89 *Italy v Commission ('Alfa Romeo')*, para 17. See also Cases T-228 and 233/99 *Westdeutsche Landesbank v Commission* [2003] ECR II-435, para 241, where the CFI confirmed that the market economy investor principle applied where the operation was one of restructuring profit-making as opposed to loss-making undertakings. The Commission's Decision in Case N 274/2005 *Huta Cynku Miasteczko Śląskie* (13 September 2005) concerning the Polish government's restructuring of the steel producer Huta Czestochowa found that the debt waiver combined with a debt for equity swap satisfied the private creditor test, since it offered public creditors a better solution than bankruptcy.

[31] 2004 Guidelines, para 15.

also allow for the funding of urgent structural measures, such as the immediate closure of a branch or the termination of a loss-making business. Rescue aid cannot, however, be used to fund structural measures which do not require immediate action, since these fall to be considered under the definition of restructuring aid. Similarly, aid which is paid following the implementation of a restructuring or liquidation plan cannot be considered rescue aid and would fall to be assessed as restructuring aid.[32]

Restructuring aid. Restructuring aid is, in effect, any aid other than rescue aid which is used to fund restructuring measures in order to support the firm's transition to a viable long-term future.[33] In many cases, it takes the form of long-term loans, recapitalizations, tax or social security relief or debt write-offs. The aid is used to reorganize and rationalize the firm's business, which may involve for example terminating loss-making activities, restructuring the existing activities. The restructuring plan will make them competitive, and diversifying into new and viable activities. It will typically involve a physical reorganization of the business, together with a financial restructuring of the firm's capital. It must be based on a 'feasible coherent and far reaching plan' for the business. Since restructuring aid is a longer-term measure than rescue aid, it carries a higher risk of competitive distortion. Accordingly, there are particularly strict criteria which must be met before the aid can be approved. In particular, there must be a significant contribution from the firm's own resources, as well as conditions aimed at putting the business on a viable long-term footing while minimizing any distortion in the marketplace.[34] **7.11**

Firm in difficulty. Rescue and restructuring aid is only provided to 'firms in difficulty'.[35] As the 2004 Guidelines indicate, there is no Community definition of the term,[36] but the Commission regards a firm as being in difficulty where it is unable, whether through its own resources or with the funds it is able to obtain from its owners/shareholders or creditors, to stem losses which, without outside intervention by the public authorities, will almost certainly condemn it to going out of business in the short or medium term.[37] This will be the case where: (1) in the case **7.12**

[32] See further section 2 below.

[33] 2004 Guidelines, para 16.

[34] See further section 3 below.

[35] It is clear from the 2004 Guidelines that both rescue and restructuring aid may only be provided to firms in difficulty (see eg para 14) although it is expressed to be a condition only in relation to restructuring aid (para 3.3).

[36] Though see the simplified definition of an undertaking in difficulty as regards SMEs, in Article 1(7) of the GBER: Reg 800/2008 [2008] OJ L214/3. However, for aid to SMEs which is not covered by the GBER, and for aid to large enterprises, the full definition in the 2004 Guidelines applies: see GBER, recital (15). Thus, para 11 of the 2004 Guidelines, setting out other signs of a firm being in difficulty, such as increasing losses and excess capacity, will need to be taken into account in deciding whether the undertaking meets the definition.

[37] 2004 Guidelines, paras 9–13. This approach was approved in Case T-349/03 *Corsica Ferries France v Commission* [2005] ECR II-2197, para 183.

of limited liability companies, more than half of the registered capital (or where members have unlimited liability, more than half of the capital as shown in the company accounts) has disappeared, and more than one quarter has been lost over the preceding 12 months; or (2) the company fulfils the criteria under national law for collective insolvency proceedings. However, there may also be other situations which indicate that a firm is in difficulty, for example increasing losses, declining turnover, excess capacity, declining cash flow, mounting debts, and declining or nil asset value. A key criterion is that the firm cannot recover its financial position from its own resources or from funds obtained from its shareholders or from the market, such that State intervention is required to protect the firm from defaulting.[38] Under the 2004 Guidelines, a newly created firm is not eligible for rescue or restructuring aid for three years following the start of operations. In addition, a firm which is part of a larger business group is not normally eligible for rescue or restructuring aid, although an exception is made where the firm suffers intrinsic difficulties which are not the product of an arbitrary allocation of costs within the group and where the difficulties are too serious to be dealt with by the group.[39]

7.13 **'One time, last time' principle.** As the 2004 Guidelines make clear,[40] it is a fundamental principle that rescue and restructuring aid may be granted only once. The rule was specifically introduced into the 1999 Guidelines in order to tighten up the requirements for approval of aid, and has been further reinforced in the 2004 Guidelines. Community policy allows only for limited State intervention to maintain a firm in the market pending a restructuring of its business, and not for repeated grants of assistance to protect the firm from normal market disciplines. As a general rule, therefore, a firm cannot benefit from rescue or restructuring aid more than once in ten years except as follows:[41]

(a) The firm may receive both rescue and restructuring aid as part of a restructuring programme.

[38] *Corsica Ferries France*, ibid, para 165. See also Decision in Case NN 101/2002 *British Energy* (27 November 2002), para 3.2.1, where British Energy 'would no longer be able to meet its liabilities to creditors as they arose'.

[39] See eg Decision in Case NN 47/2007 *Metronet rescue aid* (28 November 2007), where the Commission accepted that the Metronet companies which were in insolvency proceedings constituted 'firms in difficulty' notwithstanding that they were companies within a larger business group which were not insolvent; and Decision in Case NN 42/2005 *Rover* (7 June 2005), where the Commission held that the financial difficulties were specific to MG Rover and its subsidiary Powertrain, and that other entities within the group would not come to their rescue.

[40] 2004 Guidelines, para 72.

[41] ibid, para 73. The firm may however have received other aid, eg R&D aid: see Case N 267/2002 *Fairchild Dornier* (19 June 2002). Further reserve aid to keep the firm afloat during the same six month period would be a continuation of the initial rescue aid and would not breach the 'one time, last time' principle (see eg Decision in Case C 14/2008 *Northern Rock* [2008] OJ C135/21, paras 103–11).

(b) When a firm receives rescue aid not followed by restructuring aid and the firm was believed to be viable in the long term following the grant of rescue aid, fresh rescue or restructuring aid may be made available if it becomes necessary due to unforeseeable circumstances and at least five years have lapsed since the granting of the initial rescue aid.

(c) Fresh aid may be granted in exceptional and unforeseeable circumstances for which the company is not responsible. There have been a number of prominent (and controversial) examples of further rescue and restructuring packages being granted as a departure from the 'one time, last time' principle particularly in the financial services sector.[42] The Commission has noted that 'indiscriminate application of the 'one time, last time' principle would excessively restrict the category of aid capable of being regarded as necessary and would not allow the Commission to examine, in each particular case, whether a project for restructuring aid was necessary in order to attain Treaty objectives.'[43]

In the case of a group of companies, the ten-year rule will normally apply to all the group entities. However, if rescue and restructuring aid has been paid to a particular group subsidiary, the other group companies remain entitled to rescue and restructuring aid provided the subsequent grant of aid is ring-fenced and has not been passed to the earlier beneficiary.[44] In the case of the sale of a business, the purchaser is not bound by the 'one time, last time' principle and therefore may receive further aid for the acquired business, provided the purchaser is clearly separate from the previous firm and has acquired the business at market prices, and provided the sale is not merely a device to avoid the 'one time, last time' principle.[45]

Basis for authorization. The Commission generally considers that apart from aid envisaged by Article 87(2), the only basis on which aid for firms in difficulty can be deemed compatible is Article 87(3)(c).[46] The 2004 Guidelines provide an indication of the circumstances in which rescue and restructuring aid may be permitted under this provision. These include: (1) social and regional policy considerations; (2) SME policy; and (3) the need to maintain competition where the loss of a firm could create a monopoly or tight oligopoly.[47] This would appear to be a non-exhaustive list of cases, and the Guidelines acknowledge that there may be other 'legitimate' reasons to justify aid, although it cannot be used simply to 7.14

[42] Decision 98/490/EC *Crédit Lyonnais* [1998] OJ L221/28; Decision 98/204/EC *GAN group* [1998] OJ L78/1.

[43] Decision 2005/941/EC *Bull* [2005] OJ L342/81, para 70.

[44] 2004 Guidelines, para 75.

[45] ibid, para 76.

[46] ibid, para 19. For the (strict) conditions of authorization under Article 87(2) see Chapter 3 above.

[47] ibid, para 8.

promote the Member State's public policy objectives.[48] Aid can in no circumstances be permitted to maintain a firm artificially, particularly in a market suffering from long-term structural over capacity. As the Guidelines indicate, 'the exit of inefficient firms is a normal part of the operation of the market'.[49] However, in the exceptional circumstances of the 2008 global financial crisis, Article 87(3)(b) has been applied to large amounts of aid granted to support the financial services sector. This is discussed at paragraph 7.16 below.[50]

7.15 **Financial institutions.** Rescue and restructuring aid to financial institutions raises particularly difficult issues because of the 'moral hazard' to the banking system, ie the concept that State support which insulates the banks from risk encourages the banks to take higher risks and act less prudently than would otherwise be the case.[51] At the same time, the State may need to act quickly and decisively to restore confidence and prevent bank runs. The Commission has taken several high profile decisions, both during the 1990s[52] and more recently in the wake of the 2007 'credit crunch',[53] concerning rescue and restructuring aid in the banking sector within the framework of the 2004 Guidelines. These include a decision taken within 24 hours of notification, in the case of the UK's rescue package for the bank Bradford & Bingley.[54] Some standard central banking measures—even the provision of emergency liquidity support in circumstances where there is sufficient collateral and a penal interest rate—may well not constitute State aid at all.[55] The 2004 Guidelines also provide some relaxations in the criteria for rescue and restructuring aid, notably that rescue aid to banks may be provided in forms other than loans and guarantees. However the Commission's authorization of aid typically

---

[48] ibid, paras 8 and 20.

[49] ibid, para 4.

[50] For the Commission's normal approach to Article 87(3)(b), see Decision 98/490/EC *Crédit Lyonnais* [1998] OJ L221/28, section 10.1, where the Commission considered that State support was not 'designed to remedy serious economic disruption, since its purpose is to resolve the problems of a single recipient, [Crédit Lyonnais], as opposed to the acute problems facing all operators in the industry'; and Decisions in Cases NN 70/2007 *Northern Rock* (5 December 2007) and NN 25/2008 *WestLB risk shield* (30 April 2008) where the Commission rejected Article 87(3)(b) as grounds for authorization of rescue aid.

[51] For an early treatment of this issue, see Bagehot, *Lombard Street: a description of the money market* (1873, reprinted Wiley 1999).

[52] See eg Decision 98/490/EC *Crédit Lyonnais* [1998] OJ L221/28, which concerned bail-out measures of €20 billion.

[53] Decisions in Cases NN 70/2007 *Northern Rock* (5 December 2007), NN 25/2008 *WestLB risk shield* (30 April 2008), NN 36/2008 *Roskilde Bank* (31 July 2008) and NN 41/2008 *Bradford & Bingley* (1 October 2008); and Decision 2008/263/EC *BAWAG-PSK* [2008] OJ L83/7.

[54] See *Bradford & Bingley*, ibid, and press release IP/08/1437.

[55] Decision in Case NN 70/2007 *Northern Rock* (5 December 2007); see also the Communication on the global financial crisis, discussed in para 7.16 below, which points out (section 6) that central bank measures which form part of the monetary policy of Member States to ensure sufficient liquidity may not constitute State aid.

comes at the price of heavy divestiture and other commitments to restore the bank's future viability.[56]

The global financial crisis. In late 2008, the 'credit crunch' of the previous year developed into a global financial crisis, with the severe reduction in liquidity and in inter-bank lending threatening the viability of many leading financial institutions. A number of Member State governments adopted emergency measures to support their domestic banking systems, including the guaranteeing of retail deposits, the provision of loans to increase liquidity, and the recapitalization of banks through State investment.[57] In the Ecofin Council of 7 October 2008, the Member States agreed to take coordinated steps to restore confidence, calling on the Commission to 'act quickly and apply flexibility in state aid decisions within the framework of the single market and state aid regime'.[58] Days later, on 13 October 2008, the Commission adopted a Communication on the application of State aid rules in the context of the financial crisis.[59] The Communication states that in the highly exceptional circumstances which have arisen, the Commission is prepared to authorize State aid measures for financial institutions under Article 87(3)(b), on the basis that these measures are necessary to 'remedy a serious disturbance in the economy' of individual Member States. The Communication thus allows the Commission to adopt a more flexible approach towards rescue and restructuring aid than under the 2004 Guidelines. It indicates that the following measures are capable of being authorized:[60] 7.16

(a) schemes to guarantee retail deposits (and potentially also wholesale deposits and other debt instruments), provided these are limited in time and involve a contribution from the beneficiary financial institutions;
(b) the recapitalization of financial institutions, where the capital injection is limited to the minimum necessary and State funds are not used to pursue aggressive commercial strategies;
(c) State contributions in the winding-up of financial institutions; and
(d) the provision of other types of liquidity assistance, to the extent that these constitute State aid.

The Commission has made clear in the Communication that aid can only be authorized under Article 87(3)(b) where it satisfies the normal principles of

[56] See paras 7.25 and 7.26 below.

[57] eg, on 8 October 2008, the UK Treasury announced a package of support measures to the UK banking industry, including a Special Liquidity Scheme of £200 billion (see HM Treasury press release, 8 October 2008).

[58] Ecofin Council, Conclusions, 7 October 2008.

[59] Communication on the application of State aid rules to measures taken in relation to financial institutions in the context of the current global financial crisis ('Communication on the global financial crisis'), [2008] OJ C270/8. This Communication was supplemented by a further Communication on the recapitalization of financial institutions in the current financial crisis [2009] OJ C10/2, which provides guidelines on Member State measures to recapitalize their banks.

[60] ibid, sections 3–6.

non-discrimination and proportionality.[61] The measures described above must be temporary and must be accompanied by appropriate restructuring proposals to restore long-term viability. It is also emphasized that the use of Article 87(3)(b) in the financial sector is only possible in 'genuinely exceptional circumstances where the entire functioning of financial markets is jeopardised'.[62] Notwithstanding these strict conditions, at the time of writing a large number of aid cases had been approved on this basis.[63] On 17 December 2008, the Commission adopted a Communication under Article 87(3)(b) providing a temporary framework for Member States to support access to finance in the financial economic crisis. This is due to apply until the end of 2010.[64]

2. Rescue aid

7.17 **Basic conditions.** Rescue aid must satisfy the 'one time, last time' principle[65] and may only be granted to firms in difficulty as defined at paragraph 7.12 above. In addition, under the 2004 Guidelines, rescue aid must meet the further conditions set out in the following paragraphs.

7.18 **Form of aid.** The aid must be provided as liquidity support in the form of loans or loan guarantees at normal commercial interest rates (comparable to those available for loans to healthy firms),[66] for a period of up to six months.[67] There is an exception in the case of rescue aid in the banking sector, where subsidies other than in the form of loans or guarantees may be provided to enable a credit institution to

---

[61] In Decision in Case NN 51/2008 *Danish support scheme for banks* (10 October 2008), the Commission stated that while there is no established practice for assessing aid under Article 87(3)(b), in line with general Treaty principles it is necessary to consider the appropriateness, necessity and proportionality of the measures in question (para 41). The case concerned a Danish scheme providing, *inter alia*, a State guarantee covering depositors and creditors of banks, and involved a minimum contribution from the banks as well as behavioural commitments.

[62] Communication on the global financial crisis, para 11.

[63] The first three cases were Decisions in Cases NN 51/2008 *Danish support scheme for banks* (10 October 2008), NN 48/2008 *Guarantee scheme for banks in Ireland* (13 October 2008) and N 507/2008 *UK support scheme for financial institutions* (13 October 2008). These were followed by decisions on similar schemes in many other Member States.

[64] Communication on a temporary framework for State aid measures to support access to finance in the current financial and economic crisis, as amended on February 2009. Note that this applies equally to sectors other than the banking sector; cf position taken earlier in Communication on the global financial crisis, para 11.

[65] 2004 Guidelines, paras 25(e) and 72–7.

[66] ibid, para 25(a). Even though the State is charging a normal interest rate, there will still be an aid element since the actual interest rate available in the market to a firm in difficulty may be significantly higher than those otherwise available to financially healthy firms: Decision in Case NN 70/2007 *Northern Rock* (5 December 2007), paras 32–5.

[67] The Commission's practice regarding the restriction of rescue aid to six months is not always consistent. In Decision 2006/621/EC *France Télécom* [2006] OJ L257/11, the Commission objected that the credit line had been opened for a period of 18 months, thus exceeding the six month term in the Guidelines. However, in *Northern Rock*, ibid, the Commission accepted that the UK government's guarantees were open-ended, and stated that the relevant consideration was that the government would be submitting a restructuring plan within six months. That plan is currently the subject of a formal investigation procedure: see Decision in Case C 14/08 [2008] OJ C135/21.

carry on its banking business in accordance with applicable prudential rules. The aid must, however, still be in the form of reversible liquidity support. It cannot therefore involve structural financial measures relating to the bank's own funds (eg capital injections or debt reduction), and any aid granted in a form other than loans or loan guarantees will be taken into account in deciding on any compensatory measures under the restructuring plan.[68]

Serious social difficulties. There must be serious social difficulties, with no unduly adverse spill-over effects on other Member States.[69] Thus, it may be possible to justify aid to a large employer within an assisted area, where mass redundancies would have significant local consequences. Other cases have included the need to provide rescue aid to ensure nuclear safety and security of power supply.[70] The Commission may seek conditions in order to reduce the risks of spill-over effects in other Member States. **7.19**

Commitment to restructure, liquidate or repay. The Member State must undertake that, no more than six months after the rescue aid has been authorized, it will submit a restructuring or liquidation plan, or alternatively proof that that loan has been reimbursed or guarantee terminated.[71] The requirements of the plan, which will typically form a proposal for confirmed State support for restructuring, are discussed in more detail below in relation to restructuring aid. **7.20**

Proportionality. The aid must be no more than is necessary to keep the company in business for the period during which the aid is authorized. This is effectively a principle of proportionality. Accordingly, the approved amount is based on the liquidity needs of the company which must be calculated by reference to the formula set out in the Annex to the Guidelines.[72] Rescue aid is not intended to cover anything other than the firm's short-term liquidity requirements, and must not provide the recipient with additional funds which it could use, for example, to expand capacity.[73] **7.21**

Breach of conditions. The Commission has the right to take proceedings under Article 88(2) if the Member State fails to submit a 'credible and substantiated' restructuring or liquidation plan, or fails to provide proof that the loan or guarantee **7.22**

[68] 2004 Guidelines, n 15.

[69] ibid, para 25(b); and see eg Decision 2005/878/EC *Herlitz* [2005] OJ L324/64; and Decision in Case NN 42/2005 *Rover* (7 June 2005).

[70] Decision in Case NN 101/2002 *British Energy* (27 November 2002).

[71] 2004 Guidelines, para 25(c); and see eg Decision in Case NN 70/2007 *Northern Rock* (5 December 2007): approval was given on the basis that a restructuring plan would be submitted within six months, even though the loan/guarantee measures could extend beyond six months.

[72] 2004 Guidelines, para 24(d).

[73] Decision 2005/418/EC *Alstom* [2005] OJ L150/24. The Commission may also impose monitoring and control provisions and requirements as to the drawdown of funds: see eg Decision in Cases NN 47/2007 *Metronet rescue aid* (28 November 2007); and N 91/2005 *Computer Manufacturing Services* (7 June 2005).

has come to an end within six months.[74] It is not clear whether this necessarily precludes the possibility of the Commission initiating Article 88(2) proceedings in relation to unnotified emergency loans which are repaid within six months. Even if the loan is promptly repaid, there may still be an aid element arising from the fact that the recipient firm has had access to funds which it would not otherwise have received on the open market. Although this does not appear to be the Commission's practice, the correct analysis is that the Commission is entitled to treat short-term emergency loans which are repaid as State aid and to investigate them as such.

7.23 **Subsequent restructuring aid**. The authorization of rescue aid does not necessarily mean that aid under a subsequent restructuring plan will be approved. Rather, such aid has to be examined on its own merits.

3. Restructuring aid

7.24 **Basic conditions**. Restructuring aid can take many different forms and is not restricted to loans or loan guarantees. It does however require more careful justification than rescue aid. Since restructuring aid has a greater potential to distort competition, it can only be accepted if there are offsetting benefits, such as maintaining employment or averting a monopoly or tight oligopoly of remaining firms.[75] In addition to the basic conditions that the aid must satisfy the 'one time, last time' principle,[76] and must be limited to firms in difficulty,[77] there are strict and extensive criteria which must be satisfied before the aid can be approved. These are set out in the following paragraphs.

7.25 **Restructuring plan**. The aim of restructuring aid is to restore the long-term viability of the firm.[78] The very justification for restructuring aid is that it enables the Member State to secure the long-term viability of the business in a competitive market. It must therefore be based on a viable restructuring plan which provides a programme of measures which will restore the firm to profitability. The plan must take stock of the company's present difficulties, include a market survey of the relevant product market, and must set out best case, worst case and intermediate assumptions of the firm's prospects. The financial objectives are that the firm should in future achieve an expected return of capital which is sufficient to enable it to compete on its own merits.[79] The restructuring plan must be as short

[74] 2004 Guidelines, para 27.

[75] ibid, para 31.

[76] See para 7.13 above.

[77] 2004 Guidelines, para 33; see further para 7.12 above.

[78] Operating aid is therefore excluded: see eg Decision 1999/262/EC *Société de Banque Occidantale* [1999] OJ L103/19, in which the Commission considered that the aid would not allow the State-owned bank to return to viability.

[79] In Decision 2005/418/EC *Alstom* [2005] OJ L150/24, France's proposals for a further capital increase in the company and the consequent reduction in debt removed the Commission's initial doubts about financial viability.

as possible, and must involve the abandonment of activities which would remain structurally loss-making. The restructuring must restore the business to viability within a 'reasonable timescale'.[80] The Commission's evaluation will focus on the financial impact on the business, but may also take account of the social implications, such as jobs created or lost. The Commission's decisions indicate that it carries out a detailed evaluation of the proposed recovery measures, their achievability, and the profit forecasts of the company, and will frequently seek changes to the Member State's proposals where it has doubts about the effectiveness of the plan.[81] The restructuring plan, and any timetable for implementation, may be amended with the agreement of the Commission.[82] Any failure to implement the plan, or to modify it without the Commissioner's approval, will be treated as the misuse of aid and may be subject to Article 88(2) proceedings.[83]

Compensatory measures. In order to minimize the adverse effects on competition, appropriate compensatory measures must be taken such as the divestment of assets, reductions in capacity or the lowering of entry barriers,[84] as well as other restructuring obligations.[85] The 2004 Guidelines also introduced fixed minimum thresholds to ensure private co-financing of restructuring. The purpose of such measures is to offset the adverse effects which the aid may have on the firm's competitors. Where for example there is structural overcapacity in the market, the restructuring plan must propose additional closures (above what would be necessary to restore the firm's viability) as a compensatory measure.[86] In cases of long-term structural overcapacity, the reduction in capacity may need to be as high as 100%. Compensatory measures must, however, strike a balance between the need to mitigate the impact of the aid on competitors and the need to preserve the beneficiary company's viability.[87] The necessity for offsetting measures is assessed on a case-by-case basis. It may, for example, be inappropriate to carry out capacity closures which lead to a monopoly or a tight oligopoly of remaining competitors. Any structural measures must also be in proportion to the size and relative importance of the firm on the relevant market. For this reason, firms with low market shares may not need to be subject to any measures.[88] **7.26**

[80] 2004 Guidelines, paras 34–7. There is no definition of a 'reasonable timescale'. In many cases, five years is considered a reasonable benchmark, but this is assessed on an ad hoc basis.

[81] See eg Decision 2005/418/EC *Alstom* [2005] OJ L150/24.

[82] 2004 Guidelines, para 52.

[83] ibid, paras 47 and 54.

[84] ibid, paras 38–42.

[85] In Decision 2005/407/EC *British Energy* [2005] OJ L142/26, British Energy was required *inter alia* to be split into separate businesses to ensure transparency of accounting and to guard against cross-subsidization.

[86] Decision 1999/690/EC *Graphischer Maschinenbau* [1999] OJ L272/16; Decision 2000/7/EC *SKET Maschinen- und Anlagenbau* [2000] OJ L30/25.

[87] Decision 2005/407/EC *British Energy* [2005] OJ L142/26, para 435.

[88] The 1999 Guidelines stated that firms with 'negligible' market share would not need to be subject to compensatory measures. This provision was removed from the 2004 Guidelines,

7.27 **Proportionality.** The amount of aid must be limited to the minimum necessary to enable the restructuring to take place.[89] A 'significant contribution' is required from the firm's own resources, with funds raised either from the sale of assets or from external financing in order to demonstrate that the markets (ie both owners and creditors of the business) believe in long term viability.[90] The beneficiary's contribution must be at least 50% in the case of large firms, 40% for medium sized firms, and 25% for small firms. It must moreover be an *actual* present valuation contribution, as opposed to an undertaking to provide a share of future profits. The Commission will only accept a lower contribution in exceptional cases of 'particular hardship'.[91] Aid may not be used to finance costs (eg pricing or marketing campaigns) other than those strictly linked to the restructuring of the firm. Thus, the State cannot fund new investment which is not an intrinsic part of the restoration of the firm's long-term viability.[92]

7.28 **Specific conditions.** The Commission may impose other conditions to limit any distortions in competition.[93] Examples from the case-law include requirements to divest assets, conclude industrial partnerships, sell off shareholdings, refrain from offering lower prices, refrain from undercutting non-aided competitors, hive-off subsidiaries or branches, not to offer online contracts for mobile telephony and not to acquire or increase capacity; the monitoring of average margins to check for predatory pricing and requirements not to act as price lender; and restrictions on corporate acquisitions.[94] In cases of divestiture, a Commission-approved trustee may be required to handle the sale of the business. Member States may also be

---

following criticism that 'negligible' was not defined, but the aid beneficiary's market share remains a relevant factor in determining the need for structural changes: 2004 Guidelines, paras 40–1.

[89] 2004 Guidelines, para 43. In Decision 2003/19/EC *Schmitz-Gotha* [2003] OJ L77/41, para 67 the Commission found that the aid was in excess of the minimum necessary (upheld on appeal in Case T-17/03 *Schmitz-Gotha v Commission* [2006] ECR II-1139).

[90] In Decision 1999/647/EC *Addinol Mineralöl* [1999] OJ L260/19, the Commission considered that the contribution from private shareholders was insufficient—mentioned at p 24 (part VII) and p 25 (part VII). See also Decision 2005/941/EC *Bull* [2005] OJ L342/81, where the Commission noted the significant contribution from shareholder funds and from the sale of non-core assets. By contrast, in Decision 2003/383/EC *Technische Glaswerke Ilmenau* [2003] OJ L140/30, restructuring aid where there was no contribution was declared unlawful.

[91] 2004 Guidelines, para 44. In Decision 2000/393/EC *CBW Chemie* [2000] OJ L150/38, the Commission accepted a contribution of 19% in the circumstances of a management buyout.

[92] 2004 Guidelines, para 45.

[93] ibid, para 46.

[94] Decision 2005/418/EC *Alstom* [2005] OJ L150/24; Decision 2004/167/EC *SNCM* [2004] OJ L61/13; Decision 2005/346/EC *MobilCom* [2005] OJ L116/55; Decision 99/332/EC *Olympic Airways* [1999] OJ L128/1; Decision 2005/407/EC *British Energy* [2005] OJ L142/26. In Decision 98/490/EC *Crédit Lyonnais* [1998] L221/28, the Commission imposed extensive conditions in its approval of a second restructuring aid package to Crédit Lyonnais. The bank was required to make significant divestments to reduce its balance sheet and also to limit any expansion following its privatisation. In Decision 2005/345/EC *Bankgesellschaft Berlin* [2005] OJ L116/1, the commitments included the reduction of banking activities and the privatisation of the bank.

required to take measures to liberalize markets to allow for new entry by other EU firms.

Privatization. In the case of State-owned assets, the restructuring proposals may involve total or partial privatization of the undertaking to demonstrate its long-term viability. Article 295 of the Treaty provides that the Treaty does not prejudice the rules in Member States concerning property ownership. The Commission is thus not entitled to require that the restructuring includes disposals to the private sector. Nevertheless, a total or partial sale is a material factor for the Commission to take into account when assessing the future prospects of the business.[95] In this way, a commitment to privatize all or part of the business may form part of the Commission's decision. The State's withdrawal from the capital of a State-owned entity may also be a necessary step to limit any market distortions.[96] The Commission has indicated that privatization may be particularly appropriate in the case of 'recidivists', ie public enterprises which have already benefited from restructuring aid.[97] **7.29**

Social costs of restructuring. Restructuring aid can be used to fund social measures which result from the rationalization and restructuring of a firm's activities. This could include redundancy benefits or early retirement pensions to the firm's workforce.[98] In addition, the Commission takes a favourable view of aid for training, counselling and practical help for employees in finding alternative employment.[99] In these cases, State support will not involve aid where it is a general measure available to all sectors.[100] However, aid may be involved where the State is contributing to or paying costs which the firm itself would normally be required to fund under national legislation.[101] Where restructuring aid is used to cover social costs exclusively for the benefit of redundant employees, the aid is disregarded for the purposes of calculating compensatory measures.[102] **7.30**

[95] In Decision 98/490/EC *Crédit Lyonnais* [1998] OJ L221/28, France gave undertakings to transfer Crédit Lyonnais to the private sector following an open tender procedure. In Decision 2000/600/EC *Banco di Sicilia* [2000] OJ L256/21, para 119, the Commission considered that privatization 'should provide a definitive solution to the above-mentioned problems . . . and will ensure that in future the bank turns to its private shareholders or to the market if it requires financing'. In Decision 2005/345/EC *Bankgesellschaft Berlin* [2005] OJ L116/1, Germany's commitment to privatize the bank and the Commission's view that privatization had a sufficient prospect of success, were both material factors in evaluating the restructuring plan.

[96] See eg Decision 2005/418/EC *Alstom* [2005] OJ L150/24, where France was required to divest its capital stake in Alstom within four years.

[97] 24th Report on Competition Policy (1994), para 360.

[98] 2004 Guidelines, para 60–7.

[99] ibid, para 65.

[100] See further paras 2.121–2.126 above.

[101] Case C-241/94 *France v Commission ('Kimberly Clark')* ECR I-4551.

[102] 2004 Guidelines, para 66.

7.31 **Agricultural sector.** The 2004 Guidelines provide for a number of modifications to the assessment of aid for restructuring in the agricultural sector:[103]

(a) Compensatory measures are normally required, even in the case of SMEs.
(b) The Commission may exempt aid to SMEs under aid schemes even where the SME concerned does not meet any of the three criteria for a firm in difficulty.
(c) In cases which require a reduction in capacity, open farmland may be reused after 15 years, during which time it must be maintained in good agricultural and environmental condition for land no longer used for production purposes.[104]
(d) The reduction in capacity must be at least 5% (3% in less favoured areas) of that for which the restructuring aid is granted. When the aid measure is targeted at particular products or operations, the reduction in capacity must be 10% (8% in less favoured areas). The reduction in capacity must be achieved in the relevant market, but not necessarily by the aid beneficiary. These requirements may be waived where the total restructuring aid in the sector concerned in any consecutive 12-month period does not exceed 1% production capacity in the Member State.
(e) There is a five-year rather than a ten-year period under the 'one time, last time' principle for both rescue and restructuring aid.

7.32 **Assisted areas.** The Commission will take account of regional development needs when assessing restructuring aid in areas eligible for regional aid under Article 87(3)(a) and 87(3)(c). The mere fact that a firm is located in an assisted area does not in itself provide a strong justification for restructuring aid. The future viability of the undertaking is still the determinative criterion on which aid will be assessed. However, in these cases the 2004 Guidelines indicate that the Commission may take a 'less stringent' approach with regard to requiring compensatory measures or the size of the beneficiary's contribution.[105] Furthermore, in view of regional development considerations there may be a case for a smaller reduction in capacity, particularly in Article 87(3)(a) areas.[106]

---

[103] ibid, paras 87–98.

[104] See Council Regulation (EC) No 1782/2003, establishing common rules for direct support schemes under the common agricultural policy and establishing certain support schemes for farmers [2003] OJ L270/1, as amended [2004] OJ L161/48, Article 5.

[105] 2004 Guidelines, para 56.

[106] See eg Decision 2001/826/EC *Dampfkesselbau Hohenturm* [2001] OJ L308/28; Decision 1999/380/EC *Spindelfabrik Hartha* [1999] OJ L145/32 (where the Commission noted that 'Harthe, which has a small market share and is an SME operating in an Article 92(3)(a) area, cannot be required to reduce capacity'); Decision 99/485/EC *Hijos de Andrés Molina ('Hamsa')* [1999] OJ L193/1, para 138. Nicolaides and Kekelekis argue ('An assessment of EC State aid policy on rescue and restructuring of companies in difficulty' (2004) 25 ECLR 578–83) that here (as indeed in other aspects) the Guidelines leave too much administrative discretion with the Commission, with the result that the outcome in a particular case may depend to a large extent on the persuasive skills of the national authorities notifying the aid. However, it is difficult to see how the position could be

4. Aid for SMEs

Application of 2004 Guidelines. While the Guidelines apply as a general rule to rescue and restructuring aid to SMEs, there are some important modifications regarding restructuring aid and the approval of aid schemes, as set out in the following paragraphs. **7.33**

Restructuring aid. Restructuring aid to SMEs will not usually require compensatory measures and the restructuring plan does not need to be endorsed by the Commission, although its content must still fulfil the conditions set out in paragraph 7.24 above.[107] The reporting requirements in relation to restructuring aid are also less stringent than for larger undertakings.[108] **7.34**

Aid schemes. In addition to the general provisions regarding the approval of rescue and restructuring aid, the Guidelines provide for the authorization of rescue or restructuring aid schemes to SMEs where the scheme meets certain criteria.[109] Where an aid scheme as been approved, an individual aid granted under that scheme does not need to be notified if the SME beneficiary meets at least one of the three criteria for a 'firm in difficulty'.[110] Where the SME beneficiary operates in a market which is characterized by long-term structural overcapacity, however, the aid must always be notified individually to the Commission.[111] The aid scheme must specify the maximum aid available to any one firm, and this figure may not in any event exceed €10 million (accumulated together with all other aid from other sources).[112] There are also less onerous reporting requirements with regard to the implementation of the aid scheme.[113] Where the aid scheme does not meet the criteria set out in the Guidelines, the Commission requires individual aid to be notified for case-by-case assessment.[114] **7.35**

5. Procedural issues

Notification. The normal procedures relating to the notification and authorization of aid apply to rescue and restructuring aid.[115] There is, in addition, a simplified **7.36**

otherwise, since much will depend on the facts of the individual case and the economic impact in the area concerned.

107 ie the conditions in paras 35–7 of the 2004 Guidelines: see 2004 Guidelines, paras 57–9.

108 ibid, para 51.

109 ibid, paras 78–81. In fact, most rescue and restructuring aid, by its very nature, is individual ad hoc aid.

110 See para 7.12 above.

111 2004 Guidelines, para 79.

112 ibid, para 83.

113 ibid, para 86.

114 See eg Decision 2003/626/EC *Thuringia loan programme* [2003] OJ L223/32; Decision 2004/343/EC *France – takeover of firms in difficulty* [2004] OJ L108/38; Decision 2000/257/EC *Italian sugar beet* [2000] OJ L79/38.

115 See Chapter 16 below.

procedure for rescue aid which meets one of the criteria for a firm in difficulty, does not exceed €10 million, and is limited to the amount calculated in the formula set out on the Annex to the Guidelines.[116] In such cases, the Commission will endeavour to take a decision within one month.[117] As in other cases, the grant of unnotified (and hence unlawful) rescue and restructuring aid may still be subsequently authorized where it meets the criteria set out in the 2004 Guidelines.[118] It must be emphasized, however, that while rescue aid is by its very nature is an urgent measure, it remains subject to the requirement for prior notification in Article 88(3), and a Member State which breaches this 'stand still' requirement is at risk of proceedings in the national courts for recovery.[119]

7.37 **Reporting.** There are ongoing monitoring and reporting requirements for restructuring aid, and Member States must submit 'regular detailed reports' about the implementation of the restructuring plan.[120] In the case of large firms, a first report must be submitted within six months and thereafter at least annually. There may also be specific more frequent reporting conditions imposed on the recipient firm. Furthermore, the Commission must be kept informed of any other aid (unless *de minimis* or covered by block exemption regulations) paid to large or medium sized enterprises during the restructuring period.[121] The primary responsibility for meeting the notification and reporting requirements falls on the Member State concerned, although in practice the recipient firm is also likely to be closely involved in providing information to the Commission.

7.38 **Previous unlawful aid.** The Guidelines also state, with reference to the ECJ's judgment in *Textilwerke Deggendorf*,[122] that where rescue or restructuring aid has previously been granted unlawfully to a firm, any further aid must be assessed taking into account the cumulative effect of the old and new aid.[123] In effect, new aid can only be made available if the previous aid has been recovered.[124]

---

[116] The formula aims at estimating the negative operating cash flows of the company in the preceding year, divided by 2 to calculate the amount of aid required to keep the company in business for six months.

[117] 2004 Guidelines, para 30. As discussed at para 7.16 above, the Commission is prepared to act more swiftly in the case of emergency measures to ensure financial stability, and eg approved the UK rescue aid package for Bradford & Bingley within 24 hours (press release IP/08/1437).

[118] See eg Decision 2005/418/EC *Alstom* [2005] OJ L150/24.

[119] A significant number of recovery actions by the Commission—80 as at 2006—involve rescue and restructuring aid.

[120] 2004 Guidelines, para 49.

[121] ibid, para 50.

[122] Cases T-244 and 486/93 *Textilwerke Deggendorf v Commission* [1995] ECR II-2265, paras 53–60.

[123] ibid, para 23; and see further para 16.59 below.

[124] Thus in Decision 2005/941/EC *Bull* [2005] OJ L342/81, the Commission required the repayment of earlier grants of rescue aid before further restructuring aid could be released.

8

RESEARCH, DEVELOPMENT AND INNOVATION

Main legislation and guidelines

Commission Regulation (EC) 800/2008 on the application of Articles 87 and 88 of the Treaty declaring certain categories of aid compatible with the common market (General Block Exemption Regulation) ('GBER') [2008] OJ L 214/3.

Community Framework for State aid for Research and Development and Innovation ('R&D&I Framework') [2006] OJ C323/1

A. Introduction

R&D&I under the EC Treaty. Article 3(n) EC lists the promotion of research and technological development as one of the objectives of the Community. The manner in which this is to be achieved and the activities covered are elaborated in Articles 163 to173. Article 163 stipulates that: 'the Community shall have the objective of strengthening the scientific and technological bases of Community industry and encouraging it to become more competitive at international level, while promoting all the research activities deemed necessary . . .'.[1] Research, development **8.01**

[1] For an example of an early case based on Article 163 see Decision in Case C 37/91 *Bull* [1992] OJ C244/2.

and innovation (R&D&I) are considered very important in promoting competitiveness and delivering employment within the EU. Despite that, however, the overall investment in R&D&I as a proportion of gross domestic product (GDP) in the EU is conspicuously lower than in a number of the EU's major trading partners. With a view to addressing this problem, the European Council in 2002 agreed an ambitious target of investing 3% of GDP in research and development by 2010, compared with the average investment level at that time of 1.9%. The aim was to ensure that at least two thirds of that investment should come from the private sector.[2] But it is recognized that public sector spending still has a role to play in stimulating or leveraging private sector investment or in addressing market failures.

8.02 **EU policy frameworks.** Article 169 EC provides the basis for a multiannual framework programme for research and development. Since 1984, the objectives of the EU's own spending on R&D&I have been implemented through multi-annual framework programmes. The seventh framework programme runs from 2007 to 2013 with a budget of over €50 billion.[3] This is mostly spent on grants for financing or co-financing research, technological development and demonstration projects chosen on the basis of a competitive call for proposals published on the Commission's CORDIS webpage. EU-funded projects are intended to complement national research programmes and must therefore have a 'European added value' or cross-border element.[4] This may be present, for example, where the research programme is carried out by participants from a number of different Member States.

8.03 **State aid policy.** In general, the Commission takes a favourable approach towards aid for R&D&I bearing in mind the objectives of such aid, the associated risks and the costs. Many forms of public support for R&D&I do not constitute State aid, since they involve non-economic activities, such as the public financing of non-economic R&D&I activities by research organizations. Similarly, where public authorities go through a competitive tendering process to commission research, this too will fall outside the scope of State aid. Nevertheless, much of the public support for research does fall within the definition of State aid, and where it does the object of EU State aid policy is to achieve a balance between limiting any distortion of competition and stimulating research and innovation. The principal risk of R&D&I aid is that it may reduce the incentive for rivals to invest

---

[2] See Communication from the Commission – Investing in research: an action plan for Europe, COM (2003) 226 final, p 3.

[3] Decision 1982/2006/EC of the Parliament and Council concerning the Seventh Framework Programme of the European Community for research, technological development and demonstration activities (2007–2013), [2006] OJ L412/1.

[4] Regulation (EC) 1906/2006 of the Parliament and Council laying down the rules for the participation of undertakings, research centres and universities in actions under the Seventh Framework Programme and for the dissemination of research results (2007–2013) [2006] OJ L391/1, Article 5.

in research or innovation. That risk is most likely to occur where there is little market incentive effect, the amount of aid granted is high, the activity is close to commercialization, the beneficiary has market power or the market is concentrated.

R&D&I Framework. In 1986, the Commission adopted the first of its Frameworks for State aid for R&D,[5] establishing guidelines for approval of compatible aid. That Framework was revised in 1996[6] and then modified again in 1998.[7] It was reviewed in 2001 without changes and extended twice.[8] At the end of 2006, following lengthy consultation, the Commission adopted its current R&D&I Framework[9] which came into force on 1 January 2007 and is valid until 31 December 2013. The Framework takes into account the Commission's more targeted economic approach to the identification of market failures and the provision of investment incentives. The aim is to leverage business investment and to differentiate between eligible projects according to their proximity to the market. The most notable feature of the new Framework is the decision to extend its scope to cover activities supporting innovation in knowledge and technology. The Framework is also designed to make provision for the increasing tendency towards the creation of public-private partnerships for collaborative research, and the issues that arise concerning the ownership of, and right to access and exploit, intellectual property rights. It is applicable to all sectors covered by the EC Treaty, but does not apply to undertakings in difficulty. These are subject to the separate regime covered by the Guidelines on aid for rescue and restructuring firms in difficulty.[10] **8.04**

SME block exemption. In 2004, pursuant to the Enabling Regulation,[11] the Commission extended the scope of the existing block exemption for SMEs to include aid for R&D.[12] The decision was taken in recognition of the difficulties and costs that SMEs face in gaining access to new technological developments and intellectual property rights, and their consequentially low level of investments in R&D. As amended, the block exemption covered R&D project aid (for fundamental **8.05**

[5] Community Framework for State aid for Research and Development [1986] OJ C83/2.

[6] Community Framework for State aid for Research and Development [1996] OJ C45/5.

[7] Community Framework for State aid for Research and Development [1998] OJ C48/2.

[8] Commission Communication concerning the prolongation of the Community Framework for State Aid for Research and Development [2002] OJ C111/3 and [2005] OJ C310/10.

[9] Community Framework for State aid for Research and Development and Innovation ('R&D&I Framework') [2006] OJ C323/1.

[10] Community guidelines on State aid for rescuing and restructuring firms in difficulty [2004] OJ C244/2; see further Chapter 7 above.

[11] Council Regulation (EC) 994/98 on the application of Articles 92 and 93 of the Treaty establishing the European Community to certain categories of horizontal State aid [1998] OJ L142/1; see further Chapter 3 above.

[12] Commission Regulation (EC) 70/2001 on the application of Articles 87 and 88 of the EC Treaty to State aid to small and medium-sized enterprises [2001] OJ L10/33, as amended [2004] OJ L63/22; see further Chapter 10 below.

research, industrial research and pre-competitive development)[13] as well as aid for technical feasibility studies[14] and aid for covering the costs of obtaining and validating patents and other industrial property rights.[15] It did not, however, cover individual aid grants of any magnitude to large enterprises.[16]

8.06 **The GBER.** The SME block exemption has now been replaced by the provisions of the new General Block Exemption Regulation ('GBER').[17] This came into force on 29 August 2008 and is due to expire on 31 December 2013. The GBER provisions concerning R&D&I are similar to those set out in the amended SME block exemption, but have been brought into line with the Commission's approval policy set out in the subsequent R&D&I Framework. By way of transitional provisions, any aid granted before 31 December 2008, which does not satisfy the conditions of the GBER but does fulfil the conditions of the previous SME block exemption, is still deemed compatible with the common market and exempt from notification.[18]

8.07 **Methodology for the assessment of R&D&I aid.** The GBER, together with the R&D&I Framework, establishes the following methodology for the assessment of aid for R&D&I.

(a) A number of R&D&I measures do not constitute State aid. These are addressed in the R&D&I Framework and considered in section B below.

(b) Where there is aid, the GBER enables R&D&I aid that complies with certain substantive and transparency requirements to be implemented without prior notification and approval. The scope of the GBER is discussed in detail in section C below.

(c) Aid measures not eligible under the GBER must be notified to the Commission and approved before they may be implemented. The Commission will assess such measures on the basis of the guidelines set out in the R&D&I Framework. These are discussed in detail in section D below.

B. Existence of aid

8.08 **Non-economic activities: general principle.** For State aid to arise, all of the criteria under Article 87(1) EC must be met,[19] including the requirement that the measure must provide a benefit or advantage to 'undertakings'. That will not

---

13 ibid, Article 5a.
14 ibid, Article 5b.
15 ibid, Article 5c.
16 ibid, Article 6.
17 Commission Regulation (EC) No 800/2008 OJ L214/3.
18 ibid, Article 44(2).
19 See para 2.02 above, and Chapter 2 generally.

normally be the case where a grant or other form of public assistance is provided to bodies carrying out non-economic activities (such as universities[20] and research institutes).[21] The central question is whether the recipient of the aid carries out an economic activity consisting of offering goods or services on a market.[22] Generally speaking, where the organization's principal activities involve education, independent research and the dissemination of research results, and where any income is reinvested in the primary activities of the research, there is a presumption that the activities are non-economic in nature. By contrast, where a research organization or a not-for-profit innovation intermediary carries out activities such as renting out equipment, infrastructure or property, providing research services for businesses or carrying out contract research, these activities would be regarded as economic activities and public assistance could involve State aid.[23]

Mixed economic and non-economic activities. In some instances, a research organization may carry out both economic and non-economic activities. In such cases, the Commission considers that public funding of the non-economic activities may still fall outside the scope of the State aid rules where it is possible to distinguish the two types of activities, and where costs and funding can be clearly separated.[24] In practice, this means using a strict system of separate cost accounting in order to ensure that public funds are not used to cross-subsidize any economic activities.[25] **8.09**

Public/private collaboration. It is common practice for publicly-funded research organizations to carry out research and development either under contract for private undertakings, or through some form of collaboration or partnership arrangement.[26] In such cases, it is necessary to consider whether the private undertaking concerned obtains an advantage as a result of its association with the publicly funded body, that it would not have obtained under normal market conditions. The following paragraphs consider this question separately in relation to contract and partnership arrangements. **8.10**

---

20 eg Decision in NN 54/2006 *Přerov Logistics College* (8 November 2006); Decision in NN 152/2001 – *Digital university* (15 January 2002).

21 For a discussion concerning the distinction between economic and non-economic activities see eg Case T-155/04 *Selex Sistemi Integrati v Commission* [2006] ECR II-4797, paras 87–92 and see further paras 2.22–2.23 above.

22 Case C-222/04 *Ministero dell'Economia e delle Finanze v Cassa di Risparmio di Firenze* [2006] ECR I-289, para 123.

23 R&D&I Framework, section 3.1.2.

24 ibid, section 3.1.1; and Decision in N 543/2006 *Creation of the energy, environment and water research centre* (25 May 2007), para 15.

25 See eg Decision in N 79/2007 *R&D for the preservation of natural resources and ecosystems* (31 August 2007), para 33.

26 eg Decision in N 267/2007 *R&D&I scheme for enterprises in Sachsen-Anhalt* (11 September 2007); Decision in N 410/2005 *CENIT Programme* (28 October 2005); Decision in N 295/2005 *CASIMIR Programme* (28 October 2005); Decision in N 319/2005 *Grant for collaborative R&D* (22 December 2005).

8.11 **Contract arrangements.** Where a private undertaking enters into a contract with a publicly subsidized research organization under which the private undertaking owns the results of the research and carries the risk of failure, so long as the contract sets out the terms and conditions of the project, and the undertaking pays a market price for the service or a price which reflects the full costs and a reasonable margin, no State aid will pass to the private undertaking.[27] Conversely, where the private undertaking does not pay a market price for the research it may be inferred that it is receiving an indirect subsidy.

8.12 **Partnership arrangements.** It is possible to structure a partnership arrangement between a research organization and private undertakings to ensure that no indirect aid is transferred to the private partners.[28]

(a) First, the participating private undertakings must bear the full costs of the project.

(b) Secondly, the results of the project that have not given rise to intellectual property rights must be made widely available. Where intellectual property rights do arise as a result of the participation of the research organization, that research organization should enjoy the full economic benefit of the rights. In other words, they should have ownership over the rights and be able to license them (to third parties and/or the participating private undertakings).

(c) Thirdly, where the private undertakings acquire intellectual property rights from the research organization, they should provide the full market price for those rights, although any contribution to the costs of the research by those undertakings may be deducted.

Where these conditions are not fulfilled, the Member State may alternatively rely on an individual assessment of the collaboration project, to demonstrate that the overall arrangement adequately reflects the respective interests and contributions of the financial partners to the project. If that is the case it may be concluded that no State aid arises. If, however, the general conditions set out above are not fulfilled, and the individual assessment of the project does not indicate that there is no State aid, the value of the contribution of the research may be regarded as State aid, depending on whether the other conditions under Article 87(1) are satisfied.[29]

8.13 **Innovation intermediaries.** So-called 'innovation intermediaries' (such as incubators, technology centres and chambers of commerce) can play a part in assisting

27 R&D&I Framework, section 3.2.1.

28 ibid, section 3.2.2.

29 ibid, section 3.2.2. In particular, it would have to be shown that the contribution constituted aid from State resources, and that the behaviour of the research organization was imputable to the State: see paras 2.89–2.108 above.

SMEs to invest in R&D&I by providing services such as strategic advice, training, networking and consultancy, and facilities such as office space, data banks, equipment, testing and certification.[30] The creation of incubation or innovation centres is becoming an increasingly common method of promoting SMEs generally or innovative start-up businesses in particular sectors. Where State funds are used to promote such schemes, it will be necessary to consider the possibility of transfer of aid. Depending on how such a scheme is established, there may potential for aid to arise at three different levels: (i) aid to the providers of innovation services; (ii) aid to the centre; and (iii) aid to the users. These are considered in the next paragraphs.

Providers of innovation services. In some cases the providers of the services are private companies and therefore clearly 'undertakings'.[31] The Commission also takes the view that even where the providers of facilities are municipalities or non-profit organizations, they may be regarded as 'undertakings' where they perform activities also carried out by private real estate firms or consultancies.[32] Nevertheless, the Commission has been prepared to recognize that where the object of the innovation is exclusively to benefit the users of a centre, it may be possible to avoid State aid at the level of the providers where the subsidy for the innovation centre is strictly ring-fenced from other activities and the provider obtains no financial advantage or benefit at any stage.[33] **8.14**

Innovation centre or cluster. The second level to consider is whether the centres and the managers are direct recipients of aid. In general, where financial assistance provides some form of benefit to the operators of the innovation centre (eg by subsidizing operational costs) aid may arise.[34] However, it may be possible to structure the arrangement to avoid provision of aid to the centre itself.[35] **8.15**

Users of innovation services. The establishment of innovation centres, and the provisions of services by innovation intermediaries, will almost invariably involve aid to the users of those services or facilities. In many cases schemes may be **8.16**

30 For examples of cases of aid to intermediaries prior to the adoption of the R&D&I Guidelines see: Decision in N 318/2003 *Promotion of technology centres in Saxony-Anhalt* (21 January 2004); Case N 213/2003 *ATLAS broadband infrastructure scheme* (20 July 2004); Case NN 87/2002 *Danish Centre for Management* (25 May 2003); Decision in NN 152/2001 *Digital university* (15 January 2002).

31 See Decision in N 525/2001 *Cluster incubator scheme* (30 January 2002), concerning the creation of incubators for small start-up firms operating in the high technology sector. The aid was in form of grants to property developers chosen through a public tender, to build specific premises for eligible SMEs at lower than market rent. The Commission considered that the scheme constituted State aid to the developers but approved it under Article 87(3)(a) and (c).

32 Decision 2005/782/EC *Business, technology and incubator centres* [2005] OJ L295/44, para 28.

33 ibid, paras 26–34.

34 See eg Decision in Case C 7/2003 *SBS Incubation Fund* [2003] OJ C104/2. The UK withdrew the scheme after concerns were raised regarding assistance for the daily operation of the centre: [2005] OJ C263/39.

35 See para 8.17 below.

structured to ensure that aid to users is *de minimis*,[36] or to take advantage of the new exemption provisions under the GBER on aid for innovation advisory services and innovation support services and aid for the loan of highly qualified personnel.[37] In other cases the aid may have to be notified and assessed under the conditions set out in the R&D&I Framework.[38]

8.17 ***De minimis* aids.** Finally, aid for R&D&I may also fall within the scope of the *de minimis* block exemptions. In such cases the aid is deemed not to meet the criteria of Article 87(1). The general *de minimis* Regulation is dicussed in Chapter 2.[39] The separate *de minimis* Regulations applicable in the agriculture and fisheries sectors are addressed in Chapter 11.[40]

C. General Block Exemption Regulation ('GBER')

8.18 **Structure.** As described in more detail in Chapter 5 above, Chapter I of the GBER contains a set of common conditions and procedural provisions applicable to the various types of aid covered by the GBER. The provisions of Chapter I relevant to aid for R&D&I are addressed in section 1 below. Section 2 will then address the specific R&D&I exemptions in the GBER, as set out in Chapter II of the GBER.

1. Common and procedural provisions

8.19 **Sectoral scope of R&D&I exemptions.** The R&D provisions of the GBER apply to almost all sectors of the economy including the primary production, processing and marketing of agricultural products, the fishery and aquaculture sectors, and the coal, steel, shipbuilding and synthetic fibres sectors.[41]

8.20 **Individual notification thresholds.** Under the GBER certain aids are excluded where the value of the financial assistance exceeds specified thresholds. This varies according to the type of aid in question. For R&D&I aid, the thresholds per undertaking, project or feasibility study over which notification is required are:[42]

(a) €20 million in the case of aid for fundamental research;
(b) €10 million in the case of aid for industrial research;

[36] See Commission Regulation (EC) No 1998/2006 OJL379/5.
[37] GBER, Articles 35, 36 and 37.
[38] R&D&I Framework at para 5.6; and see para 8.50 below.
[39] See para 2.148 above.
[40] See paras 11.18–11.20 (agriculture) and 11.63 (fisheries) below.
[41] GBER, Article 1(3). These sectors remain subject to exclusions for certain other kinds of aid.
[42] ibid, Article 6(1)(e).

(c) €7.5 million for all other projects (eg experimental research); and
(d) in the case of EUREKA[43] projects, twice the sum identified in (a), (b) or (c).

In the case of a 'mixed project' involving both fundamental and industrial research, the level of eligible funding is determined according to the 'predominant' value. A project is considered to be predominantly within one category if more than 50% of the eligible costs relate to that category. In the case of doubt, the lower threshold applies.[44] A simplified notification ceiling of €5 million per undertaking per project has been introduced in relation to aid for industrial property rights costs for SMEs.[45] When calculating the level of aid, the figure used is the gross figure before deduction of tax or other charges. If aid is given in a form other than a grant, the level is calculated at the grant equivalent of the aid.[46]

Common conditions. In addition to the specific provisions referred to above on the scope of the R&D&I exemptions, the GBER contains a number of general conditions common to all types of aid within its ambit. These are set out in detail in paras 5.17–5.26 above, to which reference should be made. In summary, these provisions concern: **8.21**

(a) the exclusion of all forms of aid to certain undertakings and certain sectors;
(b) the general conditions for exemption of aid schemes and individual aid granted under such schemes, as well as for ad hoc individual aid;
(c) the basis of calculation of aid intensities;
(d) the requirement to provide documentary evidence of eligible costs;
(e) the requirement for exempted aid to be transparent;
(f) the conditions under which aid can be cumulated with other aid exempted under the GBER;
(g) the requirement for aid to have an incentive effect; and
(h) the reporting and monitoring requirements applicable to all aid exempted under the GBER.

2. Specific R&D&I exemptions

Overview. The GBER includes provisions exempting aid for R&D projects, technical feasibility studies and aid to cover industrial property rights costs for SMEs, under certain conditions. These provisions are similar to the R&D provisions in the amended SME block exemption. Unlike the SME block exemption, however, the GBER applies also to R&D aid for large undertakings. This change reflects the **8.22**

43 EUREKA was established by a Conference of Ministers from 17 countries and Members of the European Commission in July 1985. The Commission favours aid given under a coordinated framework of cross-border collaboration.

44 GBER, Article 6(1).

45 ibid, Article 6(1)(f).

46 ibid, Article 4(1).

generally favourable treatment of aid for R&D, and the recognition that the obstacles for investment and level of risk involved is not exclusively a problem for small businesses. The GBER also introduces new categories of aid for R&D&I, namely aid for young innovative enterprises, aid for innovation advisory services and support services and aid for the loan of highly qualified personnel.

8.23 **Categories of research.** The GBER draws a distinction between three categories of research project. *Fundamental research* refers to experimental or theoretical work, *industrial research* refers to planned research or investigation designed to develop new products, processes or services or making improvements to existing products, processes or services, and *experimental development* refers to the stage prior to commercialization where existing knowledge or technology is used to plan and define new products, processes or services including the development of experimental prototypes and pilot projects.[47]

8.24 **Aid for R&D projects.** The permitted aid intensity for R&D projects is determined according to the principle that the further the research activities are from the market, the less distortive is the likely effect on the market. This is reflected in the permitted aid intensities under the GBER. The basic permissible aid intensity is 100% in the case of fundamental research, 50% for industrial research and 25% for experimental development.[48] Where a project involves several different activities, the permitted aid intensity is determined separately in relation to each task. The basic aid intensities set for industrial research and experimental development may be increased by 10% where the recipient is a medium-sized enterprise, and by 20% for a small enterprise. A bonus of 15% may be added to the intensities set for industrial research and experimental development (up to a maximum aid intensity of 80%) for certain types of cross-border collaboration, collaboration with research organizations or, in the case of industrial research, where the results of the project are made publicly available.[49] Eligible costs include personnel costs, costs of instruments and equipment to the extent and period of the project, the cost of buildings and land used during the research project, the cost of contractual research, patents, know how or other third party rights bought or licensed for the purposes of the research and other directly related overheads and operating expenses. In each instance, the costs must be allocated to a specific category of the R&D.[50]

---

47 ibid, Article 30.

48 ibid, Article 31(3). This compares with the basic aid intensity levels of 100% for fundamental research, 60% for industrial research and 35% for pre-competitive development under Article 1(4) of Commission Regulation 364/2004 amending Regulation (EC) 70/2001 as regards the extension of its scope to include aid for research and development [2004] OJ L63/22. While the basic level of intensity for industrial and pre-competitive development has been lowered, the revised bonus system will raise the maximum level of eligible investment for certain types of projects.

49 ibid, Article 31(4)(b).

50 ibid, Article 31(6).

Aid for technical feasibility studies. The GBER exemption also covers contributions to the cost of technical feasibility studies that are preparatory either to industrial research or experimental development activities.[51] In the case of SMEs, the exemption applies to up to 75% of the cost of studies preparatory to industrial research activities, and up to 50% of studies preparatory to experimental development activity. In the case of large enterprises the permissible aid intensities are 65% and 40% respectively. **8.25**

Aid for industrial property rights costs for SMEs. One of the difficulties faced by SMEs is gaining access to patents and other industrial property rights to use in advancing their business. The cost for example of obtaining and validating such rights is often prohibitive for a small business. Under the GBER, the subsidization of costs related to the acquisition of industrial property rights may be exempted at the same level of aid intensity as would be permitted for the type of project aid that led to the industrial property rights concerned.[52] Eligible costs include those related to the application for a grant of the right in the first jurisdiction, the costs of translation and other requirements related to seeking validation in subsequent jurisdictions, and the costs of defending the validation of the right during the application stage (including costs relating to defending opposition proceedings).[53] **8.26**

R&D in the agricultural sector. Prior to the adoption of the GBER, aid for R&D activities in the primary agricultural sector[54] could be individually approved by the Commission, but did not benefit from automatic exemption. However, on the basis of its experience with analysing notified cases, the Commission decided that the GBER should cover aid for R&D in this sector where it is carried out by a research institution. Under Article 34 of the GBER, aid given to a research institution for R&D concerning products listed in Annex I of the Treaty is exempt from notification if four conditions are met. First, the R&D must be of general interest. Secondly, prior notice of the proposed research project is published on the internet indicating the likely timing of results. Thirdly, the results of the research must be made available on the internet for five years, and must be published there as soon as they are provided to any specific organization. Finally, the aid must be granted directly to the research institution, and must not involve the grant of non-research aid to a company producing, processing or marketing agricultural products, or provide price support for the producers of such products. Where these conditions are met, aid of up to 100% of eligible costs[55] may be provided. Where these conditions are not met (for example where the aid is granted to private undertakings), the **8.27**

---

[51] ibid, Article 32.
[52] ibid, Article 33(2).
[53] ibid, Article 33(3).
[54] ie for products listed in Annex I to the EC Treaty.
[55] Eligible costs are the same as for general R&D projects as set out in GBER Article 31(5).

aid may still benefit from the block exemption if it complies with the general provisions governing R&D for project aid, aid for technical feasibility studies or aid for industrial property rights costs for SMEs.[56]

8.28 **Aid for young innovative enterprises.** Start-up companies in particular face hurdles in funding innovative research. As part of its strategy to overcome these difficulties, aid to young innovative enterprises benefits from a specific exemption under Article 35 of the GBER. To benefit from the exemption, the enterprise must have been established for no longer than six years at the date of the grant and its R&D activities must represent at least 15% of its total operating expenses in at least one of the three preceding years (or in the last fiscal period in the case of a start-up company). Where these conditions are met the enterprise may be eligible for aid of up to a threshold of €1 million. This may be exceeded in the case of companies based in areas designated for regional development.[57] A company can only receive this type of aid once during the period in which it is eligible.[58]

8.29 **Aid for innovation advisory services and support services.** Financial assistance may be granted to innovative enterprises to cover the cost of innovation advisory and innovation support services, provided that the aid is designed to assist the recipients of the services and does not provide an unfair commercial advantage to the providers. The provisions reflect those under the R&D&I Framework[59] and reflect the Commission's experience with cases notified under its provisions. To benefit from such aid the enterprise must be an SME and the aid must not exceed more than €200,000 per beneficiary within any three-year period. Innovative advisory and support services must be purchased at market price (or in the case of a not-for-profit entity, a price which reflects its full costs plus a reasonable margin). For the recipient to be able to use the aid to cover all eligible costs, the service provider must have national or European certification. Otherwise the aid may only cover up to 75% of the costs.[60] In the case of innovation advisory services, the costs which will be treated as eligible include management consulting, technological assistance, technology transfer services, training, consultancy for acquisition, protection and trade in intellectual property rights and licensing agreements and consultancy in the use of standards.[61] For innovation support services, eligible costs include office space, data banks, technical libraries, market research, laboratory use, quality labelling, testing and certification.[62]

---

56 ibid, Article 34(7).

57 ibid, Article 35(4), setting thresholds of €1.5 million for enterprises in Article 87(3)(a) regions and €1.25 million for those in Article 87(3)(c) regions.

58 ibid, Article 35(5).

59 R&D&I Framework, section 5.6.

60 GBER Article 36(4).

61 ibid, Article 36(6)(a).

62 ibid, Article 36(6)(b).

Aid for the loan of highly qualified personnel. Another area of aid that is now eligible for exemption from notification under the GBER is aid to cover some of the costs of seconding expert staff from a research institution or a large company to provide specialist R&D&I support.[63] This type of aid is only available for SMEs. The seconded personnel must not be simply employed as a replacement to other personnel but be employed to occupy a specially created position within the SME to work on R&D&I activities. The seconded employee must have been employed for at least two years with the research institute or enterprise from which he or she is seconded. Eligible costs include all employment costs[64] including any costs for using a recruitment agency and any mobility allowance for the seconded personnel. The maximum aid intensity is 50% of eligible costs for a maximum of three years for each seconded person. **8.30**

D. Authorization under Article 87(3)

1. General principles

Scope. The R&D&I Framework sets out the circumstances in which the Commission will approve aid for R&D&I that does not fall within the ambit of the GBER. The Framework applies to aid to support R&D&I in all sectors governed by the EC Treaty, including sectors subject to specific rules on State aid, unless those rules provide otherwise.[65] Where the measure is being used to fund 'an important project of common European interest' then approval might also be granted under Article 87(3)(b). In practice, however, this provision is less frequently relied upon. Instead, the main provision under the EC Treaty under which State aid for R&D&I can be approved under the Framework is Article 87(3)(c). **8.31**

Balancing test. Generally the Commission takes a positive view of State aid for R&D&I, but will not approve financial support that unduly distorts competition. The R&D&I Framework sets out the criteria under which notified aid is assessed. A central feature of the assessment of aid under the Framework is the application of the 'balancing test' established in the Commission's State Aid Action Plan.[66] This test is designed to weigh the negative effects on competition **8.32**

---

[63] ibid, Article 37. This provision closely follows section 5.7 of the R&D&I Framework and reflects the Commission's experience with cases notified under those provisions.

[64] However, it does not cover consultancy costs covered by GBER Article 26.

[65] R&D&I Framework, section 2.1, which notes for example that special rules exist governing the compatibility of State aid to R&D in the sector of transport by rail, road and inland waterway.

[66] State Aid Action Plan – Less and better targeted State aid: a roadmap for State aid reform 2005-2009, COM(2005) 107 final, paras 11 and 20.

and trade against the positive objectives in the common interest.[67] The first limb examines whether the objective of the aid is in the common interest. The second limb involves assessment of how the aid is designed to deliver that objective, having regard to the appropriateness of the State aid, the incentive effect and the proportionality of the measure. Finally, the third limb examines whether the distortions of competition and trade are limited so that the overall balance is positive. The application of these considerations in the field of R&D&I is considered in more detail in the following paragraphs.

8.33 **Common interest.** The R&D&I Framework addresses the objective of common interest of promoting R&D&I. In this respect, there is a focus on whether there is some form of 'market failure' resulting in a reluctance or inability to invest. Examples include the existence of positive externalities and knowledge spillovers, imperfect and asymmetric information, and difficulties in coordinating R&D and finding adequate partners.[68] It is recognized at the EU level that the incentives to innovate for SMEs may be even lower, since in general they have fewer resources to invest or to protect their innovation (eg through patents).[69]

8.34 **Appropriate instrument.** Where a market failure in relation to R&D&I is identified, it is necessary to consider if State aid is the appropriate instrument to address the problem. Alternative instruments might include for example the introduction of a general tax measure favouring R&D&I, or increased funding for universities.[70]

8.35 **Incentive effect.** There is an increasing emphasis in the Commission's assessment policy upon the demonstration of the incentive effect and necessity of aid. Aid will therefore only be approved if it leads to a change in behaviour in the recipient.[71] This involves carrying out a counterfactual analysis, demonstrating that the aid will induce an undertaking to carry out a project that it otherwise could or would not carry out, or that the size, scope, speed or level of activity will be increased as

---

[67] R&D&I Framework, section 1.3.1; see also State Aid Action Plan, ibid, paras 11 and 20, further elaborated in the Commission's Consultation document on State aid for Innovation, COM(2005) 436 final.

[68] R&D&I Framework, section 1.3.2. For a recent example of such market failure see Decision in Case N 603/2007 *GENESIS programme* (4 June 2008).

[69] Community rules on State aid for innovation, SEC (2004) 1453 at para 4.1.

[70] R&D&I Framework, section 1.3.3.

[71] ibid, section 1.3.4. For example, in November 2007, the Commission opened the formal investigation procedure into proposed French R&D aid to Peugeot-Citroën for a hybrid diesel car on the basis that other car manufacturers had carried out similar projects without a subsidy: Decision in Case C 51/2007 *VHD programme* (13 November 2007) and press release IP/07/1679. The notification was withdrawn shortly thereafter. See also Decision in N 256/2004 *Intel Ireland – MSF (2002)* (2 March 2005) – notification withdrawn after Commission raised doubts about the incentive effect of the aid on a project by Intel to build a semiconductor plant in Ireland.

a result of the proposed State intervention.[72] It is assumed that the incentive test is not met where the potential beneficiary has begun the project before applying for aid[73] unless it has simply carried out a feasibility review. By contrast, there is a presumption that the incentive effect is met for certain aid measures, namely:

(a) project aid and feasibility studies where the aid beneficiary is an SME and the value of aid is below €7.5 million;
(b) aid for industrial property rights costs for SMEs;
(c) aid for young innovative enterprises;
(d) aid for innovation advisory services and innovation support services; and
(e) aid for the loan of highly qualified personnel.[74]

In other situations, the Commission will require evidence of how the planned aid will induce an increase in R&D&I activity.[75] The Commission may also take into account, in assessing the likely incentive effect of the aid, the form of the aid provided (eg direct subsidy, repayable loan, tax reduction or guarantee).[76]

Proportionality. The aid measure must be proportionate to the market failure it is intended to compensate, in the sense that there must be no less distortive means of achieving that result. It must therefore be demonstrated that the level and intensity of aid is limited to the minimum for the required R&D&I activity to be achieved.[77] In a situation where there are a number of potential candidates for carrying out an activity, there is a presumption that the proportionality test will be met if the project has been allocated on the basis of an open, transparent and non-discriminatory selection procedure.[78] **8.36**

Distortion of competition and trade. When considering what the impact on competition is likely to be, the Commission takes into account competition at two levels: (1) competition in the innovation process; and (2) the impact on the product market where the results of the R&D&I activities are exploited.[79] The main concern with granting R&D&I to undertakings is the potential effect it might have on the incentive of competitors to make their own investment plans ('crowding out effect'). Factors which will be taken into account in making this **8.37**

---

72 R&D&I Framework, section 1.3.4 and Chapter 6. See eg Decision in Case N 674/2006 *R&D NeoVal* (21 February 2007), and cf Decision in Case C 9/2007 *Large R&D aid to ITP – Trent 1000* [2007] OJ C108/18 (doubts raised by the Commission as to the incentive effect of the aid).

73 ibid, section 6; and see Decision 98/251/EC *Hoffmann-La Roche* [1998] OJ L103/28, section II(B)(c).

74 ibid, section 6.

75 ibid, section 6.

76 See Commission's *Consultation Document on State aid for Innovation* COM(2005) 436 final, para 20.

77 R&D&I Framework, section 1.3.5

78 ibid, section 7.3.4.

79 ibid, section 7.4.

assessment include the level of aid, the closeness of the activity to the market, whether the aid is granted through an open selection process on the basis of objective and non-discriminatory criteria, the extent of market exit barriers, the impact on incentives to compete for a future market, product differentiation and the intensity of competition.[80] A further concern is whether the aid may strengthen the market power of a beneficiary. Where a beneficiary has a market share of below 25%, there is a general presumption that it is unlikely to raise competition concerns. Above that level, the Commission carries out an analysis of the market taking into account, for instance, the relative market power of the beneficiary and the degree of concentration in the market, market entry barriers, the strength or otherwise of buyer power and whether the aid measure gives undertakings with a strong market position the ability to influence the selection process.[81] The Commission is also reluctant to approve aid that will support inefficient markets, such as those already characterized by overcapacity, unless the objective of the aid is to transform the growth dynamics of that industry by introducing new technologies.[82]

8.38 **Implementing the balancing test.** The R&D&I Framework contains detailed provisions intended to implement the balancing test.[83] A small category of cases may benefit from approval under Article 87(3)(b) EC. These are considered in Chapter 4 of the Framework (see section 2 below). Most R&D&I projects notified to the Commission are, however, likely to be assessed in relation to their compatibility with the provisions of Article 87(3)(c) EC. In that respect, where certain conditions are met, there will be a presumption that the measure is compatible. These cases are discussed in Chapter 5 of the Framework, which sets out specific conditions, parameters and intensities depending on the nature of the measures (section 3 below). In other instances, where aid is deemed to entail a high risk of distortion of competition, the Commission will carry out a more detailed analysis of the factual background to inform its final decision on compatibility. This analysis is addressed in Chapters 6 and 7 of the Framework (section 4 below).

2. Compatibility under Article 87(3)(b)

8.39 **Compatibility criteria.** Article 87(3)(b) may apply to cases involving important projects of common European interest.[84] Under Chapter 4 of the R&D&I Framework, the Commission sets out four conditions for approval for aid for these types of projects in the R&D&I context. First, the project (or group of projects) must be clearly defined in terms of its participants and objectives.

80 ibid, section 7.4.1.
81 ibid, section 7.4.2.
82 ibid, section 7.4.3.
83 The different types of case are summarized at section 1.4 of the Framework.
84 See paras 3.51–3.53 above.

Secondly, it must relate to a clear and identifiable European objective of interest. The common European interest must be demonstrated in concrete terms, for instance by showing that the project enables progress to be made in meeting a particular Community objective. The benefits should not be limited to the industry directly concerned, but must have wider relevance and application to the EU economy.[85] Thirdly, the aid must be necessary to achieve the objectives and provide an incentive to the parties to execute the project. This means that the types of projects that are eligible are ones involving a high level of risk. Finally, the importance of the project will be assessed in terms of its character and size. The Commission will also consider projects in a more positive light where the beneficiaries make their own significant contribution to the project and/or where the project involves undertakings or research from a significant number of Member States.

3. Presumption of compatibility under Article 87(3)(c)

Aid categories. Chapter 5 of the R&D&I Framework sets out eight types of measures that benefit from a presumption of eligibility for exemption under Article 87(3)(c), provided that specified conditions are met, including in particular permitted aid intensities and/or thresholds: **8.40**

(1) aid for R&D projects;
(2) aid for technical feasibility studies preparatory to industrial research or experimental development activities;
(3) aid for industrial property rights costs for SMEs;
(4) aid for young innovative enterprises;
(5) aid for process and organizational innovation in services;
(6) aid for innovation advisory services and for innovation support services for SMEs;
(7) aid for the loan of highly qualified personnel to SMEs; and
(8) aid for innovation clusters.

(1) Aid for R&D projects: aid intensities. R&D projects are classified in the same way as in the GBER, into fundamental research, industrial research and experimental development.[86] The basic level of aid intensity for each beneficiary of aid is 100% for fundamental research, 50% for industrial research and 25% for experimental development.[87] In the case of industrial research and experimental **8.41**

[85] eg Decisions in Cases N 837/2000 *Medea plus* (13 Febuary 2001); N 478/2003 *Medea plus (T 207)* (19 May 2004); N 116/2003 *Lithography methods for nanoelectronic components* (29 October 2003); N 207/2002 *Medea plus (A 302)* (30 October 2002); and N 62/2003 *Medea plus (T 206)* (17 September 2003); cf Decision in 2001/780/EC *Iveco* [2001] OJ L292/58, para 20—Article 87(3)(b) exemption refused on grounds that project not of common European interest.

[86] See para 8.23 above.

[87] R&D&I Framework, section 5.1.2.

development the level of aid may be increased by 10% for medium-sized enterprises, by 20% for small enterprises, and by 15% for certain forms of collaborative research where the relevant conditions are met, up to a maximum aid intensity of 80%.[88] The Commission will in certain circumstances, permit higher levels of aid intensity where it can be demonstrated that competitors located outside the EU have, or will receive, a similar level of aid for similar projects.[89] This is known as 'aid matching' and it is intended to help EU companies face international competition.

8.42 **Eligible costs.** The aid intensity for an R&D project is calculated on the basis of the eligible costs. These include the costs of personnel employed on the research project, the costs of instruments and equipment for the period in which they are used in the project, the costs of building of land used during the project, the cost of any contractual research, technical knowledge and patents acquired, the cost of any consultancy services used exclusively for the purposes of the research and any other overheads or operating expenses (such as materials and supplies) which are directly incurred as a result of the research activity.[90]

8.43 **Form of aid.** In some instances (particularly in the aeronautical sector),[91] financial assistance for a research project is provided in the form of a repayable advance, dependent on the success of the project. In such cases, an assessment must be made as to whether the loan constitutes aid. Where it does, it will require notification. Where it is possible to design the scheme in such a way that that it is possible to calculate the gross grant equivalent of the aid and where that aid fulfils the conditions for investment aid then it can be approved up to the level of intensity permissible for other types of R&D&I investment. In other cases, the Commission will assess the aid in accordance with the provisions set out in section 5.1.5 of the R&D&I Framework. In doing so, it will examine the basis on which the Member State will determine the successful outcome of the research activities and the provisions under which the loan is to be repaid. Fiscal measures are also used to encourage greater investment by companies in R&D&I.[92] The Commission will assess the incentive effect of such schemes on the basis of evaluation studies. The aid intensity of such schemes will be calculated either on the basis of individual projects or, at the level of an undertaking, as the ratio between the overall tax relief and the sum of all eligible R&D&I costs incurred in a period not exceeding three consecutive fiscal years.[93]

---

[88] ibid, section 5.1.3.
[89] ibid, section 5.1.7.
[90] ibid, section 5.1.4.
[91] eg Decision in Case N 101/2008 *R&D aid in the aeronautic sector* (1 July 2008).
[92] eg Decisions in Cases N 33/2007 *R&D tax credits for SMEs* (30 May 2008); N 34/2007 *Vaccine research relief* (30 May 2008); and N 816/2006 *R&D tax credits for SMEs* (30 May 2008).
[93] R&D&I Framework section 5.1.6.

(2) **Technical feasibility studies.** Aid for technical feasibility studies will be authorized where the aid intensity does not exceed 75% for studies preparatory to industrial research, and 50% for preparatory to experimental development studies in the case of SMEs. For large undertakings, the permitted aid intensities are 10 percentage points lower, ie 65% for studies preparatory to industrial research and 40% for preparatory to experimental development studies.[94] **8.44**

(3) **Industrial property rights costs for SMEs.** SMEs may receive aid to cover the cost of obtaining and validating patents and other industrial property rights up to the same level of aid as would have qualified as R&D aid for research activities leading to the industrial property rights concerned.[95] Eligible costs that can be covered are those associated with obtaining the grant of the right in the first jurisdiction, translation and other costs incurred to validate the right in other legal jurisdictions and the cost of defending the validity of the right.[96] **8.45**

(4) **Young innovative enterprises.** Where a small enterprise has been in existence for less than six years at the time aid is granted, it may benefit from aid of up to €1 million[97] where the aid is to assist with innovation.[98] To be authorized, either (i) it must be demonstrated on the basis of an expert's evaluation that the beneficiary will be able to develop products, services or processes that are technologically new or substantially improved compared to the state of the art in the industry in the Community, and which carry a risk of technological or industrial failure; or (ii) the beneficiary's R&D expenses must represent at least 15% of its total operating expenses in at least one of the three years prior to the grant of the aid or, in the case of a start-up company, during its current year.[99] In practice, many such schemes will now be exempt from notification under the GBER.[100] **8.46**

(5) **Process and organizational innovation in services.** Where certain conditions are met, aid for process and organizational innovation in services will be authorized[101] up to the following levels of intensity: (i) 15% for large enterprises; (ii) 25% for medium enterprises; and (iii) 35% for small enterprises. However, large enterprises are only eligible where they are collaborating with SMEs and where **8.47**

94 ibid, section 5.2.

95 See eg Decision in Case N 278/2007 *Promotion of patent protection for small enterprises* (23 August 2007).

96 R&D&I Framework, section 5.3.

97 This may be increased to €1.5 million in regions eligible for derogation under Article 87(3)(a)EC and up to €1.25 million in regions eligible for the derogation in Article 87(3)(c)EC. R&D&I Framework, section 5.4.

98 eg Decisions in Cases N 15/2008 *NESTA YIE* (20 May 2008); and N 512/2006 *Guidelines for promotion of young innovative enterprises* (29 May 2007).

99 R&D&I Framework, section 5.4.

100 GBER, Article 35.

101 See eg Decision in Case N 100/2007 *Lower Austria economic and tourism fund for supporting R&D&I* (15 November 2007).

the collaborating SMEs incur at least 30% of the eligible costs. Organizational innovation must relate to the use and exploration of informational and communication technologies to bring about changes in the organization, and the innovation must be run as a project under a qualified project manager. The result of the aided project must be the development of a standard, business model, methodology or concept that can be systematically reproduced, or possibly either certified or patented. The process or organizational innovation must be novel or substantially improved compared with the state of the art of the industry and the project must entail a clear degree of risk, for instance in terms of cost or probability of failure.[102]

8.48 (6) **Innovation advisory services and support services.** The objective of this type of measure is to enable an SME to purchase the advisory and support systems it requires to assist it with innovation.[103] Large companies are not eligible. For the measure to be authorized, the aid must not exceed a maximum of €200,000 per beneficiary within any three-year period (though it may be cumulated with *de minimis* aid in respect of different eligible expenses).[104] To avoid the risk of unqualified advisers taking advantage of the measure, the rules require that either the service providers must be certified, or the level of aid provided must be limited to 75% of eligible costs. The SME must use the aid to buy services at a market price, or (where the provider is a not-for-profit organization) at a price representing the full cost and a reasonable margin. Advisory service costs that may be covered include those for management consulting, technological assistance, technology transfer services,[105] consultancy relating to acquiring and protecting intellectual property rights and licensing agreements and consultancy on the use of standards. Innovation support may include the cost of office space, data banks, technical libraries, market research, laboratory use, quality labelling, testing and certification.[106] As discussed in section C above, in many cases such schemes will now benefit from exemption from notification under the GBER.[107]

8.49 (7) **Loan of highly qualified personnel.** SMEs may also receive aid to cover the cost of employing experienced[108] and highly qualified personnel seconded from

[102] R&D&I Framework, section 5.5.

[103] eg Decisions in Cases N 836/2006 *Mittelstandsfonds Schleswig-Holstein* (11 January 2008); N 613/2007 *Innovation advisory and support* (23 January 2008); and N 308/2007 *SME aid for innovation advisory and support services* (4 December 2007).

[104] R&D&I Framework, n 37.

[105] For an example of an earlier case approved directly under Article 87(3)(c), see Decision in Case N 558/2001 *Technology transfer in Saxony* (30 April 2002).

[106] R&D&I Framework, section 5.6.

[107] GBER, Article 36.

[108] The seconded individual must have been employed for at least two years in the research organization or large enterprise: R&D&I Framework, section 5.7. However, the Commission has approved as employment aid schemes for the employment of highly qualified graduates for R&D

a research organization or large enterprise to be employed in a newly created position, working on R&D&I activities within a SME.[109] The purpose of such aid is to facilitate access to highly qualified and skilled personnel who might be otherwise be difficult or too expensive for SMEs to employ directly for a specific project. The maximum aid intensity permissible is 50% of the personnel costs, for a maximum of three years per undertaking and per employee on secondment.[110] In many cases such aid will now benefit from exemption under the GBER.[111]

(8) **Aid for innovation clusters.** Innovation clusters are groupings of independent undertakings (innovative start-ups, SMEs, large undertakings and research organizations) operating in a particular sector and region, and designed to stimulate innovation activity by promoting intensive interaction, sharing offices and facilities, and exchanging expertise. Under the R&D&I Framework, aid may be granted to a legal entity that is responsible for the establishment, expansion, operation and management of that innovation cluster. Investment aid for facilities for training and research, open-access research infrastructure (including laboratory and testing facilities) and broadband network infrastructures is permitted up to an intensity of 15%, though a higher level of intensity is permitted in development aid regions falling under Article 87(3)(a) or 87(3)(c), or where the innovation cluster manager is an SME.[112] Operating aid for 'cluster animation' is granted to the cost of such functions as marketing for participation in the cluster, the management of open-access facilities, and the organization of training programmes, workshops and conferences. Aid to cover these costs may be granted for a limited duration of no more than five years. The permitted aid intensity, where the aid is digressive, may be as high as 100% in the first year but must have fallen progressively to zero by the end of the fifth year. Where the aid is not digressive, its intensity may not exceed 50% and may be granted for five years. Where the Member State provides convincing evidence to justify it, aid for cluster animation may be authorized for a longer period of time, not exceeding 10 years.[113] **8.50**

posts eg Decision in Case N 501/2003 *Programme for employment of innovation assistants in Berlin* (23 March 2004).

[109] eg researchers, engineers, designers and marketing managers. See Decision in Case N 473/2005 *PPARC Industry programme support scheme* (17 November 2005).

[110] R&D&I Framework, section 5.7.

[111] GBER, Article 37.

[112] ie groupings of independent undertakings such as innovative start-up companies, businesses and research organizations operating in a particular sector and region and designed to stimulate innovation through intensive interaction and sharing of facilities, knowledge and expertise. See eg Decisions in Cases N 336/2007 *Innovation clusters* (24 September 2007); N 519/2003 *Saxony–Anhalt scheme for future technologies* (13 May 2004); N 525/2001 *Cluster incubator scheme* (30 January 2002); and N 128/2000 *ÖAW, IMBA/IMP, Boehringer* (26 July 2000).

[113] R&D&I Framework, section 5.8.

4. Detailed assessment procedure

8.51 **Aid subject to a detailed assessment.** In all cases where the level of aid exceeds certain value thresholds, the Commission will carry out a more detailed assessment to ensure that the benefits in terms of additional R&D&I outweigh any harm on competition or trade. The Commission has indicated that the level of assessment will nevertheless be proportionate to the potential for distortion of the market. The fact that a case is subject to more detailed assessment therefore does not automatically imply that the Commission will open a formal investigation procedure, though in some cases this may be necessary.[114]

8.52 **Cases subject to detailed assessment.** The categories of case subject to a more detailed assessment include all those required to be individually notified to the Commission under Article 6(1)(e) of the GBER,[115] and measures covered by the R&D&I Framework where the value of the aid for projects and feasibility studies exceeds the following limits:[116]

(a) €20 million per undertaking, per project/feasibility study for fundamental research;
(b) €10 million per undertaking, per project/feasibility study for industrial research;
(c) €7.5 million per undertaking, per project/feasibility study for all other projects;
(d) €5 million per project, per undertaking for process or organisational innovation in service activity; and
(e) €5 million for innovation clusters.[117]

8.53 **Balancing test.** As described in Chapter 7 of the R&D&I Framework, the detailed assessment is carried out on the basis of the balancing test described above,[118] under which the Commission will weigh the extent to which the measure induces an undertaking to pursue R&D&I activities which it would not otherwise be in a position to carry out (or at least not to the same extent) against the potential for distortion of competition and limitation on cross-border trade.[119] In particular, in this assessment, the Commission will take into account the provisions set out in Chapter 6 of the Framework on the assessment of the necessity and incentive effect of the aid.

---

[114] ibid, section 7.1.

[115] See para 8.20 above.

[116] The threshold is twice the value in the case of EUREKA projects: see R&D&I Framework, section 7.1, n 42.

[117] ibid, section 7.1.

[118] See paras 8.32–8.37 above.

[119] R&D&I Framework, section 7.1.

5. Cumulation and reporting

Cumulation. The aid ceilings under the R&D&I Framework apply to aid granted entirely from the resources of Member States, as well as aid that is partly funded by the Community, except where specific rules apply under the EU's Research and Technology Development Framework programmes. Where the costs of a project are eligible for exemption under a regime other than the R&D&I Framework, the most favourable threshold applies to those common costs.[120] Aid for R&D&I cannot be cumulated with *de minimis* support for the same eligible expenses.[121] **8.54**

Reporting and monitoring. Member States are required to submit annual reports to the Commission on aid.[122] Beyond those requirements, for each approved R&D&I measure, information is required concerning the name of all beneficiaries, the amount of aid given per beneficiary, the aid intensity and the sector in which the assisted project is undertaken.[123] In addition, Member States will be required to demonstrate and explain how the incentive effect was verified before granting aid to a large undertaking under an approved scheme. In the case of fiscal aid, a list of beneficiaries receiving tax relief of over €200,000 must be submitted. In the case of innovation clusters, the report must describe how aid has attracted R&D&I activity.[124] There is also a reporting obligation in relation to cases not subject to individual notification (eg where it is part of an approved scheme) but where the level of aid is over €3 million. An information sheet must be completed and be submitted within 20 working days from the grant of the aid. Detailed records of aid for all R&D&I measures must be maintained for ten years.[125] **8.55**

[120] The limitation does not apply to aid granted in accordance with the Community guidelines on State aid to promote risk capital investments in small and medium-sized enterprises [2006] OJ C194/2: see further Chapter 9 below.

[121] R&D&I Framework, section 8.

[122] See para 16.127 below.

[123] R&D&I Framework, section 10.1.1.

[124] ibid, section 10.1.1. A supplementary information sheet is required for reports on individual aid: see Annex 1, Part III.6.b. of Commission Regulation 794/2004 ('Implementing Regulation') [2004] OJ L140/1, as amended.

[125] R&D&I Framework, section 10.1.3.

9

RISK CAPITAL

Main legislation and guidelines

Commission Regulation (EC) 800/2008 on the application of Articles 87 and 88 of the Treaty declaring certain categories of aid compatible with the common market (General Block Exemption Regulation) ('GBER') [2008] OJ L214/3

Community guidelines on state aid to promote risk capital investments in small and medium-sized enterprises ('Risk Capital Guidelines') [2006] OJ C194/2

A. Introduction

Definition of risk capital. The Commission defines risk capital as the provision of equity or quasi-equity finance to companies in their start-up and development phases.[1] It covers investments by individual investors or investment funds providing seed, start-up or expansion capital to new or young businesses with growth potential. It typically carries a higher investment risk, because of the nature of the businesses, but with the prospect of higher returns from the equity invested. The Commission's Risk Capital Guidelines provide a similar definition of risk capital: **9.01**

> Equity and quasi-equity financing to companies during their early-growth stages (seed, start-up and expansion phases) including informal investment by business

[1] Risk capital: a key to job creation in the European Union, SEC(1998) 552 final.

angels, venture capital, and alternative stock markets specialised in SMEs including high growth companies.[2]

For these purposes the term risk capital is not used to describe other types of investments, such as ad hoc capital injections into individual companies, which are subject to separate considerations.

9.02 **Risk capital and the Lisbon Strategy.** The Commission seeks to encourage the availability of risk capital to business start-ups and SMEs. It is acknowledged that there is a market failure—a so-called 'equity gap'—in meeting demand for capital to set up and expand new businesses, particularly innovative, high-tech enterprises.[3] Conventional sources of funding are less likely to be available because of the risk profile of the investees, the fact that they often have no track record of activity, and also the fact that the transaction costs in making the investment may outweigh the size of the investment. The Commission considers that these types of companies offer a potential for growth and job creation, and should not become over-reliant on debt finance alone. The Commission adopted a Risk Capital Action Plan in 1998,[4] setting out proposals for the development of risk capital markets to stimulate job creation. The Lisbon European Council in 2002 established the growth of risk capital as a Community objective, and set 2003 as the date for implementation of the Risk Capital Action Plan. State aid policy is one of a variety of initiatives which aim to stimulate the provision of risk capital to this sector.[5] The Commission recognizes the role that public funds may play in stimulating the provision of equity finance and improving access to finance to meet the needs of new and innovative businesses. State aid can therefore be justified as a tool to leverage private capital and address the funding gap for these types of enterprises.

9.03 **2001 Communication.** In 2001, the Commission published its Communication on State Aid and Risk Capital[6] which dealt with the application of Article 87(1) to risk capital measures, and set out guidelines for the authorization of measures under Article 87(3). The Communication acknowledged that there is 'a role for public funding of risk capital measures limited to addressing identifiable market failures'.[7] It established basic principles to identify the existence of aid within the

---

[2] Community guidelines on state aid to promote risk capital investments in small and medium-sized enterprises ('Risk Capital Guidelines') [2006] OJ C194/2, para 2.2(k).

[3] Communication to the Spring European Council, COM(2005) 24.

[4] Risk capital: a key to job creation in the European Union, SEC(1998) 552 final. See also Progress Report on the Risk Capital Action Plan, COM(2000) 658.

[5] Other initiatives include the High Growth and Innovative SME Facility under the Competitiveness and Innovation Programme: see Proposal for a Decision of the European Parliament and of the Council establishing a Competitiveness and Innovation Framework Programme (2007–2013), COM (2005) 121 final.

[6] [2001] OJ C235/3.

[7] ibid, para I.7.

meaning of Article 87(1) to investors, to the investment fund carrying out the investment, and to the investee company. It also discussed the circumstances when aid will be considered compatible with the common market. At that time, risk capital measures which potentially provided aid either to commercial co-investors or to SMEs could not be authorized on the basis of any existing policy instruments. Existing rules only provided for State aid linked to certain types of expenditure (eg fixed investments, R&D and training) rather than the financing of working capital for a new start-up or growing business. The Communication provided for the first time a basis for authorization provided that there was evidence of market failure[8] or a market gap which required State intervention. Aid could therefore be justified where it was proportionate to the presumed market failure and where any distortion of competition was minimized.[9]

2006 Guidelines. The Commission's State Aid Action Plan[10] referred to the need to facilitate start-up enterprises and announced a review of the Communication on State Aid and Risk Capital. The issue of risk capital financing was also considered in a 2006 Communication on financing SME growth.[11] In August 2006 the Commission adopted the Risk Capital Guidelines, which replaced the 2001 Communication.[12] The Guidelines apply until 31 December 2013, and set out in detail the circumstances in which aid may be present in risk capital measures, as well as the conditions for authorization where aid does arise. **9.04**

The GBER. In addition to the Risk Capital Guidelines, the new General Block Exemption Regulation came into force on 29 August 2008 and is due to last until 31 December 2013.[13] It contains provisions exempting aid in the form of risk capital schemes in favour of SMEs, provided that certain conditions are satisfied. **9.05**

Methodology for the assessment of aid for risk capital. The GBER, together with the Risk Capital Guidelines, establishes the following methodology for the assessment of aid for risk capital investments. **9.06**

[8] Defined in para XI.2 of the Communication as 'a situation in which economic efficiency is not achieved owing to imperfections in the market mechanism. A market failure may manifest itself either in the inability of the system to produce goods which are wanted (in this case a risk capital market) or by a mis-allocation of resources which could be improved in such a way that some consumers would be better off and not worse off'.

[9] ibid, para VI.6.

[10] State Aid Action Plan – Less and better targeted state aid: a roadmap for state aid reform 2005-2009, COM(2005) 107 final.

[11] Financing SME Growth – Adding European Value, COM(2006) 349 final.

[12] Risk Capital Guidelines, section 2.1.

[13] Commission Regulation (EC) 800/2008 on the application of Articles 87 and 88 of the Treaty declaring certain categories of aid compatible with the common market (General Block Exemption Regulation) ('GBER') [2008] OJ L214/3.

(a) A number of measures to promote risk capital do not constitute State aid. The existence of aid is addressed in the Risk Capital Guidelines and considered in section B below.

(b) Where there is aid, the GBER enables risk capital aid schemes in favour of SMEs that comply with certain substantive and procedural requirements to be implemented without prior notification and approval. The scope of the GBER is discussed in detail in section C below.

(c) Risk capital aid measures not eligible under the GBER may still be individually approved by the Commission under the conditions set out in the Risk Capital Guidelines. These conditions are discussed in detail in section D below.

B. Existence of aid

9.07 **General principles.** Risk capital support constitutes State aid insofar as it provides a financial advantage to undertakings. This may take a number of different forms, including the State's participation in investment funds, guarantees to risk capital investors, or fiscal incentives to funds or their managers to undertake investments. The provision of risk capital is normally a commercial activity undertaken by private investors such as venture capital funds, investment funds or 'business angels'[14] investing in higher risk start-ups which provide the potential for higher financial returns. Public funding may therefore take the place of commercial funding, potentially displacing private capital (the so-called 'crowding-out' of private investors).

9.08 **Levels at which State aid may arise.** It is generally considered that there is a risk of State aid arising in risk capital transactions at three levels: (1) private investors investing in funds or co-funding the investment; (2) the intermediary investment vehicle or investment fund through which the funding is made; and (3) the target enterprises receiving the funding. The Risk Capital Guidelines consider the application of Article 87(1) at each of these levels of the transaction.[15] While the Guidelines deal specifically with risk capital investments in SMEs, the principles set out in relation to the identification of aid are not restricted to SMEs, and are equally applicable to other types of risk capital measures.

9.09 **Investors.** State risk capital funding for SMEs will often be provided alongside private funding. In this case, there may be State aid to the investor if the State measure allows private investors to invest on terms more favourable than those applying to public investors, or on terms more favourable than would have applied

---

14 See Risk Capital Guidelines, section 2.2(s).

15 ibid, section 3.

in the absence of public funding. However, State aid will normally not arise if the public and private investments are effected *pari passu*, ie if public and private investors share exactly the same upside and downside risks and rewards and hold the same level of subordination, and normally where at least 50% of the funding is provided by private investors which are independent of the investee company.[16] Consequently, where a public body is co-funding an equity investment alongside private investors, in order to avoid potential State aid issues at the level of co-funders, it will be necessary to ensure that the public investor is obtaining the same (or at least no worse) financial returns as the private investor in proportion to its investment, and is not accepting any higher level of risk than the private investor. It is not sufficient simply to ensure that the State attracts the *maximum* private investment for the *minimum* public subordination: any degree of subordination of the public investment involves State aid.[17] Further, if a public body does not secure at least 50% co-funding from private investors, there may be a question mark over whether private investors are genuinely investing on terms which reflect normal market economy principles.[18]

Investment funds. Many risk capital measures involve a State investment in an investment fund or investment vehicle which in turn makes an equity investment in the investee company. The general rule is that the fund is an intermediary vehicle for the transfer of aid and is not itself a beneficiary of aid.[19] This is particularly likely to be the case where a new fund is set up specifically to make investments in certain beneficiary undertakings. However, the position may be different in the case of established funds with a large and diverse base of investors, since these are more likely to be seen as independent operators on the market.[20] As in the case of investee companies, there may be aid to the fund unless the State's investment is on market economy terms. Aid may also accrue to the fund's managers where their remuneration does not reflect market norms. However there is a presumption that **9.10**

---

16 ibid, section 3.2. For examples of cases where investments were not *pari passu*, see Decision in Case N 652/2007 *Northern Ireland spin-outs* (6 May 2008); Decision in Case N 521/2007 *Clusterfunds* (21 February 2008); Decision in Case N 160/2007 *Equity guarantees* (18 October 2007). See also Decision in Case N 287/2007 *BES* (23 August 2007), in which the beneficiaries were private individuals and not undertakings.

17 *Northern Ireland spin-outs*, ibid, paras 45–7.

18 For this purpose the term 'private investor' does not include publicly-owned entities which operate commercially: see Decision in Case N 263/2007 *Technology fund TGFS, Saxony* (31 January 2008), para 86, in which the Commission rejected Germany's argument that investments by the German State-owned bank 'counted' as private investments.

19 Risk Capital Guidelines, section 3.2. See also Decision in Case C 46/2000 *Viridian Growth Fund* [2001] OJ L144/23, para 28; Decision in Case N 722/2000 *Coalfields Enterprise Fund* (20 December 2001), para 3.1.2; Decision in Case N 606/2001 *Community Development Venture Fund* (9 April 2002), para 18.2; and Decision in Case N 620/2002 *SME Venture Capital Fund* (4 February 2003), para 4.1.2.

20 See eg Decision in Case N287/2007 *BES* (23 August 2007).

State aid will not arise if the manager is chosen through an open and transparent tender process.[21] In *Clusterfunds*, the failure to appoint the manager BKG by public tender gave rise to an indication of aid at the level of the fund's management.[22]

9.11 **Investee company.** Public risk capital funding will result in State aid to the investee company unless it is on market economy terms. There is a presumption of no aid where private co-funders provide at least 50% of the funding in the company on a *pari passu* basis (see para 9.09 above), since this provides strong evidence that the investment satisfies the private investor test.[23] A further important consideration in the case of a fund is how investment decisions are made. It will be necessary to show that investments are exclusively profit-driven and linked to a reasonable business plan and projection, as well as a clear and realistic exit strategy. The fund's managers will also need an investment mandate based exclusively on commercial principles.[24]

9.12 ***De minimis* aid.** Risk capital for SMEs may by its very nature fall below the *de minimis* ceiling in Regulation 1998/2006, and the specific Agriculture and Fisheries *de minimis* Regulations.[25] However, all three Regulations provide that aid comprised in risk capital measures shall not be considered transparent *de minimis* aid unless the capital provided to each target undertaking does not exceed the *de minimis* ceiling.[26] This may be difficult to satisfy where aid is provided in the form of an equity investment, and the calculation of its value is complex. Where this difficulty can be overcome, the *de minimis* rule will be applicable.[27]

C. General Block Exemption Regulation ('GBER')

9.13 **Structure.** As described in more detail in Chapter 5 above, Chapter I of the GBER contains a set of common conditions and procedural provisions applicable to the

[21] Risk Capital Guidelines, section 3.2.

[22] Decision in Case N 521/2007 *Clusterfunds* (21 February 2008), paras 94-97. See also Decision in Case N 726b/2007 *Omnibus decentralised* (22 April 2008), para 43.

[23] See eg Decision in Case N 344/2005 *NEOTEC risk capital fund* (28 October 2005), where the Commission confirmed that the schemes involved no aid.

[24] Risk Capital Guidelines, section 3.2.

[25] Commission Regulation (EC) 1998/2006 on the application of Articles 87 and 88 of the Treaty to *de minimis* aid [2006] OJ L379/5 (see further para 2.148 above), Commission Regulation (EC) 1535/2007 on the application of Articles 87 and 88 of the Treaty to *de minimis* aid in the sector of agricultural production [2007] OJ L337/35 (see further paras 11.18–11.20 below) and Commission Regulation (EC) 875/2007 on the application of Articles 87 and 88 of the EC Treaty to *de minimis* aid in the fisheries sector and amending Regulation (EC) No 1860/2004 [2007] OJ L193/6 (see further para 11.63 below).

[26] Regulation 1998/2006, Article 2(4)(c); Regulation 1535/2007, Article 3(6)(c); and Regulation 875/2007, Article 3(7)(c).

[27] Risk Capital Guidelines, section 3.3.

various types of aid covered by the GBER. The provisions of Chapter I relevant to aid in the form of risk capital are addressed in section 1 below. Section 2 will then address the specific risk capital exemption in the GBER, as set out in Chapter II of the GBER.

1. Common and procedural provisions

Sectoral scope of risk capital exemption. The risk capital provisions of the GBER apply to almost all sectors of the economy including the primary production, processing and marketing of agricultural products listed in Annex I to the Treaty, the fishery and aquaculture sectors and the steel, shipbuilding and synthetic fibres sectors.[28] The GBER does not, however, apply to risk capital aid in the coal sector.[29] **9.14**

Common conditions. In addition to the specific provisions referred to above on the scope of the risk capital aid exemption, the GBER contains a number of general conditions common to all types of aid within its ambit. These are set out in detail in paras 5.17–5.26 above, to which reference should be made. In summary, these provisions concern: **9.15**

(a) the exclusion of all forms of aid to certain undertakings and certain sectors;
(b) the general conditions for exemption of aid schemes and individual aid granted under such schemes, as well as for ad hoc individual aid;
(c) the basis of calculation of aid intensities;
(d) the requirement to provide documentary evidence of eligible costs;
(e) the requirement for exempted aid to be transparent;[30]
(f) the conditions under which aid can be cumulated with other aid exempted under the GBER;
(g) the requirement for aid to have an incentive effect;[31] and
(h) the reporting and monitoring requirements applicable to all aid exempted under the GBER.

2. Specific risk capital exemption

Schemes. The GBER only applies to risk capital aid *schemes* in favour of SMEs.[32] A risk capital aid scheme will typically involve aid which is available to SMEs satisfying certain criteria, eg those operating within a particular sector or having **9.16**

28 These sectors remain subject to exclusions for certain other kinds of aid.

29 GBER, Article 1(3).

30 The transparency condition is specifically deemed to be satisfied in the case of risk capital aid fulfilling the conditions of Article 29: ibid, Article 5(2)(b).

31 Deemed to be satisfied in the case of any aid in the form of risk capital that satisfies the substantive conditions of Article 29: ibid, Article 8(5), para 4.

32 ibid, Article 29(1), and see Article 2(2) for definition of an 'aid scheme'.

certain investment requirements. The GBER does not cover ad hoc risk capital aid to an individual enterprise.

9.17 **Investment funds.** To fall within the exemption, the aid must be provided in the form of participation in a profit-driven private equity investment fund managed on a commercial basis.[33] This will typically arise where the State is an investor in a fund providing capital to the SMEs. The GBER will not therefore apply to other types of measure, such as guarantees or fiscal incentives to risk capital investors.

9.18 **Conditions.** A number of further conditions must be met in relation to the aid scheme, in order to benefit from the exemption.[34]

(a) The fund's investment in any one target undertaking over a period of 12 months must not exceed €1.5 million.

(b) Investments must be restricted to seed, start-up, or expansion capital in the case of SMEs in assisted areas, and in the case of small undertakings in non-assisted areas. In the case of medium-sized undertakings in non-assisted areas, the investments must be for seed or start-up capital only.

(c) 70% of the risk capital measure must be in the form of an equity or quasi-equity investment in the target undertaking, as opposed to debt instruments. 'Equity' is defined as an ownership interest represented by the issue of shares. 'Quasi-equity' is a financial instrument where the return is based predominantly on the profits or losses of the target firm and which are unsecured in the event of default.[35]

(d) The Member State must ensure that at least 50% of the funding in the investment fund—30% in the case of funds targeting exclusively SMEs in assisted areas—is provided by private equity investors selected by a public tender or open invitation to participate.

(e) The risk capital measure must be profit-driven, as evidenced by a business plan for each investment, containing details of product, sales and profitability development and establishing the *ex ante* viability of the project; and a 'clear and realistic' exit strategy for each investment. The exit strategy[36] must be based on a plan to achieve maximum returns, including trade sale, write-offs, repayment of preference shares/loans, sale to another venture capitalist, sale to a financial institute and sale by public offering (including Initial Public Offerings).

---

[33] ibid, Article 29(2).

[34] ibid, Article 29(2)–(8).

[35] ibid, Article 28(1). For quasi-equity instruments, see eg Decision in Case N 160/2007 *Equity guarantees* (18 October 2007), para 80. See also Decision in Case C 33/2007 *IBG Risk capital fund Sachsen-Anhalt* [2007] OJ C246/20 on the question whether the IBG's 'silent participations' qualified as debt or as quasi-equity.

[36] Defined in Article 28(g) of the Risk Capital Guidelines.

(f) The investment fund must be managed on a commercial basis. This requires an agreement between the fund and a professional fund manager, with managers being incentivized by linking remuneration to performance. The private equity investors must be represented in the firm's decision-making structure, eg through an investors' or advisory committee. Best practice and regulatory supervision must apply to the management of the funds.

D. Authorization under Article 87(3)

1. General principles

Risk Capital Guidelines. The Risk Capital Guidelines set out the circumstances in which the Commission will approve risk capital aid that does not fall within the ambit of the GBER. As with the GBER, the Guidelines only apply to schemes providing risk capital to SMEs, and not to ad hoc measures providing capital to an individual enterprise. Also excluded are risk capital measures for firms in difficulties and for firms in the shipbuilding, coal and steel industry, any risk capital aid to export-related activities, and aid contingent upon the use of domestic in preference to imported goods.[37] **9.19**

Standard and detailed assessment procedures. While the Risk Capital Guidelines are substantially based on the 2001 Communication, they have introduced a number of modifications to reflect the intention in the State Aid Action Plan to create a more economics-based approach and to provide increased flexibility in assessing risk capital measures. The Guidelines have thus introduced two types of assessment for risk capital measures:[38] a 'rapid' (also known as a 'standard') assessment for schemes meeting certain criteria, under which the Commission will endeavour to assess the schemes rapidly within the time limits laid down by Regulation 659/1999,[39] and a detailed assessment for all other schemes, which may involve opening the formal investigation procedure. **9.20**

Cumulation. Where risk capital measures authorized under the Guidelines are combined with aid measures provided under other State aid instruments, the relevant aid ceilings are reduced by 50% (20% for enterprises located in assisted areas) for the first three years of a first risk capital investment and up to the total **9.21**

[37] ibid, section 2.1. Note that the Commission's Communication on a temporary framework for State aid measures to support access to finance in the current financial and economic crisis, 17 December 2008, as amended on 25 February 2009 provides a temporary relaxation of this for certain risk capital measures for firms in difficulty until the end of 2010; see also para 7.16 above.

[38] ibid, section 4.1.

[39] Council Regulation (EC) 659/1999 laying down detailed rules for the application of Article 93 of the EC Treaty [1999] OJ L83/1, as amended [2006] OJ L363/1. See further Chapter 16 below.

amount received. This limitation does not however apply in the case of R&D schemes under the R&D&I Framework or the GBER.[40]

2. Standard assessment

9.22 **Type of scheme.** The criteria for a standard assessment are set out in section 4 of the Guidelines. The Risk Capital scheme may include not only State participation in investment funds, but also guarantees to investors or funds provided that the public cover for any potential losses does not exceed 50% of the nominal amount of the investment, other financial instruments (which could include debt) to provide extra capital for investment, and fiscal incentives for investors, funds or managers.[41] The Commission is prepared to accept measures focusing on specific innovative technologies or sectors, such as health, IT and biotechnology.[42]

9.23 **Conditions.** To fall within the standard assessment procedure, the scheme must satisfy a number of conditions described as 'specific safe harbour thresholds'.

(a) The total investment (including any non-aid elements) must not exceed €1.5 million per SME over a 12-month period.

(b) The investment must be restricted to the seed or start-up stage for medium-sized enterprises in non-assisted areas. For medium-sized enterprises in assisted areas, or small enterprises in general, it must be restricted to financing the seed, start-up or expansion stages.

(c) At least 70% of the total budget of the scheme must be in the form of equity and quasi-equity investment rather than debt.[43]

(d) There must be significant private sector investment: private investors must provide at least 50% of the funding (30% in the case of SMEs in assisted areas).

(e) Investment decisions must be profit-driven. This will generally be the case where there is significant participation of private investors acting on a commercial basis, a detailed business plan setting out details of product, sales and profitability development and demonstrating the *ex ante* viability of the project, and a 'clear and realistic' exit strategy for each investment.

(f) The investment must be commercially managed. This will be demonstrated where there is a professional fund manager whose remuneration is linked to performance, private investors are represented in decision-making eg through

---

40 Risk Capital Guidelines, section 6. See also Decision in Case N 625/2007 *Risk capital aid scheme* (5 May 2008), in which the risk capital scheme was modified to reflect the cumulation requirements.

41 ibid, section 4.2.

42 ibid, section 4.3.7. See eg Decision in Case N 73/2005 *East Midlands media investment* (23 January 2006), which dealt with a scheme focusing on the film and digital media sector.

43 See Risk Capital Guidelines, section 2.2 for definitions of 'equity' and 'quasi-equity' investments.

an investors' or advisory committee, and best practice and regulatory supervision apply to the management of the funds.

Overlap with GBER. To a large extent, the standard assessment under the Guidelines is now less relevant than previously, since many aid schemes previously qualifying for this procedure will now qualify for block exemption under the GBER. However, there are some differences between the two regimes. In particular, the GBER does not cover the provision of debt finance, guarantees or fiscal measures, and in these cases notification for individual authorization will still be required. **9.24**

3. Detailed assessment

Purpose of procedure. In cases not falling within section 4 of the Risk Capital Guidelines, the detailed assessment procedure in section 5 of the Guidelines will be used to determine, on a case-by-case basis, whether the risk capital measures have a sufficiently positive effect to justify Article 87(3) authorization.[44] **9.25**

Type of scheme. The first question under the detailed assessment procedure concerns the type of risk capital aid scheme. The Guidelines set out seven types of scheme that may be authorized, subject to certain conditions. **9.26**

(a) Investments exceeding €1.5 million over 12 months. These require evidence of market failure to justify the higher levels of finance. A market study assessing the extent of the equity gap over the last three to five years together with future projections must be submitted.
(b) Measures providing finance for the expansion stage for medium-sized companies in non-assisted areas. These must be supported by evidence that these firms have insufficient access to risk capital.
(c) Follow-on investments into target companies. In certain circumstances, the Commission is prepared to accept further financing rounds following an initial investment to ensure continuity of financing and to avoid dilution of the public sector participation. The amount must be consistent with the initial investment and the size of the fund.
(d) Private sector participation of less than 50% (or 30% in assisted areas). Participation below this level will only be accepted where there is evidence that there is a difficulty in identifying private investors. This is particularly likely to be the case in assisted areas, where there may be greater problems in raising capital.[45]

[44] For a recent example of the approval of risk capital aid following a detailed assessment see Decision in Case N 596a/2007 *Reduction in solidarity tax on wealth* (11 March 2008).

[45] In Decision in Case NN 81/2005 *NESTA* (20 October 2005) the Commission unusually approved initial rounds of 100% public funding into beneficiary companies. This was on the basis

(e) Provision of seed capital to small enterprises. A more favourable assessment may be made in the case of the provision of seed capital to small enterprises, given the stronger likelihood that there is of a market failure in the provision of financing to these companies at the start-up stage, and the reduced risk of 'crowding-out' and any distortions of competition. In these cases, the Commission may be prepared to countenance limited, or even no, private investment and the use of debt rather than equity or quasi-equity instruments.

(f) Measures specifically involving an investment vehicle. As stated above, the investment fund or vehicle is not generally seen as an aid beneficiary in its own right. However where it is (such as in the case of an established fund with a larger investor base) the Commission is prepared to consider authorizing aid measures involving investment vehicles where there is evidence of a market failure requiring financial incentives to the vehicle.

(g) 'Scouting costs'. The Commission will also accept grants covering up to 50% of the costs to risk capital funds in identifying SMEs, prior to the due diligence phase. The grants must encourage the funds or their managers to carry out more 'scouting' activities than would otherwise be the case, the eligible costs must be limited to the scouting costs related to SMEs mainly in their seed or start-up stage, and the costs must exclude legal and administrative costs of the funds.[46]

9.27 **Balancing test.** A detailed assessment of risk capital aid is also explicitly subject to the 'balancing test' established in the Commission's State Aid Action Plan.[47] This test is designed to weigh the negative effects on competition and trade against the positive objectives in the common interest.[48] The first limb examines whether the objective of the aid is in the common interest. The second limb involves assessment of how the aid is designed to deliver that objective, having regard to the appropriateness of the State aid, its incentive effect and the proportionality of the measure. Finally, the third limb examines whether the distortions of competition and trade are limited so that the overall balance is positive. The application of these considerations to risk capital is considered in more detail in the following paragraphs.

9.28 **Common interest.** The Commission considers that there is no general risk capital market failure in the Community. It does, however, accept that there are market

that initial subsidy was necessary at the early 'profit of concept' stage in order to attract private investment for subsequent funding.

[46] See Decision in Case N 9/2006 *Risk capital funds in favour of innovative SMEs located in Mezzogiorno* (19 July 2006) where the Commission approved scouting costs in order to 'screen' potential SME applicants.

[47] State Aid Action Plan – Less and better targeted State aid: a roadmap for State aid reform 2005–2009, COM(2005) 107 final; and see para 3.28 above.

[48] Risk Capital Guidelines, section 1.3.1.

gaps for some types of investment at certain stages of enterprises' development.[49] Under the detailed assessment procedure the Commission requires evidence of the market failure being tackled at each level where aid may be present. The evidence must be based on a study showing the level of the 'equity gap' with regard to the enterprises and sectors targeted by the risk capital measure. The Guidelines give specific examples of the types of evidence that may be submitted in this respect. Where the measures target SMEs in assisted areas, the evidence must also show the regional specificities justifying the measure envisaged. This may include specific local economic data in comparison with the situation at national or Community level, and other data showing an increased degree of market failure.[50]

Appropriate instrument. It must be demonstrated that State aid is an appropriate policy instrument to encourage private risk capital investment.[51] Other policy options should also be considered. These might include promoting a culture of entrepreneurship, introducing a more neutral taxation of the different forms of SME financing, fostering market integration and easing regulatory constraints, such as limitations on investments by certain institutions and administrative procedures for setting up companies.[52] Where the Member State has considered other policy options but established the advantages of using State aid, the measures are considered to constitute an appropriate instrument.[53] **9.29**

Incentive effect. The measure must be shown to have an incentive effect, ie result in a net increase in the availability of risk capital. There will need to be evidence that public intervention is necessary to leverage private investment, and that this would not have happened in the absence of public support.[54] The incentive effect is considered to be present for measures falling within standard assessment criteria in section 4 of the Risk Capital Guidelines. But for measures outside those criteria, which require the detailed assessment procedure, the incentive effect is less obvious. The Commission therefore takes account of a number of further criteria showing the profit-driven character of investment decisions.[55] **9.30**

(a) The investment should be managed by professional fund managers, appointed following an open tender process, with proven experience and track record in capital market investments.

49 ibid, section 1.3.2.
50 ibid, section 5.2.1.
51 In Decision in Case N 287/2007 *BES* (23 August 2007) the Commission came to the view (para 98) that the notified schemes would encourage private investment.
52 Risk Capital Guidelines, section 1.3.3.
53 ibid, section 5.2.2.
54 ibid, section 1.3.4.
55 ibid, section 5.2.3.

(b) The existence of an investment committee with experienced professionals from the private sector is also viewed positively by the Commission. The investment committee's role would be to assess investment prospects in potential investee companies. Where private investors are not directly involved in the decision-making, the Commission will require evidence that funding decisions are based on sound commercial principles.[56]

(c) The Commission also encourages larger funds which can take advantage of economies of scale and spread transaction and administrative costs over larger portfolio investments as well as diversify risk.

(d) The presence of 'business angels'[57] will also be a positive factor, to the extent that the Commission may be prepared to authorize a higher degree of subordination of state funds.

9.31 **Proportionality.** The aid must be proportionate to the market failure it is intended to compensate. In the risk capital context, aid will be regarded as inefficient (and hence disproportionate) if it goes beyond what is needed to induce more risk capital provision.[58] In order to limit the extent of aid to the minimum necessary, the Commission regards as best practice an open tender, not only for the appointment of the management company, but also to attract investors.[59] The Commission may require the fund to be publicly advertised and to invite expressions of interest from potential investors.[60]

9.32 **Distortion of competition and trade.** Against the positive effects of the aid, the Commission will balance its potential negative effects in terms of distortion of competition. In particular, aid will not be authorized if there is a risk of 'crowding-out'—ie deterring other potential investors of capital.[61] A Member State will therefore need to provide evidence regarding the existence of other funds or venture capital available in the sector concerned. A further consideration is the impact of State aid at the level of the SME beneficiaries, for example whether risk capital funding may artificially keep inefficient or uncompetitive firms in business or add to the problems of over-capacity in a particular sector. This necessitates a market study of the target firms themselves.[62]

---

56 See eg Decision in Case C 33/2007 *IBG Risk capital fund Sachsen-Anhalt* [2007] OJ C246/20.

57 Risk Capital Guidelines, section 2.2(s).

58 ibid, section 1.3.5.

59 ibid, section 5.2.4.

60 See eg Decision in Case NN 81/2005 *NESTA* (20 October 2005).

61 Risk Capital Guidelines, section 5.3.1. See eg the Commission's decision to open an investigation into a Danish scheme to provide tax relief to investors trading in alternative markets: there were concerns that the measure would regularly affect other investors or equity markets: Decision in Case C 2/2007 *Danish alternative marketplaces* (24 January 2007), press release IP/07/91. The notification was subsequently withdrawn.

62 Risk Capital Guidelines, section 5.3.2.

Conditions attached to decision. Where the Commission approves a risk capital measure, it may impose conditions in its decision pursuant to Article 7(4) of Regulation 659/1999. The Guidelines indicate that such conditions may include a limit on the investment in each target enterprise, limiting investments to particular stages or tranches, a progressive increase in the participation of private investors, a requirement for the Member State to obtain an adequate return when providing seed capital, modifications to the profit and loss sharing arrangements between the public and private sector, and/or more stringent cumulation limits than would otherwise apply.[63] **9.33**

[63] ibid, section 5.4.

10

SMALL AND MEDIUM-SIZED ENTERPRISES

Main legislation and guidelines

Commission Regulation (EC) 800/2008 on the application of Articles 87 and 88 of the Treaty declaring certain categories of State aid compatible with the common market (General Block Exemption Regulation) ('GBER') [2008] OJ L214/3

A. Introduction

Role of SMEs. Small and medium-sized enterprises play a critical role in the EU's development strategy for economic growth and social welfare. The Commission sees SMEs as crucial for the development of the common market. More specifically, SMEs are regarded as important for the development of jobs and encouraging an entrepreneurial drive throughout the EU. The promotion and nurturing of SMEs allows new and smaller businesses to be created, develop and grow, which increases the pool of competitors. Better competition drives down consumer prices, increases innovation and efficiency and adds to the long term stability of the EU. The important role of SMEs has been recognized, most recently, in the Commission's Small Business Act, published in June 2008.[1] **10.01**

State aid policy. In line with the strategic importance of SMEs, the Commission has consistently taken a favourable approach to aid to encourage the development **10.02**

[1] 'Think Small First' – A 'Small Business Act' for Europe, COM(2008) 394.

and sustainability of SMEs. In particular, aid may be approved where it addresses the market failures that are known to have a significant limiting effect on the development of SMEs.[2] SMEs usually have difficulties obtaining and securing capital for all types of expenditure. This is due to financial institutions being unwilling to accept the risk against the limited guarantees that SMEs are able to provide.[3] In addition, due to their size SMEs will have limited access to certain types of information (such as new technology and new markets). SMEs consequently enjoy a favoured status in relation to State aid. As set out below, many types of aid to SMEs are block exempted, and SMEs are also generally able to enjoy the benefit of higher levels of aid intensity than larger enterprises.

10.03 **Early guidelines on aid to SMEs.** In 1992 the Commission published its first guidelines setting out criteria for the approval of aid to SMEs.[4] The guidelines identified the advantages offered to the economy by SMEs and recognized a number of market failures that significantly hampered their development and progress. Accordingly, they set out the conditions under which aid could be approved pursuant to Article 87(3)(c). A revised version of these guidelines was published in 1996.[5] Although the revised version of the guidelines stipulated that its operation would be reviewed after it had been in force for a period of three years,[6] this was overtaken by the Commission's development of a block exemption for SMEs.

10.04 **SME block exemption.** In 2001, pursuant to the Enabling Regulation,[7] the Commission adopted a block exemption for certain types of State aid to small and medium-sized enterprises.[8] This formalized the policy that had been set out in the Commission's 1992 and 1996 guidelines. It set out clear 'safe harbours' where aid that fell within the scope of the block exemption would automatically be considered to be compatible with the common market without the need for notification to and approval of the Commission. In 2003 the Commission published a number of proposals in its Recommendation concerning the definition of micro, small

[2] See Commission Regulation (EC) 800/2008 on the application of Articles 87 and 88 of the Treaty declaring certain categories of State aid compatible with the common market (General Block Exemption Regulation) ('GBER') [2008] OJ L214/3, recitals (54)–(58).

[3] See eg comments in Case XS 29/2001 *Regional aid scheme for SMEs* [2002] OJ C58/19.

[4] Community guidelines on State aid for small and medium-sized enterprises [1992] OJ C213/2.

[5] Community guidelines on State aid for small and medium-sized enterprises [1996] OJ C213/4.

[6] ibid, para 5.4.

[7] Council Regulation (EC) 994/98 on the application of Articles 92 and 93 of the Treaty establishing the European Community to certain categories of horizontal State aid [1998] OJ L142/1; see further paras 3.34–3.35 above.

[8] Commission Regulation (EC) 70/2001 on the application of Articles 87 and 88 of the EC Treaty to State aid to small and medium-sized enterprises [2001] OJ L10/33.

and medium-sized enterprises,[9] which were directed at improving the wording and application of the block exemption. As a result, the block exemption was amended in 2004.[10] In particular, the amendments extended the scope of the block exemption to cover aid to SMEs for R&D activities. In 2006 the block exemption was amended further, to bring within its scope aid to SMEs active in the processing and marketing of agricultural products.[11]

The GBER. The SME block exemption has now been replaced by the provisions of the new General Block Exemption Regulation ('GBER'). This came into force on 29 August 2008 and is due to expire on 31 December 2013.[12] The GBER contains exemptions for categories of SME aid that are similar to the exemptions in the SME block exemption (eg investment aid, and aid for the participation at fairs). In addition, the GBER covers a number of new categories of aid to SMEs, such as aid for female entrepreneurship, and aid for the early adoption of future Community environmental standards. SMEs also generally benefit from more favourable treatment under other GBER exemptions for horizontal aid and regional aid. As with the SME block exemption, aid falling within the categories specified in the GBER may be granted without prior notification to and approval of the Commission. By way of transitional provisions, any aid granted before 31 December 2008, which does not satisfy the conditions of the GBER but does fulfil the conditions of the previous SME block exemption, is still deemed compatible with the common market and exempt from notification.[13] **10.05**

Methodology for the assessment of aid to SMEs. The GBER, together with the Commission's general rules for the approval of aid measures, establishes the following methodology for the assessment of aid for SMEs. **10.06**

(a) A number of SME support measures do not constitute State aid. These are considered in section B below.
(b) Where there is aid, the GBER enables aid to SMEs that complies with certain substantive and transparency requirements to be implemented without prior notification and approval. The scope of the GBER is discussed in detail in section C below.

---

[9] Commission Recommendation 2003/361/EC concerning the definition of micro, small and medium-sized enterprises [2003] OJ L124/36.

[10] Commission Regulation (EC) 364/2004 amending Regulation (EC) 70/2001 as regards the extension of its scope to include aid for research and development [2004] OJ L63/22; see further para 8.05 above.

[11] See Commission Regulation (EC) 1857/2006 on the application of Articles 87 and 88 of the Treaty to State aid to small and medium-sized enterprises active in the production of agricultural products and amending Regulation (EC) 70/2001, recital (26) and Article 21.

[12] GBER, Article 45.

[13] ibid, Article 44(2).

(c) SME aid measures not eligible under the GBER may still be individually approved by the Commission under Article 87(2) and (3). This is considered in section D below.

10.07 **SMEs in the agriculture and fisheries sectors.** Most forms of aid to the agriculture and fisheries sectors are excluded from the scope of the GBER.[14] Instead, such aid has been the subject of separate block exemptions and guidelines, which are discussed in detail in Chapter 11 below. Reference to that chapter should be made in respect of any aid to SMEs in those sectors, that does not fall within the scope of the GBER.

B. Existence of aid

10.08 **Article 87(1) issues.** For State aid to arise, all of the criteria under Article 87(1) must be met. These are discussed in detail in Chapter 2 above. In most cases involving aid to SMEs, it will be straightforward to establish the existence of aid within Article 87(1). The doubtful cases are likely to be those where the nature of the SME's business makes it questionable whether the aid would affect trade between Member States, and cases of *de minimis* aids.

10.09 **Effect on inter-State trade.** Article 87(1) is only engaged where the aid strengthens the position of an undertaking compared with other undertakings competing in intra-Community trade. This condition has been interpreted broadly, so that it is not (for example) necessary to establish that the beneficiary itself exports its products, or even that there is any actual trade between Member States in the product or service at the time when the aid is granted.[15] But it is acknowledged that the criterion may well not be satisfied where aid is granted to undertakings in relation to products or services which by their nature are not traded between States.[16] This may well be the case for SMEs, particularly micro enterprises, providing local services for example. If this is the case, the aid is likely to fall outside the scope of Article 87(1).[17]

10.10 ***De minimis* aids.** Aid to SMEs may also fall within the scope of the *de minimis* block exemptions. In such cases, the aid is deemed not to meet the criteria of Article 87(1). The general *de minimis* Regulation is discussed in Chapter 2.[18]

[14] See para 10.13 below for the agriculture and fisheries aids that are covered by the GBER.
[15] See paras 2.143–2.144 above.
[16] See para 2.145 above.
[17] See Community guidelines on State aid for small and medium-sized enterprises [1996] OJ C213/4, para 2.1.
[18] See para 2.148 above.

The separate *de minimis* Regulations applicable in the agriculture and fisheries sectors are addressed in Chapter 11.[19]

C. General Block Exemption Regulation ('GBER')

SME-specific exemptions: GBER structure. As described in more detail in Chapter 5 above, Chapter I of the GBER contains a set of common conditions and procedural provisions applicable to the various types of aid covered by the GBER. The provisions of Chapter I relevant to aids specifically targeted at SMEs are addressed in section 1 below. Section 2 will then address the specific SME aid exemptions in the GBER, as set out in Chapter II of the GBER. **10.11**

Favourable terms in other exemptions. In addition to the exemptions specifically targeted at SMEs, which are discussed below, SMEs benefit from terms more favourable than those applicable to larger enterprises in almost all of the other exemptions contained within the GBER. In relation to *regional investment and employment aid*, SMEs are permitted to receive higher levels of aid intensity, and benefit from other favourable conditions (Article 13). In relation to *environmental aid*, SMEs are able to benefit from increased levels of aid intensity with regard to aid for investment enabling undertakings to go beyond Community standards for environmental protection (Article 18), aid for the acquisition of transport vehicles which go beyond Community standards (Article 19), aid for investment in energy saving measures (Article 21), environmental investment aid for high-efficiency cogeneration (Article 22), environmental investment aid for the promotion of energy from renewable energy sources (Article 23), and aid for environmental studies (Article 24). Similarly, SMEs benefit from higher aid intensities in the provisions on aid for *risk capital* (Article 29). In relation to *R&D&I*, SMEs are able to obtain higher levels of aid intensity than other enterprises to assist in the funding of projects (Article 31), and can obtain increased levels of aid intensity for technical and feasibility studies to industrial research or experimental development activities (Article 32). Finally, SMEs are eligible for increased levels of aid intensity for *training aid* (Article 39). The procedural and substantive conditions applicable to these exemptions are discussed in other chapters of this book. **10.12**

1. Common and procedural provisions

Sectoral scope of SME exemptions. In relation to the specific SME exemptions, the GBER provisions exclude aid to undertakings in the coal, fisheries and aquaculture sectors, and the primary production of agricultural products. The only **10.13**

[19] See paras 11.18–11.20 (agriculture) and 11.63 (fisheries) below.

relevant exceptions to these exclusions are aid for R&D&I (ie in relation to SMEs, the provisions of Articles 35 to 37) and environmental aid (ie in relation to SMEs, the provisions of Article 20) which are applicable in the coal sector and in relation to the primary production of agricultural products, insofar as the aid is not already covered by the Agriculture Block Exemption Regulation. In addition, the SME-R&D&I provisions (but not the SME-environmental aid provisions) apply to the fishery and aquaculture sectors.[20]

10.14 **Individual notification thresholds.** Under the GBER certain aids are excluded where the value of the financial assistance exceeds specified thresholds. This varies according to the type of aid in question. For the various categories of aid specific to SMEs, the thresholds per undertaking per project are:[21]

(a) €7.5 million in the case of SME investment and employment aid;
(b) €2 million in the case of consultancy aid in favour of SMEs;
(c) €2 million in the case of aid granted to SMEs for participation in fairs; and
(d) €5 million in the case of aid granted to SMEs for industrial property rights costs.

10.15 **Common conditions.** In addition to the specific provisions referred to above on the scope of the SME exemptions, the GBER contains a number of general conditions common to all types of aid within its ambit. These are set out in detail in paras 5.17–5.26 above, to which reference should be made. In summary, these provisions concern:

(a) the exclusion of all forms of aid to certain undertakings and certain sectors;
(b) the general conditions for exemption of aid schemes and individual aid granted under such schemes, as well as for ad hoc individual aid;
(c) the basis of calculation of aid intensities;
(d) the requirement to provide documentary evidence of eligible costs;
(e) the requirement for exempted aid to be transparent;
(f) the conditions under which aid can be cumulated with other aid exempted under the GBER;[22]
(g) the requirement for aid to have an incentive effect;[23] and
(h) the reporting and monitoring requirements applicable to all aid exempted under the GBER.

---

20 GBER, Article 1(3).

21 ibid, Article 6.

22 Care must be taken, especially when drafting the wording for aid schemes or granting individual aid, to ensure that cumulative thresholds are not exceeded. In previous cases, such cumulation provisions were not prevalent, as in Decision 2003/469/EC *Thuringia Working Capital Programme* [2003] OJ L157/55, where the relevant thresholds were exceeded. As a result Germany was required to recover the aid granted in excess of the thresholds.

23 Deemed to be satisfied in the case of SMEs if the beneficiary has submitted an application for aid before work on the project or activity has started: GBER, Article 8(2).

2. Specific SME exemptions

Definition of SMEs. Annex I to the GBER defines an enterprise as 'any entity engaged in an economic activity, irrespective of its legal form'. This includes self-employed persons and family businesses, as well as partnerships or associations regularly engaged in an economic activity.[24] The GBER goes on to define micro, small and medium-sized enterprises.[25] These categorizations are important for determining the levels of aid that can be authorized under different areas of the GBER. In general, the various block exemptions generally allow greater levels of aid and aid intensity to smaller enterprises. The table below sets out the definitions for each category of enterprise. 10.16

Category of enterprise	Number of employees[26]	Annual turnover (€)	Annual balance sheet total (€)
Micro	Less than 10	2 million	2 million
Small	Less than 50	10 million	10 million
Medium-sized	Less than 250	50 million	43 million

Categories of specific SME exemptions. In addition to the increased aid intensities for SMEs under the general horizontal and regional aid provisions, discussed at para 10.12 above, the GBER exempts a number of specific categories of aid that apply solely to SMEs. These are: aid for newly created small enterprises (Article 14), SME investment and employment aid (Article 15), aid for female entrepreneurship (Article 16), aid for early adaptation to Community environmental standards (Article 20), aid for consultancy (Article 26), aid for participation in fairs (Article 27), aid for industrial property rights costs (Article 33), aid for young innovative enterprises (Article 35), aid for innovation advisory services and innovation support services (Article 36), and aid for the loan of highly qualified personnel (Article 37). The conditions for exemption in each case are described below. 10.17

Aid for newly created small enterprises. Under the regional aid provisions of the GBER, aid may be granted to newly created small enterprises. The eligible expenses are the costs directly incurred in creating the enterprise, namely the legal, advisory, consultancy and administrative costs. The aid can also be used to support certain types of running costs of the enterprise in the first five years following the enterprise's creation. The aid cannot, however, be awarded to enterprises that are controlled by shareholders that had owned a failed enterprise active in the same 10.18

[24] GBER, Annex I Article 1.

[25] ibid, Annex 1 Article 2. This is based on the definitions in Commission Recommendation 2003/361/EC concerning the definition of micro, small and medium-sized enterprises [2003] OJ L124/36.

[26] Calculated on the basis of the number of AWUs (Annual Work Units): GBER, Annex 1 Article 5.

market, or adjacent markets, in the previous year. This prevents aid being given to 'phoenix' enterprises.[27]

10.19 **SME investment and employment aid.** Investment and employment aid may be granted to SMEs.[28] The maximum aid intensity is 20% in the case of small enterprises and 10% in the case of medium-sized enterprises.[29] The costs eligible for aid are (for investment aid) the eligible tangible and intangible costs or (for employment aid) the estimated wage costs of employment directly created by the investment project, over a period of two years.[30] Where the aid concerns the processing and marketing of agricultural products, different levels of aid intensity apply which vary depending on the region: 75% of eligible investments in the outermost regions, 65% of eligible investments in the smaller Aegean Islands, 50% of eligible investments in regions eligible under Article 87(3)(a) EC and 40% of eligible investments in all other regions.[31] This is to enable further assistance to be given for agricultural aid in regions of the Community where the standard of living is abnormally low or where there is serious under-employment.

10.20 **Aid for female entrepreneurship.** The GBER has introduced a new type of exempted aid in the form of 'aid for small enterprises newly created by female entrepreneurs'.[32] The origins of this exemption seem to have come from the Small Business Act,[33] which identified a clear differential between the genders in relation to entrepreneurial activity. In order to deal with this differential, the new exemption under the GBER has the clear aim of promoting female entrepreneurship in the Community, and reducing the *de facto* inequalities existing in the area of entrepreneurship.[34] The aid must be granted to a 'small enterprise newly created by female entrepreneurs'. This means that 51% or more of the capital of the enterprise must be owned by one or more women, or women are the registered owners of the enterprise, *and* a women must be in charge of the management of the enterprise.[35] The aid ceiling is €1 million per undertaking, 33% of which may be paid in any single year. The maximum aid intensity is 15% of eligible expenses incurred

[27] ibid, Article 14, addressed in more detail at paras 15.57–15.59 below.

[28] GBER, Article 15. For an example under the old SME block exemption see Decision in Case N 606/2000 *Highlands and Islands aid scheme* (14 June 2001). In regions of the Community eligible for regional aid, however, it will be preferable to use the SME provisions of the regional investment and employment aid exemption in GBER, Article 13, for which more generous aid intensities apply: see para 15.55 below.

[29] GBER, Article 15(2).

[30] ibid, Article 15(3), and see Article 12 for definitions of eligible investment and employment costs.

[31] ibid, Article 15(4).

[32] ibid, Article 16. This appeared for the first time in the final version of the text for the GBER, and did not appear in the earlier consultation drafts.

[33] 'Think Small First' – A 'Small Business Act' for Europe, COM(2008) 394, especially Section 4 'Turning principles into policy action'.

[34] GBER, recital (44).

[35] ibid, Articles 16(2) and 2(28).

in the first five years after the creation of the undertaking.[36] The eligible costs are set out in Article 16(5).[37] These include the legal, advisory, consultancy and administrative expenses directly incurred in setting up the business. In addition, a number of other types of running costs are eligible for aid, including interest on external financing, utilities bills and child care and parental costs, including parental leave.[38] As with the general category of aid for newly created small enterprises, there is a provision aimed at preventing aid to 'phoenix' enterprises, by excluding aid to enterprises that are controlled by shareholders that had owned a failed enterprise active in the same market, or adjacent markets, in the previous year.[39]

Aid for early adaptation to future Community environmental standards. SMEs have disproportionate costs in adapting to new Community environmental standards. In larger organizations, such overheads will not be sufficient to have a detrimental effect on the business, but for SMEs this can have a significant impact on their profitability, and hence their continuing viability. The GBER therefore allows aid to assist SMEs to comply with new Community environmental standards, which are not yet in force.[40] This type of aid to SMEs is new in the GBER. To benefit from exemption the investment must be implemented at least a year before the mandatory date for transposition of the standards in question. The aid intensity is set at 15% for small enterprises and 10% for medium-sized enterprises if the investment is implemented more than three years before the mandatory date of transposition. If the investment is implemented between one and three years before that date, only small enterprises are eligible for aid, and then only up to a maximum intensity of 10%. The eligible costs are the extra investment costs necessary to achieve the level of environmental protection required by the Community standard, as defined in Article 18(5).[41] **10.21**

Aid for consultancy. The GBER exempts aid to SMEs for consultancy up to a maximum aid intensity of 50% of the eligible costs. Eligible costs are the consultancy costs of services provided by external consultants. These services must not be a continuous or periodic activity, nor relate to the undertaking's usual operating costs such as routine tax consultancy services, regular legal services or advertising.[42] **10.22**

---

36 ibid, Article 16(2)–(4).

37 It is not clear why the GBER uses the term 'eligible expenses' in Article 16(4) but 'eligible costs' in Article 16(5). It is assumed that these are intended to represent the same thing.

38 GBER, Article 16(5).

39 ibid, Article 16(6).

40 cf the position taken in relation to aid for compliance with existing mandatory Community standards, that amounts in effect to operating aid rather than an environmental incentive: Decision 2001/806/EC *Aid for SME manure transport companies* [2001] OJ L305/22, paras 20–1.

41 GBER, Article 20.

42 ibid, Article 26. See eg under the old SME block exemption Case XS 182/2006 *Consultancy aid for software development* [2007] OJ C174/21.

10.23 **Aid for participation in fairs.** The GBER exempts certain types of aid assisting SMEs to participate in fairs. Fairs provide opportunities to access information that may be useful for SMEs, as well as show-casing the goods or services that SMEs can offer. Aid for SME participation in fairs is thus exempted up to a maximum aid intensity of 50% of the costs incurred in renting, setting up and running the stand for the first participation of an undertaking in any particular fair or exhibition.[43] Consistent with the Commission's previous practice, aid for subsequent participation in any particular fair or exhibition will not be covered.[44]

10.24 **R&D&I aids for SMEs.** It is recognized that SMEs may experience difficulties in gaining access to new technological developments and technology transfers, as well as highly qualified personnel.[45] For that reason, in addition to the higher aid intensities permitted for aid for R&D projects and technical feasibility studies,[46] SMEs may benefit from four specific types of R&D aid that are not available for large enterprises. These are aid for industrial property rights costs for SMEs, aid to young innovative enterprises, aid for innovation advisory and support services, and aid for the loan of highly qualified personnel.[47] The aid intensities and eligible costs for these categories of aid are addressed in detail in Chapter 8.[48]

D. Authorization under Article 87(2) and (3)

10.25 **Basis for approval.** Aid for SMEs that falls outside the GBER (and outside the special rules for agriculture and fisheries in Chapter 11) may still be notified to the Commission for approval under the provisions of Article 87(2) and (3). Of these, the main provision under which State aid for SMEs is likely to be approved is Article 87(3)(c). In addition, some forms of aid to SMEs may fall under the derogation in Article 87(3)(d) for aid to promote culture and heritage conservation, or the categories in Article 87(2) of aids which are always exempted such as social aids and disaster aid.

10.26 **Guiding principles.** The Commission has not yet set out any general guidelines for the approval of SME aid that falls outside the block exemptions. Many SME aids will, however, be covered by the specific horizontal and/or regional aid guidelines, addressed in other chapters of this book. In the remaining cases, it is

43 GBER, Article 27.

44 See Decision 2003/226/EC *Saxony SMEs* [2003] OJ L91/13, paras 66–68 and 76.

45 GBER, recital (58).

46 ibid, Articles 31 and 32.

47 ibid, Articles 33, 35, 36 and 37.

48 See paras 8.44, 8.45, 8.47 and 8.48 above.

necessary to refer simply to the general principles governing Article 87(2) and (3), as discussed in Chapter 3 above. In addition it should be noted that, as with other aids falling outside the GBER, the Commission is still likely to assess the aid in accordance with the guiding principles of the GBER. Aid that does not meet all of the criteria of the GBER should therefore be constructed in a way that is, otherwise, as similar to the GBER as possible.

11

AGRICULTURE AND FISHERIES

Main legislation and guidelines

Council Regulation (EC) 1698/2005 on support for rural development by the European Agricultural Fund for Rural Development (EAFRD) ('Rural Development Regulation') [2005] OJ L277/1

Council Regulation (EC) 1184/2006 applying certain rules of competition to the production of, and trade in, agricultural products [2006] OJ L214/7

Commission Regulation (EC) 1857/2006 on the application of Articles 87 and 88 of the Treaty to State aid to small and medium-sized enterprises active in the production of agricultural products and amending Regulation (EC) 70/2001 ('Agriculture Block Exemption Regulation') [2006] OJ L358/3

Council Regulation (EC) 1234/2007 establishing a common organisation of agricultural markets and on specific provisions for certain agricultural products ('Single CMO Regulation') [2007] OJ L299/1

Commission Regulation (EC) 1535/2007 on the application of Articles 87 and 88 of the EC Treaty to *de minimis* aid in the sector of agricultural production ('Agriculture *de minimis* Regulation') [2007] OJ L337/35

Commission Regulation (EC) 875/2007 on the application of Articles 87 and 88 of the EC Treaty to *de minimis* aid in the fisheries sector and amending Regulation (EC) No 1860/2004 ('Fisheries *de minimis* Regulation') [2007] OJ L193/6

Commission Regulation (EC) 736/2008 on the application of Articles 87 and 88 of the Treaty to State aid to small and medium-sized enterprises active in the production, processing and marketing of fisheries products ('Fisheries Block Exemption Regulation') [2008] OJ 201/16

Commission Regulation (EC) 800/2008 declaring certain categories of aid compatible with the common market in application of Articles 87 and 88 of the Treaty (General Block Exemption Regulation) ('GBER') [2008] OJ L214/3

Community guidelines for State aid in the agriculture and forestry sector 2007 to 2013 ('Agriculture Guidelines') [2006] OJ C319/1

Guidelines for the examination of State aid to fisheries and aquaculture ('Fisheries Guidelines') [2008] OJ C84/10

A. Introduction

11.01 **Definitions.** 'Agricultural products' are defined by Article 32(1) of the Treaty as 'the products of the soil, of stockfarming and of fisheries and products of first stage processing directly related to these products'. They are also listed in Annex I to the Treaty and include, for example, live animals, meat and edible meat offals, fish, crustaceans and molluscs, dairy produce, edible vegetables, cereals, oil seeds, beet sugar and cane sugar, and wine of fresh grapes.[1] However, while both Article 32(1) and Annex I encompass products of fisheries, the State aid rules which apply in the fisheries sector are substantially different to those which apply in the agriculture sector. Accordingly, this chapter deals separately with the agriculture and fisheries sectors.

11.02 **Special application of the competition rules.** The agriculture and fisheries sectors have always been subject to special treatment under the Treaty, set out in Title II of the Treaty (Articles 32 to 38).[2] This reflects the special status accorded to farmers in the Community, the justification for which has evolved over the years.[3] The special treatment of this sector extends, in principle, to the rules

[1] The list in Annex I would not seem as broad as the general definition in Article 32(1). For example, wool would seem to satisfy the general definition, yet does not appear in the list. In such circumstances, the list prevails: Case 77/83 *CILFIT* [1984] ECR 1257.

[2] Title II is currently termed simply 'Agriculture', but if the Treaty of Lisbon is ratified it will formally extend to both agriculture and fisheries: [2007] OJ C306/1.

[3] Thus, the original emphasis on the need to increase productivity yielded to greater focus on the 'multifunctional' role of agriculture as the provider of not just food and fibre, but also 'public goods' (such as environmental benefits and higher standards of animal welfare): see eg Mid-term review of

on competition. Thus, Article 36 EC provides that the Treaty rules on competition 'shall apply to production of and trade in agricultural products only to the extent determined by the Council . . . account being taken of the objectives [of the common agricultural policy].'[4] The extent to which the State aid rules have in fact been applied to the agriculture and fisheries sectors by secondary legislation is discussed further below.[5] In order to understand that discussion, however, it is necessary to understand the basic principles underlying the common agricultural policy. These are addressed in the following paragraphs.

Objectives of the common agricultural policy. The objectives of the common agricultural policy are described in Article 33(1) EC as being to increase agricultural productivity by promoting technical progress and ensuring the rational development of agricultural production, as well as the optimum utilization of the factors of production, in particular labour; to ensure a fair standard of living for the agricultural community, in particular by increasing individual earnings; to stabilize markets; to assure the availability of supplies; and to ensure that supplies reach consumers at reasonable prices. Where these objectives conflict it is for the Community institutions to reconcile such conflicts and, where necessary, grant one or more objectives temporary priority in order to satisfy the demands of economic factors or conditions.[6] **11.03**

Regional differences. A further important strand of the common agricultural policy is the recognition of regional differences within the Community. Article 33(2) EC provides that such differences must be taken into account in working out the common agricultural policy and its application. This general principle has been particularly relevant in the State aid rules, which frequently differentiate according to the region in which the aid is to be granted. **11.04**

The 'two pillars' of the common agricultural policy. Following substantial reforms under Agenda 2000,[7] the regulatory framework of the common agricultural policy is divided into two pillars. The first of these concerns price support and market management. Its key elements are the Single Common Market **11.05**

---

the common agricultural policy, COM(2002) 394. More recently, as supplies have tightened, the emphasis has switched again to food security: see eg Preparing for the 'Health Check' of the CAP Reform, COM(2007) 722. Note also that the set-aside rate was reduced to zero for 2008: Council Regulation (EC) 1107/2007 derogating from Regulation (EC) 1782/2003 establishing common rules for direct support schemes under the common agricultural policy and establishing certain support schemes for farmers, as regards set-aside for the year 2008 [2007] OJ L253/1.

[4] See also eg Community guidelines for State aid in the agriculture and forestry sector 2007 to 2013 ('Agriculture Guidelines') [2006] OJ C319/1, para 1: 'Recourse to State aid can only be justified if it respects the objectives of this policy'.

[5] See paras 11.10–11.16 for the agriculture sector, and para 11.61 for the fisheries sector.

[6] See eg Case C-311/90 *Hierl v Hauptzollamt Regensburg* [1992] ECR I-2061; and Case C-280/93 *Germany v Council* [1994] ECR I-4973.

[7] Agenda 2000: for a stronger and wider Union, COM(97) 2000.

Organisation ('Single CMO') and the regime which provides direct payments for farmers. The second pillar concerns rural development. Specific State aid rules apply under both pillars.

11.06 **Single CMO.** The Single CMO has in principle applied since 1 January 2008. It brings under one umbrella the 21 common organizations of the market which were previously in force.[8] These included, in particular, the common organizations of the market in beef and veal, milk and milk products, sheepmeat and goatmeat, cereals and the sugar sector. This amalgamation of earlier measures constitutes a central plank in the ongoing process of simplifying common agricultural policy legislation.[9] However, certain products are still unregulated by any common organisation of the market, such as potatoes (other than starch potatoes). In accordance with the EC Treaty, the Single CMO governs, in particular, the regulation of prices, aids for production and marketing of the various products, storage and carry-over arrangements and common machinery for stabilizing imports or exports.[10]

11.07 **Direct payments for farmers.** The regime which provides direct payments for farmers was substantially reformed by the mid-term review of the common agricultural policy, agreed on 26 June 2003.[11] Most direct payments are now comprised within a single farm payment.[12] This is understood to be decoupled from production, in that no specific form of production, or indeed production at all, is required for its receipt.[13] All direct payments (not just the single farm payment) are, nevertheless, dependent upon the observance of three 'cross-compliance' obligations. First, farmers must respect statutory management requirements in the areas of public, animal and plant health, environment and animal welfare.[14] Secondly, they must maintain all agricultural land in good agricultural and environmental condition.[15] Thirdly, Member States are to ensure the maintenance of land under permanent pasture.[16]

---

[8] Council Regulation (EC) 1234/2007 establishing a common organization of agricultural markets and on specific provisions for certain agricultural products ('Single CMO Regulation') [2007] OJ L299/1. For the detailed commencement provisions see ibid, Article 204.

[9] See eg Communication from the Commission on simplification and better regulation for the common agricultural policy, COM(2005) 509; and Single CMO Regulation, recital (5).

[10] Article 34(2) EC.

[11] Mid-term review of the common agricultural policy, COM(2002) 394. See also generally M Cardwell, *The European Model of Agriculture* (Oxford University Press, 2004), pp 159–74; and JA McMahon *EU Agricultural Law* (Oxford University Press, 2007), pp 250–8.

[12] As set out in Council Regulation (EC) 1782/2003 establishing common rules for direct support schemes under the common agricultural policy and establishing certain support schemes for farmers [2003] OJ L270/1.

[13] ibid, recital (28).

[14] ibid, Article 4 and Annex III (as amended by Council Regulation (EC) 21/2004 [2004] OJ L/5.8).

[15] ibid, Article 5(1) and Annex IV (as amended by Council Regulation (EC) 864/2004 [2004] OJ L206/20).

[16] ibid, Article 5(2). Different rules apply for the 'old' and 'new' Member States.

Rural development. The 'second pillar' of the common agricultural policy, rural development, was instituted under the Agenda 2000 reforms, with earlier measures being brought together under a single regime.[17] The current legislative framework is provided by the Rural Development Regulation.[18] This implements the objectives of rural development through four 'Axes'. The first is improving the competitiveness of the agricultural and forestry sector; the second is improving the environment and the countryside; the third is the quality of life in rural areas and diversification of the rural economy; and the fourth is the 'Leader'[19] initiative (which relates to local rural development action groups). The Rural Development Regulation covers the programming period from 1 January 2007 to 31 December 2013, and central to its operation is the principle of subsidiarity. Thus, within its legislative framework, Member States are responsible for implementing their rural development programmes at the appropriate territorial level, according to their own institutional arrangements.[20] Strategic guidelines are, however, provided at Community level and national strategy plans must ensure that Community aid for rural development is consistent with these guidelines.[21] **11.08**

Overall framework of State aid rules in the agriculture sectors and fisheries. The State aid rules in the agriculture sectors and fisheries will be considered in this chapter as follows. **11.09**

(a) Section B below sets out the extent to which the State aid rules have been generally applied in the agriculture sector by the Council under Article 36 of the Treaty, together with the extent to which they have been specifically applied under the regulations which govern both the common organizations of the market and rural development.
(b) Section C addresses the Agriculture *de minimis* Regulation, which sets out circumstances in which agricultural aid is sufficiently small that Article 87(1) is deemed not to apply.
(c) Section D addresses the provisions of the Agriculture Block Exemption Regulation.
(d) Agricultural aid that falls to be notified to the Commission may be authorized under the Agriculture Guidelines. These are discussed in section E.
(e) Finally, section F addresses the State aid rules in the fisheries sector.

---

17 Council Regulation (EC) 1257/1999 on support for rural development from the European Agricultural Guidance and Guarantee Fund (EAGGF) [1999] OJ L160/80.

18 Council Regulation (EC) 1698/2005 on support for rural development by the European Agricultural Fund for Rural Development (EAFRD) ('Rural Development Regulation') [2005] OJ L277/1; and see Commission Regulation (EC) 1974/2006 laying down detailed rules for the application of Council Regulation (EC) 1698/2005 [2006] OJ L368/15 (Article 57 specifically addressing State aid).

19 'Leader' is the acronym for 'Liaison entre actions de développement de l'économie rurale'.

20 Rural Development Regulation, Article 7.

21 ibid, Article 11(2); and see Council Decision 2006/144/EC on Community strategic guidelines for rural development (programming period 2007 to 2013) [2006] OJ L55/20.

B. Application of State aid rules in the agriculture sector

11.10 **General application of State aid rules.** As set out above, under Article 36 EC the Treaty rules on competition apply to production of and trade in agricultural products only to the extent determined by the Council. In the case of State aids, the determination has been made that, as a general rule, Article 88(1) and the first sentence of Article 88(3) of the EC Treaty shall apply to aid granted for production of, or trade in, the products listed in Annex I to the Treaty.[22] That means that, under Article 88(1), the Commission will keep under constant review the systems of aid existing in Member States and shall propose any appropriate measures required by the progressive development or by the functioning of the common market; and under the first sentence of Article 88(3) the Commission must be informed, in sufficient time to enable it to submit its comments, of any plans to grant or alter aid. This is a relatively light degree of control by comparison with the full provisions of Article 88 applying to other sectors.

11.11 **Common organizations of the market.** In addition, the State aid rules were applied in full to the individual common organizations of the market,[23] and this approach was continued on enactment of the Single CMO Regulation. Thus, Article 180 of the Single CMO Regulation stipulates that, save as otherwise provided in the Single CMO Regulation, Articles 87, 88 and 89 of the Treaty shall apply to the production of and trade in the following products: cereals, rice, sugar, dried fodder, seeds, hops, olive oil and table olives, flax and hemp, bananas, live plants and products of floriculture, raw tobacco, beef and veal, milk and milk products, pigmeat, sheepmeat and goatmeat, eggs, poultrymeat, ethyl alcohol of agricultural origin, apiculture products, and silkworms, as well as a miscellany of 'other products' specified in Part XXI of Annex I to the Single CMO Regulation. Specific provisions apply for the milk and milk products sector,[24] and specific national provisions include authority (for Member States which have reduced their sugar quota by more than 50% from the level fixed on 20 February 2006) to grant temporary State aid during the period for which transitional aid for beet growers is being paid under the European Community direct payments regime.[25]

---

22 Council Regulation (EC) 1184/2006 applying certain rules of competition to the production of, and trade in, agricultural products [2006] OJ L214/7.

23 eg Council Regulation (EEC) 1766/92 on the common organization of the market in cereals [1992] OJ L181/21, Article 19, and the Agriculture Guidelines, para 10.

24 Single CMO Regulation, Article 181.

25 ibid, Article 182. Sugar quotas within the European Community were reduced following the decision of the World Trade Organization Appellate Body in *European Communities – Export Subsidies on Sugar* WT/DS265/AB/R, WT/DS266/AB/R and WT/DS283/AB/R, 28 April 2005. This transitional aid under the Community direct payments regime is paid under Council Regulation (EC) 1782/2003 [2003] OJ L270/1, Title IV Chapter 10f (as amended by Council

In addition, by provisions outside the Single CMO Regulation, the State aid rules are applied to the fruit and vegetable and wine sectors.[26] However, again there are exceptions. For example, Spain and Italy were granted authority to pay up to €15 million during the 2007–2008 marketing year in order to support the adaptation of the tomato processing sector to the new fruit and vegetable regime.[27]

Common market organization derogations. Where the State aid rules are applied to a common organization of the market, but the regulations concerned contain specific provisions or derogations, it is established that the State aid rules remain subordinate to the specific provisions or derogations.[28] More generally, the Commission may not approve State aid which is incompatible with the provisions governing a common organization of the market, or which would interfere with its proper functioning.[29] **11.12**

Products outside common market organizations. As indicated in para 11.06 above, certain products are still unregulated by any common organization of the market. Nevertheless, under the general rule these are still subject to Article 88(1) and the first sentence of Article 88(3) of the EC Treaty.[30] The Commission will also take into account the risk of aid for such products benefiting the production of products subject to a common organization of the market. The danger of such cross-subsidization is considered especially great in the potato sector.[31] **11.13**

Rural development: general. As with the first pillar of the common agricultural policy, the State aid rules are applied by specific provision to the second pillar. Thus, the Rural Development Regulation stipulates that, save as otherwise provided, Articles 87, 88 and 89 of the Treaty shall apply to support for rural development by Member States.[32] As a general rule, rural development expenditure is subject to co-financing by the European Agricultural Fund for Rural Development (EAFRD), with the balance being provided by the Member States. Article 88(1) of the Rural Development Regulation expressly confirms that the State aid rules are not to apply to the financial contributions provided by Member **11.14**

Regulation (EC) 319/2006 [2006] OJ L58/32). The reference level, against which the reduction was measured, was fixed by Council Regulation (EC) 318/2006 [2006] OJ L58/1, Annex III.

26 Council Regulation (EC) 1182/2007 laying down specific rules as regards the fruit and vegetable sector [2007] OJ L273/1, Article 43; and Council Regulation (EC) 479/2008 on the common organization of the market in wine [2008] OJ L148/1, Article 127. This separate application of the State aid rules was necessitated by the fact that, on establishment of the Single CMO, the fruit and vegetable and wine sectors were subject to ongoing reform: Single CMO Regulation, recital (8) and Article 180.

27 Regulation 1182/2007 [2007] OJ L273/1, Article 43(b).

28 Case 177/78 *Pigs and Bacon Commission v McCarren* [1979] ECR 2161.

29 Agriculture Guidelines, para 11.

30 See para 11.10 above.

31 Agriculture Guidelines, para 21.

32 Rural Development Regulation, Article 88(1).

States as a counterpart of Community support. Accordingly, the State aid rules do not bite on expenditure by Member States necessary to co-finance rural development measures.

11.15 **Rural development: aid intensities and other conditions.** The Annex to the Rural Development Regulation sets out the maximum aid intensity for individual measures (for example, setting up support for young farmers is limited to €55,000). Detailed provisions govern the circumstances in which these maximum aid intensities may be exceeded. Thus, while aid for the modernization of agricultural holdings is not to exceed the percentages or amounts set out in the Annex, this prohibition is relaxed in the case of investments undertaken predominantly in the public interest and related to the conservation of traditional landscapes shaped by agricultural and forestry activities or to the relocation of farm buildings, investments relating to the protection and improvement of the environment, investments relating to the improvement of the hygiene conditions of livestock undertakings and animal welfare, and those with regard to occupational safety at the workplace.[33] Specific rules also govern rural development measures relating to compensation for natural handicaps in mountain areas and in other areas with handicaps,[34] agri-environmental and animal welfare commitments,[35] and meeting standards based on both Community and national legislation in the fields of environmental protection, public health, animal and plant health, animal welfare and occupational safety.[36]

11.16 **Rural development: notification requirements.** Any State aid intended to provide additional financing for rural development for which Community support is granted must be notified by Member States and approved by the Commission as part of its rural development programming.[37] In these circumstances, the procedure under the first sentence of Article 88(3) EC does not apply.

11.17 **Relevant Directorate General.** Where State aid falls to be notified to the Commission, notifications are dealt with by the Directorate General for Agriculture and Rural Development (DG Agri). While most recent State aid decisions in the agriculture sector are now listed on the DG Comp State aid register,[38] the DG Agri website contains a more comprehensive register of the English and French versions of decisions in the agricultural sector.

---

[33] ibid, Article 88(2).

[34] ibid, Article 37.

[35] ibid, Articles 39 and 40.

[36] ibid, Article 31.

[37] ibid, Article 89. Note also that Article 16(g) of the Rural Development Regulation expressly provides that rural development programmes should include 'the elements needed for appraisal under competition rules and, when applicable, the list of aid schemes authorised under Articles 87, 88 and 89 of the Treaty to be used for the implementation of the programmes'.

[38] See para 16.07 below.

C. *De minimis* exemption

The *de minimis* Regulations. Even where the State aid rules have been applied to the agriculture sector, aid measures will not require notification to the Commission if they fall within the *de minimis* rules. In such cases, Article 87(1) is considered not to apply. The general *de minimis* regime is governed by Regulation 1998/2006, considered in Chapter 2 above.[39] This covers aid for the processing and marketing of agricultural products.[40] The *de minimis* rules for the primary production of agricultural products are, however, set out in the Agriculture *de minimis* Regulation.[41] This reflects the fact that even low levels of State aid in the agricultural sector could fulfil the criteria of Article 87(1) of the Treaty.[42] **11.18**

Scope. The Agriculture *de minimis* Regulation extends to aid granted to undertakings in the agricultural production sector, subject to four exceptions.[43] Those exceptions are aid whose amount is fixed on the basis of price or quantity of products put on the market,[44] aid to export-related activities, aid contingent on the use of domestic over imported goods, and aid granted to undertakings in difficulty. For the purposes of the Regulation, undertakings in the sector of agricultural production must be active in the primary production of agricultural products,[45] and agricultural products are defined as the products listed in Annex I to the Treaty, with the exception of fisheries and aquaculture products.[46] **11.19**

***De minimis* aid.** The Agriculture *de minimis* Regulation exempts *de minimis* aid granted to any one undertaking up to €7,500 over any period of three fiscal years.[47] Where the total amount of aid exceeds that ceiling, then all the aid is **11.20**

---

[39] Commission Regulation (EC) 1998/2006 on the application of Articles 87 and 88 of the Treaty to *de minimis* aid [2006] OJ L379/5; and see further para 2.148 above.

[40] Save when the amount of the aid is fixed on the basis of the price or quantity of such products purchased from primary producers or put on the market by the undertakings concerned, or when the aid is conditional on being partly or entirely passed on to primary producers: ibid, Article 1(1)(c) (for the rationale for the first exclusion see n 44 below). See also Article 1(2)(b) and (c) for definitions of 'processing' and 'marketing' of agricultural products in this context.

[41] Commission Regulation (EC) 1535/2007 on the application of Articles 87 and 88 of the Treaty to *de minimis* aid in the sector of agricultural production ('Agriculture *de minimis* Regulation') [2007] OJ L337/35. This replaced the earlier exemption in Commission Regulation (EC) 1860/2004 on the application of Articles 87 and 88 of the EC Treaty to *de minimis* aid in the agriculture and fisheries sectors [2004] OJ L325/4.

[42] Agriculture *de minimis* Regulation, recital (2).

[43] ibid, Article 1.

[44] The rationale behind this exception is that, once the European Community has legislated for the establishment of a common organization of the market in a given sector of agriculture, Member States are under an obligation to refrain from taking any measure which might undermine or create exceptions to it: ibid, recital (7); Case 177/78 *Pigs and Bacon Commission v McCarren* [1979] ECR 2161, para 14; and Case C-113/00 *Spain v Commission* [2002] ECR I-7601, para 73.

[45] Agriculture *de minimis* Regulation, Article 2(1).

[46] ibid, Article 2(2).

[47] ibid, Article 3(2).

subject to the State aid rules.[48] In addition, a ceiling is imposed at Member State level: the cumulative amount of *de minimis* aid granted per Member State to undertakings in the agricultural production sector over any three fiscal years is limited to the value set out in the Annex to the Regulation (in the case of the UK this is €152,842,500).[49] Further, exemption can only be conferred where it is possible to calculate precisely the gross grant equivalent of the aid *ex ante*, without need to undertake a risk assessment (in other words, 'transparent aid').[50]

D. Agriculture Block Exemption Regulation

11.21 **Relationship with GBER.** Where aid is granted in amounts exceeding the relevant *de minimis* threshold, it may still be exempt from notification where it satisfies the conditions of one of the State aid block exemptions. All of the exemptions contained in the new General Block Exemption Regulation ('GBER'),[51] including the exemptions for aid to SMEs, apply to aid for the processing and marketing of agricultural products.[52] The GBER also applies to certain horizontal aids favouring activities in the primary production of agricultural products, namely: training aid, aid in the form of risk capital, aid for research and development, environmental aid, and aid for disadvantaged and disabled workers.[53] However, most aid for SMEs active in the production of agricultural products is governed by the specific Agriculture Block Exemption Regulation.[54] The provisions of the GBER are considered elsewhere in this book.[55] The paragraphs below address the provisions of the Agriculture Block Exemption Regulation.

---

[48] ibid, Article 3(2).

[49] ibid, Article 3(3) and Annex.

[50] ibid, Article 3(6); and see in this connection Communication from the Commission on the revision of the method for setting the reference and discount rates [2008] OJ C14/6.

[51] Commission Regulation (EC) 800/2008 declaring certain categories of aid compatible with the common market in application of Articles 87 and 88 of the Treaty (General Block Exemption Regulation) ('GBER') [2008] OJ L214/3.

[52] Save when the amount of the aid is fixed on the basis of the price or quantity of such products purchased from primary producers or put on the market by the undertakings concerned, or when the aid is conditional on being partly or entirely passed on to primary producers: ibid, Article 1(3)(c) (for the rationale for the first exclusion see n 44 above). See also Article 2(23) and (24) for definitions of 'processing' and 'marketing' of agricultural products in this context.

[53] ibid, Article 1(3)(b).

[54] Commission Regulation (EC) 1857/2006 on the application of Articles 87 and 88 of the Treaty to State aid to small and medium-sized enterprises active in the production of agricultural products ('Agriculture Block Exemption Regulation') [2006] OJ L358/3. This replaced the earlier agriculture block exemption in Commission Regulation (EC) 1/2004 on the application of Articles 87 and 88 of the EC Treaty to State aid to small and medium-sized enterprises active in the production, processing and marketing of agricultural products [2004] OJ L1/1.

[55] See Chapters 5 (environmental aid), 6 (employment and training aid), 8 (R&D&I), 9 (risk capital), 10 (SMEs) and 15 (regional aid).

Scope. The Agriculture Block Exemption Regulation covers only transparent aid granted to small and medium-sized agricultural holdings (farms) active in the primary production of agricultural products. It does not apply to aid granted for expenditure linked to the processing and marketing of agricultural products.[56] It also does not apply to aid to export-related activities or aid contingent upon the use of domestic over imported goods.[57] For these purposes the definition of SMEs is the same as that for the general regime implemented under the GBER.[58] Agricultural products are specifically defined as those listed in Annex I to the Treaty, with the exception of fishery and aquaculture products, cork products, and products intended to imitate or substitute milk and milk products.[59] Where the conditions for exemption are satisfied, then the aid is deemed compatible with the common market within the meaning of Article 87(3)(c) EC, and may be implemented without notification to the Commission.[60] Otherwise, the aid must be notified and will be assessed in accordance with the criteria laid down by the Agriculture Guidelines.[61] **11.22**

Categories of aid: introduction. The Agriculture Block Exemption Regulation applies to 14 categories of aid: investment in agricultural holdings, conservation of traditional landscapes and buildings, relocation of farm buildings in the public interest, aid for setting up of young farmers, aid for early retirement, aid for producer groups, aid in respect of animal and plant diseases and pest infestations, aid for losses due to adverse climatic events, aid towards the payment of insurance premiums, aid for land reparcelling, aid to encourage the production of quality agricultural products, the provision of technical support in the agricultural sector, support for the livestock sector and aid under certain Council Regulations. **11.23**

Agricultural holdings: aid intensities. Aid may be granted for investment in agricultural holdings within the Community for primary production of agricultural products (except the manufacture of products which imitate or substitute for milk and milk products).[62] The gross aid intensity must not exceed percentages which vary according to the measure and region.[63] Thus, it must not exceed 50% of eligible investments in less-favoured areas or in areas designated as eligible for natural **11.24**

---

56 Agriculture Block Exemption Regulation, Article 1(1). For the definition of transparent aid see Article 2(18).

57 ibid, Article 1(2).

58 See GBER, Annex I (including eg a requirement that there be fewer than 250 employees).

59 Agriculture Block Exemption Regulation, Article 2(2). The fishery and aquaculture products excluded are those covered by Council Regulation (EC) 104/2000 [2000] OJ L17/22. The products intended to imitate or substitute milk or milk products are those referred to in Council Regulation (EEC) 1898/87 [1987] OJ L182/36.

60 ibid, Article 3(1)–(3).

61 ibid, Article 3(4); and see paras 11.41–11.59 below.

62 ibid, Article 4(1) and (10).

63 ibid, Article 4(2).

handicap payments to farmers in mountain areas, payments to farmers in areas with handicaps (other than mountain areas) and Natura 2000 payments and payments linked to the Water Framework Directive.[64] (Unless expressly stated otherwise, all these areas will be collectively referred to as 'less-favoured areas' for the purposes of this chapter.) In other regions, the gross aid intensity must not exceed 40%.[65] However, in the case of investments made by young farmers within five years of setting up, a 10% increment is applied, so that the maximum percentages are raised respectively to 60% and 50%,[66] and up to 75% is available for eligible investments in the outermost regions and the small Aegean Islands.[67] Specific provisions apply where investments result in extra costs relating to the protection and improvement of the environment, the improvement of hygiene conditions of livestock enterprises or the welfare of farm animals. As has been seen, such measures are central to the vision of a 'multifunctional' model of European agriculture and they attract heightened support. Thus, it is 75% in less-favoured areas,[68] and elsewhere the ceiling is 60%.[69] Such investments must go beyond the minimum Community requirements in force or be made to comply with newly introduced minimum standards.[70]

11.25 **Agricultural holdings: other conditions.** The investments must pursue the reduction of production costs, improvement and re-deployment of production, improvement of quality, or the preservation and improvement of the natural environment or the improvement of hygiene conditions or animal welfare standards.[71] Aid may not be granted to enterprises in difficulty;[72] and it must not be granted in contravention of any prohibitions or restrictions laid down in Council regulations

---

64 ibid, Article 4(2)(a). The designation of less-favoured areas has proved controversial. In the case of some Member States, the vast majority of their utilized agricultural area has been so designated and this has attracted the criticism of the Court of Auditors: see eg Court of Auditors Special Report No 4/2003 concerning rural development: support for less-favoured areas. On the enactment of the Rural Development Regulation, agreement could not be reached as to revised designations, with the result that the earlier lists of less-favoured areas will not be repealed until 1 January 2010: Rural Development Regulation, Article 93. The Natura 2000 network of conservation sites was established under Council Directive 79/409/EEC (Wild Birds Directive) [1979] OJ L103/1 and Council Directive 92/43/EEC (Habitats Directive) [1992] OJ L206/7. The Water Framework Directive will lead to the implementation of river basin management plans: Directive 2000/60/EC of the European Parliament and of the Council establishing a framework for Community action in the field of water policy [2000] OJ L327/1.

65 Agriculture Block Exemption Regulation, Article 4(2)(b).

66 ibid, Article 4(2)(c).

67 ibid, Article 4(2)(d). For the areas that qualify see Council Regulation (EC) 2019/93 [1993] OJ L184/1.

68 ibid, Article 4(2)(e).

69 ibid.

70 ibid. This is consistent with the 'provider gets' principle: see eg Commission Communication – Directions towards sustainable agriculture [1999] OJ C173/2, 17.

71 ibid, Article 4(3).

72 ibid, Article 4(5).

establishing common organizations of the market.[73] Further, aid must not, as a rule, be limited to specific agricultural products,[74] and it must not be granted in respect of the purchase of production rights, animals and annual plants, the planting of annual plants, drainage works or irrigation equipment and irrigation works, unless this leads to a reduction of previous water use by at least 25%, and simple replacement investments.[75] On the other hand, aid may be granted for the purchase of land (other than land for construction purposes) costing up to 10% of the eligible expenses of the investment.[76] The maximum amount per individual enterprise is limited to €400,000 over any period of three fiscal years, except where the enterprise is situated in a less-favoured area, in which case the maximum amount is raised to €500,000.[77]

Conservation of traditional landscapes and buildings. Aid may be granted for up to 100% of the real costs incurred for investments or capital works intended for the conservation of non-productive heritage features located on agricultural holdings, such as archaeological or historical features. Such costs may include reasonable compensation for the work undertaken by the farmer himself, or his workers, up to €10,000 per annum.[78] Again the gross aid intensity varies depending on whether or not the farm is situated within a less-favoured area. If the farm is situated in a less-favoured area, the ceiling is 75%, while otherwise the ceiling is 60%. In either case the investment should not entail any increase in production capacity. If there is an increase in production capacity, the aid rates applicable to investments in agricultural holdings are to apply as regards eligible expenses resulting from undertaking the relevant work using normal contemporary materials. Additional aid may be granted at a rate of up to 100% to cover the extra costs incurred by using traditional materials necessary to maintain the heritage features of the building.[79] **11.26**

Relocation of farm buildings in the public interest. Aid may be granted for up to 100% of the actual costs incurred where a relocation in the public interest consists of the dismantling, removal and re-erection of existing facilities.[80] Where the relocation results in the farmer benefiting from more modern facilities, he must contribute a percentage of the increase in value of the facilities concerned after relocation, this percentage being at least 60% or, in less-favoured areas, **11.27**

[73] ibid, Article 4(6).
[74] ibid, Article 4(7). Member States are, however, permitted to *exclude* certain products where there is overcapacity or a lack of market outlets.
[75] ibid.
[76] ibid, Article 4(8).
[77] ibid, Article 4(9).
[78] ibid, Article 5(2).
[79] ibid, Article 5(3).
[80] ibid, Article 6(2).

at least 50%.[81] On the other hand, if the beneficiary is a young farmer, the contribution is reduced respectively to 55% or 45%. The same differentiated contribution rates (in respect of both less-favoured areas and young farmers) apply where the relocation results in an increase in production capacity.[82]

11.28 **Aid for setting up young farmers and aid for early retirement.** The Agriculture Block Exemption Regulation covers both aid for setting up young farmers and aid for early retirement.[83] In the case of aid for early retirement, it is expressly provided that the cessation of commercial farming activities must be permanent and definitive,[84] and in both cases the detailed criteria set out in the Rural Development Regulation must be satisfied.[85]

11.29 **Young farmers: detailed criteria.** The detailed criteria governing aid for setting up young farmers require that the beneficiaries be less than 40 years old, and must be setting up for the first time on an agricultural holding as head of the holding.[86] They must also possess adequate occupational skills and submit a business plan for the development of their farming activities.[87] The maximum amount of support is €55,000.[88]

11.30 **Early retirement: detailed criteria.** The detailed criteria governing aid for early retirement are complex. Aid is available not only to farmers who decide to stop their agricultural activity for the purpose of transferring their holding to other farmers, but also to farm workers who decide to stop all farm work definitively upon the transfer of the holding.[89] In the case of transferors, they must be not less than 55 years old but not yet of normal retirement age at the time of the transfer or not more than ten years younger than the normal retirement age in the Member State concerned at the time of the transfer.[90] They must also stop all commercial farming activity definitively and have practised farming for the ten years preceding the transfer.[91] The transferee must either succeed the transferor by setting up as a young farmer or be a farmer of less than 50 years old or a private law body and take over the agricultural holding to increase the size of their holding.[92] In the case of farm workers, the criteria similarly require that they must be not less than

---

81 ibid, Article 6(3).
82 ibid, Article 6(4).
83 ibid, Articles 7 and 8.
84 ibid, Article 8(b).
85 ibid, Articles 7 and 8(a).
86 Rural Development Regulation, Article 22(1)(a).
87 ibid, Article 22(1)(b) and (c).
88 ibid, Article 22(2) and Annex.
89 ibid, Article 23(1).
90 ibid, Article 23(2)(a).
91 ibid, Article 23(2)(b) and (c).
92 ibid, Article 23(3).

55 years old, but not yet of normal retirement age or not more than ten years younger than the normal retirement age in the Member State concerned.[93] In addition, they must have devoted at least half of their working time to farm work during the preceding five years, either as a farm helper or farm worker; they must have worked on the agricultural holding for at least the equivalent of two years full-time during the four-year period preceding the early retirement of the transferor; and they must belong to a social security scheme.[94] The maximum duration of early retirement support is 15 years and it shall not continue, in any event, beyond the seventieth birthday of the transferor and the normal retirement age of the farm worker.[95] The maximum amount of support is €18,000 per transferor per year, subject to a total amount of €180,000, or €4,000 per worker per year, subject to a total amount of €40,000.[96]

Producer groups. A further exempt category is start-up aid for the constitution of producer groups or producer associations.[97] Provided that they are entitled to financial assistance under the legislation of their own Member State, this covers aid to producer groups or producer associations involved in the production of agricultural products and/or associations of producers responsible for the supervision of the use of geographical indications and designations of origin or quality marks in conformity with Community law.[98] The internal rules of the producer group or association must require producers to remain members for at least three years and to give at least 12 months' notice of withdrawal. They must also provide common rules on production, relating, in particular, to such matters as product quality or the use of organic or other practices designed to protect the environment.[99] The agreements concluded in the framework of the producer group or association must, in any event, comply fully with all relevant provisions of competition law and, in particular, Articles 81 and 82 of the Treaty.[100] The total **11.31**

[93] ibid, Article 23(4)(a).

[94] ibid, Article 23(4)(b) – (d). These requirements may present difficulties where there had been diversification away from traditional farming on the agricultural holding.

[95] ibid, Article 23(5).

[96] ibid, Article 23(6) and Annex.

[97] Agriculture Block Exemption Regulation, Article 9. The promotion of farming cooperatives in the UK was strongly advocated in the Curry Report: Policy Commission on the Future of Farming and Food, *Farming and food: a sustainable future* (London, 2002), 34–5.

[98] ibid, Article 9(2). For the Community law concerned see eg Council Regulation (EC) 509/2006 on agricultural products and foodstuffs as traditional specialities guaranteed [2006] OJ L93/1; and Council Regulation (EC) 510/2006 on the protection of geographical indications and designations of origin for agricultural products and foodstuffs [2006] OJ L93/12. This shift to quality production has become a central plank of common agricultural policy reform, conforming with public expectations: see eg Commission *Europeans, agriculture and the common agricultural policy: Special Eurobarometer 294* (Brussels, 2008) 7.

[99] Agriculture Block Exemption Regulation, Article 9(2).

[100] ibid.

amount of aid granted to a producer group or association must not exceed €400,000.[101]

11.32 **Aid in respect of animal and plant diseases and pest infestations.** Aid to compensate farmers for the costs of prevention and eradication of animal or plant diseases or pest infestations falls under the Agriculture Block Exemption Regulation, provided that the gross intensity does not exceed 100% and the aid is granted in kind by means of subsidized services which do not involve direct payments of money to producers.[102] Exemption is also conferred on aid to compensate farmers for losses caused by animal or plant diseases or pest infestations.[103] In this case, there is a specific requirement that compensation must be calculated only: in relation to the market value of animals killed or plants destroyed by the disease or pest infestation or of animals killed or plants destroyed by public order as part of a compulsory public prevention or eradication programme; and in relation to income losses due to quarantine obligations and difficulties in restocking or replanting.[104] As with aid for the costs of prevention and eradication of animal or plant diseases or pest infestations, up to 100% compensation may be paid,[105] but the aid must be limited to losses caused by diseases for which an outbreak has been formally recognized by public authorities.[106] In all cases payments must be made as part of a public programme at Community, national or regional level for the prevention, control or eradication of the disease or pest concerned.[107]

11.33 **Aid for losses due to adverse climatic events.** The Agriculture Block Exemption Regulation extends to aid to compensate farmers for losses of plants or animals or farmbuildings caused by adverse climatic events which can be assimilated to natural disasters.[108] This may not exceed 80% (or 90% in less-favoured areas) of the reduction in income from the sale of the product resulting from the adverse climatic event.[109] The same intensities apply to damage suffered by farm buildings and farm equipment.[110] The adverse climatic event which can be assimilated to a natural disaster must be formally recognized as such by public authorities.[111] As from 1 January 2010, the amount of compensation offered is to be reduced by 50%, unless the farmer has taken out insurance covering at least 50% of his average

101 ibid, Article 9(7).
102 ibid, Article 10(1).
103 ibid, Article 10(2).
104 ibid, Article 10(2)(a).
105 ibid, Article 10(2)(b).
106 ibid, Article 10(2)(c).
107 ibid, Article 10(4).
108 ibid, Article 11.
109 ibid, Article 11(2).
110 ibid, Article 11(6).
111 ibid, Article 11(7).

annual production or production-related income and the statistically most frequent climatic risks in the Member State or region concerned.[112] As from 1 January 2011, aid for losses caused by drought may be paid only by a Member State which has fully implemented the Water Framework Directive in respect of agriculture and which ensures that the costs of water services provided to agriculture are recovered through an adequate contribution from the sector.[113]

Aid towards the payment of insurance premiums. The Community institutions have shown increased interest in insurance as a form of risk management.[114] This may be regarded, not least, as a policy response to climate change. At the same time, certain forms of insurance support to farmers have the advantage that they are not subject to World Trade Organization domestic support reduction commitments.[115] Consistent with this, the block exemption includes aid for insurance premiums, with different degrees of intensity.[116] The aid must not exceed 80% of their cost where the policy specifies that it covers only against losses caused by adverse climatic events which can be assimilated to natural disasters.[117] The percentage rate is reduced, however, to 50% where the policy specifies that it covers against such losses and against other losses caused by climatic events and/or losses caused by animal or plant diseases or pest infestations.[118] Importantly, the aid must not constitute a barrier to the operation of the internal market for insurance services.[119] Any amounts received under insurance schemes are to be deducted in calculating losses both in respect of animal and plant diseases and pest infestations and in respect of adverse climatic events.[120] **11.34**

Aid for land reparcelling. Such aid is exempt up to 100% of actual costs, provided that it is granted towards and limited to legal and administrative costs (including survey costs).[121] **11.35**

Aid to encourage the production of quality agricultural products. As has been seen, the promotion of quality agricultural products has been accorded high priority by the Community institutions; and the mid-term review of the common **11.36**

[112] ibid, Article 11(8).

[113] ibid, Article 11(9). For the Water Framework Directive see Directive 2000/60/EC of the European Parliament and of the Council [2000] OJ L327/1.

[114] See eg Commission *Working document: risk management tools for EU agriculture with a special focus on insurance* (Brussels, 2001); and DG Agri and JRC, *Agricultural insurance schemes* (Brussels, 2006). For consideration of the State aid implications of a compulsory insurance scheme see Case C-355/00 *Freskot v Elliniko Dimosio* [2003] ECR I-5263.

[115] See the Uruguay Round Agreement on Agriculture, Annex 2 paras 7 and 8.

[116] Agriculture Block Exemption Regulation, Article 12.

[117] ibid, Article 12(2)(a).

[118] ibid, Article 12(2)(b).

[119] ibid, Article 12(3).

[120] ibid, Articles 10(3)(a) and 11(3)(a).

[121] ibid, Article 13.

agricultural policy saw the addition of a specific food quality chapter to the regulatory framework for rural development.[122] Aid to cover the costs of a broad range of service activities is exempted, insofar as the costs are related to the development of quality agricultural products.[123] Examples include aid to 100% of the costs of: market research activities; product conception and design; the introduction of quality assurance schemes; and charges levied by recognized certifying bodies for the initial certification of quality assurance and similar schemes.[124] A further example is aid in respect of participation by farmers in food quality schemes under the Rural Development Regulation, but this is limited to €3,000 per holding.[125] Moreover, this last example is the only form of aid that can involve direct payments of money to producers; otherwise, the aid is to be granted in kind by means of subsidized services.[126]

11.37 **Provision of technical support in the agricultural sector.** The Agriculture Block Exemption Regulation also encompasses aid for the provision of technical support in the agricultural sector.[127] This includes aid for the education and training of farmers and farm workers, farm replacement services, consultancy services provided by third parties and the production of publications such as catalogues or websites.[128] The aid may cover up to 100% of the costs, but must be granted in kind by means of subsidized services as opposed to direct payments of money to producers.[129]

11.38 **Support for the livestock sector.** A further exempt category is support for enterprises active in the livestock sector.[130] This reflects the shocks suffered by that sector over recent years, not least the Bovine Spongiform Encephalopathy (BSE) crisis.[131] Specific forms of exempt support include aid at a rate of up to 100% to cover the administrative costs of the establishment and maintenance of herd books, aid at a rate of up to 70% of the costs of tests performed by or on behalf of third parties to determine the genetic quality or yield of livestock (but not controls undertaken by the owner or routine controls of milk quality), and, until 31 December 2011, aid at a rate of up to 40% for the introduction at farm level of innovative animal breeding techniques or practices (but not costs relating to the

[122] See now Rural Development Regulation, Article 20(c).
[123] Agriculture Block Exemption Regulation, Article 14(2).
[124] ibid, Article 14(2)(a), (b) and (d).
[125] ibid, Article 14(2)(f), and see Rural Development Regulation, Article 32 and Annex.
[126] Agriculture Block Exemption Regulation, Article 14(5).
[127] ibid, Article 15.
[128] ibid, Article 15(2).
[129] ibid, Article 15(3).
[130] ibid, Article 16.
[131] For an account of the extensive measures necessary to address the shock of BSE, and for the costs of those measures, see Court of Auditors Special Report No 19/98 concerning the Community financing of certain measures taken as a result of the BSE crisis [1998] OJ C383/1.

introduction or performance of artificial insemination).[132] In addition, there is exemption for various costs which may be incurred in the disposal of fallen stock and carcasses, provided that the Member State concerned has in place a consistent programme monitoring and ensuring safe disposal.[133] Thus, aid is permitted at a rate of up to 100% of the costs of removal of fallen stock, and 75% of the costs of destruction of such carcasses. Alternatively, aid is permitted up to an equivalent amount towards the costs of premiums paid by farmers for insurance covering the costs of removal and destruction of fallen stock.[134] Similarly, aid is permitted at a rate of up to 100% for costs of removal and destruction where the aid is financed through fees or compulsory contributions.[135] Special rules apply in respect of transmissible spongiform encephalopathies (TSE) and BSE. Aid is fully exempt for the costs of removal and destruction of fallen stock where there is an obligation to perform TSE tests; and the costs of TSE tests are also fully exempt.[136] In the case of compulsory BSE testing of bovine animals slaughtered for human consumption, total direct and indirect support, including Community payments, must not exceed €40 per test.[137] Again aid shall not involve direct payments of money to producers.[138]

Other aid. Finally, the Agriculture Block Exemption Regulation covers aid under three Council regulations.[139] In particular, aid is permitted in the milk sector for the supply of milk products to pupils,[140] and, under Regulation 1782/2003, national aid is permitted for rice and for up to 50% of the costs associated with establishing multiannual crops intended for bio-mass production on set-aside land.[141] **11.39**

Cumulation. The various aid ceilings apply whether or not the support for the aided project or activity is financed entirely by the Member State or is partly financed by the Community.[142] Aid exempted is not to be cumulated with other State aid, financial contributions provided by the Member States or financial contributions by the Community in relation to the same eligible costs, if such cumulation would result in an aid intensity exceeding the maximum laid down by **11.40**

[132] Agriculture Block Exemption Regulation, Article 16(1)(a)–(c).

[133] ibid, Article 16(2). A free service for the collection and disposal of animal carcasses and slaughterhouse waste amounts to State aid: Case C-126/01 *GEMO* [2003] ECR I-13769.

[134] ibid, Article 16(1)(d).

[135] ibid, Article 16(1)(e).

[136] ibid, Article 16(1)(f) and (g).

[137] ibid, Article 16(1)(g).

[138] ibid, Article 16(3).

[139] ibid, Article 17.

[140] Under the Single CMO Regulation, Article 102 (replacing Council Regulation (EC) 1255/1999 [1999] OJ L160/48, Article 14(2)).

[141] Regulation 1782/2003 [2003] OJ L270/1, Articles 87 and 107(3), the latter provision only being applicable where a Member State has chosen to retain certain levels of arable support coupled to production. This is not the case in the UK.

[142] Agriculture Block Exemption Regulation, Article 19(1); and see para 11.14 above.

the Agriculture Block Exemption Regulation.[143] Further, aid exempted by the Agriculture Block Exemption Regulation is not to be cumulated with *de minimis* support in respect of the same eligible expenditure or investment project, if such cumulation would again result in an aid intensity exceeding the maximum laid down by the Agriculture Block Exemption Regulation.[144]

E. Agriculture Guidelines

11.41 **Scope.** Where aid is not covered by the GBER, the Agriculture Block Exemption Regulation or the *de minimis* rules, it must be notified and is assessed under the Agriculture Guidelines.[145] These replace and consolidate earlier guidelines, in particular the 2000 Community guidelines for State aid in the agriculture sector.[146] Unlike the Agriculture Block Exemption Regulation and the Agriculture *de minimis* Regulation, the Agriculture Guidelines extend not just to the production of agricultural products, but also to the processing and marketing of such products.[147] For these purposes agricultural products mean, in addition to those listed in Annex I to the Treaty, cork products and products intended to imitate or substitute milk and milk products, but fishery and aquaculture products are excluded.[148] The Agriculture Guidelines also contain rules for the forestry sector, including aid for the afforestation of agricultural land. The Guidelines do not, however, apply to aid in the fisheries and aquaculture sector.[149]

11.42 **General principles.** As has been seen, the Commission may not approve a State aid which is incompatible with the provisions governing a common organization

[143] ibid, Article 19(2).

[144] ibid, Article 19(3).

[145] Community guidelines for State aid in the agriculture and forestry sector 2007 to 2013 ('Agriculture Guidelines') [2006] OJ C319/1.

[146] [2000] OJ C28/2. Other guidelines which have been consolidated include the Community guidelines for State aid concerning TSE tests, fallen stock and slaughterhouse waste [2002] OJ C324/2.

[147] Agriculture Guidelines, para 5; and see paras 7 and 8 for definitions of 'processing' and 'marketing' (very similar to those applicable to *de minimis* aid—see n 40 above). It is emphasized, however, that State aid rules applying to agricultural processing and marketing companies should be harmonized with those applying to non-agricultural companies, and that aid in favour of agricultural processing and marketing should normally only be declared compatible with Article 87(2) or (3) EC if it meets the criteria for compatibility applicable to other enterprises: ibid, paras 17 and 19.

[148] Agriculture Guidelines, para 6. This conforms with the definition in Article 2(2) of the Agriculture Block Exemption Regulation. Again the products intended to imitate or substitute milk or milk products are those referred to in Council Regulation (EEC) 1898/87 [1987] OJ L182/36; and the fishery and aquaculture products excluded are those covered by Council Regulation (EC) 104/2000 [2000] OJ L17/22.

[149] Agriculture Guidelines, para 5. For the guidelines in respect of the fisheries and aquaculture sector see Guidelines for the examination of State aid to fisheries and aquaculture [2008] OJ C84/10; and para 11.69 below.

of the market or which would interfere with its proper functioning.[150] Nor will the Commission authorize aid to export-related activities or aid contingent on the use of domestic over imported goods.[151] Finally, since environmental protection requirements are to be integrated into both agricultural and competition policy under Articles 3 and 6 EC, particular attention is to be given to environmental issues in future aid notifications, even where the aid schemes are not specifically concerned with environmental issues.[152]

Structure. The Agriculture Guidelines contain four main sections. The first three of these are directed to the agricultural sector, being respectively rural development measures, risk and crisis management and other types of aid; and the fourth is directed to the forestry sector. **11.43**

1. Rural development measures

Agricultural holdings. Aid for investment in agricultural holdings is compatible with Article 87(3)(c) EC if it is linked to the primary production of agricultural products and meets all the conditions of Article 4 of the Agriculture Block Exemption Regulation.[153] Aid may also be granted in respect of specific products and in respect of drainage works or irrigation equipment and irrigation works which do not lead to a reduction of previous water use of 25%. The maximum amounts per individual enterprise as set out in the Agriculture Block Exemption Regulation do not apply.[154] Similarly, provided that it meets the relevant conditions of the Agriculture Block Exemption Regulation, aid may also be declared compatible if it is for the conservation of traditional landscapes and buildings, for the relocation of farm buildings in the public interest and for investments resulting in extra costs relating to the protection and improvement of the environment, the improvement of hygiene conditions of livestock enterprises or the welfare of farm animals.[155] In 'new' Member States the Agriculture Guidelines permit aid of 75% for the extra costs of investments to **11.44**

---

150 Agriculture Guidelines, para 11; and see para 11.12 above.

151 ibid, para 12.

152 ibid, para 22.

153 ibid, paras 27 and 29; and see para 11.24 above.

154 ibid, para 29.

155 ibid, paras 30–2. For the relevant conditions see Agriculture Block Exemption Regulation, Article 5 (conservation of traditional landscapes and buildings), Art 6 (relocation of farm buildings in the public interest) and Article 4(2)(e) (the protection and improvement of the environment, the improvement of hygiene conditions of livestock enterprises or the welfare of farm animals). In the case of the conservation of traditional landscapes and buildings, the limit of €10,000 p.a. may be exceeded in duly justified circumstances: Agriculture Guidelines, para 30. In the case of the protection and improvement of the environment, the improvement of hygiene conditions of livestock enterprises or the welfare of farm animals, specific rules govern the maximum aid intensity of investment expenditure incurred after the dates for compliance with newly introduced standards: ibid, para 32.

implement the Nitrates Directive.[156] For the ten Member States which acceded on 1 May 2004, the aid may not continue beyond 31 December 2008; for the two Member States which acceded on 1 January 2007, this deadline is extended until 31 December 2010.[157] In all other Member States the permitted aid intensity is 40% (or 50% in less-favoured areas).[158] Whether or not the aid is granted in an 'old' or 'new' Member State, investments which result in an increase in production capacity are excluded.[159] Further, no aid is to be authorized for investments to comply with existing Community or national standards, except in the case of young farmers as part of their business plan, when the maximum aid intensity is 50% (or 60% in less-favoured areas).[160]

11.45 **Processing and marketing of agricultural products.** Notwithstanding the promotion of diversification under the Rural Development Regulation, aids granted to promote the diversification of primary producers into other activities connected with the processing and marketing of agricultural products are to be treated in the same way as aid granted to agricultural processing and marketing firms that are independent of primary producers.[161] Similarly, if the diversified activities are not connected with the production, processing and marketing of agricultural products (such as agri-tourism), they are not covered by the Agriculture Guidelines, and instead continue to be assessed in accordance with the usual principles applicable to the assessment of aids outside the agricultural sector.[162]

11.46 **Processing and marketing of agricultural products: conditions.** The Agriculture Guidelines state that aid for investment granted to companies active in the processing and marketing of agricultural products may be declared compatible with Article 87(3)(a) or (c) of the Treaty if it satisfies Article 4 of the block exemption for small and medium-sized enterprises, the State aid rules governing national regional investment aid, or the 2007–2013 Regional Aid Guidelines.[163] Where the 2007–2013 Regional Aid Guidelines apply, the maximum aid intensity may be increased to 50% in regions eligible under Article 87(3)(a) of the Treaty and

---

[156] ibid, para 33 and Council Directive 91/676/EEC concerning the protection of waters against pollution caused by nitrates from agricultural sources [1991] OJ L375/1. For a Commission report in this regard see On the implementation of the Nitrates Directive see On implementation of Council Directive 91/676/EEC concerning the protection of waters against pollution caused by nitrates from agricultural sources for the period 2000–2003, COM(2007) 120 final.

[157] Agriculture Guidelines, para 33.

[158] ibid, para 34.

[159] ibid, paras 33 and 34.

[160] ibid, para 35. For business plans see Rural Development Regulation, Article 22(1)(c).

[161] Agriculture Guidelines, para 41(d).

[162] ibid, para 41(e).

[163] ibid, para 42(a)–(c). The first two of these conditions referred to provisions that have since been superseded by the provisions of the GBER, namely Commission Regulation (EC) 70/2001 and Commission Regulation 1628/2006. It is unclear how these conditions are now intended to apply.

to 40% in other regions eligible for regional aid, provided that the beneficiary is an SME; and to 25% in regions eligible under Article 87(3)(a) of the Treaty and to 20% in other regions eligible for regional aid, provided that the beneficiary has less than 750 employees and/or less than €200 million turnover.[164] In regions not eligible for regional aid, companies that are not SMEs but which have less than 750 employees and/or less than €200 million turnover may receive aid up to 20% of eligible investments listed in the 2007–2013 Regional Aid Guidelines.[165] Otherwise, unless specifically provided, the Commission will only authorize aid for investments for companies active in the processing and marketing of agricultural products with 750 employees and more and a turnover of €200 million and more if they fulfil all the conditions of those guidelines.[166] No aid may be granted for the manufacture and marketing of products which imitate or substitute milk and milk products.[167] Aid for investments with eligible expenses in excess of €25 million, or where the actual amount of aid will exceed €12 million, must be specifically notified to the Commission.[168]

Environmental and animal welfare aid. In order to be authorized by the Commission, environmental aid schemes in the agricultural sector must give sufficient priority to the elimination of pollution at source and to the correct application of the polluter pays principle.[169] In addition, in order to qualify for environmental and animal welfare aid, farmers must meet the 'cross-compliance' obligations imposed by Regulation 1782/2003.[170] State aid should not normally be paid simply for respecting these obligations.[171] Aid for agri-environmental or animal welfare commitments may be approved under Article 87(3)(c) EC if, in particular, it fulfils all the requirements as set out in Articles 39 and 40 respectively of the Rural Development Regulation.[172] For example, as a general rule, the commitments must be undertaken for a period between five and seven years.[173] Aid over and above the amounts fixed in the Annex to the Rural Development Regulation may in principle only be authorized if granted for demonstrated additional costs and/or income foregone where the case is exceptional (taking into account special **11.47**

[164] ibid, para 42(c).

[165] ibid, para 42(d).

[166] ibid, para 43.

[167] ibid.

[168] ibid, para 45.

[169] ibid, para 49(b). On the polluter pays principle generally see eg N de Sadeleer, *Environmental principles: from political slogans to legal rules* (Oxford University Press, 2002) pp 21–60.

[170] Agriculture Guidelines, para 49(d); and see para 11.07 above.

[171] Agriculture Guidelines, para 49(d).

[172] ibid, para 51.

[173] The Rural Development Regulation, Articles 39(3) and 40(2). If exceptionally a Member State proposes to grant State aid for commitments of a shorter duration, it should provide a detailed justification, including a demonstration that the full environmental effects can be realized in the a shorter time proposed: Agriculture Guidelines, para 58.

circumstances to be duly justified) and where exceptional benefits for environmental protection can be shown.[174] Aid may also be approved under Article 87(3)(c) EC if it fulfils all the conditions set out in Article 38 of the Rural Development Regulation (relating to Natura 2000 payments and payments linked to the Water Framework Directive).[175] Otherwise, aid in favour of environmental protection will be examined by the Commission on the basis of the Environmental Aid Guidelines, which the Agriculture Guidelines expressly declare to be applicable to the agriculture sector.[176]

11.48 **Compensation for handicaps in certain areas.** Until 1 January 2010 the Commission will approve aid compensating for regional handicaps under Article 87(3)(c) EC if, in particular, it fulfils all the specified conditions of Regulation 1257/1999,[177] the precursor to the current Rural Development Regulation.[178] These include, for example, a requirement that farmers undertake to pursue their farming activity in a less-favoured area for at least five years from the first payment of a compensatory allowance. As from 1 January 2010, the successor provisions of the Rural Development Regulation (Articles 37 and 88(3)) will come into force,[179] and it will be these conditions which must be observed. Again there is a requirement that farmers undertake to pursue their farming activity in the designated areas for at least five years from the first payment. In all cases Member States must demonstrate the handicaps in question and provide proof that the amount of compensation to be paid avoids any overcompensation.[180] Further, the level of the compensatory payment must be proportionate to the economic impact of the handicaps,[181] and only the economic impact of permanent handicaps that lie outside human control can be taken into account when calculating the amount of compensatory payments.[182]

11.49 **Meeting standards.** The Commission will approve aid to meet standards under Article 87(3)(c) EC if, in particular, it fulfils all the conditions of Articles 31 and 88(5) of the Rural Development Regulation.[183] Article 31 provides support to farmers towards part of the costs incurred and income foregone as a result of compliance

---

[174] ibid, para 54.

[175] ibid, para 60. For Natura 2000 payments and payments linked to the Water Framework Directive see para 11.24 above.

[176] ibid, para 62; the latest version of these are the Community guidelines on State aid for environmental protection [2008] OJ C82/1, on which see further Chapter 5 above.

[177] [1999] OJ L160/80 (the specified conditions being set out in Article 14(1), the first two indents of Article 14(2) and Article 15).

[178] Agriculture Guidelines, para 70.

[179] Rural Development Regulation, Article 94.

[180] Agriculture Guidelines, para 73(a).

[181] ibid, para 73(b).

[182] ibid, para 73(c).

[183] ibid, para 77.

with standards in the fields of environmental protection, public health, animal and plant health, animal welfare and occupational safety. The standards must be newly introduced in national legislation implementing Community law and must impose new obligations or restrictions on farming practice which have a significant impact on typical farm operating costs and concern a significant number of farmers. The detailed rules include a requirement that any such aid must be flat-rate, temporary and degressive, granted on an annual basis for a maximum duration of five years from the date that the standard becomes mandatory under Community law.[184] Article 88(5), as has been seen, permits additional aid over and above the maximum amount fixed in the Annex to the Rural Development Regulation (€10,000 per holding) where it helps farmers to comply with national legislation which exceeds Community standards.[185] The additional aid must not, however, cover more than 80% of the costs incurred and income foregone by farmers. Moreover, taking into account all Community support, the total amount of support must not exceed €12,000 per holding.[186] Support may only be granted in relation to standards which, if calculated for an average farm of the sector and Member State concerned, can be shown to be the direct cause of an increase in operating costs for the product or products concerned of at least 5% or of an income loss equal to at least 10% of net profits from the products or products.[187] Further, there must be such an increase in operating costs or loss of income for at least 25% of all farms in the sector or subsector in the Member State concerned.[188]

Other rural development and ancillary measures. The Agriculture Guidelines also provide for the approval of aid for other rural development and ancillary measures. These measures include aid for the setting up of young farmers,[189] aid for early retirement or the cessation of farming activities,[190] aid for producer groups (with a focus on 'start-up' aids for SMEs)[191] aid for land reparcelling[192] aid to encourage the production of quality agricultural products to primary producers, and to companies active in the processing and marketing of agricultural products (support being limited to SMEs),[193] the provision of technical support in **11.50**

184 Rural Development Regulation, Article 31(2).

185 See para 11.15 above.

186 Agriculture Guidelines, para 78. This amount is not to be exceeded over any five-year period in the case of compensation granted for meeting more than one standard.

187 ibid, para 79.

188 ibid, para 80.

189 ibid, para 84. This must fulfil the conditions set out in Article 22 of the Rural Development Regulation.

190 ibid, para 87. This must fulfil the conditions set out in Article 23 of the Rural Development Regulation.

191 ibid, para 90.

192 ibid, para 96.

193 ibid, paras 98–9.

the agricultural sector (again support being limited to SMEs[194] and aids in the livestock sector (again support being limited to SMEs).[195]

2. **Risk and crisis management**

11.51 **General.** Good risk and crisis management is understood to be a key tool for a sustainable and competitive agricultural sector in the Community.[196] State aid is considered appropriate for such measures, provided that no undue distortions of competition ensue.[197] The focus, nonetheless, is upon support to those involved in primary production, since companies active in processing and marketing of agricultural products would normally have much greater opportunities to hedge risks.[198]

11.52 **Aid compensating for damage to agricultural production.** In the case of all aids to compensate for damage to agricultural production or the means of agricultural production, the Commission may not generally approve proposals submitted more than three years after the occurrence of the event, and aid must not be paid out more than four years following the event.[199] This type of aid is divided into four categories: aid to make good the damage caused by natural disasters or exceptional circumstances, aid to compensate for losses caused by adverse weather conditions, aid for combating animal and plant diseases, and aid towards the payment of insurance premiums. The first category applies to the whole of the agriculture sector, but the others are confined to support granted to primary production.

11.53 **(1) Natural disasters or exceptional circumstances.** Aid to make good the damage caused by natural disasters or exceptional circumstances is permitted within Article 87(2)(b) of the Treaty, but a restrictive interpretation is placed on the notions of both 'natural disaster' and 'exceptional occurrence'.[200] Circumstances that have qualified as natural disasters include earthquakes, avalanches, landslides and floods;[201] and circumstances that have qualified as exceptional circumstances include war and strikes, but not, as a general rule, outbreaks of plant or animal diseases.[202] Once the existence of a natural disaster or an

[194] ibid, para 103.
[195] ibid, para 109.
[196] ibid, para 112. See generally Communication from the Commission to the Council on risk and crisis management in agriculture, COM(2005) 74; and see also, with particular reference to insurance, para 11.34 above.
[197] Agriculture Guidelines, para 113.
[198] ibid, para 114.
[199] ibid, para 119.
[200] ibid, para 121; and see further paras 3.12–3.19 above.
[201] ibid, para 121.
[202] ibid, para 122.

exceptional occurrence has been demonstrated, aid will be permitted up to 100%. This may include compensation from loss of income, but any payments received under insurance policies should be deducted.[203] A direct causal link must be shown between the damage caused by the exceptional occurrence and the State aid.[204]

(2) **Adverse weather conditions.** Aid to compensate farmers for losses caused by adverse weather conditions may be permitted, even though the severity of the adverse weather conditions is insufficient to amount to a natural disaster.[205] The Treaty basis for authorization is therefore Article 87(3)(c) as opposed to Article 87(2)(b). The aid must, nonetheless, fulfil all the conditions of Article 11 of the Agriculture Block Exemption Regulation.[206] For losses suffered as from 1 January 2010, the Commission will derogate from the benefits conferred by taking out insurance contained in Article 11(8) of the Agriculture Block Exemption Regulation only if a Member State can convincingly show that, despite all reasonable efforts, affordable insurance covering the statistically most frequent climatic risks in the Member State or region concerned was not available at the time of the damage.[207] **11.54**

(3) **Animal and plant diseases.** Where a farmer loses livestock as a result of animal disease or his crops are affected by plant disease, this would not normally amount to either a natural disaster or exceptional occurrence, but aid may still be permitted under Article 87(3)(c) EC.[208] In this case, the aid must fulfil all the conditions of Article 10 of the Agriculture Block Exemption Regulation.[209] In addition, State aid for TSE tests and fallen stock may be declared compatible with Article 87(3)(c) if fulfils all the conditions of Article 16 of the Agriculture Block Exemption Regulation.[210] **11.55**

(4) **Insurance premiums.** Finally, aid towards the payment of insurance premiums also qualifies, provided that it fulfils all the conditions of Article 12 of the Agriculture Block Exemption Regulation and is not in favour of either large companies or, as already seen, companies active in the processing and marketing of agricultural products.[211] **11.56**

---

[203] ibid, para 123.

[204] ibid; and see para 3.14 above.

[205] ibid, para 125.

[206] ibid, para 126; and for Article 11 of the Agriculture Block Exemption Regulation see para 11.33 above.

[207] ibid, para 130.

[208] ibid, para 132.

[209] ibid, para 133; and for Article 10 of the Agriculture Block Exemption Regulation see para 11.32 above.

[210] ibid, para 134; and for Article 16 of the Agriculture Block Exemption Regulation see para 11.38 above. For a Commission decision in this context see Decision in Case N 283/2003 *TSE testing of fallen cattle aged over 24 months* (20 August 2003).

[211] ibid, paras 140 and 142; and for Article 12 of the Agriculture Block Exemption Regulation see para 11.34 above.

11.57 **Aid for closing production, processing and marketing capacity.** The Commission will approve aid for the closing of capacity under Article 87(3)(c) EC, either in sectors where excess capacity exists or, even if excess capacity does not exist, where the aid is in the interest of the sector as a whole (a condition which can be met for animal or human health, sanitary or environmental reasons). In the former case, the aid for capacity reduction must be part of a programme for the restructuring of the sector, with defined objectives and a specific timetable.[212] The duration of aid schemes should normally be limited to not more than six months for collecting applications for participation and a further 12 months for actually closing down.[213] Legally binding commitments must be obtained from the beneficiary that the closure is definitive and irreversible and that the beneficiary will not recommence the same activity elsewhere.[214] The commitments must also bind future purchasers of the facility.[215] This type of aid is only open to farmers who have actually been producing and in respect of production capacities that have actually been in constant use for the five years prior to closure.[216] In order to avoid erosion and other negative effects on the environment, open farmland or orchards taken out of production should, as a general rule, be afforested, although, alternatively, it is possible that they may be re-used after 15 years.[217] The amount of aid should be strictly limited to compensation for loss of the value of the assets, together with an incentive payment of up to 20% of that value.[218] Since continuing economic operators in the sector ultimately benefit from closure aid, the sector must provide a cash contribution of at least 50% of the actual public expenditure incurred, except where capacity is closed for health or environmental reasons.[219] If a Member State introduces a scheme for closing capacity, it must undertake not to grant aid for new production capacities in the sector for five years following termination of the closure programme.[220]

3. Other types of aid

11.58 **Other types of aid.** The Agriculture Guidelines also cover other types of aid, in particular aids for employment,[221] aid for research and development[222] and aid for

[212] ibid, para 144(a) and (b).
[213] ibid, para 144(c).
[214] ibid, para 144(f).
[215] ibid.
[216] ibid, para 144(g).
[217] ibid, para 144(h). Pending re-use, the land in question must be maintained in good agricultural and environmental condition (for which see Regulation 1782/2003 [2003] OJ L270/1 Article 5(1) and para 11.07 above).
[218] ibid, para 144(l).
[219] ibid, para 144(m).
[220] ibid, para 144(n).
[221] ibid, para 147.
[222] ibid, para 148.

advertising of agricultural products.[223] In the case of aid for advertising of agricultural products, there is again emphasis on 'added-value' production.[224] Accordingly, the advertising campaign must be earmarked for quality products,[225] Community-recognized denominations (whether protected designations of origin, protected geographical indications or other designations of origin which are protected under Community legislation) or national or regional quality labels.[226] In the case of national or regional quality labels, the origin of the product may be mentioned, but only as a subsidiary message, so as not to reinforce the preferences of domestic consumers in favour of products from their Member State.[227] The rate of direct aid may not exceed 50%, but where the sector contributes to at least 50% of the costs the aid rate may rise to 100%.[228] Aid for advertising up to 100% is also permitted if generic in character and for the benefit of all producers of the product concerned (although in this case no mention may be made of product origin).[229]

4. Forestry sector

Aids for the forestry sector. The Agriculture Guidelines depart from the earlier **11.59**
2000 guidelines in providing a specific policy on aids in the forestry sector.[230] The Commission will approve aid up to 100% under Article 87(3)(c) EC where the Member State can demonstrate that the measures directly contribute to maintaining or restoring ecological, protective and recreational functions of forests,

---

223 ibid, paras 153–9.

224 See para 11.36 above.

225 Defined by reference to Article 32 of the Rural Development Regulation.

226 See eg Council Regulation (EC) 509/2006 [2006] OJ L93/1; and Council Regulation (EC) 510/2006 [2006] OJ L93/12; and see generally eg C Macmaolain, *EU Food law: protecting consumers and health in a common market* (Hart Publishing, 2007), pp 102–22. The importance of such denominations may be judged by the extensive litigation that they have generated: see eg the Feta cheese litigation commencing with Cases C-289, 293 and 299/1996 *Denmark v Commission* [1999] ECR I-1541.

227 Agriculture Guidelines, paras 152(f) and 155. For the risk of advertising being incompatible with the Treaty on this basis see Case 249/81 *Commission v Ireland* [1982] ECR 4005; Case 222/82 *Apple and Pear Development Council v Lewis* [1983] ECR 4083; and Case C-325/00 *Commission v Germany* [2002] ECR I-9977. But Community legislation has long permitted reference to the origin of the product to meet specific policy objectives, a classic example being designations of origin and geographical indications: see now Council Regulation (EC) 510/2006 [2006] OJ 93/12, Art 2. On this aspect see Decision in Case N 653/2007 *Welsh red meat* (28 May 2008).

228 Agriculture Guidelines, para 156.

229 ibid, para 157.

230 ibid, paras 175–82. Forestry has been included here notwithstanding that Annex I to the Treaty cannot be regarded as covering in general terms trees and forestry products, even though some of those products taken in isolation might fall within its scope: Cases C-164-165/97 *European Parliament v Council* [1999] ECR I-1139. However, it may also be noted that the specific policy on aids in the forestry sector is without prejudice to the possibility of applying other State aid rules applicable to all sectors of trade and industry: Agriculture Guidelines, para 182.

biodiversity and a healthy forest ecosystem.[231] Such measures encompass planting, pruning and felling of trees and other vegetation in forests; maintaining and improving the soil quality in forests and ensuring a balanced and healthy tree growth; preventing, eradicating and treating pests, pest damage and tree diseases; restoration and maintenance of natural pathways, landscape elements and features and the natural habitat for animals; constructing, improving and maintaining forest roads; the costs of information materials and activities; and the purchase of forestry land used or to be used as nature protection areas.[232] Provided that it meets all the conditions laid down in Articles 43 to 49 of the Rural Development Regulation, the Commission may also permit aid for the afforestation of agricultural and non-agricultural land, the establishment of agroforestry systems on agricultural land, Natura 2000 payments, forest-environment payments, restoration of forestry potential and the introduction of prevention actions as well as non-productive investments.[233] The Commission may also authorize aid for the additional costs and income foregone due to the use under voluntary commitments of environmentally friendly forestry technology going beyond the relevant mandatory requirements.[234] Provided that specified conditions in the Agriculture Block Exemption Regulation are fulfilled, authorization may extend to aid for the purchase of forestry land, aid for training forest owners and forest workers and for consultancy services and aid for the setting up of forestry associations.[235]

F. Fisheries

11.60 **Definition of fisheries products.** Although, as has been seen, certain fishery products fall within Annex I to the EC Treaty,[236] for the purposes of the State aid rules the definition generally applied is that contained in Regulation 104/2000 on the

[231] ibid, para 175; and see Decision in Case N 204/2007 *English woodlands grants scheme* (27 July 2007).

[232] ibid.

[233] ibid, para 176. Conditions include the exclusion of Christmas trees in the case of first afforestation of agricultural and non-agricultural land and in the case of first establishment of agroforestry systems on agricultural land: Rural Development Regulation, Articles 43(3)(b), 44(3) and 45(2). For the Natura 2000 network see para 11.24 above. In these cases the Agriculture Guidelines require the maximum intensities stipulated in the Annex to the Rural Development Regulation to be respected (para 176).

[234] ibid, para 177. The maximum amounts stipulated in the Annex to the Rural Development Regulation may be exceeded if the aid is granted for demonstrated additional costs and/or income foregone, in exceptional cases taking into account specific circumstances to be duly justified, the commitments leading to a demonstrable and significant positive effect on the environment.

[235] ibid, paras 178–80. For the specified conditions in the Agriculture Block Exemption Regulation see in the case of the purchase of forestry land, Article 4; in the case of training and consultancy services, Article 15; and, in the case of forestry associations, Article 9.

[236] See para 11.01 above.

common organization of the markets in fishery and aquaculture products.[237] This definition covers both products caught at sea or in inland waters and specified products of aquaculture. These include live fish; fresh, chilled and frozen fish (subject to limited exceptions); dried, salted and smoked fish; crustaceans; molluscs; and pasta containing more than 20% by weight of fish, crustaceans, molluscs or other aquatic invertebrates.

General application of State aid rules. Just as with agriculture, under Article 36 EC the rules on competition apply to fisheries only to the extent determined by the Council.[238] However, again as with agriculture, the legislative framework for the fisheries sector does generally apply these rules. Thus Article 32 of Regulation 104/2000 stipulates that, notwithstanding any provisions to the contrary adopted under Articles 36 and 37 of the Treaty, Articles 87, 88 and 89 of the Treaty shall apply to the production of and trade in fishery products.[239] Similar provision is made under Article 7 of Regulation 1198/2006 on the European Fisheries Fund.[240] **11.61**

Legislative framework. Again as with agriculture, the general application of the State aid rules has historically been tempered by a block exemption and by *de minimis* rules, with guidelines covering the assessment of cases falling outside these provisions. The first such legislative package was adopted in 2004, with a block exemption Regulation,[241] a combined agriculture and fisheries *de minimis* Regulation[242] and guidelines.[243] A new Fisheries *de minimis* Regulation was adopted in 2007,[244] and the new Fisheries Guidelines were issued in April 2008.[245] In August 2008 the new Fisheries Block Exemption Regulation entered into force. As with the Agriculture Block Exemption Regulation, it is due to expire on **11.62**

[237] Council Regulation (EC) 104/2000 on the common organisation of the markets in fishery and aquaculture products [2000] OJ L17/22, Article 1.

[238] See para 11.10 above.

[239] [2000] OJ L17/22.

[240] Council Regulation (EC) 1198/2006 [2006] OJ L223/1, although note that Article 7(2) exempts from the State aid rules any financial contributions from Member States to operations co-financed by the European Fisheries Fund, which are provided as part of an operational programme. See also Council Regulation (EC) 744/2008 instituting a temporary specific action aiming to promote the restructuring of the European Community fishing fleets affected by the economic crisis [2008] OJ L202/1, Article 4.

[241] Commission Regulation (EC) 1595/2004 on the application of Articles 87 and 88 of the EC Treaty to State aid to small and medium-sized enterprises active in the production, processing and marketing of fisheries products [2004] OJ L291/3.

[242] Commission Regulation (EC) 1860/2004 on the application of Articles 87 and 88 of the EC Treaty to *de minimis* aid in the agriculture and fisheries sectors [2004] OJ L325/4.

[243] Guidelines for the examination of State aid to fisheries and aquaculture [2004] OJ C299/5.

[244] Commission Regulation (EC) 875/2007 on the application of Articles 87 and 88 of the EC Treaty to *de minimis* aid in the fisheries sector and amending Regulation (EC) 1860/2004 ('Fisheries *de minimis* Regulation') [2007] OJ L193/6.

[245] Guidelines for the examination of State aid to fisheries and aquaculture ('Fisheries Guidelines') [2008] OJ C84/10.

31 December 2013.[246] In addition, some forms of aid in the fisheries sector are now covered by the GBER.

11.63 ***De minimis* exemption.** The Fisheries *de minimis* Regulation applies to aid granted to undertakings in the fisheries sector, subject to exceptions that are similar to those in the agriculture sector. Thus, it does not apply to aid whose amount is fixed on the basis of price or quantity of products put on the market, aid to export-related activities, aid contingent on the use of domestic over imported goods or aid granted to undertakings in difficulty. In addition, there are two further exclusions specific to the fisheries sector: aid serving to increase fishing capacity, unless for modernization over the main deck, and aid for the purchase or construction of fishing vessels.[247] However, the definition of undertakings covered by the exemption is wider: unlike the agriculture sector the exemption applies not only to undertakings active in the production of fisheries products, but also those active in their processing and marketing.[248] A significant departure from the earlier legislation is that the Fisheries *de minimis* Regulation now exempts aid granted to any one undertaking up to €30,000 over any period of three fiscal years.[249] The detailed provisions are similar to the Agriculture *de minimis* Regulation. Accordingly, where the total amount of aid exceeds that ceiling, then all the aid is subject to the State aid rules.[250] A ceiling is also imposed at Member State level, with the cumulative amount of *de minimis* aid that may be granted to undertakings in the fisheries sector over any three fiscal years being, in the case of the UK, €102,725,000.[251] Finally, exemption can again only be conferred where it is possible to calculate precisely the gross grant equivalent of the aid *ex ante*, without need to undertake a risk assessment.[252]

11.64 **The GBER.** The GBER does apply to the fisheries sector in limited cases, namely training aid, aid in the form of risk capital, aid for R&D&I, and aid for disadvantaged and disabled workers.[253] In the majority of cases, however, the relevant block exemption will be the new Fisheries Block Exemption Regulation.

11.65 **Fisheries Block Exemption Regulation: general.** The Fisheries Block Exemption Regulation applies to transparent aid to SMEs active in the production, processing

---

246 Commission Regulation (EC) 736/2008 on the application of Articles 87 and 88 of the Treaty to State aid to small and medium-sized enterprises active in the production, processing and marketing of fisheries products ('Fisheries Block Exemption Regulation') [2008] OJ 201/16, Article 27.

247 Fisheries *de minimis* Regulation, Article 1.

248 ibid, Article 2(a).

249 ibid, Article 3(1)(2). The ceiling had previously been €3,000 over any period of three years.

250 ibid, Article 3(3).

251 ibid, Article 3(4) and Annex.

252 ibid, Article 3(7).

253 GBER, Article 1(3)(a).

or marketing of fisheries products.[254] It does not, however, apply to aid fixed on the basis of price or quality of products put on the market; aid to export-related activities; aid contingent upon the use of domestic over imported goods; aid granted to undertakings in difficulties; aid schemes which do not explicitly exclude the payment of individual aid[255] in favour of an undertaking which is subject to an outstanding recovery order following a previous Community decision declaring an aid illegal and incompatible with the common market; or ad hoc aid[256] in favour of an undertaking which is subject to such an order.[257] In addition, the exemption excludes aid for individual projects with eligible expenses in excess of €2 million, or where the amount of aid exceeds €1 million per beneficiary per year.[258]

Conditions. Ad hoc aid fulfilling all the conditions of the Fisheries Block Exemption Regulation is compatible with the common market under Article 87(3)(c) EC and exempt from the notification requirement of Article 88(3) EC, provided that the requisite information has been provided and the aid contains an express reference to the Regulation.[259] In the case of an aid scheme there is the additional requirement that any individual aid that could be awarded under the scheme must fulfil all the conditions of the Regulation;[260] and individual aid granted under such a scheme must directly fulfil all the conditions of the Regulation.[261] In all cases aid measures are only exempt as far as they explicitly provide that, during the grant period, the beneficiaries must comply with the rules of the common fisheries policy. Where these conditions are not met, the aid must be notified and assessed in accordance with the criteria laid down in the Fisheries Guidelines. **11.66**

Cumulation. For the purposes of the Fisheries Block Exemption Regulation the total amount of public support measures should be taken into account, whether or not that support is financed by local, regional, national or Community sources.[262] On the other hand, aid exempted under the Fisheries Block Exemption Regulation is not to be cumulated with any other aid exempted under its provisions, *de minimis* aid under the Fisheries *de minimis* Regulation or any other Community funding in relation to the same eligible costs if such cumulation **11.67**

---

254 Fisheries Block Exemption Regulation, Article 1(1). The definition of SMEs is that found in the GBER: ibid, Article 2(g).

255 Individual aid means ad hoc aid and notifiable awards of aid on the basis of an aid scheme: ibid, Article 2(c).

256 Ad hoc aid means individual aid not awarded on the basis of an aid scheme: ibid, Article 2(d).

257 ibid, Article 1(2).

258 ibid, Article 1(3).

259 ibid, Article 3(1). For the requisite information see ibid, Article 25.

260 ibid, Article 3(2).

261 ibid, Article 3(3).

262 ibid, Article 6(1).

would exceed the highest aid intensity or aid amount applicable to that aid under the Fisheries Block Exemption Regulation.[263]

11.68 **Categories of aid.** The following categories of aid may benefit under the Fisheries Block Exemption Regulation:[264] aid for the permanent cessation of fishing activities; aid for the temporary cessation of fishing activities; aid for socio-economic compensation for the management of the fleet; aid for productive investments in aquaculture; aid for aqua-environmental measures; aid for public health measures; aid for animal health measures; aid for inland fishing; aid for processing and marketing; aid for collective action; aid for measures intended to protect and develop aquatic fauna and flora; aid for investments in fishing ports, landing sites and shelters; aid for development of new markets and promotional campaigns; aid for pilot projects; aid for modification for reassignment of fishing vessels; aid for technical assistance; and tax exemptions in accordance with Directive 2003/96/EC.[265] In the case of all but the last category, detailed conditions must be satisfied by reference to the legislative framework governing the European Fisheries Fund;[266] and aid intensity is governed by the same framework.[267]

11.69 **Fisheries Guidelines.** The new Fisheries Guidelines, which took effect as from 1 April 2008, apply to the entire fisheries sector and concern the exploitation of aquatic resources and aquaculture. They include the means of production, processing and marketing of the resultant products, but exclude recreation and sport fishing which does not result in the sale of fishery products.[268] State aid can only be justified if it is in accordance with the objectives of Community competition policy and the common fisheries policy. It must not be protective in its effect: rather, it must serve to promote the rationalization and efficiency of the production and marketing of fishery products.[269] In order to be approved, the aid measure must contain some incentive element or require some counterpart on the part of the beneficiary.[270] The maximum duration of aid schemes is to be limited to ten years.[271] Measures of particular relevance to the Fisheries Guidelines include aid for investment on board fishing vessels, aid to make good damage caused by

---

263 ibid, Article 6(3).

264 ibid, Articles 8–24.

265 Directive 2003/96/EC restructuring the Community framework for the taxation of energy products and electricity [2003] OJ L283/51.

266 ie Regulation 1198/2006 [2006] OJ L223/1; and Commission Regulation (EC) 498/2007 laying down detailed rules for the implementation of Council Regulation (EC) 1198/2006 [2007] OJ L120/1.

267 Regulation 1198/2006 [2006] OJ L223/1, Annex II.

268 Fisheries Guidelines, paras 1.1 and 5.3.

269 ibid, para 3.1.

270 ibid, para 3.3.

271 ibid, para 3.6. By way of exception, a Member State may provide justification for an aid scheme with a duration in excess of ten years.

natural disasters, exceptional occurrences or specific adverse climatic events, and tax relief and labour-related costs concerning Community fishing vessels operating outside Community waters.[272] In the case of natural disasters and exceptional occurrences, aid of up to 100% may be permitted to compensate for material damage, with the existence of a natural disaster or exceptional occurrence being assessed on a case-by-case basis taking into account Commission practice and the ECJ's jurisprudence.[273] Not every adverse climatic event is to be considered a natural disaster or exceptional occurrence, but aid up to 100% can be approved under Article 87(3)(c) EC if the level of damage reaches 30% of the annual turnover of the undertaking concerned in the previous three years.[274]

Relevant Directorate General. State aid notifications in the fisheries sector are dealt with by the Directorate General for Maritime Affairs and Fisheries (DG Fish). While most recent State aid decisions in the agriculture sector are now listed on the DG Comp State aid register,[275] the DG Fish website contains a more comprehensive register of the decisions in the fisheries sector since 1997. **11.70**

[272] ibid, paras 4.3–4.5.
[273] ibid, para 4.4, and see para 11.53 above for similar provisions in the Agriculture Guidelines.
[274] ibid, para 4.4.
[275] See para 16.07 below.

12

TRANSPORT

Main legislation and guidelines

Council Regulation (EEC) 1191/69 on action by Member States concerning the obligation inherent in the concept of a public service in transport by rail, road and inland waterway [1969] OJ L156/1

Council Regulation (EEC) 1192/69 on common rules for the normalisation of the accounts of railway undertakings [1969] OJ L156/8

Council Regulation (EEC) 1107/70 on the granting of aids for transport by rail, road and inland waterway [1970] OJ L130/1

Council Regulation (EEC) 2408/92 on access for Community air carriers to intra-Community air routes [1992] OJ L 240/8

Regulation (EC) 1370/2007 of the European Parliament and of the Council on public passenger transport services by rail and by road and repealing Council Regulations (EEC) 1191/69 and 1107/70 [2007] OJ L315/1

Commission Regulation (EC) 800/2008 on the application of Articles 87 and 88 of the Treaty declaring certain categories of aid compatible with the common market (General Block Exemption Regulation) ('GBER') [2008] OJ L214/3

Decision 2005/842/EC on the application of Article 86(2) of the EC Treaty to State aid in the form of public service compensation granted to certain undertakings entrusted with the operation of services of general economic interest ('Article 86(2) Decision') [2005] OJ L312/67

Commission guidelines on the application of Articles 92 and 93 of the EC Treaty and Article 61 of the EEA agreement to State aids in the aviation sector ('1994 Aviation Guidelines') [1994] OJ C350/5

Framework on State aid to shipbuilding ('Shipbuilding Framework') [2003] OJ C317/11

Community guidelines on State aid to maritime transport ('Maritime Guidelines') [2004] OJ C13/3

Community Guidelines on financing of airports and start-up aid to airlines departing from regional airports ('2005 Aviation Guidelines') [2005] OJ C312/1

Community guidelines on State aid for railway undertakings ('Rail Guidelines') [2008] OJ C184/13

A. Introduction

12.01 **Treaty provisions: overview.** The transport sector is subject to special provisions under the EC Treaty, set out in Title V of the Treaty (Articles 70 to 80). These include specific rules on State aid, in Articles 73 and 76, which apply alongside the general Treaty State aid provisions in Articles 86 to 88.[1] But not all modes of transport fall within these rules. Article 80(1) confirms that Title V applies only to transport by rail, road and inland waterways. Consideration of the State aid rules for rail, road and inland waterways therefore needs to take account of both the *lex specialis* in Articles 73 and 76 and the *lex generalis* in Articles 86 to 88. By contrast, in relation to sea and air transport, Article 80(2) simply provides that the Council may adopt specific provisions for these two transport modes. Some legislation has been adopted on the basis of Article 80(2),[2] but this does not include any provisions displacing or derogating from the normal Treaty rules on State aid. In relation to the aviation and maritime transport sectors, therefore, the general rules in Articles 86 to 88 apply. These overlapping Treaty provisions are discussed in more detail in the following paragraphs.

12.02 **Existence of aid.** Nothing in Title V of the Treaty derogates from the basic definition of aid contained in Article 87(1), which applies to the entire transport sector

[1] ie they do not displace those rules or exempt any sector from the general State aid rules: Cases 209–213/84 *Asjes* [1986] ECR 1425, paras 41–2, and see further paras 12.03–12.04 below.

[2] Including Regulations 2408/92 and 3577/92, considered below in sections C and D respectively.

as for all other sectors.[3] Therefore if a State measure in the transport sector does not constitute aid (particularly on the grounds that it compensates for the costs of providing a public service, within the test set out in the *Altmark* case),[4] it will not engage either Article 73 or 76. It is only if a measure does constitute aid within that definition that, in respect of inland transport, Articles 73 and 76 become relevant. Equally, however, if a measure is in any event compatible on the basis of Article 73 and the secondary legislation implementing that Article, then it will not be necessary to consider whether it is aid under Article 87(1).

Article 73 and secondary legislation. Article 73 provides that: **12.03**

> Aids shall be compatible with this Treaty if they meet the needs of coordination of transport or if they represent reimbursement for the discharge of certain obligations inherent in the concept of a public service.

The Court has confirmed that the effect of this provision is not to *exempt* rail, road and inland waterway transport from the State aid rules of the Treaty: Articles 86 to 88 EC continue to apply in principle to these sectors.[5] Rather, the role of Article 73 is to provide for those sectors a specific basis on which certain types of aid may be compatible with the Treaty, in derogation from the rules that would otherwise apply in that respect.[6] However, at present, Article 73 cannot be applied directly; its application is defined exhaustively by the secondary implementing legislation[7] in Regulations 1191/69 and 1107/70.[8] Regulation 1191/69 sets out the conditions under which Member States may impose public service obligations in relation to inland transport, and how public services can be compensated. Regulation 1107/70 contains the rules on the grant of State aid to rail, road and inland waterways, especially in relation to coordination measures and the imposition of obligations. Both Regulations will be repealed on 3 December 2009 when Regulation 1370/2007[9] comes into force. After the entry into force of Regulation1370/2007, Article 73 EC will be directly applicable as a legal basis for establishing the compatibility of aid not covered by the Regulation.[10]

---

[3] As confirmed in Council Regulation (EEC) 1107/70 on the granting of aids for transport by rail, road and inland waterway [1970] OJ L130/1, Article 2.

[4] Case C-280/00 *Altmark* [2003] ECR I-7747, discussed at paras 2.67–2.73 above.

[5] See Case 156/77 *Commission v Belgium* [1978] ECR 1881, para 10.

[6] See also Case C-280/00 *Altmark* [2003] ECR I-7747, para 34.

[7] ibid, paras 96–109; see also Case T-157/01 *Danske Busvognmaend v Commission* [2004] ECR II-917, para 100.

[8] Council Regulation (EEC) 1191/69 on action by Member States concerning the obligation inherent in the concept of a public service in transport by rail, road and inland waterway [1969] OJ L156/1, as amended [1991] OJ L169/1; and Regulation 1107/70 [1970] OJ L130/1.

[9] Regulation (EC) 1370/2007 of the European Parliament and of the Council on public passenger transport services by rail and by road and repealing Council Regulations (EEC) 1191/69 and 1107/70 [2007] OJ L315/1.

[10] ibid, Article 9(2).

12.04 **Article 76.** By contrast to Article 73 and the secondary legislation referred to above, which provides for the *compatibility* of certain State aid in the transport sector, Article 76 sets out a *prohibition* specifically applicable to road, rail and inland waterways. Article 76(1) prohibits Member States from granting support or protection to undertakings or industries through favourable transport rates or conditions, unless authorized by the Commission. Under Article 76(2), in examining such rates or conditions, the Commission must take into account the objectives of any appropriate regional economic policy and the needs of underdeveloped areas. It should also take account of the problems of areas seriously affected by political circumstances on the one hand, and the effects of such rates and conditions on competition between the different modes of transport on the other. The Commission has a wide discretion to balance regional, economic and political concerns against the competitive effect of transport rates and conditions.[11] There is, however, little case-law relating to Article 76, which has rarely been applied in practice.

12.05 **Article 86(2).** As set out in Chapter 3 above, Article 86(2) allows aid to be approved where it is necessary for the performance of a service of general economic interest. However due to the application of Article 73 and Regulations 1191/69 and 1107/70, public service compensation in the road, rail and inland waterways sectors will be assessed in the first instance against those provisions rather than Article 86. As a result the Commission's Article 86(2) Decision does not cover land transport.[12] Public service compensation in the aviation and maritime sectors can, however, be assessed under Article 86(2), and the Article 86(2) Decision specifically allows certain types of public service compensation for airports, ports, maritime and air services where certain thresholds and conditions are met. In addition, Article 86(2) will continue to be relevant to cases in any transport sector which involve measures in favour of undertakings entrusted with a service of general economic interest, but which do not involve the payment of compensation as such.[13]

12.06 **Article 87(2) and (3).** As with Article 87(1), the provisions of Article 87(2) and (3) apply equally in the transport sector as for other sectors, and are thus available as a basis for the authorization of aid which falls outside the compatibility rules of Article 73 and Regulations 1191/69 and 1107/70. Any relevant secondary legislation, such as the new General Block Exemption Regulation ('GBER'), will also

---

[11] Case 1/69 *Italy v Commission* [1969] ECR 277, para 4.

[12] Decision 2005/842/EC on the application of Article 86(2) of the EC Treaty to State aid in the form of public service compensation granted to certain undertakings entrusted with the operation of services of general economic interest [2005] OJ L312/67, Article 2(2). See further paras 3.27–3.77 above.

[13] See Decision in Case N 540/2000 *Reform of the motorway concession system in France* (4 October 2000).

apply to the transport sector on this basis.[14] A significant amount of aid in the transport sectors has thus been approved under the heads of social aid, restructuring aid, environmental aid, training aid and aid to deal with natural disasters or other occurrences. Regional aid is also particularly important in the transport sector, as many transport schemes are viewed as generating and promoting regional development, which is a key element of the Community's transport policy.

Community transport policy. In addition to the relevant primary and secondary legislation referred to above, State aid decisions in the transport sector should take account of the Community's general transport policy. The main objective of the Commission's White Paper on Transport Policy[15] is the guarantee of safe, efficient and high quality transport services. This is in part a response to the progressive liberalization undergone by the sector since the 1980s.[16] The policy also aims to remove disparities between transport undertakings in different Member States which could result in substantial distortions in competition. State aid is identified as the means of promoting these objectives. For example by supporting transport systems to connect remote regions with the rest of the EU and neighbouring third countries, such measures are seen as improving the economic competitiveness of those regions. State aid is also seen as playing a role in promoting environmentally friendly modes of transport and transport systems. Member States' governments have put the Community transport policy at the heart of any future socio-economic development of the EU, and State aid is seen as having an important role in driving that policy forward. **12.07**

Relevant Directorate General. The Directorate General for Energy and Transport (DG Tren) deals with State aid notifications in the transport sector, although such notifications must still comply with the general procedural requirements set out in Regulations 659/199 and 794/2004.[17] In addition certain supplementary information is required when notifying restructuring aid in the aviation section, aid for transport infrastructure, aid for maritime transport and aid for **12.08**

[14] See Commission Regulation (EC) 800/2008 on the application of Articles 87 and 88 of the Treaty declaring certain categories of aid compatible with the common market (General Block Exemption Regulation) ('GBER') [2008] OJ L214/3. Indeed certain provisions of the GBER apply specifically to the transport sector: see para 12.13 below.

[15] European Transport Policy for 2010: time to decide, COM(2001) 370 final, reviewed in 2006 in Keep Europe Moving – Sustainable mobility for our continent – Mid Term Review of the European Commission Transport White Paper, COM(2006) 314 final.

[16] The aviation sector began this liberalization process in the 1980s with the first Community liberalization package which removed governmental intervention in relation to the introduction of tariffs. The maritime, road and inland waterways sectors have been gradually liberalized over the last 20 years. Rail liberalization has gathered momentum over the past ten years, and the recent adoption of the third rail liberalization package will see a greater opening up of the rail sector in the EU.

[17] See further Chapter 16 below.

combined transport.[18] While many transport decisions are listed on the DG Comp State aid register, a more comprehensive list of decisions in the transport sector dating from 1999 can be found on the website of DG Tren.

B. Inland transport—rail, road and inland waterways

1. Common legislative framework

12.09 **Overview.** As noted in section A above, the lawfulness of State aid for inland transport is governed not only by the general rules contained in Articles 86 to 88 EC, but also by the provisions of Article 73 as implemented by Regulations 1191/69 and Article 1107/69.[19] Regulation 1191/69 sets out the conditions under which Member States can impose public service obligations and how public services can be compensated. Regulation 1107/70 contains the rules on the granting of State aid, especially in relation to coordination measures and the imposition of obligations. Both these Regulations are to be repealed on 3 December 2009 when Regulation 1370/2007[20] comes into force. The following paragraphs explain generally the application of these Regulations. Sections 2 to 4 below address their specific application to rail, road and inland waterways.

12.10 **Regulation 1191/69.** Regulation 1191/69[21] sets out the framework within which Member States are able to compensate undertakings for public service obligations in the inland transport sectors. In particular, it defines the conditions under which Member States should impose public service obligations on public transport operators, and sets out in detail how such obligations may be compensated. Article 17(2) of the Regulation exempts Member States from the obligation contained in Article 88(3) to notify the Commission of compensation payments in relation to public service obligations, provided that they comply with the Regulation.[22] In consequence, many public service compensation schemes in rail, road and inland waterways have not been notified to the Commission on the basis that they fulfil the conditions of the Regulation.

---

[18] Commission Regulation (EC) 794/2004 implementing Council Regulation (EC) 659/1999 laying down detailed rules for the application of Article 93 of the EC Treaty [2004] OJ L140/1, as amended [2008] OJ L82/1, Annex 1 Part III.13.

[19] Regulation 1191/69 [1969] OJ L156/1; Regulation 1107/70 [1970] OJ L130/1.

[20] Regulation 1370/07 [2007] OJ L315/1.

[21] Regulation 1191/69 [1969] OJ L156/1.

[22] They must, however, 'promptly' forward to the Commission details of any compensation payments, a procedure similar to the reporting procedure established under the General Block Exemption Regulation—see para 5.26 above.

Regulation 1107/70. Insofar as Regulation 1191/69 does not apply, Regulation 1107/70 sets out exhaustively[23] the circumstances in which aid may be granted pursuant to Article 73 in order to compensate for public service obligations, or in order to coordinate inland transport. In relation to the latter, the Commission has consistently taken the position that the concept of aid meeting the needs of coordination of transport refers to the need for government intervention arising in the absence of a competitive market or in the presence of market failures.[24] Article 3(1) of the Regulation therefore sets out the types of coordinating aid that will be considered compatible under Article 73 of the Treaty. Article 3(2) lists the limited circumstances in which aid compensating for public service obligations, that does not fall within Regulation 1191/69, may nevertheless be permitted under Article 73. Unlike Regulation 1191/69, however, the measures listed in Article 3 are not exempt from notification under Article 88(3) EC, but must be duly notified to the Commission under that provision in order that the Commission can verify that the conditions of Regulation 1107/70 are satisfied.[25] The only exception is a narrow category of 'payments by States and public authorities to railway undertakings made by reason of any failure to achieve harmonisation . . . of the rules governing the financial relations between railway undertakings and States', in relation to which aid may be granted without the obligation to notify.[26] **12.11**

Regulation 1370/2007. On 23 October 2007 the Council and the European Parliament adopted the text for a new Regulation dealing with public service obligations for road and rail transport. This will enter into force on 3 December 2009, and will repeal Regulations 1191/69 and 1107/70 (save for freight transport services in relation to which Regulation 1191/69 will continue to apply until 3 December 2012). Regulation 1370/2007 sets out the framework under which Member States can grant compensation for the operation of public passenger services. The Regulation specifically applies to the provision of road and rail passenger services. However Member States have the discretion to extend its application to public transport by inland waterways.[27] Where it applies, the effect of the Regulation is to require Member States to enter into public service contracts where they wish to grant undertakings exclusive rights or compensation for the **12.12**

---

[23] Case C-280/00 *Altmark* [2003] ECR I-7747, paras 101–9.

[24] eg Decision in Case N 464/2003 *Company Neutral Revenue Scheme (CNRS)* (16 December 2003); Decision in Case N 810/2002 *Incentive scheme for railway freight transport* (10 December 2003); Decision in Case N 335/2003 *Aid for the setting up of rolling-motorway services in Friulia-Venezia-Giulia* (3 March 2004); Decision in Case N 64/2003 *Aid in support of combined transport* (1 October 2003); Decision in Case N 219/2001 *Intermodal transport on the River Danube* (20 June 2001).

[25] Regulation 1107/70 [1970] OJ L130/1, Article 5(1).

[26] ibid, Articles 4 and 5(2). There is, however, an annual reporting obligation: ibid, Article 5(2).

[27] Regulation 1370/2007 [2007] OJ L315/1.

discharge of public service obligations. The contracts must specify clearly and objectively how the public service compensation is to be calculated and the nature of any exclusive rights. The compensation must also be calculated in a way that prevents overcompensation, taking into account both the costs incurred and revenues generated in complying with the public service obligations, as well as a reasonable profit.[28] Public service compensation for public passenger services complying with the Regulation is exempt from the prior notification requirement under Article 88(3) EC.[29]

12.13 **The GBER.** Article 19 of the GBER specifically exempts aid for the acquisition of new transport vehicles which go beyond Community environmental standards or increase the level of environmental protection where there are no Community standards. Retrofitting of transport vehicles with the aim of increasing environmental protection will also be exempted. In order to qualify for exemption the aid intensity must not be more than 35%, although this can be increased to 55% for small enterprises and 45% for medium-sized enterprises. The aid must also fulfil the conditions set out in Article 18(2) of the GBER, which reiterate that the aid must result in an increase in the level of environmental protection.[30]

2. Rail

12.14 **Existence of aid.** Much public financing for railways has not been notified.[31] In some cases, this is because the measures simply do not constitute State aid within Article 87(1). In particular, the Commission considers that where railway infrastructure can be used by all potential users in a fair and non-discriminatory manner, and access to the infrastructure is charged for at a rate in accordance with Community legislation,[32] the construction of that infrastructure is not an economic activity, and the public financing of the infrastructure therefore does not constitute State aid.[33] In addition, insofar as the sector is not yet fully liberalized, State support will not be deemed to fall within Article 87(1).[34] However with the adoption of the 'third liberalisation package' in October 2007[35] the Community's

[28] ibid, Articles 3 and 4; see also Article 6 which defines how public service contracts must be awarded.

[29] ibid, Article 9.

[30] See also para 5.29 above; and note the similar provisions in the 2008 Environmental Aid Guidelines, for aid falling outside the GBER: para 5.42 above.

[31] State Aid Scoreboard – Autumn 2007 update, COM(2007) 719 final, p 15.

[32] ie Council Directive 91/440/EEC on the development of the Community's railways [1991] OJ L237/25, as amended [2001] OJ L75/1.

[33] Decision in Case N 478/2004 *Coràs Iompair Eireann* (7 June 2006), paras 24–34. There may, however, be aid where the infrastructure measure has the economic effect of enabling railway undertakings to benefit from charges below the normal commercial rates: Case C-382/99 *Netherland v Commission* [2002] ECR I-5153, para 66. See further paras 2.22–2.23 above.

[34] Cases C-15/98 and C-105/99 *Sardegna Lines* [2000] ECR I-8855, paras 68–70.

[35] Directive 91/440/EEC [1991] OJ L237/25, as amended [2001] OJ L75/1, is regarded as the 'first liberalisation package'. The 'second liberalisation package' was embodied in Directive

rail sector will move towards full liberalization. By 1 January 2010 all international passenger traffic will be open to competition as railway undertakings will have the right to access the rail infrastructure in all Member States. This means that, in the future, more financing in the rail sector is likely to be regarded as State aid.

Regulation 1192/69. A further reason for the non-notification of aid in the railway sector is the secondary legislation exempting certain types of compensation from the notification requirement contained in Article 88(3) EC. In addition to the common legislative framework for the inland transport sector set out in section 1 above, Regulation 1192/69[36] applies specifically to rail transport, and provides that Member States may compensate railway undertakings for burdens which, in other sectors, are normally borne by the State. This process of compensation is referred to in the Regulation as the 'normalisation of the accounts' of the railway undertakings. Railway undertakings are required to show the compensation they have received in respect of each class in a table annexed to their annual accounts.[37] Compensation within the Regulation does not, however, have to be notified to the Commission pursuant to Article 88(3) EC.[38] **12.15**

Rail Guidelines. In April 2008, the Commission adopted Community Guidelines on State aid for the railway undertakings ('Rail Guidelines').[39] The main objective of the Guidelines is to provide guidance on the compatibility with the Treaty of State aid to railway undertakings.[40] In particular, the Guidelines are based on the principles established in the three successive railway liberalization packages,[41] which aimed to create railway undertakings as independent commercial companies which were not directly linked to or dependent on infrastructure management. The Guidelines therefore aim to improve the transparency of public financing **12.16**

2004/51/EC [2004] OJ L164/164, which further amended Directive 91/440/EEC. The 'third liberalisation package' comprised (i) Regulation (EC) 1371/2007 of the European Parliament and of the Council on rail passengers' rights and obligations [2007] OJ L315/14; (ii) Directive 2007/58/EC of the European Parliament and of the Council amending Council Directive 91/440/EEC on the development of the Community's railways and Directive 2001/14/EC on the allocation of railway infrastructure capacity and the levying of charges for the use of railway infrastructure [2007] OJ L315/44; (iii) Directive 2007/59/EC of the European Parliament and of the Council on the certification of train drivers operating locomotives and trains on the railway system in the Community [2007] OJ L315/51.

36 Council Regulation (EEC) 1192/69 on common rules for the normalisation of the accounts of railway undertakings [1969] OJ L156/8.

37 ibid, Article 10.

38 ibid, Article 13(2). As with Article 17(2) of Regulation 1191/69, however, Member States must 'promptly' forward to the Commission details of compensation amounts paid under the Regulation.

39 [2008] OJ C184/19.

40 ibid, para 15. A 'railway' undertaking is defined in Directive 91/440/EEC [1991] OJ L237/25, Article 2 as 'any public or private undertaking the principal business of which is to provide services for the transport of goods and/or passengers by rail with a requirement that the undertaking must ensure traction'.

41 ibid, para 9 and n 35 above.

and legal certainty with regard to the Treaty rules in the context of opening markets for railway undertakings.[42] Specifically, they address the public financing of railway undertakings by means of infrastructure funding, aid for the purchase of and renewal of rolling stock, debt cancellation by States with a view to the financial rejuvenation of railway undertakings, aid for restructuring railway undertakings, aid for transport coordination and State guarantees for railway undertakings. However they do not deal with aspects of public service compensation covered by the new Regulation 1370/2007, for which the Commission has not yet developed any decision making practice.[43] Nor do they consider public financing for infrastructure managers.[44]

12.17 **Aid for railway infrastructure.** To the extent that financing of railway infrastructure constitutes aid at all,[45] it may be authorized under Article 3(1)(b) of Regulation 1107/70. This permits, in the context of the coordination of transport, aid for infrastructure granted to undertakings which have to bear expenditure relating to the infrastructure used by them, while other undertakings are not subject to a like burden. In assessing whether aid for infrastructure falls within that provision, the Commission will consider whether or not the recipient of the aid can provide funding itself for the development of the infrastructure.[46] An example of authorization under Regulation 1107/70 is the approval of an aid scheme in Saxony-Anhalt for the acquisition, maintenance, construction and development of railway infrastructure for freight transport.[47] In particular the Commission found that the development of the infrastructure would benefit the common interest as it would encourage the movement of freight from road to rail.[48] As noted at para 12.12 above, on 3 December 2009 Regulation 1107/70 will be repealed and Regulation 1370/2007 will enter into force. After that date, Article 73 will be available as a direct legal basis for the authorization of infrastructure aid of this nature.[49] The Commission's approach in this respect is set out in the section of the Rail Guidelines addressing aid for the coordination of transport.[50] Railway infrastructure aid has also been approved under Article 87(3)(b) where it constitutes an important project of common European interest,[51] and could also in principle be authorized under Article 87(3)(c).

[42] ibid, para 15.
[43] ibid, para 21.
[44] ibid, para 15.
[45] See para 12.14 above.
[46] Decision in Case N 308/2002 *German aid for rail infrastructure* (18 September 2002), para 36; Decision in Case N 170/2004 *Private railway sidings* (6 October 2004), paras 42 and 43.
[47] Decision in Case N 95/2007 *Aid for railway infrastructure in Saxony-Anhalt* (30 July 2007).
[48] ibid, paras 21 and 27.
[49] At least, until common rules on the allocation of infrastructure costs enter into force: Regulation 1370/2007 [2007] OJ L315/1, Article 9(2).
[50] See para 12.23 below.
[51] Decision in Case N 687/2002 *Channel Tunnel Rail Link* (30 April 2003).

Aid for rolling stock. Aid for the purchase and renewal of rolling stock has been reviewed by the Commission under a number of different heads: aid for coordination of transport, aid for restructuring, aid for SMEs, aid for environmental protection, regional aid and compensation for public service obligations. In particular the Commission is likely to approve aid for the purchase of rolling stock where it is in line with the Commission's policy to promote rail, especially through the better use of the infrastructure and trans-European networks. Consequently the Commission has approved under Article 87(3)(c) a scheme guaranteeing loans to Czech railways for the purchase of new passenger rolling stock. The loans amounted to State aid as they benefited the Czech railways, which were competing with other modes of transport. But the Commission did not consider that the aid adversely affected competition, since the extent of the aid was limited compared to the total turnover of the Czech railways. Further, the aid would result in the general promotion of rail transport.[52] **12.18**

Regional aid and rolling stock. Under the 2007–2013 Regional Aid Guidelines, expenditure on the purchase of transport equipment (movable assets) is not eligible for aid for initial investment.[53] In the Rail Guidelines, however, the Commission explains that there should be a derogation from this rule for rail passenger transport (but not freight transport). This is because it considers the costs of acquisition of rolling stock in the rail passenger sector to be admissible expenditure within the meaning of the Regional Aid Guidelines. For this derogation to be applicable, four cumulative conditions must be met: (1) the rolling stock concerned must be used exclusively for the provision of urban, suburban or regional passenger transport services in a specific region or for a specific line serving several regions; (2) rolling stock must remain exclusively assigned to the specific region or line; (3) replacement rolling stock must meet the latest interoperability, safety and environmental standards applicable to the network concerned; and (4) there must be evidence that the project contributes to a coherent regional development strategy.[54] **12.19**

Aid for restructuring of railway undertakings. When reviewing aid for restructuring of railway undertakings, the Commission will in principle apply the 2004 Rescue and Restructuring Guidelines.[55] These were applied in the *Metronet* case, where the Commission authorized loan facilities of up to £897 million granted by the UK authorities to Metronet, a company charged with maintaining, replacing and upgrading the majority of London Underground.[56] Specific considerations **12.20**

[52] Decision in Case N 770/2006 *Loan guarantee for railway rolling stock* (10 May 2007).
[53] Guidelines on National Regional Aid for 2007–2013 [2006] OJ C54/13, para 50 n 48.
[54] Rail Guidelines, paras 34–6.
[55] Community Guidelines on State aid for rescuing and restructuring firms in difficulty [2004] OJ C244/2 (considered in detail in Chapter 7 above); and see Rail Guidelines, para 62.
[56] Decision in Case NN 47/2007 *Metronet rescue aid* (28 November 2007).

apply, however, to the rail freight sector. The Rail Guidelines set out the conditions on which aid for to a railway undertaking allowing it to overcome difficulties in its freight operations might be compatible with the common market, even where such aid is not directly covered by the 2004 Rescue and Restructuring Guidelines.[57] In particular the restructuring must transform the freight activity from a protected activity enjoying exclusive rights to one which is competitive on the open market.[58]

12.21 **State guarantees.** The Commission's Notice on State guarantees[59] sets out the legal requirements applicable to State guarantees in the rail transport field. The Commission has consistently taken the view that unlimited State guarantees in a sector which is open to competition are incompatible with the Treaty. When State guarantees are granted to undertakings with a presence in both competitive and non competitive markets, the Commission requires the removal of the unlimited guarantee granted to the undertaking as a whole.[60] The Rail Guidelines acknowledge, however, that several railway undertakings still enjoy unlimited guarantees as a result of legacy monopolies established before the liberalization of the rail sector. Since these guarantees to a large extent constitute existing aid, the Commission has invited the Member States concerned to notify their guarantee arrangements as well as any measures to remove the unlimited guarantees.[61] This suggests that the Commission will no longer accept the existence of such unlimited guarantees, unless they can be clearly justified.

12.22 **Debt cancellation.** Directive 91/440/EEC, which set out the first rail liberalization package, specifically required Member States to set up mechanisms to help reduce the indebtedness of railway undertakings 'to a level that does not impede sound financial management and to improve their financial situation'.[62] Article 9(3) of the Directive envisages the grant of State aid in accordance with Articles 73, 87 and 88 EC to cancel the debts of railway undertakings. The Rail Guidelines confirm that this type of aid should generally be assessed on the basis of the 2004 Rescue and Restructuring Guidelines. However if the cancelled debts concern transport coordination, compensation for public service obligations or the setting of accounting standards, then the compatibility of the aid will be examined under Article 73 EC and its implementing regulations.[63] The Commission

[57] Rail Guidelines, paras 62–84.

[58] ibid, para 80.

[59] Commission Notice on the application of Article 87 and 88 of the EC treaty to State aid in the form of guarantees [2000] OJ C71/14; see further paras 2.42–2.43 above.

[60] Decision 2005/145/EC *State aid granted by France to EDF* [2005] OJ L49/9, paras 119–36.

[61] Rail Guidelines, paras 118–23.

[62] Directive 91/440/EEC [1991] OJ L237/25, as amended [2001] OJ L75/1, Article 9.

[63] Rail Guidelines, paras 52–3.

also takes the view that aid of this nature may be authorized under Article 87(3)(c) provided that five conditions are met. These conditions relate to (1) the duration of the debt, (2) the need for the debt to be linked directly to rail transport activities, (3) the indebtedness must hinder the financial management of the undertaking, (4) proportionality, and (5) the cancellation of the debt must not give an undertaking a competitive advantage. When these conditions are met, the debt is considered as contributing to the objective of Article 9 of Directive 91/440/EEC without unduly distorting competition and inter-State trade, and can therefore be considered compatible with the common market.[64]

Aid for coordinating rail transport services. As with aid for rail infrastructure, aid which has been granted to meet the needs of coordination of rail transport, within the meaning of Article 73 EC, must fulfil the requirements of Article 3(1)(b) of Regulation 1107/70. Following the entry into force of Regulation 1370/2007 and the repeal of Regulation 1107/70 in December 2009, this type of aid will be capable of authorization directly on the basis of Article 73, insofar as the aid is not covered by the other provisions of Regulation 1370/2007. In that respect, the Commission has made it clear that while in principle aid that meets the needs of transport coordination must be considered compatible with the Treaty, for an aid measure to be considered to 'meet the needs' of transport coordination within Article 73 a number of conditions must be satisfied.[65] First, the measure must be necessary and proportionate. Below certain aid intensity thresholds, there is a presumption of necessity and proportionality; but above those thresholds the necessity and proportionality of the aid must be specifically demonstrated.[66] Secondly, the distortion of competition must not jeopardise the general interests of the Community. Third, the aid must be limited to a maximum of five years to allow the Commission to re-examine it after that period. **12.23**

3. Road

Overview. Regulation 881/92[67] liberalized road freight transport across Member States from 1 January 1993. Road freight cabotage (the movement of goods within a Member State) has been liberalized since 1 January 1998 under the terms of Regulation 3118/93.[68] Unlike the rail transport sector, there is no specific implementing legislation or guidance applying the State aid rules to road transport. **12.24**

---

[64] ibid, paras 55–61.

[65] ibid, paras 95–9.

[66] ibid, paras 107–11.

[67] Council Regulation (EEC) 881/92 on access to the market in the carriage of goods by road within the Community to or from the territory of a Member State or passing across the territory of one or more Member States [1992] OJ L95/1.

[68] Council Regulation (EEC) 3118/93 laying down the conditions under which non-resident carriers may operate national road haulage services within a Member State [1993] OJ L279/1.

Aid for road transport schemes is therefore subject to Article 73 and its implementing legislation, as well as Articles 86 to 88. The following paragraphs consider the main issues that have arisen in this sector.

12.25 **Existence of aid.** Several of the issues considered in Chapter 2 above have arisen in relation to road transport measures. In particular, many State aid measures in the road transport sector relate to public service compensation. Where such compensation fulfils the *Altmark* test, it is not State aid within Article 87(1).[69] A measure may also escape classification as aid to the extent that it applies to businesses operating only at a local level, such that there is no effect on inter-State trade.[70] The Court has, however, repeatedly rejected attempts to classify road transport aids as general measures, where the Member State simply relies on an objective such as environmental protection, without establishing that the logic of the aid system strictly flows from that objective.[71]

12.26 **Approval of public service compensation schemes.** In the cases where public service compensation is aid within Article 87(1), certain schemes are exempt from notification under Regulation 1191/69, as discussed at para 12.10 above. However the Commission will still examine compensation schemes where it is alleged that the conditions of Regulation 1191/69 have not been met. In 2007, following an investigation into compensation for Maltese bus operators, the Commission found that the measures (to the extent that they were State aid at all) complied with Regulation 1191/69.[72] By contrast, a formal investigation procedure has been opened in relation to compensation payments to Irish bus operators following concerns that funding was not available on an equal basis for all potential operators.[73] The Commission has also opened proceedings against the Czech Republic for failing to advertise a tender to the provision bus services in Southern Moravia in accordance with the provisions of Regulation 1191/69.[74] Failure to comply with the secondary legislation implementing Article 73 is, of course, not fatal to the approval of a State aid. In its decision on a compensation payment of €1 million to bus operators in Wittenberg, the Commission held that Regulation 1191/69 was inapplicable and that the conditions of Regulation 1107/70

[69] Case C-280/00 *Altmark* [2003] ECR I-7747, discussed at paras 2.67–2.73 above. See Decision N 604/2005 *Public bus services in Wittenberg* (16 May 2006) for a case in which the *Altmark* criteria were held not to be satisfied.

[70] See Decision 2001/605/EC *Renove II [2001]* OJ L212/34, para 29 (other parts of the decision annulled in Case C-409/00 *Spain v Commission ('Spanish trucks II')* [2003] ECR I-1487), and para 2.145 above.

[71] eg Case T-55/99 *CETM v Commission* [2000] ECR II-3207; *Spanish trucks II*, ibid; and see further para 2.129 above.

[72] Decision in Case NN 53/2006 *Aid to bus operators in Malta* (21 March 2007).

[73] Decision in Case C 31/2007 *Irish bus operators* [2007] OJ C217/44.

[74] Decision in Case C 3/2008 *Southern Moravian bus companies* [2008] OJ C43/19.

were not satisfied. However the aid was approved under Article 87(3)(c) since it was intended to improve the quality of public transport in the area, and the bus operators had been selected by an open, transparent and non-discriminatory public tender process.[75] In addition, aid might be approved under Article 86(2), as was the case for a French scheme extending operating concessions for motorways.[76]

Environmental aid. The Commission has on a number of occasions examined whether aid given for the purchase of vehicles may be approved under Article 87(3)(c) on environmental grounds. In 2002 the Commission initially approved a Spanish scheme which provided aid for the purchase of electric and hybrid powered vehicles in the Castile Leon region.[77] In 2007 the Commission agreed to the extension of the scheme which enabled individuals and companies to apply for grants of up to 30% of extra costs of the new vehicles compared to conventional vehicles. The scheme was found to be compatible with Article 87(3)(c).[78] An Italian scheme to encourage companies to replace older and more polluting lorries with more environmentally friendly lorries was approved under Article 87(3)(c) and the 2001 Environmental Aid Guidelines.[79] Similarly the Commission has approved Danish and Italian aid schemes enabling lorry and bus operators to retrofit anti-pollution filters.[80] However, as noted at para 12.13 above, Article 19 of the GBER now exempts aid for the acquisition of transport vehicles which improve or promote environmental protection beyond Community standards. It is therefore possible that environmental aid schemes such as those noted above will in the future be designed so as to comply with the conditions of Article 19, and therefore be exempted from notification. **12.27**

4. Inland waterways

Overview. Cabotage traffic on inland waterways has been liberalized since 1993.[81] **12.28**
Regulation 1356/96 further liberalized inland transport between Member States

[75] Decision N 604/2005 *Public bus services in Wittenberg* (16 May 2006).

[76] Decision in Case N 540/2000 *Reform of the motorway concession system in France* (4 October 2000).

[77] Decision in Case N 203/2002 *Electric and hybrid vehicles* (18 September 2002).

[78] Decision in Case N 212/2007 *Electric and hybrid vehicles* (15 June 2007).

[79] Decision in Case N 463/2007 *Commercial vehicles — environmental protection* (15 January 2008).

[80] Decision in Case N 573/2005 *Lorries — environmental protection* (21 December 2006); Decision in Case N 400/2006 *Lombardia — installation of particulate filters on diesel buses* (6 December 2006).

[81] Pursuant to Council Regulation (EEC) 3921/91 laying down the conditions under which non-resident carriers may transport goods or passengers by inland waterway within a Member State [1991] OJ L373/1.

from 1 August 1996.[82] While a large proportion of recent inland waterways aid schemes are part of intermodal schemes (discussed in section 5 below), the Commission has considered some pure inland waterway schemes. These have mainly been assessed under Article 73 and its implementing Regulation 1107/70 and the provisions of Article 87, especially Article 87(3)(c). Aid to inland waterways is generally compatible with the objectives of Europe's transport policy in that it encourages the use of inland transport as a competitive alternative to road transport. Consequently the Commission often considers that any distortion of competition arising from the aid is outweighed by its contribution to the objectives of the common European interest.

12.29 **Approved schemes.** Aid for inland waterways is frequently approved on environmental grounds. The Commission thus recently approved a French aid scheme which provided funding for environmental measures, fleet modernization and improved safety. In particular the Commission considered that the scheme promoted and revived the occupation of inland waterway carriers and facilitated investment in new vessels which would save energy and reduce pollution.[83] A similar scheme was approved for the purchase of low-emission engines, transhipment equipment and navigational equipment in the Czech Republic.[84] The Commission has also approved two Belgian schemes to promote inland waterway transport on environmental grounds, taking account also of the Community policy of encouraging intermodal transport.[85]

5. Intermodal transport

12.30 **Definition.** 'Intermodal transport' refers to two separate but interrelated activities. Primarily, it is the term used to describe the efficient movement of goods, using two or more modes of transport, in an integrated transport chain. Each mode of transport has its own advantages in relation to capacity, high levels of safety, flexibility, low energy consumption and low environmental impact. Intermodal transport therefore allows each mode to contribute to a transport chain which is more efficient, cost effective and sustainable. Within the context of European transport policy 'intermodal' also refers to the shift from road to other modes

---

[82] Council Regulation (EC) 1356/96 concerning common rules applicable to the inland carriage of goods or of persons by waterways between Member States, with a view to carrying out in this transport the freedom to provide services [1996] OJ L175/7.

[83] Decision in Case N 651/2007 *French scheme to boost inland water transport* (2 July 2008).

[84] Decision in Case N 358/2007 *Czech Republic scheme for inland waterway transport* (20 May 2008).

[85] Decisions in Cases N 53/2006 *Haven van Zeebrugge - estuarine navigation* (12 October 2006) and N 720/2006 *Port de Bruxelles - navigation intérieure* (18 July 2007). On intermodal transport see next section.

of transport. The Commission's White Paper on Transport Policy[86] thus encourages the use of rail and other environmentally friendly modes of transport, such as short sea shipping and inland transport, as alternatives to road haulage. This not only reduces congestion, but improves road safety and has benefits for the environment.

Application of State aid rules. When State aid rules are applied to intermodal transport two types of schemes will be reviewed: (1) schemes which allow the development of efficient transport chains and (2) schemes which facilitate an efficient shift from road to alternative modes of transport. Often these two types of schemes will be interrelated. Article 73 is therefore applicable to these intermodal or combined transport schemes. Initially Article 3(1)(e) of Regulation 1107/70 had specifically allowed temporary aids for infrastructure and fixed and moveable facilities which were designed to facilitate the development of combined transport. However this provision ceased to apply after 31 December 1997.[87] As a result the Commission considered that, in the absence of specific secondary legislation on State aid to combined transport, Article 73 could be directly applied in this respect.[88] However since the ECJ's confirmation that Article 73 is *not* directly applicable,[89] the Commission has assessed intermodal schemes under Article 87(3)(c). As with inland waterways, aid for intermodal transport is generally regarded as compatible with the promotion of the Europe's transport policy and the specific aim of moving freight off the road and onto other more environmentally friendly modes of transport. **12.31**

Approved schemes. The Commission has approved, under Article 87(3)(c), an Italian aid scheme for logistics undertakings organizing combined transport services departing or arriving from a railway station or intermodal centre located in the Friulia-Venezia Giulia region,[90] and another Italian scheme aimed at promoting road-sea combined transport services on long distance routes in Sicily and other ports in Italy and the EU.[91] An Austrian scheme which encouraged the **12.32**

[86] European Transport Policy for 2010: time to decide, COM(2001) 370 final, reviewed in 2006 in Keep Europe Moving – Sustainable mobility for our continent – Mid Term Review of the European Commission Transport White Paper, COM(2006) 314 final.

[87] Article 3(1)(e) was inserted into Regulation 1107/70 by Regulation 1658/82 [1982] OJ L184/1, and amended by Regulation 3578/92 [1992] OJ L364/11 to permit such aid under the Regulation until 31 December 1995. Regulation 543/97 [1997] OJ L84/6 subsequently extended this to 31 December 1997.

[88] Decisions in Cases N 79/97 *Stimuleringsregeling Gecombineerd Goederenvervoer* (20 October 1997); and N 577/1999 *Subsidy for rail terminals in the port of Rotterdam* (4 October 2000).

[89] In Case C-280/00 *Altmark* [2003] ECR I-7747: see para 12.03 above.

[90] Decision in Case N 436/2004 *Friuli-Venezia Giulia – Measures to develop intermodality* (22 March 2006).

[91] Decision in Case N 551/2003 *Measure to encourage combined road-sea transport of freight in Sicily* (6 October 2004).

development of combined transport and a shift away from road transport was also approved under Article 87(3)(c).[92] In France the Commission has approved under Article 87(3)(c) a scheme aimed at reducing the disadvantages of having to load and unload goods using combined transport as opposed to door to door transport. Under the scheme operators will be paid a flat rate aid for each intermodal transport unit which is transhipped at a land or port terminal located in France.[93]

C. Air transport

12.33 **Policy.** Up until the 1980s national airlines that were wholly or partially owned by the Member State governments were prevalent in the airport transport sector. Such airlines typically benefited from considerable subsidies and preferential rights.[94] With the gradual liberalization of the sector between 1987 and 1997 many national airlines were not economically strong enough to withstand an open market and suffered heavy losses. Applying State aid to bolster failing national carriers was therefore a natural consideration for many Member State governments. Consequently there was initially a need for stricter application for the State aid rules to avoid distortions in competition. However, this strict approach had to be tempered following the terrorist attacks of 11 September 2001. These left air carriers facing increased security costs and a dramatic fall in passengers, which resulted in many European airlines facing economic hardship. Most Member States considered intervening to provide financial support for the ailing airlines. The application of the State aid rules in the aviation sector has therefore had to balance the need to maintain undistorted competition with the need to ensure that the European air sector can operate effectively in what has become an economically volatile environment.

12.34 **1994 Aviation Guidelines.** The first Guidelines on State aid in favour of air carriers were published in 1984 to coincide with the Commission's proposed liberalization programme for air transport.[95] These were replaced by the 1994

[92] Decision in Case N 196/2006 *Aid for transhipment systems in intermodal transport* (13 September 2006).

[93] Decision in Case N 159/2008 *French aid scheme to promote combined transport* (17 June 2008).

[94] See Report by the Commission to the Council and the European Parliament on the evaluation of aid schemes established in favour of Community air carriers, SEC(1992) 431 final, which lists all subsidies granted by Member States to national carriers.

[95] Memorandum No 2 on civil aviation: progress towards the development of a Community air transport policy, COM(84) 72 final, Annex IV: Guidelines and criteria for the evaluation of State aid in favour of air carriers on the basis of Articles 92 and 93 of the EC Treaty.

Aviation Guidelines.[96] The Guidelines set out the situations in which operating aid will be approved, and consider the application of the Article 87(3)(a) and (c) exemptions to the aviation sector, aid elements in the privatization of national carriers, and the grant of exclusive rights for activities ancillary to air transport. This refers mainly to duty free shops, but extends also to activities such as flight schools, airport facilities, franchises and airport charges.[97]

2005 Aviation Guidelines. The 1994 Aviation Guidelines did not address State infrastructure investment in airports, as at the time the Commission considered that infrastructure development was a general measure of economic policy which was not covered by the State aid rules.[98] This assumption was, however, no longer valid following the liberalization and restructuring of the aviation sector. In its 29th Report on Competition Policy the Commission noted that due to the increasingly important commercial role played by airports coupled with combined transport and transport infrastructure user charges, it was reviewing its traditional approach on the application of the State aid rules to infrastructure.[99] In addition, there was increased recognition of the importance of regional airports and the disadvantages suffered by these compared to the major hubs. These two factors led to the adoption of the 2005 Aviation Guidelines.[100] These do not replace the 1994 Guidelines, but supplement them by specifying how the State aid rules apply to various means of financing airports for airlines serving regional airports. **12.35**

Operating aid. The 1994 Aviation Guidelines confirm that direct operational subsidization of air routes will only be approved where it compensates public service obligations, or where the aid is of a social character exempted by Article 87(2)(a).[101] In relation to public service obligations, aid will however only be approved if the relevant rules contained in Regulation 2408/92 are observed.[102] With regard to social aid, the Guidelines note that aid will be allowed where it is of direct benefit to the end consumer. To this end aid will be allowed where it covers specific categories of passengers or a route servicing underprivileged regions. As discussed in the next paragraph, a number of measures favouring air transport have been approved as being aid of a social character. **12.36**

[96] Commission guidelines on the Application of Articles 92 and 93 of the EC Treaty and Article 61 of the EEA agreement to State aids in the aviation sector [1994] OJ C350/5.

[97] 1994 Aviation Guidelines, para 10.

[98] ibid, para 12; and see 25th Report on Competition Policy (1995), para 175.

[99] 29th Report on Competition Policy (1999), para 299.

[100] Community Guidelines on financing of airports and start-up aid to airlines departing from regional airports [2005] OJ C312/1.

[101] 1994 Aviation Guidelines, paras 14–24. For a case of prohibited operating aid see Decision 2004/393/EC *Charleroi airport - Ryanair* [2004] OJ L137/1.

[102] Council Regulation (EEC) 2408/92 on access for Community air carriers to intra-Community air routes [1992] OJ L240/8; and see para 12.42 below.

12.37 **Social aid.** A number of measures affecting the airline industry have been approved under the social aid exemption in Article 87(2)(a),[103] particularly aid schemes assisting inhabitants in remote islands. On this basis, a French scheme assisting young students and trainees with air travel costs from the French overseas departments to the French mainland was found to be compatible with Article 87(2)(a). The grants were made directly to the individuals concerned and as they favoured air services operating between the French mainland and the overseas departments, this generated additional demand for those services.[104] The Commission also approved on this basis a social aid scheme involving air services to the smaller Sicilian islands.[105]

12.38 **Rescue and restructuring aid.** Recapitalization that complies with the private investor test will fall outside the scope of Article 87(1).[106] Where Article 87(1) is engaged, rescue and restructuring aid may be approved under the provisions of the 2004 Guidelines on Rescue and Restructuring Guidelines, which in principle apply to the aviation sector.[107] However, the 2004 Guidelines are expressly subject to any specific sectoral rules that apply,[108] which include the provisions in the 1994 Aviation Guidelines on restructuring aid.[109] The 1994 Aviation Guidelines envisaged that, after the completion of the common aviation market in 1997, restructuring aid would not be authorized save 'in very exceptional cases and under very stringent conditions'.[110] In any event, however, the 1994 Aviation Guidelines provide that any restructuring aid must comply with a number of detailed conditions, including that the aid must form part of a comprehensive programme and be of limited duration; the programme must be self-contained in the sense that no further aid is necessary for the duration of the programme or is envisaged in the future; the objective of the aid must not be to increase capacity and the offer of the airline concerned to the detriment of its competitors; the Member State must allow the company to be run according to commercial principles; the aid must be proportionate and only used for the purposes of the restructuring programme; and the aid must be transparent.[111]

---

[103] See paras 3.07–3.11 above for detailed discussion of the conditions under this provision.

[104] Decision in Case NN 25/2005 *Mobility passport* (20 April 2005); see also similar scheme for Réunion: Decision in Case N 656/2006 *Réunion social aid scheme* (4 December 2006).

[105] Decision in Case N 399/1999 *Italia* (3 September 1999).

[106] See paras 2.33 *et seq* above, and note in particular the recent judgment in Case T-301/01 *Alitalia* (judgment of 9 July 2008), upholding the Commission's finding of aid in relation to the recapitalization of Alitalia in the late 1990s.

[107] Community Guidelines on state aid for rescuing and restructuring firms in difficulty [2004] OJ C244/2.

[108] ibid, para 21.

[109] 1994 Aviation Guidelines, paras 38–41; and see para 7.08 above.

[110] ibid, paras 38(2) and 41, applied in Case T-301/01 *Alitalia* (judgment of 9 July 2008).

[111] ibid, para 38.

Start-up aid. The 2005 Aviation Guidelines acknowledge that in order to promote the development of small regional airports especially in more remote regions of the Community, start-up aid may be necessary for routes operating to and from remote regions. The Guidelines set out detailed conditions for the approval of such aid, including conditions that the aid must normally relate to routes linking certain regional airports to other EU airports, that the aid should only apply to the opening of new routes or new schedules which will increase passenger volumes, and should not encourage traffic simply to be transferred from one airline to another, and that the aid must be granted on a transparent and non-discriminatory basis.[112] On the basis of the Guidelines, the Commission approved start-up aid to support new routes from Malta International Airport, with the object of enhancing access to air transport services in Malta.[113] Similarly the Commission approved plans to grant a subsidy to Ryanair to start an air service between the airports of Toulon and London Stansted.[114] In both of these decisions the Commission concluded that the aid would be granted in a transparent and non-discriminatory manner. It should also not be forgotten that the Commission allowed Ryanair to retain some aid that it received from Charleroi Airport for the launch of new routes provided certain conditions were met. In particular, the aid had to serve as an incentive for the opening of the new routes and be proportionate to that objective. It also had to be accompanied by a mechanism for imposing penalties should the carrier fail to comply with its commitments. The Commission also stipulated that the aid had to be non-discriminatory, such that it would be available in the future to any airline established at Charleroi.[115] **12.39**

11 September 2001. The airline industry was dramatically affected by the 11 September 2001 terrorist attacks. The attacks prompted the insurance industry to review its risk exposure and withdraw almost all war and terrorism cover at short notice. This resulted in the Commission's adopting a Communication in October 2001 in which the Commission acknowledged that some aid could be justified under Article 87(2)(b) to compensate airlines for these extraordinary events.[116] In particular the Commission identified two instances when aid would be appropriate: aid to cover the losses incurred as a result of American airspace being closed for four days, and aid to compensate for the extra costs of insurance cover.[117] The Commission subsequently approved aid for airlines and for private **12.40**

[112] 2005 Aviation Guidelines, paras 77–81 set out the detailed compatibility criteria.

[113] Decision in Case N 640/2006 *Air route development scheme for Malta* (22 November 2006).

[114] Decision in Case N 563/2005 *Aid to Ryanair for the air service between Toulon and London* (22 June 2006).

[115] Decision 2004/393/EC *Charleroi airport - Ryanair* [2004] OJ L137/1.

[116] Communication on the repercussions of the terrorist attacks in the United States on the air transport industry, COM(2001) 574.

[117] ibid, paras 35–40.

providers of insurance against terrorist risks in the UK, Luxembourg, Portugal, Sweden, Belgium, Austria, Denmark, France, Spain, and Germany.[118] In the *Olympic Airways* case, however, the CFI held that approval could not be limited to compensation for the losses incurred from 11 to 14 September, provided that there was a direct causal connection between the loss and the events of 11 September, and that the loss could accurately be evaluated. On that basis the Court partially annulled the Commission's decision in relation to Greek aid consequent upon the 11 September attacks, to the extent that the Commission had found certain parts of the aid incompatible with the common market.[119]

12.41 **Infrastructure**. Before the adoption of the 2005 Aviation Guidelines, the Commission had authorized public grants for improving infrastructure at the airports of Manchester and Elba, on the grounds that the measures concerned did not constitute State aid within the meaning of Article 87(1).[120] In the 2005 Aviation Guidelines, however the Commission stated that in the case of public funding of an infrastructure:

> it is not possible to rule out the possibility that particular cases may contain elements of aid. For example, there might be aid if the infrastructure in question were allotted to a predetermined manager which gained undue advantage therefrom, or if an unjustifiable difference between the sale price and a recent construction price were to give the purchaser an undue advantage.[121]

Where there is aid, the 2005 Aviation Guidelines confirm that it may be compatible under Article 87(3)(a), (b) or (c) or Article 86(2).[122] In particular the Commission will examine whether construction and operation of the infrastructure meets a clearly defined objective of general interest (regional development, accessibility, etc) and is necessary and proportional to the objective which has been set. It will also take into account whether the infrastructure has satisfactory medium-term prospects for use, and whether all potential users of the infrastructure have access to it in an equal and non-discriminatory manner. The Commission has

[118] Decisions in Cases NN 90/2001 *UK* (23 October 2001); NN 140/2001 *Luxembourg* (28 November 2001); NN 144/2001 *Portugal* (28 November 2001); NN 139/2001 *Sweden* (11 December 2001); NN 141/2001 *Belgium* (11 December 2001); NN 153/2001 *Austria* (20 December 2001); NN 146/2001 and NN 161/2001 *Denmark* (20 December 2001); NN 157/2001 *France* (20 December 2001); NN 143/2001 *Spain* (20 December 2001); and NN 162/2001 *Germany* (20 December 2001).

[119] Case T-268/06 *Olympiaki Aeroporia Ypiresies ('Olympic Airways') v Commission* (judgment of 25 June 2008).

[120] Decisions in Cases NN 109/1998 *Manchester Airport* (14 June 1999) and N 638/1998 *Subsidy to Aerelba* (30 March 1999).

[121] 2005 Aviation Guidelines, para 59.

[122] ibid, para 61.

approved Irish and UK infrastructure aid schemes under Article 87(3)(a) and (c), on the basis of conditions in the 2005 Aviation Guidelines.[123]

Public service compensation. As noted at para 12.05 above, public service compensation in the aviation sector can be approved directly on the basis of Article 86(2). In addition to the general requirements of that provision, such compensation will only be approved where it complies with the provisions of Regulation 2408/92, which sets out in detail the scope of the public service obligations which Member States may impose in the aviation sector.[124] In principle, such compensation must still be notified to the Commission under Article 88(3), insofar as it does indeed constitute State aid.[125] However, under the terms of the Article 86(2) Decision, two types of public service compensation may be granted without notification: (1) compensation for air links to islands on which average annual traffic does not exceed 300,000 passengers during the two financial years preceding the assignment of the SGEI; and (2) compensation for airports for which average annual traffic during the two financial years preceding the assignment of the SGEI does not exceed one million passengers.[126] In both cases, where the compensation complies with the provisions of Regulation 2408/92 and the conditions set out in the Decision, the aid is exempt from the requirement of notification in Article 88(3) EC. In addition the exemption contained in Article 2(1)(a) of the Article 86(2) Decision relating to undertakings with an annual turnover of less than €100 million is also applicable to all transport sectors including the aviation sector. **12.42**

D. Maritime transport

Background. It has been estimated that in 1979 that the EU registered shipping vessels represented 29.6% of the total global fleet. By the 1990s this figure had dropped to 14–15%.[127] This dramatic decline was fuelled in part by the liberalization of the maritime sector, which began in the mid 1980s and was completed **12.43**

[123] Decisions in Cases N 353/2006 *Regional airports capital expenditure grant scheme* (26 September 2006) and NN 21/2006 *City of Derry airport* (16 May 2006).

[124] Regulation 2408/92 [1992] OJ L240/8, Article 4. This includes conditions that the relevant routes must either serve remote regions or must be 'thin' routes to a regional airport in the Member State, and that the obligation should ensure the adequate provision of scheduled air services satisfying fixed standards of continuity, regularity, capacity and pricing, which the air carrier would not assume if it were solely considering its own commercial interest.

[125] See para 12.02 above.

[126] Article 86(2) Decision, Article 2(1)(c) and (d).

[127] S Bilal and P Nicolaides (eds), *Understanding State Aid Policy in the European Community: Perspectives on Rules and Practice* (Brill 1999), p 129.

by 1999,[128] and by the high wages and social charges that were in place in many Member States.[129] The Commission therefore recognized that State aid had an important role to play in developing the competitiveness of the Community's fleet within the global shipping market. This policy was reflected in successive sets of guidelines on the application of the State aid rules to Community shipping companies (discussed below). Today it is estimated that 34% of the global fleet is made up of vessels owned by EU companies—indeed the top three global container shipping lines are European. This resurgence in European shipping interests is in part the result of the Commission adopting a State aid policy which was focused on rebuilding Europe's maritime sector. However while Europe's maritime sector has seen a rebirth, it still has to grow in order to compete effectively on the world stage. As a result the pragmatic application of the State aid rules continues to be important.

12.44 **Early guidelines on maritime transport aid.** In 1989 the Commission published guidelines on the application of State aid to Community shipping companies, establishing the principle that State aid should enable Community shipowners to compete on a level playing field with their global competitors.[130] This first set of guidelines was replaced by a second set of guidelines in 1997, which established a more liberal State aid regime for maritime transport than existed for other sectors, based on the policy objective of regenerating European shipping.[131] These 1997 Guidelines were in turn replaced in 2004 by the current Maritime Guidelines.

12.45 **Maritime Guidelines.**[132] The Maritime Guidelines confirm that State aid to the European shipping industry continues to be justified. Building on the approach adopted in 1997, they set out the parameters within which State aid to maritime transport will be approved by the Commission under Article 87(3)(c) and Article 86(2). The Maritime Guidelines are applicable to the 'transport of goods and persons

[128] In Cases C-15/98 and C-105/99 *Italian Republic and Sardegna Lines v Commission* [2000] ECR I-8855, a 1997 decision concerning aid for Sardinian shipping companies was annulled for failure to take into account the fact that until 1 January 1999 island cabotage in the Mediterranean was excluded from the liberalization of maritime transport services within Member States: see further para 2.145 above.

[129] Meanwhile the importance of maritime sector to the EU's economy continues to grow. In 2006 the European Commission estimated that maritime transport is responsible for almost 90% of the European Union's external trade and more than 40% of its internal trade. As a result approximately 3.5 billion tonnes of freight is loaded and unloaded at EU ports every year: see *Maritime Transport Policy – Improving the competitiveness, safety and security of European Shipping*, Commission, October 2006.

[130] Financial and fiscal measures concerning shipping operations with ships registered in the Community, SEC(89) 921 final.

[131] Community guidelines on State aid to maritime transport [1997] OJ C205/5.

[132] Community guidelines on State aid to maritime transport (Maritime Guidelines) [2004] OJ C13/3.

by sea'.[133] However unlike the earlier guidelines, the Maritime Guidelines also address State aid for dredging and towage activities. For towage activities to benefit from aid, more than 50% of a tug company's annual activity must amount to maritime transport. Similarly dredging companies are entitled to fiscal aid where more than 50% of their activities are maritime transport.[134]

Fiscal measures. The Maritime Guidelines allow Member States to grant Community shipowners substantial tax relief where it facilitates the development of employment within the Community shipping sector.[135] This generous regime which has evolved since the adoption of the 1989 Guidelines initially resulted in a number of Member States exempting shipowners from paying corporation tax. Eventually Member States replaced corporation tax for shipowners with a 'tonnage tax' directly related to the amount of tonnage that the shipowner operated, irrespective of the company's actual profits and losses. The Commission has approved such schemes in the Netherlands, Germany, the United Kingdom, Spain, Denmark, Finland, Ireland, France, Belgium, Italy and Lithuania.[136] The Commission is currently reviewing an amendment to the Danish tonnage tax scheme to determine whether proposed changes to the scheme would affect its original assessment of the scheme,[137] and is also investigating Poland's proposed tonnage tax scheme.[138] **12.46**

Social costs. The generous corporate tax environment in which Community shipowners can operate is further enhanced by the fact that Member States are also able to reduce the burden of social costs for shipowners.[139] In some cases, such measures will constitute employment law measures that fall outside Article 87(1).[140] Even where measures do constitute aid, however, the Maritime Guidelines state that in order to promote employment in shipping, reduced social contributions and income tax rates will be allowed for Community seafarers on board ships registered in a Member State. 'Community seafarers' are defined as (1) Community/EEA citizens working on board vessels providing scheduled **12.47**

---

133 ibid, section 2.

134 ibid, section 3.1.

135 ibid, section 3.2.

136 Decisions in Cases NN 738/1995 *Netherlands* (20 March 1996); N 396/1998 *Germany* (25 November 1998); N 790/1999 *UK* (12 July 2000); N 736/2001 *Spain* (27 February 2002); N 572/2002 *Spain – Biscay* (5 February 2003); N 563/2001 *Denmark* (12 March 2002); N 195/2002 *Finland* (16 October 2002); N 504/2002 *Ireland* (11 December 2002); N 737/2002 *France* (13 May 2003); Decision 2005/417/EC *Belgium* [2005] OJ L150/1; N 114/2004 *Italy* (20 October 2004); and N 330/2005 *Lithuania* (19 July 2006).

137 Case C 5/07 *Danish tonnage tax modification* [2007] OJ C135/6.

138 Case C 34/07 *Polish tonnage tax scheme* [2007] OJ C300/22.

139 Maritime Guidelines, section 3.2.

140 See Cases C-72 and 73/91 *Sloman Neptun* [1993] ECR I-887, discussed at paras 2.90 and 2.103 above.

passenger services between ports of the Community and (2) in all other cases, all seafarers liable to taxation and/or social security contributions in a Member State. Within this context the Commission has approved schemes in Italy, Germany, Sweden and the Netherlands relieving shipowners from paying social contributions for their ships' crews.[141] However the Commission adopted a negative decision in respect of measures planned by the Irish government, on the grounds that ships other than those registered in a Member State would benefit from the measures.[142] It has also initiated the formal investigation procedure in relation to the extension of a Danish scheme exempting shipowners from having to pay income tax and social security contributions for seafarers employed by dredging and cable-laying companies.[143] More generally, the Commission has insisted on the dismantling of any nationality clause attached to schemes exempting shipowners from payment of the social contributions of their seafarers.[144]

12.48 **Investment aid.** Investment aid for fleet renewal must comply with the Shipbuilding Framework, discussed in section E below, and will rarely be approved in cases other than aid supporting a restructuring which leads to a reduction in fleet capacity.[145] Other investment aid may, however, be permitted under the Maritime Guidelines, but only if the investment is required to improve environmental and safety standards of vessels beyond the mandatory standards laid down in international conventions, and only where the aid also complies with the applicable Community provisions on shipbuilding.[146]

12.49 **Training and employment aid.** The provisions of the GBER on training and employment aid are applicable to the maritime transport sector.[147] In particular, the GBER notes that training aid in the maritime sector may reach 100% intensity if it is applied to specific or general training schemes where the trainee is a non-crew member and the training takes place on Community registered vessels.[148] Where training aid is not exempted under the GBER, the Maritime Guidelines consider when such aid may be approved. In particular the Commission will take a favourable

141 See eg Decisions in Cases N 350/1997 *Italy* (13 May 1998); N 396/1999 *Italy* (18 March 1999); Case N 519/2002 *Italy – maritime cabotage* (6 September 2002); Case N 599/2003 *Italy – maritime cabotage* (3 February 2004); NN 94/2002 *Germany* (30 December 2002); NN 19/2004 *Germany* (22 September 2004); N 749/2006 *Sweden* (27 June 2007); N 447/ 2005 *Netherlands – commercial cruising vessels* (21 March 2007).

142 Decision 1999/651/EC *Refund of shipowners' social security contributions* [1999] OJ L257/15.

143 Decision in Case C 22/2007 *Extension of the DIS regime to cable laying and dredging activities* [2007] C213/22.

144 2006 Report on Competition Policy, para 59.

145 See eg Decision 2002/868/EC *Italian single hull tankers* [2002] OJ L307/49.

146 Maritime Guidelines, section 5; and see eg Decision in Case N 225/2006 *Maritime innovation* (24 April 2007).

147 GBER, Article 1(3).

148 ibid, Article 39(2).

attitude towards non-discriminatory on-board training schemes; aid for research and development focusing on quality, productivity, safety and environmental protection; and aid aimed at improving the skills of Community officers.[149] On this basis the Commission has approved a ten-year German training aid scheme providing funding to shipping companies to train mechanics and assistant officers.[150] The Commission also approved the SMarT training scheme for seafarers in the UK which had a funding budget of £24 million.[151]

Restructuring aid. The Maritime Guidelines confirm that in reviewing restructuring aid in the maritime sector the Commission will follow its guidelines on restructuring aid.[152] Following formal investigation proceedings, the Commission found that restructuring aid granted to Brittany Ferries was in large part compatible with the guidelines then applicable. A proposal to grant an additional FRF 80 million to Brittany Ferries was, however, rejected as being unnecessary to guarantee the company's long term viability.[153] **12.50**

Short sea shipping. The Commission has held that development activities that shift traffic from road to other transport modes are in the common interest within the meaning of Article 87(3)(c) of the Treaty.[154] Consistent with this approach, the Maritime Guidelines acknowledge the importance of start-up aid to encourage the establishment of new short sea routes as an alternative to road transport. In 2002 the Commission approved such a scheme allowing France to provide start-up funding for new short sea shipping services.[155] Then in 2003 the Community set up the Marco Polo programme, which provides Community funding to short sea transport schemes.[156] A scheme may benefit from both funding under the Marco Polo programme as well as additional public funding, as long as this does not constitute unlawful State aid, and as long as the combined public subsidy does not exceed 30% for modal shift actions, 35% for new operations, and 50% for common learning action. In this context, the Maritime Guidelines state that aid to short sea shipping must (1) not exceed three years in duration; (2) relate to shipping services connecting Community ports and permitting road cargo to be **12.51**

[149] Maritime Guidelines, section 7.

[150] Decision in Case N 376/2004 *Seafarers' skills* (16 November 2004).

[151] Decision in Case N 499/2001 *Support for maritime training (SMarT) scheme* (2 October 2001).

[152] The current version being the Community Guidelines on state aid for rescuing and restructuring firms in difficulty [2004] OJ C244/2, discussed in detail in Chapter 7 above.

[153] Decision 2002/15/EC *Britanny Ferries* [2002] OJ L12/33.

[154] Decision in N 121/99 *Austria* (8 July 1999); Decision in Case N 598/98 *Aid for purchase of a crane for Born rail terminal* (9 December 1998).

[155] Decision 2002/610/EC *French short sea shipping* [2002] OJ L196/31.

[156] Regulation (EC) 1382/2003 of the Parliament and Council on the granting of Community financial assistance to improve the environmental performance of freight transport system (Marco Polo Programme) [2003] OJ L196/1.

moved wholly or partly by sea; and (3) cover either up to 30% of the operational costs of the service in question, or up to 10% of any investment in transhipment equipment. These principles were applied by the Commission when it approved a UK 'Waterborne Freight Grant' scheme. This aimed to encourage the modal shift of freight from road to water by granting aid to coastal, short-sea and inland waterway services.[157]

12.52 **Public service compensation.** As noted at para 12.5 above, public service compensation in the maritime transport sector can be approved directly on the basis of Article 86(2). In addition to the general requirements of that provision, where the compensation is for maritime cabotage services,[158] it will only be approved where it complies with the provisions of Regulation 3577/92, which sets out in detail the scope of the public service obligations which Member States may impose in respect of maritime cabotage.[159] In addition it should be noted that Regulation 1370/2007 gives the Member States the discretion to apply the provisions relating to public service compensations to public passenger national sea waters. In respect of international maritime transport services, the Maritime Guidelines indicate that public service obligations may only be imposed where they are necessary to meet imperative public transport needs, and that they should be limited to a reasonable period (normally in the order of six years).[160] In both the case of maritime cabotage and international maritime transport, where compensation for such obligations constitutes State aid,[161] it must in principle be notified to the Commission under Article 88(3).[162] However, as with the aviation sector, under the terms of the Article 86(2) Decision two types of public service compensation may be granted without notification: (1) compensation for maritime links to islands on which average annual traffic does not exceed 300,000 passengers during the two financial years preceding the assignment of the SGEI; and (2) compensation for ports for which average annual traffic during the two financial years preceding the

---

157 Decision in Case N 206/2003 *UK WFG* (20 April 2004); see also Decision in Case N 649/2001 *Freight facilities grant* (20 December 2001).

158 ie the provision of maritime transport services between ports within the same Member State.

159 Council Regulation (EEC) 3577/92 applying the principle of freedom to provide services to maritime transport within Member States (maritime cabotage) [1992] OJ L364/7, Article 4. In particular, the public service obligations must be limited to the ports to be served, the regularity, continuity and frequency of the service, the capacity required for the service, the rates to be charged for the service and the manning of the vessels used on the service; and any compensation for public service obligations must be available to all Community shipowners.

160 Maritime Guidelines, section 9.

161 See para 12.02 above.

162 For an example of a decision applying Article 86(2) to a notified aid see Decision in Case N 62/2005 *Maritime transport - Friuli Venezia Giulia* (21 February 2007), approving aid for the provision of regular scheduled passenger ferry services between the Friuli Venezia Giulia region of Italy and Slovenia and Croatia.

assignment of the SGEI does not exceed 300,000 passengers.[163] In both cases, where the compensation complies with the provisions of Regulation 3577/92 and the conditions set out in the Decision, the aid is exempt from the requirement of notification in Article 88(3) EC. In addition the exemption contained in Article 2(1)(a) of the Article 86(2) Decision relating to undertakings with an annual turnover of less than €100 million is also applicable to all transport sectors including the maritime sector.

Port infrastructure. As with other infrastructure support, many measures granting aid for the development of port infrastructure will not fall within Article 87(1).[164] Insofar as such measures do constitute aid, there are no specific guidelines on the circumstances in which the aid may be approved. However in a consultation on port policy, the Commission has suggested that such guidelines should be introduced.[165] In particular, the Commission recognizes that EU ports may be less competitive than non-EU ports given the high costs incurred arising from European labour and environmental legislation. However the Commission also acknowledges that State aid to ports might affect competition in the internal market.[166] As a result the Commission has stated that State aid to ports must be properly authorized and sufficiently transparent.[167] **12.53**

E. Shipbuilding

1. Background

Overview. For a period recently, commercial shipbuilding enjoyed a record surge in activity, however, generally, the shipbuilding industry has been characterized by worldwide production overcapacity and depressed prices. This is partly due to the cyclical nature of the industry, but is also caused by significant subsidies given in non-EU countries[168] which have led to significant market distortions. As a result European shipyards have suffered adverse effects in the form of decreasing market shares, reduced capacity utilization and unemployment. International trade rules are difficult to apply in this sector. Action taken through the OECD and the WTO routes (discussed below) has proved to be ineffective. The Maritime Policy Green Paper states that it is therefore important to use the anti-dumping rules to **12.54**

[163] Article 86(2) Decision, Article 2(1)(c) and (d).

[164] See eg Decision in Case N 510/2005 *Poland – port infrastructure* (10 July 2007).

[165] Commission Port Policy Consultation 2006–2007, p 11.

[166] ibid, p 18.

[167] ibid, p 9.

[168] An EU Commission Report in 2003, found that Korean yards had reduced prices to as much as 39% below normal price: see 7th Commission report to the Council on the situation in world shipbuilding, COM(2003) 232 final.

the fullest extent possible.[169] However, anti-dumping rules are also often difficult to apply in this sector due to the fact that commercial vessels are generally not 'imported', ships are rarely produced in series, and applying a penalty is difficult if not impossible. As a result, the Commission has commented that the shipbuilding sector is 'practically the only industry with little, if any, effective protection against unfair pricing'.[170]

12.55 **OECD and WTO action.** In 2002, a group involving 26 countries started negotiations, in the framework of the OECD, to establish a framework for the restoration of normal competitive conditions in the shipbuilding market and especially to deal with the problem of government subsidies and unfair pricing leading to market distortions. However, due to a lack of common ground (particularly in relation to pricing), negotiations were suspended in 2005.[171] Also in 2002 the EU initiated a WTO dispute settlement proceeding against the Republic of Korea. This ultimately found that Korea had provided export subsidies explicitly prohibited by the 1994 WTO agreement on subsidization through specific advanced payments, refund guarantees and pre-shipment loans. However, in relation to the main part of the proceedings, relating to restructuring subsidies, the WTO found in Korea's favour.

12.56 **Temporary Defence Mechanism.** 2002 also saw the adoption by the EU of a Temporary Defence Mechanism ('TDM') Regulation[172] which authorized direct operating aid of up to 6% of the contract value before aid, to be granted to EU shipyards until 31 March 2004 (subsequently extended until 31 March 2005). Aid to EU shipyards that could show that they had suffered strong adverse effects caused by Korean competition could be approved in relation to container ships, chemical and products tankers and liquefied natural gas carriers. Following a complaint by Korea, the WTO subsequently held that the TDM Regulation did not respect the EU's obligation to use exclusively the WTO dispute settlement system. By the time this decision was reached in April 2005, however, the TDM had already expired.[173]

---

[169] Commission Green Paper 'Towards a future Maritime Policy for the Union: A European vision for the oceans and seas', COM(2006) 275 final, p 41.

[170] See <http://ec.europa.eu/trade/issues/sectoral/industry/shipbuilding/index_en.htm>.

[171] Previous OECD negotiations had led to an agreement between the main shipbuilding nations in 1994, but this never entered into force as the US refused to ratify it.

[172] Council Regulation (EC) 1177/2002 concerning a temporary defence mechanism to shipbuilding [2002] OJ L172/1.

[173] The Commission later relied on this WTO decision when refusing to approve aid notified after 31 March 2005, even though contracts were entered into before the 31 March deadline, stating that the provisions of the Regulation had to be interpreted in a manner consistent with international law: see Decision 2007/581/EC *Temporary defensive mechanism to shipbuilding* [2007] OJ L219/25.

LeaderSHIP 2015. In response to the competitive challenges being faced by the European shipbuilding industry, the industry launched the LeaderSHIP 2015 initiative aimed at improving the future competitiveness and prosperity of European shipbuilding and establishing a level playing field at world level. The work carried out within this initiative played a key role in the introduction, in 2004, of a new set of rules regulating State aid in the shipbuilding sector. **12.57**

2. Community State aid rules

Framework on State aid to shipbuilding. State aid to the shipbuilding sector has been the subject of specific Community measures since the early 1970s. The current rules are contained in the Shipbuilding Framework[174] which came into force on 1 January 2004. In July 2008 the Commission extended the application of the Shipbuilding Framework until 31 December 2011, as there had still been few cases in which it had been applied and the Commission wished to gain more experience, particularly in relation to the application of the provisions on innovation aid.[175] **12.58**

Scope. The Shipbuilding Framework covers all aid granted to shipbuilding, which includes aid to any shipyard, related entity, shipowner and third party which is granted, directly or indirectly, for building, repair or conversion of ships (in this context meaning self-propelled seagoing commercial vessels[176])[177]. Aid related to military vessels is excluded from the application of the State aid rules.[178] The Framework sets out special rules for innovation aid, closure aid, export credits, development aid and regional aid. It also extends existing horizontal rules (eg those relating to research and development aid, rescue and restructuring aid, training aid, employment aid, environmental aid, aid to SMEs and *de minimis* aid) to shipbuilding. **12.59**

---

[174] Framework on State aid to shipbuilding [2003] OJ C317/11. This replaced Council Regulation (EC) 1540/98 establishing new rules on aid to shipbuilding [1998] OJ 202/1. By contrast with the current Shipbuilding Framework which does not permit operating aid, Regulation 1540/98 did permit contract-related operating aid (up to a maximum of 9%) for contracts entered into before 31 December 2000. Vessels had to be delivered by 31 December 2003, although there have been a number of decisions relating to requests to extend this deadline, eg Decision 2006/946/EC *ENVC* [2006] OJ L383/16.

[175] See Communication from the Commission concerning the prolongation of the Framework on State aid to shipbuilding [2008] OJ C173/3. The State Aid Action Plan states that the Commission must decide whether the Framework is necessary or whether the sector should merely be governed by the normal State aid rules: State Aid Action Plan: Less and better targeted state aid: a roadmap for state aid reform 2005–2009, COM(2005) 107 final, para 65.

[176] As defined at para 10(d) of the Shipbuilding Framework.

[177] Shipbuilding Framework, para 11.

[178] Where a shipyard is used for military production as well as civil production, the Commission will consider what proportion of the aid was granted to the military production before applying State aid rules to aid relating specifically to the civil production: see eg Decision 2005/246/EC *State aid to Hellenic Shipyards* [2005] OJ L75/44.

12.60 **Innovation aid.** The EU shipbuilding industry continues to be the technological world leader, with all major innovations coming from Europe.[179] At the time the Shipbuilding Framework was adopted, shipbuilding was the only sector eligible for innovation aid.[180] To be approved under the Shipbuilding Framework, innovation aid should be a true incentive to innovate and carry out projects that would not be carried through in the absence of public support.[181] The maximum aid intensity is 20%, and aid will only be available in relation to the industrial application of innovative products and processes.[182] This may include the development and design of a new class of vessel, innovative components and systems of a ship, and innovative processes regarding production, planning logistics or design.[183] Eligible costs must be limited to supporting expenditure on investments, design, engineering and testing activities directly and exclusively related to the innovative part of the project.[184] In exceptional cases, additional production costs that are strictly necessary to validate the technical innovation are eligible for aid.[185] These may include, for example, incremental and overhead labour costs or costs of the construction and installation of a new component or system.[186] The aid scheme should ensure the necessity of the aid, for example by providing that no aid will be granted if, at the time of the application, the shipyard and the purchaser have already concluded a binding agreement to implement the project.[187]

12.61 **Closure aid.** Aid to defray the costs related to total or partial closure of shipyards may be approved where the capacity reduction is of a genuine and irreversible nature.[188] Costs eligible for aid include redundancy payments, costs of vocational retraining or counselling for workers, and costs incurred for the redevelopment of the yard. Companies receiving partial closure aid must not have benefited from

---

[179] Towards a future Maritime Policy for the Union: A European vision for the oceans and seas, COM(2006) 275 final, pp 8–9.

[180] Innovation aid for shipbuilding was first introduced by Reg 1540/98 [1998] OJ 202/1. Other sectors are now also eligible for innovation aid under the new R&D&I Framework: see Chapter 8 above.

[181] Press release IP/03/1607; and see similar provisions in the R&D&I Framework discussed at para 8.34 above.

[182] Shipbuilding Framework, para 15(a). Schemes usually provide that the innovative character will be checked on a case by case basis by an independent expert.

[183] Decisions in cases N 452/2004 *Scheme on innovation aid to shipbuilding* (16 February 2005); N 719/2006 *Innovation aid scheme for shipbuilding* (1 February 2007); N 752/2006 *Innovation aid scheme to shipbuilding in Italy* (30 April 2007).

[184] Shipbuilding Framework, para 15(b).

[185] ibid.

[186] Decisions in Cases N 452/2004 *Scheme on innovation aid to shipbuilding* (16 February 2005); and N 423/2004 *Aid to shipbuilding companies/grant* (16 March 2005).

[187] See eg Decisions in Cases N 719/2006 *Innovation aid scheme for shipbuilding* (1 February 2007); N 752//2006 *Innovation aid scheme to shipbuilding in Italy* (30 April 2007).

[188] Shipbuilding Framework, para 16. In order to establish the irreversible nature of a closure, the Member State must ensure the facilities remain closed for a period of at least ten years (para 21).

rescue or restructuring aid within the last ten years, save in 'exceptional and unforeseeable circumstances for which the company is not responsible'.[189]

Export credits. Under paragraph 23 of the Framework, aid in the form of state-supported credit facilities may be approved where it complies with the terms of the 1998 OECD Arrangement on Guidelines for Officially Supported Export Credits[190] and with its Sector Understanding on Export Credit for Ships.[191] Measures approved by the Commission have included an 'interest make-up' financing scheme granting interest compensation to banks that financed the purchase or conversion of a vessel built by a German shipyard,[192] and interest rate support to shipowners from any nationality on condition that they commission the new building or conversion of a vessel to a Spanish shipyard.[193] It should be noted, however, that compliance with the OECD Arrangement is not a guarantee of approval. Thus aid will not be justified where it involves the matching of illegal aid from other Member States, notwithstanding the existence of a matching clause in the OECD Arrangement.[194] **12.62**

Development aid. Aid granted as development assistance to a developing country may be approved where it complies with the terms of the 1998 OECD Arrangement on Guidelines for Officially Supported Export Credits and with its Sector Understanding on Export Credit for Ships.[195] The Commission will additionally verify the particular development content of the proposed aid, verify that aid is necessary and verify that the offer of development is open to bids from different yards in line with procurement rules.[196] Development criteria recognized by the Commission include the improvement of 'Search and Rescue' capabilities in Vietnam,[197] the rational and sustainable exploitation of fisheries in Indonesia,[198] the maintenance of internal waterways in Bangladesh,[199] and preventing pollution and increasing ship movements in harbours in Ghana.[200] According to the **12.63**

---

[189] Shipbuilding Framework, para 19.

[190] As revised from time to time. The most recent version is the 2008 revision, TAD/PG(2007)28/FINAL (21 December 2007).

[191] The latest version is the 2007 Sector Understanding, TAD/PG(2007)27 (10 October 2007).

[192] See decision in Case N 20/2004 *CIRR ship financing* (14 July 2004).

[193] See decision in Case N 760/2006 *Extension of export financing scheme - Spanish shipbuilding* (8 March 2007).

[194] Commission Decision 2005/122/EC *Dutch shipyards* [2005] OJ L39/48.

[195] Shipbuilding Framework, para 24.

[196] ibid, para 25.

[197] Decision in Case N 185/2005 *Aid to Vietnam* (20 July 2005).

[198] Decision in Case N 262/2006 *Aid to Indonesia – shipbuilding* (7 June 2006).

[199] Decision in Case N 517/2004 *Shipbuilding – development aid to Bangladesh* (16 March 2005).

[200] Decision in Case N 450/2004 *Development aid to Ghana – tugboats* (2 February 2005).

OECD criteria a minimum concessionality level[201] of 35% has to be achieved by shipbuilding projects in Lower Middle Income Countries; the minimum concessionality level for Least Developed Countries is 50%.[202]

12.64 **Regional aid.** Regional aid to shipbuilding may only be approved where it is granted for investment in upgrading or modernizing existing yards (not linked to a financial restructuring of the yard), with the objective of improving the productivity of existing installations. Projects accepted by the Commission as complying with this requirement include the construction of a new production line for panels and building additional sites for section construction (allowing more efficient vessel construction),[203] the extension of production areas to address existing layout problems and the installation of energy distribution rails,[204] the purchase and installation of a harbour mobile crane, production machines, new cutting technology, and a chamber jet to speed up cleaning of steel plates,[205] the fitting out of halls,[206] and the extension of halls to provide shelter to activities previously being carried out outdoors.[207] The aid must be limited to support eligible expenditure as defined in the applicable Community guidelines on regional aid.[208] The aid intensity must not exceed 22.5% for Article 87(3)(a) regions and 12.5% for Article 87(3)(c) regions.[209] The Commission often expresses concern where it believes that the investment will lead to an increase in capacity, and has stated that one of the objectives of the Shipbuilding Framework is to ensure that investment for the mere creation of new capacity is not supported by State aid.[210] However the Commission may approve aid where a capacity increase is found to be purely a side effect of the productivity improvements and is not disproportionate to the productivity increase.[211]

[201] The concessionality level is a measure of the 'softness' of a credit reflecting the benefit to the borrower compared to a loan at market rate. The manner in which this is calculated is set out in para 37 of the OECD Arrangement on Guidelines for Officially Supported Export Credits.

[202] OECD Arrangement on Guidelines for Officially Supported Export Credits, para 35; and see Decisions in Cases N 262/2006 *Aid to Indonesia – shipbuilding* (7 June 2006); N 185/2005 *Aid to Vietnam* (20 July 2005); N 517/2004 *Shipbuilding – development aid to Bangladesh* (16 March 2005).

[203] Decision 2007/402/EC *Investment aid for Volkswerft Stralsund* [2007] OJ L151/33.

[204] Decision 2007/529/EC *Regional aid to shipyard Komárno* [2007] OJ L195/36.

[205] Decision in Case N 35/2007 *Investment aid to Peene-Werft* (27 June 2007); and Decision 2007/529/EC *Regional aid to shipyard Komárno* [2007] OJ L195/36.

[206] Decision in Case N 35/2007 *Investment aid to Peene-Werft* (27 June 2007).

[207] Decision 2007/255/EC *Investment aid for Rolandwerft* [2007] OJ L112/32.

[208] See Chapter 15 below.

[209] Shipbuilding Framework, paras 26(b) and (c).

[210] See eg press release IP/07/896.

[211] See eg Decisions 2007/529/EC *Regional aid to shipyard Komárno* [2007] OJ L195/36, at paras 47–54; 2007/402/EC *Investment aid for Volkswerft Stralsund* [2007] OJ L151/33, at para 64; and 2007/255/EC *Investment aid for Rolandwerft* [2007] OJ L112/32, paras 76–83.

Other forms of aid. The Shipbuilding Framework extends the current horizontal aid rules to the shipbuilding sector.[212] For example, any shipbuilding aid aimed at research and development will be reviewed in accordance with the R&D&I Framework,[213] and aid aimed at restructuring will be reviewed in accordance with the Rescue and Restructuring Guidelines.[214] An example of the latter is the Commission's investigation into operating aid granted to two Polish shipyards: Szczecin and Gdynia. In November 2008, the Commission concluded that aid granted to these shipyards did not comply with the 2004 Rescue and Restructuring Guidelines, but rather constituted illegal operating aid which had to be repaid.[215] The General Block Exemption Regulation ('GBER') also applies to the shipbuilding sector, with the exception of regional aid to that sector.[216] **12.65**

Ship financing. Ship financing schemes must be free of State aid. Any state guarantee schemes for shipbuilding financing will be reviewed under the Notice on State guarantees.[217] **12.66**

[212] Shipbuilding Framework, para 12.

[213] Discussed in Chapter 8 above; and see eg Decisions in Cases N 43/2006 *CETENA and INSEAN* (4 July 2006); and N 423/2004 *Aid to shipbuilding companies/grant* (16 March 2005).

[214] Discussed in Chapter 7 above; and see eg Decision in Case N 561/2006 *Restructuring aid to constructions mécaniques de Normandie* (10 July 2007).

[215] Decisions in Cases C 17/2005 *Restructuring aid for Gdynia shipyard* (6 November 2008) and C 19/2005 *Restructuring aid for Szczecin shipyard* (6 November 2008); see press release IP/08/1642. The Polish authorities undertook that the recovery of the illegal aid would be made through a sale of the yards' assets.

[216] GBER Article 1(3).

[217] Discussed at para 2.42–2.43 above. See eg Decisions in Cases N 35/2006 *Guarantee scheme for shipbuilding – France* (16 May 2006); N 253/2005 *Guarantee scheme for shipbuilding – Netherlands* (20 July 2005); N 325/2006 *Prolongation of shipbuilding guarantee scheme* (25 August 2006).

13

MEDIA AND COMMUNICATIONS

Main legislation and guidelines

Treaty on European Union, Protocol on the System of Public Broadcasting in the Member States ('Broadcasting Protocol') [1997] OJ C340/109

Notice from the Commission on the application of the competition rules to the postal sector and on the assessment of certain State measures relating to postal services [1998] OJ C39/2

Communication on the application of the State aid rules to public service broadcasting ('Broadcasting Communication') [2001] OJ C320/5

Commission Communication on certain legal aspects relating to cinematographic and other audiovisual works ('Cinema Communication') [2002] OJ C43/6

Community framework for State aid in the form of public service compensation ('Article 86(2) Framework') [2005] OJ C297/4

A. Introduction

13.01 **The Lisbon Agenda.** The media and communications sectors are of central importance to the objective of creating a 'knowledge based economy' agreed as part of the Lisbon Agenda by the European Council in March 2000. Although the creation of a successful economy is important to EU policy in this area, such policy also takes into account broader aims such as 'social, economic and territorial cohesion'[1] and the transmission of 'European cultural identities'.[2] The application of State aid rules in the media and communications sectors thus has to take account of public service and cultural objectives while ensuring that distortions of competition are minimized. These objectives may not always easily be reconciled, and a number of the Commission's decisions in these areas have been appealed to the European Court in recent years.

13.02 **Areas within media and communications.** This chapter considers in turn the application of the State aid rules in relation to the broadcasting, broadband, postal services, and film/audiovisual sectors. Each of these has very specific features and the Commission has produced guidance on how the rules apply in each area (with the exception of the relatively new broadband area). While that guidance takes into account the specific context of each area, it is clear that the Commission has sought to maintain a coherent approach across all of these areas and to ensure consistency with the application of the State aid rules in other sectors. The 'telecommunications' sector as such is not addressed specifically in this chapter, but important telecommunications cases are discussed in the sections of this chapter dealing with broadcasting and broadband.

13.03 **Basis for approval.** A great deal of State aid is authorized in respect of the media and communications sectors. In relation to broadcasting and postal services, where providing universal access to services on a fair and affordable basis is a key consideration, the Commission's analysis of compatibility with the State aid rules tends to take place under the rules on services of general economic interest ('SGEIs') in Article 86(2) EC. In relation to broadband, however, Article 87(3)(c) (relating to aid to facilitate the development of certain economic activities or of certain economic areas) has in practice been the main basis for an assessment of compatibility, and in the film and audiovisual area the derogation under Article 87(3)(d) (relating to the promotion of culture and heritage conservation) plays a more prominent role.

---

[1] Directive 2008/6/EC of the European Parliament and Council amending Directive 97/67/EC with regard to the full accomplishment of the internal market of Community postal services [2008] OJ L52/3, recital (5).

[2] Commission Staff Working Paper on certain legal aspects relating to cinematographic and other audiovisual works SEC(2001) 619, section 1.1.

B. Broadcasting

Overview. This section considers the Community's policy towards public funding for public service broadcasters against the background of increasing competition from other broadcasters and the developing activities of broadcasters, including the promotion of digital switchover. In most cases, where State aid has arisen, it has been approved in the context of Article 86(2). Some cases, however, have been considered under Article 87(2) and (3). **13.04**

1. Policy and legislation

Role of broadcasting. State aid policy in the broadcasting sector must take account of the fact that broadcasting plays a role in the EU that goes beyond the provision and receipt of economic services, to address broader 'democratic, social and cultural needs'.[3] As the Commission said in its Communication on SGEIs: **13.05**

> The broadcast media play a central role in the functioning of modern democratic societies, in particular in the development and transmission of social values. Therefore, the broadcasting sector has, since its inception, been subject to specific regulation in the general interest. This regulation has been based on common values, such as freedom of expression and the right of reply, pluralism, protection of copyright, promotion of cultural and linguistic diversity, protection of minors and of human dignity, consumer protection.[4]

Market development. State aid policy in this sector has also been affected by the major changes in the competitive landscape since the original Treaty provisions were agreed. In particular, State monopoly broadcasting regimes in Member States have given way over time to a more diverse environment in which the range of both public service and commercial broadcasting services has expanded enormously. Indeed, the division between public service and commercial broadcasting itself has blurred to an extent, with some broadcasters active in both segments. The application of the State aid rules in this sector must therefore ensure a 'level playing field'[5] between broadcasters while allowing Member States sufficient latitude to fund public service broadcasting effectively. **13.06**

Broadcasting Protocol. The specific nature of broadcasting is recognized by an interpretative protocol on the system of public service broadcasting added to the EC Treaty by the Treaty of Amsterdam, maintained in substantially the same form **13.07**

---

[3] Treaty on European Union, Protocol on the System of Public Broadcasting in the Member States [1997] OJ C340/109.

[4] Communication from the Commission on Services of General Interest in Europe [2001] OJ C17/4, 22; see also Article 16 EC on SGEIs generally.

[5] Communication from the Commission on the application of State aid rules to public service broadcasting ('Broadcasting Communication') [2001] OJ C320/5, para 1.3.

by the Treaty of Lisbon.[6] This 'Broadcasting Protocol' provides that the Treaty provisions:

> shall be without prejudice to the competence of Member States to provide for the funding of public service broadcasting and insofar as such funding is granted to broadcasting organisations for the fulfilment of the public service remit as conferred, defined and organised by each Member State, and insofar as such funding does not affect trading conditions and competition in the Union to an extent which would be contrary to the common interest, while the remit of that public service shall be taken into account.

Effectively, the Broadcasting Protocol is a specific application of the more general provisions of Article 86(2), discussed in Chapter 3.

13.08 **Broadcasting Communication.** In 2001, the Commission published a Communication on the application of the State aid rules to public service broadcasting (the 'Broadcasting Communication').[7] This sets out in detail the Commission's approach to State support in this area. The Commission is currently reviewing this Communication, with a view to revising it to reflect technological changes (in particular the growth of new media), as well as new legislation, developments in the Commission's decisional practice since 2001, and the jurisprudence of the European Court. On 4 November 2008 the Commission published for comment a revised draft Communication.[8] In this draft, the Commission comments that public service broadcasters must be able to take advantage of digitization and the diversification of new distribution platforms, but cautions against pay-services where these may conflict with the principle of universality and the notion of public service broadcasting. The Commission is expected to publish its revised Communication during 2009.

2. Existence of aid

13.09 **Issues.** In determining whether Article 87(1) applies to any form of State funding, a key issue is the existence of an economic advantage, particularly in cases involving public service compensation and the *Altmark* test. In addition, questions may arise as to whether the measure involves the use of State resources and has a sufficient effect on competition and trade. Another set of issues relates to whether any particular grant of aid can be said to be part of an existing aid scheme.

13.10 **Economic advantage.** State support to public service broadcasters provides an economic advantage not available to private operators or other public service broadcasters not included in the scheme, which have to rely on other sources

[6] Treaty on European Union, Protocol on the System of Public Broadcasting in the Member States [1997] OJ C340/109.

[7] [2001] OJ C320/5.

[8] Press release IP/08/1626.

of revenue.[9] There may also be spill-over effects benefiting the purely commercial activities of the public service broadcaster or of its commercial subsidiaries.[10] Aid to broadcasters may, in addition, provide indirect benefits to other operators. So, for example the Commission considered that proposed State funding for transmission fees payable to the operators of digital transmission networks by commercial broadcasters for the carriage of their channels in North Rhine-Westphalia would give the network operator an indirect advantage, enabling it to charge higher fees.[11] By contrast in Sweden, where the main public service broadcaster was charged the same (cost-based) transmission fee as private broadcasters for the transmission of its channels, there was no indirect economic advantage to the network operator and therefore no aid.[12] Grants for consumers may also amount to State aid to undertakings in certain circumstances: for example, grants for the purchase of digital decoders may have indirect benefits for the producers of such decoders, operators of the digital networks, broadcasters whose channels are carried on those networks and cable TV operators.[13]

Public service compensation. No economic advantage will arise if the State support is regarded as compensation for public service obligations, within the meaning of the *Altmark* judgment.[14] The conditions set out in *Altmark* are, however, very strict and most subsequent Commission decisions concerning State support in the broadcasting sector have not found the conditions to be satisfied.[15] **13.11**

---

[9] Decision in Case E 3/2005 *Financing of public sector broadcasters in Germany* (24 April 2007), para 184; Decision 2004/838/EC *France 2 and France 3* [2004] OJ L361/21, para 49 (appeal in Case T-144/04 *TF1 v Commission* held inadmissible by Order of 19 May 2008). cf Decision in Case NN 64/2005 *Digital replacement licences* (25 January 2006) where the Commission accepted that market value had been paid for the licences in question, so that no economic advantages arose.

[10] Decision in Case E 3/2005 *Financing of public sector broadcasters in Germany* (24 April 2007), para 188.

[11] Decision in Case C 34/2006 *North Rhine-Westphalia DTT* (23 October 2007), paras 83–5: this aid was considered to be incompatible with Articles 87(3) and 86(2). On indirect beneficiaries see generally para 2.31 above.

[12] Decision 2007/258/EC *Digital terrestrial television in Sweden* [2007] OJ L112/77, paras 100–6.

[13] Decision in Case N 270/2006 *Digital decoder subsidy* (24 January 2007), paras 30–45; Decision 2007/374/EC *Digital decoders – Italy* [2007] OJ L147/1 (under appeal in Case T-96/07 *Telecom Italia v Commission*); Decision in Case N 103/2007 *Subsidies for DTT decoders/installation in Sora* (25 September 2007).

[14] Case C-280/00 *Altmark* [2003] ECR I-7747, considered at paras 2.67–2.73 above.

[15] Decision in Case N 37/2003 *BBC Digital Curriculum* (1 October 2003), para 23; Decision 2004/838/EC *France 2 and France 3* [2004] OJ L361/21, paras 55–6 (appeal in Case T-144/04 *TF1 v Commission* held inadmissible by Order of 19 May 2008); Decision 2004/339/EC *RAI* [2004] OJ L119/1, paras 95–8. In contrast see Cases T-309/04 etc *TV2/Danmark v Commission* (judgment of 22 October 2008) in which the CFI held that the Commission in Decision 2005/217/EC *TV2/Danmark* [2006] OJ L85/1, para 71 had wrongly assessed compliance with the second and fourth *Altmark* criteria. Several appeals are still pending concerning the related, subsequent, Decision in Case N 313/2004 *Recapitalisation of TV2/Danmark* (6 October 2004); see Case T-12/05 TV *Danmark and Kanal 5 Denmark v Commission* and Case T-16/05 *Viasat Broadcasting UK v Commission.*

Difficulties have arisen particularly in showing that the compensation mechanism has been established in advance in an objective and transparent manner (the second condition) and that the level of compensation has been determined by reference to the costs that a typical well run undertaking would incur (the fourth condition). It remains to be seen whether the *BUPA* judgment of the Court[16] will give rise to a more relaxed approach to the application of these criteria, and a consequent shift in the analysis from the question of whether aid is justified under Article 86(2), to the question of whether there is aid at all under Article 87(1).

13.12 **State resources and imputability.** In many cases it will be easy to identify the use of State resources in public support for broadcasters, as well as the imputability of the measure to the State. The grant of aid to broadcasters through direct subsidies or loans, or through fiscal measures, is therefore not likely to raise difficult questions of the involvement of State resources. Some cases, however, will not be so straightforward. The Commission takes the view that funding of the BBC out of the licence fee system involves State resources, since although it is collected by the BBC, the BBC is entitled to retain it (or an equivalent sum) under the arrangements agreed with the UK government. This means that the licence fee is under public control.[17] By contrast, an obligation imposed on cable operators to transmit public service channels at no cost to the broadcasters does not involve the transfer of State resources to the broadcasters, since the revenue foregone is that of the cable operators, not the State.[18] Charging transmission fees at below the market rate is a transfer of State resources where the network is managed by the State.[19] Where, however, a broadcasting network is managed by an entity whose decisions are not attributable to the State even though the entity is a public undertaking, the acceptance of late payments for use of the network does not amount to State aid.[20]

---

[16] Case T-289/03 *BUPA v Commission* (judgment of 12 February 2008), discussed at para 2.74 above.

[17] Decision in Case N 631/2001 *BBC licence fee* (22 May 2002), para 20. See also Decision 2005/217/EC *TV2/Danmark* [2006] OJ L85/1, paras 57–9, upheld in this respect but annulled on other grounds on appeal in Cases T-309/04 etc *TV2/Danmark v Commission* (judgment of 22 October 2008).

[18] Decision 2008/136/EC *Ad hoc financing of Dutch public service broadcasters* [2008] OJ L49/1, para 91.

[19] Decision 2005/217/EC *TV2/Danmark* [2006] OJ L85/1, para 66, upheld in this respect but annulled on other grounds on appeal in Cases T-309/04 etc *TV2/Danmark v Commission* (judgment of 22 October 2008).

[20] Case T-442/03 *SIC v Commission* (judgment of 26 June 2008), paras 93–114.

Effect on competition and trade. State financing of public service broadcasters will generally affect competition in the common market.[21] Public service broadcasters compete with private broadcasters for audience share, which in turn impacts on advertising revenue.[22] Public funding may also distort competition in the market for rights such as sports rights,[23] in the market for the sale of programmes and programming,[24] in new media markets where other providers already offer online services,[25] and in other markets in which public service broadcasters are active such as film production,[26] and electronic learning materials.[27] Public funding for digital switchover may distort competition between digital platforms and, if granted to those broadcasters already in the market, might distort competition to the detriment of new entrants.[28] State aid to public service broadcasters will also normally affect trade between Member States.[29] Even if the public service broadcaster does not itself export, the market has a number of international features. In particular, the acquisition of rights and sale of programming take place at international level.[30] Advertising may have a cross-border element especially for common-language areas, and the ownership structures of broadcasters may extend to more than one Member State.[31] **13.13**

Existing/new aid. In many instances, the financing scheme for broadcasters has pre-dated the membership of the EU of the relevant Member State, and therefore amounts to existing aid. Such aids are not subject to the formal notification procedures but are kept under review by the Commission. Alterations (other than purely formal) to existing aid schemes do, however, require prior notification.[32] Key questions which have arisen in a number of broadcasting cases are (1) whether the change proposed amounts to an 'alteration' which would, if severable, require **13.14**

---

[21] Broadcasting Communication [2001] OJ C320/5, paras 17–18.

[22] Decision in Case E 3/2005 *Financing of public service broadcasters in Germany* (24 April 2007), paras 182–90.

[23] Decision 2004/838/EC *France 2 and France 3* [2004] OJ L361/21, paras 59–61 (appeal in Case T-144/04 *TF1 v Commission* held inadmissible by Order of 19 May 2008); Decision in Case E 3/2005 *Financing for public service broadcasters in Germany* (24 April 2007), para 185.

[24] Decision in Case E 3/2005 *Financing of public service broadcasters in Germany* (24 April 2007), paras 182–90.

[25] ibid, para 188.

[26] ibid.

[27] Decision in Case N 37/2003 *BBC Digital Curriculum* (1 October 2003), para 24.

[28] Decision in Case C 34/2006 *North Rhine-Westphalia DTT* (23 October 2007), para 124.

[28] Broadcasting Communication [2001] OJ C320/5, para 61.

[29] ibid, para 18.

[30] Decision 2004/339/EC *RAI* [2004] OJ L119/1, para 91.

[31] ibid, paras 91–4; Decision 2004/838/EC *France 2 and France 3* [2004] OJ L361/21, paras 59–61 (appeal in Case T-144/04 *TF1 v Commission* held inadmissible by Order of 19 May 2008).

[32] See further para 16.16 below.

notification; or (2) whether the change is non-severable and is such that it affects the substance of the original scheme so as to transform the whole funding mechanism into a new aid, which requires notification under Article 88(3).

13.15 **Examples.** Changes to schemes for financing broadcasters which have been held by the Commission not to involve new aid or not to affect the character of the existing aid include transferring responsibility for broadcasting matters from federal to State authorities;[33] altering the methodology for calculating public service broadcasters' costs and compensation levels;[34] changing the rules for distribution among public service broadcasters;[35] and increases in the level of the licence fee including rebasing increases on the national consumer prices index,[36] provided that the public service mission has not been substantially changed.[37] Similarly, the introduction of new channels may be treated as within the scope of existing aid, especially where no new additional reimbursable public service cost was incurred.[38] Offering programme-related material and accompanying activities on the internet and broadcasting via new digital platforms may also be treated as sufficiently close to the original scheme and therefore within the existing aid scheme as long as those activities are consistent with and supportive of the initial public service broadcasting obligations.[39] But where the BBC sought to distribute educational materials on the internet, the Commission held that the scheme could not constitute existing aid, since it was a digression from the markets on which the BBC had been active, and therefore the use of State resources to fund the service amounted to new aid.[40] New tax exemptions and capital injections may also amount to new aid.[41]

3. Authorization under Article 86(2)

13.16 **Article 86(2) conditions.** Article 86(2) EC forms the usual basis for an assessment of compatibility of State aid in the broadcasting sector. As set out in Chapter 3, the case-law and Commission practice (including in particular the guidance in the

33 Decision in Case E 3/2005 *Financing of public service broadcasters in Germany* (24 April 2007), paras 192–216.

34 Decision in Case E 14/2005 *RTP compensation payment* (22 March 2006), paras 58–80; Decision in Case E 3/2005 *Financing of public service broadcasters in Germany* (24 April 2007), paras 192–216.

35 Decision in Case E 14/2005 *RTP compensation payment* (22 March 2006), paras 70–4.

36 Decision in Case E 4/2005 *RTE and TG4* (27 February 2008), paras 65–78.

37 Decision in Case E 3/2005 *Financing for public service broadcasters in Germany* (24 April 2007), para 206; Decision in Case E 10/2005 *France: licence fee* (20 April 2005), para 21; Decision in Case E 9/2005 *RAI* (20 April 2005), para 42.

38 Decision in Case E 14/2005 *RTP compensation payment* (22 March 2006), paras 67–9.

39 Decision in Case E 3/2005 *Financing of public service broadcasters in Germany* (24 April 2007), paras 207–11.

40 Decision in Case N 37/2003 *BBC Digital Curriculum* (1 October 2003), paras 27–36.

41 Decision 2004/339/EC *RAI* [2004] OJ L119/1.

Article 86(2) Framework)[42] indicates that five conditions should be satisfied for the application of this provision: (1) existence of a genuine SGEI; (2) entrustment of the SGEI task; (3) absence of overcompensation; (4) necessity and proportionality; and (5) the development of trade must not be affected contrary to the interests of the Community.[43] In practice, as in other sectors, decisions in the broadcasting sector have tended to focus on the first four of these conditions. The Commission's application of these is discussed in more detail below.

Existence of SGEI. Member States are entitled to define, confer and organize their public service remit in the broadcasting sector. The Commission's role in this regard is thus limited to identifying 'manifest errors' in the exercise of this competence by Member States.[44] The definition of the public service in question must, however, be sufficiently precise to enable the Commission and Member States' authorities to monitor compliance.[45] To date, the Commission has given Member States a significant degree of latitude to define the scope of the public service. In the *BBC Digital Curriculum* case a complainant had argued that the services in question were vague and insufficiently precise. The Commission allowed the UK authorities to provide further information to explain the scope of what was being proposed, and was prepared to approve the aid under Article 86(2) on the basis that a more detailed 'commissioning plan' would be produced before the launch of the service in question that would more closely define the scope of the public service.[46] Similarly, in the case of State aid to the Italian public service broadcaster RAI, the Commission was prepared to accept a remit of a 'qualitative and rather wide nature' as sufficiently defined 'in so far as it does not explicitly include any commercial activities such as advertising or the sale of programmes'.[47] In the case of funding to TV2 in Denmark, the Commission took the view that support for Danish cinema production fell within the scope of public service broadcasting, on the basis that TV2 acquired the distribution rights to broadcast the films in question on public service television. The CFI, endorsing the Commission's decision on this point (though it annulled it on other grounds), noted that Member States were entitled to define broadcasting SGEIs in broad and qualitative terms, covering the broadcasting of full-spectrum programming, and that this was not called into question by the fact that the broadcaster also engaged in commercial activities such as advertising. The CFI also confirmed the Commission's assessment of the 13.17

[42] Community framework for State aid in the form of public service compensation [2005] OJ C297/4.

[43] See further paras 3.80–3.92 above. See also Broadcasting Communication, para 29; and Case T-442/03 *SIC v Commission* (judgment of 26 June 2008), paras 144–56.

[44] Broadcasting Communication, para 36; and *SIC v Commission*, ibid, paras 195–204.

[45] Broadcasting Communication, paras 38–9.

[46] Decision in Case N 37/2003 *BBC Digital Curriculum* (1 October 2003), paras 42–4.

[47] Decision 2004/339/EC *RAI* [2004] OJ L119/1, para 117.

SGEI defined by Denmark, and held that the fact that the programming was similar to that of commercial television channels did not invalidate that public service remit.[48] The Commission was also prepared to accept that an internet site that informed users about TV2's public service television programmes fell within the scope of TV2's public service broadcasting remit, although further commercial internet services such as the provision of games and chatrooms did not, since they did not differ from similar commercial products and did not 'address the democratic, social and cultural needs of society'.[49]

13.18 **Entrustment.** The Commission needs to be satisfied that the defined public service has been effectively assigned to the recipient of the State support under consideration by means of an 'official act'.[50] Although the Commission can be expected to scrutinize this aspect in some detail, it does not tend to take a formalistic approach. Hence, in the *BBC News 24* case the Commission found that, although the services in question were not defined in the BBC's Charter, a letter from the Secretary of State to the BBC entrusting it with the service in question was sufficient to constitute entrustment.[51] The Commission may also consider the extent to which the entrusted task is effectively supervised by an independent operator, such as a parliamentary commission or committee,[52] or a regulator.[53] A requirement that the public service operator present an annual report on compliance with its public service obligations also helps to address this point.[54]

13.19 **Overcompensation, necessity and proportionality.** The Commission recognizes that State support is normally necessary for an undertaking to carry out public service broadcasting tasks that have been entrusted to it. It will, however, analyse carefully whether such funding is proportionate to the fulfilment of the public service mission in question, and the related question of the existence of any

---

48 Decision 2005/217/EC *TV2/Danmark* [2006] OJ L85/1, para 86 and Cases T-309/04 etc *TV2 Danmark v Commission* (judgment of 22 October 2008), paras 114–123.

49 Decision 2005/217/EC *TV2/Danmark*, ibid, paras 90–3. The CFI did not go into this level of detail in Cases T-309/04 etc *TV2/Danmark v Commission*, ibid. See also Decision 2006/513/EC *Berlin-Brandenburg DTT* [2006] OJ L200/14, para 125: no genuine SGEI where commercial broadcasters not charged with any public service task.

50 Broadcasting Communication [2001] OJ C320/5, para 40.

51 Decision in Case NN 88/98 *BBC News 24* (14 December 1999), paras 62–71.

52 Decision 2004/838/EC *France 2 and France 3* [2004] OJ L361/21, paras 76–9 (appeal in Case T-144/04 *TF1 v Commission* held inadmissible by Order of 19 May 2008); Decision 2004/339/EC *RAI* [2004] OJ L119/1, para 119.

53 Decision 2004/339/EC *RAI* [2004] OJ L119/1, para 119.

54 Decision 2005/217/EC *TV2/Danmark* [2006] OJ L85/1, para 96, upheld in this respect but annulled on other grounds on appeal in Cases T-309/04 etc *TV2/Danmark v Commission* (judgment of 22 October 2008); Decision 2004/838/EC *France 2 and France 3* [2004] OJ L361/21, para 77 (appeal in Case T-144/04 *TF1 v Commission* held inadmissible by Order of 19 May 2008).

overcompensation. In that respect, it is clear that any State aid in question should not exceed the net costs of the public service mission, taking also into account other direct or indirect revenues derived from the public service task.[55]

Assessment of funding arrangements. In order to determine the issues of necessity and proportionality, and verify that no overcompensation exists, the Commission will normally undertake a detailed assessment of the specific funding arrangements in each case.[56] This will often involve a forensic examination of the relevant undertaking's accounts.[57] The Broadcasting Communication contains detailed provisions on the way in which accounts should be kept in order to enable the Commission to carry out that assessment.[58] It also deals with the specific nature of funding in the broadcasting sector, including the fact that many broadcasters maintain 'dual-funding' systems whereby public service broadcasting is financed both through both State funds and through revenues from commercial activities such as advertising.[59] **13.20**

Examples of schemes approved under Article 86(2). Examples of public funding schemes approved under Article 86(2) include licence fees levied on the owners of television sets[60] or electricity consumers,[61] regular investment grants and capital injections,[62] tax relief or use of a different methodology for calculating tax,[63] **13.21**

[55] Broadcasting Communication, para 57. On 27 February 2008 the Commission closed investigations in relation to the State funding of the Flemish broadcaster VRT, and the Irish broadcaster RTE, after the Belgian and Irish governments respectively agreed to define sufficiently precisely the public service remits and to put in place adequate financial control mechanisms, including *ex ante* reviews of additional services to preclude over-compensation: see Decision in Cases E 4/2005 *RTE and TG4* (27 February 2008); and E 8/2006 *VRT* (27 February 2008). A few months later the Commission announced that it had opened the Article 88(2) procedure to investigate whether financial support proposed to be granted to Channel 4 to assist it in meeting the costs of digital switchover met the test of proportionality and did not lead to over-compensation: Case C 13/2008 *Channel 4 - digital switchover* [2008] C137/16.

[56] cf Case T-442/03 *SIC v Commission* (judgment of 26 June 2008), paras 219–56 in which the CFI held that the Commission had failed to carry out the necessary verification.

[57] Decision 2004/339/EC *RAI* [2004] OJ L119/1, paras 120–51.

[58] Broadcasting Communication, paras 49–56; see also the requirements set out in Commission Directive 2006/111/EC on the transparency of financial relations between Member States and public undertakings as well as on financial transparency within certain undertakings [2006] OJ L318/17.

[59] Broadcasting Communication, paras 42–62.

[60] Decision in Case E 3/2005 *Financing for public service broadcasters in Germany* (24 April 2007), paras 27–36.

[61] Decision in Case E 14/2005 *RTP compensation payment* (22 March 2006), para 35.

[62] Decision 2004/838/EC *France 2 and France 3* [2004] OJ L361/21, paras 28–30 (appeal in Case T-144/04 *TF1 v Commission* held inadmissible by Order of 19 May 2008).

[63] Decision in Case E 3/2005 *Financing of public service broadcasters in Germany* (24 April 2007), paras 41–6: in that case the tax authorities levied tax based on assumed profitability percentage given the difficulty of allocating costs between PSB and commercial activities.

guarantees,[64] and the provision of free technical services.[65] Short term or one-off support has included recapitalization,[66] a package of loans, debt rescheduling, capital injections,[67] and bond issue backed by government guarantee,[68] funding to cover restructuring costs,[69] and grants to help public broadcasters to secure broadcasting rights.[70] In the *TV2/Danmark* case the Commission originally approved a number of similar measures under Article 86(2), including in particular ad hoc transfers to cover the costs of digitalization of production systems and related costs. In October 2008 the decision was annulled by the CFI for errors in the assessment of the *Altmark* criteria. At the time of writing, the Commission is in the process of reconsidering its decision in this case.[71]

4. Authorization under Article 87(2) and (3)

13.22 **Assessment under Article 87(2) and (3).** As noted at para 13.16 above, State aid in the broadcasting sector is normally assessed for compatibility under Article 86(2). Nevertheless, each of the derogations set out in Article 87(2) and (3) EC[72] may in principle apply in the case of State aid in the broadcasting sector.[73] Even where these provisions apply, however, the Commission has stated that its substantive analysis of compatibility will be conducted on the basis of the general considerations set out in the Broadcasting Communication.[74]

13.23 **Examples.** In several cases, the Commission has found that subsidies to enable low-income consumers to purchase equipment enabling them to receive digital broadcasting fell within the scope of Article 87(2)(a) (relating to aid having a

64 Decision in Case E 3/2005 *Financing of public service broadcasters in Germany* (24 April 2007), paras 47–9.

65 Decision 2008/136/EC *Ad hoc financing of Dutch public service broadcasters* [2008] OJ L49/1, para 60.

66 Decision in Case N 313/2004 *Recapitalisation of TV2/Danmark* (6 October 2004), paras 11–20, under appeal in Case T-12/05 *TV Danmark and Kanal 5 Denmark v Commission* and Case T-16/05 *Viasat Broadcasting UK v Commission.*

67 Decision in Case N 279/2008 *France Télévisions* (16 July 2008), approval of capital injection to assist meeting the costs of the public service mission following the French government's decision to prohibit advertising being carried on public service channels.

68 Case T-442/03 *SIC v* Commission (judgment of 26 June 2008), paras 115–29.

69 Decision in Case NN 8/2007 *RTVE workforce reduction measures* (7 March 2007), paras 9–22.

70 Decision 2008/136/EC *Ad hoc financing of Dutch public service broadcasters* [2008] OJ L49/1, para 38.

71 Decision 2005/217/EC *TV2/Danmark* [2006] OJ L85/1 and Cases T-309/04 etc *TV2/Danmark v Commission* (judgment of 22 October 2008).

72 On which see further Chapter 3 above.

73 Unusually, the Commission approved emergency funding for the Danish broadcaster TV2 under its 2004 Guidelines on rescue and restructuring aid: Decision in Case N 287/2008 *TV2/Danmark* (4 August 2008).

74 Broadcasting Communication, para 27.

social character).[75] Aid measures to support the transition from analogue to digital broadcasting have also been regarded as compatible under Article 87(3)(c) (aid to facilitate the development of certain economic activities or certain economic areas).[76] But the Commission has rejected the application of Article 87(3)(b) (aid to promote the execution of an important project of common European interest) in this context, on the basis that the measures in question were not supported jointly by a number of Member States.[77] Article 87(3)(d) EC (relating to aid to promote culture and heritage conservation) seems on its face to be particularly relevant to support in the broadcasting sector. However, the Commission takes the approach that this provision must be interpreted restrictively and a distinction made between the cultural, social and democratic needs of society identified in the Broadcasting Protocol; only measures aimed at promoting culture, narrowly defined, are deemed by it to fall within the scope of Article 87(3)(d) EC.[78] This follows the Commission's approach in the *BBC News 24* case, where it took the view that 'the provision of a 24-hour news channel is aimed more at fulfilling the information needs of UK citizens than at promoting culture or national heritage within the meaning of Article 87(3)(d)'.[79] On the basis of that approach, the educational and democratic needs of society are not covered by Article 87(3)(d), though, as the Commission acknowledges, 'State aid to public broadcasters often does not differentiate between those three needs'.[80]

The limits of Article 87(2) and (3). The limits of these provisions were demonstrated when the Commission considered Italian subsidies for the purchase of digital decoders.[81] Italy sought to rely on Article 87(2)(a), (b), (c) and (d). All of these arguments were rejected by the Commission. Since the measure was not compatible under Article 86(2) either, the aid was unlawful and had to be recovered from the indirect beneficiaries of the aid, namely digital terrestrial broadcasters and cable network operators. **13.24**

[75] Decisions in Cases N 622/2003 *Austrian fund for digitalization* (16 March 2005), paras 22–4; and N 546/2006 *French digital television* (6 December 2006), paras 25–30 approving a fund of €140 million for low income groups to purchase digital reception equipment.

[76] Decision in Case N 622/03 *Fund for digitalisation* (16 March 2005), paras 29–40; see also Decision 2006/513/EC *Berlin-Brandenburg DTT* [2006] OJ L200/14, paras 91–120.

[77] Decision in Case N 622/03 *Fund for digitalisation* (16 March 2005), paras 26–8; see further para 13.24 below.

[78] Broadcasting Communication, para 26.

[79] Decision in Case NN 88/98 *BBC News 24* (14 December 1999), para 36; see also Decision 2006/513/EC *Berlin-Brandenburg DTT* [2006] OJ L200/14, paras 121–2.

[80] Broadcasting Communication, para 27.

[81] Decision 2007/374/EC *Digital decoders – Italy* [2007] OJ L147/1, under appeal in Case T-96/07 *Telecom Italia Media v Commission.*

C. Broadband

1. Policy

13.25 **Lisbon Agenda.** The European Council, meeting in Lisbon in March 2000, set as a strategic goal for the EU the strengthening of employment, economic reform and social cohesion as part of a 'knowledge based economy'. Central to the Lisbon Agenda is the programme for building knowledge infrastructures, in particular the provision of telecommunications and internet access across the Community, so that 'Businesses and citizens . . . have access to an inexpensive, world-class communications infrastructure and a wide range of services'.[82] Access to broadband at affordable prices is recognized as being of critical importance to the Community as a whole and to urban and rural regeneration, by improving competitiveness and stimulating economic activity and employment.[83]

13.26 ***e*Europe action plans.** Three action plans have been developed to implement the Lisbon Agenda in the field of information and communications building on the *e*Europe initiative launched in 1999.[84] Consistent with those action plans, the European Council Meeting of March 2003 called on Member States to put in place national broadband/high speed internet strategies.[85] The *i*2010 Action Plan, covering the period from 2005 to 2010, underlines the Commission's active support for the widespread availability of broadband services and identifies as an objective 'the creation of a Single European Information Space offering affordable and secure high bandwidth communications, rich and diverse content and digital services'.[86]

13.27 **Public funding requirements.** Each of the *e*Europe initiatives has recognized that investment in new technology and infrastructure should in principle come from the private sector. Public funding may be required in cases of market failure, particularly in rural areas where (primarily for cost reasons) private investment is unlikely, and in cases where political objectives such as territorial coverage need to be ensured.[87] Research shows that there is a digital divide between urban and

[82] Lisbon European Council 23–24 March 2000: Presidency Conclusions, paras 8–11.

[83] Seville European Council 21–22 June 2002: Presidency Conclusions; Brussels European Council 20-21 March 2003: Presidency Conclusions.

[84] *e*Europe 2002 An Information Society for All Action Plan (June 2000); *e*Europe 2005 An Information Society for All Action Plan, COM(2002) 263; and *i*2010 – A European Information Society for growth and employment, COM(2005) 229.

[85] Brussels European Council 20-21 March 2003: Presidency Conclusions, para 38.

[86] *i*2010 Annual Information Society Report, COM(2007) 146, section 3.3.

[87] See eg *e*Europe 2005 An Information Society for All Action Plan, COM(2002) 263, section 3.1.4.

rural areas and that public intervention accelerates broadband deployment in less profitable areas.[88]

Public funding schemes. Public funding for broadband development may in practice be aimed at the public generally, or at public services, or at end-users including businesses and residential users. Schemes examined by the Commission include schemes to build a high bandwidth, fully managed, network for public services,[89] the provision of a free broadband wireless network,[90] investment in passive network infrastructure (ducts, fibre, street cabinets) allowing private operators to have open access to provide retail broadband applications,[91] investment in backhaul infrastructure to support local loop unbundling,[92] funding to provide high speed symmetrical broadband services for SMEs coupled with information and communication policy aimed at users,[93] access grants to telecommunications network operators to upgrade local exchanges enabling them to provide ADSL services,[94] tax credits for investment in broadband infrastructure,[95] the build and operation of a 'backbone' network linking business parks with a series of local access networks,[96] and investment in wireless broadband services not served for topographical and economic reasons by ASDL or leased lines.[97] **13.28**

Structure of publicly funded schemes. As the above examples demonstrate, State supported broadband schemes typically fund investment in, or provide a grant for, the development of infrastructure. The physical development of the infrastructure and the subsequent management and operation of it may be outsourced to one or more commercial businesses following a public procurement procedure. The entity responsible for the roll-out of the network is often called the 'technology partner'. Typically, the technology partner or, if different, the infrastructure manager will conclude wholesale contracts with service providers who will in turn supply retail services to end customers such as residential and business users. The public funder's interests may be protected through being held in a special purpose vehicle or a joint venture which may be jointly controlled with any private investors. **13.29**

---

[88] Bridging the Broadband Gap, COM(2006) 129, section 4.3.

[89] Decision in Case N 46/2007 *Welsh public sector network scheme* (30 May 2007), para 3.

[90] Decision in Case NN 24/2007 *Prague municipal wireless network* (30 May 2007), para 8.

[91] Decision 2008/729/EC *Amsterdam Citynet* [2008] OJ L247/27, paras 14–26; see also Decision in Case N 213/2003 *Atlas broadband infrastructure scheme* (20 July 2004), paras 4–13.

[92] Decision in Case N 118/2006 *Development of rural broadband* (7 June 2006), paras 11–13.

[93] Decision in Case N 126/2004 *Broadband for SMEs in Lincolnshire* (14 December 2004), paras 8–13; see also Decision in Case N 890/2006 *France – Sicoval* (10 July 2007), paras 13–28.

[94] Decision in Case N 222/2006 *Digital divide in Sardinia* (22 November 2006), paras 8–9.

[95] Decision in Case N 398/2005 *Development tax benefit for broadband* (16 May 2006), para 9.

[96] Decision in Case N 131/2005 *FibreSpeed broadband project in Wales* (22 February 2006), paras 14–18. As amended: see Case N 692/2007 *Amendment of N 131/2005 FibreSpeed broadband project Wales* (10 January 2008).

[97] Decision in Case N 57/2005 *Regional innovative broadband support in Wales* (1 June 2005), paras 9–14.

2. Existence of aid

13.30 **Issues.** The issues which have arisen in determining whether State support for the development and use of broadband amounts to State aid include whether the finance supports infrastructure within the responsibility of the State, whether the finance would have been made by a private investor, and whether it amounts to compensation for the provision of a public service that falls within the *Altmark* test. By contrast, the involvement of State resources in broadband support projects has generally been easy to identify and has not raised difficult issues.

13.31 **Beneficiaries of broadband funding.** Broadband funding may provide advantages to a range of potential direct and indirect beneficiaries of the scheme. *Infrastructure providers* may receive an opportunity to build out an infrastructure on conditions not otherwise available on the market. *Network operators and third party service providers* may be able to offer broadband connectivity at prices lower than those which would have prevailed under normal market conditions. An open public procurement procedure to select the infrastructure builder or technology partner, or network operator, might remove any economic advantage, but this may not be the case if there is a negotiated phase in the tender process, or if the award criteria include qualitative elements rather than being based solely on the economically most advantageous bid.[98] Even where the profits made by the infrastructure builder or technology partner are controlled,[99] the ability to build and acquire ownership of a new infrastructure may be regarded as an economic advantage.[100] *Service providers* may also benefit from being able to lease capacity from the infrastructure created under the scheme, rather than entering the market using more expensive market solutions such as satellite or leased line offerings.[101] *End-users* who are businesses may also benefit,[102] although Article 87(1) will not apply where the benefit is purely to members of the public[103] or public sector bodies,[104] as they are not 'undertakings'.[105]

---

[98] Decision in Case N 126/2004 *Broadband for SMEs in Lincolnshire* (14 December 2004), para 27; Decision in Case N 222/2006 *Digital divide in Sardinia* (22 November 2006), para 45.

[99] Decision in Case N 157/2006 *South Yorkshire digital region broadband project* (22 November 2006), para 31.

[100] Decision in Case N 746/2006 *North Yorkshire NYNET Project* (21 February 2007), para 26.

[101] *North Yorkshire NYNET Project*, ibid, para 28. The position may be different where schemes are localised and small-scale: see Decision in Case N 46/2007 *Welsh public sector network scheme* (30 May 2007), para 19.

[102] *North Yorkshire NYNET Project*, ibid, para 29.

[103] eg a scheme enabling citizens to access public sector websites through wireless hotspots: Decision in Case NN 24/2007 *Prague municipal wireless network* (30 May 2007), paras 34–5 Note that this scheme was amended considerably to remove elements which might have involved State aid such as allowing commercial exploitation in competition with existing broadband service providers.

[104] eg a scheme to link public sector bodies: Decision in Case N 46/2007 *Welsh public sector network scheme* (30 May 2007), paras 17–19.

[105] See further on the concept of an 'undertaking' paras 2.22 *et seq* above.

Private investor test. As discussed in Chapter 2, public funding is not regarded as State aid where a private investor would also have made the investment.[106] This principle was applied in the *Amsterdam Citynet* case, where the Commission decided that the investment by the Municipality of Amsterdam, along with private investors, in a project to build ducts, fibre and street cabinets as part of rolling out a fibre-to-home telecommunications access network was not State aid.[107] The Commission concluded that the two private sector companies involved had invested on equal terms with the Municipality of Amsterdam, and had not made their decision based on earlier project research undertaken by the City authorities; moreover, all investing parties would have to share any losses in the event of an underperforming business. However, the private investor test was not satisfied where, for example, the rate of return was below market rates[108] and too low for a private investor,[109] or where the pricing policy of the aid beneficiary was determined by governmental policy instead of commercial objectives,[110] or where the purpose of the investment was to lower entry barriers to boost competitive supply of electronic communication services.[111] 13.32

Public service compensation. As in the case of aid for broadcasting, no economic advantage will arise if the State support is regarded as compensation for public service obligations within the meaning of the *Altmark* judgment.[112] This was considered in two cases involving investments made by French regional authorities in public open access broadband communications networks, in regions which consisted mainly of rural and remote areas. In each case, the French regional authority awarded a concession contract, following an open tender procedure, for the construction of the infrastructure, allowing third party service providers to provide broadband services to the general public including businesses and public sector users on transparent and non-discriminatory terms. The Commission considered that the investments linked to network infrastructures qualified as compensation for SGEIs and that in each case the *Altmark* criteria were met.[113] But the *Altmark* criteria were not satisfied in cases where infrastructure was aimed 13.33

[106] See paras 2.33 *et seq* above.

[107] Decision 2008/729/EC *Amsterdam Citynet* [2008] OJ L247/27, paras 87–135.

[108] Decision in Case N 284/2005 *Metropolitan Area Network Broadband Program* (8 March 2006), paras 41–2.

[109] Decision in Case N 213/2003 *Atlas broadband infrastructure scheme* (20 July 2004), para 30.

[110] ibid.

[111] Decision in Case N 284/2005 *Metropolitan Area Network Broadband Program* (8 March 2006), paras 41–2.

[112] Case C-280/00 *Altmark* [2003] ECR I-7747, considered at paras 2.67–2.73 above.

[113] Decision in Cases N 381/2004 *Pyrénées-Atlantiques telecommunications network* (16 November 2004), paras 51–87, and N 382/2004 *Limousin telecommunications network* (3 May 2005), paras 45–79. In both cases, the Commission noted that broadband services offered to the end-users did not qualify as SGEIs, so investment linked to such services would not be covered by the *Altmark* test.

at providing high speed broadband connections for operators to provide to large businesses rather than mass market end users,[114] or where the relationship between the provider of wholesale broadband services and the municipal financing authority was more akin to a classic public-private partnership, without any clear entrustment of an SGEI mandate to enable broadband access to the general public, citizens and businesses in rural and remote areas.[115]

13.34 **General infrastructure measures.** It has sometimes been argued that State investment in broadband infrastructure is not State aid, but is a general (non-selective) infrastructure measure. The Commission accepts that where the investment made by the public authority is in respect of a service which falls within the responsibility of the State towards the general public and is limited to meeting the requirements of that service, the funding may not fall within Article 87(1). Rather, it may be likened to the provision of certain transport infrastructure, which is open to all potential users on non-discriminatory terms, and is not normally provided by the market on a commercial basis.[116] But funding a scheme for broadband services for commercial users located in business parks and which would benefit businesses rather than serving the general public will not qualify as a general measure.[117] The same applies to public investment in infrastructure which duplicates investments made by businesses[118] or which supports services which are already provided by the market.[119]

13.35 **Effect on infrastructure competition.** Where the effect of the investment is to facilitate the provision of broadband services on terms which are different from those available under market-led solutions, there is potentially a distortion of competition in respect of infrastructure. New entrants who might otherwise have invested in broadband infrastructure might be deterred from doing so.[120] Public funding may also distort competition to the detriment of existing suppliers whose investment decisions would have been made of the basis of others investing, if at

[114] Decision in Case N 284/2005 *Metropolitan Area Network Broadband Program* (8 March 2006), paras 37–40.

[115] Decision 2007/175/EC *Broadband infrastructure in Appingedam* [2007] OJ L86/1, paras 38–42. It should be added that in no case to date has a Member State invoked Article 86(2) as a justification for State aid in the broadband sector.

[116] Decision in Case N 284/2005 *Metropolitan Area Network Broadband Program* (8 March 2006), paras 35–6.

[117] Decision in Case N 213/2003 *Atlas broadband infrastructure scheme* (20 July 2004), paras 31–2.

[118] Decision in Case NN 24/2007 *Prague municipal wireless network* (30 May 2007), para 36: there were already at least 49 local private wi-fi operators in Prague so the investment could not qualify as public service infrastructure outside the scope of State aid control.

[119] Decision in Case N 284/2005 *Metropolitan Area Network Broadband Program* (8 March 2006), paras 37–40.

[120] Decision in Case N 746/2006 *North Yorkshire NYNET Project* (21 February 2007), para 30.

all, on a market basis.[121] Even where the intervention is made because of market failure, for example because the sparse nature of the population or the topography of the area makes investment uneconomic, it cannot be assumed that market initiatives would not become viable in the longer term.[122]

Effect on downstream competition. Broadband investment may also affect competition in downstream markets. For example, new cable-based broadband infrastructure could distort competition at the wholesale level to the detriment of those providing market-led solutions such leased lines and satellite,[123] and may also impact on competition at the retail level. In cases where a selected service provider is obliged to offer services to end-users, that provider may enjoy a first mover advantage over prospective competitors at the retail level.[124] Aid to support the promotional efforts undertaken by business councils to encourage small businesses to use IT and e-business may distort competition to the disadvantage of consultancy firms.[125] There may also be distortions of competition where the scheme is only available to businesses in certain regions or active in certain electronic communications markets; business end-users may receive an advantage over competitors in other areas or using other technologies.[126] **13.36**

Effect on trade. An effect on trade is normally readily established, particularly since those active in the markets for electronic communications services compete with service providers from other Member States, and their activities are subject to trade between Member States.[127] It has also been suggested that there is an effect on trade between businesses benefiting from broadband investment and their competitors in other Member States.[128] **13.37**

3. Authorization under Article 87(3)

Role of Article 87(3). Aid schemes to promote broadband coverage and usage may, depending on their terms and the intended beneficiaries, be supported through **13.38**

[121] Decision in Case N 126/2004 *Broadband for SMEs in Lincolnshire* (14 December 2004), para 27.

[122] Decision in Case N 264/2006 *Broadband for rural Tuscany* (13 September 2006), para 26.

[123] Decision in Case N 284/2005 *Metropolitan Area Network Broadband Program* (8 March 2006), para 51; Decision in Case N 157/2006 *South Yorkshire digital region broadband Project* (22 November 2006), para 34.

[124] Decision in Case N 264/2006 *Broadband for rural Tuscany* (13 September 2006), para 26.

[125] Decision in Case N 214/2005 *Scheme for promoting SMEs' use of IT and e-business* (15 July 2005), section 3.1.

[126] Decision in Case N 157/2006 *South Yorkshire digital region broadband project* (22 November 2006), paras 35–6; Decision in Case N 284/2005 *Metropolitan Area Network Broadband Program* (8 March 2006), para 51.

[127] *South Yorkshire digital region broadband project*, ibid, para 37.

[128] Decision in Case N 264/2006 *Broadband for rural Tuscany* (13 September 2006), para 28; Decision in Case N 126/2004 *Broadband for SMEs in Lincolnshire* (14 December 2004), para 29.

structural funds under the European Regional Development Fund (ERDF) in eligible regions, especially in rural and remote areas.[129] Alternatively, public funding may be permissible under the provisions on regional aid, aid to SMEs or *de minimis* aids.[130] If none of those applies at all or to the extent that beneficiaries of the aid scheme include parties other than those covered by those provisions,[131] then it is necessary to consider whether the aid qualifies for approval under Article 87(3) by reason of its other features. In all cases to date, save one,[132] the Commission has approved the proposed funding (modified as necessary) and has relied on Article 87(3)(c).[133]

13.39 **Application of Article 87(3)(c).** The general criteria for applying Article 87(3)(c) are discussed in Chapter 3. This section focuses on the specific application of those criteria to public investment in broadband deployment and uptake. After considering the Commission's overall approach in this sector, the paragraphs below address in turn the Commission's approach to the various elements of the 'balancing test' that is now applied for all assessments under Article 87(3), namely whether the aid measure is aimed at a well-defined objective of common interest, whether the aid is well designed to deliver the objective of common interest, and whether the aid is proportional. The aid will be approved if, having regard to these considerations, the overall balance is positive.[134]

13.40 **Overall approach.** In assessing cases of public funding for broadband networks, the Commission takes into account the extent of broadband coverage in the relevant area to ensure that the aid is kept to the minimum possible to encourage private investment. In rural and scarcely populated zones such as mountainous or other isolated areas where no broadband services or only expensive alternatives such as leased line or satellite services are available (sometimes referred to as 'white' areas), State support for broadband is generally deemed compatible if certain proportionality conditions are respected.[135] State funding where basic broadband

---

[129] See Guidelines on Criteria and Modalities of Implementation of Structural Funds in Support of Electronic Communications, SEC(2003) 895, section 4.

[130] See Chapter 2, para 2.148 (*de minimis* aid), Chapter 10 (SMEs) and Chapter 15 (regional aid).

[131] Decision in Case N 214/2005 *Scheme for promoting SMEs' use of IT and e-business* (15 July 2005), section 3.3 (some beneficiaries not SMEs, but scheme approved under Article 87(3)(c) as aid for non-SMEs was a minimum incentive to guarantee the implementation of the scheme); Decision in Case N 126/2004 *Broadband for SMEs in Lincolnshire* (14 December 2004), paras 31–3 (measure cannot be assessed under Regional Aid Guidelines as not all areas are assisted areas under the Guidelines); Decision in Case N 746/2006 *North Yorkshire NYNET Project* (21 February 2007), para 34 (some but not all areas eligible for regional development assistance).

[132] Decision 2007/175/EC *Broadband infrastructure in Appingedam* [2007] OJ L86/1.

[133] For a recent example see Decision in Case N 115/2008 *Broadband in rural areas of Germany* (2 July 2008), paras 40–1.

[134] See further on the balancing test para 3.28 above.

[135] Decision in Case N 475/2007 *Ireland: National Broadband Scheme* (25 November 2007), paras 37–47; Decision in Case N 250/08 *Alto Adige, Italy* (3 July 2008) IP/08/1095; Decision in Case N 497/2008 *Broadband in Lazdijai and Alytus, Lithuania* (17 August 2008). The Commission's

services are partly already covered by at least one operator ('grey' areas), will be more critically analysed. In 'black' areas, characterized by the availability of different broadband services of at least two competing infrastructures (such as telephone and cable TV networks), State aid will be harder to justify given the greater likelihood that State intervention would exclude or harm existing and future private investments.[136]

Common interest objective. The public funding scheme must reflect Community policy on the deployment of broadband set out in paras 13.25–13.27 above. In addition, the aid must address specific market failure objectives such as the lack of private investment in rural or under-served areas,[137] and the Member State must demonstrate the achievement of cohesion and economic development objectives.[138] **13.41**

Well-designed aid. It must be shown that other measures would not achieve the desired result. The Commission has recognized that tariff and access regulation could be another instrument of State intervention, particularly to achieve price reductions, but has consistently held that such *ex ante* regulation is not sufficient to facilitate the supply of broadband services in remote and under-served regions. Moreover, demand side measures in favour of broadband (such as vouchers, tax advantages or other schemes to encourage use) do not address problems on the supply side.[139] The 'well-designed aid' condition also requires that the scheme must provide the right incentives to operators. This is usually demonstrated by expressions of interest in participating in the project from commercial enterprises at the various levels of supply involved. **13.42**

Proportionality. The scheme must achieve an appropriate balance between the resulting benefits and any disadvantages which might lead to distortions of competition and disincentives for the private sector to invest. While the relevant factors vary depending on the scheme, the Commission will typically consider factors such as whether the service providers are selected pursuant to an open tender in accordance with EC public procurement rules,[140] whether the scheme is **13.43**

press release on Case N 497/2008 also noted that more than half of the 38 cases relating to public investment in broadband approved since 2003 related to rural areas: IP/08/1170.

136 Decision in Case NN 24/2007 *Prague municipal wireless network* (30 May 2007), para 38 and n 26. See also speech of Commissioner Neelie Kroes 'Broadband Rollout and Competition Policy – What Role for Public Funding' Brussels (15 May 2007).

137 Decision 2007/175/EC *Broadband infrastructure in Appingedam* [2007] OJ L86/1, paras 72–80. The aid was deemed unlawful because market failure could not be demonstrated: over 70% of the Dutch territory had access to broadband and there were already two suppliers in Appingedam.

138 Decision in Case N 746/2006 *North Yorkshire NYNET Project* (21 February 2007), para 39; see also Decision in Case N 201/2006 *National broadband project* (4 July 2006), paras 51–3.

139 *North Yorkshire NYNET Project*, ibid, para 42; Decision in Case N 284/2005 *Metropolitan Area Network Broadband Program* (8 March 2006), paras 72–3.

140 Decision in Case N 126/2004 *Broadband for SMEs in Lincolnshire* (14 December 2004), para 42; Decision in Case N 222/2006 *Digital divide in Sardinia* (22 November 2006), para 45: the

technology neutral and the reasons why not,[141] whether the scheme allows open access to the infrastructure on transparent and non-discriminatory terms to all interested wholesale broadband providers,[142] whether the acquisition of infrastructure is achieved on the most economically efficient basis—for example whether the infrastructure provider has the freedom to lease or build, including incorporating existing infrastructure,[143] and whether any price distortion with existing service providers is minimized for example by requiring retail prices or tariffs to be comparable with those offered by existing service providers.[144] The Commission will also consider whether there is any mechanism to ensure that there is no over-compensation. In this context, the Commission has approved schemes which include clawback provisions enabling the public funder to recover profits in excess of an agreed rate of return[145] or requiring the excess to be contributed to other agreed cost reducing measures;[146] or reverse payment mechanism to ensure that the public funding is diminished as demand for the new services grows.[147]

D. Postal services

1. Policy and legislation

13.44 **The role of postal services in the EU.** Postal services form a critical part of the media and communications sector within the EU. They are viewed by the European Parliament and the Council of the European Union as constituting 'an essential instrument for communication and information exchange'[148] and as playing a 'vital role which contributes to the objectives of social, economic and

Italian authorities had not received any response to the open tender and then negotiated with the three main operators.

141 *Digital Divide in Sardinia*, ibid, para 45: justified on the basis that ADSL technology was appropriate given the topography of the region and the absence of cable networks.

142 Decisions in Cases N 157/2006 *South Yorkshire digital region broadband project* (22 November 2006) para 43; and N 307/2004 *Broadband in Scotland* (16 November 2004), para 45.

143 Decision in Case N 746/2006 *North Yorkshire NYNET Project* (21 February 2007), para 44.

144 Decision in Case N 126/2004 *Broadband for SMEs in Lincolnshire* (14 December 2004), para 44; and *NYNET*, ibid, para 44.

145 Decisions in Cases N 222/2006 *Digital divide in Sardinia* (22 November 2006), para 45; and N 157/2006 *South Yorkshire digital region broadband project* (22 November 2006), para 51.

146 Decision in Case N 746/2006 *North Yorkshire NYNET Project* (21 February 2007), para 44.

147 Decisions in Cases N 126/2004 *Broadband for SMEs in Lincolnshire* (14 December 2004) paras 18 and 42; and N 307/2004 *Broadband in Scotland* (16 November 2004), paras 24 and 45. Subsequently, the Commission approved an extension to the scheme to cover a limited number of households not reached under the earlier scheme: Decision in Case N 14/2008 *Broadband in Scotland – extending broadband reach* (30 April 2008).

148 Directive 2008/6/EC of the European Parliament and of the Council of 20 February 2008 amending Directive 97/67/EC with regard to the full accomplishment of the internal market of Community postal services [2008] OJ L52/3, recital (5).

territorial cohesion in the Union.'[149] It is pointed out that postal services 'make universal access to essential local services possible',[150] and are vital for all economic and social activities.[151]

Liberalization. The liberalization of the postal sector has sought to promote competition between different providers of postal services, while ensuring the effective provision of services of general economic interest throughout the Community. The liberalization process has been pursued primarily through a series of postal directives: Directive 97/67/EC (the 'First Postal Directive'),[152] Directive 2002/39/EC (the 'Second Postal Directive')[153] and most recently Directive 2008/6/EC (the 'Third Postal Directive').[154] The Postal Directives leave Member States with a broad margin of discretion, while setting out the general approach which they should follow in this area. In particular, they set out the requirements of a universal postal service that each Member State must guarantee (essentially, the permanent provision of a minimum level of deliveries and collections at all points in a Member State's territory, on a fair, non-discriminatory and affordable basis), set minimum quality standards for national and intra-Community mail, provide a framework for harmonization of technical standards, require transparent accounts to be maintained, provide for means of financing the universal service, and mandate the creation of independent national regulatory authorities in each Member State. **13.45**

Application of the State aid rules. The Postal Directives do not affect the obligation on Member States to respect the ordinary competition and State aid rules.[155] In an effort to increase the level of legal certainty in this area the Commission issued a notice in 1998 which considered the application of the competition and State aid rules to the postal sector.[156] Since then, however, there have been considerable developments in the law on the application of the State aid rules to public **13.46**

[149] ibid.

[150] ibid.

[151] Notice from the Commission on the application of the competition rules to the postal sector and on the assessment of certain State measures relating to postal services [1998] OJ C39/2, preface.

[152] Directive 97/67/EC of the European Parliament and of the Council on common rules for the development of the internal market of Community postal services and the improvement of quality of service [1998] OJ L15/14.

[153] Directive 2002/39/EC of the European Parliament and of the Council amending Directive 97/67/EC with regard to the further opening to competition of Community postal services [2002] OJ L176/21.

[154] Directive 2008/6/EC of the European Parliament and of the Council amending Directive 97/67/EC with regard to the full accomplishment of the internal market of Community postal services [2008] OJ L52/3.

[155] ibid, recital (59).

[156] Notice from the Commission on the application of the competition rules to the postal sector and on the assessment of certain State measures relating to postal services [1998] OJ C39/2.

service compensation,[157] and in practice decisions in the postal sector often tend to refer instead to the more general Article 86(2) Framework.[158]

13.47 **State funding in the postal sector: general policy issues.** State support in the postal sector potentially takes a range of forms including direct payments,[159] exemption from taxes,[160] overpayment for services received,[161] the provision of State guarantees,[162] the grant of exclusive rights[163] and the public funding of pensions for staff employed by the postal operator in question.[164] These illustrate that State aid is common in the postal sector. Traditionally, postal incumbents in many Member States have provided not only a universal postal service, but also basic retail banking services, a means of obtaining State benefit payments and, more generally, a way for individuals to access State services at a local level. A complete commercialization of the activities undertaken by State incumbents would inevitably mean that certain of those activities would be cut back, on the basis that they would be unprofitable. Vulnerable groups within society such as the old or the poor would be likely to be particularly adversely affected by reductions in the scope of services provided, or in the number of locations in which they could be accessed. Many State aids in the postal sector are intended to address this form of market failure by providing support for social objectives that would not otherwise be economically viable.

13.48 **Overview of Commission approach.** Numerous measures aimed at providing financial support for the provision of a universal postal service or supporting rural networks of post offices have been cleared by the Commission.[165] In addition, measures providing financial support for the provision of post office card accounts aimed at the 'un-banked' (especially old age pensioners)[166] and the provision of services out of post offices such as the processing of social benefit and tax payments

---

[157] See Chapters 2 and 3 above.

[158] See eg Decisions in Cases N 166/2005 *Rural network support* (22 February 2006), para 37; N 822/2006 *Post Office debt payment funding* (7 March 2007), paras 39–46; and N 388/2007 *Post Office Limited transformation programme* (28 November 2007), para 36.

[159] See eg Decision in Case N 388/2007 *Post Office Limited transformation programme* (28 November 2007).

[160] Decisions in Cases 2002/782/EC *Poste Italiane* [2002] OJ L282/29; and N 763/2002 *Increase in the capital of La Poste* (23 July 2003).

[161] *Poste Italiane*, ibid.

[162] Decision in Cases N 763/2002 *Increase in the capital of La Poste* (23 July 2003); and E 12/2005 *Unlimited State guarantee to Poczta Polska* (24 April 2007).

[163] Decision in Case C 36/2007 *Deutsche Post* [2007] OJ C245/21.

[164] ibid.

[165] See eg Decisions in Cases N 650/01 *Equity injection to An Post* (12 March 2002); and N 784/2002 *Government support to Post Office* (27 May 2003). Note however comments at para 13.51 below.

[166] Decision in Case N 514/2001 *Universal banking services* (13 February 2002).

and the processing of national identity and licensing schemes[167] have been found to be compatible with Article 86(2) EC. By contrast, State support that goes beyond covering the additional costs of providing services of general economic interest or risks cross-subsiding the competitive activities of a postal operator will not be looked on favourably by the Commission.[168]

2. Existence of aid

Issues. Much state support in the postal sector constitutes compensation for the additional costs of providing services of general economic interest. The question of whether this falls within Article 87(1) has therefore been a major issue. Further key issues have been the private investor test and the question of whether funding involves State resources. By contrast, as discussed further below, the potential for competition to be distorted and the effect on trade between Member States is not normally difficult to establish. **13.49**

Private investor test. As discussed in Chapter 2, public funding is not regarded as State aid where a private investor would also have made the investment.[169] In the case of capital injections granted by the Italian State to Poste Italiane, the Commission concluded that, in view of the recipient's record of heavy losses, the Italian state could not expect a return that would have been acceptable to a private investor.[170] In considering the provision of certain loan facilities by the UK to the Post Office, the Commission took into account not only prevailing interest rates but also the fact that the security provided for loans in question could not in practice be realised without closing down the Post Office's network, a step which commercial lenders would be unlikely to find realistic.[171] The application of the private investor test in the postal sector is further complicated by the fact that networks of the type maintained by postal incumbents will not normally have an exact counterpart in the private sector against which costs can be compared. This issue was considered by the European Court in the *Chronopost* cases, where one of the points was whether logistical and commercial assistance provided by La Poste to its subsidiary SFMI-Chronopost was made under normal market conditions. The Commission found that the support by La Poste was of a type that a private **13.50**

---

[167] Decision in Case N 822/2006 *Debt payment funding to Post Office Limited for 2007-2008* (7 March 2007).

[168] See eg Decision in Case C 18/2007 *DHL Leipzig* (2 July 2008).

[169] See paras 2.33 *et seq* above.

[170] Decision 2002/782/EC *Poste Italiane* [2002] OJ L282/29, para 102.

[171] Decision in Case N 388/2007 *Post Office Limited transformation programme* (28 November 2007), para 29.

investor would also have been prepared to make under similar circumstances, and the ECJ ultimately upheld this approach.[172]

13.51 **Public service compensation.** As in the case of aid for broadcasting and broadband development, no economic advantage will arise if the State support for postal services is regarded as compensation for public service obligations within the meaning of the Court's case-law. In the wake of the ECJ's judgment in *Ferring*,[173] setting out a broad principle in this respect, the Commission adopted a number of decisions finding that State support in the postal sector did not constitute aid within Article 87(1).[174] Since the tightening of the criteria for public service compensation, in the subsequent *Altmark* judgment,[175] it has been more difficult to establish that payment for postal services falls outside Article 87(1). This is primarily because of the fourth *Altmark* condition, which states that where an undertaking which is to discharge public service obligations in a given case is not chosen pursuant to a public procurement procedure, the level of compensation needed must be determined on the basis of an analysis of the costs which a typical well-run undertaking within the same sector would incur, taking into account the receipts and a reasonable profit from discharging those obligations. The main difficulty in satisfying this condition in relation to the postal sector is that Member States tend to entrust the fulfilment of public service obligations in the postal sector to incumbent postal operators without organizing a tender. It is also difficult to establish what the costs of a typical undertaking within the sector would be, given the complexity of the tasks involved and the limited nature of competition: quite simply, there is often no obvious comparator against which costs can reliably be bench marked. These difficulties mean that State support in the postal sector tends to constitute State aid within the meaning of Article 87(1), assuming the other conditions are met, and that Member States therefore have to rely on approval of the measure under (in practice) Article 86(2).[176]

13.52 **State resources.** The use of State resources in cases in this sector is not usually difficult to identify. Even where the resources do not derive directly from central

---

172 Cases C-341-342/06 P *Chronopost* (judgment of 1 July 2008), paras 159–64; and see earlier judgment in Cases C-83, 93 and 94/01 P *Chronopost v Ufex* [2003] ECR I-6993, paras 31–8, both discussed further at para 2.58 above.

173 Case C-53/00 *Ferring v ACOSS* [2001] ECR I-9067, considered at para 2.66 above.

174 And that even if it did, Article 86(2) EC would apply: see Decisions in Cases N 252/2002 *Reinvention of the urban Post Office Network* (18 September 2002), paras 59–60; and N 784/2002 *Government support to Post Office* (27 May 2003), paras 71–2.

175 Case C-280/00 *Altmark* [2003] ECR I-7747, considered at paras 2.67–2.73 above.

176 See eg Decision in Case N 822/2006 *Debt payment funding to Post Office Limited for 2007–2008* (7 March 2007) and Decision in Case NN 24/2008 *Poste Italiane* (30 April 2008). Note, however, that in Case T-266/02 *Deutsche Post v Commission* (judgment of 1 July 2008) the Court annulled the Commission's finding that public service compensation in favour of Deutsche Post amounted to aid within Article 87(1), on the ground that it had not established the existence of an economic advantage.

government, they can nevertheless often be traced back to government instructions. Thus in a decision on the UK's rural network support funding of the Post Office, certain of the funds in question were deemed to constitute State funding since they had originally come to the Post Office from Royal Mail following a direction by the government.[177] Voluntary contributions which are not under the control of the State will not, however, constitute State resources.[178]

Effect on competition. The Commission will readily find that State support in the postal sector is capable of distorting competition. Funding granted by the UK government for the purpose of reconfiguring the urban Post Office counter network was deemed by the Commission to be capable of distorting competition by helping to sustain the Post Office's retail network and making the creation and operation of rival retail networks more difficult.[179] Similarly, an unlimited State guarantee to a Polish postal operator that went beyond its reserved area was likely to distort competition.[180] Such measures are deemed to be capable of distorting competition not only in relation to postal services but also in relation to the provision of other products and services such as lottery tickets, bureau de change services,[181] and the provision of financial services.[182] **13.53**

Effect on trade. Postal operators that receive State support tend to be large undertakings that actually or potentially compete with other postal operators within the Community both at a national level and internationally. In addition, as noted in the foregoing paragraph, postal operators may provide a variety of other goods and services through their network, and State support may therefore also affect trade between Member States in respect of those goods and services.[183] **13.54**

3. Authorization under Article 86(2)

Article 86(2) conditions. There is no reason in principle why a State aid measure in the postal sector could not be approved on the basis of the exceptions set out in Article 87(2) and (3) EC. In practice, however, the Commission's decisions have focused on Article 86(2) EC.[184] As set out in Chapter 3, the case-law and **13.55**

[177] Decision in Case N 166/2005 *Rural network support* (22 February 2006), paras 31–4.

[178] See eg Decision in Case N 514/2001 *Universal banking services* (13 February 2002), para 23.

[179] Decision in Case N 252/2002 *Reinvention of the urban Post Office Network* (18 September 2002), para 51.

[180] Decision in Case E 12/2005 *Unlimited State guarantee to Poczta Polska* (24 April 2007), para 32.

[181] Decision in Case N 252/2002 *Reinvention of the urban Post Office Network* (18 September 2002), para 91.

[182] Decision 2002/782/EC *Poste Italiane* [2002] OJ L282/29, para 116.

[183] ibid, paras 114–18.

[184] In Decision in Case E 12/2005 *Unlimited State guarantee to Poczta Polska* (24 April 2007), paras 48–52, the Commission briefly considered Article 87(3)(a), (b), (c) and (d) EC before dismissing these as possible grounds of justification; and in Decision in Case NN 83/2006 *Measures in favour of Royal Mail and Post Office Limited* (21 February 2007), para 52, the Commission expressed its doubts as to whether Article 87(3)(c) could apply.

Commission practice (including in particular the guidance in the Article 86(2) Framework) indicates that five conditions should be satisfied for the application of this provision: (1) existence of a genuine SGEI; (2) entrustment of the SGEI task; (3) absence of overcompensation; (4) necessity and proportionality; and (5) the development of trade must not be affected contrary to the interests of the Community.[185] In practice, as in other sectors, decisions in the postal sector have tended to focus on the first four of these conditions. The Commission's application of these is discussed in more detail below.

13.56 **Existence of SGEI.** Member States have a wide discretion in defining services of general economic interest, and the Commission will not intervene unless it considers that the relevant State entity has made a manifest error in the qualification of the relevant services.[186] Hitherto, the concept of an SGEI has been accepted in relation to the distribution of post throughout the national territory at uniform tariffs,[187] the maintenance of loss-making rural offices in order to ensure the provision of a universal service,[188] and the provision of universal access to basic cash and banking facilities, particularly in rural areas.[189] The relevant services should, however, be clearly defined: the Commission has in the past objected to a State support mechanism that would have allowed a postal operator to make use of funding for all purposes 'connected with' the provision of the relevant SGEI.[190]

13.57 **Entrustment.** The undertaking receiving support must have been 'entrusted' with the operation of the SGEI in question. In a number of cases in the postal sector, the SGEI has been entrusted by way of a ministerial instruction.[191] There are, however, a variety of other means by which entrustment may legitimately take place.[192]

---

185 See further paras 3.80–3.92 above.

186 See, for instance, Decision in Case N 388/2007 *Post Office Limited transformation programme* (28 November 2007), para 39.

187 Case C-320/91 *Corbeau* [1993] ECR I-2533, para 15; Decision in Case N 822/2006 *Post Office debt payment funding* (7 March 2007), paras 32–5. See also Decision in Case NN 24/2008 *Poste Italiane* (30 April 2008)—SGEI described simply as the provision of a universal postal service in Italy.

188 Decision in Case N 166/2005 *Rural network support 2006–2008* (22 February 2006), para 39; Decision in Case N 388/2007 *Post Office Limited transformation programme* (28 November 2007), para 38.

189 Decision in Case N 388/2007 *Post Office Limited transformation programme* (28 November 2007), para 14.

190 ibid, para 17; this issue was resolved by the UK withdrawing the relevant part of its notification.

191 See for instance Decision in Case N 166/2005 *Rural network support funding to Post Office Limited for 2006–2008* (22 February 2006), para 45; Decision in Case N 388/2007 *Post Office Limited transformation programme* (28 November 2007), para 41; Decision in Case N 822/2006 *Post Office debt payment funding* (7 March 2007), para 37.

192 See further para 3.86 above.

Overcompensation, necessity and proportionality. The Commission can be expected to undertake a detailed analysis of the costs and receipts of the SGEI to determine whether the aid is necessary and proportionate, and whether there is any overcompensation.[193] Since the services of general economic interest that benefit from State support in this area are often loss making, the Commission will often be satisfied that no overcompensation has taken place if it is clear that the losses made by the relevant service exceed the level of aid granted.[194] **13.58**

E. Film and audiovisual sector

1. Policy

Cultural importance. The Commission recognizes the important role that European audiovisual works, and particularly cinema, play in promoting and shaping the diversity of European culture and national identities.[195] The European Parliament and Council have also recognized that 'the development of the European film industry is of vital importance for Europe in view of its significant potential in the fields of access to culture, economic development and job creation'.[196] On this basis, a range of measures have been introduced over the years at a European level to help facilitate the promotion of this sector. On the regulatory side, the Television Without Frontiers initiative[197] was recently modernized with the introduction of the Audiovisual Media Services Directive in December 2007.[198] This is a response to technological developments, and is designed to create a new level-playing field in Europe for emerging audiovisual media services (video on demand, mobile TV, audiovisual services on digital TV). In addition, the MEDIA 2007 programme, with a budget of €755 million over seven years (2007–2013), provides a series of support measures for the European audiovisual industry. These include 'i2i Audiovisual', which aims to help audiovisual production companies to access financing from banks and other financial institutions, by supporting some of the **13.59**

---

193 See eg Decision in Case NN 24/2008 *Poste Italiane* (30 April 2008).

194 See eg Decision in Case N 388/2007 *Post Office Limited transformation programme* (28 November 2007), para 81.

195 See eg Commission Staff Working Paper on certain legal aspects relating to cinematographic and other audiovisual works, SEC(2001) 619 (11 April 2001), section 1.1.

196 Recommendation of the European Parliament and of the Council of 16 November 2005 on film heritage and the competitiveness of related industrial activities [2005] OJ L323/57, recital (6).

197 Introduced in 1989 with the aim of achieving the free movement of television programmes, and requiring that European works accounted for at least half of transmission time.

198 Directive 2007/65/EC of the European Parliament and of the Council of 11 December 2007 amending Council Directive 89/552/EEC on the coordination of certain provisions laid down by law, regulation or administrative action in Member States concerning the pursuit of television broadcasting activities [2007] OJ L332/27. This entered into force on 19 December 2007; Member States have two years to implement its provisions in their national law.

costs of guarantees required by such institutions and/or part of the costs of bank financing.

13.60 **Public funding requirements.** At the same time as recognizing the cultural importance of audiovisual works, European authorities acknowledge that it is often difficult for producers of such works to attract the commercial backing that is necessary in order for such projects to come to fruition. In their decision implementing the MEDIA 2007 programme, the European Parliament and Council referred to the 'almost complete lack' of companies specializing in providing loan financing in the audiovisual sector as a major obstacle to competition throughout the EU.[199] It is therefore recognized that public support measures are essential if this industry is to survive and prosper. Indeed, it has even been suggested that, in the absence of public support for film production in most Member States, most European productions would already have disappeared.[200] Across Europe, an estimated €1.6 billion is spent on national film support each year.[201]

13.61 **Common forms of aid.** The most common forms of aid granted to film and audiovisual works are direct grants and subsidies, although tax incentive schemes are also becoming increasingly commonplace. Tax incentives recently approved by the Commission include enhanced tax deductions and payable film tax credits for film production companies,[202] and tax relief incentives for companies for individuals who invest in film and audiovisual productions.[203] The Commission has also approved loans corresponding to 25% of the total project costs up to a maximum of £600,000,[204] as well as potentially recoupable loans for development and production.[205] It should be noted, however, that funds provided directly from Community programmes such as the MEDIA 2007 programme do not constitute State resources and are therefore not State aid.[206]

---

199 Decision 1718/2006/EC *MEDIA 2007* [2006] OJ L327/12, para 13.

200 Jérôme Broche, Obhi Chatterjee, Irina Orssich and Nóra Tosics, 'State Aid for films – a policy in Motion?' Competition Policy Newsletter 2007(1) 44; the article goes on to state that, in the four years from 2002 to 2005, Member States provided over €6.5 billion of State aid for film production.

201 See press release IP/08/1580.

202 Decision in Case N 461/2005 *UK film tax incentive* (22 November 2006).

203 For example see Decision in Case N 151/2006 *Tax relief for investment in films* (16 May 2006), whereby investors could write off for tax purposes 80% of the amount invested; see also Decision in Case N121/2007 *Tax measures to encourage the production of audiovisual works* (16 July 2007), whereby companies subject to Belgian tax law could deduct annually 150% of the value of its investment from its taxable income (subject to a maximum deduction of €750,000).

204 Decisions in Cases N 504/2006 *Northern Ireland film production fund* (1 September 2006) and N 353/03 *Northern Ireland film production fund* (10 December 2003).

205 Decision in Case N 593/2006 *Northern Ireland Screen Fund* (21 February 2007).

206 See Commission Communication on certain legal aspects relating to cinematographic and other audiovisual works [2002] OJ C43/6, section 2.3(b); and see further para 2.99 above.

2. Existence of aid

Issues. The existence of aid has tended to be relatively easily established in the Commission's decisions in the film and audiovisual sector: the aid is usually available only to certain undertakings and it is well established that aid for film and audiovisual works affects trade between Member States. Issues that have arisen, however, include the question of whether tax incentives to encourage individuals to invest in such works constitute State aid, the application of the private investor test, and the involvement of State resources. **13.62**

Economic advantage. In relation to measures aimed at encouraging investment in the film and audiovisual sectors, tax incentives aimed at individuals will not amount to aid at the level of the investor. They may, however, constitute indirect aid to the investee companies in the film and audiovisual sector. Thus in a case involving an Irish tax relief scheme for corporate and individual taxpayers to invest in film production, the Commission considered there to be aid to the film production companies, since the measure would enable them to raise capital more easily.[207] **13.63**

Private investor test. As discussed in Chapter 2, public funding is not regarded as State aid where a private investor would also have made the investment.[208] One case considered by the Commission in this sector involved the creation of an investment fund, operated with 100% public investment, which would co-invest in film projects together with private investors. The Commission was satisfied that both private and public investors were investing on a fully commercial basis, and that they received equal terms with regard to risks, rewards, fiscal treatment and all other conditions. The Commission consequently found that the measure respected the market economy investor principle and did not involve State aid.[209] However, in another case decided just a few months earlier, also involving an investment club with a public investment fund co-investing with private investors, the Commission found that the private investor test was not satisfied. The Commission was concerned that private investors might be limited to 30% of the overall investment, and that the private investments might not be made at arms length in view of the specific sectoral focus of the measure.[210] **13.64**

---

[207] Decision in Case N 387/2004 *Tax relief for investment in film* (1 December 2004), sections 3.1.2.1 and 3.1.2.2; and see further paras 2.26 and 2.30 above.

[208] See paras 2.33 *et seq* above.

[209] Decision in Case N 194/2006 *Screen East Content Investment Fund* (7 June 2006). See also Decision in Case C 8/2008 *Ciudad de la Luz studios* (13 February 2008), in which the Commission expressed doubts that the private investor test was satisfied and asked Spain to provide further information to enable it to reach a final decision.

[210] Decision in Case N 73/2005 *East Midlands media investment* (23 January 2006), para 33. The Commission went on to consider the State aid in this case under the Communication on State aid and risk capital [2001] OJ C235/3, discussed further in Chapter 9 above.

13.65 **State resources.** An obligation on national television broadcasters to invest sums in financing audiovisual and cinematic productions has been found not to involve State resources and therefore did not constitute State aid.[211] In the same case, a system whereby money was available to cinemas for modernization or the creation of new cinemas was also found not to involve State resources. Whilst the scheme was administered by a public body, the sums available were in fact financed entirely by contributions imposed on the companies benefiting under the scheme. The companies could not receive more than they had paid in. The scheme therefore acted essentially as a means of requiring companies to put money aside to be used for improving their infrastructure.[212]

13.66 **Effect on competition and trade.** The potential beneficiaries of aid schemes in this sector tend to be restricted to film projects/producers meeting certain specified eligibility criteria. These beneficiaries compete with others involved in the production of audiovisual works, including those who do not benefit from the scheme. Moreover, films are traded at an international level and films from one Member State will be in competition with films from all other Member States and may attract audiences internationally.[213] In those circumstances, aid schemes benefiting national film producers are very likely to have the requisite effect on competition and trade within the meaning of Article 87(1).

3. Authorization under Article 87(3)

13.67 **Role of Article 87(3).** Aid granted to this sector may qualify for approval under the provisions on aid to SMEs,[214] employment and training aid or *de minimis*[215] aids, all of which are considered elsewhere in this book.[216] Where none of these apply, then it is necessary to consider whether the aid can be approved under Article 87(3) by reason of its other features.

[211] Decision in Case NN 84/2004 and N 95/2004 *Support measures in the cinema and audiovisual sectors* (22 March 2006), paras 390–8. See AG Kokott in Case C-222/07 *Unión de Televisiones Comerciales Asociadas (UTECA)* (opinion of 4 September 2008).

[212] *Support measures in the cinema and audiovisual sectors*, ibid, paras 242–8.

[213] See eg Decision in Case N 695/2006 *German Film Fund* (20 December 2006), para 23; Decision in Case N 291/2007 *Netherlands Film Fund* (10 July 2007), para 37.

[214] See eg Decision in Case NN 84/2004 and N 95/2004 *Support measures in the cinema and audiovisual sectors* (22 March 2006), para 423; see also Cases XS 301/2007 *Línea Industria audiovisual* [2008] OJ C11/13; XS 171/2005 *Audio visual industry sector development project* [2006] OJ C177/14; and XS 67/2002 *Cornwall film fund for SMEs* [2003] OJ C154/16.

[215] See Decision N 194/2006 *Screen East Content Investment Fund* (7 June 2006), para 18; Decision in Case NN 84/2004 and N 95/2004 *Support measures in the cinema and audiovisual sectors* (22 March 2006), where the *de minimis* exemption was applied to a variety of different support mechanisms within the overall scheme; see sections 9, 13, 18, 27, 28 and 37 of the Decision.

[216] See Chapter 2, para 2.148 (*de minimis* aid), Chapter 6 (employment and training aid), Chapter 10 (SMEs) and Chapter 15 (regional aid). The Commission has also previously examined an aid measure in this sector under its Communication on State aid and risk capital [2001] OJ C235/3: Decision in Case N 73/2005 *East Midlands media investment* (23 January 2006).

Article 87(3)(d). As discussed above, the film and audiovisual sector is seen as having a vital role to play in the preservation of European cultural diversity. It is therefore unsurprising that the overwhelming majority of aid schemes approved by the Commission in this sector have been found to be compatible with the common market under the application of the cultural derogation in Article 87(3)(d). In 1998 the European Commission issued a decision relating to an aid scheme for French cinema production, in which it set out four criteria against which an aid scheme should be assessed under Article 87(3)(d): (1) the aid must be directed to a cultural product; (2) the producer must be free to spend at least 20% of the film budget in other Member States without suffering any reduction in aid; (3) the aid intensity must not exceed 50% of the production budget (difficult and low budget films are excluded from this limit); and (4) aid supplements for specific filmmaking activities (eg post-production) are not allowed.[217] **13.68**

Cinema Communication. The four criteria set out above were subsequently enshrined in the Commission's Cinema Communication,[218] which sets out the criteria under which the cultural derogation under Article 87(3)(d) can be applied to State aid to production activity in the film and audiovisual sectors. It provides that the Commission must verify first that the scheme respects the 'general legality' principle: ie it must not be contrary to provisions of the EC Treaty in fields other than State aid.[219] The Commission must then go on to examine whether the four criteria identified in the French cinema production decision, set out above, are satisfied. In principle the Communication only applies to national aid schemes, however the Commission has also applied it by analogy to individual aid measures on numerous occasions.[220] **13.69**

Review of Cinema Communication. The period of application of the Communication was extended in 2004[221] and again in June 2007 (when its application was extended until 31 December 2009).[222] On 28 January 2009 the **13.70**

[217] Decision in Case N 3/1998 *France – support for cinema production* (29 July 1998).

[218] Commission Communication on certain legal aspects relating to cinematographic and other audiovisual works ('Cinema Communication') [2002] OJ C43/6.

[219] Indeed, this principle should in fact apply to *any* aid authorized by the Commission: see Case 73/79 *Commission v Italy* [1980] ECR 1533, para 11, and para 3.30 above.

[220] See eg Decisions in Cases N 40/2007 *Eurovize* (29 June 2007); N 624/2006 *Aid to SEN FILM – Slovakia* (24 October 2006); N 623/2006 *Aid to ALEF Film & Media Group – Slovakia* (24 October 2006); N 393/2006 *Jakubisko Film Slovakia* (19 July 2006).

[221] Communication from the Commission to the Council, the European Parliament, the Economic and Social Committee and the Committee of the Regions on the follow-up to the Commission communication on certain legal aspects relating to cinematographic and other audiovisual works (Cinema Communication) [2004] OJ C123/1.

[222] Commission Communication concerning the prolongation of the application of the Communication on the follow-up to the Commission communication on certain legal aspects relating to cinematographic and other audiovisual works (Cinema Communication) [2007] OJ C134/5.

Commission announced a further extension until 31 December 2012, in order to allow further consideration of the territoriality requirements for State aid approval. In doing so, the Commission also noted a number of emerging trends that will require some refinement of the assessment criteria in due course, such as support for aspects other than film and TV production (eg digital projection and film distribution), more regional support schemes and competition among some Member States to attract inward investment from large-scale, mainly US, film production companies.

13.71 **General legality principle.** The Commission must verify that the eligibility conditions of the State aid schemes do not contain clauses contrary to the EC provisions in fields other than State aids.[223] This means that principles such as freedom of establishment, freedom to provide services and free movement of goods must be respected. Thus schemes must not reserve aid for nationals only, or require beneficiaries to have the status of national undertaking established under national commercial law.[224] This stipulation has, however, been interpreted loosely. An aid scheme with eligibility tests referring specifically to German origin was held not to be discriminatory on the basis that 'German' could relate not just to nationality but also residence or cultural background.[225] Likewise, an aid scheme where the beneficiaries were production companies with a permanent branch in Catalonia was held to comply, as production companies established in other EU Member States could benefit from the scheme if they committed to opening a branch in Catalonia once the aid was approved.[226]

13.72 **Cultural content.** The Cinema Communication requires that each Member State must ensure that the content of the aided production is cultural according to verifiable national criteria.[227] Aid schemes must therefore include a means of testing the cultural content of the production in question. The format of such tests is left entirely open for the Member States to decide, but the Commission will carefully review the criteria used to satisfy itself that they do in practice achieve their intended aim of ensuring cultural content. Cultural tests accepted by the Commission have tended to consist of a number of cultural criteria including for example: the language of the film/screenplay,[228] the film locations, the nationality or residency of leading characters; the national nature of the subject matter (eg whether it addresses national cultural, social or political issues); the nationality

[223] Cinema Communication, section 2.3(a).

[224] ibid.

[225] Decision in Case N 695/2006 *German Film Fund* (20 December 2006), para 27.

[226] Decision in Case N 268/2006 *State aid for producing first or second films by new directors* (20 September 2006).

[227] Cinema Communication, section 2.3(b)(1).

[228] Note however, that in its Decision in Case N 461/2005 *UK film tax incentive* (22 November 2006), the Commission stated that as English was widely spoken internationally, it could be argued that the use of English would not necessarily guarantee that a film would be culturally British (para 41).

of the author; and the nature of the storyline (eg whether the theme concerns art/artists or historical figures/events).[229] Alternatively, schemes may simply make provision for a body to assess the cultural requirement in relation to each application for funding. Where a test of eligibility for financial aid combines both cultural and non-cultural elements, the Commission will need to be satisfied that there is a safeguard ensuring that a minimum level of cultural elements need to be fulfilled.[230] In the *UK film tax incentive* case,[231] the Commission was not satisfied that the cultural test implemented by the UK authorities actually achieved in practice the aim of ensuring cultural content, and the scheme was only approved once the UK had amended the test to the satisfaction of the Commission. The Commission, however, has taken the view that cinematic co-productions which meet the terms of the European Convention on Cinematographic Co-Production will automatically be deemed to satisfy the cultural content requirement and do not additionally need to pass the relevant national cultural tests.[232] The same applies to co-productions qualifying under bilateral co-production agreements, as they have the same objective as the Convention.[233]

Territoriality. The Cinema Communication requires that the producer must be free to spend at least 20% of the film budget in other Member States without suffering any reduction in the aid provided for under the scheme. The Commission will thus accept aid schemes with territoriality criteria corresponding to up to 80% of the production budget of the aided film or TV work.[234] There has, however, been a considerable degree of debate regarding this issue. The Commission expressly acknowledges in the Cinema Communication that territoriality requirements fragment the internal market and may constitute a barrier to the free circulation of workers, goods and services across the EC. There is therefore a tension between the promotion of national film industries and the achievement of a free market. The justification adopted by the Commission for the inclusion of such a requirement is that it may be necessary to ensure the continued presence of human skills and technical expertise required for cultural creation.[235] Nevertheless, as part of its ongoing review of the Cinema Communication the Commission conducted **13.73**

[229] See Decisions in Cases N 461/2005 *UK film tax incentive* (22 November 2006); N 695/2006 *German Film Fund* (20 December 2006); N 291/2007 *Netherlands Film Fund* (10 July 2007); N 605/2007 *Financial Incentives for the Audiovisual Industry Regulations* (28 November 2007); and N 742/2007 *Audiovisual support scheme* (13 February 2008).

[230] See eg Decision in Case N 60/2008 *Support for cinema in Sardinia* (16 July 2008), para 62.

[231] Decision in Case N 461/2005 *UK film tax incentive* (22 November 2006).

[232] eg *UK film tax incentive*, ibid, paras 38–9; Decision in Case N 695/2006 *German Film Fund* (20 December 2006), paras 32–4; and Decision in Case NN 6/2006 *UK film development and production funds* (11 December 2007), paras 112–13.

[233] *UK film tax incentive*, ibid, paras 38–9.

[234] Cinema Communication, section 2.3(b)(2).

[235] ibid, section 2.3(b).

a study focusing on the use of territorialization clauses. The final report was published in May 2008.[236] The Commission, finding that the report was not conclusive on the economic and cultural impact of such clauses in film support schemes, determined that further reflection was required before proposing a modification of the existing territorialization criterion. It has therefore announced a further three-year extension to the Cinema Communication to allow for such further reflection (among other things).[237]

13.74 **Aid intensity.** The aid intensity must in principle be limited to 50% of the production budget with a view to stimulating normal commercial initiatives inherent in a market economy and avoiding a bidding contest between Member States.[238] However, no aid intensity limit applies to 'difficult and low budget' films. It is for the Member States to establish its definition of 'difficult and low budget' films according to national parameters. The Commission will have to be satisfied that they have established satisfactory definitions. The definitions of 'difficult' films accepted by the Commission have tended to be definitions focusing on films that would have little if any prospect of commercial success, either because of their experimental nature or because they represent a high level of commercial risk.[239] Aid intensities exceeding 50% have been accepted for 'difficult' films with budgets as high as £8 million.[240] The Commission is likely to review the threshold for films to be labelled as 'low budget' films by reference to the typical value of other films in the region in question.[241] Accepted thresholds for 'low budget' films have included budget limits of as much as €2 million.[242] The Commission has previously determined that, in general, short films are low budget films and they can also be seen to be difficult films as they do not find much of an audience, making it very difficult to sell and to finance them.[243]

13.75 **Aid supplements related to production.** Aid supplements for specific film-making activities (eg post-production) are not allowed. This criterion seeks to ensure that

[236] 'Study on the Economic and Cultural Impact, notably on Co-productions, of Territorialisation Clauses of State aid Schemes for Films and Audiovisual Productions', A final report for the European Commission, DG Information Society and Media, 21 May 2008.

[237] See para 13.70 above.

[238] Cinema Communication, section 2.3(b)(3).

[239] See eg Decision in Case N 605/2007 *Financial Incentives for the Audiovisual Industry Regulations* (28 November 2007); Decision in Case N 695/2006 *German Film Fund* (20 December 2006);

[240] Decision in Case N 461/2005 *UK film tax incentive* (22 November 2006).

[241] See eg Decision in Case N 291/2007 *Netherlands Film Fund* (10 July 2007)—threshold was over 25% below the average budget of supported film productions in the Netherlands; and Decision in Case N 233/2008 *Latvian support scheme* (16 July 2008)—threshold was below the median film budgets for the same categories of films.

[242] *Netherlands Film Fund,* ibid.

[243] Decision in Case N 415/06 *State Aid for the production of short films* (26 July 2006); Decision in Case N 142/02 *Scheme of aid to cinema production and film related activities* (9 April 2002).

the aid has a neutral incentive effect, and does not attract those specific activities into (or protect those activities in) the Member State granting the aid.[244] The Cinema Communication thus applies only to aid directed at production activity. However, in cases where the aid scheme is not directed at production activity, but still bears some relation to production (ie most pre-production activity and some post-production activity such as promotion or distribution), the Commission in assessing the compatibility of the aid scheme will still apply the criteria of the Cinema Communication by analogy.[245] Such cases, by their very nature, are the most likely to give rise to consideration of the existence of aid supplements for specific film-making activities. Where no territorial conditions apply to supplementary aid to specific activities in pre- or post-production, the aid is likely to have a neutral incentive regarding those activities in the country in question and therefore would be deemed to comply with the Cinema Communication.[246] Aid granted for the development of feature length films has previously been found to constitute an aid supplement for a specific film-making activity. However, since the aid involved no obligation or incentive for expenditure in France, it was found to be compatible with the Cinema Communication.[247] A similar approach was also taken in the same decision in relation to aid for the creation of original music for a film[248] and aid for distribution of expensive, high quality films,[249] both of which were identified as aid supplements. Aid granted for the promotion of films abroad, on the other hand, was found not to constitute an aid supplement as, strictly speaking, it did not relate to specific film-making activity.[250]

Activity unrelated to production. Where the activity bears no relation to production, such as measures relating to the broadcasting of the work, the Cinema Communication will not be relevant and the Commission will assess the 13.76

[244] Cinema Communication, section 2.3(b)(4). Note that even in the absence of aid supplements the Commission may have concerns in some cases where there are doubts over the neutrality of the incentive effect of the aid: see Decision in Case N 605/2007 *Financial Incentives for the Audiovisual Industry Regulation* (28 November 2007), paras 47–9.

[245] Decision in Cases NN 84/2004 and N 95/2004 *Support measures in the cinema and audiovisual sectors* (22 March 2006), p 57; Decision in Case N 291/2007 *Netherlands Film Fund* (10 July 2007), para 40; Decision in Case NN 6/2006 *UK film development and production funds* (11 December 2007), para 276; Decision in Case N 562/2007 *Aid for the creation and production of films in Spain* (2 April 2008); Decision in Case N 742/2007 *Audiovisual support scheme* (13 February 2008), para 45.

[246] *Netherlands Film Fund*, para 65; and Decision in Case N 60/2008 *Support for cinema in Sardinia* (16 July 2008), para 74 relating to the creation of screenplays.

[247] Decision in Cases NN 84/2004 and N 95/2004 *Support measures in the cinema and audiovisual sectors* (22 March 2006), para 110.

[248] ibid, para 123.

[249] ibid, para 153.

[250] ibid, para 315.

compatibility of the scheme under the general principles of Article 87(3)(d)[251] (or, in appropriate cases, other derogations such as 87(3)(c)—see next paragraph). Aid that has been approved under Article 87(3)(d) includes support for film festivals, exhibitions, seminars, education and training.[252] Such derogations will however be interpreted strictly. The Commission recently expressed the view that Article 87(3)(d) could not apply to State aid providing the construction and operation costs of a new, large film studio complex as there was no evidence that it aided the promotion of culture.[253]

13.77 **Articles 87(3)(c).** In cases where neither the provisions on horizontal or *de minimis* aids,[254] nor Article 87(3)(d) apply, the other exception that is most likely to be applied is Article 87(3)(c).[255] In a Spanish case involving direct grants to support the costs of subtitling and/or dubbing (as well as promotion) in the Basque language, the Commission held that neither the Cinema Communication nor the general cultural derogation in Article 87(3)(d) applied as the measure concerned a specific post-production activity, which was linked to the commercialization of the works. The cultural derogation had to be applied restrictively, and was not engaged simply because the scheme related to a language little-spoken in the Community. Instead, the Commission applied the derogation under Article 87(3)(c), finding that the measure was in the common interest and that it satisfied the necessity and proportionality tests.[256] Another measure approved under Article 87(3)(c) was a selective aid scheme to support modernization and creation of cinemas.[257]

---

[251] See eg *Support measures in the cinema and audiovisual sectors*, ibid, para 13. The application of Article 87(3)(d) is discussed in detail in Chapter 3. For broadcasting, specifically, see also section B above.

[252] See eg Decisions in Cases N 60/2008 *Support for cinema in Sardinia* (16 July 2008); and N 233/08 *Latvian support scheme* (16 July 2008).

[253] Decision in Case C 8/2008 *Ciudad de la Luz studios* (13 February 2008), paras 108–14.

[254] See para 13.67 above.

[255] Note, however, that the Cinema Communication at p 8 also states that Article 87(3)(a) may also apply. See for example Decision in Case N 94/203 *Modification of aid scheme N 708/98: ZEC – Audiovisual activities* (12 August 2003), extending an existing authorised tax assistance scheme in the Canary Islands to audiovisual production activity. See also Decision in Case C 8/2008 *Ciudad de la Luz studios* (13 February 2008) where the Commission is considering the possible classification of aid as regional aid. In that case, Spanish authorities argue that, in terms of regional development and cohesion, the contribution to the revenues and employment of the province of Alicante were sizeable. However, the Commission has requested further information before reaching a decision on the issue.

[256] Decision in Case N 481/2007 *Promotion of movies and DVDs in Basque* (13 November 2007), para 33.

[257] Decision in Cases NN 84/2004 and N 95/2004 *Support measures in the cinema and audiovisual sectors* (22 March 2006), paras 250–5 on pp 95–6.

14

ENERGY, COAL AND STEEL

Main legislation and guidelines

Council Regulation (EC) 1407/2002 on State aid to the coal industry [2002] OJ L205/1

Commission Regulation (EC) 800/2008 on the application of Articles 87 and 88 of the Treaty declaring certain categories of aid compatible with the common market (General Block Exemption Regulation) ('GBER') [2008] OJ L214/3

Community guidelines on State aid for environmental protection ('2008 Environmental Aid Guidelines') [2008] OJ C82/1

Commission Communication relating to the methodology for analysing State aid linked to stranded costs ('Communication on stranded costs') SG(2001) D/290869

A. Introduction

General. The energy, coal and steel sectors are all sectors in which the grant of **14.01** State aid has been a highly sensitive subject. To start with, they are sectors which for various reasons have tended to be characterized by a high level of governmental involvement. In addition, all three sectors have been subject to specific Treaty rules which have ousted or circumscribed the normal rules applicable under Articles 87 and 88 EC. In the energy sector, account must be taken of the impact of the Euratom Treaty on aid to the nuclear fuel industry. In the coal and steel sectors, State aid was historically governed not by Articles 87 and 88 EC, but by Article 4(c) of the ECSC Treaty. Notwithstanding the demise of the ECSC, all three sectors remain subject to specific rules, which are discussed in the following sections.

14.02 **National v Commission policy.** Government intervention and direction, across Europe, has had an important role to play in the development of State aid policy in relation to the energy, coal and steel sectors. European governments, notably in the newer Member States, continue to be central to managing the transition of these sectors from direct governmental control to arms-length regulation as privatized industries. European State aid policies for these sectors have mirrored national policy considerations, which have included energy security, economic development, employment and regional development. Over time the Commission has successfully placed the question of the economic rationality of supporting these sectors at the top of the list of its policy consideration, leading to privatizations, rationalization and closures. More recently, the tension between the more politically based national objectives and the Commission's long-term economics-based policies has resurfaced in the guise of a debate about 'energy security'. Member States have argued that in an increasingly uncertain world the development of these three 'strategic' sectors cannot be left to the uncertainty of the market. Environmental protection has also emerged as a key policy consideration for both Member States and the Commission.

14.03 **Non-nuclear energy.** Section B below addresses the application of the State aid rules to the energy sector, with the exception of nuclear energy and coal. While this sector is frequently the beneficiary of State support, many measures are structured in such a way as to avoid (or attempt to avoid) the application of the State aid rules altogether, by ensuring that State resources are not involved, or by attempting to frame legislation as a general measure. Where State aid does exist, however, it will often be approved under the provisions of the Environmental Aid Guidelines or, in certain circumstances, the rules on stranded costs.

14.04 **Nuclear energy.** In the nuclear sector, discussed in section C below, there is a complex relationship between the rules on State aid in Articles 87 and 88 EC, and the provisions of the Euratom Treaty which (by contrast to the ECSC Treaty) is unlimited in duration. In a number of cases, this difficulty has been circumvented by finding the measure in question not to constitute State aid. In other cases, aid has been held to be compatible. To date, the Commission has not ever found an existing or proposed measure of State support for the nuclear industry to constitute incompatible State aid.

14.05 **Coal and steel.** The European Coal and Steel Community ('the ECSC'), established by the Treaty of Paris in 1951, created a common market for coal and steel.

The ECSC Treaty provided separate rules for State aid in the coal and steel sectors. In particular, in contrast to the EC Treaty, the ECSC prohibited the Member States from granting subsidies or aid, in any form whatsoever, in the steel and coal sectors.[1] However, in the 1970s and 1980s, the Community decided that aid to the coal and steel industry would be required to achieve the large-scale restructuring of the two industries. The Commission therefore used its powers under ECSC Article 95 to put in place rules for aid to the coal and steel industries. The expiry of the ECSC Treaty in July 2003 resulted in the Commission considering aid to the coal and steel sectors against the same criteria used for all other forms of aid. Nevertheless, some specific rules remain, which are discussed in sections D (coal) and E (steel) below.

B. Non-nuclear energy

Overview. As the EU and Member States seek to address climate change concerns and meet the EU's Kyoto Protocol commitments, aid to assist the development of renewable energy or 'green fuels' has increased in importance. Many such measures will not constitute aid at all (section 1 below). Where aid within Article 87(1) does arise, it will often fall under the new General Block Exemption Regulation ('GBER') or will be capable of authorization by the Commission under the 2008 Environmental Aid Guidelines (section 2 below). Outside of the field of renewable energy, State aid for the energy sector will normally only be authorized in two main groups of cases. The first is cases involving stranded costs (section 3 below). The second is where authorization is sought for rescue and/or restructuring aid. That is addressed in Chapter 7 above.[2] **14.06**

1. Existence of aid

Article 87(1) issues. The concept of aid is discussed in detail in Chapter 2. Energy sector aids raise many of the issues discussed in that chapter. The aids may not be granted to 'undertakings', or might compensate for the costs of an SGEI. The establishment of a 'green energy' purchase obligation may fall outside Article 87(1) where it does not involve support through state resources. Exemptions from **14.07**

[1] ECSC Article 4(c). However, in the 1970s and 1980s the Community decided that aid to the coal and steel industry would be required to achieve the large-scale restructuring of the two industries. The Commission used its powers under ECSC Article 95 to put in place rules for aid to the coal and steel industries.

[2] The main example of an approval of this type of case in the energy sector is the Decision in Case NN 101/2002 *British Energy* (27 November 2002).

energy tax may be justified by the nature or general scheme of the system. These issues are considered in more detail in the next paragraphs.

14.08 **Beneficiaries of aid.** Article 87(1) only applies to aid to undertakings.[3] Subsidies to encourage individuals and bodies not carrying on economic activities (eg schools) to invest in renewable energy or energy conservation are therefore not State aid.[4]

14.09 **Compensation for SGEIs.** The production of energy may involve public service obligations, such as a security of supply obligation. On this basis, the Commission approved a Slovenian scheme that supported an electricity plant by offering a guaranteed purchase price for electricity produced using Slovenian brown coal. The Commission considered that the scheme fulfilled all four of the *Altmark* conditions and therefore did not constitute aid within Article 87(1).[5] Similar reasoning was applied to an Irish scheme for electricity generation.[6]

14.10 **Purchase obligations: *PreussenElektra*.** The seminal case on the application of Article 87(1) to a 'green energy' purchase obligation was the ruling of the ECJ in *PreussenElektra* in 2001.[7] In that case, the Court established that an obligation imposed by German law, on private electricity suppliers, to purchase electricity from renewable energy sources at a set minimum price, did not constitute State aid. Although the measure conferred an 'undeniable' advantage on certain undertakings, namely the suppliers of electricity from renewable energy sources, that advantage did not involve any direct or indirect transfer of State resources since the burden fell entirely on the private electricity supply undertakings.[8]

14.11 **Subsequent cases.** Since *PreussenElektra* the Commission has adopted decisions in a number of similar cases where 'green energy' purchase obligations have been held not to constitute State aid. These cases have included several Belgian measures requiring electricity distributors to purchase a prescribed quantity of 'green certificates' each year, certifying compliance with requirements to purchase specified percentages of their electricity needs from renewable sources.[9] The same conclusion was reached in relation to German laws that benefited the producers of renewable energy by obliging energy grid operators to connect green electricity generation to the national grid, purchase green electricity in priority over other

---

[3] See paras 2.22 *et seq* above.

[4] See Decision in Case N 94/2007 *Aid for the use of renewable energies* (22 March 2007), and earlier related decisions referred to therein.

[5] Decision 2007/580/EC *Slovenian green electricity scheme* [2007] OJ L219/9, paras 98–123.

[6] Decision in Case N 475/2003 *New electricity generation capacity* (16 December 2003).

[7] Case C-379/98 *PreussenElektra* [2001] ECR I-2099.

[8] See further para 2.93 above.

[9] Decision in Case N 550/2000 *Green electricity certificates* (25 July 2001); Decision in Case N 415a/2001 *Green certificate mechanism* (28 November 2001); Decision in Case N 14/2002 *Federal renewable energy scheme* (2 August 2002); and Decision in Case N 254/2006 *Panneaux photovoltaïques* (24 October 2006).

forms of energy, and pay a minimum price for green electricity that was above the market price for non-renewable electricity.[10] The common feature of the Belgian and German measures was that while they conferred a benefit on the producers of green electricity, this support was not through financial assistance from the State. By contrast, a Slovenian scheme requiring electricity network operators to purchase electricity from renewable sources at above the market price was held to be State aid. Under that scheme, the network operators recouped their losses via a parafiscal levy imposed on the consumption of electricity.[11]

Exemptions from energy taxes. In general 'selective taxation' schemes are likely to be considered State aid measures even when they are related to wider environmental objectives. This is the view the Court took in *Adria-Wien Pipeline*,[12] reasoning that an energy tax introduced with environmental protection in mind, but that distinguished between manufacturing and other sectors, was selective. While ecological considerations underlay the legislation, they did not justify treating the consumption of natural gas or electricity by undertakings supplying services differently from the consumption of energy by undertakings manufacturing goods.[13] But the Commission held that German legislation taxing energy products used for heating and fuel purposes, but not those used for mineralogical and dual-use processes, was consistent with the nature and logic of the German energy tax system, and was therefore not aid.[14] **14.12**

2. Authorization of aid for renewable energy

Community policy. Increased use of renewable energy sources (defined in Directive 2001/77 as non-fossil energy sources including wind, solar, geothermal, wave, tidal, hydropower, biomass, landfill gas, sewage treatment plant gas and biogases)[15] is one of the Community's main environmental priorities as well as an economic and energy-related priority. Directive 2001/77 requires Member States to take steps to encourage greater consumption of electricity produced from renewable energy sources, and to publish a report every five years setting out setting out targets for **14.13**

---

[10] Decision in Case NN 27/2000 *German feed-in laws for renewable electricity* (22 May 2002) and Decision in Case NN 68/2000 *Law on the protection of electricity generated from CHP* (22 May 2002).

[11] Decision 2007/580/EC *Slovenian green electricity scheme* [2007] OJ L219/9. The aid was, however, declared compatible with the common market as it complied with the 2001 Environmental Aid Guidelines.

[12] Case C-143/99 [2001] ECR I-8365.

[13] ibid, para 52. See also the decisions in relation to a Finnish differentiated energy tax rate, favouring manufacturing industry: Decisions in Case NN 75/2002 (1 August 2002) and N 892/2006 (28 February 2007).

[14] N 820/2006 *Tax exemption for certain energy intensive processes* (7 February 2007).

[15] Directive 2001/77/EC of the European Parliament and of the Council on the promotion of electricity produced from renewable energy sources in the internal electricity market [2001] OJ L283/33, Article 2(a).

the use of renewable energy for the next ten years.[16] Subsequently the target has been set for renewable energy to account for 20% of overall EU energy consumption by 2020.[17]

14.14 **The GBER.** The GBER provides a block exemption for aid to assist undertakings investing in the production of energy from renewable energy sources. The costs eligible for exemption are the additional costs borne by the beneficiary compared with production from a conventional power plant or conventional heating system with the equivalent capacity. The maximum aid intensity is 45% for large enterprises, 55% for medium-sized enterprises and 65% for small enterprises.[18]

14.15 **2008 Environmental Aid Guidelines.** Aid falling outside the GBER may still be authorized by the Commission where it satisfies the criteria in the 2008 Environmental Aid Guidelines. Both the 1994 and 2001 Environmental Aid Guidelines[19] were used by the Commission to authorize aid for the production of renewable energy. This approach has been maintained in the 2008 Environmental Aid Guidelines,[20] which contain detailed rules regarding the treatment of aid for renewable energy. The Commission takes the view that such aid qualifies for special treatment because of the difficulties these sources of energy have sometimes encountered in competing effectively with conventional sources. In particular, aid may be necessary where the technical processes available do not allow renewable energy to be produced at unit costs comparable to those of conventional sources.[21]

14.16 **Investment aid.** The 2008 Environmental Aid Guidelines provide for investment aid to support renewable energy production to be approved up to an intensity of 60% for large enterprises, 70% for medium-sized enterprises, 80% for small enterprises and 100% for aid provided following a competitive bidding process on non-discriminatory criteria.[22]

14.17 **Operating aid.** The 2008 Environmental Aid Guidelines state that operating aid may be justified in order to cover the difference between the cost of producing

---

[16] ibid, Article 3(2).

[17] An Energy Policy for Europe, COM(2007) 1 final, section 3.5.

[18] Commission Regulation (EC) 800/2008 on the application of Articles 87 and 88 of the Treaty declaring certain categories of aid compatible with the common market (General Block Exemption Regulation) ('GBER') [2008] OJ L214/3, Art 23. See further Chapter 5 above for the other relevant conditions of the GBER. Chapter 5 also discusses the exemption and authorization of other energy-related measures, such as aid for energy saving, aid for high-efficiency cogeneration and aid for energy-efficient district heating, which are not addressed in this chapter.

[19] Community guidelines on State aid for environmental protection [1994] OJ C72/3 and Community Guidelines on State aid for environmental protection [2001] OJ C37/3.

[20] Community Guidelines on State aid for environmental protection ('2008 Environmental Aid Guidelines') [2008] OJ C82/1.

[21] ibid, para 48.

[22] ibid, paras 102–6; and see para 5.47 above.

energy from renewable energy sources and the market price of that energy.[23] Three options are set out for the approval of operating aid for renewable energy.[24]

(a) Option 1. Member States may grant operating aid to compensate for the difference between the production cost of renewable energy and the market price for the form of power concerned. Operating aid may then be granted until the plant has been fully depreciated under normal accounting rules. Any further energy produced by the plant will not qualify for any assistance.
(b) Option 2. Member States may support renewable energy sources by using market mechanisms such as green certificates or tenders. These mechanisms allow renewable energy producers to benefit indirectly from guaranteed demand for their energy at a price above the market price for conventional power. Where such mechanisms constitute State aid, the Member State must show that support is essential to ensure the viability of the renewable energy sources concerned, does not result in overcompensation, and does not dissuade renewable energy producers from becoming more competitive.
(c) Option 3. In the case of aid which is gradually reduced, the aid intensity must not exceed 100% of the extra costs in the first year but must have fallen in a linear fashion to zero by the end of the fifth year. In the case of aid which does not decrease gradually, the aid intensity must not exceed 50% of the extra costs.

In addition, Member States may grant operating aid to new plants producing renewable energy that is calculated on the basis of the external costs avoided. This is the cost that the public would pay for the same quantity of energy from a conventional source. This type of aid will, however, be subject to more detailed scrutiny by the Commission.[25]

Energy production. The Commission has approved a number of schemes in various countries supporting investment in renewable energy production on the basis of the applicable Environmental Aid Guidelines. These have included in particular a number of schemes in the Netherlands, such as direct grants for energy producers to support investment in projects contributing to the reduction of carbon dioxide emissions,[26] a tax exemption scheme for the use of renewable gas,[27] a tax relief programme for the Dutch Offshore Wind Park which allowed investors accelerated depreciation of their investments,[28] and subsidies for the production **14.18**

[23] ibid, para 107.
[24] ibid, paras 108–11.
[25] ibid, para 161; see further paras 5.60 *et seq* above.
[26] Decision in Case N 304/2000 *CO_2 reduction plan* (7 August 2000).
[27] Decision in Case N 168a/2001 *Modifications energy tax 2001* (28 November 2001).
[28] Decision in Case N 707/2002 *Stimulating renewable energy* (19 March 2003).

of energy from renewable sources or using Combined Heat and Power ('CHP') technology.[29] In the UK, the Commission approved a scheme providing capital grants for offshore wind projects, biomass and energy crop power projects and small-scale biomass heat and CHP projects.[30]

14.19 **Biofuels.** Under the 2001 Environmental Aid Guidelines, biofuels were regarded as renewable energy sources and a number of biofuel aid schemes were approved on that basis. These schemes tended to take the form of excise tax reductions, and were notified by Austria,[31] the Czech Republic,[32] Estonia,[33] Hungary,[34] Italy,[35] Ireland,[36] Lithuania,[37] the Netherlands,[38] Sweden[39] and Belgium.[40] The 2008 Environmental Aid Guidelines are more restrictive, and only permit aid for the production of sustainable biofuels.[41]

14.20 **Market mechanisms.** 'Green certificates' are a popular market mechanism used to encourage the production of energy from renewable sources, by subsidizing producers of renewable energy. The certificates are tradable environmental commodities that represent proof that a specified quantity of electricity was generated from a renewable energy resource. In the Commission's view, a number of measures introducing 'green certificates' and similar trading allowances may constitute State aid. However these have been generally been approved under the relevant Environmental Aid Guidelines.[42]

[29] Decision in Case N 478/2007 *Netherlands renewable energy scheme* (21 December 2007). The subsidies were designed to compensate for the difference between the production costs of renewable and CHP electricity and the market price of conventional energy.

[30] Decision in Case N 504/2000 *Renewables obligation and technologies* (28 November 2001).

[31] Decision in Case NN 43/2004 *Tax exemption for biofuels* (5 October 2005).

[32] Decision in Case N 206/2004 *State aid for the promotion of biofuels* (30 June 2004) and Case N 223/2005 *Aid to biofuels* (5 July 2005).

[33] Decision in Case N 314/2005 *Tax exemption for biofuels* (27 July 2005).

[34] Decision in Case N 427/2004 *Tax exemption for biofuels* (16 March 2005).

[35] Decisions in Cases N 582/2004 *Aid to biofuels/tax benefit* (21 June 2005); and N 326/07 *Tax reduction biodiesel* (11 March 2008).

[36] Decision in Case N 599/2004 *Tax exemption for biofuels* (2 March 2005).

[37] Decision in Case N 44/2005 *Excise tax reduction on biofuels* (27 July 2005).

[38] Decision in Case N 570/2005 *Tax reduction biofuel* (22 December 2005).

[39] Decision in Case N 187/2004 *Excise duty exemption for biofuels* (1 June 2005).

[40] Decision in Case N 334/2005 *Excise reduction for biofuels* (23 December 2005).

[41] 2008 Environmental Aid Guidelines, para 101.

[42] Decision in Case NN 30b/2000 *Zero rate for green electricity* (28 November 2001); Decision in Case N 550/2000 *Green electricity certificates* (25 July 2001) and Decision in Case N 415a/2001 *Green certificate mechanism* (28 November 2001); Decision in Case N 826/2001 *AER I to IV* (15 January 2002) and Decision in Case N 553/2001 *Renewable energy sources* (15 January 2002).

3. Stranded costs

Communication on stranded costs. On 19 February 1997, Directive 96/92 liberalizing the electricity market[43] entered into force. The Directive itself allowed Member States to adopt transitional measures derogating from some of its provisions, in order to allow their electricity undertakings to adjust to the newly liberalized market.[44] However, many Member States also wished to grant aid to electricity undertakings to compensate for the cost of commitments that could no longer be honoured in the light of the price decreases generated by the introduction of competition (so-called 'stranded costs'). The Commission agreed that additional measures were needed to allow aid to be granted to electricity undertakings in certain cases. It therefore adopted a Communication[45] setting out its approach to aid in this field. Under the Communication, aid measures to compensate for stranded costs are, in certain circumstances, permitted under Article 87(3)(c) to enable the liberalization of the market, and to ensure security of supply, the smooth operation of the Community economy and the interests of environmental protection.[46] 14.21

Definition of stranded costs. Stranded costs are commitments or guarantees of operation given before the entry into force of Directive 96/92, that might not be honoured on account of the Directive's provisions.[47] Examples include long-term purchase contracts and investments undertaken with a guarantee of sale because of the existence of a monopoly. 14.22

Eligibility criteria. The Communication only applies to stranded costs that fulfil a number of criteria.[48] In particular, the commitments or guarantees in question must pre-date 19 February 1997, the date of entry into force of Directive 96/92.[49] They must be irrevocable, and must 'run the risk' of not being honoured on account of the provisions of the Directive.[50] The latter condition requires a specific causal link to be established between the Directive and the difficulty of honouring the relevant commitments or guarantees: commitments or guarantees 14.23

43 Directive 96/92/EC concerning common rules for the internal market in electricity [1997] OJ L27/20.

44 ibid, Article 24. Prior authorization of the Commission is required for derogations under this provision. These transitional rules are no longer included in the new Electricity Directive: Directive 2003/54/EC concerning common rules for the internal market in electricity and repealing Directive 96/92/EC [2003] OJ L176/37.

45 Commission Communication relating to the methodology for analysing State aid linked to stranded costs ('Communication on stranded costs') SG (2001) D/290869.

46 ibid, para 4.

47 Directive 96/92/EC [1997] OJ L27/20, Article 24.

48 Communication on stranded costs, para 3.

49 ibid, para 3.1.

50 ibid, paras 3.3 and 3.4.

that could have been honoured irrespective of the entry into force of the Directive are not regarded as stranded costs.[51] Moreover, the commitments or guarantees must not only become non-economical as a result of the Directive, but must also 'significantly affect the competitiveness of the undertaking concerned'.[52] Eligible costs must be limited to the minimum level necessary to allow the undertakings to honour the commitments or guarantees in question, so must be calculated to take into account the most economic solution to the difficulty. This may involve the termination of commitments or guarantees, where that is possible, or the disposal of assets giving rise to stranded costs.[53]

14.24 **Compatibility criteria.** In addition to the above criteria regarding the costs that are eligible for aid, the Communication sets out a number of criteria that the aid itself should meet if it is to be approved under Article 87(3)(c).[54] As the purpose of the aid is to offset eligible stranded costs, the amount of aid must not exceed the amount of those costs,[55] and the maximum aid (as well as the detailed arrangements for calculating and financing the aid) must be specified in advance.[56] The calculation of the amount of the aid must provide for changes in competition which alter the amount of eligible costs.[57] Aids of a degressive nature are viewed particularly favourably by the Commission.[58] No rescue or restructuring aid may be cumulated with aid for stranded costs.[59]

14.25 **Examples.** To date, the Commission has adopted decisions in relation to stranded costs arising in a number of Member States.[60] In several of those cases, the Commission concluded that the scheme or elements of the scheme did not fall within Article 87(1), for example where relevant payments were made by consumers rather than through State resources.[61] In other cases stranded costs were authorized under Article 87(3)(c) as complying with the provisions of the

---

51 ibid, para 3.3.
52 ibid, para 3.3.
53 ibid, para 3.11.
54 ibid, paras 4.1–4.6.
55 ibid, para 4.1.
56 ibid, para 4.5.
57 ibid, para 4.2.
58 ibid, para 4.4.
59 ibid, para 4.6.
60 Including Austria – Case N 34/1999 *Compensation of stranded costs* (25 July 2001); Belgium – Case C 31/2002 *Transitional regime for the electricity market* [2002] OJ C222/2; Greece – Case N 133/2001 *Stranded costs* (16 October 2002); Italy – Decision 2006/941/EC [2006] *AEM Torino* OJ L366/62; Hungary – Decision C 41/2005 *Hungarian stranded costs* (4 June 2008); the Netherlands – Case N 597/1998 *Electricity market – stranded costs* (25 July 2001); Poland – Case C 43/2005 *Polish stranded costs* (25 September 2007); Portugal – Case N 161/2004 *Stranded costs* (22 September 2004); Spain – Case NN 49/1999 *Competition transition costs* (25 July 2001); and the UK – Case N 661/1999 *Competitive transition charge* (27 February 2002).
61 The UK scheme and part of the Belgian, Greek and Polish schemes.

Communication on stranded costs.[62] In two cases the Commission has found the aid or part of the aid to be unlawful.[63]

C. Nuclear energy

Policy considerations. Aid to the nuclear power industry is designed to meet a wide range of policy concerns, including concerns that at various periods have dominated the political debate across the Community. Chief among these are concerns relating to potential health risks, the safety of nuclear reactors and decommissioning issues. The spectre of the 1986 Chernobyl disaster continues to inform public debate in this field. More recently, an increasingly significant consideration is energy security, in particular the need for Europe to reduce its reliance on energy sources outside the Community to provide for its energy needs. **14.26**

EC and Euratom Treaties. Aid to the nuclear industry in governed by both Article 87 EC and the Euratom Treaty, the aims of which include the development of nuclear power in the Community. However, the relationship between the two Treaties in this respect remains unclear. Under Article 305(2) EC, the provisions of the EC Treaty may not derogate from those of the Euratom Treaty. But this wording (particularly compared with the different wording of Article 305(1) in relation to the ECSC Treaty) implies that the EC Treaty, including the State aid rules, may apply to the nuclear sector insofar as this is not inconsistent with the Euratom provisions.[64] **14.27**

Key decisions. The following paragraphs consider the key Commission decisions approving aid to the nuclear industry. These relate to the UK government's rescue and restructuring aid packages for British Energy, and its aid for the establishment of the Nuclear Decommissioning Authority. **14.28**

***British Energy* rescue and restructuring packages.** British Energy Plc (BE) is one of the largest electricity generators in the UK, with nuclear energy making up 83% of its output. On 9 September 2002 a rescue aid package was put in place by the UK government to BE, necessitated by a general fall in electricity prices, BE's lack of hedging and unplanned power station outages, and BE's high non-avoidable costs. The Commission did not object to the rescue package, but a condition of that decision was that the UK had to submit a restructuring or liquidation **14.29**

[62] The Austrian, Netherlands, Portuguese, Spanish and Italian schemes (although the Italian decision was conditional on repayment of previous unlawful aid) and part of the Greek and Polish schemes.

[63] The Hungarian scheme and part of the Polish scheme.

[64] See also AG Reischl in Cases 188–190/80 *France, Italy and UK v Commission* [1982] ECR 2545, para 30; and Decision 2005/407/EC *British Energy* [2005] OJ L142/26, para 239.

plan for BE, or demonstrate repayment of the aid. In March 2003 the UK did submit a restructuring plan, the main aim of which was to restructure BE's costs and establish a stable capital structure so that BE could continue as a financially viable entity. The Commission initiated the formal investigation procedure under Article 88(2), and received comments from a large number of interested parties, including British Nuclear Fuels Limited (BNFL), competing power suppliers and Greenpeace.

14.30 ***British Energy* decision.**[65] Most of the elements of the restructuring package were not considered to involve aid. Some did not involve State resources (eg asset disposal requirements). The modification of BNFL's supply contracts with BE, and standstill agreements reached with BE's creditors, were consistent with the private creditor test and in any event were not imputable to the State. The deferral of local taxes, subject to payment of interest at an appropriate rate, was likewise not held to be aid. However the proposal for the UK government to take on financial responsibility for part of BE's liabilities to BNFL for the reprocessing and management of spent nuclear fuel did constitute aid. The aid was nevertheless approved under Article 87(3)(c) subject to the fulfilment of a number of detailed conditions. The Commission also noted that the intervention of the UK authorities was fully consistent with the objectives of the Euratom Treaty, particularly in relation to the maintenance of the nuclear plants as an extensive energy resource, while at the same time ensuring safety and security.

14.31 *Nuclear Decommissioning Authority (NDA).* Only 18 months after its *British Energy* decision the Commission adopted another highly political decision approving the transfer of assets from BNFL to the NDA, a newly created body established to manage the decommissioning of public sector nuclear assets in the UK. The assets transferred included the Magnox nuclear power plants and the THORP and SMP plants on the Sellafield site. Since it was very likely that the value of the assets transferred would not be sufficient to pay for the costs of their decommissioning, the UK government had undertaken to cover the shortfall. It was this guarantee in particular that triggered the Commission's Article 88(2) investigation.

14.32 ***NDA* decision.**[66] The polluter-pays principle set out in Article 174 EC requires the cost of pollution to be internalized by polluters. Operators of nuclear plants should therefore, in principle, cover the decommissioning costs for their plants. It was clear, therefore, that the State guarantee constituted an advantage. More difficult, however, was the determination of which of the successive operators of the nuclear sites received that advantage, by being relieved of their pollution costs,

[65] *British Energy*, ibid.

[66] Decision 2006/643/EC *Nuclear Decommissioning Authority* [2006] OJ L268/37.

in circumstances where there was no Community-wide system for allocating decommissioning costs to the successive owners of a nuclear plant. The Commission considered two methodologies for the allocation of such costs: one system where decommissioning liabilities were treated as investment costs, and a second system treating such liabilities as operating costs. Whichever method was adopted, however, the same conclusion was reached: that the scheme did not involve aid to BNFL, but did involve aid to the NDA. The aid was, however, approved under Article 87(3)(c), but again subject to detailed conditions. As with its *British Energy* decision, the Commission also considered that the aid was designed to facilitate the objectives of the Euratom Treaty, specifically ensuring the decommissioning and management of nuclear waste in a way that protected the health and safety of workers and the general population.

D. Coal

General. Coal, together with steel, was subject to a different regime under the ECSC Treaty, which lapsed on 23 July 2002. However, the special characteristics of the coal industry required the continuation of a special regime in the field of State aid. The importance of coal as an indigenous source of energy has been widely recognized,[67] justifying the grant of aid to reduce the Community's dependence on external supplies of primary energy sources. At the same time, imported coal has become more competitive, and the Community industry has had to embark on a major restructuring to improve efficiency. Following the lapse of the ECSC Treaty, the Council therefore adopted Regulation 1407/2002 on State aid to the coal industry[68] trying to strike a balance between the need to maintain coal-producing capability to guarantee access to reserves, and the need to restructure the European coal industry. The Regulation is valid until 31 December 2010.[69] In its recent report on the application of Regulation 1407/2002, the Commission expressed its satisfaction with how the regime has worked in practice and indicated that there is no intention to amend it before its expiry in 2010.[70] **14.33**

67 See eg Commission Green Paper 'Towards a European Strategy for the security of energy supply', COM(2000)769, Annex 3.

68 Council Regulation (EC) No 1407/2002 on State aid to the coal industry [2002] OJ L205/1. See also Communication from the Commission concerning certain aspects of the treatment of competition cases resulting from the expiry of the ECSC Treaty [2002] OJ C152/5 for some transitional provisions.

69 ibid, Article 14(3).

70 Communication from the Commission to the European Parliament, the Council, the European Economic and Social Committee and the Committee of the Regions – Commission Report on the Application of Council Regulation (EC) No 1407/2002 on State Aid to the Coal Industry COM(2007) 253.

14.34 **Scope of the Regulation.** Regulation 1407/2002 applies to aid granted in the coal industry. 'Coal' includes high-grade, medium-grade and low-grade category A and B coal.[71] Aid may cover costs in connection with coal for the production of electricity, the combined production of heat and electricity, the production of coke and the refuelling of blast furnaces in the steel industry.[72]

14.35 **Reduction of activity.** Aid may be granted for the reduction of activity, where it is intended to cover the current production losses of production units. The aid measure must form part of a closure plan which has been submitted to the Commission by 31 October 2002 and which does not extend beyond 31 December 2007.[73] The amount must not exceed the difference between production costs and foreseeable revenue for a year,[74] and must not result in the coal being priced lower than imported coal or distort competition in the market.[75]

14.36 **Accessing coal reserves.** Aid may be granted to maintain access to coal reserves. In this case, aid may be granted either towards initial investment or current production, but not for both.[76] In relation to aid to cover initial investment the aid must be earmarked for existing production units which have not received aid under Article 3 of Decision No 3632/93/ECSC[77] or which have received aid authorized by the Commission under Article 3 having demonstrated that they were able to achieve a competitive position vis-à-vis prices for coal of a similar quality from third countries.[78] Production units have to draw up an operating plan and a financing plan showing that the aid granted to the investment project in question will ensure the economic viability of these production units.[79] The aid notified and actually paid shall not exceed 30% of the total costs of the relevant investment project which will enable a production unit to become competitive in relation to prices for coal of a similar quality from third countries.[80] Initial investment aid may only be granted if the Member State wishing to grant aid has submitted a plan for accessing coal reserves to the Commission by 31 October 2002.[81] Current production aid must satisfy the same conditions as closure aid, but the deadline of 31 December 2007 does not apply.[82] The operation of the production units must form part of a plan for accessing coal reserves and aid must be granted to those

[71] Regulation 1407/2002, Article 2(a).
[72] ibid, Article 3(2).
[73] ibid, Articles 4(a) and 9(4).
[74] ibid, Article 4(b).
[75] ibid, Articles 4(c) and 9(4).
[76] ibid, Article 5(1).
[77] Commission Decision No 3632/93/ECSC establishing Community rules for State aid to the coal industry [1993] OJ L329/12.
[78] Regulation 1407/2002, Article 2(a).
[79] ibid, Article 5(2)(b).
[80] ibid, Article 5(2)(c).
[81] ibid, Article 9(5).
[82] ibid, Article 5(3).

units which afford the best economic prospects.[83] As with initial investment aid, a plan for accessing coal reserves must have been presented to the Commission by 31 October 2002.[84]

Overall ceiling for reduction of activity and accessing coal reserves. Aid for the reduction of activity and aid for current production must follow a downward trend.[85] The overall aid for the coal industry in respect of the reduction of activity and access to coal reserves, granted for any year after 2003, may not exceed the amount authorized by the Commission under Articles 3 and 4 of Decision No 3632/93/ECSC for the year 2001.[86] **14.37**

Exceptional costs. Aid may also be granted to undertakings carrying (or having carried) out an activity in connection with coal production to enable them to cover the costs arising from the rationalization and restructuring of the coal industry that are not related to current production.[87] Such costs may have been incurred by a single or several undertakings and are detailed in the Annex to the Regulation. They range from social payments to workers to rehabilitation of former mining sites and contributions for the supply of water and the removal of waste water. **14.38**

Application in practice. The Commission has approved a number of measures on the basis of Regulation 1407/2002. These have included, in particular, UK aid to support redundancy payments to miners arising out of the closure of the Selby coal-mining complex,[88] and aid to maintain access to coal reserves in mines considered to have a viable future,[89] as well as closure aid for the last two operational French coal mines.[90] **14.39**

E. Steel

General. Alongside coal, aid to the steel sector was governed by the ECSC Treaty which lapsed on 23 July 2002. However the sector is characterized by structural overcapacity, and special rules have therefore been maintained in place. Any investment in the steel sector is likely to be regarded as aid, since the Commission **14.40**

[83] ibid, Article 5(3)(a)– (b).

[84] ibid, Article 9(6).

[85] ibid, Article 6(1).

[86] ibid, Article 6. Article 3 of Decision 3632/93/ECSC concerns operating aid, whereas Article 4 concerns aid for the reduction of activity: see Decision authorising the United Kingdom to grant aid to the coal industry for 2001 [2001] OJ L241/10 for the UK; Decision on German aid to the coal industry for 2000 and 2001 [2001] OJ L127/55 for Germany; Decision authorising France to grant aid to the coal industry for 2001 [2001] OJ L239/35 for France; and Decision on the granting by Spain of aid to the coal industry in 2001 [2002] L82/11.

[87] Regulation 1407/2002, Article 7.

[88] Decision in Case N 20/2003 *UK Coal Selby Complex* (27 May 2003).

[89] Decision in Case N 814/2002 *Initial investment costs in the UK coal industry* (24 June 2003).

[90] Decision in Case N321/2004 *State aid to the French coal industry* (19 January 2005).

considers that an investor operating under normal market conditions would not be prepared to invest in the steel sector because profitability could not be guaranteed in view of the risk involved.[91] Decisions adopted in 1991[92] and 1996[93] blocked aid to this sector except in three circumstances: research and development, environmental protection and closure aid. Under the current State aid rules, regional aid to the steel sector is excluded from the scope of the GBER,[94] and aid to the steel sector is also excluded from approval under the 2004 Rescue and Restructuring Guidelines. The Environmental Aid Guidelines, R&D&I Framework and Risk Capital Guidelines do, however, apply to the steel sector, and the Commission continues to permit closure aid for the steel sector in certain circumstances.

14.41 **Closure aid**. As has been clear from the Commission's policy from the mid-1990s, no restructuring aid is permitted for undertakings in the steel industry.[95] On the other hand, closure aid may be allowed under Article 87(3)(c) in favour of steel firms which permanently cease production of steel products, up to a maximum of the residual book value of the plants to be closed.[96] In order to be eligible for aid, the firms must have existed before 1 January 2002, must have been producing steel products up to the date of notification of the aid and must not have reorganized their production or plant structure since 1 January 2002.[97] Aid may also cover redundancy or early retirement payments to workers of steel firms proceeding to partial or total closure of steel plants, up to a maximum of 50% of those payments.[98]

14.42 **Accession Treaties**. Under the Europe Agreements agreed between the 12 new Member States that joined the EU between 2004 and 2007 and the Community, the accession States agreed to comply with Community rules on State aid through their adoption of the *acquis communautaire*.[99] A number of States were granted a five-year transitional period to allow steel companies to finalize restructuring and fully integrate into the European internal market for steel. This was the case for the Czech Republic, Hungary, Poland, Slovakia and Slovenia.[100] This exemption from the general State aid rules was conditional on the fulfilment of certain obligations: namely that the beneficiaries would become viable in the long term; that

[91] Decision 2005/137/EC *Carsid* [2005] OJ L47/28.
[92] Decision 3855/91/ECSC *Community rules for aid to the steel industry* [1991] OJ L362/57.
[93] Decision 2496/96/ECSC *Community rules for aid to the steel industry* [1996] OJ L338/42.
[94] GBER, Article 1 (3)(e).
[95] Communication from the Commission — Rescue and restructuring aid and closure aid for the steel sector [2002] OJ C70/21, para 1.
[96] ibid, para 2.2.
[97] ibid, para 2.2.
[98] ibid, para 2.1.
[99] See further Chapter 4 above.
[100] M Lienemeyer, 'State aid for restructuring the steel industry in the new Member States', Competition Policy Newsletter, Number 1, Spring 2005, p 95.

the aid granted was the minimum necessary to achieve the desired objectives; and that a link existed between the aid measure and a general global rationalization and reduction in capacity in the steel industry. The Czech Republic and Poland did not complete the restructuring of their steel industries within the transitional, period and were granted extended periods for this, which were incorporated in their Accession Treaties.

Czech Republic. Protocol 2 of the Accession Treaty[101] sets out exemptions from the application of Articles 87 and 88 EC, enabling the Czech Republic to grant restructuring aid to the steel sector until 31 December 2006, provided that certain conditions are met. Annex 1 to the Protocol lists the three Czech companies that are entitled to receive restructuring aid.[102] The Protocol stipulates that those companies are not permitted to pass on the aid in the event of a merger, or take on the assets of any company not listed in Annex 1 that is declared bankrupt in the period up to 31 December 2006.[103] Any additional aid for the purpose of restructuring the Czech steel industry is prohibited by the Protocol. This has the effect of allowing the Commission to investigate any aid granted before accession for the restructuring of the Czech steel industry between 1997 and 2006.[104] On that basis, the Commission investigated a number of aid measures put in place for the Czech steel producer Třinecké Železárny, a company not listed in Annex 1 to the Protocol. It found, however, that a share purchase transaction satisfied the private investor test, and that the training aid element of the package was covered by the provisions of the training aid block exemption then in force.[105] **14.43**

Poland. As with the provisions for the Czech Republic, Protocol 8 of the Accession Treaty[106] entitled Poland to grant restructuring aid to the steel sector until 31 December 2006, again provided that certain conditions are met. Annex 1 to the Protocol lists the eight Polish companies that are eligible for restructuring aid.[107] The Protocol stipulates that those companies are not permitted to pass on the aid in the event of a merger, or take on the assets of any company not listed in Annex 1 that is declared bankrupt in the period up to 31 December 2006.[108] As with the Czech Republic, any additional aid for the purpose of restructuring the Polish steel industry is prohibited by the Protocol. This has the same effect of the equivalent provisions in Protocol 2: that the Commission may investigate any aid **14.44**

[101] [2003] OJ L236/934.

[102] Nová Hut' a.s, Vítkovice Steel a.s and Válcovny Plechu a.s.

[103] Protocol 2, point 4.

[104] Decision in Case C 45/2004 *Třinecké Železárny* (8 September 2006), paras 36–43.

[105] ibid, paras 44–64.

[106] [2003] OJ L236/948.

[107] Polskie Huty Stali SA, Huta Andrzej SA, Huta Bankowa Sp. z o.o, Huta Batory S.A., Huta Bucez S.A., Huta L.W. Sp. z o.o., Huta Łabędy S.A. and Huta Pokoj SA.

[108] Protocol 8, point 4.

granted before accession for the restructuring of the Czech steel industry between 1997 and 2006.[109] On that basis, the Commission opened the formal investigation procedure in relation to the restructuring of one of Poland's main steel producers, Huta Częstochowa. Certain of the measures were found not to constitute State aid, and others were compatible with the common market under the terms of the R&D Framework then applicable. But the Commission decided that some €4 million of restructuring aid given to the company between 1997 and 2002 was incompatible and unlawful, and required its repayment.[110]

109 Decision 2006/937/EC *Huta Cz stochowa* [2006] OJ L366/1, paras 104–9.
110 ibid, paras 110–47.

15

REGIONAL AID

Main legislation and guidelines

Commission Regulation (EC) 800/2008 on the application of Articles 87 and 88 of the Treaty declaring certain categories of aid compatible with the common market (General Block Exemption Regulation) ('GBER') [2008] OJ L214/3

Guidelines on National Regional Aid for 2007–2013 ('2007–2013 Guidelines') [2006] OJ C54/13

A. Introduction

Background. The origins of competition policy control of regional aids date back to the 1960s. They were closely linked with two concerns: first, the extent of regional disparities in the European Community and the potential role for a common policy to address this; and second, competitive outbidding for mobile investment projects. These factors have been important in the evolution of regional aid discipline. The European Commission views regional aid control as a complement to Community **15.01**

Cohesion policy, a common policy which now accounts for over one-third of the EU budget; and curbing incentive competition between potential locations remains an important strand of regional aid control. The criteria applied by the Commission when examining the compatibility of regional aid have been progressively codified in guidelines, most recently those adopted in 2006 to cover the period 2007–2013.[1] The overall impact of these guidelines is to allow general investment aid to large undertakings only in designated regional aid areas and to set maximum aid intensities as a percentage of eligible expenditure for all undertakings (including SMEs).

15.02 **Definition of regional aid.** Regional aid is aid which is restricted to, or targeted at (for example by higher award values), certain geographical areas within a Member State. In certain circumstances, a measure which is restricted to a given region, but which is implemented by devolved regional authorities that are deemed to have institutional, procedural and economic autonomy, may be regarded as a general measure and therefore not aid within the meaning of Article 87(1). This situation is discussed in Chapter 2 above;[2] this chapter addresses only those measures that are aids within Article 87(1).

15.03 **Basis for approval.** Regional aid may be approved on the legal basis of Article 87(3)(a) and (c). The difference in the scope of these provisions is discussed in detail in section C below. Many cases of regional aid will now fall under the General Block Exemption Regulation ('GBER'), which allows certain types of aid to be granted without notification to the Commission. Aid not falling under the GBER must, however, be submitted for approval by the Commission before it may be implemented. In most cases, however, where prior approval is necessary, regional aid is offered under aid schemes or programmes which are approved as a whole, thereby avoiding the need for approval of each individual award on a case-by-case basis.

15.04 **Early history of regional aid control.** Until the late 1990s, regional aid was not assessed in a systematic manner. In the 1970s and early 1980s Commission policy was developed on the basis of published 'principles,' which set out how the Commission proposed to interpret Article 87(3). These formed the basis for Commission intervention as regards the geographic coverage of assisted areas, award values and forms of aid. However, there was no detailed rationale for the principles, which were often unclear and which were applied inconsistently, leading to growing resentment among national policymakers. This, together with a number of inter-related developments, notably enlargement to include Spain and Portugal, the Single European Act and moves to complete the internal market

[1] Guidelines on National Regional Aid for 2007–2013 ('2007–2013 Guidelines') [2006] OJ C54/13.

[2] See paras 2.123–2.125 above.

by 1992, put pressure on the Commission for a more transparent approach, culminating in the publication of the 1988 Communication on regional aid.[3] Importantly, this made explicit reference to the two Article 87(3) derogations relevant to regional aid (paragraphs (a) and (c)), building on the then-recent case-law,[4] and outlined how the areas eligible under each of these derogations would be defined. However, Commission control of regional aid continued to be applied in a somewhat ad hoc fashion and subject to political pressures. There were lengthy transitional arrangements where the Commission sought reductions in assisted area coverage, and the timings of Commission reviews under Article 88(1) were sensitive to national and local election schedules. Moreover, many Member States were critical of aspects of the methodology which were perceived to be too prescriptive regarding the selection of assisted areas under Article 87(3)(c). Another major issue was the lack of consistency between the national assisted areas and those eligible for Community Cohesion policy.

2000–2006 Guidelines. In the course of the early 1990s, the Commission had **15.05** been informally piloting an approach to controlling the geographical coverage of Article 87(3)(c) areas, using percentage population coverage as a benchmark and providing the Member States with greater flexibility in the actual choice of areas. The regional aid guidelines adopted in 1998, and covering the period 2000–2006,[5] formalized this practice as well as replacing and consolidating the large number of existing texts relating to regional aid.

Policy underlying 2000–2006 Guidelines. The policy underlying the Guidelines **15.06** is significant.[6] In particular, successive Treaty amendments had reinforced the importance of economic and social cohesion in the Community. There was now a decade of experience with the reformed Structural Funds, and increased emphasis on the need for coherence between national and Community regional policies. The Commission's regular surveys on State aid expenditure had also highlighted concerns regarding the budgetary capacity of the less prosperous Member States to compete with richer ones for mobile investment. In addition, the regulatory environment for State aids generally had shifted to a more proactive, rather than essentially reactive, approach. Finally, in the 1990s, so-called 'Europe Agreements' had been concluded with countries in central and eastern Europe and the Baltic states as a precursor to accession. Some changes to regional aid discipline were thus perceived to be needed to accommodate up to a dozen mainly poorer

[3] Commission communication on the method for the application of Article 92(3)(a) and (c) to regional aid [1988] OJ C212/2.

[4] Case 248/84 *Germany v Commission* [1987] ECR 4013.

[5] Guidelines on national regional aid ('2000–2006 Guidelines') [1998] OJ C74/9.

[6] For a historical perspective on the development of policy see F Wishlade, *Regional State Aid and Competition Policy in the EU* (2003) Kluwer Law International, The Hague.

Member States into a system of regional aid control, without diluting that system of control. Reflecting this, the 2000–2006 Guidelines were in line with a policy framework trend of becoming more rigorous over time and consistent with an increasingly formal approach to State aid control. An important component of this was that the Guidelines required existing regional aid schemes to be brought into line with the new provisions by 1 January 2000.

15.07 **Multisectoral Frameworks.** From a Commission perspective, a persistent problem in regional aid control has been the assessment of large awards to large projects. The approach to regional aid control generally has been to devise policy frameworks within which aid schemes could be authorized, thereby avoiding the need for case-by-case analysis of individual awards. In the case of very large projects, however, this allowed substantial amounts of aid to be awarded without any opportunity for Commission scrutiny of its competitive effects. The Commission addressed this issue in 1998, in the first so-called 'Multisectoral Framework'.[7] The essence of the Framework was that projects or awards which met specified size and sectoral criteria had to be notified to the Commission and evaluated individually. In practice the 1998 Multisectoral Framework proved to be administratively cumbersome and had little impact on award values because of the way in which the evaluation criteria were designed. As a result, it was superseded by the 2002 Multisectoral Framework.[8] This has now been incorporated, substantially unchanged, into the 2007–2013 Guidelines.

15.08 **2007–2013 Guidelines and block exemptions.** In December 2005 a new set of regional aid guidelines was adopted, covering the period from 2007–2103 (the '2007–2013 Guidelines').[9] Their aim was to refocus regional aid on the most deprived regions of the enlarged EU.[10] Complementing the 2007–2013 Guidelines, a regional aid block exemption was adopted in 2006 exempting a number of categories of regional aid from the duty to notify aid under Article 88(3).[11] That block exemption has now been superseded by the provisions of the GBER.[12] This came into force on 29 August 2008 and is due to last until 31 December 2013.

7 Multisectoral framework on regional aid for large investment projects [1998] OJ C107/7.

8 Multisectoral framework on regional aid for large investment projects ('2002 Multisectoral Framework') [2002] OJ C70/8, as amended [2003] OJ C263/3.

9 Guidelines on National Regional Aid for 2007–2013 ('2007–2013 Guidelines') [2006] OJ C54/13.

10 Press release IP/05/1653.

11 Commission Regulation (EC) No 1628/2006 of 24 October 2006 on the application of Articles 87 and 88 of the Treaty to national regional investment aid [2006] OJ L302/29.

12 Council Regulation (EC) 800/2008 declaring certain categories of aid compatible with the common market in application of Articles 87 and 88 of the Treaty (General Block Exemption Regulation) ('GBER') [2008] OJ L214/3.

Methodology for the assessment of regional aid. Together, the 2007–2013 Guidelines and the GBER establish the following methodology for the assessment of new regional aid. 15.09

(a) First, the 2007–2013 Guidelines set out the criteria for determining the demarcation of the eligible areas and associated award values for 2007–2013.[13] The principles followed in the demarcation of assisted areas under the Guidelines are discussed in detail in section C below.
(b) The GBER enables aids that meet transparency and other requirements, and that comply with the regional aid maps approved under the 2007–2013 Guidelines, to be implemented without prior notification and approval. The scope of the GBER is discussed in detail in section D below.
(c) Any measures not eligible under the GBER, in particular, operating aids and other measures which do not meet the transparency criteria, are assessed under the provisions of the 2007–2013 Guidelines. These are discussed in detail in section E below.

Before addressing these, however, Section B below provides an overview of the 2000–2006 Guidelines and 2002 Multisectoral Framework, since a number of decisions under those rules remain outstanding.[14]

B. 2000–2006 Guidelines and 2002 Multisectoral Framework

1. 2000–2006 Guidelines

Scope. The 2000–2006 Guidelines[15] superseded all existing documents relating to regional aid control. They covered all sectors except agriculture, fisheries and coal.[16] They were principally concerned with the regulation of regional aid schemes open to all firms in the sectors concerned. However, they were also used as the basis for assessing ad hoc aid. 15.10

Population coverage. A core principle was that regional aid areas should cover less than 50% of the Community population. In practice, the Commission set a ceiling of 42.7% of the population. The Article 87(3)(a) regions were determined on 15.11

13 2007–2013 Guidelines, paras 12–32.

14 Indeed decisions frequently continue to be taken under those rules where they relate to unnotified aid granted before 2007—see eg Decision in Case NN 17/2008 *Digital Display Devices* (16 April 2008).

15 Guidelines on national regional aid [1998] OJ C74/9.

16 2000–2006 Guidelines, para 2(1).

the basis of 'top-down' criteria by the Commission;[17] these covered about 21% of the EU15 population. The remainder represented the coverage of Article 87(3)(c) areas and was distributed among the Member States according to internal disparities in GDP per head and unemployment rates, subject to adjustments concerning transitional arrangements, minimum and maximum coverage of Article 87(3)(c) areas, low population density areas and the constraints of the overall ceiling.[18] This process resulted in a population ceiling for each Member State.[19] These ranged from 100% of the population in the case of Greece, Ireland and Portugal, to 15% in the case of the Netherlands.

15.12 **Article 87(3)(a) areas.** These were defined by the Commission as NUTS II regions[20] where gross domestic product (GDP) as measured in purchasing power standards (PPS) was less than 75.0% of the EU15 average for the last three years[21] for which data were available.[22]

15.13 **Article 87(3)(c) areas.** These were not defined by the Commission but rather were selected by the Member States, subject to the population ceilings and the constraints on the area designation methodology imposed by the Guidelines.[23] The map proposals were subject to intense scrutiny by the Commission, which often required amendments to the maps prior to approval. Details of the approved maps were contained in letters to the Member States.[24]

15.14 **Forms of aid.** Regional aid granted under the Guidelines could take a number of forms, such as grants, soft loans, interest-rate rebates, guarantees, tax exemptions and social security concessions.[25] The aid generally had to be linked to an initial investment[26] or job creation.[27] Operating aid would only exceptionally be approved, and then only in Article 87(3)(a) or designated low population density areas under Article 87(3)(c).[28]

---

17 ibid, para 3.5(2).

18 ibid, Annex III.

19 National ceilings for regional aid coverage under the derogations provided for in Article 87(3)(a) and (c) of the Treaty for the period 2000 to 2006 [1999] OJ C16/5.

20 NUTS is a common classification of territorial units for statistical purposes comprising a five-tier hierarchy. NUTS II is equivalent to a French region or a Spanish autonomous community. In the UK, NUTS II regions are mainly groups of counties.

21 1993–1995.

22 2000–2006 Guidelines, para 3.5(2).

23 ibid, para 3.10.

24 These were not published in the Official Journal, but are available on the European Commission's State aid register on the DG COMP website.

25 2000–2006 Guidelines, para 4.2(2).

26 ibid, para 4.4.

27 ibid, paras 4.11–4.14.

28 ibid, paras 4.15–4.17.

Eligible expenditure. Aid schemes had to require applications for aid to be submitted before the start of the project.[29] Initial investment referred to investment in fixed capital relating to the setting up of a new establishment, the extension of an existing one, the starting up of an activity involving a fundamental change in the products or production process of an existing establishment through rationalization, diversification or modernization. Replacement investment was explicitly excluded.[30] The value of eligible investment was calculated on a standard base comprising land, buildings, and plant and machinery.[31] Eligible expenditure could include intangible assets arising from technology transfer through the acquisition of patents, licences and know-how, subject to a maximum of 25% of the standard base in the case of large firms.[32] Aided assets had to be retained for a minimum period of five years[33] and aided jobs maintained for the same period.[34] **15.15**

Aid intensities. Beneficiaries were required to contribute a minimum of 25% of project costs.[35] The level of aid was expressed as a percentage of reference costs, depending on the type of aid.[36] The award ceilings stipulated in the Guidelines ranged from 65% net grant-equivalent (NGE)[37] in the so-called 'outermost regions'[38] eligible under Article 87(3)(a) to 10% NGE in Article 87(3)(c) areas with both GDP higher than the EU15 average and an unemployment rate lower than the EU average.[39] In the case of small and medium-sized enterprises (SMEs), the relevant ceilings were increased by 15 percentage points (gross)[40] in Article 87(3)(a) areas and 10 percentage points (gross) in Article 87(3)(c) areas.[41] Aid for job creation had to respect the relevant ceilings expressed as a percentage of the wage cost of the person hired over a period of two years.[42] In practice, the actual rates applicable were negotiated with the Commission and did not always reach these ceilings. Aid could not be cumulated in respect of the same costs, but where investment was eligible for regional aid and for aid for other purposes, the aid ceiling applicable was the higher of the two.[43] **15.16**

---

29 ibid, para 4.2(3).
30 ibid, para 4.4.
31 ibid, para 4.5.
32 ibid, para 4.6.
33 ibid, para 4.10.
34 ibid, para 4.14.
35 ibid, para 4.2.
36 ibid, paras 4.5, 4.6 and 4.13.
37 The value of aid after tax has been taken into account.
38 The outermost regions are the Canaries, Madeira, the Azores, Guadeloupe, Martinique, Réunion and French Guiana.
39 2000–2006 Guidelines, para 4.8.
40 This represents the pre-tax value of aid.
41 2000–2006 Guidelines, para 4.9.
42 ibid, para 4.13.
43 ibid, para 4.20.

2. 2002 Multisectoral Framework

15.17 **Purpose.** The rationale for the 2002 Multisectoral Framework was that while large investments could contribute effectively to regional development, such investments are less affected by region-specific problems in disadvantaged areas.[44] In addition, where such projects are supported by State aid, there is an increased risk of trade distortion.[45] The objective of the Framework was therefore to introduce a further level of aid discipline for large projects, even where awards were made under approved regional aid schemes. This was achieved by reducing maximum rates of award for all projects involving eligible investment of more than €50 million and by subjecting particularly large awards to notification.

15.18 **Scope.** The 2002 Multisectoral Framework applied only to regional investment aid examined under Article 87(3)(a) and (c) and was without prejudice to the assessment of aid proposals under other Treaty provisions.[46] It applied to aid granted until 31 December 2006; from 1 January 2007, provisions on large investment projects were incorporated into the 2007–2013 Guidelines.[47]

15.19 **Sectoral issues.** The 2002 Multisectoral Framework prohibited regional investment aid to the synthetic fibres sector[48] and the steel industry.[49] It also proposed the compilation of a list of all sectors in which serious structural problems prevailed, and in which regional investment aid would generally not be authorized.[50] Subsequently, owing to methodological difficulties, the Commission decided to postpone the adoption of such a list. At the same time, it decided not to include the shipbuilding sector within the scope of the 2002 Multisectoral Framework.[51]

15.20 **Reduction of aid levels.** Aid levels were subject to a formula, similar in operation to a progressive tax regime, whereby the larger the aided investment, the lower the rate of award. This formula was applied automatically by awarding bodies administering regional aid as follows:

Eligible expenditure	**Aid ceiling**
Up to €50 m	100% of regional aid ceiling
For the part between €50 m and €100 m	50% of regional aid ceiling
For the part exceeding €100 m	34% of regional aid ceiling

44 2002 Multisectoral Framework, para 13.
45 ibid, para 14.
46 ibid, para 4.
47 2007–2013 Guidelines, para 105.
48 2002 Multisectoral Framework, para 42(b).
49 ibid, para 27.
50 Paras 28–34 of 2002 Multisectoral Framework, original version.
51 Commission communication on the modification of the Multisectoral Framework on regional aid for large investment projects (2002) with regard to the establishment of a list of sectors facing structural problems and on a proposal of appropriate measures pursuant to Article 88 paragraph 1 of the EC Treaty, concerning the motor vehicle and the synthetic fibres sector [2003] OJ C263/3.

In the motor vehicle sector however, for aid amounts exceeding €5 million, the maximum aid intensity for regional investment aid was 30% of the relevant regional aid ceiling.[52]

Reporting. Regional aid for investments exceeding €50 million had to be reported to the Commission on the basis of the standard form in Annex A to the framework within 20 working days.[53] This information provided the basis for case summaries published by the Commission under the so-called 'transparency system'.[54] These are listed as category 'MF' followed by a serial number and the year of registration (for example MF 1/2003). **15.21**

Individual notification. All cases of regional aid where the aid amount was more than that which a €100 million investment could receive (ie 75% of the prevailing regional aid ceiling) had to be individually notified to and approved by the Commission before they could be implemented,[55] irrespective of whether they would otherwise be covered by an approved aid scheme. In practice, and as intended by the Commission, relatively few aid proposals were notified. Indeed, there is evidence of some 'clustering' of award levels just below the threshold at which notification would be required.[56] **15.22**

Eligibility. Individually notifiable projects were ineligible for aid if either (1) the aid beneficiary accounted for more than 25% of the sales of the product (or would do so after the investment),[57] or (2) the capacity created by the project was more than 5% of the market measured using apparent consumption data, except in the case of rapidly growing markets.[58] The burden of proving that neither of these situations pertained lay with the Member State concerned.[59] If neither of these situations applied, then the maximum allowable rate of award was that determined by the matrix above. This apparently created the paradox that if either of the ineligibility conditions was satisfied, aid above the notification threshold would be prohibited in its entirety, even if aid slightly below that threshold could have been granted under an approved aid scheme.[60] The only option to avoid total prohibition would then be to withdraw a notification if an investigation seemed likely. This appears to have happened in the case of a notified proposed aid **15.23**

52 2002 Multisectoral Framework, para 42, as amended.

53 ibid, para 36.

54 Available on the State aid register on the DG Comp website: see also para 16.08 below.

55 2002 Multisectoral Framework, para 24.

56 For an overview of reported cases see F Wishlade, *All's well that ends well? Recent developments in EU competition policy and regional aid control,* paper to the EoRPA Regional Policy Research Consortium, European Policies Research Centre, University of Strathclyde (2007).

57 2002 Multisectoral Framework, para 24(a).

58 ibid, para 24(b).

59 ibid, para 24.

60 See also U Soltesz, 'The New Multisectoral Framework – Overkill or an "Appropriate Measure"' [2005] ECLR 98–105.

to Intel (Ireland)[61] where the Commission intimated its intention to open the investigative procedure. In response, the Irish authorities withdrew the notification in May 2005 and in December 2005 they awarded aid at a level just below the notification threshold.[62] However, more recently, the Commission has made clear that breaching the market share and capacity limits does not result in aid being prohibited altogether, but rather the amount of aid being reduced to a level below the notification threshold.[63]

15.24 **Assessment of notified projects.** Around 20 cases have been considered by the Commission under the notification requirements of the 2002 Multisectoral Framework; about half of these have been notified by Germany or Portugal. The majority of aid proposals have been approved without recourse to the investigative procedure.[64] However, it is worth noting that under the special arrangements for the motor vehicle sector a significant number of awards escaped notification. Indeed, the motor vehicle sector accounts for around a third of cases reported to the Commission under the transparency mechanism. Moreover, the five largest awards reported were all made to motor vehicle manufacturers and all exceeded the notification threshold by a wide margin.[65] By the end of 2007, when the 2002 Multisectoral Framework expired (although some cases were still outstanding), the investigative procedure had only been opened in one instance: the *IBIDEN Hungary* case. In that case, the Commission prohibited the planned aid in excess of the notification threshold.[66]

C. Demarcation of regions under 2007–2013 Guidelines

15.25 **General.** Regional aid is designed to promote the economic development of disadvantaged areas defined on the basis of Article 87(3)(a) and (c). This effectively restricts the use of investment aid to large firms to those located in designated areas; it also determines the areas in which SMEs may benefit from higher rates of award. Under the current Guidelines, the regional aid maps were defined for the period 2007–2013, with limited scope for review. The Guidelines establish a

61 Case N 256/2004 *Intel Ireland – MSF (2002)* (2 March 2005).

62 Case MF 48/2007.

63 See Decision 2008/830/EC *IBIDEN Hungary* [2008] OJ L295/34, para 107.

64 Some of these have involved aid amounts exceeding €100 million – see eg Decisions in Cases N 872/2006 *Qimonda* (30 January 2008) and N 810/2006 *AMD* (18 July 2007).

65 eg in Case MF 1/2004, Autoeuropa was awarded assistance exceeding €69 million where the notification threshold for projects in other sectors would have been around €20 million.

66 See Decision 2008/830/EC *IBIDEN Hungary* [2008] OJ L295/34.

percentage of the Community population to be eligible for regional aid[67] and list the regions eligible on the basis of Article 87(3)(a)[68] (see section 1 below). Regarding Article 87(3)(c), the Guidelines set out the criteria for designating assisted areas, a task undertaken by the Member States, subject to Commission approval (see section 2 below). The resulting maps form an integral part of the Guidelines and determine the geographical coverage of regional aid and rates of award for most aid types (see section 3 below).

Population ceiling. The 2007–2013 Guidelines retain the principle that regional aid should be 'exceptional' and that the population coverage of the assisted areas should be substantially less than the non-assisted areas.[69] The Commission set an initial limit of 42% of the EU25 population.[70] After the application of a 'safety net' to ensure that no Member State lost more than 50% of the population covered in 2000–2006,[71] and following the accession of Bulgaria and Romania, this resulted in a ceiling of 46.6% of the EU27 population. **15.26**

1. Article 87(3)(a) areas

Scope. Article 87(3)(a) of the Treaty provides that: **15.27**

> aid to promote the economic development of areas where the standard of living is abnormally low or where there is serious underemployment

may be considered compatible with the common market. The Court has held that:

> . . . the use of the words 'abnormally' and 'serious' in the exemption contained in article [87](3)(a) shows that it concerns only areas where the economic situation is extremely unfavourable in relation to the Community as a whole.[72]

For its part, the Commission has taken the view that GDP per head measured in purchasing power standards (PPS) 'is capable of reflecting synthetically both phenomena mentioned' (ie standards of living and underemployment).[73] This is a questionable interpretation both of the Treaty provisions and the statistical indicators: Article 87(3)(a) does not require low standards of living and underemployment to be present simultaneously; GDP(PPS) per head measures neither phenomenon. Nevertheless, it is clear from successive communications and

---

67 2007–2013 Guidelines, para 1.2.

68 ibid, Annex V.

69 ibid, para 12.

70 ibid, para 13.

71 ibid, para 14.

72 Case 248/84 *Germany v Commission* [1987] ECR 4013, para 19; Case C-113/00 *Spain v Commission ('Extremadura')* [2002] ECR I-7601, para 65.

73 2007–2013 Guidelines, n 19.

guidelines since 1988 that this interpretation is now well entrenched in State aid policy and practice and is further supported by the use of the same indicators for Community Cohesion policy.

15.28 **Categories of assisted areas.** For the 2007–2013 period, there are three categories of Article 87(3)(a) regions: (1) the standard Article 87(3)(a) areas; (2) the outermost regions; and (3) the so-called 'statistical effect' regions. These are the areas that are in principle eligible for regional aid, although Member States are not obliged to designate them as such in their regional aid maps.[74]

15.29 **'Standard' Article 87(3)(a) regions.** As in the case of the 2000–2006 Guidelines, the 2007–2013 Guidelines define Article 87(3)(a) areas as NUTS II regions with GDP per head, measured in purchasing power standards (PPS), of less than 75% of the EU average on the basis of the latest three years' data available.[75] For the 2007–2013 Guidelines, the EU25 average was used and the data concerned the period 2000–2002. The accession of Bulgaria and Romania from 1 January 2007 did not affect the eligibility criteria. Based on this definition, Article 87(3)(a) regions cover the following areas: all of Estonia, Latvia, Lithuania, Malta, Poland, Slovenia and the French *Départements d'Outre Mer*; most of Hungary and the Czech and Slovak Republics; and parts of Germany, Greece, Spain, Italy and the United Kingdom.[76] Bulgaria and Romania are also now covered by Article 87(3)(a) in their entirety.[77] The standard Article 87(3)(a) areas and the outermost regions together account for around 32.2% of the EU27 population.[78]

15.30 **Outermost regions.** In recognition of the special handicaps relating to remoteness, the outermost regions defined in Article 299 of the Treaty are deemed to have Article 87(3)(a) status, irrespective of whether they meet the GDP per head criterion.[79] Of the seven regions concerned, two—the Canaries and Madeira—are above the qualifying GDP threshold.

15.31 **'Statistical effect' regions.** The 2007–2013 Guidelines contain transitional arrangements for so-called 'statistical effect' regions. These are regions with GDP(PPS) per head above the EU25 qualifying threshold, but which would have qualified as Article 87(3)(a) regions if enlargement had not taken place—ie if the qualifying threshold had retained the EU15 average as the basis for designation.

---

[74] For example, the Lüneburg region in Germany was designated a statistical effect region on the basis of the 2007–2013 Guidelines (see Annex V), but the German authorities opted not to include the entire region in the national assisted areas map.

[75] 2007–2013 Guidelines, para 18.

[76] ibid, Annex V.

[77] Decisions in Cases N 1/2007 *Bulgaria* [2007] OJ C73/17 and N 2/2007 *Romania* [2007] OJ C73/17.

[78] Author's calculations.

[79] 2007–2013 Guidelines, para 17.

Statistical effect regions are defined as NUTS II areas where GDP(PPS) per head is between 75% and 82.2% of the EU25 average.[80] These are eligible for regional aid under Article 87(3)(a) until 31 December 2010.[81] In 2010, the Commission will review the position of these regions on the basis of the latest GDP data available from Eurostat. If the relative GDP of any of the regions has fallen below 75% of the EU25 average, the regions concerned will continue to be eligible under Article 87(3)(a). Otherwise, the statistical effect regions will become eligible under Article 87(3)(c) from January 2011. Statistical effect regions cover most of Greece, parts of Belgium, Germany, Spain, Italy, Austria, Portugal and the United Kingdom.[82] Together they account for about 3.4% of the EU27 population.[83]

2. Article 87(3)(c) areas

Scope. Article 87(3)(c) of the Treaty provides that: **15.32**

> aid to facilitate the development of certain economic activities or of certain economic areas, where such aid does not adversely affect trading conditions to an extent contrary to the common interest

may be considered to be compatible with the common market. The Court has held that, by contrast with Article 87(3)(a), the exemption in Article 87(3)(c):

> . . . permits the development of certain areas without being restricted by the economic conditions laid down in article [87](3)(a) . . . . That provision gives the Commission the power to authorise aid intended to further the economic development of areas of a Member State which are disadvantaged in relation to the national average.[84]

Determination of Article 87(3)(c) areas. Article 87(3)(c) areas have been determined under the 2007–2013 Guidelines on the basis of a two-stage process. First, the Commission set a ceiling on coverage for each Member State, expressed as a percentage of the national population which could have Article 87(3)(c) status. Second, the Guidelines set criteria pursuant to which Member States could designate their Article 87(3)(c) areas. In addition, there were transitional arrangements for some areas. On the basis of those criteria, the Member States selected their Article 87(3)(c) areas in regional aid maps, which were then submitted to the Commission for approval. **15.33**

---

80 ibid, para 18.

81 ibid, para 19.

82 ibid, Annex V.

83 Author's calculations.

84 Case 248/84 *Germany v Commission* [1987] ECR 4013, para 19; Case C-113/00 *Spain v Commission ('Extremadura')* [2002] ECR I-7601, para 65.

15.34 **Population coverage.** The Article 87(3)(c) coverage for each Member State was calculated under the Guidelines on the following basis.

(a) Economic development areas. Each Member State automatically received a population 'quota' equal to the population of areas that had 'outgrown' Article 87(3)(a) status—that is, regions which would have ceased to qualify under Article 87(3)(a), even without the impact of enlargement on EU average GDP per head. Northern Ireland was added to this group, even though it had not qualified under Article 87(3)(a) during 2000–2006.[85] Over a quarter of the populations of Hungary and Ireland are deemed to be economic development areas, which also cover smaller parts of Greece, Spain, Finland and the United Kingdom. Together, these areas cover around 3.6% of the EU27 population.[86]

(b) Low population density areas. Each Member State automatically received an allocation equal to the population of NUTS III areas with a population density of fewer than 12.5 inhabitants per km^2.[87] These areas are mainly in Sweden and Finland and cover less than 0.4 % of the EU27 population.[88]

(c) Residual quota. The population eligible on the basis of Article 87(3)(a) and the economic development and low population density areas were deducted from the initial ceiling of 42% of the EU25 population to produce a residual quota for distribution among the Member States.[89] This was allocated on the basis of a key which took account of regional variations in GDP per head and unemployment rates set in a national and a Community context.[90]

(d) Safety net. Final adjustments were made such that losses in coverage in relation to the previous period were limited to a maximum of 50% of the population covered in 2000–2006. This resulted in an overall coverage higher than the initial ceiling of 42% of the EU25 population.

15.35 **Main designation criteria.** Within the Article 87(3)(c) population quota, the principal areas which could be designated for aid were specified by the Guidelines as follows.

(a) Economic development areas.[91] Member States could opt to designate these areas for Article 87(3)(c). In practice several such regions were not included in their entirety, and the 'surplus' population used to designate other areas.

---

85 2007–2013 Guidelines, para 25.
86 Author's calculations.
87 2007–2013 Guidelines, para 26. NUTS III is equivalent to a French *département* or Italian provincia. In the UK, NUTS III regions are a mix of counties, unitary authorities and districts.
88 Author's estimate.
89 2007–2013 Guidelines, para 27.
90 ibid, Annex IV.
91 ibid, para 30(a), and see para 15.34(a) above.

(b) Low population density areas.[92] These were essentially made up of NUTS II regions with a population density of fewer than eight inhabitants per km^2 or NUTS III regions with a population density of fewer than 12.5 per km^2. However, some flexibility in the precise choice of areas was allowed, provided that the overall population coverage of low population density areas was not increased. It should be noted that this differs from the definition of low population density areas used to determine the population quota (see para 15.34(b) above). This was to enable Member States to include small areas in 'non-qualifying' NUTS III areas by excluding population centres in eligible NUTS III areas in order to make geographical coverage more relevant to the aims of policy, rather than simply following administrative boundaries.

(c) Contiguous zones with a minimum population of 100,000.[93] These had to be within NUTS II or III regions where either GDP per head was less than the EU25 average or where the unemployment rate was more than 115% of the national average. In practice, this provision accounted for most of the population designated under Article 87(3)(c).[94]

(d) NUTS III areas with a population of less than 100,000 where either GDP per head is less than the EU25 average or the unemployment rate is more than 115% of the national average.[95]

(e) Islands and 'other regions categorised by similar geographical isolation' where either GDP per head is higher than the EU25 average or the unemployment rate is more than 115% of the national average.[96]

(f) Islands with fewer than 5,000 inhabitants and other communities with fewer than 5,000 inhabitants characterized by similar geographical isolation.[97]

(g) Border areas. These were defined as all or parts of NUTS III regions that are adjacent to regions eligible for Article 87(3)(a) and those which share a land border, or a sea border of less than 30km, with a country that is not a member of the EEA or EFTA.[98]

(h) Areas undergoing restructuring. These were defined as contiguous zones with a minimum population of 50,000 which are undergoing major structural change or are in serious relative decline 'compared with other comparable regions'.[99]

---

92 ibid, para 30(b).

93 ibid, para 30(c).

94 See F Wishlade, *All's well that ends well? Recent developments in EU competition policy and regional aid control,* paper to the EoRPA Regional Policy Research Consortium, European Policies Research Centre, University of Strathclyde (2007) for a full discussion of Member States' approaches to area designation under the 2007–2013 Guidelines.

95 2007–2013 Guidelines, para 30(d).

96 ibid, para 30(e).

97 ibid, para 30(f).

98 ibid, para 30(g).

99 ibid, para 30(h).

15.36 **Localized regional disparities.** In addition to the main designation criteria above, there was scope for Member States to target very localized regional disparities by designating areas smaller than the NUTS III level. However, aid under this category is restricted to SMEs, to eligible investments of less than €25 million and to areas with a minimum population of 20,000.[100]

15.37 **Transitional arrangements.** A number of areas lose Article 87(3)(c) eligibility as a result of the 2007–2013 Guidelines, which allow some of those areas to continue to be eligible, but only until 31 December 2009.[101] However, the combined total of areas eligible for regional investment aid must not exceed 66% of the national population eligible on 31 December 2006. Aid is subject to a ceiling of 10% of eligible investment. The following countries had the scope to designate areas under the phasing-out provisions: Czech Republic, Denmark, Spain, France, Ireland, Italy, Cyprus, Luxembourg, Netherlands, Portugal and Slovakia. Around 3.6 % of the EU27 population qualified under this provision.[102]

3. Regional aid maps

15.38 **General.** National authorities were responsible for drawing up regional aid map proposals identifying areas with Article 87(3)(a) and 87(3)(c) status, subject to the population ceilings and the area designation criteria specified in the Guidelines. The Guidelines do not create an obligation to define a regional map, to exhaust the population ceiling for Article 87(3)(c) areas or to offer aid at the maximum levels stipulated. In the course of 2006–2007, regional aid map proposals were notified to the Commission by all 27 Member States and were examined in accordance with the Article 88(3) procedure. The decisions by which the Commission approves the regional aid maps are construed as forming an integral part of the 2007–2013 Guidelines, and having binding force, on condition that the Guidelines have been accepted by the Member States.[103] This acceptance was secured from all EU25 Member States during the course of 2006.[104] Details of the approved regional aid maps were published in the Official Journal.[105]

[100] ibid, para 31.

[101] ibid, para 95.

[102] Author's calculations.

[103] 2007–2013 Guidelines, para 97, and Case C-242/00 *Germany v Commission* [2002] ECR I-5603, para 35.

[104] State aid: Guidelines on national regional aid for 2007–2013: Acceptance by 24 Member States of the Commission's proposal of appropriate measures pursuant to Article 88(1) of the Treaty [2006] OJ C153/13; and Decision in Case C 25/2006 *Guidelines on national regional aid for 2007–2013 – appropriate measures – Germany* [2006] OJ C320/16.

[105] Decisions in Cases N 492/2006 *Austria* [2007] OJ C34/5; N 745/2006 *Belgium* [2007] OJ C73/15; N 1/2007 *Bulgaria* [2007] OJ C73/17; N 814/2006 *Cyprus* [2007] OJ C68/28; N 510/2006 *Czech Republic* [2006] OJ C280/7; N 693/2006 *Denmark* [2007] OJ C141/6; N 466/2006 *Estonia* [2006] OJ C286/6; N 359/2006 *Finland* [2007] OJ C34/2; N 343/2006

Function of maps. The regional aid maps define the areas eligible for regional investment aid and aid for newly created enterprises. They also set the maximum aid intensity for initial investment, and define the scope of any group exemption exempting regional aid from the notification obligation under Article 88(3).[106] They do not, however, define the areas eligible for operating aid schemes. These are assessed on a case-by-case basis following notification by the Member State concerned pursuant to Article 88(3).[107] **15.39**

Aid intensities. Aid intensities are calculated in gross grant-equivalent (GGE) terms.[108] The intensity of the aid must be adapted to take account of the nature and severity of the regional problem. As a result, rates are higher in Article 87(3)(a) regions than in Article 87(3)(c) areas,[109] and are increased further for the outermost regions (OMR).[110] The main provisions for maximum rates are summarized in the table below.[111] **15.40**

	Large enterprises	Medium-sized enterprises	Small enterprises	OMR
Article 87(3)(a) GDP per head <45% EU25 av	50%	60%	70%	+20%[112]
Article 87(3)(a) GDP per head <60% EU25 av	40%	50%	60%	+20%
Article 87(3)(a) GDP per head <75% EU25 av	30%	40%	50%	+20%
Article 87(3)(a) statistical effect	30%→20%	40%→30%	50%→40%	
OMR with GDP per head >75% EU25 av	30%	40%	50%	
Article 87(3)(c)	15%/10%	25%/20%	35%/30%	

France [2007] OJ C94/34; N 459/2006 *Germany* [2006] OJ C295/6; N 408/2006 *Greece* [2006] OJ C286/5; N 487/2006 *Hungary* [2006] OJ C256/7; N 374/2006 *Ireland* [2006] OJ C292/11; N 324/2007 *Italy* [2008] OJ C90/4; N 447/2006 *Latvia* [2006] OJ C287/26; N 641/2006 *Lithuania* [2006] OJ C286/6; N 523/2006 *Luxembourg* [2006] OJ C280/8; N 631/2006 *Malta* [2006] OJ C275/35; N 249/2007 *Netherlands* [2007] OJ C176/10; N 531/2006 *Poland* [2006] OJ C256/7; N 727/2006 *Portugal* [2007] OJ C68/26; N 2/2007 *Romania* [2007] OJ C73/17; N 434/2006 *Slovenia* [2006] OJ C256/6; N 469/2006 *Slovak Republic* [2006] OJ C256/6; N 626/2006 *Spain* [2007] OJ C35/4; N 431/2006 *Sweden* [2007] OJ C34/4; and N 673/2006 *United Kingdom* [2007] OJ C55/2.

106 2007–2013 Guidelines, para 98.

107 ibid, para 96.

108 This contrasts with the use of net grant-equivalent (ie the after-tax value) under previous Guidelines. This change follows the judgment in Case T-298/97 *Alzetta Mauro and others v Commission* [2000] ECR II-2319.

109 2007–2013 Guidelines, para 42.

110 ibid, para 45.

111 ibid, paras 44–9.

112 In fact there are currently no OMRs with a GDP of less than 45% per head.

Statistical effect regions, ie areas losing Article 87(3)(a) eligibility at 31 December 2010, will qualify for a maximum rate of 20% GGE from 1 January 2011.[113] In general, in Article 87(3)(c) areas, the maximum rate of award is 15% of eligible expenditure. However, in NUTS III regions where GDP per head is higher than the EU25 average and the unemployment rate is lower than the EU25 average[114] the rate is lowered to 10%.[115] This reduction in the standard rate does not apply in the following cases: low population density regions; Article 87(3)(c) areas adjoining an Article 87(3)(a) region; and NUTS III regions, or parts thereof, which share a land border with a country which is not a member of the European Economic Area or EFTA.[116] Actual rates of award are set out in the Commission decisions approving the regional aid maps.[117]

15.41 **Validity of maps and scope for review.** In principle, the approved regional aid maps should apply throughout the period 2007–2013. However, Member States may initiate a mid-term review and propose changes to eligible areas or aid intensities. These must be notified to the Commission by 1 April 2010. Any changes of region should not exceed 50% of the total coverage allowed for that Member State under Article 87(3)(c). Changes in eligible areas remain subject to the overall population ceiling for the Member State concerned, but Member States may at any time notify to the Commission a request to add further regions to the list until such time as the relevant population ceiling is reached. There are no transitional arrangements for areas losing eligibility following any mid-term review, except in the case of the statistical effect regions.[118]

D. General Block Exemption Regulation ('GBER')

15.42 **GBER and old regional aid block exemption.** On 24 October 2006, the Commission used its powers under the Enabling Regulation[119] to adopt a block exemption regulation in the field of regional aid.[120] As noted at para 15.08 above, the regional aid block exemption has since 29 August 2008 been superseded by the GBER. However, regional aid granted before 31 December 2008, which

[113] 2007–2013 Guidelines, para 46.

[114] Based on averages for the latest three years and using Eurostat data.

[115] 2007–2013 Guidelines, para 47.

[116] ibid, para 48.

[117] See n 105 above.

[118] 2007–2013 Guidelines, para 104, and see para 15.31 above

[119] Council Regulation (EC) 994/98 on the application of Articles 92 and 93 of the Treaty establishing the European Community to certain categories of horizontal State aid [1998] OJ L142/1; see further paras 3.34–3.35 above.

[120] Commission Regulation (EC) No 1628/2006 on the application of Articles 87 and 88 of the Treaty to national regional investment aid [2006] OJ L302/29.

does not satisfy the conditions of the GBER but does fulfil the conditions of the old regional aid block exemption is deemed compatible and exempt from notification.[121] As with the old regional aid block exemption, the GBER exempts regional investment and employment aid that is offered in compliance with the approved regional aid map and fulfils all the conditions of the block exemption. On substantive regional aid issues, the provisions of the GBER are essentially the same as those of the old regional aid block exemption, the principal differences being twofold. First, the GBER contains more onerous requirements for showing an 'incentive effect' for aid to large firms. Secondly, aid to newly created enterprises in assisted areas has now been brought within the ambit of the GBER, rather than being subject to prior notification and approval on the basis of the 2007–2013 Guidelines.

Structure. As described in more detail in Chapter 5 above, Chapter I of the GBER contains a set of common conditions and procedural provisions applicable to the various types of aid covered by the GBER. The provisions of Chapter I relevant to regional aid are addressed in section 1 below. Sections 2 and 3 will then address the specific regional aid exemptions in the GBER, as set out in Chapter II of the GBER. **15.43**

1. Common and procedural provisions

Sectoral scope of regional aid exemptions. The GBER does not apply to regional aid to the fisheries and aquaculture, shipbuilding, coal, steel and synthetic fibres sectors. Nor does it apply to activities linked to the primary production of agricultural products or activities in the fishery and aquaculture sectors, but it does apply to the processing and marketing of agricultural products.[122] The GBER also excludes regional aid schemes which are targeted at specific sectors of economic activity within manufacturing or services.[123] **15.44**

Individual notification thresholds. Under the GBER certain aids are excluded where the value of the financial assistance exceeds specified thresholds. No individual notification threshold is specified for regional aid to newly created enterprises. But regional investment aid awarded in favour of large investment projects must be notified to the Commission if the total amount of aid from all sources exceeds 75% of the maximum amount of aid an investment with eligible costs of €100 million could receive, applying the standard aid threshold in force for large **15.45**

---

[121] GBER, Article 44(2).
[122] ibid, Article 1(3).
[123] Though schemes aimed at tourism activities are not considered as targeted at specific sectors: ibid Article 1(4).

enterprises in the relevant approved regional aid map on the date the aid is to be granted.[124]

15.46 **Common conditions.** In addition to the specific provisions on the scope of the regional aid exemptions, the GBER contains a number of general conditions common to all types of aid within its ambit. These are set out in detail in paragraphs 5.17–5.26 above, to which reference should be made. In summary these provisions concern:

(a) the exclusion of all forms of aid to certain undertakings and certain sectors;
(b) the general conditions for exemption of aid schemes and individual aid granted under such schemes, as well as for ad hoc individual aid;
(c) the basis of calculation of aid intensities;
(d) the requirement to provide documentary evidence of eligible costs;
(e) the requirement for exempted aid to be transparent;
(f) the conditions under which aid can be cumulated with other aid exempted under the GBER;
(g) the requirement for aid to have an incentive effect;[125] and
(h) the reporting and monitoring requirements applicable to all aid exempted under the GBER.

2. Regional investment and employment aid

15.47 **Aid schemes and ad hoc aid.** The exemption in the GBER for regional investment and employment aid primarily applies to aid *schemes*.[126] However ad hoc aid which is only used to supplement aid granted on the basis of a regional investment and employment aid scheme, and which does not exceed 50% of the total aid to be granted for the investment, is exempt from the Article 88(3) notification requirement, provided that the aid awarded directly fulfils all the conditions of the GBER.[127]

15.48 **Compliance with regional aid map.** The aid must be granted in areas eligible for regional aid, as determined by the approved regional aid map, and must be within the prevailing aid ceiling in the region concerned, as also specified by the regional aid map.[128]

15.49 **Eligible investments.** An eligible investment is defined as either (1) investment in tangible or intangible assets relating to the setting up of a new establishment, the extension of an existing establishment, the diversification of the output into new

124 ibid, Article 6(2).
125 Although it is not clear how this provision should apply to aid for newly created enterprises.
126 GBER, Article 13(1), and see Article 2(2) for definition of an 'aid scheme'.
127 ibid, Article 13(1).
128 ibid, Article 13(2).

additional products or a fundamental change in the overall production process of an existing establishment; or (2) the acquisition of capital assets directly linked to an establishment where the establishment has closed or would have closed had it not been purchased and the assets are bought by an independent investor. The acquisition of shares alone in an undertaking does not constitute initial investment.[129]

Eligible assets. Land, buildings, plant, machinery and equipment are all eligible tangible assets. In the transport sector, expenditure on transport equipment is not eligible for investment aid.[130] Intangible assets are those related to technology transfer through the acquisition of patent rights, licences, know-how or unpatented technical knowledge.[131] Intangible assets are eligible provided that they are purchased from third parties under market conditions, regarded as depreciable assets and used exclusively in the establishment receiving the regional aid.[132] Aided investments must be maintained in the recipient region for at least five years (three years in the case of SMEs) after the whole investment is completed. This does not preclude the replacement of plant or equipment which has become outdated within the period due to rapid technological change, provided the economic activity is retained in the region concerned for the minimum period.[133] For large undertakings, intangible assets are eligible up to a limit of 50% of total eligible expenditure; for SMEs, there is no limit. Except in the case of SMEs and takeovers, all assets must be purchased new.[134] **15.50**

Takeovers. In the case of acquisition of an establishment, only the cost of buying assets from third parties under market conditions is eligible for regional investment aid. Where the acquisition is accompanied by initial investment, this expenditure is added to the cost of the purchase. If the assets acquired have already been aided prior to the takeover, these assets are deducted from eligible expenditure.[135] **15.51**

Leasing. Costs related to the acquisition of assets under lease, other than land and buildings, are only taken into account if the arrangement takes the form of financial leasing and contains an obligation to purchase the asset at the end of the agreement. For the lease of land and buildings, the agreement must extend at least five years after the anticipated date of completion of the investment project (three years in the case of SMEs).[136] **15.52**

129 ibid, Article 12(1).
130 ibid, Article 2(10).
131 ibid, Article 2(11).
132 ibid, Article 12(2).
133 ibid, Article 13(2).
134 ibid, Article 13(7).
135 ibid.
136 ibid.

15.53 **Aid calculated on the basis of wage costs.** Where the aid is calculated on the basis of wage costs, the jobs concerned must be directly created by an investment project within three years of the completion of the investment. The investment must lead to a net increase in the number of employees in the establishment concerned, compared with the average over the previous 12 months. Employment must be maintained for a minimum period of five years, three years in the case of SMEs.[137]

15.54 **Own resources.** The beneficiary must provide a financial contribution of at least 25% of eligible costs (whether tangible or intangible assets or acquisition costs in the case of takeover), either through its own resources or by external financing, in a form which is free of any public support. Where the maximum aid intensity approved under the regional aid map exceeds 75%, the financial contribution of the beneficiary is reduced accordingly.[138]

15.55 **Aid ceilings.** The aid ceilings are calculated either as a percentage of the tangible and intangible costs, or as a percentage of the estimated wage costs of the person hired, calculated over a period of two years, for jobs directly created by the investment project, or a combination of the two, provided that the aid does not exceed the most favourable amount resulting from either calculation.[139] The prevailing regional aid ceilings[140] may be raised by 10 percentage points in the case of medium-sized enterprises and 20 percentage points in the case of small enterprises.[141] In the field of marketing and processing of agricultural products, aid intensities derogate from these rates. The following ceilings apply to SMEs: 75% of eligible investment in the outermost regions; 65% of eligible investments in the smaller Aegean Islands;[142] 50% of eligible investment in other Article 87(3)(a) regions and 40% in Article 87(3)(c) areas;[143] for undertakings with fewer than 750 employees and/or turnover of less than €200 million, aid intensities may be set at 25% in Article 87(3)(a) regions and 20% in Article 87(3)(c) areas.[144]

15.56 **Aid values.** For calculating aid intensity, all figures used are taken before any deduction of tax or other charge.[145] Where aid is awarded in a form other than

[137] ibid, Article 12(3).

[138] ibid, Article 13(6).

[139] ibid, Article 13(5).

[140] As set out in the Commission decisions approving the regional aid maps: see paras 15.38–15.40 above.

[141] GBER, Article 13(4). These supplements do not apply to large investment projects or to aid for the transport sector.

[142] As defined in Council Regulation (EC) No 1405/2006 laying down specific measures for agriculture in the small Aegean Islands [2006] OJ L265/1.

[143] GBER, Articles 13(9) and 15(4).

[144] ibid, Article 13(9).

[145] ibid, Article 4(1).

a grant, the aid amount is calculated as a grant-equivalent. Aid payable in several instalments is discounted at the moment of the granting of the aid. The interest rate used for discounting purposes is the reference rate applicable at the time of the grant.[146] Where aid takes the form of tax exemptions or reductions in future taxes due, discounting of aid tranches takes place on the basis of the reference rates applicable at the time the tax advantages become effective.[147]

3. Aid for newly created small enterprises

Scope of exemption. Aid for newly created small enterprises is intended to support business start-ups and the early stage of development of small enterprises in the assisted areas. Only small enterprises are eligible for aid,[148] and the aid cannot, however, be awarded to enterprises that are controlled by shareholders that had owned a failed enterprise active in the same market, or adjacent markets, in the previous year. This prevents aid being given to 'phoenix' enterprises, and also prevents inefficiencies created by supporting unsuccessful enterprises.[149] **15.57**

Eligible expenses. Eligible expenses are legal, advisory, consultancy and administrative costs directly related to the creation of the enterprise, and the following costs incurred within five years of start-up: interest on external finance and a dividend on own capital employed, not exceeding the reference rate; rental of production facilities and equipment; energy, water, heating, taxes (except VAT and corporate taxes on business income) and administrative charges; and, depreciation, leasing production facilities and equipment and wage costs, including compulsory social security charges (provided that these are not already aided).[150] **15.58**

Aid ceilings. In Article 87(3)(a) regions the Commission will approve aid schemes which provide up to €2 million per firm. That figure is reduced to €1 million per firm in Article 87(3)(c) areas. In both cases, the annual amounts of aid must not exceed 33% of those aid ceilings.[151] The aid intensity must not exceed 35% of eligible expenses incurred in the first three years and 25% in the two subsequent years. The aid intensity must not exceed 25% of eligible expenses incurred in the first three years and 15% in the two subsequent years. These aid intensities are increased by 5% in Article 87(3)(a) regions with GDP per head of less than 60% of the EU25 average, in regions with a population density of less than 12.5 inhabitants **15.59**

---

[146] These are published periodically by the Commission. See Commission notice on current State aid recovery interest rates and reference/discount rates for 25 Member States applicable as from 1 January 2007 [2007] OJ C317/2.

[147] GBER, Article 4(2).

[148] ibid, Article 14(2).

[149] ibid, Article 14(6).

[150] ibid, Article 14(5).

[151] ibid, Article 14(3).

per km^2 and in islands with a population of fewer than 5,000 or other communities of the same size suffering from similar isolation.

E. Authorization under Article 87(3)

15.60 **Scope.** The 2007–2013 Guidelines set out the circumstances in which the Commission will approve regional State aid that does not fall within the ambit of the GBER. The Guidelines cover three categories of aid: regional investment aid (sections 1 and 2 below);[152] operating aid (section 3 below);[153] and aid for newly created enterprises (section 4 below).[154] The provisions for those categories of aid apply to all sectors apart from coal and fisheries. They do not apply to agricultural production as specified in Annex I to the Treaty, but they do apply to the processing and marketing of such products. Aid for the steel and synthetic fibres industries is prohibited,[155] and regional aid for firms in difficulty may only be provided in accordance with the Guidelines on State aid for rescue and restructuring firms in difficulty.[156]

15.61 **Basic principle.** In general, regional aid should be part of a multisectoral scheme which forms part of a regional development strategy with clearly defined objectives. Where, exceptionally, ad hoc aid is proposed, the onus is on the Member State to demonstrate that the project contributes towards a coherent regional development strategy.[157]

1. Regional investment aid

15.62 **Residual scope of Guidelines.** In practice, the majority of regional investment aid schemes will fall within the scope of the GBER, not least since most of the assessment criteria (for example, compliance with the regional aid map and accompanying aid intensities, eligible expenditure and eligible investments) under the Guidelines are identical to those under the GBER. The principal exceptions are aids that do not meet the transparency criteria in the GBER or the strict requirements for incentive effect in the case of large enterprises, ad hoc aid that does not merely supplement aid under an exempted scheme and aid to large projects that exceeds the individual notification threshold. In addition to the general considerations in this section, special provisions apply to large investment projects—defined

[152] 2007–2013 Guidelines, paras 33–75.
[153] ibid, paras 76–83.
[154] ibid, paras 84–91.
[155] ibid, para 8.
[156] ibid, para 9.
[157] ibid, para 10.

as those involving eligible expenditure exceeding €50 million. These are discussed separately (see section 2 below).

Form of aid. Unlike the GBER which applies only to 'transparent' aid in defined forms, the form of aid eligible for authorization under the Guidelines is flexible. Aid may take the form of grants, low-interest loans or interest rebates, State guarantees, the purchase of a shareholding or an alternative provision of capital on favourable terms, exemptions or reduction in taxes, social security or other compulsory charges or the supply of land, or goods or services at favourable prices.[158] **15.63**

Compliance with regional aid map. Regional aid schemes or ad hoc regional aid must be compliant with the approved regional aid map and the prevailing regional aid ceilings.[159] Regional aid ceilings are set out in the Commission decisions approving the regional aid maps.[160] The prevailing regional aid ceilings refer to the intensity of the aid calculated either as a percentage of the tangible and intangible costs or as a percentage of the estimated wage costs of the person hired, calculated over a period of two years, for jobs directly created by the investment project. It may also be a combination of the two, provided that the aid does not exceed the most favourable amount resulting from either calculation.[161] **15.64**

Timing of application. Aid may only be granted under aid schemes if the beneficiary has submitted an application for aid and the awarding authority has subsequently confirmed in writing, prior to project start that, subject to detailed verification, the project in principle meets the eligibility criteria. An express reference to these two conditions—the submission of application and written confirmation of provisional eligibility—must be included in all aid schemes. In addition, where the project is subject to individual notification to the Commission, the awarding authority must indicate in writing that eligibility is contingent on Commission approval of the aid proposal. In the case of ad hoc aid, the awarding authority must, prior to the project's start, have issued a letter of intent, conditional on Commission approval, to award aid. If these conditions are not met the whole project is ineligible for aid.[162] **15.65**

Other substantive conditions. As with the GBER, the Guidelines apply to both to aid in the form of material and immaterial investment costs and to aid in the form of wage costs for jobs directly created by the investment project.[163] The Guidelines set out substantive conditions relating to eligible investments, eligible **15.66**

158 ibid, para 37.
159 ibid, para 106.
160 See paras 15.38–15.40 above.
161 2007–2013 Guidelines, para 72.
162 ibid, para 38.
163 ibid, para 36.

assets, takeovers, leasing, wage costs, own resources, aid ceilings and aid values that are identical to those set out in the GBER and discussed in paras 15.47–15.56 above.[164] They are therefore not repeated here.

15.67 **Cumulation.** The aid ceilings set out in the Guidelines refer to total public support for the aided project regardless of whether financed from local, regional or national sources. Where the expenditure eligible for regional aid is eligible in whole or in part for aid for other purposes, the common portion is subject to the most favourable ceiling under the applicable rules.[165] Where a Member State allows for State aid under one scheme to be combined with aid under other schemes, it must specify, in each scheme, the method by which it will ensure compliance with the cumulation limits.[166] Regional aid cannot be combined with *de minimis* support in respect of the same eligible expenditure if this would result in the aid intensities fixed by the Guidelines being exceeded.[167]

2. Large investment projects

15.68 **General.** The provisions on large investment projects in section 4.3 of the 2007–2013 Guidelines incorporate the provisions of the 2002 Multisectoral Framework, with a few specific changes which are discussed below. As with the Multisectoral Framework, the purpose of these specific provisions is to require notification of certain aids to large projects, even where these would not normally fall to be notified under an approved regional aid scheme.

15.69 **Scope.** A large investment is an initial investment with an eligible expenditure exceeding €50 million.[168] The eligible expenditure taken into account to establish whether the threshold is met is either the investment cost or the wage cost, whichever is the higher.[169] In order to prevent large projects being artificially subdivided, a large investment project is considered to be a single investment where the initial investment is undertaken in a period of three years by one or more companies and consists of fixed assets combined in an economically indivisible way. To assess whether an investment is economically indivisible, the Commission takes into account the technical, functional and strategic links and immediate geographical proximity. Economic indivisibility is assessed separately from ownership. This implies that the assessment of whether a large project constitutes a single investment is the same, irrespective of whether the project is carried out by one undertaking, by several undertakings sharing the investment costs or by several

[164] ibid, paras 33–59 generally.
[165] ibid, para 73.
[166] ibid, para 74.
[167] ibid, para 75.
[168] ibid, para 60.
[169] ibid, para 61.

undertakings bearing the costs of separate investments within the same investment project (for example, in the case of a joint venture).[170]

Aid ceilings. Regional investment aid for large projects is subject to an adjusted regional aid ceiling. As with the 2002 Multisectoral Framework, the formula applied is similar in operation to a progressive tax regime, whereby the larger the investment, the lower the rate of award. The starting point for the adjustment is the prevailing regional aid ceiling for large firms, as specified in the Commission decisions approving the regional aid maps;[171] SME bonuses do not apply to large investment projects, irrespective of firm size.[172] This formula is applied automatically by awarding bodies administering regional aid, subject to the notification requirements. **15.70**

Eligible expenditure	**Aid ceiling**
Up to €50 m	100% of regional aid ceiling
For the part between €50 m and €100 m	50% of regional aid ceiling
For the part exceeding €100 m	34% of regional aid ceiling

By contrast with the 2002 Multisectoral Framework, the motor industry is now subject to the same award matrix.

Reporting. Regional aid granted on the basis of existing schemes for non-notifiable large investment projects must be reported to the Commission on the basis of the standard form in Annex III to the Guidelines within 20 working days of the award.[173] Member States must maintain detailed records on the granting of aid to all large investment projects. Such records must contain all the information necessary to establish that the maximum allowable aid intensity has been respected and must be maintained for ten years from the granting of the aid.[174] **15.71**

Individual notification. Member States are required to notify individually to the Commission any aid where the amount proposed is more than the maximum which an investment with eligible expenditure of €100 million could receive according to the reduction formula referred to in para 15.70 above. The notification thresholds, expressed in amount of aid, for a range of prevailing regional aid ceilings are as follows.[175] **15.72**

Prevailing ceiling	10%	15%	20%	30%	40%	50%
Notification threshold	€7.5m	€11.25m	€15m	€22.5m	€40m	€37.5m

[170] ibid, para 60.
[171] See n 105 above.
[172] 2007–2013 Guidelines, para 67.
[173] ibid, para 65.
[174] ibid, para 66.
[175] ibid, para 64.

15.73 **Commission assessment of individually notified projects.** If the beneficiary has (or will have after the investment) more than 25% of the sales of the product(s) concerned or if the production capacity created by the project is more than 5% of the market for the product concerned,[176] except where annual average growth rate for the last five years is above the annual average growth rate of EEA GDP, then the 2002 Multisectoral Framework indicated that the aid would be prohibited in its entirety, although there appeared to be some uncertainty about whether this prohibition would be applied in practice.[177] This uncertainty has been removed from the 2007–2013 Guidelines which makes clear that the Commission decision refers to aid amounts in excess of the notification threshold. Importantly, the 2007–2013 Guidelines introduce an element of discretion in cases where the market share or capacity thresholds are exceeded. In such cases the Commission will open a formal investigation under Article 88(2).[178] It will subsequently only approve the aid once it has verified that the aid is necessary to provide an incentive effect for the investment, and that the benefits of the aid measure outweigh the resulting distortion of competition and effect on trade between Member States.[179] Prior to the entry into force of 2007–2013 Guidelines, the Commission was to have drawn up guidance on the criteria it would take into account in making this assessment.[180] In November 2008 the Commission initiated a consultation on draft guidance for the handling of such projects.

3. Operating aid

15.74 **Scope.** Operating aid, ie aid aimed at reducing a firm's current expenses, is normally prohibited. However, under the 2007–2013 Guidelines, such aid may be granted in Article 87(3)(a) regions provided that it is justified in terms of its contribution to regional development, and provided that its level is proportional to the handicaps it seeks to alleviate. Member States are responsible for demonstrating the existence and scale of any such handicaps. In addition, certain specific forms of operating aid can be authorized in the low population density and least populated areas.[181] Operating aid should in principle only be granted in respect of a pre-defined set of eligible expenditures (such as replacement investment,

[176] Measured using apparent consumption data, this being defined as production, plus imports, minus exports.

[177] See para 15.23 above.

[178] 2007–2013 Guidelines, para 68. To avoid a formal investigation, the burden of proof that the market share and production capacity situations do not pertain lies with the Member States: ibid, para 70.

[179] ibid, para 68.

[180] ibid, n 63.

[181] ibid, para 76.

transport or labour costs) and limited to a certain proportion of those costs.[182] Operating aid intended to promote exports is excluded.[183]

Financial and intragroup services.[184] These are ineligible for operating aid, unless such aid is granted under general schemes which are open to all sectors and which are designed to offset additional transport and employment costs.[185] **15.75**

Temporary and degressive. In general, because operating aid is intended to overcome bottlenecks and delays in regional development, operating aid should be temporary and reduced over time.[186] For this reason too, the Commission will only authorize operating aid for the duration of the 2007–2013 Guidelines.[187] **15.76**

Outermost and least-populated regions. By way of exception to the general principle that operating aid should be temporary and non-degressive, the Commission may authorize operating aid in the outermost regions, which is neither limited in time nor progressively reduced, insofar as it is intended to offset the additional costs involved in pursuing economic activity arising from the permanence and combination of insularity, small size, difficult topography and climate, and dependence on a few products.[188] Moreover, the Commission considers that, except in the case of financial and intragroup activities, operating aid of up to 10% of the turnover of the beneficiary may be awarded without the need for specific justification.[189] In the least-populated regions, the Commission may authorize ongoing aid intended to reduce or prevent the continuing depopulation of these regions.[190] These are defined as NUTS II regions, or parts thereof, where the population density is eight inhabitants per km^2 or less and includes adjacent and contiguous smaller areas meeting the same population density criterion. The onus is on the Member State to demonstrate that the aid is necessary and appropriate to prevent or reduce continuing depopulation.[191] **15.77**

---

[182] ibid, para 77.

[183] ibid, para 78.

[184] Defined in Section J (codes 65, 66 and 67) and Section K (code 74) of the NACE code.

[185] 2007–2013 Guidelines, para 78. See Decisions in Cases N 376/2006 *ZEC* (20 December 2006) and N 421/2006 *Zona Franca da Madeira* (27 June 2007) where such activities were excluded from the scope of the schemes approved.

[186] 2007–2013 Guidelines, para 79.

[187] ibid, para 82.

[188] ibid, para 80. See eg Decision in Case N 542/2006 *Exonération des charges sociales patronales* (23 October 2007) where the concession is permanent; however, the French authorities undertake to re-notify the measure before 31 December 2013.

[189] 2007–2013 Guidelines, n 74. See Decision in Case N 293/2007 *Reduced excise duty for locally produced beer in Madeira* (10 October 2007).

[190] 2007–2013 Guidelines, para 80.

[191] See EFTA Surveillance Authority (ESA) Decision 228/06/COL *Regionally-differentiated social security contributions in Norway* (19 July 2006). ESA applies the same rules on regional aid to members of the EEA that are not members of the EU (namely, Norway, Iceland and Liechtenstein).

15.78 **Transport aid.** In the outermost regions and the low population density regions, the Commission may authorize transport aid which is not progressively reduced nor limited in time.[192] The low population density regions are those included in the approved regional aid map on the basis of the low population density criterion;[193] these are more extensive than the least populated regions referred to in the foregoing paragraph. Transport aid may serve only to compensate for the additional cost of transport; although the amount of aid may be calculated on a representative basis, systematic over-compensation must be avoided. Aid may only be given in respect of transport within the national borders and may not be given to activities with no alternative location (products of extractive industries, hydroelectric power stations, etc).[194] In the outermost regions only, aid may cover the cost of transporting primary commodities, raw materials or intermediate products from the place of their production to the place of final processing in the region concerned. In all cases, the amount of aid must be objectively quantifiable in advance, on the basis on an aid-per-passenger or aid-per-ton/kilometre ratio. The estimate of the additional cost must be based on the most economical form of transport and the shortest route between the place of production or processing and commercial outlets using that form of transport; external costs to the environment should also be taken into account.

15.79 **Reporting.** An annual report must show the operation of the aid ratios. In addition, Member States are required to provide a single report in respect of each NUTS II region in which operating aid is granted which provides a breakdown of total expenditure, or estimated income foregone, for each operating aid scheme approved in the region concerned and which identifies the ten largest beneficiaries of operating aid in the region, specifying the amount of aid and the sector of activity.[195]

4. Aid for newly created small enterprises

15.80 **General.** The provisions on aid for newly created enterprises reflect the perception that the economic development of assisted areas is hindered by relatively low levels of economic activity and by lower than average levels of business start-ups. Aid for newly created small enterprises is intended to support business start-ups and the early stage of development of small enterprises in the assisted areas and can be granted in addition to regional investment aid.[196]

---

192 2007–2013 Guidelines, para 81.

193 ibid, para 30b.

194 See Decisions in Cases N 886/2006 *Finnish regional transport subsidy* (10 May 2007); and N 152/2007 *Swedish regional transport subsidy* (23 October 2007).

195 2007–2013 Guidelines, para 83.

196 For examples of approved measures see Decisions in Cases N 203/2007 *Newly created enterprises in Murcia* (10 July 2007); and N 384/2007 *Start-up aid for the creation of small enterprises* (3 October 2007).

Residual application following GBER. The conditions for eligible enterprises, eligible expenses and aid ceilings are virtually identical to those set out in the GBER and discussed in paras 15.57–15.59 above.[197] They are therefore not repeated here. In most cases where the Guidelines apply, therefore, the aid is likely to fall within the scope of the GBER and will not require notification. The Guidelines will apply, however, in some residual cases where the aid does not satisfy the formal requirements of the GBER, in particular where the aid is granted in a form that does not meet the GBER's transparency criteria. The Guidelines also do not contain the same requirement to demonstrate an incentive effect that is a condition of the GBER.[198] **15.81**

[197] 2007–2013 Guidelines, paras 86–91generally.

[198] Insofar as the GBER does require this to be demonstrated formally for this category of aid: see query at n 125 above.

PART III

ENFORCEMENT AND REMEDIES

16

SUPERVISION BY THE COMMISSION

Main legislation and guidelines

Council Regulation (EC) 659/1999 laying down detailed rules for the application of Article 93 of the EC Treaty ('Procedural Regulation') [1999] OJ L83/1, as amended [2006] OJ L363/1

Commission Regulation (EC) 794/2004 implementing Council Regulation (EC) No 659/1999 laying down detailed rules for the application of Article 93 of the EC Treaty ('Implementing Regulation') [2004] OJ L140/1, as amended [2008] OJ L82/1

Commission Communication to the Member States on the accelerated clearance of aid schemes for SMEs and of amendments of existing schemes [1992] OJ C213/10

Commission Notice – Towards an effective implementation of Commission decisions ordering Member States to recover unlawful and incompatible State aid ('Recovery Notice') [2007] OJ C272/4

A. Overview of Commission procedure

16.01 **Article 88 EC.** Article 88 sets out the Community system for the enforcement of State aid. The Commission must apply this procedure in investigating aid and determining its compatibility, whatever the type of instrument granting the aid. Article 88 provides as follows:

> 1. The Commission shall, in cooperation with Member States, keep under constant review all systems of aid existing in those States. It shall propose to the latter any appropriate measures required by the progressive development or by the functioning of the common market.
> 2. If, after giving notice to the parties concerned to submit their comments, the Commission finds that aid granted by a State or through State resources is not compatible with the common market having regard to Article 87, or that such aid is being misused, it shall decide that the State concerned shall abolish or alter such aid within a period of time to be determined by the Commission.
>
>   If the State concerned does not comply with this decision within the prescribed time, the Commission or any other interested State may, in derogation from the provisions of Articles 226 and 227, refer the matter to the Court of Justice direct.
>
>   On application by a Member State, the Council may, acting unanimously, decide that aid which that State is granting or intends to grant shall be considered to be compatible with the common market, in derogation from the provisions of Article 87 or from the regulations provided for in Article 89, if such a decision is justified by exceptional circumstances. If, as regards the aid in question, the Commission has already initiated the procedure provided for in the first subparagraph of this paragraph, the fact that the State concerned has made its application to the Council shall have the effect of suspending that procedure until the Council has made its attitude known.
>
>   If, however, the Council has not made its attitude known within three months of the said application being made, the Commission shall give its decision on the case.
> 3. The Commission shall be informed, in sufficient time to enable it to submit its comments, of any plans to grant or alter aid. If it considers that any such plan is not compatible with the common market having regard to Article 87, it shall without delay initiate the procedure provided for in paragraph 2. The Member State concerned shall not put its proposed measures into effect until this procedure has resulted in a final decision.

16.02 **Division of competences.** The effect of Article 88(3), as interpreted by the Court, is to create a division of competences between the Commission and the national courts. The Commission has exclusive jurisdiction to determine whether aid is compatible with the common market,[1] save in the 'exceptional circumstances'

[1] Case C-354/90 *FNCEPA v France* [1991] ECR I-5505, para 14; Case C-39/94 *SFEI v La Poste* [1996] ECR I-3547, para 42; Case C-143/99 *Adria-Wien Pipeline* [2001] ECR I-8365, para 29;

referred to in the third and fourth subparagraphs of Article 88(2), where the Council may intervene,[2] and subject to review by the CFI and ECJ.[3] National courts have an important role in safeguarding the jurisdiction of the Commission through the so-called 'standstill clause' in Article 88(3), as well as enforcing Commission decisions,[4] but neither they nor national competition authorities have the competence to pronounce upon the application of any of the principles of compatibility set out in Article 87(2) and (3).[5] Furthermore, although the Court itself has not yet pronounced on the question of the direct effect of Article 86(2), it seems likely that the Commission has exclusive jurisdiction to apply this provisions in the field of State aid, such that there is no scope for its application in the national courts.[6]

Regulation 659/1999 ('Procedural Regulation'). Prior to 1999, the detailed rules for the application of Article 88 by the Commission were developed through the Commission's decisional practice and the case-law of the Court. In the interests of ensuring effective and efficient procedures under Article 88, as well as increasing transparency and legal certainty, that case-law and Commission practice was codified in the so-called 'Procedural Regulation', adopted by the Council pursuant to Article 89.[7] This entered into force on 16 April 1999, and since then has applied not only to all new State aid procedures registered by the Commission, but also to all procedures pending before the Commission on that date.[8] The provisions of the Procedural Regulation are also regarded as superseding earlier conflicting case-law.[9] **16.03**

Regulation 794/2004 ('Implementing Regulation'). Article 27 of the Procedural Regulation empowers the Commission to adopt detailed implementing provisions concerning notification of aid, annual reports, time limits and the interest rate applicable to the recovery of aid. Those implementing provisions have subsequently been specified in the so-called 'Implementing Regulation', Commission **16.04**

Case C-451/03 *Servizi Ausiliari Dottori Commercialisti* [2006] ECR I-2941, para 71.

[2] See paras 3.101–3.106 above.

[3] See Chapter 17 below.

[4] See Chapter 18 below.

[5] Case 78/76 *Steinike und Weinlig v Germany* [1977] ECR 595, paras 8–10.

[6] See para 3.69 above.

[7] Council Regulation (EC) 659/1999 laying down detailed rules for the application of Article 93 of the EC Treaty [1999] OJ L83/1, as amended [2006] OJ L363/1. The Court has confirmed that the Procedural Regulation represents a codification of the Commission practice and Court case-law: Case C-400/99 *Italy v Commission ('Tirrenia')* [2005] ECR I-3657, para 23.

[8] Case T-366/00 *Scott v Commission* [2003] ECR II-1763, paras 52–3, confirmed in Case C-276/03 P *Scott v Commission* [2005] ECR I-8437; Case C-368/04 *Transalpine Ölleitung* [2006] ECR I-9957, para 34.

[9] See Case T-351/02 *Deutsche Bahn v Commission* [2006] ECR II-1047, para 53.

Regulation 794/2004,[10] which was recently amended by Commission Regulation 271/2008.[11]

16.05 **The different State aid procedures.** Article 88 and the Procedural Regulation distinguish between four types of aid: new aid, unlawful aid, misused aid and existing aid. *New aid* must be notified to the Commission prior to its implementation, and may not be put into effect until the Commission has taken a decision. The Commission may decide that the measure is not aid, or that the aid is compatible with the common market, on the basis of a preliminary review of the measure (also referred to as the Article 88(3) procedure). Alternatively it may open the formal investigation procedure (also referred to as the Article 88(2) procedure) before adopting a decision. New aid which is implemented without notification and approval constitutes *unlawful aid*. In relation to unlawful aid, the preliminary and formal procedures apply as with notified new aid, but the Commission has additional powers to suspend or recover the aid which has been granted. *Misused aid* triggers the formal investigation procedure, and the Commission has very similar powers of suspension and recovery to those set out for unlawful aid. *Existing aid* does not have to be notified, but is subject to continuous review by the Commission. If the aid is subsequently deemed incompatible with the common market, the Commission may propose appropriate measures to the Member State and, if those measures are not accepted, open the formal investigation procedure. These procedures are addressed in detail in the remainder of this chapter.

16.06 **Directorates General responsible for State aid control.** Within the Commission, State aid control under the provisions of Article 88 and the Procedural Regulation is carried out by four Directorates General. DG Energy and Transport (DG Tren) deals with State aid in the areas of transport and coal. DG Agriculture and Rural Development (DG Agri) and DG Fisheries and Maritime Affairs (DG Fish) deal with State aid in the agriculture and fisheries sectors respectively. All other sectors are handled by DG Competition (DG Comp).

16.07 **State aid register.** Since 1 January 2000, State aid cases have all been listed on a central register on the State aid section of the DG Comp website, where they are classified into what are now 12 categories:

N – notified aid
NN – unnotified aid

[10] Commission Regulation (EC) 794/2004 implementing Council Regulation (EC) No 659/1999 laying down detailed rules for the application of Article 93 of the EC Treaty [2004] OJ L140/1.

[11] Commission Regulation (EC) 271/2008 amending Regulation (EC) 794/2004 implementing Council Regulation (EC) No 659/1999 laying down detailed rules for the application of Article 93 of the EC Treaty [2008] OJ L82/1.

C – cases in which the Commission has opened the formal investigation procedure
E – existing aid
X – General Block Exemption Regulation cases
XA – agriculture block exemption cases
XE – employment block exemption cases
XF – fisheries sector block exemption cases
XP – SME block exemption cases concerning the processing and marketing of agricultural products
XR – regional block exemption cases
XS – SME block exemption cases
XT – training block exemption cases

The category letter is followed by a serial number and the year of registration (for example N 1/2007). In exceptional cases, a large case comprising a number of State aid measures may be split into two or more cases, identified as 'a', 'b', etc (for example NN 62b/2006). During the lifetime of a State aid case, the matter may take on different case numbers. Thus an 'N' case may get a new 'NN' number if the Commission receives information that the aid was unlawfully granted; and 'N', 'NN' and 'E' cases are reclassified under a 'C' number if a formal investigation procedure under Article 88(2) is opened.

Transparency system. The 2007–2013 Regional Aid Guidelines contain reporting requirements for non-notifiable aid granted on the basis of existing schemes for large investment projects, and the R&D&I Framework contains similar provisions for individual R&D&I aid of over €3 million which is part of an approved scheme.[12] The State aid register contains tables summarizing the information provided by Member States under both of these provisions. **16.08**

B. Notification of new aid

1. Types of aid that must be notified

The 'standstill clause'. Article 88(3) provides that the Commission is to be notified of any plans to grant or alter aid before those plans are implemented. The aid may not be implemented until it has been approved. This provision, reproduced in Article 3 of the Procedural Regulation, is generally known as the 'standstill clause'. The effect is that all aid which falls within the conditions set out in Article 87(1)[13] **16.09**

[12] See respectively paras 15.71 and 8.54 above.
[13] Procedural Regulation, Article 1(a).

must be notified and approved before implementation. A measure that does not satisfy all of the conditions of Article 87(1), as set out in Chapter 2, does not have to be notified. In practice, however, to ensure legal certainty a Member State may notify such a measure with a request for a decision confirming that the measure does not constitute aid.[14]

16.10 **Aids that are compatible with the common market.** The obligation to notify applies even where the Member State considers the measure to be compatible with the common market pursuant to the provisions of Article 87(2) or (3). The same applies for aids which are covered by Article 86(2): while that provision represents a derogation from the rules of the Treaty, it does not prevent classification of the measure as State aid within the meaning of Article 87(1).[15] The Court has thus held that even where a case is covered by Article 86(2), the obligations to notify aid and suspend implementation of the aid until approval still apply.[16]

16.11 **Block exemption cases.** As set out elsewhere in this book, the Commission currently applies a Regulation ('GBER') covering a number of categories of horizontal and regional aid, as well as specific block exemptions in the agriculture and fisheries sector, and block exemptions for *de minimis* aids. Where the conditions of these block exemptions are satisfied, the aid is exempted from the obligation to notify.

16.12 **Existing and new aid.** The other major category of case where notification is not required is existing aid, since the notification requirement only applies to new aid. The distinction between existing aid and new aid is, however, not always straightforward and is therefore considered in detail in the next section.

2. Distinction between new and existing aids

16.13 **Existing aid.** There are five categories of 'existing aid', as defined in Article 1(b) of the Procedural Regulation:

(a) aid which existed at the time of the entry into force of the Treaty in the respective Member States (for the first 12 States to join the EU, between 1958 and 1986).[17]

---

[14] As discussed below at para 16.115, a belief that the measure is not within Article 87(1) does not exonerate a State from the obligation to recover a payment, if it is subsequently found to be aid.

[15] Case C-172/03 *Heiser* [2005] ECR I-1627, para 51.

[16] Case C-332/98 *France v Commission ('CELF')* [2000] ECR I-4833, paras 31–3, rejecting the ingenious argument of the French government that Article 86(2) had the effect of disapplying the suspensory effect of Article 88(3), even if the aid still had to be notified. See also Cases C-261-262/01 *Van Calster* [2003] ECR I-12249, para 61; and *Heiser*, ibid.

[17] This was in 1958 for Belgium, France, Germany, Luxembourg, Italy and the Netherlands; 1973 for Denmark, Ireland and the UK; 1981 for Greece and 1986 for Spain and Portugal.

Different provisions apply to Austria, Finland and Sweden, which acceded on 1 January 1995;[18] the Czech Republic, Estonia, Cyprus, Latvia, Lithuania, Hungary, Malta, Poland, Slovenia and Slovakia, which acceded on 1 May 2004;[19] and Bulgaria and Romania, which acceded on 1 January 2007;[20]

(b) aid which has been authorized by the Commission or Council;

(c) aid which has been notified to the Commission but where, after two months, the Commission has not taken a decision, such that the aid is deemed to have been authorized;

(d) aid for which the limitation period of ten years from the date of grant has expired; and

(e) aid which did not constitute aid at the time it was put into effect, and only became an aid due to the evolution of the common market, without having been altered by the Member State.

New aid. The question of whether an aid is to be classified as existing or new aid is determined objectively.[21] All aid schemes and individual aids that are not existing aids constitute new aid. This includes individual aids which are awarded on the basis of an existing aid scheme, but which are required to be notified to the Commission prior to implementation. Alterations to existing aids are also regarded as new aid which must be notified.[22] **16.14**

---

18 As set out in the Act of Accession of Austria, Finland and Sweden [1994] OJ C241. Article 144 of the Act provides that only the aids applied in the new Member States prior to accession, and communicated to the Commission by 30 April 1995, are deemed to be existing aids. Article 172(5) of the Act provides that decisions taken by the EFTA Surveillance Authority prior to accession remain valid for the purposes of Article 87 unless the Commission decides otherwise under Article 88. However aids granted during 1994 which, in contravention of the EEA Agreement, were not notified to the EFTA Surveillance Authority or were granted before approval are not considered as existing aids under Article 88.

19 As set out in the Act of Accession of those new Member States, Annex IV points 3 and 4 and the Appendix to that Annex [2003] OJ L236/797. This lists as existing aid, for all sectors other than transport and agriculture: (a) aid measures put into effect before 10 December 1994, (b) aid measures listed in the Appendix to the Annex, and (c) aid measures assessed by the State aid monitoring authority of the new Member State prior to accession, and found to be compatible with the *acquis*, and to which the Commission did not raise an objection following the procedure specified in point 3(2) of Annex IV. In the transport and agriculture sectors, aids in effect prior to accession are regarded as existing aid until the end of the third year from the date of accession provided that they are communicated to the Commission within four months of the date of accession. See also list of measures considered as existing aid in these Member States, published in the State aid register on the DG Comp website.

20 As set out in the Act of Accession of Bulgaria and Romania, Annex V points 2 and 3(b) and the Appendix to that Annex [2005] OJ L157/268. This contains the same provisions as set out above in relation to the ten new Member States acceding on 1 May 2004, save that in relation to Romania category (c) concerning aid measures assessed by the State aid monitoring authority only applied after such date as the Commission determined that Romania's State aid enforcement record in the period prior to accession had reached a satisfactory level. See also list of measures considered as existing aid in these Member States, published in the State aid register on the DG Comp website.

21 Case C-295/97 *Rinaldo Piaggio* [1999] ECR I-3735, paras 47–8.

22 ibid, Article 1(c) and (e).

16.15 **Aid schemes.** The Procedural Regulation defines two types of aid schemes. The first is a scheme on the basis of which individual aid may be granted to undertakings defined in a general and abstract manner, without further implementing measures being required. The second is an act on the basis of which aid not linked to a specific project may be awarded to one or more undertakings for an indefinite period of time and/or for an indefinite amount.[23] Specific grants of aid pursuant to an existing aid scheme are not regarded as new aid. However there will be new aid where a grant departs from the conditions of a scheme, or where the approval of the original scheme is subject to conditions that require specific grants to be notified. The Commission may also, following its approval of an aid scheme, adopt a reservation for a particular sector. In such a case a grant of aid in that reserved sector, even if within the terms of the originally approved aid scheme, will constitute new aid which must be notified.[24]

16.16 **Alteration of existing aid.** An alteration to existing aid constitutes new aid and must be notified. This requirement, which is set out explicitly in Article 88(3) as well as in the Procedural Regulation,[25] is interpreted strictly.[26] Article 4(1) of the Implementing Regulation thus defines an alteration to existing aid as 'any change, other than modifications of a purely formal or administrative nature which cannot affect the evaluation of the compatibility of the aid measure with the common market'. Any substantive change in a system of aid will therefore normally constitute an alteration to the aid.[27] Whether there is such a change depends not on the financial amount of aid at any given point, but rather on whether the provisions establishing the aid have been altered.[28] For this reason, in *Namur-Les Assurances*, an enlargement of the field of activity of the aid beneficiary was not regarded as an alteration to the aid, since it did not affect the arrangements put in place by the legislation granting the aid in 1939.[29] On the other hand an increase in the ceilings of assets that may benefit from an aid scheme, which entails an increase in the potential beneficiaries of the scheme, does constitute a notifiable alteration.[30]

[23] Procedural Regulation, Article 1(d).

[24] See Case C-313/90 *CIRFS v Commission* [1994] ECR I-4635, para 35.

[25] Procedural Regulation, Article 1(c).

[26] See AG Warner in Case 177/78 *Pigs and Bacon Commission v McCarren* [1979] ECR 2161, p 2204.

[27] AG Lenz in Case C-44/93 *Namur-Les Assurances v OND* [1994] ECR I-3829, opinion para 77; AG Fennelly in Cases C-15/98 and C-105/99 *Italy and Sardegna Lines v Commission* [2000] ECR I-8855, opinion para 62.

[28] *Namur-Les Assurances*, ibid, judgment para 28; Case T-35/99 *Keller and Keller Meccanica v Commission* [2002] ECR II-261, para 61.

[29] *Namur-Les Assurances*, ibid, judgment para 29.

[30] Case T-35/99 *Keller and Keller Meccanica v Commission* [2002] ECR II-261, para 62. The Court rejected the argument that the increase was designed to take account of a devaluation of the lira, on the basis that on the facts the increase was disproportionate to the monetary depreciation: para 63.

The Court has also rejected arguments that loans granted to repay debts secured by a guarantee from a different public body constituted intervention under the existing guarantee.[31] However one type of alteration is permitted: the Implementing Regulation confirms that an increase in the original budget of an existing aid scheme by up to 20% is not considered to be an alteration to existing aid.[32]

Severability of alterations to aid scheme. If the Commission is not informed of an alteration to an aid scheme that it has approved, the question arises whether the failure to notify taints the entire scheme, such that the whole scheme is regarded as new aid that may not be implemented prior to a new approval, pursuant to Article 88(3). This in turn has implications for any remedies flowing from the application of Article 88(3), such as the recovery of unlawful aid by the Commission or national courts. The Procedural Regulation does not explicitly address this question. However the Court has ruled that an alteration will only transform the original scheme into a new aid scheme where the alteration affects the 'actual substance' of the original scheme. Where, on the other hand, the alteration is severable from the initial scheme only the alteration itself will be notifiable as a new aid.[33] **16.17**

Evolution of the common market. Article 1(b)(v) of the Procedural Regulation includes as existing aids measures which have become aid due to the evolution of the common market. That must be understood as a change in the economic and legal framework of the sector concerned.[34] It does not apply if the measure is classified as aid following a change in the Commission's approach.[35] If the Commission's change of approach leads it to reclassify a measure which it had previously approved, however, that particular measure will be regarded as existing aid under Article 1(b)(ii).[36] Article 1(b)(v) also specifies that where a measure becomes aid following the liberalization of an activity by Community law, it is not considered as existing aid after the date fixed for liberalization.[37] **16.18**

---

[31] Case T-318/00 *Freistaat Thüringen v Commission* [2005] ECR II-4179, paras 195, 232, 247 and 281.

[32] Implementing Regulation, Article 4 and recital (4).

[33] Cases T-195 and 207/01 *Government of Gibraltar v Commission* [2002] ECR II-2309, paras 109–11. See also Cases 91 and 177/83 *Heineken Brouwerijen* [1984] ECR 3435, para 21.

[34] Cases C-182/03 and C-217/03 *Belgium and Forum 187 v Commission* [2006] ECR I-5479, para 71. One example might be the transformation of airports into competing commercial entities: see Decision in Case NN 86/2001 *Aer Rianta* (5 October 2001), para 3.

[35] Cases T-269, 271 and 272/99 *Diputación Foral de Guipúzcoa v Commission* [2002] ECR II-4217, para 80; Cases T-346-348/99 *Diputación Foral de Álava v Commission* [2002] ECR II-4259, para 84; Cases C-182/03 and C-217/03 *Belgium and Forum 187 v Commission*, ibid, para 71.

[36] As was the situation in *Belgium and Forum 187 v Commission*, ibid. See also the discussion in Cases T-50/06 etc *Ireland v Commission* (judgment of 12 December 2007).

[37] cf Cases T-298/97 etc *Mauro Alzetta v Commission* [2000] ECR II-2319, paras 143–4, where the Court came to the opposite view on the basis that liberalization cannot be regarded as a material alteration to an aid system, such that it renders the aid notifiable.

16.19 **Legal basis for aid.** The distinction between new and existing aid may involve consideration of the proper legal basis for the measure in question. A Sardinian agricultural aid scheme established in 1988 did not escape classification as new aid simply because it referred back to a 1928 law. In the first place, the 1928 law had itself been amended and supplemented by subsequent legislation. In any event, however, it was apparent from the information before the Court that the contested aid measures were not based on that law, but rather were based directly on the 1988 legislation.[38]

3. Notification procedure

16.20 **Responsibility of Member States.** The obligation to notify is imposed on the Member States alone.[39] Notification cannot be made by the undertaking receiving the aid. This was made clear in *P&O European Ferries (Vizcaya) v Commission* where a central issue was the question of whether an agreement had been notified properly.[40] In the course of discussions with the Commission concerning the unnotified original agreement, P&O itself had supplied the Commission with a new agreement, on the basis of which the Commission had taken its initial decision. In subsequent proceedings concerning (*inter alia*) the recoverability of the aid, both the CFI and the ECJ held that the provision of the new agreement by P&O did not constitute notification for the purposes of Article 88(3).[41]

16.21 **Formal notification.** In some cases, a Member State may engage in informal discussions before a State aid notification is submitted. These could even last for a number of years.[42] If the State decides to continue with the aid, however, it must make its formal notification in 'sufficient time' for the Commission to reach its decision prior to implementation of the measure,[43] since the prohibition on implementation of the aid continues until the Commission has either approved the aid, or is deemed to have done so. Even if the Commission has started its investigation on the basis of a third party complaint, the Member State should make a formal notification in order to protect itself from the consequences of a decision declaring the aid unlawful.[44]

---

[38] Cases C-346 and 529/03 *Atzeni v Regione autonoma della Sardegna* [2006] ECR I-1875, para 52.

[39] Procedural Regulation, Article 2(1).

[40] Cases T-116 and 118/01 *P&O European Ferries (Vizcaya) v Commission* [2003] ECR II-2957, upheld on appeal in Cases C-442 and 471/03 P *P&O European Ferries (Vizcaya) v Commission* [2006] ECR I-4845 (discussed further below at para 16.112).

[41] CFI, ibid at para 64; ECJ, ibid at paras 102–7.

[42] In one recent case discussions with the Commission commenced in 1998, but the aid scheme was not formally notified to the Commission until 2003: Decision in Case N 46/2003 *Irish risk equalization scheme* (13 May 2003), upheld in Case T-289/03 *BUPA v Commission* (judgment of 12 February 2008).

[43] Procedural Regulation, Article 2(1).

[44] See eg Cases T-116 and 118/01 *P&O European Ferries (Vizcaya) v Commission* [2003] ECR II-2957 and Cases C-442 and 471/03 P *P&O European Ferries (Vizcaya) v Commission* [2006] ECR I-4845, discussed further below at para 16.112.

Electronic notification procedure. The notification procedure is governed by the Procedural Regulation, and the detailed provisions laid down in the Implementing Regulation, as amended. The notification forms are now all contained in the Commission's SANI web application[45] and all notifications must now be made electronically on that system. Similarly, all correspondence in connection with a notification must be sent electronically via the Commission's secured Public Key Infrastructure ('PKI') email system.[46] Other means of communication may only be used by agreement with the Commission, in exceptional circumstances.[47] **16.22**

Standard notification form. The Implementing Regulation establishes a compulsory standard notification form. Article 2 of the Regulation provides that this form, set out at Part I of Annex I to the Regulation, must be used for all notification of new aid, save for coal sector aids and alterations to existing aid covered by the simplified procedure.[48] Part III of Annex I contains notification forms which must be used to provide specified supplementary information, in cases where the aid is covered by specific regulations or guidelines. **16.23**

Simplified notification form. A simplified notification form is set out in Annex II to the Implementing Regulation. This must be used for three types of alteration to existing aids: (a) increases in the budget of an authorized aid scheme exceeding 20%, (b) the prolongation of an existing authorized scheme by up to six years, with or without an increase in its budget, and (c) the tightening of the criteria for an authorized aid scheme, a reduction of the aid intensity or a reduction of eligible expenses. **16.24**

Required information. Article 2(2) of the Procedural Regulation requires a State aid notification to provide all necessary information to enable the Commission to take its decision, whether on the basis of a preliminary review or a formal investigation. This should be easier for Member States to do since the adoption of the standard notification form, which is very comprehensive and requires the provision of a large amount of information including the legal basis for the aid, its objectives, the aid beneficiaries, the amount of aid, the form of the aid and its method of financing (for example through parafiscal charges or public enterprises). Article 2(2) must, however, also be read in the light of the fact that the Commission is required to initiate the formal investigation procedure if doubts are raised as to the compatibility with the common market of a measure.[49] It is only during the formal investigation procedure that the Commission is expected to be fully **16.25**

45 State Aid Notification Interactive.
46 Implementing Regulation, Article 3(3).
47 ibid, Article 3(4).
48 ibid, Article 4.
49 Case T-357/02 *Freistaat Sachsen v Commission* [2007] ECR II-1261, para 138.

informed of all the details of the case.[50] For that reason, in relation to the preliminary review procedure, the Court has held that it is sufficient if the notification contains enough information to enable the Commission to form a *prima facie* view of the compatibility of the aid with the Treaty, and to decide to initiate the formal investigation procedure in cases of doubt.[51]

16.26 **Third parties.** The Member State does not have to make its notification known to interested parties: this is the task of the Commission where it decides to open the formal investigation procedure.[52]

16.27 **Alteration to initial plans notified to Commission.** If an aid plan initially notified to the Commission is subsequently amended before the Commission takes a decision, the Commission must be informed of the amendments. This will normally take place in the course of the discussions with the Commission following the notification.[53]

16.28 **Withdrawal of notification.** A Member State may withdraw its notification at any time before the Commission takes a decision on the measure. If the Commission has already opened the formal investigation procedure at the time of withdrawal, that procedure must be closed.[54] A notification is also deemed to have been withdrawn if the Member State has not provided information requested by the Commission within the prescribed period, unless before expiry of that period the time-limit has been extended by agreement of both the Commission and the Member State, or the Member State has sent the Commission a reasoned statement explaining that the information requested is not available or has already been provided.[55] If a notification is deemed to be withdrawn on these grounds, the Commission is required to inform the Member State.[56]

C. Preliminary review procedure

16.29 **Preliminary examination of the measure.** The Commission is required to acknowledge receipt of a notification without delay,[57] and examine the notification as soon as it is received.[58] It must take account of all matters brought to its notice, whether

[50] See Case T-95/96 *Gestevision Telecinco v Commission* [1998] ECR II-3407, para 51; Case T-46/97 *SIC v Commission* [2000] ECR II-2125, para 70.

[51] Case C-99/98 *Austria v Commission* [2001] ECR I-1101, paras 52–6; Case T-357/02 *Freistaat Sachsen v Commission* [2007] ECR II-1261, para 139.

[52] Procedural Regulation, Article 6(1) and Cases 91 and 177/83 *Heineken Brouwerijen* [1984] ECR 3435, para 15. See further paras 16.42 and 16.46 below.

[53] Cases 91 and 177/83 *Heineken Brouwerijen*, ibid, paras 17–18.

[54] Procedural Regulation, Article 8.

[55] ibid, Article 5(3).

[56] ibid.

[57] ibid, Article 2(1).

[58] ibid, Article 4(1).

by the Member State itself or other persons concerned by the aid, such as complainants.[59] In particular, where the Member State alleges that the measure is existing aid rather than new aid, the Commission must undertake an adequate examination of that question, so as to be able to reach at least a provisional conclusion.[60] Where the measure is brought to its attention by way of a complaint rather than a notification, the Commission must conduct a 'diligent and impartial' examination of that complaint, which may require it to examine matters not expressly raised by the complainant.[61]

Standstill requirement during procedure. It follows from the standstill clause in Article 88(3) that, throughout the preliminary review procedure, the Member State may not put the planned aid into effect.[62] That is so even where the aid is urgent: the Court has held that the interest of a Member State in a rapid decision is satisfied by the two-month time limit laid down in Article 4(5) of the Procedural Regulation.[63] **16.30**

Rights of Member States. The Commission may not initiate the formal investigation procedure in respect of a measure without discussing its concerns with the Member State which has implemented the measure. Thus in the *Tirrenia* case the Court partially annulled the Commission's decision to open the Article 88(2) procedure, on the grounds that certain measures were included in that decision which had not ever been discussed with the Italian authorities.[64] **16.31**

Rights of third parties (including complainants). Third parties do not enjoy the same rights as Member States in the preliminary review procedure. Rather, the right of a complainant has thus been described as the more limited right to be 'associated' with the preliminary review procedure 'in an adequate manner taking into account the circumstances of the case at issue'.[65] In many cases, the Commission may engage in a dialogue with third parties such as complainants, as part of its duty of sound administration.[66] But it is not under any obligation in general to give third parties an opportunity to state their views, or to conduct an **16.32**

---

59 Case C-204/97 *Portugal v Commission* [2001] ECR I-3175, para 35.

60 Case C-400/99 *Italy v Commission ('Tirrenia')* [2005] ECR I-3657, para 54; and see further para 16.43 below.

61 Case C-367/95 P *Commission v Sytraval and Brink's France* [1998] ECR I-1719, para 62.

62 ibid, para 37.

63 Cases T-239 and 323/04 *Italy and Brandt v Commission* [2007] ECR II-3265, paras 86–9. Note that in exceptional cases the Commission may act very swiftly, eg the decision taken within 24 hours of the notification of the UK's rescue package for Bradford & Bingley: see paras 7.15 and 7.36 above.

64 Case C-400/99 *Italy v Commission ('Tirrenia')* [2005] ECR I-3657, paras 29–34. cf the earlier contrary view adopted in Cases T-195 and 201/01 *Government of Gibraltar v Commission* [2002] ECR II-2309, para 144.

65 Case C-521/06 P *Athinaïki Techniki v Commission* (judgment of 17 July 2008), para 38.

66 Case T-95/03 *Asociación de Estaciones de Servicio v Commission* [2006] ECR II-4739, para 139.

exchange of views and arguments with complainants.[67] Similarly, while in some cases the Commission might send a complainant the comments submitted by the Member State concerned, it is not bound to do so by any principle of 'transparency'.[68] Greater protection is given, however, where a complaint of unlawful or misused aid has been sent to the Commission, and where the Commission considers that 'there are insufficient grounds for taking a view on the case'. In such a case it is required under Article 20(2) of the Procedural Regulation to inform the complainant of this. The Court has recently held that the Commission must then also allow the complainant to submit additional comments within a reasonable period, before it reaches its final decision following the preliminary review procedure.[69]

16.33 **Requests for information.** Where the Commission considers that information provided by the Member State with regard to a notified measure is incomplete, it must request all necessary additional information.[70] If the Member State concerned does not provide the information requested within the period requested, or provides incomplete information, the Commission must send a reminder, allowing an appropriate further period to respond.[71] If the Member State still does not provide the information requested, the notification may be deemed to be withdrawn.[72] As with the notification itself, all correspondence in connection with the notification is now required to be transmitted electronically.[73]

16.34 **Two-month time limit.** The Commission's decision in the preliminary review procedure must be taken within two months from the receipt of a 'complete' notification by the Member State.[74] The purpose of this short time limit is to provide legal certainty by informing the Member State quickly as to the compatibility with the Treaty of a particular aid, and (save where extended as set out below) the time limit is binding on all parties to the preliminary examination procedure.[75]

16.35 **'Complete' notification.** The notification is considered complete if, within two months from its receipt, or from the receipt of any additional information requested, the Commission does not request further information. The period may be extended with the consent of both the Commission and the Member

[67] Case C-367/95 P *Commission v Sytraval and Brink's France* [1998] ECR I-1719, paras 58–9.
[68] Case T-266/94 *Skibsvaerftsforeningen v Commission* [1996] ECR II-1399, para 259.
[69] Case C-521/06 P *Athinaïki Techniki v Commission* (judgment of 17 July 2008), paras 39–40.
[70] Procedural Regulation, Article 5(1).
[71] ibid, Article 5(2).
[72] ibid, Article 5(3): see para 16.28 above.
[73] Implementing Regulation, Article 3(4).
[74] Procedural Regulation, Article 4(5). According to the Commission's statistics, the average duration of the preliminary review procedure following a 'complete' notification is around 1.8 months. However, most notifications are not considered 'complete' and the Commission asks for further information. This increases the average duration of the procedure for notified cases as a whole to 5.2 months: see State Aid Scoreboard, Spring 2008 update, COM(2008) 304 final, pp 41–2.
[75] Cases T-239 and 323/04 *Italy and Brandt v Commission* [2007] ECR II-3265, paras 87–9.

State concerned.[76] However, the Commission may not artificially extend the period by making a trivial request for further information close to the deadline. As discussed above, the notification is sufficient if it contains the information necessary for the Commission to form a *prima facie* view of the compatibility of the aid. If that is provided, the notification must be regarded as complete.[77] This point is illustrated by *Austria v Commission* where the Court annulled a decision to open the Article 88(2) procedure on the grounds that it was taken long after the two-month period had expired.[78] A letter containing a single question on an subsidiary aspect of the plan, and representing less than 2% of the total investment, was held not necessary to enable the Commission to form a *prima facie* opinion on the compatibility of the aid with the Treaty. In reality, the purpose of the letter 'was not to obtain clarification of matters raised in its [earlier] letter, but to gain for the Commission extra time in which to consider other aspects of the plan to grant aid. The additional time which the Commission sought to gain in that way therefore amounted to an artificial extension of the preliminary review phase.'[79]

Shorter time-limits. In appropriate cases, the Commission may fix a shorter time-limit.[80] One example is cases of alterations to existing aid notified on the simplified notification form, where the Commission will use its 'best endeavours' to take a decision within a month.[81] This procedure replaces the 'accelerated clearance' procedure.[82] **16.36**

Decisions following preliminary review. The Commission must take one of three decisions at the end of the preliminary review phase. These are often referred to as Article 4(2), Article 4(3) and Article 4(4) decisions, respectively. First, the Commission may find that the notified measure does not constitute aid.[83] Secondly, it may decide that, insofar as the measure falls within Article 87(1), there is no doubt that the measure is compatible with the common market. This is also referred **16.37**

---

[76] Procedural Regulation, Article 4(5).

[77] Case T-357/02 *Freistaat Sachsen v Commission* [2007] ECR II-1261, para 139.

[78] Case C-99/98 *Austria v Commission* [2001] ECR I-1101; but cf Case T-176/01 *Ferriere Nord v Commission* [2004] ECR II-3931, paras 61–4, upheld on appeal in Case C-49/05 *Ferriere Nord v Commission* (judgment of 8 May 2008) concerning a similar time period for a notification made under the ECSC Treaty.

[79] Case C-99/98 *Austria v Commission*, ibid, paras 61–5. See also Case T-357/02 *Freistaat Sachsen v Commission* [2007] ECR II-1261, paras 140–56, where a notification was found to be complete notwithstanding the fact that further information was subsequently requested by the Commission.

[80] Procedural Regulation, Article 4(5).

[81] Implementing Regulation, Article 4(2).

[82] Case T-357/02 *Freistaat Sachsen v Commission* [2007] ECR II-1261, para 52. The accelerated clearance procedure was formerly set out in the Communication to the Member States on the accelerated clearance of aid schemes for SMEs and of amendments of existing schemes [1992] OJ C213/10.

[83] Procedural Regulation, Article 4(2).

to as a 'decision not to raise objections'.[84] Thirdly the Commission may find that the measure raises doubts as its compatibility with the common market (which may include cases where the Commission has doubts as to the classification of the measure as aid).[85] In that case it must initiate the formal investigation procedure.[86] In the 2000–2006 period, only 5% of notified aid proceeded to the formal investigation procedure, with the vast majority of cases being dealt with by a decision following the preliminary review procedure only.[87] Whichever decision is adopted, it must be addressed to the Member State concerned and notified to that State without delay.[88]

16.38 **Deemed authorization of notified aid.** Where an aid has been notified, and the Commission has not taken any decision at the end of the two-month period, it is deemed to have authorized the aid, and the measure thereafter constitutes existing aid.[89] The Member State concerned may then implement the measure in question, after giving the Commission prior notice,[90] unless the Commission takes a decision on the measure within 15 working days after receiving the notice,[91] and communicates the decision to the Member State concerned.[92] A mere objection to the implementation of the aid is not sufficient to prevent deemed authorization: if the Commission has concerns about the measure, it must initiate the formal investigation procedure.[93]

16.39 **Application of the 15-day rule.** The *Commission v Spain* case gives a good example of the application of the 15-day rule in Article 4(6) of the Procedural Regulation.[94] The Spanish government had notified several measures in 1999, following which the Commission requested further information. That information was provided on 24 May 2000, whereupon the Commission fell silent. It was not contested that the two-month time limit expired without interruption, so that from 25 July 2000

---

84 ibid, Article 4(3).

85 Case C-400/99 *Italy v Commission ('Tirrenia')* [2005] ECR I-3657, para 47.

86 Procedural Regulation, Article 4(4).

87 Commission's State Aid Scoreboard, spring 2007 update, COM(2007) 347 final, p 4. The figure was much higher for unlawful aid, with around 40% of cases going to the formal investigation procedure. See also Spring 2008 update, COM(2008) 304 final, pp 37–8, giving similar figures for the decisions taken during 2007.

88 Procedural Regulation, Article 25.

89 Procedural Regulation, Articles 1(b)(iii) and 4(6), which codify the principle established in Case 120/73 *Lorenz* [1973] ECR 1471, paras 4–5. Aid authorized pursuant to this procedure became known as 'Lorenz aid'.

90 If it does not do so, the aid measure may be treated as unnotified new aid: Case C-278/00 *Greece v Commission* [2004] ECR I-3997, paras 31–3.

91 Procedural Regulation, Article 4(6).

92 Case C-398/00 *Spain v Commission* [2002] ECR I-5643, paras 28–35.

93 See Case C-99/98 *Austria v Commission* [2001] ECR I-1101, paras 84–6.

94 Case C-398/00 *Spain v Commission* [2002] ECR I-5643.

it was open to the Spanish authorities to implement the measure, subject to giving notice to the Commission. That notice was sent in a fax at 17.49 on Friday 28 July 2000. On 17 August 2000 the Commission adopted a decision to initiate the formal investigation procedure, and that decision was notified to the Spanish government by letter dated 22 August 2000, received the following day on 23 August 2000. The Court held that the period of 15 working days in Article 4(6) of the Procedural Regulation started running the working day after the fax was received, ie 31 July 2000. The period therefore expired on 21 August 2000.[95] Although the decision to open the Article 88(2) procedure had already been taken by that date, the decision could not take effect until it became enforceable against the Member State, which was at the time of its notification. Accordingly, since the decision was not received by the Spanish authorities until 23 August 2000 it fell outside the period of 15 working days, and was annulled on that ground alone.[96] It is to be expected, however, that errors of this nature are less likely to arise following the new rules on electronic transmission of documents,[97] and the consequent streamlining of the State aid procedure.

Limited scope of the preliminary review procedure. The Court has consistently held that the preliminary review procedure under Article 88(3) EC is intended merely to allow the Commission to form a *prima facie* view of the measure.[98] This applies equally to the more detailed rules of the preliminary review procedure now set out in Article 4 of the Procedural Regulation. The Commission is therefore only entitled to close the case after a preliminary review if it can reach a firm view that the measure is not aid, or is compatible with the common market, without requiring a detailed examination of the matter. If the Commission considers that the measure does constitute incompatible aid, or has serious difficulties in determining whether the measure is compatible with the common market, it must open the formal investigation procedure.[99] This is a strict legal requirement, in respect of which the Commission has no discretion: once it encounters serious difficulties, the Commission must initiate the formal procedure, and may not decline to do so on the grounds of third party interests, considerations of **16.40**

[95] ibid, paras 23–7.

[96] ibid, paras 28–35.

[97] Implementing Regulation, Article 3(4).

[98] Case 84/82 *Commission v Germany* [1984] ECR 1451, para 11; Case C-367/95 P *Commission v Sytraval and Brink's France* [1998] ECR I-1719, para 38; Case C-204/97 *Portugal v Commission* [2001] ECR I-3175, para 32.

[99] *Commission v Germany*, ibid, para 13; *Commission v Sytraval and Brink's France*, ibid, para 39; *Portugal v Commission*, ibid, para 33; Case C-521/06 P *Athinaïki Techniki v Commission* (judgment of 17 July 2008), para 34.

procedural economy or any other ground of administrative convenience.[100] Failure to initiate the formal investigation procedure, when the circumstances indicate that the Commission should have done so, will render its decision liable to annulment, particularly by complainants aggrieved at the clearance of the aid in this preliminary phase.[101]

16.41 **Indicators of 'serious difficulties'**. The existence of serious difficulties must be determined on an objective basis,[102] though the Commission maintains a certain margin of discretion in identifying and evaluating the circumstances of the case to determine whether or not they present serious difficulties.[103] A good indicator is the extent of discussion required with the Member State following the notification. It is normal for contact to take place between the Member State and the Commission following notification of an aid, and for further information to be submitted concerning the measure. Such contacts do not themselves imply that the formal investigation procedure should be opened.[104] However, if extensive discussions with the Member State are required before the approval of aid, or if the time spent on the preliminary review far exceeds the time normally spent, this indicates that the preliminary review procedure is not appropriate.[105] The extension of the preliminary review procedure due to the Member State's delay in providing information requested,[106] and the absence of complete information necessary to assess the measure,[107] are also indicators of the existence of serious difficulties in assessing the measure. However, the size of an investment or aid scheme cannot in itself constitute a serious difficulty.[108]

---

[100] Case T-73/98 *Société Chimique Prayon-Rupel v Commission* [2001] ECR II-867, paras 44–5; and see Case T-95/03 *Asociación de Estaciones de Servicio v Commission* [2006] ECR II-4739, para 139.

[101] See eg Case T-46/97 *SIC v Commission* [2000] ECR II-2125; Case C-204/97 *Portugal v Commission* [2001] ECR I-3175; *Société Chimique Prayon-Rupel v Commission*, ibid.

[102] Case T-49/93 *SIDE v Commission* [1995] ECR II-2501, para 60; Case T-73/98 *Société Chimique Prayon-Rupel v Commission*, ibid, para 48.

[103] Case T-95/03 *Asociación de Estaciones de Servicio v Commission* [2006] ECR II-4739, para 139.

[104] See AG Van Gerven in Case C-225/91 *Matra v Commission* [1993] ECR I-3203, opinion paras 42–4.

[105] See Case 84/82 *Commission v Germany* [1984] ECR 1451, paras 14–15 (extensive bilateral negotiations between Belgian government, substantial amendments to original plan and 16-month period between notification and favourable decision); Case T-46/97 *SIC v Commission* [2000] ECR II-2125 (decision adopted more than 39 months after the first complaint, and nearly 33 months after the complaint had been finalized); Case T-73/98 *Société Chimique Prayon-Rupel v Commission* [2001] ECR II-867, para 107 (at least eight months between notification and decision, during which the Commission was forced to make three separate official requests for information, and delays by the Member State in providing information required). Each case will, however turn on its own facts and the mere fact of an excessively long procedure may not of itself suffice to show serious difficulties: see Case T-95/03 *Asociación de Estaciones de Servicio v Commission* [2006] ECR II-4739, paras 133–42.

[106] *Société Chimique Prayon-Rupel v Commission*, ibid, para 100.

[107] Case C-198/91 *William Cook v Commission* [1993] ECR I-2487, paras 35–8; Case T-49/93 *SIDE v Commission* [1995] ECR II-2501, paras 67–9, 75.

[108] Case C-225/91 *Matra v Commission* [1993] ECR I-3203, para 36.

D. Formal investigation procedure

1. Opening the procedure

Decision opening the procedure. The decision to initiate the formal investigation procedure must summarize the relevant issues of fact and law, including a preliminary assessment as to the aid character of the proposed measure, and the Commission's doubts as to its compatibility with the common market. The decision must also invite the Member State concerned and interested parties to submit comments within a prescribed period, usually no longer than a month.[109] Notwithstanding its preliminary nature, the decision constitutes a formal 'decision' within the meaning of Article 249 EC.[110] The full text of the decision in its authentic language version is published in the Official Journal (OJ), accompanied (where necessary) by a summary in the language of that OJ.[111] **16.42**

Legal consequences of decision opening procedure. The decision initiating the formal procedure under Article 88(2) has different consequences according to whether the Commission has decided that the aid is new or existing aid. The importance of this was considered in *Tirrenia*, where the Commission initiated the formal investigation procedure in relation to Italian aid for ferry services operated by the Tirrenia group. The Italian authorities applied for partial annulment of the decision. In an interlocutory judgment in 2001, the Court held that the application was admissible, contrary to the submissions of the Commission. It pointed out that where the measure is new aid, the Member State is under a continuing obligation under Article 88(3) EC and Article 3 of the Procedural Regulation not to implement the measure before it is approved. However, where the Commission initiates the Article 88(2) procedure on the basis that the measure is existing aid which it wishes to re-examine, the Member State is not under any obligation to suspend the measure, and the Commission cannot require it to do so. Thus where a Member State regards a measure as existing aid, but the Commission opens the Article 88(2) procedure with the provisional classification of the measure as new aid, that decision has independent legal effects despite the provisional nature of the Commission's conclusions. In particular, it entails legal and commercial uncertainty for the aid beneficiaries and businesses dealing with those undertakings, as well as raising the possibility of proceedings in the national **16.43**

---

[109] Procedural Regulation, Articles 6(1) and 88(2) EC. See further para 16.46 below on the notice requirement.

[110] Cases T-195 and 207/01 *Government of Gibraltar* [2002] ECR II-2309, para 74.

[111] Procedural Regulation, Article 2(2).

courts for infringement of Article 88(3). For these reasons, Court held that the decision could legitimately be the subject of an application for annulment.[112]

16.44 **Legitimate expectations arising from decision opening procedure.** The Member State and interested parties may have legitimate expectations on the basis of the decision initiating the procedure, which the Commission must take into account in the formal investigation procedure. The Commission may not, therefore, base its decision in matters which, in the light of the decision initiating the procedure, the parties were not aware they should address.[113] For the same reason, if the Commission proposes to rely on new guidelines which have been adopted since the initiation of the formal investigation procedure, which will alter its analysis of the aid, and on which the Member State concerned and interested parties have not had the opportunity to comment, it must re-open the consultation procedure on that point.[114]

16.45 **Purpose of procedure.** The aim of the formal investigation procedure, by contrast with the preliminary review procedure, is twofold. First, it is designed to enable the Commission to be fully informed of all the facts of the case by carrying out consultations before reaching its final decision. Secondly, the procedure is intended to protect the rights of potentially interested third parties by allowing them to make their views known.[115] For this reason, the procedure for consultation, set out in the following paragraphs, is a particularly important part of the obligations on the Commission in the formal investigation of a State aid.

16.46 **Notice to submit comments.** As noted above,[116] the Commission is required to give notice to 'interested parties' (or, in the words of Article 88(2), 'parties concerned') to submit comments, which it does in the decision opening the procedure. This does not require the Commission to give individual notice to particular persons, such as the aid beneficiaries.[117] *A fortiori*, the Commission cannot be held responsible for the failure by the relevant Member State to send the aid recipients a copy

---

[112] Case C-400/99 *Italy v Commission ('Tirrenia' - admissibility)* [2001] ECR I-7303, paras 45–65. (In the substantive judgment, reported at [2005] ECR I-3657, the Court did indeed annul the decision in part: see para 16.31 above.) This ruling was followed by the CFI in Cases T-195 and 207/01 *Government of Gibraltar* [2002] ECR II-2309, paras 68–88, despite the Commission's attempt to distinguish the *Tirrenia* case on the grounds that (*inter alia*) it had required suspension of the aid, whereas no such requirement was imposed in the *Gibraltar* decision.

[113] See Case T-176/01 *Ferriere Nord v Commission* [2004] ECR II-3931, para 88, upheld on appeal in Case C-49/05 *Ferriere Nord v Commission* (judgment of 8 May 2008).

[114] Case T-176/01 *Ferriere Nord v Commission*, ibid, paras 75–81 (though finding that on the facts of case the Commission had not derived any new principles or criteria from the new guidelines, so there was no failure to consult).

[115] See Case T-171/02 *Regione autonoma della Sardegna v Commission* [2005] ECR II-2123, para 32.

[116] At para 16.42.

[117] See Case 323/82 *Intermills v Commission* [1984] ECR 3809 para 17; Case T-354/99 *Kuwait Petroleum v Commission* [2006] ECR II-1475, paras 81–2.

of the letter initiating the Article 88(2) procedure.[118] The Commission must, nevertheless, set out its concerns in the decision opening the Article 88(2) procedure in sufficient detail that the interested parties can comment properly during the formal investigation procedure.[119] This is particularly important where the identity of the aid beneficiaries is in doubt. Thus in *EURL Le Levant 001*, the Court emphasized that in order for aid recipients to be able to exercise their rights of defence, the beneficiaries of aid must be identified in the decision or (at the very least) at a later stage in the procedure, prior to the adoption of the final decision:

> The identification of the beneficiary of the aid is necessarily one of the 'relevant issues of fact and law' within the meaning of the first sentence of Article 6(1) of Regulation No 659/1999 which must, under that provision, be contained in the decision to open the procedure if that is possible at that stage of the procedure, since it is on the basis of that identification that the Commission will be able to adopt the recovery decision.
>
> In the absence of an indication that a party is a beneficiary of the aid in dispute, either in the decision to open the procedure or at a later stage in the formal investigation procedure prior to adoption of the final decision finding that the aid is incompatible with the common market, that type of interested party cannot be regarded as having been duly called on to submit his comments, because he may legitimately believe that such comments are not necessary, since he is not named as the beneficiary of the aid to be recovered. [120]

In that case, the decision opening the Article 88(2) had given the impression that the only beneficiary of an investment aid was the operator of the cruise vessel in which the investment was made. By contrast, the final negative decision referred to the investors as the direct beneficiaries, and ordered recovery of the aid from those investors. The Court held that this infringed Article 88(2) and Article 6(1) of the Procedural Regulation.[121]

Interested parties. The 'interested parties' entitled to submit comments are defined in the Procedural Regulation as 'any Member State and any person, undertaking or association of undertakings whose interests might be affected by the granting of aid, in particular the beneficiary of the aid, competing undertakings and trade associations'.[122] This codifies the principle set out in the *Intermills* case[123] and followed in numerous subsequent judgments. The question has arisen, however, as to the interpretation of the words 'in particular'. While it is clear that the **16.47**

[118] Case T-109/01 *Fleuren Compost v Commission* [2004] ECR II-127, para 47.

[119] Case T-354/99 *Kuwait Petroleum v Commission* [2006] ECR II-1475, para 83.

[120] Case T-34/02 *EURL Le Levant 001 v Commission* [2006] ECR II-267, paras 82–3.

[121] ibid, paras 77–98. cf Case T-354/99 *Kuwait Petroleum v Commission* [2006] ECR II-1475, paras 83–9, where the decision opening the Article 88(2) procedure did provide sufficient information for the applicant oil companies to submit their comments.

[122] Procedural Regulation, Article 1(h).

[123] Case 323/82 *Intermills v Commission* [1984] ECR 3809, para 16.

reference to the aid beneficiary and competing undertakings or associations is not intended to be exhaustive, the interests of undertakings falling outside these categories may need to be carefully examined. The Court has applied the criterion of whether the aid affects the undertaking's competitive position on the market. It is therefore not sufficient that the undertaking simply pays taxes which are used to finance the contested measure.[124] 'Interested parties' is also relevant to the issue of standing to bring proceedings in the European Cout. This is considered further in Chapter 17 below, to which further reference should be made.

2. The Commission's investigation

16.48 **Diligent examination of facts.** The Commission must conduct a diligent and impartial examination of the case.[125] This involves in particular carrying out an appropriate examination into the facts of the case, resolving any contradictions which it may uncover.[126] The Commission is entitled to engage outside consultants,[127] and a failure to obtain an expert report has been criticized by the CFI where it would have been particularly useful because of the inherent uncertainty involved in a specific crucial determination, such as that of the market value of real estate.[128]

16.49 **Rights of third parties (including complainants).** As with the preliminary review procedure,[129] a distinction is drawn between the position of the Member State which has implemented the contested measure, and the position of interested third parties. The Court has underlined that the procedure for reviewing State aid is a procedure initiated in respect of the Member State responsible for the aid.[130] Therefore, while third parties have the right to submit comments on the measure, and are a source of information for the Commission,[131] the Commission is not required to conduct an exchange of views with third parties;[132] nor is it required to give third parties access to its file, or copies of the comments submitted by other

[124] Case T-188/95 *Waterleiding Maatschappij 'Noord-West Brabant' v Commission* [1998] ECR II-3713, paras 67–8.

[125] Case C-367/95 P *Commission v Sytraval and Brink's France ('Sytraval')* [1998] ECR I-1719, para 62; Cases T-228 and 233/99 *Westdeutsche Landesbank v Commission* [2003] ECR II-435, paras 167–8; and Case T-266/02 *Deutsche Post v Commission* (judgment of 1 July 2008), para 92 (annulling a decision for overlooking detailed information provided by the German government).

[126] Case T-366/00 *Scott v Commission* [2007] ECR II-797, para 136.

[127] Case T-106/95 *FFSA v Commission* [1997] ECR II-229, para 102, and Cases T-371/94 and T-394/94 *British Airways and British Midland Airways v Commission* [1998] ECR II-2405, para 72.

[128] Case T-366/00 *Scott v Commission* [2007] ECR II-797, para 137.

[129] See paras 16.31–16.32 above.

[130] Cases C-74-75/00 P *Falck and Acciaierie di Bolzano v Commission* [2002] ECR I-7869, para 81; Case T-109/01 *Fleuren Compost v Commission* [2004] ECR II-127, para 42; Case T-198/01 *Technische Glaswerke Ilmenau v Commission* [2004] ECR II-2717, para 191.

[131] *Technische Glaswerke Ilmenau v Commission*, ibid, para 192 and the case-law there cited.

[132] See Case C-367/95 P *Commission v Sytraval and Brink's France* [1998] ECR I-171, para 59; Case T-109/01 *Fleuren Compost v Commission* [2004] ECR II-127, para 43.

parties to the procedure.[133] This even applies to the beneficiary of the aid, which is not regarded as having rights of defence as such, on the grounds that the State aid procedure is not initiated 'against' the recipient of the aid.[134] The beneficiary of aid is thus in the same position as other third parties in this respect.[135] The same is true of a local authority which has granted the aid: it is considered only to be an interested party in the procedure.[136] Nevertheless, the Commission cannot assume that there is an identity of interest between the Member State and the recipient of aid, in particular with regard to the calculation of the value of aid to be recovered.[137] Moreover, the Commission may in certain circumstances be obliged to take into account the observations of the aid beneficiary even after the expiry of the time laid down by the decision to open the procedure.[138]

Rights of the Member State concerned. The rights of the Member States concerned by a formal investigation procedure are more extensive, consistent with the fact that it is the party directly engaged by the investigation. As far as the Member State implementing the measure is concerned, the procedure is referred to as an 'adversarial' procedure.[139] In accordance with the rights of defence in such a procedure, which requires in particular a fair hearing, Article 6(2) of the Procedural Regulation requires that the comments received by third parties must be submitted to the Member State concerned, so that it may make its views known on those observations. Insofar as the Member State is not given the opportunity to comment on specific allegations, these may not be incorporated by the Commission in a decision against that State.[140] If this principle is infringed, it will lead to the annulment of the decision where the Member State can show that, but for the infringement of its procedural rights, the outcome of the procedure might have been different.[141] These obligations of consultation do not, however, require the Commission to inform the Member State concerned—or, *a fortiori*, third parties—of its position on the legal assessment of the aid before adopting the decision.[142] **16.50**

[133] Case T-198/01 *Technische Glaswerke Ilmenau v Commission* [2004] ECR II-2717, para 197.

[134] Cases C-74–75/00 P *Falck and Acciaierie di Bolzano v Commission* [2002] ECR I-7869, para 83; Case T-109/01 *Fleuren Compost v Commission* [2004] ECR II-127, para 44; *Technische Glaswerke Ilmenau v Commission*, ibid, paras 193–4.

[135] *Technische Glaswerke Ilmenau v Commission*, ibid, para 195.

[136] Cases T-228 and 233/99 *Westdeutsche Landesbank v Commission* [2003] ECR II-435, para 122.

[137] Case T-366/00 *Scott v Commission* [2007] ECR II-797, para 59.

[138] *Scott v Commission*, ibid, para 56; Case T-34/02 *EURL Le Levant 001 v Commission* [2006] ECR II-267, para 96.

[139] Case T-198/01 *Technische Glaswerke Ilmenau v Commission* [2004] ECR II-2717, para 197.

[140] *Technische Glaswerke Ilmenau v Commission*, ibid, para 201.

[141] Case 234/84 *Belgium v Commission* [1986] ECR 2263, paras 27–30; Case 40/85 *Belgium v Commission* [1986] ECR 2321, paras 28–31; Case 259/85 *France v Commission* [1987] ECR 4393, paras 12–13.

[142] See Case T-198/01 *Technische Glaswerke Ilmenau v Commission* [2004] ECR II-2717, para 198.

16.51 **Responsibility to provide information.** It is the responsibility of the Member State and the aid beneficiary (or potential beneficiary) to ensure that the Commission is fully informed of the facts of the case. In particular, they must put forward any arguments which suggest that the aid falls within one of the exceptions provided in the Treaty and is therefore compatible with the common market.[143] The Commission does not have an obligation to consider of its own motion what should have been submitted to it;[144] in particular, it is not required to consider of its own motion whether aid might benefit from a derogation in Article 87(2) or (3), if this has not been raised by the Member State concerned.[145]

16.52 **Requests for information.** The Commission has the same powers to request information as it does in relation to the preliminary review procedure.[146] Indeed, in some cases failure to do so may be fatal to the Commission's decision. In its recent *SIC* judgment the CFI partially annulled a Commission decision for failure to require a Member State to disclose contractual external audit reports, in order to verify the accuracy of other reports that were not systematically accompanied by an audit statement, and whose reliability was therefore in doubt.[147]

16.53 **Length of investigation.** It is a general principle of Community law that an administrative procedure should be of reasonable duration. The fundamental requirement of legal certainty also precludes the Commission from postponing the exercise of its powers indefinitely. These principles apply as much to a State aid procedure as to other types of Commission procedure.[148] In addition to these general principles, the Procedural Regulation contains the specific requirement that the Commission must take its decision as soon as its doubts as to the compatibility of the measure have been removed. Furthermore, it must 'endeavour' to adopt a decision within an indicative period of 18 months from the opening of the formal investigation procedure, which may be extended by agreement between the Commission and the Member State concerned.[149] That 18-month period is, however, 'an objective to be observed and not a mandatory time-limit'.[150] It is therefore necessary to consider on the facts of each case whether the Commission has failed to act within a reasonable time. In that respect, the Court has held that

[143] Case T-176/01 *Ferriere Nord v Commission* [2004] ECR II-3931, paras 93–4, upheld on appeal in Case C-49/05 *Ferriere Nord v Commission* (judgment of 8 May 2008).

[144] Case T-109/01 *Fleuren Compost v Commission* [2004] ECR II-127, para 49.

[145] See Case C-261/89 *Italy v Commission* [1991] ECR I-4437, para 23.

[146] See para 16.33 above.

[147] Case T-442/03 *SIC v Commission* (judgment of 26 June 2008), para 225 and paras 232–56.

[148] See Case T-171/02 *Regione autonoma della Sardegna v Commission* [2005] ECR I-2123, para 53; and Case T-190/00 *Regione Siciliana v Commission* [2003] ECR II-5015, para 136.

[149] Procedural Regulation, Article 7(6).

[150] Case T-190/00 *Regione Siciliana v Commission* [2003] ECR II-5015, para 139; see also Case C-49/05 *Ferriere Nord v Commission* (judgment of 8 May 2008), paras 48–51.

a period of 22 months does not unreasonably exceed that time limit.[151] In another case, where a long procedure was attributable mainly to the delays of the Member State concerned in providing its comments and information requested by the Commission, the Court held that a total period of 33½ months was not an excessively long time.[152] Once the 18-month time period (plus any agreed extension) has expired, the Member State may call upon the Commission to take a decision on the basis of the information available to it. In such a case the decision must be taken within two months. If the information is not sufficient to establish the compatibility of the aid, the decision will be a negative one.[153]

Excessive haste not in itself a procedural error. At the other extreme, the Commission cannot be criticized for acting with excessive haste: the particularly speedy adoption of a decision cannot, by itself, justify annulment of the decision. A claim for annulment might lie, however, if the Commission's undue haste caused it to breach procedural rules, or to adopt a decision containing errors of law or inadequate reasoning.[154] **16.54**

Examination of aid schemes. In the case of an aid scheme under which individual aids are granted, the Commission is generally not in a position to identify exactly the amount of aid received by individual recipients. For that reason, it is not required to examine each particular case in which the regime applies, but is entitled to confine its examination to the characteristics of the programme in order to determine whether it amounts to aid.[155] The specific circumstances of individual recipients can be assessed at the stage of recovery.[156] **16.55**

3. The final decision

Decisions to close the formal investigation procedure. The formal investigation procedure may be closed by one of four formal decisions: a no-aid decision, a positive **16.56**

[151] *Regione Siciliana*, ibid, para 139; *Ferriere Nord*, ibid, para 51.

[152] Case T-171/02 *Regione autonoma della Sardegna v Commission* [2005] ECR II-2123, paras 57–60. See however press release EO/08/2 concerning the intervention of the European Ombudsman in a case where the Commission took almost seven years to adopt a new decision on aid to the Sardinian shipping sector, after its original decision was annulled in Cases C-15/98 and C-105/99 *Italy and Sardegna Lines v Commission* [2000] ECR I-8855. The new decision was finally adopted in July 2007: Decision 2008/92/EC *Aid to the Sardinian shipping sector* [2008] OJ L29/24.

[153] Procedural Regulation, Article 7(7).

[154] See Cases T-371 and 394/94 *British Airways and British Midland Airways v Commission* [1998] ECR II-2405, para 71.

[155] Case C-75/97 *Belgium v Commission* [1999] ECR I-3671, para 48; Case C-310/99 *Italy v Commission* [2002] ECR I-2289, paras 89–91; Case C-278/00 *Greece v Commission* [2004] ECR I-3997, para 24; Cases C-182 and 217/03 *Belgium and Forum 187 v Commission* [2006] ECR I-5479, para 82; Case T-354/99 *Kuwait Petroleum v Commission* [2006] ECR II-1475, para 67.

[156] *Italy v Commission*, ibid, para 91; *Kuwait Petroleum v Commission*, ibid, para 67.

decision, a conditional decision or a negative decision.[157] As with a decision following the preliminary review procedure, the final decision must be addressed to the Member State concerned and notified to it without delay.[158] On occasion, however, the procedure may be closed without a formal decision, where the procedure has become devoid of purpose.

16.57 **'No aid' and positive decisions.** There are two types of decision approving the aid unconditionally. First, the Commission may find that the measure does not constitute aid, on the basis that the conditions in Article 87(1) are not satisfied by the measure.[159] Secondly, it may find that the measure is aid, but is compatible with the common market. This is referred to as a 'positive decision'.[160]

16.58 **Conditional decision.** The third type of decision is where the Commission considers the measure compatible with the common market only on certain conditions. In that case it may also set out obligations to enable compliance with those conditions to be monitored. This is referred to as a 'conditional decision'.[161] The conditions may include, for example, the requirement to implement an agreed restructuring plan.[162]

16.59 ***Deggendorf* condition.** Another common condition is based on the so-called *Deggendorf* principle, whereby the Commission may require the Member State to recover from an undertaking aid previously declared to be unlawful, before new aid is paid to the same company.[163] The Commission now routinely requests a commitment from the Member State to suspend the payment of new aid to any beneficiary that still has at its disposal an earlier unlawful aid that was declared incompatible by a Commission decision.[164] In the absence of such a commitment, the suspension of such aid will be incorporated as a condition in any final compatibility decision.[165] The Commission intends to integrate this principle into all future State aid rules and decisions.[166]

---

157 Procedural Regulation, Article 7(1).

158 ibid, Article 25.

159 ibid, Article 7(2).

160 ibid, Article 7(3).

161 ibid, Article 7(4).

162 See eg Case T-349/03 *Corsica Ferries France v Commission* [2005] ECR II-2197.

163 Cases T-244 and 486/93 *Textilwerke Deggendorf ('TWD') v Commission* [1995] ECR II-2265, paras 53–60. The *Deggendorf* principle has been extended by the Commission in recent years to cover cases where the beneficiary of new aid belongs to the same 'economic unit' as the beneficiary of the old aid: Decision 2006/598/EC *Reduction of greenhouse gas emissions (Lazio)* [2006] OJ L244/8; appeal pending in Case T-303/05 *AceaElectrabel v Commission*.

164 See Part I, point 11 of the standard new aid notification form annexed to the Implementing Regulation.

165 See eg Decision 2006/941/EC *AEM Torino* [2006] OJ L366/62.

166 Recovery Notice paras 76–7.

Non-compliance with conditions: aid already paid. Any aid paid contrary to the stipulated conditions may (depending on the circumstances) trigger the procedure for misuse of aid,[167] or may lead the Commission to open a formal investigation into new aid.[168] The Commission will also be entitled to bring infringement proceedings directly before the Court pursuant to Article 88(2) EC and Article 23 of the Procedural Regulation.[169] **16.60**

Non-compliance with conditions: aid still payable. The issue of a failure to comply with the conditions for a future payment of aid was considered in the *Aer Lingus* case.[170] The Commission had approved aid to be paid to the Aer Lingus group in three tranches, subject to a number of conditions. Prior to the payment of the second tranche, it was established that the conditions for that payment were not met. The Commission granted a derogation from its earlier decision and approved the second payment, without opening the formal Article 88(2) procedure. That decision was challenged by Ryanair. The Court held that failure to comply with the conditions in a conditional decision leads to a presumption that further payment of aid is incompatible with the common market. The aid must therefore be suspended until adoption of a decision by the Commission granting a formal derogation from the condition in question. If the deviation from its original decision is relatively minor, and the Commission has no doubts as to whether the aid is still compatible with the common market, the Commission may vary its decision on the basis of the preliminary review procedure. This might be the case in particular where the approved aid is to be paid in tranches over a relatively long period of time. In such a case the Commission should have a power to manage and monitor the implementation of the aid and deal with unforeseeable developments without reopening the Article 88(2) procedure. However where the derogation from its original decision is not minor, or where the variation would give rise to doubts as to the compatibility of the aid, the Commission must reopen the formal Article 88(2) procedure before departing from its original decision.[171] **16.61**

Negative decision. Finally, the Commission may adopt a 'negative decision' finding that the aid is not compatible with the common market and may not be put into effect.[172] A negative decision ordering the abolition or alteration of aid must specify precisely the aspects of aid regarded as incompatible.[173] **16.62**

---

167 See para 16.69 *et seq* below.

168 See Case C-294/90 *BAe and Rover v Commission* [1992] ECR I-493, para 13.

169 ie without being required to comply with the preconditions of Article 226 EC: see further Chapter 17 below.

170 Case T-140/95 *Ryanair v Commission ('Aer Lingus')* [1998] ECR II-3327.

171 ibid, paras 85–90. The Court went on to find that on the facts the Commission was entitled to vary its decision without reopening the Article 88(2) procedure.

172 Procedural Regulation, Article 7(5).

173 Case 70/72 *Commission v Germany* [1973] ECR 813, paras 20–1.

16.63 **Time limit for compliance.** A Member State should be given a period for compliance with the decision where the repayment of an unlawful aid or the abolition of an existing aid is concerned. These situations are discussed below.[174] In the case of new aid (whether notified or unnotified) that has not yet been implemented, it is not strictly necessary to specify a time period, since the measure simply cannot be put into effect.[175] For this reason, most earlier Commission decisions of this type did not contain a time period for compliance. More recently, however, the Commission has adopted the practice of specifying a period of two months within which the Member State must inform the Commission of the measures taken to comply with it (see also para 16.93 below on the time limits for compliance with recover decisions).

16.64 **Case closure without formal decision.** The formal investigation procedure may also be terminated without a decision, where continuing the procedure serves no useful purpose. That will be the case where the measure the subject of the investigation has been discontinued or withdrawn.[176] This also occurred where during the course of the formal investigation procedure the aid recipient ceased all economic activities, and its capital was transferred to the State free of charge. The Commission noted that in those circumstances a decision on the classification of the measures as aid, and their compatibility, would have no practical effect.[177]

4. Revocation and annulment

16.65 **Revocation under the Procedural Regulation.** A positive decision (whether taken following the preliminary review procedure, or following the formal investigation procedure) finding that the notified measure does not constitute aid, or that the measure is compatible with the common market, or that the measure is compatible subject to certain conditions, may be revoked by the Commission under Article 9 of the Procedural Regulation. Revocation is only possible where the decision was based on incorrect information provided during the investigation, which was a determining factor for the decision. Before revoking the decision the Commission must open the formal investigation procedure and give the Member State concerned the opportunity to submit its comments. In such a case most of the special provisions applicable to unlawful aid also apply, namely the powers to adopt an information injunction and to order interim suspension of the aid, and the power to recover aid already granted.

---

[174] See paras 16.93 (recovery of unlawful aid) and 16.126 (existing aids).

[175] Case 173/73 *Italy v Commission* [1974] ECR 709, paras 7–9.

[176] eg Decision 2006/743/EC *AZ and AZ Vastgoed* [2006] OJ L307/194; in similar vein see the Decision in Case C 25/2006 *Guidelines on national regional aid for 2007-13 – appropriate measures – Germany* [2006] OJ C320/16, where Germany initially failed fully to accept the regional aid measures proposed by the Commission, but subsequently did so following the opening of the formal investigation procedure.

[177] Decision 2006/238/EC *Mines de potasse d'Alsace* [2006] OJ L86/20, paras 16–17.

Revocation under general principles of law. A negative decision may not be revoked under Article 9 of the Procedural Regulation.[178] But the Commission's right to revoke a decision is not restricted to the situations referred to in Article 9. Rather, the Court has held that this provision is merely a specific expression of the general principle of law which allows retrospective withdrawal of an unlawful administrative act which has created subjective rights. That right exists in particular if the act was adopted on the basis of false or incomplete information provided by the party concerned, but the act may also be revoked in other situations provided that the institution which adopted the act complies with reasonable time limits, and respects the legitimate expectations of the beneficiaries of the act.[179] **16.66**

Examples of revocation. The power to revoke a decision was used in the *Verlipack* case, where the initial decision cleared a capital injection on the basis that it was consistent with the actions of a provider of risk capital operating under normal market conditions. That assessment was based, in particular, upon a simultaneous investment by a private company, Heye. Following complaints to the Commission, it later discovered that the 'private' investment in fact originated from public loans to Heye. The Commission therefore initiated the Article 88(2) procedure, following which it revoked its original decision and found the capital injection to constitute State aid incompatible with the common market.[180] In *González y Díez* the Court also upheld the partial revocation of a negative Commission decision, and its replacement with a new decision declaring parts of the aid to be compatible with the common market.[181] On the other hand, the revocation procedure cannot be used to amend a decision on the basis of new facts which have come to light since the decision was taken. The Commission therefore rejected an attempt by Germany to use the procedure to obtain approval for an increased aid intensity for aid to the timber company Kronoply, based on a new study on the development of the relevant market.[182] **16.67**

Procedure following annulment. If a Commission decision taken on the basis of Article 88(2) is annulled by the European Court, the Commission is required under Article 233 to take the necessary measures to comply with the judgment. This requires the Commission to take account not only of the *dispositif* of the **16.68**

[178] Case T-25/04 *González y Díez v Commission* [2007] ECR II-3121, para 96.

[179] ibid, para 97. Presumably the correct course would be to submit a fresh notification.

[180] Decision 2001/856/EC *Verlipack* [2001] OJ L320/28. The decision was subsequently upheld by the Court in Case C-457/00 *Belgium v Commission ('Verlipack')* [2003] ECR I-6931.

[181] Case T-25/04 *González y Díez v Commission* (judgment of 12 September 2007), rejecting arguments of procedural flaws, but annulling one part of the second decision on the grounds of manifest error of assessment.

[182] See Case T-130/02 *Kronoply v Commission* [2003] ECR II-4857, rejecting as inadmissible Kronoply's application to annul the Commission's refusal to revoke its earlier decision. An attempt to achieve the same result by a renotification of the measure was also unsuccessful: Decision 2006/262/EC *Kronoply* [2006] OJ L94/50.

judgment, but also the relevant reasoning of the Court.[183] The Commission may, depending on the facts of the case, be able to take a fresh decision based on the same information without going through the entire Article 88(2) procedure again, and without further consultation with the Member State.[184] In other cases, however, it will not be possible to take a new decision without opening (or reopening) the Article 88(2) procedure. That will obviously be the case where a favourable decision has been annulled for failure to initiate the Article 88(2) procedure; it is also likely to be the case where a favourable decision has resulted from a misapplication of Article 87(1),[185] or an error in the assessment of the compatibility of aid in the course of an Article 88(2) procedure.[186] Either way, however, the Commission's new decision must be taken within a reasonable timeframe. In *Alitalia II* the Court considered that a period of seven months between its judgment in *Alitalia I* and the adoption of a new decision was not excessive.[187]

E. Unlawful and misused aids

16.69 **Overview of procedure.** Aid is unlawful where it is implemented without notification to and approval by the Commission under Article 88(3).[188] By contrast, 'misused' aid refers to a situation where the aid has been approved by the Commission, but where the beneficiary has used it in contravention of the Commission's approval decision.[189] In both cases, however, special procedural provisions apply, as set out in Articles 10 to16 of the Procedural Regulation. These include slightly different powers and obligations in the investigation of the matter, the power to prescribe interim measures, and the requirement to require recovery of aid which has been granted unlawfully or which has been misused.

16.70 **Unlawful and misused aids: procedural differences.** The special procedural provisions outlined in the foregoing paragraph apply in the same way to both unlawful

[183] Case T-301/01 *Alitalia v Commission ('Alitalia II')* (judgment of 9 July 2008), paras 97–8.

[184] See Case C-415/96 *Spain v Commission* [1998] ECR I-6993 paras 34, 40; and *Alitalia II*, ibid, paras 99–147.

[185] See eg T-14/96 *Bretagne Angleterre Irlande (BAI) v Commission* [1999] ECR II-139, annulling the Commission's decision, following the Article 88(2) procedure that no State aid was present. The Commission then reopened the procedure and adopted a negative decision, which was in turn the subject of a (this time unsuccessful) application for annulment in Cases T-116 and 118/01 *P&O European Ferries (Vizcaya) v Commission* [2003] ECR II-2957. cf Case T-301/01 *Alitalia v Commission ('Alitalia II')* (judgment of 9 July 2008) where the CFI upheld the Commission's decision not to reopen the Article 88(2) procedure, after annulment of its decision based on misapplication of the private investor test.

[186] eg Decision 2000/199/EC *Heracles* [2000] OJ L66/1, para 26.

[187] Case T-301/01 *Alitalia v Commission ('Alitalia II')* (judgment of 9 July 2008), para 156.

[188] Procedural Regulation, Article 1(f).

[189] ibid, Article 1(g).

and misused aids, save for two differences which arise from the fact that, unlike unlawful aid, aid which has possibly been misused is aid which has been previously approved by the Commission.[190] The first is that the provisions on interim recovery of aid apply only to unlawful aid. The second is the range of decisions open to the Commission following its investigation. In the case of unlawful aid, the Commission may adopt any decision that would have been available had the aid been notified, including decisions to close the procedure following a preliminary review. By contrast, where misused aid is concerned, the Commission must either open the formal investigation procedure or close its file informally.

1. The investigation of unlawful or misused aids

16.71 **Complaint.** The Commission may initiate an investigation into alleged unlawful or misused aid on the basis of information 'from whatever source'.[191] In practice, however, most such investigations will be triggered by a complaint from a competitor of the beneficiary of the aid. If a complaint is received, the Commission is under a duty to conduct a diligent and impartial examination of the matter,[192] which may include considering issues not raised by the complainant.[193]

16.72 **Information requests.** As in the case of a preliminary or formal investigation of a notified aid, the Commission may where necessary request information from the Member State concerned,[194] and the Member State is required to provide that information in order to enable the Commission to take its decision.[195] In a case of unlawful or misused aid, however, where following a reminder the Member State does not provide the information requested, or does not provide complete information, the Commission has the additional power under Article 10 of the Procedural Regulation to take a decision requiring information to be provided. Such a decision is known as an 'information injunction'. The Commission must specify the information to be provided and the period within which it is to be supplied. If the Member State continues to withhold information notwithstanding an information injunction, the Commission may proceed to a decision on the basis of the information available to it;[196] and if that information is insufficient to establish either that the measure does not constitute aid, or that the aid is compatible with the common market, then the decision will be a negative one.

---

[190] See Procedural Regulation, recital (15).

[191] ibid, Article 10(1).

[192] Case T-95/96 *Gestevision Telecinco v Commission* [1998] ECR II-3407 paras 53, 72; Case T-157/01 *Danske Busvognmænd v Commission* [2004] ECR II-917, para 44; Case T-167/04 *Asklepios Kliniken v Commission* [2007] ECR II-2379, para 81.

[193] Case T-95/96 *Gestevision Telecinco*, ibid, para 53.

[194] Procedural Regulation, Articles 10(2) and 5(1) and (2).

[195] ibid, Articles 10(2) and 2(2).

[196] ibid, Article 13(1). See also eg Case C-301/87 *France v Commission ('Boussac')* [1990] ECR I-307, para 22; and Case T-274/01 *Valmont v Commission* [2004] ECR II-3145, para 55.

The corollary of this procedural framework is that the Commission may only adopt such a decision if it has used the full range of its powers in Article 10 to request and (if necessary) require the provision of information. If it has not done so, it may not rely on the incompleteness of the information before it in order to justify a defective decision.[197] This safeguard is required to avoid (insofar as possible) a situation arising where the Member State's failure to cooperate has unwarranted negative consequences for the aid recipient.[198]

16.73 **Length of investigation.** When it is investigating an allegedly unlawful or misused aid measure, the Commission is not bound by the timetables set out for the preliminary and formal examination of a notified aid.[199] This corresponds with the case-law of the Court, which considered it inappropriate to impose a strict time limit in such cases.[200] The only exception to this is where the Commission has adopted a recovery injunction requiring interim repayment of the aid pending is final decision. In such a case the Commission's decision must be taken within the time-limits applicable to notified aid.[201]

16.74 **Requirement to act within a reasonable period of time.** The absence of a general timetable for the investigation of unlawful or misused aid does not mean, however, that the Commission is absolved from any duty to act promptly. In the first place, the Procedural Regulation requires it to act on information concerning unlawful or misused aid 'without delay'.[202] In addition, the Court has held that the Commission must act upon a complaint within a reasonable period of time, and cannot prolong indefinitely its preliminary investigation.[203] Whether or not the duration of the investigation is reasonable must be determined on the facts of each case, in particular its complexity and importance for the parties, its context, and the various procedural stages to be followed by the Commission.[204]

16.75 **Examples.** An extreme example of delay was provided in *Gestevision Telecinco*, where the Commission's failure to do adopt a decision, 47 months after the first complaint and 26 months after the second complaint, was held to justify a declaration for failure to act under Article 232, on the basis that those periods considerably

---

197 *Valmont v Commission*, ibid, paras 54–60; Case T-366/00 *Scott v Commission* [2007] ECR II-797, paras 144 and 146; Case T-196/02 *MTU Friedrichshafen v Commission* [2007] ECR II-2889, paras 39–41.

198 *Scott v Commission*, ibid, para 149.

199 Procedural Regulation, Article 13(2).

200 See eg Case T-95/96 *Gestevision Telecinco v Commission* [1998] ECR II-3407, paras 76–9.

201 Procedural Regulation, Article 11(2).

202 ibid, Articles 10(1) and 16.

203 Case T-95/96 *Gestevision Telecinco v Commission* [1998] ECR II-3407, paras 73–4; Case T-395/04 *Air One v Commission* [2006] ECR II-1343, para 61; Case T-95/03 *Asociación de Estaciones de Servicio v Commission* [2006] ECR II-4739, para 121.

204 *Air One v Commission*, ibid, para 61; *Asociación de Estaciones de Servicio v Commission*, ibid, para 122; Case T-167/04 *Asklepios Kliniken v Commission* [2007] ECR II-2379, para 81.

exceeded the period of deliberation which was reasonably necessary to assess the aid measures.[205] In another case, the Court found a period of 28 months for the preliminary examination of a complaint to be unreasonably long, and a breach of the Commission's duty to conduct a diligent examination.[206] On the other hand an investigation of less than six months in a relatively complex case concerning several Italian airports was held to be not an unreasonable period of time.[207] In another complaint concerning the financing of all German public sector hospitals, the Court took into account the fact that the proceedings in the *Altmark* case, concerning the financing of public services, were ongoing at the time of the complaint, and held that the Commission was entitled to defer its consideration of the complaint pending clarification of the legal issues by the Court. A period of six months following the publication of the *Altmark* judgment was too short for the Commission to be able to complete its preliminary examination of the contested measures.[208]

Consequences of excessive delay. While excessive delay does not of itself render unlawful a decision ultimately adopted by the Commission,[209] it might contribute to the annulment of the decision on other grounds. Where, for example, the Commission approves an aid under the preliminary review procedure, the length of time for that procedure may indicate that the formal investigation procedure should have been initiated.[210] If, by contrast, the Commission adopts a negative decision, excessive delay in the administrative procedure may bar recovery of any unlawful aid.[211] **16.76**

2. Interim measures

Suspension injunction. In both cases of alleged unlawful aid and cases of alleged misuse of aid, the Commission has the power to suspend the aid until it has taken a decision on the compatibility of the measure with the common market. A decision suspending aid is known as a 'suspension injunction', and may only be adopted after giving the Member State concerned the opportunity to submit its comments.[212] The Commission is not, however, required in every case to require suspension of the aid,[213] and in practice the suspension injunction is rarely used.[214] **16.77**

205 Case T-95/96 *Gestevision Telecinco v Commission* [1998] ECR II-3407, para 75.
206 T-95/03 *Asociación de Estaciones de Servicio v Commission* [2006] ECR II-4739, para 129.
207 Case T-395/04 *Air One v Commission* [2006] ECR II-1343, paras 62–7.
208 Case T-167/04 *Asklepios Kliniken v Commission* [2007] ECR II-2379, paras 86–91.
209 T-95/03 *Asociación de Estaciones de Servicio v Commission* [2006] ECR II-4739, para 130.
210 See paras 16.40–16.41 above.
211 See para 16.117 below.
212 Procedural Regulation, Articles 11(1) and 16.
213 C-75/97 *Belgium v Commission ('Maribel bis/ter')* [1999] ECR I-3671, para 74.
214 The only recent example was the Commission's decision on 20 October 2005 to require Greece to suspend the further grant of State aid in the form of a reduction in the tax base of companies in various sectors, by up to 35% of their profits. The Commission simultaneously initiated the

16.78 **Recovery injunction.** Where unlawful aid has been implemented by a Member State, the Commission has the further power under Article 11(2) of the Procedural Regulation to adopt a decision known as a 'recovery injunction' requiring the Member State provisionally to recover the aid, pending its decision on the compatibility of the aid with the common market. This power derogates from the principle that the Commission may not order recovery of aid simply because it has been implemented without notification and approval.[215] It therefore only applies to unlawful aid (not misused aid) implemented after the entry into force of the Procedural Regulation, and then only where three strict criteria are fulfilled:[216]

(a) according to established practice, there must be no doubt that the measure does indeed constitute aid within Article 87(1);
(b) there must be an urgency to act; and
(c) there must be a serious risk of substantial and irreparable damage to a competitor.

These strict conditions make the application of the recovery injunction very limited in practice, and to date it has not yet been used by the Commission in any case.

16.79 **Procedure for recovery.** Where a recovery injunction is adopted, recovery must be effected on the basis of the same procedure that applies to recovery of aid following a final decision. That includes, for example, the payment of interest on the aid. However the Commission may authorize the Member State to couple the refunding of aid with the payment of rescue aid to the firm concerned.[217]

16.80 **Non-compliance with suspension or recovery injunction.** If a Member State fails to comply with either a suspension injunction or a recovery injunction the Commission is entitled, while carrying out its investigation of the substance of the aid, to bring the matter before the Court and apply for a declaration that the failure to comply constitutes an infringement of the Treaty.[218]

3. Decisions in respect of unlawful or misused aids

16.81 **Decisions following preliminary review.** Where alleged unlawful aid is concerned, the Commission may adopt any of the decisions available following the preliminary review of a notified measure. In other words, it may find that the measure does not constitute aid or is compatible with the common market, or it

formal investigation procedure, which ultimately resulted in a negative decision ordering recovery: Decision 2008/723/EC *Tax exempt reserve fund* [2008] OJ L244/11.

[215] See para 16.89 below.

[216] Procedural Regulation, Article 11(2).

[217] ibid.

[218] ibid, Article 12.

may decide to open the formal investigation procedure.[219] In addition, the Commission may simply decide that there are insufficient grounds for taking a view on the case, and therefore close its file without a formal decision.[220] By contrast, where it is alleged that existing aid has been misused, the Commission has only two options following its preliminary review of the matter: either it must open the formal investigation procedure, or it must close the file informally.[221]

Decisions following formal investigation. If the Commission decides to initiate the formal investigation procedure pursuant to Article 88(2) then, in respect of both unlawful and misused aids, it is required to close the procedure by means of one of the four types of decision set out in Article 7 of the Procedural Regulation.[222] The major difference between a decision taken following notification and a decision on an unlawful or misused aid is that, in the latter case, a negative decision carries with it the consequence of recovery of the aid. This is addressed in detail in the next section. **16.82**

Revocation of decision. The rules set out at paras 16.65–16.67 above relating to the revocation of decisions on notified aid apply equally to decisions relating to unlawful or misused aid.[223] **16.83**

4. Recovery of aid

Overview. The recovery of aid is an issue which has generated a huge amount of case-law, primarily resulting from Member States' reluctance to enforce the repayment of aid which has been unlawfully granted. The chronic problem with recovery as a matter of State aid enforcement is highlighted in the Commission's Recovery Notice,[224] which notes that there is practically not a single case in which recovery has been completed within the deadline set out in the recovery decision.[225] Likewise the Commission's State Aid Scoreboard shows that of the 119 recovery decisions adopted between 2000 and June 2007, only 75 had been closed by December 2007.[226] Paradoxically, however, the principles for the recovery of aid, as contained in the case-law of the Court and relevant legislation (in particular the Procedural Regulation and the Implementing Regulation) are relatively clear. **16.84**

---

219 ibid, Article 13(1).

220 ibid, Article 20(2) and Case T-351/02 *Deutsche Bahn v Commission* [2006] ECR II-1047, para 114.

221 ibid, Articles 16 and 20(2).

222 Procedural Regulation, Article 13(1).

223 Procedural Regulation, Article 13(3).

224 Commission Notice 'Towards an effective implementation of Commission decisions ordering Member States to recover unlawful and incompatible State aid' [2007] OJ C272/4.

225 ibid, para 3.

226 State Aid Scoreboard, Spring 2008 update, COM(2008) 304 final, pp 30–1, noting also that of the pending recovery cases, five related to decisions taken more than eight years ago.

The general principles are set out in the following paragraphs. Section 5 below then addresses the possible defences to the recovery of aid, and the cases in which the Commission may refrain from ordering recovery.

(a) Powers and duties of the Commission

16.85 **Logical consequence of unlawfulness.** The Court first confirmed the power of the Commission to order recovery in the *Commission v Germany* case in 1973.[227] Under the provisions of the Procedural Regulation, if the Commission adopts a negative decision in relation to an unlawful or misused aid, it is now not only empowered but *required* in principle to order recovery of the aid.[228] It follows that the Commission is not required to provide any specific reasons, in its decision, justifying the exercise of that power.[229] The Court has consistently held that recovery of unlawful aid is the logical consequence of a finding that the aid is unlawful,[230] irrespective of the form in which the aid was granted.[231] A recovery order cannot therefore be regarded as disproportionate to the objectives of the Treaty with regard to State aid.[232]

16.86 **Restoration of status quo ante.** The aim of ordering recovery is to restore the previous situation and eliminate the distortion of competition caused by the unlawful aid.[233] A Commission recovery decision is thus not penal in character.[234] Rather, by repaying the aid, the recipient forfeits the advantage which it had enjoyed over its competitors, and the situation prior to payment of the aid is restored.[235] It is no answer to suggest that, absent the aid, the undertaking would have arranged its affairs differently so as to secure other benefits under the generally applicable legal provisions (for example the ordinary tax scheme). Re-establishing the status quo

---

227 Case 70/72 *Commission v Germany* [1973] ECR 813, para 13.

228 Procedural Regulation, Article 14(1). The corollary of this is that recovery is *only* permitted following the Article 88(2) procedure: the Commission cannot simply order recovery of aid on the basis that (for example) it was granted contrary to a condition of a previous decision: Case C-294/90 *BAe and Rover v Commission* [1992] ECR I-493, paras 11–13.

229 Case C-75/97 *Belgium v Commission ('Maribel bis/ter')* [1999] ECR I-3671, para 82; Case C-148/04 *Unicredito Italiano* [2005] ECR I-11137, para 99.

230 Case C-142/87 *Belgium v Commission ('Tubemeuse')* [1990] ECR I-959, para 66; C-169/95 *Spain v Commission* [1997] ECR I-135, para 47; *Belgium v Commission ('Maribel bis/ter')*, ibid, para 64; Case C-310/99 *Italy v Commission* [2002] ECR I-2289, para 98.

231 Case C-183/91 *Commission v Greece* [1993] ECR I-3131, para 16; C-404/97 *Commission v Portugal* [2000] ECR I-4897, para 38.

232 Cases C-278-280 *Spain v Commission* [1994] ECR I-4103, para 75.

233 Case C-75/97 *Belgium v Commission ('Maribel bis/ter')* [1999] ECR I-3671, para 64; Case C-310/99 *Italy v Commission* [2002] ECR I-2289, para 98; Case C-277/00 *Germany v Commission* [2004] ECR I-3925, para 76. It is not, however, necessary to demonstrate that the aid will be able to restore the market situation: see Case C-305/89 *Italy v Commission ('Alfa Romeo')* [1991] ECR I-1603, para 41.

234 Case T-366/00 *Scott v Commission* [2007] ECR II-797, para 94.

235 *Belgium v Commission ('Maribel bis/ter')*, ibid, para 66; Case C-310/99 *Italy v Commission*, ibid, para 99.

merely allows account to be taken of the transaction actually carried out, and the aid consequences flowing from that.[236]

No margin of appreciation. Recovery, where required, must be ordered in full. The Commission does not have a margin of appreciation as to the amount to be recovered. Thus it may not, out of sympathy with the beneficiary, order recovery of an amount less than the value of the aid received. Equally, since recovery of aid is not a penalty,[237] the Commission cannot sanction a particularly serious infringement of the State aid rules by ordering recovery of an amount in excess of the value of the benefit received by the recipient of the aid.[238] **16.87**

Uncertainty as to grant of aid. Recovery of any aid may legitimately be ordered even where the Commission is uncertain, at the time of the decision, as to whether the aid has actually been paid to the beneficiaries.[239] But the Commission cannot order recovery where the aid is purely hypothetical, as in the *MTU Friedrichshafen* case where on the basis of the information available the Commission simply concluded that it 'cannot be ruled out' that there had been a transfer of State resources to the alleged aid beneficiary.[240] **16.88**

Cases where unnotified aid is subsequently approved. It has long been established that the Commission cannot order State aid to be repaid solely on grounds that it was not notified under Article 88(3).[241] Therefore if aid is implemented before approval, contrary to Article 88(3), but the Commission subsequently finds it to be compatible with the common market, it has no power to order recovery as part of its final decision.[242] In such a case (save for the exceptional cases where the Commission has adopted a recovery injunction in the course of its investigation) a complainant's only means of obtaining repayment of the aid is through proceedings in the national courts.[243] **16.89**

(b) Role of Member States

Obligations of Member States. Under Article 249 EC, decisions are binding in their entirety upon their addressees. The Court has also confirmed that a **16.90**

---

236 Case C-148/04 *Unicredito Italiano* [2005] ECR I-11137, paras 113–19.

237 Case C-75/97 *Belgium v Commission*]1999] ECR I-3671, para 65.

238 Case T-366/00 *Scott v Commission* [2007] ECR II-797, paras 95–6.

239 Case C-364/90 *Italy v Commission* [1993] ECR I-2097, paras 48–9.

240 Case T-196/02 *MTU Friedrichshafen v Commission* [2007] ECR II-2889, paras 46–8.

241 Case C-301/87 *France v Commission ('Boussac')* [1990] ECR I-307, paras 19–22; Case C-354/90 *FNCEPA v France* [1991] ECR I-5505, para 13. Case C-39/94 *SFEI v La Poste* [1996] ECR I-3547, para 43; Case C-261-262/01 *Van Calster* [2003] ECR I-12249, paras 73–6.

242 For the view that this is an error in the Court's case-law, see J Flynn, 'The Role of National Courts' in Biondi, Eeckhout and Flynn (eds), *The Law of State Aid in the European Union*, Oxford University Press 2004, nn 28 and 51 and text thereto (pp 328 and 334).

243 See paras 18.16–18.17 below.

Commission decision addressed to a Member State is binding on all the organs of that State, including the courts of that State.[244] A Member State to which a recovery decision is addressed is therefore obliged to execute the decision. The national authorities are also bound by Article 10 EC to facilitate the achievement of the Community's tasks and to abstain from any measures that could jeopardise the attainment of the Treaty objectives. A Member State's failure to take appropriate steps to recover aid, in cooperation with the Commission, may therefore be regarded in addition as a breach of its obligations under Article 10.[245]

16.91 **Responsible body.** Community law does not stipulate which institution of a Member State is responsible for the implementation of a recovery decision. It is therefore for the Member State concerned to designate the bodies that will be responsible. Certain Member States have designated a single central body with the task of overseeing the recovery process, but this is not a universal practice, nor is it required as a matter of law.

16.92 **National procedural rules.** Unless the Commission's decision is suspended by the European Court under Article 242 EC, recovery of aid should take place 'without delay' and in accordance with the procedures under the national law of the Member State concerned (including interim relief procedures) provided that these allow the immediate and effective execution of the Commission's decision.[246] This means that, as long as the national procedures do not adversely affect the scope and effectiveness of Community law, a Member State is free to choose the means of fulfilling the obligation to recover to comply with the Commission's decision.[247] In addition, the Court has laid down three further conditions which must be satisfied by measures to recover aid: (1) they must be suitable for re-establishing the conditions of competition distorted by the grant of aid, (2) they must be sufficiently transparent to enable the Commission and other interested parties to identify that the first condition is satisfied, and (3) they must be unconditional and immediately applicable.[248] The simplest and most obvious way of recovering the funds is by a cash payment. This also lends itself easily to supervision by the Commission. But a Member State is entitled to recover unlawful aid by other means provided that these conditions are satisfied.[249]

[244] Case 249/85 *Albako Margarinefabrik Maria von der Linde v Bundesanstalt für landwirtschaftliche Marktordnung* [1987] ECR 2345, para 17.

[245] Case C-441/06 *Commission v France* [2007] ECR I-8887, paras 45–54.

[246] Procedural Regulation, Article 14(3). See further paras 18.29–18.33 below.

[247] Case C-209/00 *Commission v Germany* [2002] ECR I-11695, para 34; Case C-404/00 *Commission v Spain* [2003] ECR I-6695, paras 22–4.

[248] Case C-209/00 *Commission v Germany*, ibid, paras 43 and 58.

[249] ibid, paras 43, 57–8. These conditions were not satisfied on the facts of the case, where a decision ordering recovery of aid was purportedly implemented by an agreement for the State shareholder in the beneficiary company to receive an additional share of the company's surpluses in the event of its liquidation or a change in the shareholders' holdings in the capital, and where that agreement was

Time limit for compliance. Historically, when the Commission adopted a recovery decision, it specified a time limit of two months within which the Member State concerned was required to inform it of the measures taken to comply with the decision. More recently, and in the light of its experience with the implementation of recovery decisions,[250] the Commission has recognized that two months is too short a deadline in the majority of cases. It has therefore decided to specify two time limits in recovery decisions: a first time limit of two months following the entry into force of the decision, within which the Member State must inform the Commission of the measures either taken or planned, and a second time limit of four months following the entry into force of the decision, within which the decision must have been actually executed. If the Member State encounters serious difficulties with either of these deadlines, and provides an adequate justification to the Commission, the Commission may agree to extend the deadlines.[251] **16.93**

(c) Calculation of repayment

Calculation of the aid to be recovered. In many cases the calculation of the amount of aid to be recovered may entail complex calculations which take into account the detailed provisions of national tax and social security legislation. The national authorities are generally best placed to carry out those calculations,[252] particularly where an aid scheme is involved.[253] For that reason, the Commission is not required to specify the exact amount of aid to be recovered. Rather, it is legitimate for the Commission to limit itself to an order declaring that there is an obligation to repay, and leave it to the national authorities to calculate the exact amount to be repaid.[254] If the Decision does not quantify the aid, however, it must at least contain sufficient parameters to enable the Member State (in cooperation with the Commission if necessary) to carry out the calculation without excessive difficulty.[255] Where the Commission does fix the amount of aid to be recovered, it may have to resort to an approximate evaluation where, in the circumstances of the case (for example in a land sale where a significant period of time has elapsed **16.94**

to be annulled with retroactive effect if the CFI were to annul *or* confirm the decision, or if it were to consider that the agreement did not implement the decision.

250 See comments at para 16.84 above.

251 Recovery Notice paras 40–2.

252 Case C-441/06 *Commission v France* [2007] ECR I-8887, para 39.

253 Recovery Notice para 38.

254 Case C-480/98 *Spain v Commission ('Magefesa')* [2000] ECR I-8717, paras 25–6; Case C-441/06 *Commission v France* [2007] ECR I-8887, para 29; Case C-419/06 *Greece v Commission ('Olympic Airways')* (judgment of 14 February 2008), para 44. The methodology for calculating the grant equivalent of aid and the aid element resulting from interest subsidy schemes is set out in the Communication from the Commission on the revision of the method for setting the reference and discount rates [2008] OJ C14/6.

255 *Commission v France*, ibid, para 29; Decision 2006/621/EC *France Télécom* [2006] OJ L257/11, para 258.

since the sale took place) it is not possible to determine the precise value of the aid.[256]

16.95 **Interest on the recovered aid.** The aid to be recovered by a Member State pursuant to a recovery decision must now include compound interest from the date on which the unlawful aid was first put at the disposal of the beneficiary, until the date of its recovery.[257] In *Keller and Keller Meccanica* the question arose as to the starting point for the calculation of interest on aid arising from soft loans. The aid element in the loan consisted of the reduced rate of interest. The applicant beneficiaries argued that this advantage only impacted on their financial position on the first anniversary of the loans. Accordingly, they said, the interest should only accrue from those dates. The Court rejected this argument and held that the interest was to run from the dates on which the loans were granted.[258]

16.96 **Interest rate.** The rate of interest for the recovery of unlawful aid is fixed by the Commission for each Member State, according to the methodology set out in Article 9 of the Implementing Regulation. It is an annual percentage rate, specified for each calendar year, and published in the Official Journal and on the DG Competition website.[259] The interest rate in force at the time of the Commission's decision is normally applied to the whole period on which interest is charged. If, however, more than a year has elapsed between the date on which the unlawful aid was first put at the disposal of the beneficiary and the date of the recovery of the aid, the rate is recalculated at yearly intervals, taking as a basis the rate in force at the time of recalculation.[260]

16.97 **Effect of tax.** The aid calculation may take into account, where appropriate, any tax paid by the aid beneficiary in respect of the aid, by recovering only the net amount received by the beneficiary.[261] In such cases, however, the Commission considers that the national authorities should ensure that the beneficiary does not enjoy a further tax deduction by claiming that the reimbursement has reduced his

[256] Case T-366/00 *Scott v Commission* [2007] ECR II-797, para 96.

[257] Implementing Regulation, Article 11, implementing Procedural Regulation, Article 14(2). The Implementing Regulation was the first legislative embodiment of this principle, which departed from the Commission's original practice of requiring simple interest only. In Case T-369/00 *Département du Loiret (France) v Commission* [2007] ECR II-851 the Court partially annulled the first Commission decision (taken in 2000) that capitalized interest, without giving any reasons for this change of practice. In exceptional cases, however, it might be appropriate not to include interest: see Case C-480/98 *Spain v Commission ('Magefesa')* [2000] ECR I-8717, paras 36–40.

[258] T-35/99 *Keller and Keller Meccanica SpA v Commission* [2002] ECR II-261, paras 106–8.

[259] Implementing Regulation, Articles 9(1) and 10, as amended following the methodology set out in the Communication from the Commission on the revision of the method for setting the reference and discount rates [2008] OJ C14/6. The interest rates applicable since 1997 are available at <http://ec.europa.eu/comm/competition/state_aid/legislation/reference. html>.

[260] ibid, Article 11(3).

[261] Case T-459/93 *Siemens v Commission* [1995] ECR II-1675, paras 82–5.

taxable income, since this would mean that the net amount of the recovery was lower than the net amount initially received.[262]

(d) Who should repay

Identification of undertakings liable to recovery. The aid must be recovered from the undertakings that actually benefited from it.[263] Accordingly, the Commission's practice is to identify in its recovery decisions, where possible, the identity of the undertaking(s) from whom the aid must be recovered.[264] Difficult questions may arise, however, regarding repayment of aid where the assets of the aid beneficiary have been transferred to another undertaking, or where the aid indirectly benefits undertakings other than the direct recipient of the aid. In such cases it is necessary to consider carefully who bears the obligation to repay the aid. **16.98**

Sale of aid beneficiary or its assets. As Advocate General Van Gerven noted in the *Alfa Romeo* case, the repayment of aid granted illegally is not a sanction but a civil law liability arising out of the unlawful payment of aid. As such that liability may be transferred to another undertaking.[265] That may occur, for example, if the purchaser of an aid beneficiary, or of assets of that company, receives the benefit of an aid. If recovery from the purchaser in that situation were not possible, then a recovery decision by the Commission could easily be frustrated by transferring the aid beneficiary or its assets to another undertaking during the course of the Commission's investigation.[266] It follows that where the Commission can prove that assets have been sold at a price lower than their market value, especially to a successor company set up to circumvent the recovery order, the recovery order can be extended to that third party.[267] However where the sale of the aid beneficiary or its assets has taken place following an open tender under non-discriminatory competitive conditions and at market price, the purchaser cannot be regarded as having benefited from State aid.[268] In such a case, the purchaser is not liable to repay aid which was granted to its predecessor. Instead, the previous situation **16.99**

262 Recovery Notice para 50.

263 Case C-303/88 *Italy v Commission ('ENI-Lanerossi')* [1991] ECR I-1433, para 57; Case C-277/00 *Germany v Commission* [2004] ECR I-3925, para 75.

264 Recovery Notice para 32.

265 Case C-305/89 *Italy v Commission ('Alfa Romeo')* [1991] ECR I-1603, opinion para 22.

266 See comments in Cases C-328/99 and 399/00 *Italy v Commission* [2003] ECR I-4035, paras 77–8.

267 Case C-277/00 *Commission v Germany* [2004] ECR I-3925, para 72. The sale of shares in a company should, similarly, not frustrate recovery of an aid: see Cases C-328/99 and C-399/00 *Italy v Commission* [2003] ECR I-4035, para 83. This principle may encourage the inclusion of indemnification clauses in share or asset purchase agreements, but those clauses themselves may constitute State aid or an unlawful attempt to circumvent a recovery order: see Soltész and Schädle, 'How to Deal with the Risk of State Aid Recovery in M&A Practice – Reps and Warranties in Conflict with the EC State Aid Regime?' [2008] ECLR 139.

268 See para 2.32 above.

must be restored through repayment by the seller of the aid beneficiary,[269] or from the beneficiary itself where it has retained its own legal personality notwithstanding the sale.[270] In order to determine whether this is the case for a given transaction, the Commission may need to consider a number of issues including the purpose of the transaction, the price paid, the identity of the shareholders or owners of the purchaser and seller respectively, the timing of the transaction and its economic logic.[271]

16.100 **Bankrupt beneficiaries.** The bankruptcy of an aid beneficiary does not automatically extinguish the obligation on the Member State to recover the aid.[272] The Member State could, for example, register the liability relating to the repayment of the aid in the schedule of liabilities of the insolvent company,[273] and the Commission considers that it should, indeed, immediately do so.[274] The Member State should also dispute any refusal by the insolvency administrator to reject its claims, and appeal any decision to allow a continuation of the insolvent beneficiary's activity beyond the time limits set in the recovery decision.[275] If hive-off companies have been created to continue some of the activities of the aid beneficiary following its insolvency, those companies may also be required to repay the aid, insofar as it is established that they have benefited from it. That could be the case if the hive-off companies have received assets of the insolvent company without paying the market price, or if the hive-off companies were created with the specific purpose of evading the obligation to repay the aid.[276] On the other hand, as with any sale of assets of an aid beneficiary (see foregoing paragraph) if the purchaser of assets of a bankrupt beneficiary has paid market value, and the transaction is economically rational, that will indicate that the purchaser has not benefited from the aid, and is therefore not liable to repay it.[277]

---

[269] Case C-390/98 *Banks v Coal Authority* [2001] ECR I-6117, paras 77–8. On the facts of that case, however, the aid could not be repaid by the seller since it was identifiable, from an economic standpoint, with the provider of the aid: the State was both seller and aid provider: see para 79. See also Case C-305/89 *Italy v Commission ('Alfa Romeo')* [1991] ECR I-1603, para 40, permitting the recovery of aid to Alfa Romeo from its holding company Finmeccanica, after Alfa Romeo had been sold to Fiat for what AG Van Gerven observed (at para 22) was 'a price found by the Commission to be appropriate'.

[270] Case C-277/00 *Germany v Commission* [2004] ECR I-3925, paras 80–1.

[271] Cases C-328/99 and 399/00 *Italy v Commission* [2003] ECR I-4035, para 78.

[272] Case C-42/93 *Spain v Commission* [1994] ECR I-4175, para 33; Case C-261/99 *France v Commission* [2001] ECR I-2537, para 15. Though it may do so where the beneficiary has no recoverable assets: see para 16.106 below.

[273] Case C-277/00 *Germany v Commission* [2004] ECR I-3925, para 85; Case T-318/00 *Freistaat Thüringen v Commission* [2005] ECR II-4179, para 332.

[274] Recovery Notice para 64.

[275] ibid, paras 65–6.

[276] Case C-277/00 *Germany v Commission* [2004] ECR I-3925, para 86.

[277] ibid; and Case T-318/00 *Freistaat Thüringen v Commission* [2005] ECR II-4179, paras 326–46.

Indirect aid beneficiary. The Procedural Regulation requires the aid to be recovered 'from the beneficiary'.[278] It follows that in cases where the true beneficiary of aid is not the direct recipient of the financial subsidy, but another undertaking, repayment must be ordered against the second undertaking. That was the result in *Verlipack*, where State aid was granted in the form of a loan to Heye on condition that it was allocated to the recapitalization of Verlipack. The CFI upheld the Commission's decision requiring the aid to be recovered from Verlipack itself rather than Heye.[279] The corollary of this is that, in such a case, the Commission is not be entitled to order recovery from the intermediate undertaking unless it has also identified that undertaking as a beneficiary. **16.101**

Aid schemes. When the Commission adopts a recovery decision regarding an aid scheme, it may not be in a position to identify, in the decision itself, all the undertakings that have received unlawful aid. In such a case this will have to be done at the start of the implementation process by the Member State concerned.[280] **16.102**

5. Defences (and non-defences) to recovery

General policy. Article 14(1) of the Procedural Regulation prohibits the Commission from requiring recovery of the aid if this would be contrary to a general principle of Community law. Indeed, the Commission is required to take automatically into account any exceptional circumstances which indicate that Article 14(1) applies in a given case.[281] This raises the question of what circumstances require the Commission not to order recovery, or provide a defence to recovery if it is ordered. In rare cases, the Commission itself has forgone recovery in the light of the circumstances of the case. More usually, however, the parameters of the available defences have been tested by the case-law of the Court in relation to infringement actions against Member States, and actions for the annulment of Commission decisions. In such actions, Member States and aid beneficiaries have relied on a variety of arguments to justify non-compliance or annulment (as appropriate), including in particular the impossibility of recovery, legitimate expectations and legal certainty. Hitherto, however, the Court has adopted a very strict approach to such arguments, and has required recovery in all but the most exceptional of cases. **16.103**

[278] Procedural Regulation, Article 14(1) discussed further at para 2.31 above.

[279] Case C-457/00 *Belgium v Commission ('Verlipack')* [2003] ECR I-6931, paras 55–62. See also Case T-318/00 *Freistaat Thüringen v Commission* [2005] ECR II-4179, para 315.

[280] Case C-310/99 *Italy v Commission* [2002] ECR I-2289, para 91; and Recovery Notice para 35.

[281] Even if these are not mentioned by the Member State in question: Decision 2006/621/EC *France Télécom* [2006] OJ L257/11, para 262.

(a) Unlawfulness of decision

16.104 **Challenge to lawfulness of decision.** A Member State cannot resist recovery simply on the basis that it disputes the lawfulness of the Commission's decision.[282] Nor is it sufficient that it has brought an action for annulment of the decision, since an action for annulment does not have automatic suspensory effect. In the absence of interim measures, therefore, the obligation to recover the aid remains.[283] If the Member State wishes to avoid recovery of the aid on the basis of the illegality of the decision, it must *both* bring an action for annulment against the decision under Article 230 EC, *and* obtain an order from the Court under Article 242 or 243 requiring interim suspension of the obligation to recover.[284] This has important ramifications: if it fails to bring an action for annulment, the Member State will not be able to raise the alleged illegality of the decision in subsequent proceedings, whether in the national or the European Courts.[285]

16.105 **Non-existence of decision.** In extreme cases, the Commission's decision may contain such serious and manifest defects that it can be deemed non-existent. If that is the case, the Member State will be able to avoid recovery even if it has not brought an application for annulment against the decision and obtained interim measures.[286] However the cases of non-existence of a decision will be very rare, and to date no State aid decision has been annulled on this ground.

(b) Impossibility

16.106 **Practical impossibility.** A Member State may resist an action for failure to comply with a decision if it is in practice absolutely impossible to carry out the recovery order.[287] The burden of proof rests on the Member State to show that the decision

[282] Case C-261/99 *France v Commission* [2001] ECR I-2537, para 18; Case C-404/00 *Commission v Spain* [2003] ECR I-6695, para 40; Case C-419/06 *Commission v Greece ('Olympic Airways')* (judgment of 14 February 2008), para 52.

[283] Article 242 EC; Case 63/97 *Commission v Greece* [1988] ECR 2875, paras 10–12; Case C-404/97 *Commission v Portugal* [2000] ECR I-4897, para 57; Case C-261/99 *Commission v France* [2001] ECR I-2537, para 26; Cases C-485–490/03 *Commission v Spain* [2006] ECR I-11887, paras 5–8 and 24. Where a decision is subject to litigation before the national or Community Courts, however, the Commission may in 'duly justified cases' accept the repayment of the aid into an escrow account, rather than a repayment to the Member State: Recovery Notice para 70.

[284] See Chapter 17 below for discussion of these procedures.

[285] By virtue of the principle in Case C-188/92 *TWD Textilwerke Deggendorf* [1994] ECR I-883: see further paras 17.13 and 18.30 below.

[286] Case C-404/97 *Commission v Portugal* [2000] ECR I-4897, para 35; Case C-261/99 *Commission v France* [2001] ECR I-2537, para 19; Case C-404/00 *Commission v Spain* [2003] ECR I-6695, para 41; Case C-207/05 *Commission v Italy* (judgment of 1 June 2006), para 43.

[287] Case 52/84 *Commission v Belgium* [1986] ECR 89, para 14; Case C-280/95 *Commission v Italy* [1998] ECR I-259, para 13; Case C-404/97 *Commission v Portugal* [2000] ECR I-4897, para 39; Case C-99/02 *Commission v Italy* [2004] ECR I-3353, para 16; Case C-207/05 *Commission v Italy* (judgment of 1 June 2006), para 45; Cases C-485-490/03 *Commission v Spain* [2006] ECR I-11887, para 72. If implementation of the decision was impossible at the time of the decision, then this will not only be a defence to infringement proceedings by the Commission, but will also be a

could not have been complied within the time limit provided, or at all.[288] The case-law of the Court has, moreover, strictly circumscribed the scope of this defence. Thus it is not sufficient to rely simply on the 'mere apprehension' of difficulties in implementing the decision.[289] Moreover, the Court has consistently drawn a distinction between absolute impossibility of recovery, and practical difficulties in recovery. It has hence rejected claims to impossibility in cases where the aid will have to be recovered from huge numbers, even thousands, of small undertakings who have been granted tax exemptions,[290] or where recovery will entail examining the individual situation of a large number of undertakings.[291] The financial difficulties of aid beneficiaries, if the aid were to be recovered, also does not render recovery impossible.[292] If necessary, it appears that the State has to liquidate the company. Only if the company is liquidated and has no recoverable assets can the State claim that recovery is absolutely impossible.[293] Absolute impossibility of recovering aid would probably also arise where a State-owned company having benefited from unlawful State aid is subsequently sold at market price. In that case, the purchase price reflects the consequences of the previous aid, and it is the seller rather than the buyer of the company who keeps the benefit of the aid. In that case, repayment of the aid should be sought from the seller, which would however be impossible where the seller is, from an economic standpoint, identical with the provider of the aid, ie the State, as in that case the State would merely be repaying itself.[294]

Impossibility of calculation. In cases where aid has been granted by means of a State guarantee or other potential financial support, the financial impact of the measure may be very difficult to quantify. In the *France Télécom* case, concerning a loan proposal that was never implemented, the Commission went further and decided that the circumstances of the case rendered it impossible either to quantify the aid precisely in the Decision, or to incorporate in the Decision parameters **16.107**

ground for the annulment of the decision: Case C-75/97 *Belgium v Commission ('Maribel bis/ter')* [1999] ECR I-3671, para 86.

288 Case 213/85 *Commission v Netherlands* [1988] ECR 281, para 24; Case 63/87 *Commission v Greece* [1988] ECR 2875, para 14.

289 Case C-52/95 *Commission v France* [1995] ECR I-4443, para 38; Case C-280/95 *Commission v Italy* [1998] ECR I-259, para 16; Case C-278/00 *Greece v Commission* [2004] ECR I-3997, para 112; Case C-298/00 P *Italy v Commission* [2004] ECR I-4087, paras 77–8.

290 See eg Case C-6/97 *Italy v Commission* [1999] ECR I-2981, para 32; Case C-75/97 *Belgium v Commission ('Maribel bis/ter')* [1999] ECR I-3671, para 90.

291 Case C-99/02 *Commission v Italy* [2004] ECR II-3353, para 23.

292 Case 63/97 *Commission v Greece* [1988] ECR 2875, para 14; Case C-404/97 *Commission v Portugal* [2000] ECR I-4897, para 53.

293 Case C-499/99 *Commission v Spain* [2002] ECR I-6031, paras 37–8. For an example see Decision 2002/897/EC *Ingenieur- und Gewerbebau* [2002] OJ L314/72. See further para 16.100 above.

294 Case C-390/98 *Banks* [2001] ECR I-6117, paras 77–9.

enabling France to calculate the aid. For this and other reasons the Commission decided not to order recovery.[295]

16.108 **Legal impossibility.** A Member State may not rely on provisions, practices or circumstances existing in its internal legal system in order to justify a failure to comply with its obligations under Community law.[296] It is therefore irrelevant that the domestic legal order contains no express provisions designating or establishing a concrete procedure for the execution of a decision ordering the recovery of incompatible aid.[297] Likewise, a Member State cannot plead, as making it absolutely impossible to implement the Commission's decision, the obligations to which the competent administrative authority is subject under the national rules governing the protection of legitimate expectations. Similarly, a provision laying down a time limit for the revocation of an administrative act must, like all the relevant provisions of national law, be applied in such a way that the recovery required by Community law is not rendered practically impossible and the interests of the Community are taken fully into consideration.[298]

16.109 **Solution in cases of practical difficulties.** The strict rules on impossibility do not, however, mean that there is no mechanism for resolving practical problems in the recovery of aid. If the State does discover that there are unforeseen practical difficulties to recovery of the aid, or becomes aware of consequences of recovery which have been overlooked or not envisaged by the Commission, the proper course is to submit these problems to the Commission together with proposals for suitable amendments to the decision. In such cases, the Commission and the Member State are required by the duty of cooperation in Article 10 EC to work together to overcome the difficulties, while fully observing the Treaty State aid rules.[299] It is not, however, sufficient for the Member State simply to inform the Commission of the legal, political or practical difficulties involved in implementing the decision, without taking any real step to recover the aid from the undertakings concerned, and without proposing to the Commission any alternative arrangements for implementing the decision which could have enabled those difficulties to be overcome.[300]

[295] Decision 2006/621/EC *France Télécom* [2006] OJ L257/11, paras 257–61, discussed further at para 2.44 above.

[296] Case C-5/89 *Commission v Germany* [1990] ECR I-3437, para 18.

[297] Cases C-485-490/03 *Commission v Spain* [2006] ECR I-11887, para 73.

[298] Case C-5/89 *Commission v Germany* [1990] ECR I-3437, para 19.

[299] See eg Case 52/84 *Commission v Belgium* [1986] ECR 89, para 16; Case C-183/91 *Commission v Greece* [1993] ECR I-3131, para 19; Case C-404/97 *Commission v Portugal* [2000] ECR I-4897, para 40; Case C-278/00 *Greece v Commission* [2004] ECR I-3997, para 114.

[300] Case C-404/00 *Commission v Spain* [2003] ECR I-6695, para 47; Case C-99/02 *Commission v Italy* [2004] ECR I-3353, para 18; Case C-415/03 *Commission v Greece* [2005] ECR I-3875, para 43; Case C-207/05 *Commission v Italy* (judgment of 1 June 2006), para 48.

(c) Legitimate expectations

Who may claim. Member States may not rely on the legitimate expectation of aid recipients that aid will not be recovered, to justify a failure to implement a Commission recovery decision. Otherwise, national authorities would in effect be able to rely on their own unlawful conduct in order to deprive decisions taken by the Commission of their effectiveness.[301] That does not prevent the recipient of aid from relying on legitimate expectations, particularly in the context of a recovery procedure in the national courts,[302] but also in an application for annulment of the decision.[303] However, whether in the national or Community court, a claim of legitimate expectations in relation to State aid will only succeed in exceptional circumstances, as explained in the following paragraphs. **16.110**

Unnotified aid in general. The Court has consistently held that, in principle, undertakings to which an aid has been granted may not entertain a legitimate expectation that it is lawful, unless it has been granted in accordance with the Article 88 procedure. A diligent businessman is regarded as being normally able to determine whether that procedure has been followed.[304] This principle applies equally where the aid beneficiaries are small undertakings.[305] It also applies to third parties who may be affected by the aid, such as creditor banks who have been given a State guarantee in respect of a loan to the aid beneficiary.[306] Even where the Member State has failed to inform the aid beneficiary that the aid was the subject of a Commission investigation, or has incorrectly told the beneficiary that the aid would be approved by the Commission, the beneficiary will not be permitted to rely on its legitimate expectations in an application for annulment of the decision.[307] Nor can the Commission's inaction in respect of similar aid measures create any legitimate expectation that an aid is lawful.[308] On the other hand **16.111**

301 Case C-5/89 *Commission v Germany* [1990] ECR I-3437, para 17; Case C-183/91 *Commission v Greece* [1993] ECR I-3131, para 18; Case C-169/95 *Spain v Commission* [1997] ECR I-135, para 48; C-310/99 *Italy v Commission* [2002] ECR I-2289, para 104; Case C-99/02 *Commission v Italy* [2004] ECR I-3353, para 21.

302 Case C-5/89 *Commission v Germany* [1990] ECR I-3437, para 16; Case C-310/99 *Italy v Commission* [2002] ECR I-2289, para 103; Case T-109/01 *Fleuren Compost v Commission* [2004] ECR II-127, paras 136–7.

303 Case T-55/99 *CETM v Commission* [2000] ECR II-3207, para 122; Case T-6/99 *ESF Elbe-Stahlwerke v Commission* [2001] ECR II-1523, para 183.

304 Case C-5/89 *Commission v Germany* [1990] ECR I-3437, para 14; Case C-169/95 *Spain v Commission* [1997] ECR I-135, para 51; Cases C-183 and 187/02 P *Demesa v Commission* [2004] ECR I-10609, para 44; Cases C-346 and 529/03 *Atzeni v Regione autonoma della Sardegna* [2006] ECR I-1875, para 64.

305 Cases T-298/97 etc *Mauro Alzetta v Commission* [2000] ECR II-2319, para 172; Case T-109/01 *Fleuren Compost v Commission* [2004] ECR II-127, para 141.

306 Cases C-204 and 270/97 *EPAC v Commission* [2000] ECR II-2267, para 144; C-329/93 and C-62-63/95 *Germany v Commission* [1996] ECR I-5151, opinion of AG Cosmas paras 100 and 102.

307 Case T-109/01 *Fleuren Compost v Commission* [2004] ECR II-127, paras 141, 143.

308 Case C-148/04 *Unicredito Italiano* [2005] ECR I-11137, para 105.

repeated inaction by the Commission in respect of the aid in question might, in certain circumstances, justify the non-repayment of aid.[309]

16.112 **Unnotified aid erroneously approved by Commission.** Articles 14 and 16 of the Procedural Regulation 659/99 only allow the Commission to require recovery as a consequence of a negative decision taken in relation to unlawful or misused aid. Therefore if the Commission approves an unnotified aid measure (or finds there to be no aid), it has no jurisdiction to require recovery. Any remedy lies with the national court.[310] A recovery order may be possible, however, if a favourable decision is annulled and subsequently replaced by a negative decision. This occurred in the *P&O Ferries* saga concerning the purchase by the Basque authorities of travel vouchers to be used on P&O's ferry route between Bilbao and Portsmouth. The original agreement was not notified to the Commission, who investigated the matter following a complaint by BAI. In the course of the Article 88(2) procedure, following discussions with the Commission, P&O sent the Commission a new agreement. The Commission considered that the new agreement did not confer State aid on P&O, and closed its file in 1995 on that basis. Following the annulment of that decision,[311] the Commission reopened the Article 88(2) procedure and concluded that the new agreement *did* grant P&O State aid, which had to be recovered. P&O and the Diputación Foral de Vizcaya then argued that the aid should not have to be recovered, since it was not paid until after the Commission's 1995 decision. Rejecting that argument, the Court held that since the agreement had never formally been notified to the Commission, it was unlawful aid. On that basis, neither Article 14 of the Procedural Regulation nor the principle of legitimate expectations prevented recovery of the aid.[312]

16.113 **Notified aid erroneously approved by Commission.** Neither the CFI nor the ECJ in *P&O Ferries* ruled on whether recovery is possible if an aid measure has been properly notified to the Commission, has been approved on that basis, and has subsequently been implemented before the annulment of the favourable decision. Nor does the Procedural Regulation itself provide an answer to this question. Early case-law suggested that if a measure is properly notified and approved by the Commission, then aid subsequently paid should be non-recoverable at least on

[309] See Case C-39/94 *SFEI v La Poste* [1996] ECR I-3547, opinion of AG Jacobs at para 76 and judgment at para 70.

[310] See also para 16.89 above.

[311] Case T-14/96 *Bretagne Angleterre Irlande (BAI) v Commission* [1999] ECR II-139.

[312] Cases T-116 and 118/01 *P&O European Ferries (Vizcaya) v Commission* [2003] ECR II-2957, paras 188-213, upheld on appeal in Cases C-442 and 471/03 P *P&O European Ferries (Vizcaya) v Commission* [2006] ECR I-4845. See also Case C-169/95 *Spain v Commission* [1997] ECR I-135, paras 51–4; and Case C-199/06 *CELF* (judgment of 12 February 2008), paras 56–69 confirming the absence of legitimate expectations on more general grounds discussed in the next paragraph, in a case relating to unnotified aid.

the basis of the principle of legitimate expectations.[313] More recently, however, the Court has confirmed that where an action for annulment has been brought against a positive Commission decision, and pending the ruling by the European Court on that action, the recipient of aid cannot rely on any legitimate expectation of the lawfulness of the aid.[314] The position therefore seems to be that the Commission may order recovery of aid paid following a positive decision, if that decision has been annulled and subsequently replaced by a negative decision.

Assurances by Commission. The case-law of the Court has indicated that in some cases aid beneficiaries might be able to rely on specific assurances by the Commission, so as to found a legitimate expectation that an aid is lawful and will not be recovered.[315] To date, however, no such claim has succeeded in a State aid case before the European Court. **16.114**

(d) Legal certainty

Uncertainty as to the law. In many cases a Member State will not notify a measure simply because it does not consider the measure to amount to State aid. As is apparent from Chapter 2, the concept of aid is complex and there may be considerable doubt as to whether a given measure is indeed within the scope of Article 87(1). Advocate General Darmon has commented in that respect that 'the doubts with which some undertakings may be assailed, when faced with "atypical" forms of aid, as to whether notification is necessary should not be made light of'.[316] That does not, however, necessarily prevent recovery if the measure is (contrary to the belief of the Member State or aid beneficiary) found to be aid.[317] In an exceptional case, however, a situation of uncertainty as to the lawfulness of aid might justify a decision not to recover aid. Thus in the *France Télécom* case, where the Commission made a novel finding of aid on highly unusual facts, it considered that a diligent operator could have had confidence in the lawfulness of the Member State's conduct. On that basis it decided that recovery would be contrary to the principle of legitimate expectations.[318] **16.115**

Indeterminate nature of obligation. Where an essential parameter of the prohibition declared by the Commission in a decision under Article 88(2) is unclear, **16.116**

---

[313] See Case T-67/94 *Ladbroke Racing v Commission* [1998] ECR II-1, para 182.

[314] Case C-199/06 *CELF* (judgment of 12 February 2008), para 68. The case concerned unnotified aid, but the comments appear to be of general application.

[315] Case T-129/96 *Preussag Stahl v Commission* [1998] ECR II-609, para 78; Cases T-127/99, T-129/99 and T-148/99 *Diputación Foral de Álava and others v Commission* [2002] ECR II-1275 para 231; Case T-6/99 *ESF Elbe-Stahlwerke Feralpi v Commission* [2001] ECR II-1523, para 185.

[316] Case C-5/89 *Commission v Germany* [1990] ECR I-3437, opinion para 26.

[317] Case C-75/97 *Belgium v Commission ('Maribel bis/ter')* [1999] ECR I-3671, para 69; Case T-55/99 *CETM v Commission* [2000] ECR II-3207, para 128.

[318] Decision 2006/621/EC *France Télécom* [2006] OJ L257/11, paras 262–63; for the facts of the case see para 2.44 above.

Member States do have a good defence to enforcement proceedings. Thus, in *Commission v Germany*[319] the Commission's action for infringement was dismissed, as the geographical scope of its decision had not been fixed with sufficient precision and remained indeterminate until further consultations had taken place between the Commission and the German government.

16.117 **Delay in investigation.** The requirement of legal certainty also prevents the Commission from indefinitely delaying the exercise of its powers in an investigation. For that reason, excessive delay by the Commission in deciding that an aid is unlawful may, in certain circumstances, establish a legitimate expectation on the part of the beneficiary, which precludes the Commission from ordering recovery of the aid.[320] That occurred in *RSV v Commission* in respect of aid to a sector which had been receiving aid for many years with the approval of the Commission, where the specific aid in question was to meet the additional costs of an operation which had already received authorized aid. In those circumstances, a period of 26 months taken by the Commission to reach its decision did create a legitimate expectation by the beneficiary, and the Commission could not then require recovery.[321] It is likely, however, that absent special features of this nature it will be difficult to establish a legitimate expectation of non-recovery based on delay.[322]

(e) Limitation period

16.118 **Ten-year limitation period.** Article 15 of the Procedural Regulation provides that the powers of Commission to recover aid are subject to a limitation period (sometimes referred to as a 'prescription period') of ten years, following which the aid is deemed to be existing aid. The provisions of this Article apply to any definitive action ordering recovery of aid taken after the entry into force of the Procedural Regulation, including in respect of aid granted before that date.[323]

16.119 **Interruption and suspension of limitation period.** Article 15(2) specifies that the ten-year period begins on the day on which the aid is awarded to the beneficiary, either as individual aid, or as a grant under an aid scheme. If the Commission or a Member State (at the Commission's request) takes any action regarding the aid, even a simple request for information,[324] that interrupts the limitation period and

---

[319] Case 70/72 *Commission v Germany* [1973] ECR 813, para 23.

[320] Case C-298/00 P *Italy v Commission* [2004] ECR I-4087, para 90; Case T-109/01 *Fleuren Compost v Commission* [2004] ECR II-127, para 145; and in respect of recovery in the national courts Case C-39/94 *SFEI v La Poste* [1996] ECR I-3547, opinion of AG Jacobs at para 76 and judgment at para 70.

[321] Case 223/85 [1987] ECR 4617, paras 14–17.

[322] See Case C-298/00 P *Italy v Commission* [2004] ECR I-4087, para 90; Case T-109/01 *Fleuren Compost v Commission* [2004] ECR II-127, paras 147–8.

[323] Case T-366/00 *Scott v Commission* [2003] ECR II-1763, para 53.

[324] Case T-369/00 *Département du Loiret v Commission* [2003] ECR II-1789, paras 76–82; *Scott v Commission*, ibid.

starts time running again. That is the case even if the aid beneficiary is unaware of the measures which have interrupted the limitation period.[325] The limitation period is also suspended while proceedings are pending before the European Court.

F. Existing aid

Special procedural regime. The categories of existing aid are set out at para 16.13 above. All types of existing aid are governed by the special procedural regime set out in Articles 17 to 19 of the Procedural Regulation. These provisions reflect the previous case-law of the Court, which prevented the Commission from directly re-examining an authorized aid scheme under the Treaty rules applicable to new aids. The purpose of this is to protect legitimate expectations and legal certainty from the point of view of both the Member States and undertakings, by precluding the Commission from calling into question at any time individual aid granted in strict conformity with an approved aid scheme.[326] **16.120**

Identification of existing aid. The specific procedural regime for existing aid means that it is important, particularly in a case of a State aid complaint, to identify whether the measure in question is new or existing aid. The Commission is not, however, expected to be omniscient as to the payment of aid under existing schemes. It is therefore the responsibility of the Member State concerned to inform the Commission if it considers an aid measure to be part of an existing aid scheme. If it fails to do so, the Member State cannot later impugn the Commission's decision to initiate the formal procedure under Article 88(2) without considering first whether the aid was existing aid.[327] If on the other hand the Member State does claim that the measure is existing aid, the Commission may not proceed to examine the aid under the rules on new aid until it has first decided whether the aid is covered by the aid scheme, and satisfies the conditions in any decision approving it.[328] In that process, if the Commission has doubts as to the conformity of individual aids with an existing scheme, it should order the Member State to supply, within a specified period, any information and **16.121**

[325] *Scott v Commission*, ibid, paras 58–60; upheld on appeal in Case C-276/03 P *Scott v Commission* [2005] ECR I-8437, paras 26–36.

[326] Case C-47/91 *Italy v Commission ('Italgrani')* [1994] ECR I-4635, para 24; Case C-278/95 P *Siemens v Commission* [1997] ECR I-2507, para 31.

[327] Case T-176/01 *Ferriere Nord v Commission* [2004] ECR II-3931, paras 52–4, upheld on appeal in Case C-49/05 *Ferriere Nord v Commission* (judgment of 8 May 2008); Case T-190/00 *Regione Siciliana v Commission* [2003] ECR II-5015, paras 76–8.

[328] Case C-278/95 P *Siemens v Commission* [1997] ECR I-2507, para 31; Case C-321/99 P *ARAP v Commission* [2002] ECR I-4287, para 83.

documentation necessary for it to examine the matter.[329] It is only if the Commission then decides that the aid does not fall under the existing aid scheme, or if the Member State fails to supply the information, that the Commission may examine the aid under the new aid procedure.[330]

16.122 **Implementation of existing aid, subject to review.** Existing aid may be implemented as long as the Commission has not found it to be incompatible with the common market.[331] As far as existing aid is concerned, therefore, the initiative lies with the Commission.[332] To that end, the Commission is required by Article 88(1) to keep under constant review all systems of existing aid. In order to do so, the Commission must obtain any necessary information from the Member State concerned, and the Commission and the Member State are required to cooperate in the review of the aid.[333] That involves an obligation of regular and periodic cooperation, from which neither the Commission nor a Member State may release itself unilaterally.[334]

16.123 **Preliminary view that existing aid is incompatible.** Where the Commission considers that an existing aid scheme is no longer compatible with the common market, whether as a result of its periodic review of that scheme or otherwise (for example after receiving a complaint), it must inform the Member State of its preliminary view, and give it the opportunity to submit comments within a period of a month. That period may be extended by the Commission where necessary.[335]

16.124 **Proposal for appropriate measures.** If the Commission, in the light of any information submitted to it by the Member State, concludes that the existing aid scheme is not compatible with the common market, it must issue a recommendation proposing appropriate measures to the Member State concerned. That may propose, in particular, substantive amendment of the aid scheme, procedural amendment of the scheme or abolition of the scheme altogether.[336]

16.125 **Consequences of proposal for appropriate measures.** If the Member State accepts the proposed measures and informs the Commission, that is recorded by the Commission and the Member State is then bound to implement the measures.[337]

[329] Case C-47/91 *Italy v Commission ('Italgrani')* [1994] ECR I-4635, para 34. This kind of order is known as an *Italgrani* injunction.

[330] See *Italgrani*, ibid, para 35.

[331] Case C-387/92 *Banco Exterior de España* [1994] ECR I-877, para 20; Case C-298/00 P *Italy v Commission* [2004] ECR I-4087, para 47.

[332] Case C-44/93 *Namur-Les Assurances v OND* [1994] ECR I-3829, para 11.

[333] Procedural Regulation, Article 17(1).

[334] Case C-135/93 *Spain v Commission* [1995] ECR I-1651, para 24.

[335] Procedural Regulation, Article 17(2).

[336] ibid, Article 18.

[337] ibid, Article 19(1); Case C-311/94 *Ijssel-Vliet* [1996] ECR I-5023, paras 42–3.

Where the Member State does not accept the proposal, and the Commission (taking account of the Member State's arguments) still considers that those measures are necessary, it is required to initiate the formal investigation procedure. The procedure then follows the same course as with the formal investigation of a new notified aid.[338] It follows that, as with new notified aid (but by contrast to the position for unlawful or misused aid), the Commission may not order recovery or suspension of the aid. Rather, if it does reach a negative decision, the Commission is limited to ordering abolition of the aid.

Transitional period. Since the procedure for existing aids is based on cooperation between the Member State and Commission, where the Commission orders abolition of the aid it must allow the Member State concerned a period of time to comply with that decision.[339] In some cases, it may be appropriate to specify a transitional period of some years. This occurred in relation to Luxembourg's special tax rules for so-called '1929' holding companies, which the Commission found to be State aid incompatible with the common market. It recognized, however, that the legislation had been adopted in 1929 and had not been significantly modified since then. Holding companies had established themselves in Luxembourg, entering into investments as well as medium- and long-term employment and other contracts on the basis of that legislation, and the longevity of the scheme might have given the beneficiaries the impression that it would not be terminated at short notice. The abolition of the special rules would also lead to difficult and complex business reorganization operations which would take some time to complete, and would also have serious consequences for Luxembourg's economy. For these reasons, while the abolition of the aid scheme applied immediately for new beneficiaries, the Commission set a transitional period of almost 4½ years for the abolition of the rules as regards existing beneficiaries.[340] A similar timescale was set for the progressive elimination of Spanish tax credits favouring export-related investments.[341] The case for setting a transitional period is likely to be even stronger where an aid has previously been approved by the Commission, giving rise to legitimate expectations on the part of the undertakings concerned. On that basis, in *Belgium and Forum 187*, the Court annulled a Commission decision finding a tax scheme to constitute aid, insofar as it did not lay down transitional measures for compliance. The Commission had adopted two earlier decisions finding that the contested tax regime was not aid, and had subsequently confirmed this assessment in a reply to a written question in the European Parliament. 16.126

[338] ibid, Article 19(2).

[339] Case 173/73 *Italy v Commission* [1974] ECR 709, para 7.

[340] Decision 2006/940/EC *1929 holding companies* [2006] OJ L366/47.

[341] Decision in Case E 22/2004 *Direct tax incentives in favour of export related investments* (22 March 2006).

In those circumstances, the Court found that the decision breached legitimate expectations that a reasonable transitional period would be granted.[342]

G. Monitoring and compliance

16.127 **Annual reports.** Where the Commission adopts a conditional decision, it may impose regular reporting as part of the conditions for approval of the aid, breach of which may lead to infringement proceedings in the ECJ.[343] In all other cases, Article 21 of the Procedural Regulation requires annual reports to be submitted by Member States in respect of existing aid schemes. If a Member State fails to comply with this requirement, despite a reminder, the Commission may propose appropriate measures in respect of the scheme.[344]

16.128 **On-site monitoring.** Where the Commission has serious doubts as to whether decisions not to raise objections, positive decisions or conditional decisions with regard to individual aid are being complied with, it may order a monitoring visit, after giving the Member State concerned the opportunity to submit its comments. The Member State must then allow the Commission to undertake the visit.[345] The officials authorized by the Commission are empowered for this purpose to enter any premises and land of the undertaking concerned, to ask for oral explanations on the spot, and to examine books and other business records and take, or demand, copies.[346] The Commission is required to inform the Member State concerned, in good time and in writing, of the visit and of the identities of the authorized officials and experts. If the Member State has justified objections to the Commission's choice of experts, the experts must be appointed by agreement with the Member State.[347] Officials from the Member State concerned may also be present at the monitoring visit.[348] Where an undertaking opposes a monitoring visit ordered by the Commission, the Member State must cooperate with the Commission and give it the assistance required to enable its officials and experts to carry out the visit.[349] Any report produced as a result of the visit must be provided to the Member State concerned.[350]

342 Cases C-182 and 217/03 *Belgium and Forum 187 v Commission* [2006] ECR I-5479, in particular paras 155–67.

343 Whether directly under Article 88(2) EC and Procedural Regulation, Article 23(1), or under the normal rules of Article 226 EC. For an example of the latter see Case C-69/05 *Commission v Luxembourg* (judgment of 12 January 2006).

344 Procedural Regulation, Articles 21(2) and 18.

345 ibid, Article 22(1).

346 ibid, Article 22(2).

347 ibid, Article 22(3).

348 ibid, Article 22(4).

349 ibid, Article 22(6).

350 ibid, Article 22(5).

Referral to ECJ. If a Member State does not comply with a conditional or negative decision, particularly a recovery decision, the Commission may refer the matter to the ECJ directly under Article 88(2).[351] That does not, however, prejudice its ability to bring proceedings under the normal provisions of Article 226 EC. These procedures are considered further in Chapter 17 below. 16.129

[351] Article 88(2) EC and Procedural Regulation, Article 23(1).

17

ENFORCEMENT IN THE EUROPEAN COURT

Main legislation and guidelines

Statute of the Court of Justice

Rules of Procedure of the Court of Justice

Rules of Procedure of the Court of First Instance

Council Regulation (EC) 659/1999 laying down detailed rules for the application of Article 93 of the EC Treaty ('Procedural Regulation') [1999] OJ L83/1, as amended [2006] OJ L363/1

A. Introduction

17.01 **Main forms of action.** State aid cases normally come in front of the European Court by way of one of three procedural routes. First, where a Member State does not comply with its Treaty obligations under the State aid rules, the Commission may take enforcement action in the ECJ. Many such cases will be brought under the specific procedure set out in Article 88(2) EC. In some cases, however, the normal infringement procedure in Article 226 EC will apply. Secondly, the decisions of the Commission in the State aid field are open to actions for annulment in the CFI under Article 230 EC. An appeal lies to the ECJ from the CFI's judgment in such cases, on points of law only. Finally, where national courts apply the State aid rules, they may refer points of law to the ECJ under Article 234 EC. This chapter addresses the first two of those types of action. Preliminary references are addressed in Chapter 18 below.[1]

17.02 **Other forms of action.** This chapter will also briefly describe three further forms of action, which are less frequently used in the State aid field: enforcement proceedings by one Member State against another under Article 227 EC, actions against the Commission for failure to act under Article 232 EC, and actions for damages against the Community under Article 288(2) EC.

17.03 **Relative importance.** State aid cases account for a relatively small proportion of the caseload of the ECJ. In 2006, of the 535 new cases introduced in the ECJ, only 20 concerned State aid. Five of these were direct actions brought by the Commission, six were appeals against judgments of the CFI and nine were references for a preliminary ruling. In the CFI, State aid cases are significantly more prominent, though their numerical importance has been decreasing in recent years. At the end of 2006, 164 of the total of 1,029 pending cases concerned State aid, down from a peak of 227 out of 872 at the end of 2002. In 2006, only 28 new State aid actions were lodged with the CFI, out of a total of 438 new cases.

B. Actions against Member States

17.04 **Overview.** Where a Member State fails to comply with its obligations under the EC Treaty, the Commission may bring enforcement proceedings under Article 226 EC. In most cases, however, enforcement proceedings will arise in relation to a failure to comply with a Commission decision such as a recovery decision. In such

[1] For more detailed treatment of these forms of action and those referred to in the next paragraph, see generally Anderson and Demetriou, *References to the European Court* (Sweet and Maxwell, 2002); Lasok, *European Court Practice and Procedure* (Tottel, forthcoming 2009).

cases, the Commission may bring proceedings under the procedure provided by Article 88(2), second subparagraph. As it is now generally accepted that in certain circumstances, the Commission will be obliged to make use of the Article 88(2) procedure rather than the more general procedure under Article 226, it is appropriate to set out the criteria demarcating the two types of enforcement procedures at the beginning of this section. The procedure applicable in enforcement proceedings and defences available to Member States will then be examined in turn.

1. Distinction between Articles 226 and 88(2)

Article 226 EC. Article 226 is the general legal basis for infringement actions by the Commission against Member States. It provides: **17.05**

> If the Commission considers that a Member State has failed to fulfil an obligation under this Treaty, it shall deliver a reasoned opinion on the matter after giving the State concerned the opportunity to submit its observations.
>
> If the State concerned does not comply with the opinion within the period laid down by the Commission, the latter may bring the matter before the Court of Justice.

Article 88(2) EC. The first and second subparagraphs of Article 88(2) set out a specific procedure to be followed where the Commission considers that a Member State has granted State aid incompatible with the common market. Those subparagraphs provide as follows: **17.06**

> If, after giving notice to the parties concerned to submit their comments, the Commission finds that aid granted by a State or through State resources is not compatible with the common market having regard to Article 87, or that such aid is being misused, it shall decide that the State concerned shall abolish or alter such aid within a period of time to be determined by the Commission.
>
> If the State concerned does not comply with this decision within the prescribed time, the Commission or any other interested State may, in derogation from the provisions of Articles 226 and 227, refer the matter to the Court of Justice direct.

Obligation to use Article 88(2) procedure. The procedure under Article 88(2) for the investigation of potential aids, which is discussed in detail in Chapter 16 above, contains guarantees which are specifically adapted to the special problems created by State aid with regard to competition in the common market.[2] In particular, Article 88(2) provides for a formal investigation in which all 'parties concerned' may make submissions, followed by a Commission decision. Enforcement proceedings may then be brought for non-compliance with that decision. In this respect, the procedure is fuller and more formal than the infringement procedure under Article 226, which requires only a letter of formal notice to the Member State concerned, followed by a reasoned opinion. Furthermore, only the Commission **17.07**

[2] Case 290/83 *Commission v France* [1985] ECR 439, paras 16–17.

(or in exceptional circumstances the Council) has jurisdiction to determine the compatibility of aid with the common market. For these reasons, the ECJ has ruled that the Commission must, whenever it wishes to establish that an aid scheme is incompatible with the common market, use the procedure laid down in Article 88(2) EC, and may not circumvent the procedural safeguards of that provision by bringing proceedings under Article 226 EC.[3]

17.08 **Choice of Article 88(2) or Article 226 procedure.** Once the Article 88(2) administrative procedure has resulted in a final decision, it makes sense for the Commission to have a direct route to bring the matter before the Court, rather than having to go through a further pre-litigation procedure under Article 226 EC. Thus the second subparagraph of Article 88(2) provides for infringement proceedings to be brought by the Commission or any interested State directly in the ECJ, where a Member State has failed to comply with a decision. Article 23 of the Procedural Regulation underscores that this may be either a conditional or a negative decision.[4] That does not prevent the Commission[5] from bringing infringement proceedings under Article 226 for non-compliance with a State aid decision, but given the extra procedural requirements that this would entail there is little reason why it would choose to do so.

17.09 **Obligation to use Article 226 procedure.** Article 226 remains the appropriate procedure for infringement actions in two situations. First, breaches of the obligation to notify the Commission of aid intended to be paid and of the standstill obligation laid down in the last sentence of Article 88(3) are brought by way of the normal Article 226 procedure.[6] Secondly, the compatibility of an aid scheme in relation to Community rules other than Article 87 is assessed under the Article 226 procedure.[7] This may include, for example, cases where the Commission alleges a breach of the provisions on the common organization of the market in

---

[3] *Commission v France*, ibid, paras 17–19; and see Cases C-356/90 and C-180/91 *Belgium v Commission* [1993] ECR I-2323, paras 17–18.

[4] Council Regulation (EC) 659/1999 laying down detailed rules for the application of Article 93 of the EC Treaty ('Procedural Regulation') [1999] OJ L83/1, as amended [2006] OJ L363/1, Article 23(1).

[5] Note that the Article 226 procedure is not available to a Member State, by contrast with the procedure in the second subparagraph of Article 88(2) EC.

[6] Case 169/82 *Commission v Italy* [1984] ECR 1603, paras 4 and 11; Case C-35/88 *Commission v Greece* [1990] ECR I-3125, para 34; Case C-61/90 *Commission v Greece* [1992] ECR I-2407, para 25; but contrast Case 173/73 *Commission v Italy* [1974] ECR 709, para 9, where it was held that the Commission was entitled to dispense with the pre-litigation procedure required under Article 226 where it had in fact issued a decision after following the Article 88(2) procedure with regard to a State aid adopted without notification.

[7] Case 290/83 *Commission v France* [1985] ECR 439, para 17.

agricultural products,[8] or a breach of the prohibition of discriminatory taxation contained in Article 90 EC.[9]

2. The enforcement procedure in the ECJ

Uniform procedure. Irrespective of whether proceedings are initiated under Article 88(2) or Article 226, once a case reaches the ECJ the procedure is in substance identical, governed in the normal way by Article 226 and the case-law thereunder. **17.10**

Relevant date for assessing failures to fulfil obligations. Where proceedings are brought under Article 226, the relevant date for assessing the alleged failure to fulfil obligations is the date prescribed by the Commission in its reasoned opinion. When Article 88(2) is applied, the relevant date on which compliance by the Member State falls to be assessed is that provided for in the Commission's decision adopted under the first subparagraphs of Article 88(2) or, where appropriate, one subsequently fixed by the Commission.[10] Where the Commission subsequently imposes further deadlines in correspondence, it is those later deadlines which will be referred to by the ECJ if they are reasonable.[11] **17.11**

Defences available to Member States. The defences available to a Member State in relation to the recovery of unlawful aid (including in infringement proceedings before the Court) are set out in Chapter 16 above.[12] Those principles will also apply by analogy, insofar as appropriate, to the (rare) infringement actions where the Member State's failure does not relate to the failure to recover unlawful aid. As is apparent from the discussion in Chapter 16, only two effective defences are available to Member States faced with an infringement action, namely the absolute impossibility of implementing the decision, and, in certain cases, the requirements of legal certainty. But no generalizations should be drawn from this approach as regards defences put forward by individuals such as aid beneficiaries: Member States are in a stronger position than individuals, which justifies a more restrictive approach as regards the defences which are available to them. They are in particular in a better position to challenge the validity of adverse decisions of the Commission and, as privileged applicants, can also challenge legislative acts. They can also submit problems which they encounter in the execution of **17.12**

---

[8] Case 72/79 *Commission v Italy* [1980] ECR 1411, paras 11–12; Case C-35/88 *Commission v Greece* [1990] ECR I-3125, paras 10–12.

[9] Case 277/83 *Commission v Italy* [1985] ECR 2049, paras 14–16.

[10] Case C-378/98 *Commission v Belgium* [2001] ECR I-5107, para 26; Case C-99/02 *Commission v Italy* [2004] ECR I-3353, para 24; Cases C-485-490/03 *Commission v Spain* [2006] ECR I-11887, para 53.

[11] Case C-207/05 *Commission v Italy* (judgment of 1 June 2006), paras 33–5; Case C-232/05 *Commission v France* (judgment of 5 October 2006), paras 33–4.

[12] See paras 16.103–16.119 above.

Commission decisions to the Commission. The beneficiary of an unlawful State aid may therefore be able to raise defences to recovery in the European and national courts which are not available to the Member State in an infringement action.

17.13 ***TWD* principle.** A Member State which does not apply to annul the validity of a Commission decision addressed to it cannot raise any indirect challenge to the lawfulness of such a decision in the context of an infringement action.[13] The underlying reason for this, as the Court stated in its judgment in the *TWD* case, is the consideration that the periods within which applications for annulment under Article 230 must be lodged are intended to safeguard legal certainty by preventing Community measures which involve legal effects from being called in question indefinitely.[14] The system of remedies set up by the Treaty distinguishes between actions under Articles 226 and 227, which are directed at obtaining a declaration that a Member State has failed to fulfil its obligations, and those under Articles 230 and 232, which are directed to obtaining judicial review of measures adopted by the Community institutions or of failure on their part to act. Those remedies have different objectives and are subject to different rules. In the absence of a provision of the Treaty expressly permitting it to do so, a Member State cannot, therefore, properly plead the unlawfulness of a decision addressed to it as a defence in an action for a declaration that it has failed to fulfil its obligations in failing to implement that decision.[15]

17.14 **Relief circumscribed by reasoned opinion or decision.** The case-law in relation to Article 226 proceedings unequivocally states that the relief sought in the ECJ cannot go beyond remedying the breaches of Community law specified in the reasoned opinion. Likewise, in the context of Article 88(2), the proceedings can only relate to the failure by the Member State concerned to comply with a Commission decision requiring it to discontinue or alter an aid measure.[16] The conduct of a Member State against which an action of this kind is brought must therefore be assessed solely in the light of the obligations imposed on it by the relevant decision.[17]

---

[13] Case 156/77 *Commission v Belgium* [1978] ECR 1881, para 20; Case 52/83 *Commission v France* [1983] ECR 3707, para 10; Case 183/91 *Commission v Greece* [1993] ECR I-3131, para 10; Case C-188/92 *TWD Textilwerke Deggendorf* [1994] ECR I-833, para 15; Case C-207/05 *Commission v Italy* (judgment of 1 June 2006), para 41.

[14] *TWD Textilwerke Deggendorf*, ibid, para 16.

[15] Case C-404/97 *Commission v Portugal* [2000] ECR I-4897, para 34; Case C-261/99 *Commission v France* [2001] ECR I-2537, para 18; Case C-207/05 *Commission v Italy* (judgment of 1 June 2006), para 42.

[16] Case 156/77 *Commission v Belgium* [1978] ECR 1881; Case 213/85 *Commission v Netherlands* [1988] ECR 281, para 7.

[17] *Commission v Netherlands*, ibid, para 8.

Failure to notify Commission of action taken to comply. In an action under Article 88(2) the Commission will frequently include a separate plea in its claims seeking a declaration that a Member State has not only failed to comply with its obligations to implement the relevant decision, but has also failed to notify the Commission of the measures it has adopted. This may constitute either a separate breach of an obligation specifically imposed in a Commission decision, or a breach of Article 10 of the EC Treaty. However, where the ECJ finds that the Member State has in fact breached its primary obligation of complying with a Commission decision, it does not examine the form of order sought for failing to notify the Commission.[18] **17.15**

Remedies available. Article 226 EC may serve as the basis for an order requiring a Member State specifically to obtain repayment of aid. In *Commission v Germany*, the Court rejected submissions that it was limited to finding a failure to fulfil Treaty obligations and could not order the Member State to take specific steps. According to the Court, the Commission is competent, when it has found that aid is incompatible with the common market, to decide that the State concerned must abolish or alter it. To be of practical effect, that may include an obligation to require repayment of aid granted in breach of the Treaty, so that in the absence of measures for recovery the Commission may bring the matter before the Court.[19] **17.16**

Article 228 EC and financial penalties. The process of complying with a judgment declaring that a Member State has failed to fulfil its obligations must be initiated at once, and must be completed as soon as possible.[20] Where the judgment is not complied with by a Member State, the Commission can bring a renewed action under Article 228, this time seeking an order requiring the Member State to pay a penalty payment. In accordance with the Commission's Communication on the application of Article 228,[21] the penalty sought will normally comprise two elements. The first element is a penalty by day of delay after the delivery of the Article 228 judgment, and the second element is a lump sum penalizing the continuation of the infringement between the first judgment on non-compliance and the Article 228 judgment. **17.17**

[18] Case C-348/93 *Commission v Italy* [1995] ECR I-673, para 31; Case C-207/05 *Commission v Italy* (judgment of 1 June 2006), para 53.

[19] Case 70/72 *Commission v Germany* [1973] ECR 813, paras 10–13.

[20] Case 169/87 *Commission v France* [1988] ECR 4093; Case C-387/97 *Commission v Greece* [2000] ECR I-5047, para 82.

[21] Communication from the Commission on the application of Article 228 of the EC Treaty, SEC/2005/1658.

17.18 *Olympic Airways*. While the Article 228 procedure has been used on a number of occasions in other fields,[22] it was not used in the State aid field until the *Olympic Airways* case brought by the Commission in 2007, and currently pending before the ECJ.[23] This arose from a 2002 decision that Greece had misused approved aid, that it had given Olympic Airways unnotified new aid, and ordering recovery of the aid. In 2005, following an action by the Commission, the ECJ confirmed that Greece had failed to recover the aid contrary to the Commission's decision.[24] By 2007 Greece had still not recovered the aid. The Commission has therefore brought an Article 228 action requesting that the Court of Justice impose a lump-sum penalty of €10,512 per day since the 2005 judgment and until implementation of the Commission's 2002 decision, as well as a further penalty of €53,611 per day from this second judgment until effective implementation of the 2002 decision.

3. Actions by Member States against other Member States

17.19 **Procedure**. Under Article 227 EC, Member States may bring actions against other Member States who fail to fulfil obligations under the EC Treaty. The procedure is analogous to the one under Article 226, in that a Member State must first bring the matter before the Commission, which in turn gives the other Member State an opportunity of submitting its observations both orally and in writing, before delivering a reasoned opinion setting out its position on the matter. If the Commission does not deliver a reasoned opinion within three months of being seized of a case, the complainant Member State may still bring an action in the ECJ. The possibility of bringing proceedings in the ECJ is likewise not affected by whether the Commission's reasoned opinion is supportive or not.

17.20 **Practical importance.** Resort to Article 227 is extremely rare. While there are some examples outside the State aid field,[25] there are none concerned with State aids.

---

[22] Case C-278/01 *Commission v Spain* [2003] ECR I-14141 concerning the quality of bathing water (periodic penalty of € 624,150 per year and per 1% of bathing areas in Spanish inshore waters which have been found not to conform to the applicable limit values); Case C-304/02 *Commission v France* [2005] ECR I-6263 concerning fisheries control obligations (lump sum penalty of € 20 million and a periodic penalty of € 57,761,250 for each period of six months at the end of which the judgment has not yet been fully complied with); Case C-177/04 *Commission v France* [2006] ECR I-2461 concerning product liability (periodic penalty of € 31,650 for each day of delay in taking the necessary measures to comply fully with the judgment); Case C-119/04 *Commission v Italy* [2006] ECR I-6885 concerning the rights of former foreign-language assistants (no penalty imposed).

[23] Case C-369/07 *Commission v Greece ('Olympic Airways')*.

[24] Case C-415/03 *Commission v Greece* [2005] ECR I-3875.

[25] Case 141/78 *France v United Kingdom* [1979] ECR 2923 concerning fisheries and Case C-388/95 *Belgium v Spain* [2000] ECR I-3123. In Case C-459/03 *Commission v Ireland* [2006] ECR I-4635 concerning a dispute between Ireland and the United Kingdom relating to the MOX plant at Sellafield, proceedings under Article 227 EC were narrowly avoided by the Commission taking action under Article 226 EC.

C. Actions for annulment of decisions

Article 230 EC. Article 230 sets out the parameters of an action for annulment as follows: 17.21

> The Court of Justice shall review the legality of acts adopted jointly by the European Parliament and the Council, of acts of the Council, of the Commission and of the ECB, other than recommendations and opinions, and of acts of the European Parliament intended to produce legal effects vis-à-vis third parties.
>
> It shall for this purpose have jurisdiction in actions brought by a Member State, the European Parliament, the Council or the Commission on grounds of lack of competence, infringement of an essential procedural requirement, infringement of this Treaty or of any rule of law relating to its application, or misuse of powers.
>
> The Court of Justice shall have jurisdiction under the same conditions in actions brought by the Court of Auditors and by the ECB for the purpose of protecting their prerogatives.
>
> Any natural or legal person may, under the same conditions, institute proceedings against a decision addressed to that person or against a decision which, although in the form of a regulation or a decision addressed to another person, is of direct and individual concern to the former.
>
> The proceedings provided for in this article shall be instituted within two months of the publication of the measure, or of its notification to the plaintiff, or, in the absence thereof, of the day on which it came to the knowledge of the latter, as the case may be.

Decisions of Commission and Council. In the vast majority of cases, proceedings for annulment will be directed against decisions of the Commission, which plays the main role in supervising the application of the State aid rules. However, decisions of the Council under the third subparagraph of Article 88(2) can also be challenged by way of an action for annulment.[26] 17.22

Overview. This section starts by briefly describing the rules governing the allocation of jurisdiction as between the ECJ and CFI. It then turns to the three basic issues which generally arise as regards the admissibility of actions for annulment: the requirement of a challengeable act, standing, and timing of the action. Finally, the main grounds of review and the consequences of annulment will be examined. 17.23

1. Competent Court

Allocation of jurisdiction. Until 2004, challenges to Commission decisions brought by private parties and infra-State entities were heard in the CFI, whereas Member States, as privileged applicants, were entitled to bring their cases directly 17.24

[26] Case C-122/94 *Commission v Council* [1996] ECR I-881; and Case C-309/95 *Commission v Council* [1998] ECR I-655.

in the ECJ. Since 2004, challenges to decisions in the State aid field have, at first instance, been subject to the exclusive jurisdiction of the CFI.[27]

17.25 **Parallel proceedings under Article 234 EC.** Parallel proceedings in front of the CFI and the ECJ may continue to arise where an action for annulment is brought under Article 230 in the CFI and at the same time a national court seised of the same matter decides to refer a question to the ECJ under Article 234.[28] This situation might occur for example where recovery of aid has been ordered by the Commission, and the beneficiary challenges the validity of the decision of the Commission while recovery proceedings are initiated in the national courts. In such cases, Article 54(3) of the Statute of the Court of Justice gives both jurisdictions the power of suspending the proceedings.

2. Challengeable acts

17.26 **Meaning of 'act'.** The action for annulment can, according to the wording of Article 230, only be brought to review the legality of 'acts' of the Community institutions. The acts which Community institutions may be prompted to take are listed in Article 249 EC, which provides that the institutions may 'make regulations and issue directives, take decisions, make recommendations or deliver opinions'. That list is however not exhaustive, as a number of types of innominate acts have evolved over time.[29] In order to ascertain whether measures are acts within the meaning of Article 230, it is necessary to look to their substance rather than their form, as well as the intention of those who drafted them.[30] For this reason, whether or not the measure satisfies certain formal requirements is irrelevant for its classification as a challengeable act under Article 230.[31]

17.27 **Final decision.** Only a measure which produces binding legal effects may be the subject of an action for annulment under Article 230. Thus intermediate measures, whose purpose is merely to prepare for the final decision, are not challengeable.[32] In addition, as Article 249(5) EC provides that 'Recommendations and opinions shall have no binding force', these acts cannot be challenged by way of action for annulment.

[27] See Article 51 of the Statute of the Court of Justice, as amended by Council Decision 2004/407/EC amending Articles 51 and 54 of the Protocol on the Statute of the Court of Justice [1994] OJ L132/5.

[28] See eg the parallel cases Case C-66/02 *Italy v Commission* [2005] ECR I-10901 and Case C-148/04 *Unicredito Italiano* [2005] ECR I-11137.

[29] See eg Case C-27/04 *Commission v Council* [2004] ECR I-6649, paras 44–51.

[30] Case C-249/02 *Portugal v Commission* [2004] ECR I-10717, para 35; Case C-521/06 P *Athinaïki Techniki v Commission* (judgment of 17 July 2008), paras 42–3.

[31] *Atinaïki Techniki*, ibid, para 44.

[32] Case 60/81 *IBM v Commission* [1981] ECR 2639, paras 9–10; Case C-147/96 *Netherlands v Commission* [2000] ECR I-4723, paras 26–7; *Athinaïki Techniki*, ibid, para 42.

Confirmatory acts. A decision that is purely confirmatory of an earlier decision is not a measure open to legal challenge.[33] This rule is based on the concern that the time limits for bringing an action should not be allowed to recommence once they have expired. An action against a confirmatory decision is therefore inadmissible only insofar as the decision confirmed has become final in relation to the person concerned through not having been challenged before the Court within the required period. Where the confirmed decision has not become final, the person concerned is entitled to challenge the original decision, the confirmatory decision or both.[34] **17.28**

Identifying the decision. Under Article 25 of the Procedural Regulation, decisions adopted by the Commission in the field of State aid must in principle be addressed to the Member States. That is also the case where the decisions concern a complaint regarding State aid, and the Commission refuses to initiate the procedure under Article 88(2) on the ground that the measures are not State aid or are compatible with the common market. In such a case the decision which is susceptible to challenge is the decision addressed to the Member State, not the letter to the complainant informing them of that decision.[35] But where the Commission, in breach of its duties under Article 25, fails to address a decision to the relevant Member State, it may not rely on that to avoid challenge. In the *Deutsche Bahn* case the Commission had sent Deutsche Bahn a letter rejecting its complaint regarding a tax exemption for aviation kerosene, on the basis that the exemption derived from a Council Directive and was not State aid. No letter was sent to the German State. The Court considered that the letter constituted a decision under Article 4(2) of the Procedural Regulation, which could be challenged by Deutsche Bahn in the absence of any formal decision addressed to the Member State.[36] The better course in such circumstances, however, is to challenge the Commission's decision to close its file, which even if not communicated to the Member State in question must be regarded as a decision under Article 4(2) of the Procedural Regulation.[37] **17.29**

---

[33] Case 26/76 *Metro v Commission* [1977] ECR 1875, para 4; Cases 166 and 220/86 *Irish Cement v Commission* [1988] ECR 6473, para 16; Case C-480/93 P *Zunis Holding v Commission* [1996] ECR I-1, para 14.

[34] Cases 193 and 194/87 *Maurissen and Union Syndicale v Court of Auditors* [1989] ECR 1045, para 26; Case T-64/92 *Chavane de Dalmassy v Commission* [1994] ECR-SC II-723, para 25; T-188/95 *Waterleiding Maatschappij v Commission* [1998] ECR II-3713, para 108.

[35] Case C-367/95 P *Commission v Sytraval and Brink's France* [1998] ECR I-1719, para 45; Case T-46/97 *SIC v Commission* [2000] ECR II-2125 para 45; and see Case C-521/06 P *Athinaïki Techniki v Commission* (judgment of 17 July 2008), para 47.

[36] Case T-351/02 *Deutsche Bahn v Commission* [2006] ECR II-1047, paras 34–63.

[37] Case C-521/06 P *Athinaïki Techniki v Commission* (judgment of 17 July 2008), paras 47–62.

17.30 **Examples.** In the State aid field, substantive Commission decisions provided for in the Procedural Regulation, such as decisions declaring aid to be compatible or incompatible with the common market, or finding that the measure does not constitute State aid, are clearly challengeable acts.[38] The same applies for decisions imposing suspension and recovery injunctions.[39] Decisions of the Council under Article 88(2), third subparagraph, deeming aid to be compatible with the common market are also challengeable.[40] By contrast, the initiation of the formal investigation procedure under Article 88(2) does not constitute a challengeable act where it relates to *existing aids* as the Member State in issue can maintain the aid notwithstanding the Commission's investigation, and the initiation of the investigation thus does not produce legal effects.[41] But where *new unnotified aid* is concerned, that produces legal effects for the Member State, aid beneficiaries and third parties. In such a case, therefore, the decision to open the formal investigation procedure can be challenged.[42] The right to contest a decision to initiate the formal procedure under Article 88(2) does not, however, diminish the rights of interested parties to challenge the Commission's final decision at the end of that procedure, and to rely in support of their action on defects at any stage of the procedure leading to that decision.[43]

3. Standing

(a) *Privileged applicants*

17.31 **Member States and institutions.** Article 230 draws a clear distinction between the right of action available to Member States and Community institutions on the one hand and that available to natural or legal persons on the other. Member States and Community institutions are privileged applicants in that the exercise of their right of action is not conditional on proof of an interest in bringing proceedings.[44] Thus Member States can not only (and frequently do) bring actions for the

---

[38] This is the case also for a decision finding a measure to be State aid, but approving it as being compatible with the common market: Case T-233/04 *Netherlands v Commission* (judgment of 10 April 2008), paras 37–42 (under appeal on this point in Case C-279/08 P *Commission v Netherlands*).

[39] Case C-400/99 *Commission v Italy ('Tirrenia – admissibility')* [2001] ECR I-7303, para 51.

[40] Such a decison was annulled in Case C-110/02 *Commission v Council* [2004] ECR I-6333.

[41] Cases C-182 and 217/03 R *Belgium and Forum 187 v Commission* [2003] ECR I-6887, para 119.

[42] Case C-400/99 *Commission v Italy ('Tirrenia – admissibility')* [2001] ECR I-7303, paras 63–5; and see Case C-400/99 *Commission v Italy ('Tirrenia')* [2005] ECR I-3657, paras 15–17; and see further para 16.43 above.

[43] Case T-25/04 *González y Díez v Commission* [2007] ECR II-3121, para 92.

[44] Case 45/86 *Commission v Council* [1987] ECR 1493, para 3. cf Case C-242/00 *Germany v Commission* [2002] ECR I-5603, para 46, rejecting an action brought by Germany against a decision of the Commission on the basis that the decision did not by itself have a scope unfavourable to Germany and thus did not adversely affect it. This case is however probably best seen as turning on the absence of a properly challengeable act, rather than as suggesting a limitation on the standing of Germany.

annulment of negative Commission decisions, but may also bring actions for the annulment of the authorization of aid in other Member States. For example where the Commission authorizes aid following a preliminary review only, another Member State may challenge the decision not to initiate the formal procedure.[45] A Member State may also challenge a decision approving aid as compatible with the common market, on the grounds that the Member State disputes the classification of the measure as State aid at all.[46]

(b) Non-privileged applicants: overview

Criteria. The standing of non-privileged applicants in Article 230 proceedings is affected by two distinct, if often in practice closely related, sets of circumstances. First, a non-privileged applicant must show that he has an interest in seeing the contested measure annulled. Secondly, the applicant must be sufficiently directly and individually concerned to be granted standing. The paragraphs below outline these two criteria in general terms. Subsections (c) to (e) then consider in more detail the specific situations of different classes of applicants. **17.32**

Interest in bringing proceedings. An action for annulment brought by a natural or legal person is not admissible unless the applicant has an interest in seeing the contested measure annulled.[47] The burden of proof in this respect lies on the applicant.[48] The interest in bringing proceedings must be vested and present[49] and is evaluated as at the date on which the action is brought.[50] If the interest upon which an applicant relies concerns a future legal situation, he must demonstrate that the prejudice to that situation is already certain. Therefore, an applicant cannot rely upon future uncertain circumstances to establish his interest in applying for annulment of the contested act.[51] **17.33**

Challenged act must continue to produce effects. Where a challenged act is no longer in force, or has been withdrawn by the Commission, the action for **17.34**

---

[45] Case 84/82 *Germany v Commission* [1984] ECR 1451.

[46] Case T-233/04 *Netherlands v Commission* (judgment of 10 April 2008), paras 37–42 (under appeal on this point in Case C-279/08 P *Commission v Netherlands*).

[47] Cases T-480/93 and T-483/93 *Antillean Rice Mills v Commission* [1995] ECR II-2305, para 59; Case T-102/96 *Gencor v Commission* [1999] ECR II-753, para 40; Case T-212/00 *Nuove Industrie Molisane v Commission* [2002] ECR II-347, para 33.

[48] Case C-206/89 R *S v Commission* [1989] ECR 2841, para 8; Case T-141/03 *Sniace v Commission* [2005] ECR II-1197, para 31.

[49] Case T-138/89 *NBV and NVB v Commission* [1992] ECR II-2181, para 33; Case T-141/03 *Sniace v Commission* [2005] ECR II-1197, para 25; Case T-301/01 *Alitalia v Commission ('Alitalia II')* (judgment of 9 July 2008), para 35.

[50] Case 14/63 *Forges de Clabecq v High Authority* [1963] ECR 357; Case T-141/03 *Sniace v Commission* [2005] ECR II-1197, para 25.

[51] Case T-138/89 *NBV and NVB v Commission* [1992] ECR II-2181, para 33; Case T-141/03 *Sniace v Commission* [2005] ECR II-1197, para 26.

annulment of that act will normally be devoid of purpose and inadmissible.[52] In one case in the fisheries field, however, an intention to prevent a repetition of the alleged illegality in future acts was accepted as being sufficient to constitute an interest in challenging an act which was no longer applicable.[53]

17.35 **Direct and individual concern.** In addition to the condition of interest in bringing proceedings, a non-privileged applicant must be able to show that he is directly and individually concerned by the decision.[54] In order for *direct concern* to exist, the contested Community act must directly affect the legal situation of the individual and, to the extent that implementation measures are required, leave no discretion to the addressees of that measure who are entrusted with the task of implementing it, such implementation being purely automatic and resulting from Community provisions without the application of other intermediate rules.[55] Persons other than those to whom a decision is addressed may, according to a formula laid down in the seminal *Plaumann* case,[56] claim to be *individually concerned* only if that decision affects them by reason of certain attributes which are peculiar to them or by reason of circumstances in which they are differentiated from all other persons and by virtue of those factors distinguishes them individually just as in the case of the person addressed.[57]

(c) Grantors and beneficiaries of State aid

17.36 **Grantors of aid.** A decision finding aid to be unlawful has a direct and individual effect on the grantor of aid, which therefore has an interest of its own in challenging the decision.[58] Where the grantor of aid is a governmental authority of a Member State of the EC, it will in any event be a privileged applicant, which may apply for annulment as a matter of course. However, for the purposes of jurisdiction to bring proceedings under the second paragraph of Article 230, the term 'Member State' does not include governments of regions or autonomous communities. Therefore a regional authority is not entitled to bring proceedings under

[52] Case T-239/94 *EISA v Commission* [1997] ECR II-1839, para 34.

[53] Case 207/86 *Apesco v Commission* [1988] ECR 2151, paras 14–15.

[54] See generally AG Ruiz-Jarabo Colomer in Case C-106/98 P *Comité d'entreprise de la Société française de production v Commission* [2000] ECR I-3659, para 15.

[55] Cases 41/70 to 44/70 *International Fruit Company v Commission* [1971] ECR 411, paras 23–9; Case 92/78 *Simmenthal v Commission* [1979] ECR 777, paras 25–6; Case 333/85 *Mannesmann-Röhrenwerke v Council* [1987] ECR 1381, para 14; Case C-152/88 *Sofrimport v Commission* [1990] ECR I-2477, para 9; Case C-404/96 *Glencore Grain v Commission* [1998] ECR I-2435, para 41; Case C-486/01 P *Front national v Parliament* [2004] ECR I-6289, para 34.

[56] Case 25/62 *Plaumann v Commission* [1963] ECR 95.

[57] ibid, para 107; Case C-198/91 *Cook v Commission* [1993] ECR I-2487, para 20; Case C-78/03 P *Commission v ARE* [2005] ECR I-10737, para 33; Case C-176/06 P *Stadtwerke Schwäbisch Hall v Commission* (judgment of 29 November 2007), para 19.

[58] Case T-214/95 *Vlaams Gewest v Commission* [1998] ECR II-717, paras 29–30.

the second paragraph of Article 230.[59] However a regional authority may be a legal personality within the meaning of the fourth paragraph of Article 230.[60]

Beneficiaries: unfavourable decisions. An actual beneficiary of an aid will generally have standing to challenge a decision of the Commission declaring that aid to be incompatible with the Common market.[61] In such a case, the beneficiary will have both an interest in bringing proceedings seeking the annulment of the aid, and will be directly and individually concerned by the contested decision.[62] The fact that the Commission's decision concerning the aid measure is only addressed to the Member State is of no relevance in this context.[63] **17.37**

Beneficiaries: favourable decisions. The position is more difficult where the decision under challenge is favourable, since it must be shown that the appeal will, if successful, benefit the appellant.[64] The beneficiary of the aid may nevertheless have sufficient interest if it challenges a decision declaring aid compatible with the common market on the grounds that the measure in question does not constitute State aid at all.[65] But in such a case the undertaking has to show concrete negative consequences of the finding that there was aid, in order to demonstrate that it has a sufficient interest in bringing proceedings. Examples of this may be pending actions in the national courts based on the last sentence of Article 88(3),[66] or the imposition of conditions in a decision approving the aid.[67] Where no sufficient interest can be shown for an action for annulment, the aid recipient may still challenge the existence of aid in national proceedings, and may ask the national court to make a preliminary ruling on the matter.[68] **17.38**

Potential beneficiaries. By contrast with the position of actual beneficiaries, an undertaking cannot contest a Commission decision prohibiting a general aid scheme solely on the basis that it is a potential beneficiary of the scheme. Such a decision **17.39**

---

[59] Case C-95/97 *Région wallonne v Commission* [1997] ECR I-1787; Case C-180/97 *Regione Toscana v Commission* [1997] ECR I-5245.

[60] Case T-214/95 *Vlaams Gewest v Commission* [1998] ECR II-717, para 28.

[61] See Cases C-15/98 and C-105/99 *Italy and Sardegna Lines v Commission* [2000] ECR I-8855, paras 34–6; Case C-298/00 P *Italy v Commission* [2004] ECR I-4087, paras 38–9.

[62] Cases T-239 and 323/04 *Italy and Brandt v Commission* [2007] ECR II-3265, paras 43–4.

[63] See Case 730/79 *Philip Morris v Commission* [1980] ECR 2671, where admissibility was not even challenged by Commission.

[64] Case T-301/01 *Alitalia v Commission ('Alitalia II')* (judgment of 9 July 2008), para 36.

[65] Case T-141/03 *Sniace v Commission* [2005] ECR II-1197, para 23; *Alitalia II*, ibid, para 42.

[66] *Sniace v Commission*, ibid, paras 29–30; see also Case T-136/05 *Salvat père & fils v Commission* [2007] ECR II-4063, paras 34–8.

[67] Case T-301/01 *Alitalia v Commission ('Alitalia II')* (judgment of 9 July 2008), where the Court held at paras 42–7 that the annulment of the finding of aid would have legal consequences for Alitalia, even though the parties disputed the precise nature of those consequences. See also paras 377–88 on the admissibility of a challenge to the conditions themselves.

[68] Case T-141/03 *Sniace v Commission* [2005] ECR II-1197, para 40.

entails legal effects only for a class of persons envisaged in a general and abstract manner.[69]

(d) Competitors and complainants

17.40 **Competitors generally.** The requirements for competitors to be individually concerned for the purposes of the rules on State aid vary considerably depending on the stage of proceedings in which an action is brought and the objective of that action. In the *ARE* case,[70] the ECJ summarized the conditions under which (potential) competitors of the beneficiary may be able to bring an action against Commission decisions, where the Commission does not object to the Member State measures. In this regard there are two basic types of action: on the one hand, actions aimed at bringing about the formal investigation procedure; on the other hand, actions challenging the Commission's actual decision in the case.

17.41 **Challenge to failure to open formal investigation procedure.** If the action is aimed at compelling the formal investigation procedure, on the ground that competitors will be able to enforce their rights to participate in this procedure, it is not necessary to show that the undertaking is substantially affected by the grant of aid;[71] rather, it is sufficient if the applicants are persons, undertakings or associations whose interests *might be affected*.[72] The capacity to bring an action in this respect is made relatively extensive in order to safeguard the procedural rights of potential competitors in the formal procedure which are guaranteed under Article 88(2).[73] The category of parties able to bring proceedings to force the formal review procedure to be opened thus encompasses not only actual competitors, but all 'interested parties' (or, in the words of Article 88(2), 'parties concerned'). These are defined in the Procedural Regulation as 'any Member State and any person, undertaking or association of undertakings whose interests might be affected by the granting of aid, in particular the beneficiary of the aid, competing undertakings and trade associations'.[74] It follows that it is not necessary for the applicant to

---

[69] Cases 67, 68 and 70/85 *Van der Kooy v Commission* [1988] ECR 219, para 15; Cases C-15/98 and C-105/99 *Italy and Sardegna Lines v Commission* [2000] ECR I-8855, para 33.

[70] Case C-78/03 P *Commission v ARE* [2005] ECR I-10737, para 34 *et seq.*

[71] Case T-395/04 *Air One v Commission* [2006] ECR II-1343, para 36.

[72] Case C-78/03 P *Commission v ARE* [2005] ECR I-10737, paras 35–6; Case T-95/96 *Gestevision Telecinco v Commission* [1998] ECR II-3407, para 65; and Case T-167/04 *Asklepios Kliniken v Commission* [2007] ECR II-2379, para 49.

[73] Case C-198/91 *Cook v Commission* [1993] ECR I-2487, paras 23–6; Case C-225/91 *Matra v Commission* [1993] ECR I-3203, paras 17–20; Case C-367/95 P *Commission v Sytraval and Brink's France* [1998] ECR I-1719, paras 47–8; Case C-78/03 P *Commission* v *ARE* [2005] ECR I-10737, paras 34–5; Case T-95/03 *Asociación de Estaciones de Servicio v Commission* [2006] ECR II-4739, paras 45–7.

[74] Procedural Regulation, Article 1(h); and see Case 323/82 *Intermills v Commission* [1984] ECR 3809, para 16; *Commission v Sytraval and Brink's France*, ibid, para 41; and *Commission v ARE*, ibid, para 36. See further para 16.47 above.

establish a precise definition of the market, or to show that it is in actual and direct competition with each and every beneficiary of the alleged aid.[75]

Merits challenge to approval decision. The situation is different where the action seeks to have an approval decision annulled on substantive grounds. In that case, it will not be sufficient that the applicant is an 'interested party' or a 'party concerned'. It must, rather, demonstrate that it is directly and individually concerned.[76] This requires that its market position is 'substantially'[77] or 'significantly'[78] affected by the aid which is the subject of the contested decision. This criterion serves to identify competitors who, as a result of aid which is approved, are distinguished individually in such a manner that they fulfil the requirements for admissibility in the *Plaumann* case, referred to above. It is also relevant to consider the degree of involvement of the applicant in the administrative procedure, although that of its own is not sufficient where the applicant is not substantially or significantly affected by the aid.[79] These conditions cannot be set aside on the basis of a claimed right to effective judicial protection. An individual who is not directly and individually concerned by a Commission decision relating to State aid, and whose interest consequently could not be affected by the State measure affected by that decision, cannot invoke the right to judicial protection in relation to that decision.[80] Nor can these conditions be avoided by attempting to characterize an action as a procedural challenge to the failure to open the formal investigation procedure, when the reality of the matter is that it is a substantive challenge to the merits of the decision.[81] **17.42**

[75] Case T-167/04 *Asklepios Kliniken v Commission* (judgment of 11 July 2007), paras 54–5.

[76] Case C-176/06 P *Stadtwerke Schwäbisch Hall v Commission* (judgment of 29 November 2007), paras 18–19 and 24.

[77] Case C-78/03 P *Commission v ARE* [2005] ECR I-10737, paras 68–70; Case T-95/03 *Asociación de Estaciones de Servicio v Commission* [2006] ECR II-4739, para 48; Case C-260/05 P *Sniace v Commission* [2007] ECR I-10005, para 54.

[78] Case 169/84 *Cofaz v Commission* [1986] ECR 391, para 25; Order in Case C-409/96 P *Sveriges Betodlares and Henrikson v Commission* [1997] ECR I-7531, para 45; Case T-395/04 *Air One v Commission* [2006] ECR II-1343, para 32.

[79] See *Cofaz v Commission*, ibid, paras 24–5; Case T-11/95 *BP Chemicals v Commission* [1998] ECR II-3235, para 72; Case C-260/05 P *Sniace v Commission* [2007] ECR I-10005, paras 55–7.

[80] *Sniace v Commission*, ibid, para 65.

[81] See Case C-176/06 P *Stadtwerke Schwäbisch Hall v Commission* (judgment of 29 November 2007), where the ECJ overruled the conclusion of the CFI that an application for annulment was admissible as being a procedural challenge; on the contrary, the ECJ held, it was a substantive challenge and the applicants therefore had to satisfy the test of direct and individual concern. Since they had not demonstrated that they were substantially affected by the alleged aid, this test was not satisfied and their application for annulment in the CFI was therefore inadmissible. See also Case T-254/05 *Fachvereinigung Mineralfaserindustrie v Commission* (judgment of 20 September 2007), para 48; and Case T-375/03 *Fachvereinigung Mineralfasterindustrie v Commission* (judgment of 20 September 2007), para 65.

17.43 **Meaning of 'substantial' or 'significant' effect of aid.** In basic terms, every advantage which is conferred on selectively determined market operators affects the market position of all competitors who do not enjoy this advantage. However, a competitor's market position is also positively or negatively influenced by many other factors. Thus, the mere fact that the decision at issue may have some influence on competitive relationships on the relevant market cannot in itself suffice to allow every trader in any competitive relationship with the beneficiary to be regarded as being directly and individually concerned by that decision.[82] Therefore, an undertaking cannot rely solely on its status as a competitor of the undertaking which benefits from the decision in question, but must additionally show that its circumstances distinguish it in a similar way to the undertaking in receipt of the aid,[83] by demonstrating the magnitude of the prejudice to its position on the market.[84]

17.44 **Evidence.** The CFI has stressed that it is not for the European Court, when considering whether an application is admissible, to carry out a detailed investigation into the competitive relationship between the applicants and the undertakings in receipt of the aid. It is accordingly for the applicants alone to adduce pertinent evidence to show that the Commission's decision may adversely affect their legitimate interests by seriously jeopardizing their position on the market in question.[85] In this respect, although a loss of turnover following the aid may be indicative of a substantial effect on the applicant,[86] that is not a decisive criterion, and other factors may be relevant. These could include any loss of opportunity to make a profit, the number of producers on the market, any production overcapacity on the market, and the nature of the aid.[87]

17.45 **Parallel national proceedings.** The possible existence of an adequate domestic remedy (eg challenging the payment of the aid by the Member State) does not affect standing in European Court for the purposes of an action for annulment.[88]

(e) Representative bodies

17.46 **Representative bodies.** An association of undertakings which is not the addressee of the contested measure has standing to bring an action for annulment only in two cases. The first is where the association, in bringing its action, has substituted

[82] Cases 10/68 and 18/68 *Eridania v Commission* [1969] ECR 459, paras 7–8; Case C-525/04 P *Spain v Commission* [2007] ECR I-9947, para 32.

[83] *Spain v Commission*, ibid, para 33.

[84] Case C-106/98 P *Comité d'entreprise de la Société française de production v Commission* [2000] ECR I-3659, paras 40–1. See also Case C-176/06 P *Stadtwerke Schwäbisch Hall v Commission* (judgment of 29 November 2007), paras 31–2.

[85] Case C-525/04 P *Spain v Commission* [2007] ECR I-9947, para 41.

[86] Case T-117/04 *Vereniging Werkgroep Commerciële Jachthavens Zuidelijke Randmeren v Commission* [2006] ECR II-3861, para 59.

[87] Case C-525/04 P *Spain v Commission* [2007] ECR I-9947, paras 34–9.

[88] Case T-95/96 *Gestevision Telecinco v Commission* [1998] ECR II-3407, para 68.

itself for one or more of the members whom it represents, on condition that those members were themselves in a position to bring an admissible action.[89] The second is where there are 'special circumstances', such as the role which the association has played in the procedure leading to the adoption of the contested measure, or because its negotiating position is affected by that measure.[90]

Meaning of 'special circumstances'. It is clear that the mere fact that the association made a complaint to the Commission and in that connection corresponded and had meetings with the Commission cannot constitute circumstances peculiar to the applicant sufficient to distinguish it individually from all other persons.[91] The seminal cases where special circumstances were found to exist are *Van der Kooy*[92] and *CIRFS*.[93] In *Van der Kooy*, the ECJ found that the Landbouwschap, in its capacity as negotiator of gas tariffs, had taken an active part in the procedure under Article 88(2) by submitting written comments to the Commission and by keeping in close contact with the responsible officials throughout the procedure. It was one of the parties to the contract which established the tariff disallowed by the Commission and, in that capacity, was mentioned several times in the Commission decision. The role of the applicant in *CIRFS* was also very substantial. CIRFS was an association whose membership included the main international manufacturers of synthetic fibres. It had pursued, in the interest of those manufacturers, a number of actions connected with the policy of restructuring the sector defined by the Commission. In particular, it had been the Commission's contact in negotiations to introduce restrictive rules in the sector and to extend and adapt them and it had pursued negotiations with the Commission in particular by submitting written representations to it and by keeping in close contact with the responsible departments. **17.47**

Number of undertakings represented. The number of undertakings represented by a body will also in certain circumstances be taken into account, at any event in determining the level of detail required to be supplied regarding the individual members' market position. For example, in *Vereniging Werkgroep Commerciële Jachthavens*, the applicants represented merely six of approximately 1,200 marinas **17.48**

[89] Case 282/85 *DEFI v Commission* [1986] ECR 2469, para 16; Case C-6/92 *Federmineraria v Commission* [1993] ECR I-6397, para 17; Case T-117/04 *Vereniging Werkgroep Commerciële Jachthavens Zuidelijke Randmeren v Commission* [2006] ECR II-3861, para 50.

[90] Case C-313/90 *CIRFS v Commission* [1993] ECR I-1125, paras 29–30; Case T-55/99 *CETM v Commission* [2000] ECR II-3207, para 23; *Vereniging Werkgroep Commerciële Jachthavens Zuidelijke Randmeren*, ibid, para 65; Case T-95/03 *Asociación de Estaciones de Servicio v Commission* [2006] ECR II-4739, para 42.

[91] Case T-398/94 *Kahn Scheepvaart v Commission* [1996] ECR II-477, para 42.

[92] Cases 67/85, 68/85 and 70/85 *Van der Kooy v Commission* [1988] ECR 219.

[93] Case C-313/90 *CIRFS v Commission* [1993] ECR I-1125.

operating in the Netherlands. Therefore, they represented only a tiny proportion of the harbours which might be concerned by the aid at issue. In such a situation, each of the applicants should have set out in what respect aid granted to such and such a harbour might prejudice its own activities, for example, by risking loss of custom or reduction in the profit margin.[94]

17.49 **Other examples.** In *CETM*,[95] the Spanish Confederation of Goods Transporters, a trade association, did have standing to protect the individual interests of certain of its members who had received the aid and were required to repay under the contested decision, but only as regards the aid to those members which had as their main business the transport of goods by road. In *Asociación de Estaciones de Servicio de Madrid*,[96] Spanish associations of service station owners were also held to have standing, having shown that aid granted to hypermarkets to break into the service station market was likely to have a significant effect on the position of one or more of their members. The members represented more than a quarter of all service stations in Spain and, in particular, 85% of the service stations in the Madrid region and 70% of those in Catalonia. The purpose of the aid measure was to facilitate the entry of hypermarkets into the Spanish market for the retail supply of petroleum products in order to promote competition in that market. Such an increase was held to be likely to substantially alter the competitive situation on the market to the disadvantage of other service station operators. The applicants relied in particular on the case of several service stations operated by their members which had suffered a significant drop in their sales leading, in certain cases, to the closing-down of their businesses as a result of the opening of a service station by a neighbouring hypermarket. In *Forum 187*,[97] the applicant, who represented the interests of 30 'coordination centres' the entitlement of which to benefit from a disputed aid regime was limited in time, and eight centres with pending applications for renewal of aid, was held to have standing on the basis of the standing of its members.

4. Timing of actions for annulment

17.50 **Two-month time limit.** Under Article 230(5), actions for annulment must be brought within two months of the publication of the measure, its notification to the applicant, or, in the absence thereof, the day on which it came to the knowledge of the latter, as the case may be. That time limit is extended by ten days on account of distance, pursuant to Article 102(2) of the Rules of Procedure of

[94] Case T-117/04 *Vereniging Werkgroep Commerciële Jachthavens Zuidelijke Randmeren v Commission* [2006] ECR II-3861, para 60.

[95] Case T-55/99 *CETM v Commission* [2000] ECR II-3207, para 24.

[96] Case T-95/03 *Asociación de Estaciones de Servicio v Commission* [2006] ECR II-4739, para 49.

[97] Cases C-182/03 and C-217/03 *Belgium and Forum 187 v Commission* [2006] ECR I-5479, paras 53–64.

the CFI. An application may be brought out of time only if the existence of unforeseeable circumstances or of *force majeure* can be shown.[98]

Moment time begins to run. A decision declaring notified aid to be compatible with the common market is notified only to its addressee, namely the Member State. As regards parties other than the Member State, publication in the Official Journal (OJ) will thus play a crucial role in determining when time begins to run. Under Article 26 of the Procedural Regulation, all decisions of the Commission under that Regulation are published (whether in full or in Summary form) in the OJ. The effect of Article 230(5) is that time will begin to run at the latest with publication of the measure. The knowledge of the applicant is only relevant where a measure has not been published at all.[99] Thus if the Commission does not notify the decision to the applicant, but does publish the decision in the OJ, it is only the date of publication in the OJ which starts time running for the applicant, even if he had knowledge of the full text of the decision before that date.[100] The publication of a summary of the decision in the OJ, together with a link to the Commission's website on which the full text of the decision is published, is sufficient to constitute publication within the meaning of Article 230(5).[101] In the absence of either publication or notification, it is the responsibility of a party who has knowledge of a decision concerning it to request the whole text of the decision within a reasonable period. Subject to that reservation, the two-month period does not start to run until the third party concerned has been able to obtain an exact knowledge of the content and grounds of the measure in question so as to be able to exercise his right of action.[102] 17.51

No need for act to produce effects immediately. The fact that the effects of an act do not materialize until a subsequent date determined in the act does not preclude an individual from being directly affected by it before that date. As applicants are required to comply with the period for bringing an action prescribed in the fifth paragraph of Article 230 EC, any other interpretation would have the consequence that the institution which adopted the act would be able to prevent an individual from bringing an action for annulment by postponing the date of applicability.[103] 17.52

[98] Article 45 of the Statute of the Court of Justice. See also Case T-392/05 *MMT v Commission* (order of 11 December 2006), paras 35–6 suggesting that in certain very limited cases an 'excusable mistake' may also be relied upon.

[99] Case C-122/95 *Germany v Council* [1998] ECR I-973, para 35; Case T-296/97 *Alitalia v Commission ('Alitalia I')* [2000] ECR II-3871, para 61.

[100] *Alitalia I,* ibid, paras 61–4; Case T-190/00 *Regione Siciliana v Commission* [2003] ECR II-5015, para 31.

[101] Case T-321/04 *Air Bourbon v Commission* [2005] ECR II-3469, para 34.

[102] Cases T-432-434/93 *Socurte v Commission* [1995] ECR II-503, para 49.

[103] Case T-40/04 *Bonino v Parliament and Council* [2005] ECR II-2685, paras 46–7.

5. Grounds of review

(a) Overview

17.53 **General.** The European Court has jurisdiction under Article 230(2) to review decisions of the Commission and the Council on grounds of lack of competence, infringement of an essential procedural requirement, infringement of the EC Treaty or of any rule of law relating to its application, or misuse of powers. These grounds are interpreted as including, in addition, the power to annul decisions on the basis of a manifest error of facts.

17.54 **Scope of review.** The legal concepts in Articles 87 and 88 are subject to review by the courts. In particular, the concept of State aid is a legal one which must be interpreted on the basis of objective factors. Therefore, the European Court must in principle, having regard both to the specific features of the case before them and to the technical or complex nature of the Commission's assessments, carry out a comprehensive review as to whether a measure falls within the scope of Article 87(1).[104] In that respect, the European Court is the only institution capable of providing a binding interpretation of Community law. The Commission's own views as to the interpretation of legal concepts will have persuasive but no binding value.[105] On the other hand, the Commission benefits from a wide discretion when it comes to the assessments of complex economic and social factors which have to be carried out in the State aid context, and for which the Community judicature cannot substitute its own assessment.[106] A constant challenge to practitioners is thus distinguishing those concepts which are likely to be held to be justiciable from those where the Commission enjoys a wide discretion.

17.55 **New factual matters.** The lawfulness of the Commission's assessment is to be judged by reference to the information available to the Commission when the decision was adopted.[107] Accordingly, the applicant may not rely on factual arguments which were unknown to the Commission and which could have been (but were not) submitted to it during the administrative procedure.[108] Save in entirely

[104] Case C-83/98 P *France v Ladbroke Racing and Commission* [2000] ECR I-3271, para 25; Cases C-341-342/06 P *Chronopost v Ufex* (judgment of 1 July 2008), para 141.

[105] Case C-301/96 *Germany v Commission* [2003] ECR I-9919, paras 80–1.

[106] Cases T-298/97 etc *Mauro Alzetta et al v Commission* [2000] ECR II-2319, para 130; and Case C-310/99 *Italy v Commission* [2002] ECR I-2289, para 46. See also Cases C-341-342/06 P *Chronopost v Ufex* (judgment of 1 July 2008), para 143 noting the limited power of review of a complex economic appraisal. cf Case T-266/02 *Deutsche Post v Commission* (judgment of 1 July 2008), para 90 noting the absence of discretion where no such complexity arises.

[107] Case 234/84 *Belgium v Commission* [1986] ECR 2263, para 16; Case C-241/94 *France v Commission* [1996] ECR I-4551, para 33; Case C-197/99 P *Belgium v Commission* [2003] ECR I-8461, para 86; Cases C-341-342/06 P *Chronopost v Ufex* (judgment of 1 July 2008), para 90; and see also conclusions on the merits at paras 141–64.

[108] Case C-367/95 P *Commission v Sytraval and Brink's France ('Sytraval')* [1998] ECR I-1719, para 60; Case C-197/99 P *Belgium v Commission* [2003] ECR I-8461, para 87; Case T-109/01

exceptional cases, this rule applies even where the applicant did not in fact participate in the investigation procedure provided for in Article 88(2).[109] This principle also applies where the Commission has decided to raise no objections to an aid measure without initiating the Article 88(2) procedure.[110] However there is an obvious exception to this principle where the Commission itself unreasonably prevented additional information from being provided to it, or unreasonably rejected tenders of additional information.[111]

New legal arguments. By contrast with the position in relation to new *factual* matters, nothing prevents an applicant from raising before the CFI, in relation to the annulment of the Commission's final decision, new *legal* arguments not raised during the administrative procedure.[112] That is so even where the applicant itself participated in the formal investigation procedure and could have made those arguments in the course of that procedure.[113] **17.56**

(b) Infringement of procedural rights

Procedure. Even though a wide discretion has been conferred on the Commission in the State aid field, the European Court is required to verify whether or not it has observed the procedural guarantees and apply strict standards in this regard. The procedure applicable to Commission investigations of State aid is set out in detail in Chapter 16 above. It includes, in particular, obligations to take into account the submissions of the Member State concerned as well as the submissions of third parties, including in particular the aid beneficiary, and the duty to conduct a diligent and impartial investigation within specified time-limits or (where no time-limits apply) within a reasonable time. **17.57**

Burden of proof. It is for the applicant to particularize in detail any complaint of procedural failures, setting out precisely the illegality and how it affected the applicant. It is not sufficient to make summary claims that the Commission acted unmethodically, expressed differing views without justification or did not respond to the documents submitted by the applicant, without substantiating them by more detailed information or any evidence.[114] **17.58**

Fleuren Compost v Commission [2004] ECR II-127, para 49; Case T-366/00 *Scott v Commission* [2007] ECR II-797, para 45.

[109] Cases T-111 and 133/01 *Saxonia Edelmetalle and ZEMAG v Commission* [2005] ECR II-1579, para 69; Case T-217/02 *Ter Lembeek International v Commission* [2006] ECR II-4483, para 85.

[110] Case C-390/06 *Nuova Agricast* (judgment of 15 April 2008), paras 55–60.

[111] Case T-366/00 *Scott v Commission* [2007] ECR II-797, para 46 *et seq.*

[112] Cases T-111 and 133/01 *Saxonia Edelmetalle and ZEMAG v Commission* [2005] ECR II-1579, para 68, and the cases there cited.

[113] Case T-16/96 *Cityflyer v Commission* [1998] ECR II-757, para 39.

[114] Case T-95/03 *Asociación de Estaciones de Servicio v Commission* [2006] ECR II-4739, para 143.

17.59 **Annulment not automatic.** Infringements of procedural requirements will only result in annulment where, but for the irregularity, the outcome might have been different.[115] Thus, for example, the mere adoption of a decision after the expiry of a reasonable period is not in itself sufficient to render unlawful a decision taken by the Commission at the conclusion of an initial examination conducted under Article 88(3).[116] If it is alleged that non-compliance by the Commission with a procedural requirement caused loss to the applicants, that is not in principle relevant in the context of an action for annulment, though it may, if made out, form the basis of a separately pleaded action for damages under Article 288(2).[117]

(c) Manifest error of assessment

17.60 **Review of facts.** The European Court can review the Commission's findings of fact to consider whether on the material before the Commission such findings were open to the Commission. Where it appears that there is abuse of power or manifest error of assessment, including a case where it is clear that the Commission has exercised its discretion in a way which is outside the object and purpose of the legislation, the Court may annul the Commission's decision.[118] Absent such a manifest error or misuse of powers, the Court will not interfere with the Commission's factual findings.

17.61 **Review of economic evidence.** While the Court recognizes that the Commission has a margin of discretion with regard to economic matters, and that the Court must not substitute its own economic assessment for that of the Commission, that does not mean that it must entirely refrain from reviewing the Commission's interpretation of information of an economic nature. On the contrary, the Court has emphasized that it must not only establish whether the evidence relied on by the Commission is factually accurate, reliable and consistent, but also whether that evidence contains all the information which must be taken into account, and whether it is capable of substantiating the Commission's conclusions.[119]

17.62 **Types of mistake.** The European Court will investigate any factual mistakes which are apparent from the face of the record of the Commission's investigation. Examples of such mistakes include the Commission using a basis other than the

[115] Case C-142/87 *Belgium v Commission* [1990] ECR I-959, para 48; Case C-288/96 *Germany v Commission* [2000] ECR I-8237, paras 99 and 101.

[116] Case T-378/02 R *Technische Glaswerke Ilmenau v Commission* [2003] ECR II-2921, para 65, and the cases there cited.

[117] Case T-95/03 *Asociación de Estaciones de Servicio v Commission* [2006] ECR II-4739, para 132; and see para 17.80 *et seq* below.

[118] Case 84/82 *Commission v Germany* [1984] ECR 1451 per AG Slynn at pp 1499–500; Case 187/85 *Fediol* [1988] ECR 4155, para 6; Case C-288/96 *Germany v Commission* [2000] ECR I-8237, para 26.

[119] Case C-525/04 P *Spain v Commission* [2007] ECR I-9947, paras 56–8.

market value of an asset transferred to an aid beneficiary,[120] obvious calculation errors,[121] failing accurately to verify the basis for its assessments,[122] failing to take into account pertinent facts[123] or relevant information provided by the Member State in question,[124] failing to resolve obvious discrepancies,[125] and errors in determination of the amount of aid to be recovered.[126] Moreover, while the Court has accepted that in matters which involve a complex economic appraisal it is not entitled to substitute its own economic assessment for that of the Commission,[127] the CFI (in particular) is increasingly willing to assess the merits of the detailed facts of a decision, including accounting data.[128]

Ex post **correction of factual mistakes.** To the extent that the Commission corrects a factual mistake, even after proceedings are initiated, the CFI has held that the mistake in issue can no longer of itself justify the annulment of the contested decision.[129] This can, however, only be case where the mistake in issue was not the sole object of the proceedings, and where the mistake does not involve an issue of a complex economic evaluation. Where a complex assessment is involved, the Court will not allow the Commission to argue that, notwithstanding an error, it would have reached the same conclusion. This was the case in *Alitalia v Commission*,[130] where the CFI found a manifest error of assessment in that the Commission had wrongly considered that certain insolvency costs should be excluded from the calculation of the internal rate of return for the purpose of the private investor test. It had further committed a manifest error in considering that adjustments made to a restructuring plan, which reduced risks inherent in the plan and increased profitability of the undertaking, had no impact on the calculation of the minimum and internal rate. The Commission argued that on any basis, a re-evaluation on the minimum rate and internal rate on the basis of the final version of the restructuring plan would still show that a private investor would not have made the investment. The CFI however refused to consider this: it was not for the European Courts to reassess the minimum rate and the internal rate for the investment or to decide whether a private investor would have made the proposed investment at the time when the contested decision was adopted. **17.63**

120 Case T-366/00 *Scott v Commission* [2007] ECR II-797, para 106.
121 ibid, paras 101–3 and 109–13.
122 ibid, para 115.
123 ibid, para 120.
124 Case T-266/02 *Deutsche Post v Commission* (judgment of 1 July 2008), paras 79–96.
125 Case T-366/00 *Scott v Commission* [2007] ECR II-797, paras 120 and 156.
126 ibid, para 96.
127 Case T-296/97 *Alitalia v Commission ('Alitalia I')* [2000] ECR II-3871, para 105.
128 See eg Case T-366/00 *Scott v Commission* [2007] ECR II-797, paras 97–109.
129 ibid, para 103.
130 Case T-296/97 *Alitalia v Commission ('Alitalia I')* [2000] ECR II-3871, paras 150 and 169. The Court subsequently upheld the new decision taken by the Commission: Case T-301/01 *Alitalia v Commission ('Alitalia II')* (judgment of 9 July 2008).

17.64 **Burden of proof.** In line with the procedural principles generally applicable in Community law, the applicant must prove the facts relied upon in its action. This applies not only as regards matters of fact but also as regards matters of national law, which must, akin to what applies in English courts, be pleaded and proved specifically.[131] Where an administrative practice is alleged to exist, the information submitted by the applicants must make it possible to establish the existence of such a practice. It is not sufficient merely to show that the national authorities would under applicable legislation have been capable of acting in the way alleged, with general examples of the alleged practice.[132]

(d) Reasoning

17.65 **Article 253 EC.** The Commission's duty to give proper reasons for a decision is enshrined in the Treaty. Article 253 thus provides:

> Regulations, directives and decisions adopted jointly by the European Parliament and the Council, and such acts adopted by the Council or the Commission, shall state the reasons on which they are based and shall refer to any proposals or opinions which were required to be obtained pursuant to this Treaty.

17.66 **Nature of obligation.** The obligation to state reasons is an essential legal and procedural requirement, distinct from the question whether the reasons are correct, which goes to the substantive legality of the contested measure.[133] Failure to state reasons may thus lead to the annulment of a decision even where that decision was in fact correct.[134] Inadequate reasons cannot be rectified by the provision of better reasons at the judicial stage.[135] An infringement of Article 253 must be raised by the Court of its own motion as a matter of public policy, where the parties fail to do so.[136]

17.67 **Content of statement of reasons.** The statement of reasons required under Article 253 must be appropriate to the nature of the measure in question, and must show clearly and unequivocally the reasoning of the institution which

[131] Case T-95/03 *Asociación de Estaciones de Servicio v Commission* [2006] ECR II-4739, para 75.

[132] ibid, paras 81–6.

[133] Case C-17/99 *France v Commission* [2001] ECR I-2481, para 35; Case C-310/99 *Italy v Commission* [2002] ECR I-2289, para 48.

[134] Case T-95/03 *Asociación de Estaciones de Servicio v Commission* [2006] ECR II-4739, para 107.

[135] Case C-351/98 *Spain v Commission* [2002] ECR I-8031. The elaboration of the reasoning in judicial proceedings may, however, be a factor taken into account in determining whether the Court is effectively able to review the decision: see Cases C-341-342/06 P *Chronopost v Ufex* (judgment of 1 July 2008), paras 111–12.

[136] Cases T-50/06 etc *Ireland v Commission* (judgment of 12 December 2007), para 47: the applicants raised a total 23 pleas alleging, *inter alia*, the wrongful classification of the measure as new aid and breaches of Article 87, but the Court of its own motion annulled the decision on the basis that the Commission had not set out sufficient reasoning for its finding that Article 1(b)(v) of the Procedural Regulation was inapplicable.

adopted the measure, so as to inform the persons concerned of the justification for the measure and to enable the Court to exercise its powers of review.[137]

Level of detail required. It is not necessary for the Commission's reasoning to go into all the relevant facts and points of law; nor is the Commission obliged to adopt a position on all the arguments relied on by the parties concerned.[138] Rather, it is sufficient if it sets out the facts and the legal considerations having decisive importance in the context of the decision.[139] In considering that context, it is necessary to take account of the particular circumstances of each case, in particular the content of the measure, the nature of the reasons relied on and the interest which the addressee, or other parties to whom it is of direct and individual concern,[140] may have in obtaining explanations.[141] For example, the decision may be reasoned in summary manner where the context is well known to the Member State and where the decision fits into a well-established line of decisions, such as the long line of cases relating to aids supposedly aimed at overcoming the hardship caused by the division of Germany.[142] The Court has also recently confirmed that where complex technical appraisals are concerned, it would be excessive to require a specific statement of reasons for each of the technical choices or each of the figures on which the Commission's reasoning is based.[143] **17.68**

Change in Commission's approach. By contrast, where the Commission for the first time implements a new policy, it is under an increased duty to explain the reasons underlying its decision. Accordingly, it was held that when the Commission for the first time applied interest on a compound basis in calculating the sums of aid to be recovered, it ought to have both expressly indicated in the contested decision that it had decided to capitalize the interest, and justified its approach, especially since the imposition of compound interest had significant financial consequences on the amount of the aid to be recovered.[144] **17.69**

---

[137] Case C-367/95 P *Commission v Sytraval and Brink's France ('Sytraval')* [1998] ECR I-1719, paras 63 and 67; Case C-351/98 *Spain v Commission ('Spanish trucks')* [2002] ECR I-8031, para 82.

[138] Case C-56/93 *Belgium v Commission* [1996] ECR I-723, para 86; *Sytraval*, ibid, para 63; Case C-301/96 *Germany v Commission* [2003] ECR I-9919, para 87.

[139] Case T-459/93 *Siemens v Commission* [1995] ECR II-1675, para 31, upheld on appeal in Case C-278/95 *Siemens v Commission* [1997] ECR I-2507, para 16. See also Case T-214/95 *Vlaamse Gewest v Commission* [1998] ECR II-717, para 63; Case T-55/99 *CETM v Commission* [2000] ECR II-3207, para 104; Cases T-204 and 270/97 *EPAC v Commission* [2000] ECR II-2267, para 35.

[140] Case T-369/00 *Département du Loiret v Commission* [2007] ECR II-1789, para 35.

[141] Case C-303/88 *Italy v Commission* [1991] ECR I-1433, para 52; Case C-310/99 *Italy v Commission* [2002] ECR I-2289, para 48; Cases T-50/96 etc *Ireland v Commission* (judgment of 12 December 2007), para 50.

[142] Cited in C-156/98 *Germany v Commission* [2000] ECR I-6857, para 105.

[143] Cases C-341-342/06 P *Chronopost v Ufex* (judgment of 1 July 2008), para 108.

[144] Case T-369/00 *Département du Loiret v Commission* [2007] ECR II-1789, paras 43–4; see also Case 73/74 *Fabricants de papiers peints v Commission* [1975] ECR 1491, paras 31–4; and Cases T-50/06 etc *Ireland v Commission* (judgment of 12 December 2007). cf Cases C-341-342/06 P

17.70 **Whether measure constitutes State aid.** Where the characterization of a measure as aid is in issue, the Commission must state the reasons which led it to consider that the measure falls within the scope of Article 87(1).[145] For these purposes it is not sufficient simply to quote the words of the relevant Treaty provisions without discussing the characteristics of the aid itself.[146] Conversely, where the decision is that there is no State aid, there must be adequate explanation of this. A Commission decision finding that no State aid as alleged by a complainant exists must at least provide the complainant with an adequate explanation of the reasons for which the facts and points of law put forward in the complaint have failed to demonstrate the existence of State aid. The Commission is not required, however, to define its position on matters which are manifestly irrelevant or insignificant or plainly of secondary importance.[147]

17.71 **Contradictions in operative part of decision.** Since a Commission decision constitutes a single whole, each of its parts must be read in the light of the others.[148] The CFI has thus held that the operative part of a decision is indissociably linked to the statement of reasons and must be read together with it.[149] It accordingly rejected the argument that there was a contradiction between the operative part and reasoning in a decision where the operative part seemed wider in scope than the reasons. There is no breach as long as the applicant was able to comprehend its intended scope from the detailed reasons.[150] Indeed, in its recent *BUPA* judgment the Court held that the failure even to mention reliance on Article 86(2) in the operative part of the judgment did not constitute an error of law, when it was clear from the reasoning in a decision that this Treaty provision was applied by the Commission.[151]

17.72 **Examples of annulment.** While a plea of breach of Article 253 is often added to bolster the most hopeless cases, and the European Court generally takes a

Chronopost v Ufex (judgment of 1 July 2008), para 94 (fact that decision was one of the first dealing with a complex factual issue did not of itself justify going into the detail of the relevant calculations, if the Commission took the view that the complainants' grounds in that regard were misconceived).

145 Case T-16/96 *Cityflyer Express v Commission* [1998] ECR II-757, para 66; Cases T-204 and 270/97 *SIC v Commission* [2000] ECR II-2267, para 36; Case T-217/02 *Ter Lembeek International v Commission* [2006] ECR II-4483, para 236.

146 Case 248/84 *Germany v Commission* [1987] ECR 4013, paras 21–2.

147 Case C-367/95 P *Commission v Sytraval and Brink's France ('Sytraval')* [1998] ECR I-1719, para 64; Cases C-341-342/06 P *Chronopost v Ufex* (judgment of 1 July 2008), para 89.

148 Cases T-50/06 etc *Ireland v Commission* (judgment of 12 December 2007), para 60.

149 Case T-289/03 *BUPA v Commission* (judgment of 12 February 2008), para 260.

150 Cases T-204/97 and T-270/97 *EPAC v Commission* [2000] ECR II-2267, para 39; Cases T-298/97 etc *Mauro Alzetta v Commission* [2000] ECR II-2319, paras 163–5.

151 Case T-289/03 *BUPA v Commission* (judgment of 12 February 2008), para 260.

sceptical stance as regards unparticularized pleas of this nature, there are numerous examples of decisions being annulled for lack of reasoning.[152] In *Alitalia v Commission*,[153] for example, the Commission assessed the private investor test by reference to a minimum rate of return of 30%. That was the same as the one used in the only relevant precedent, concerning Iberia. Alitalia had maintained throughout the administrative procedure that its situation was different from that of Iberia, and this was accepted to an extent by the Commission. In those circumstances the Commission was under an obligation to explain why it considered it necessary to apply to the Alitalia case the same minimum rate of 30% as had been fixed in the Iberia decision, when the risk factors present in the latter were not present or were present to a lesser extent. Similarly, in the *Spanish trucks* case,[154] it was held that a failure to classify aid as investment or operating aid in order to determine whether aid could be authorized under the Environmental Aid Guidelines constituted a breach of the obligation to give reasons. Because the aid in question was not clearly classified, Spain was not in a position fully to defend its rights.[155] More recently in *Ireland v Commission*,[156] the Court annulled a partially negative decision on the grounds that the Commission had given no reasons at all for its decision that a measure was new aid, rather than existing aid under Article 1(b)(v) of the Procedural Regulation.

(e) Misuse of powers

Misuse of powers. There is a misuse of powers where a Community institution adopts a measure with the exclusive or main purpose of achieving an end other than that stated or evading a procedure specifically prescribed by the Treaty for dealing with the circumstances of the case.[157] It will usually be difficult to establish a misuse of powers, which requires some degree of bad faith to be shown on the part of the Commission. The mere fact that the Commission does not make use **17.73**

152 See eg Case 248/84 *Germany v Commission* [1987] ECR 4013, paras 21–2 (insufficient to simply quote words of Article 87(1) without discussing characteristics of aid programme to show incompatibility with the common market); Case C-367/95 P *Commission v Sytraval and Brink's France ('Sytraval')* [1998] ECR I-1719 (failure to deal with a number of objections raised by the complainants); Case C-204/97 *Portugal v Commission* [2001] ECR I-3175, paras 40–51 (failure to explain why the aspects of the complaint regarding discriminatory taxation, and link between that and the State aid granted, were unfounded).

153 Case T-296/97 *Alitalia v Commission ('Alitalia I')* [2000] ECR II-3871, paras 124–36; cf subsequently Case T-301/01 *Alitalia v Commission ('Alitalia II')* (judgment of 9 July 2008), upholding the new decision of the Commission which did set out in detail the reasons why the same rate of return applied to Alitalia.

154 Case C-351/98 *Spain v Commission ('Spanish trucks')* [2002] ECR I-8031.

155 *Spanish trucks*, ibid, para 83. The same result was reached in a subsequent case on almost identical facts: Case C-409/00 *Spain v Commission ('Spanish trucks II')* [2003] ECR I-1487, paras 93–100.

156 Cases T-50/06 etc *Ireland v Commission* (judgment of 12 December 2007).

157 Case C-310/99 *Italy v Commission* [2002] ECR I-2289, para 47.

of procedural devices normally available to it is certainly not sufficient; a claim of misuse of powers on the basis of a failure to obtain an expert report on the question of the private investor test has thus been roundly rejected by the CFI.[158]

6. Consequences of annulment

17.74 **Effect of annulment.** Under Article 231, where an action for annulment is well-founded the Court must declare the contested act void. It follows that the decision challenged is retroactively extinguished, and any implementation of that is deemed to have been unlawful.[159] Following the annulment of a Commission or Council decision, the matter is remitted to the institution concerned. That institution is then required, under Article 233 EC, to take the necessary measures to comply with the judgment. The European Court has no jurisdiction to issue directions to Community institutions, or to assume the role assigned to those institutions. It is therefore for the Commission or Council, as appropriate, to adopt the measures required to comply with the judgment.[160]

17.75 **No power to adopt declarations.** It follows that the CFI, in an action for annulment, is confined to ordering the total or partial annulment of the decision in question. It is not entitled to declare in the *dispositif*, for example, that a measure is lawful or that State aid should not be recovered.[161] But that may, of course, be the inevitable consequence of the reasoning in the judgment.

D. Action for failure to act

17.76 **Article 232 EC.** Article 232 lays down the following framework for an action for failure to act:

> Should the European Parliament, the Council or the Commission, in infringement of this Treaty, fail to act, the Member States and the other institutions of the Community may bring an action before the Court of Justice to have the infringement established.
>
> The action shall be admissible only if the institution concerned has first been called upon to act. If, within two months of being so called upon, the institution concerned has not defined its position, the action may be brought within a further period of two months.

---

158 Case T-234/95 *DSG v Commission* [2000] ECR II-2603.

159 Case C-199/06 *CELF* (judgment of 12 February 2008), paras 61–3. See further paras 16.113 above and 18.17 below on the consequences of that for a decision that has been implemented prior to its annulment.

160 Cases T-50/06 etc *Ireland v Commission* (judgment of 12 December 2007), para 43; Case T-301/01 *Alitalia v Commission ('Alitalia II')* (judgment of 9 July 2008), para 97; and see further paras 16.68 above.

161 *Ireland v Commission*, ibid, para 44.

> Any natural or legal person may, under the conditions laid down in the preceding paragraphs, complain to the Court of Justice that an institution of the Community has failed to address to that person any act other than a recommendation or an opinion.
>
> The Court of Justice shall have jurisdiction, under the same conditions, in actions or proceedings brought by the ECB in the areas falling within the latter's field of competence and in actions or proceedings brought against the latter.

Admissibility conditions. The concept of an act, as used in the third paragraph of Article 232, is the same as that used in the first paragraph of Article 230.[162] Just as the fourth paragraph of Article 230 allows individuals to bring an action for annulment against a measure of an institution not addressed to them provided that the measure is of direct and individual concern to them, the third paragraph of Article 232 EC must be interpreted as also entitling them to bring an action for failure to act only against an institution which they claim has failed to adopt a measure which would have concerned them in the same way.[163] **17.77**

Application in State aid context. In the State aid context Article 232 may be relied upon by, for example, a competitor of an aid recipient, where the Commission has failed to take any decision following its preliminary review of the aid under Article 88(3),[164] or, by analogy, following a formal investigation under Article 88(2). In this respect the Court has held that the adoption of an abstract decision of general scope, such as Decision 2005/842/EC on the application of Article 86(2) to State aid in the form of public service competition granted to certain undertakings entrusted with the operation of services of general economic interest,[165] does not constitute a definition of position by the Commission on a specific complaint, for the purposes of Article 232 EC.[166] The action for failure to act is also the appropriate means for obtaining a declaration that the failure by the Commission to take the necessary measures to comply with a judgment of the Court is unlawful.[167] **17.78**

Remedy. The European Court is not competent to issue directions to the Commission in the context of an action based on Article 232 (for example, directions to the Commission to define its position on a complaint). All that the CFI or ECJ can do is determine whether there has been a failure to act. It is then for the **17.79**

[162] Case 15/70 *Chevalley v Commission* [1970] ECR 975, para 6.

[163] Case C-68/95 *T Port* [1996] ECR I-6065, para 59; Case T-395/04 *Air One v Commission* [2006] ECR II-1343, para 25; Case T-167/04 *Asklepios Kliniken v Commission* [2007] ECR II-2379, para 45.

[164] Case T-95/96 *Gestevisión Telecinco v Commission* [1998] ECR II-3407, paras 57–70; Case T-17/96 *TF1 v Commission* [1999] ECR II-1757, paras 26–36; *Air One*, ibid, paras 27–41.

[165] On which see further paras 3.72–3.77 above.

[166] Case T-167/04 *Asklepios Kliniken v Commission* [2007] ECR II-2379, para 77.

[167] Cases T-297/01 and T-298/01 *SIC v Commission* [2004] ECR II-743, para 45.

Commission to take the measures necessary to comply with the Court's order.[168] However where, after the action has been brought, the Commission then does carry out the contested act, the subject-matter of the action ceases to exist and there is no longer any need to adjudicate.[169] That is so even where the Commission's decision is unfavourable to the applicant: Article 232 refers to failure to act in the sense of failure to take a decision or to define a position, not the adoption of a measure different from that desired or considered necessary by the applicant.[170]

E. Action for damages

17.80 **Article 288(2) EC.** Article 288(2) provides for a damages action against the Community in the following terms:

> In the case of non-contractual liability, the Community shall, in accordance with the general principles common to the laws of the Member States, make good any damage caused by its institutions or by its servants in the performance of their duties.

17.81 **CFI as the competent court.** While Article 235 EC states that the 'Court of Justice shall have jurisdiction in disputes relating to compensation for damage provided for in the second paragraph of Article 288', it is clear from Article 225 EC, read in combination with Article 51 of the Statute of the Court of Justice, that actions for damages must always be commenced in the CFI, and may reach the ECJ on appeal only. The reference to the 'Court of Justice' in Article 235 EC must in effect be read as not referring to one Community Court or the other but to the Community institution comprising both the ECJ and the CFI.[171]

17.82 **Conditions of liability.** Liability is governed by 'the general principles common to the laws of the Member States', as developed by the European Court. Three conditions are generally recognized as having to be met for liability to arise: the rule of law infringed must be intended to confer rights on individuals; the breach must be sufficiently serious; and there must be a direct causal link between the breach and the damage suffered.[172] The burden of proving a causal link between the alleged fault on the part of the institution and the injury pleaded falls on

[168] Case T-74/92 *Ladbroke Racing Deutschland v Commission* [1995] ECR II-115, para 75; Case T-127/98 *UPS Europe v Commission* [1999] ECR II-2633, para 50; Case T-395/04 *Air One v Commission* [2006] ECR II-1343, para 24.

[169] Case C-44/00 P *Sodima v Commission* [2000] ECR I-11231, para 83, and the cases there cited; Case T-105/96 *Pharos v Commission* [1998] ECR II-285, paras 41–2.

[170] *Sodima v Commission*, ibid, para 83.

[171] See, by analogy with Article 238 EC, Case C-294/02 *Commission v AMI Semiconductor Belgium* [2005] ECR I-2175, para 49.

[172] See eg Case C-312/00 P *Commission v Camar and Tico* [2002] ECR I-11355, para 53; Case C-472/00 P *Commission v Fresh Marine* [2003] ECR I-7541, para 25.

the applicant.[173] In the field of State aid, establishing such a causal link between an unlawful act and any loss (most likely in the form of a diminution in profits) will not be easy.[174]

Limitation period of five years. Under Article 46 of the Statute of the Court of Justice, proceedings under Article 288(2) are time-barred after a period of five years from the occurrence of the event giving rise thereto. The period of limitation is interrupted if proceedings are instituted or if, prior to such proceedings, an application is made by the aggrieved party to the relevant institution. In the latter case, proceedings under Article 288(2)[175] must be instituted within the period of two months provided for in Article 230. The period of limitation for an action for liability of the Community cannot begin until all the requirements governing an obligation to provide compensation for damage are satisfied and, in particular, until the relevant damage has materialized.[176] **17.83**

Practical importance. Only very few cases have thus far been brought under Article 288(2) in the State aid field. It has yet to be seen whether an action under Article 288(2) might be used to bring a question of validity of an allegedly unlawful act in front of the European Court where the strict standing requirements for Article 230 are not met. A competitor of a beneficiary would, under Article 230, have to show that a State aid measure would significantly affect his competitive position in order to obtain standing in an action challenging the validity of a decision clearing the aid measure in question. By contrast, Article 288(2) has no standing requirement and it would appear that, while the burden for showing individual rights, a sufficiently serious breach, and causation is a high one, it may in some cases be more easily discharged than the individual concern test in the context of Article 230. In particular, there is no need to show that the adverse effects of the allegedly unlawful State aid measure are significant, as long as they are real. If the requirements of Article 228(2) were satisfied, it is difficult to see how the CFI could avoid giving a ruling on the validity of the contested measure. **17.84**

Actions against the Council. While proceedings will in most instances be directed against decisions of the Commission, which plays the main role in supervising the application of the State aid rules, decisions of the Council under Article 88(2), third subparagraph, can equally be challenged by way of an action for annulment, and may in principle also give rise to claims for damages by competitors of benefi- **17.85**

[173] Cases C-363–364/88 *Finsider v Commission* [1992] ECR I-359, para 25, Case C-362/95 P *Blackspur DIY v Council and Commission* [1997] ECR I-4775, para 31; Case T-230/95 *BAI v Commission* [1999] ECR II-123, para 30.

[174] Case 40/75 *Société des Produits Bertrand v Commission* [1976] ECR 1; Case T-230/95 *BAI v Commission* [1999] ECR II-123.

[175] Case C-282/05 P *Holcim (Deutschland) v Commission* [2007] ECR I-2941, para 36.

[176] Cases 256/80 etc *Birra Wührer v Council and Commission* [1982] ECR 85, para 10.

ciaries. Thus, in *GAEC*,[177] a French farming group brought an action under what is now Article 288(2) for damages after the Council had decided that certain aid payments to German competitors should be deemed compatible with the common market. It was argued that that decision was unlawful and that, by distorting competition in favour of German farmers, it had caused loss to the claimants. The Court rejected the claim, but only on the basis that no sufficient causal link had been made out between the loss complained about and the aid in issue.

F. Appeals to the ECJ

17.86 **Grounds of appeal.** An appeal to the ECJ against a judgment of the CFI is limited to points of law only, and must be based on the lack of jurisdiction of the CFI, a breach of procedure which adversely affects the interests of the applicant, or an infringement of Community law.[178] No appeal lies against the CFI's assessment of the facts. However the ECJ has consistently stated that it is entitled to censure a distortion by the CFI of the evidence before it, for example where the CFI's assessment of the evidence is manifestly incorrect,[179] or where the CFI has substituted its own reasoning for that of the contested decision.[180] In such a case, the question of whether the evidence has been distorted is regarded as a question of law which is subject to review by the ECJ.[181] The question of whether the reasoning of the CFI is sufficient is also a question of law which may be raised before the ECJ.[182]

17.87 **Content of arguments.** A party may not put forward for the first time before the ECJ a plea in law which it has not raised before the CFI.[183] That does not mean, however, that the appellant should simply repeat the grounds of its application to the CFI: indeed, the ECJ is not competent simply to re-examine the case raised before the CFI. Rather the appellant should set out precisely the contested

177 Case 253/84 *GAEC de la Ségaude v Council and Commission* [1987] ECR 123.

178 Article 225 EC and Article 58 of the Statute of the Court of Justice. See also Case C-260/05 P *Sniace v Commission* [2007] ECR I-10005, para 49; and Case C-320/05 P *Olsen v Commission* (order of 4 October 2007), para 47.

179 *Sniace v Commission*, ibid, paras 35–7; and see *Olsen v Commission*, ibid, paras 70 and 150–1 on the meaning of 'manifest' in this context.

180 Cases C-442 and 471/03 P *P&O European Ferries (Vizcaya) v Commission* [2006] ECR I-4845, paras 60–7. cf Case C-525/04 P *Spain v Commission* [2007] ECR I-9947, paras 54–5, where no distortion was alleged, and thus a plea based on the CFI's assessment of the evidence was inadmissible.

181 Case C-320/05 P *Olsen v Commission* (order of 4 October 2007), para 69.

182 ibid, para 111.

183 Cases C-183 and 187/02 P *Demesa v Commission* [2004] ECR I-10609, paras 59–64. cf the position in the CFI with respect to legal points not raised during the administrative procedure, para 17.56 below.

elements of the judgment under appeal, and the legal arguments which support the appeal in those respects.[184]

Effect of successful appeal. Article 61 of the Statute of the Court of Justice provides that if the appeal is successful the ECJ must quash the decision of the CFI. It may then either give final judgment in the matter itself,[185] or refer the proceedings back to the CFI for judgment.[186] In the latter case, the CFI is bound by the judgment of the ECJ on points of law. Although a number of appeals have been made to the ECJ against decisions of the CFI, only a very few have actually been successful.[187] **17.88**

G. Overarching procedural matters

Competent forum for procedural matters. Procedural applications are generally decided upon by way of order by the President of the CFI or the ECJ, as appropriate, who may refer the decision to the Court.[188] If a case has already been allocated to a Chamber, the Rules of Procedure of both the CFI and the ECJ provide that the powers of the President are to be exercised by the President of the Chamber.[189] As cases brought in the CFI are allocated to a Chamber as soon as the proceedings are initiated,[190] this means that applications in the CFI will usually be heard by the President of a Chamber rather than the President of the CFI. By contrast, cases brought in the ECJ are allocated to Chambers of the ECJ only once the written procedure is completed,[191] with the consequence that procedural applications are generally determined by the President of the ECJ, who will, where appropriate, informally seek the view of the Reporting Judge and the Advocate General. **17.89**

---

184 Case C-320/05 P *Olsen v Commission* (order of 4 October 2007), paras 48–9.

185 eg C-176/06 P *Stadtwerke Schwäbisch Hall v Commission* (judgment of 29 November 2007); and Cases C-341-342/06 P *Chronopost v Ufex* (judgment of 1 July 2008).

186 eg Cases C-83, 93-94/01 P *Chronopost v Ufex* [2003] ECR I-6993. For a hybrid case see Case C-521/06 P *Athinaïki Techniki v Commission* (judgment of 17 July 2008) where the ECJ on appeal gave final judgment on admissibility, following a successful appeal on the issue, but remitted the case to the CFI for judgment on the substance of the application for annulment.

187 These include Cases C-83, 93 and 94/01 P *Chronopost v Ufex and others* [2003] ECR I-6993, Case C-176/06 P *Stadtwerke Schwäbisch Hall v Commission* (judgment of 29 November 2007), C-408/04 P *Commission v Salzgitter* (judgment of 22 April 2008); Cases C-341-342/06 P *Chronopost v Ufex* (judgment of 1 July 2008); and Case C-521/06 P *Athinaïki Techniki v Commission* (judgment of 17 July 2008).

188 Article 93(2) of the Rules of Procedure of the ECJ; Article 116(1) of the Rules of Procedure of the CFI.

189 Article 9(4) of the Rules of Procedure of the ECJ; Article 16 of the Rules of Procedure of the CFI.

190 Article 13(1) of the Rules of Procedure of the CFI.

191 Article 44 of the Rules of Procedure of the ECJ.

1. Interim measures

17.90 **Articles 242 and 243 EC.** Article 242 on the one hand lays down the general rule that actions before the European Court have no suspensory effect,[192] but on the other hand permits the Court to suspend the application of a challenged act. More generally, Article 243 allows the Court to prescribe 'any necessary interim measures' in cases before it.

17.91 **Conditions.** Article 83(2) of the ECJ's Rules of Procedure and Article 104(2) of the CFI's Rules of Procedure provide that an application for interim measures must state the subject-matter of the proceedings, the circumstances giving rise to urgency and the pleas of fact and law establishing a *prima facie* case (*fumus boni juris*) for the interim measures applied for.[193] Those conditions are cumulative, so that an application for interim measures must be dismissed if any one of them is absent.[194] Where appropriate, the judge hearing the application must also balance the interests involved.[195] A claim for interim measures is not self-standing and can only accompany separate proceedings, usually under Article 230 or 232.

17.92 ***Prima facie* case.** The threshold for the demonstration of a *prima facie* case is fairly low. Such a case will be established where the President of the Court cannot rule out the possibility that the Commission erred in law,[196] or where the pleas in law raised by the applicant do not prima facie appear to be wholly unfounded.[197] The same standard applies to arguments of inadmissibility: for an application to be dismissed as inadmissible at the interim measures stage it is necessary to show that the admissibility of the main application is wholly excluded or wholly unfounded.[198]

17.93 **Urgency.** The urgency of an application for interim measures must be assessed in relation to the necessity for an order granting interim relief in order to prevent serious and irreparable damage, or at least harm reparable only with difficulty,[199]

---

[192] Thus, a Member State which has been ordered to withdraw aid is not entitled to refuse to comply with the decision simply by virtue of having lodged an application for annulment: Case 63/97 *Commission v Greece* [1988] ECR 2875, paras 10–12.

[193] Case C 149/95 P(R) *Commission v Atlantic Container Line* [1995] ECR 2165, para 22; Case C-110/97 R *Netherlands v Council* [1997] ECR I-1795, para 24.

[194] Case C-268/96 P(R) *SCK and FNK v Commission* [1996] ECR I-4971, para 30; Case C-7/04 P(R) *Commission v Akzo and Akcros* [2004] ECR I-8739, para 28.

[195] Case C-107/99 R *Italy v Commission* [1999] ECR I-4011, para 59; Cases C-182/03 R and C-217/03 R *Belgium and Forum 187 v Commission* [2003] ECR I-6887, para 97.

[196] Case T-378/02 R *Technische Glaswerke Ilmenau v Commission* [2003] ECR II-2921, para 74; Cases T-195 and 207/01 *Gibraltar v Commission* [2001] ECR II-3915, paras 80–2.

[197] *Technische Glasworke Ilmenau v Commission*, ibid, para 75.

[198] Cases T-195 and 207/01 *Gibraltar v Commission* [2001] ECR II-3915, paras 47 and 55.

[199] Cases C-182/03 R and C-217/03 R *Belgium and Forum 187 v Commission* [2003] ECR I-6887, para 141.

to the party requesting the interim measure.[200] It is for that party to prove that it cannot wait for the outcome of the main proceedings without suffering damage of this kind.[201] However, it is not necessary for the imminence of the damage to be demonstrated with absolute certainty. Rather, it is sufficient, especially when the occurrence of the damage depends on the concurrence of a series of factors, to show that damage is foreseeable with a sufficient degree of probability. However, the applicant is required to prove the facts forming the basis of its claim that serious and irreparable damage is likely.[202]

Pecuniary loss. While it is established that damage of a pecuniary nature cannot, save in exceptional circumstances, be regarded as irreparable, or even as being reparable only with difficulty, if it can ultimately be the subject of financial compensation, it is also settled case-law that an interim measure is justified if it appears that, without that measure, the applicant would be in a position that could jeopardize its existence before final decision in the main action or irremediably alter its position in the market.[203] The assessment of the financial viability of an applicant may take into consideration among other matters the characteristics of the group to which it is linked by way of its shareholders, so that an undercapitalized member of a healthy group of companies will not be able to plead its impecuniosity.[204] **17.94**

Own interests must be affected. In order to prove that the condition of urgency is satisfied, the applicant is required to demonstrate that the suspension of operation applied for is necessary for the protection of his own interests. The applicant cannot plead harm to an interest which is not personal to him, such as harm to a general interest or the rights of third parties, whether individuals, such as employees, or a Member State. Such interests can be taken into account, where appropriate, only when the balance of the interests involved is being examined.[205] **17.95**

Balancing exercise. Where, in connection with an application for suspension of operation, the judge hearing the application for interim relief, before whom the **17.96**

200 Cases T-195 and 207/01 *Gibraltar v Commission* [2001] ECR II-3915, para 95; *Belgium and Forum 187*, ibid, para 130.

201 Case T-181/02 R *Neue Erba Lautex v Commission* [2002] ECR II-5081, para 82 and the cases there cited; Case T-316/04 R *Wam v Commission* [2004] ECR II-3917, para 26; Case T-455/05 R *Componenta v Commission* [2006] ECR II-38, para 34.

202 Case C-278/00 R *Greece v Commission* [2000] ECR I-8787, para 15; *Neue Erba Lautex v Commission*, ibid, para 83 and the cases there cited; *Componenta v Commission*, ibid, para 34.

203 *Neue Erba Lautex v Commission* ibid, para 84; Case T-169/00 R *Esedra v Commission* [2000] ECR II-2951, para 45; Case T-316/04 R *Wam v Commission* [2004] ECR II-3917, para 29. For a recent illustration of the strict approach taken by the Court in this respect see (in a different field) Case T-246/08 R *Melli Bank v Council of the European Union* (27 August 2008).

204 Case C-12/95 P *TRAMASA v Commission* [1995] ECR I-467, para 12; Case C-43/98 P(R) *Camar v Commission and Council* [1998] ECR I-1815, para 36; Case T-420/05 R *Vischim v Commission* (order of 4 April 2006), para 81.

205 Case T-316/04 R *Wam v Commission* [2004] ECR II-3917, para 28 and the cases there cited; Case T-455/05 R *Componenta v Commission* [2006] ECR II-38, para 35.

risk of serious and irreparable damage to the applicant is pleaded, weighs up the various interests involved, he must determine whether the possible annulment of the decision at issue by the Court giving judgment in the main action would make it possible to reverse the situation that would be brought about by its immediate implementation and, conversely, whether suspension of operation of that decision would be such as to prevent the contested decision from being fully effective in the event of the main application being dismissed.[206]

17.97 **Right of appeal.** Any person whose application for interim measures has been dismissed by the CFI may appeal to the ECJ within two weeks from the notification of the decision dismissing the application.[207] The appeal is heard and determined by the President of the ECJ sitting alone under the summary procedure referred to in Article 39 of the Statute of the Court of Justice.

2. Intervention

17.98 **Principle.** Article 40 of the Statute of the Court of Justice provides that Member States and Community institutions, as well as (save in certain specified circumstances) any other person establishing an interest in the result of any case, have the right to intervene in proceedings before the European Court.

17.99 **Procedure.** An application to intervene must be made within six weeks of the publication of the notice of proceedings in the Official Journal.[208] In the CFI, an intervener who applies out of time may submit his observations during the oral procedure on the basis of the Report for the Hearing.[209] The application for intervention is served on the parties to the proceedings who have an opportunity of submitting their written or oral observations on the application. Where an application is dismissed by the CFI, reasons must be given, so as to allow the ECJ to scrutinize the reasoning on appeal.[210]

17.100 **Content of intervention.** An application to intervene must be limited to supporting the form of order sought by one of the parties, and under Article 116(3) of the Rules of Procedure of the CFI and Article 93(4) of the Rules of Procedure the intervener must accept the case as it finds it at the time of the intervention. However, those provisions do not preclude an intervener from putting forward arguments different from those raised by the party it is supporting, providing that they do not alter the framework of the dispute and that the intervention is still

[206] Case C-180/96 R *United Kingdom v Commission* [1996] ECR I-3903, para 89; Cases C-182/03 R and C-217/03 R *Belgium and Forum 187 v Commission* [2003] ECR I-6887, para 142.

[207] Article 57(2) of the Statute of the Court of Justice.

[208] Article 93(1) of the Rules of Procedure of the ECJ; Article 115(1) of the Rules of Procedure of the CFI.

[209] Article 116(6) of the Rules of Procedure of the CFI.

[210] ibid, Article 116(1).

intended to support the form of order sought by that party.[211] Applying those principles in the *BUPA* judgment, the CFI regarded as admissible the interveners' arguments that the contested measure satisfied the *Altmark* test and thus did not constitute State aid within the meaning of Article 87(1), even though the Commission (which the interveners were supporting) had not defended the case on that basis.[212] Indeed, the CFI went on to uphold the decision on that ground.

Right of appeal. Any person whose application to intervene has been dismissed by the CFI may appeal to the ECJ within two weeks from the notification of the decision dismissing the application.[213] The appeal is heard and determined by the President of the ECJ sitting alone under the summary procedure referred to in Article 39 of the Statute of the Court of Justice. **17.101**

Access to the file and confidentiality. In principle, an intervener should receive a copy of every document served on the parties. The President may, however, on application by one of the parties, omit secret or confidential documents.[214] In its application, the party must accurately identify the particulars or passages to be excluded, and why.[215] An application for confidential treatment which is insufficiently detailed as to the particulars it covers will be dismissed,[216] and account will be taken of the reasons provided in support of an application for confidential treatment in situations where it is not sufficiently clear from the examination of the particulars covered by the application that they are confidential.[217] Such consideration is, in the interests of the proper administration of justice, *a fortiori* necessary in cases where the confidential treatment sought concerns a substantial amount of information.[218] The intervener may oppose the grant of confidentiality, stating the reasons for which confidentiality with regard to those matters should be refused. Applications for confidential treatment are upheld to the extent **17.102**

[211] Case T-289/03 *BUPA v Commission* (judgment of 12 February 2008), para 153.

[212] ibid, para 154. cf para 155, finding another part of the intervention inadmissible on the grounds that it contradicted the decision, and raised an argument not put in issue by either BUPA or the Commission.

[213] Article 57(1) of the Statute of the Court of Justice.

[214] Article 93(3) of the Rules of Procedure of the ECJ; Article 116(2) of the Rules of Procedure of the CFI; Case T-143/96 *Volkswagen and Volkswagen Sachsen v Commission* (order of 3 July 1998) para 15; Case T-266/02 *Deutsche Post v Commission* (order of 13 January 2005) para 19; Case T-336/04 *TVDanmark and Kanal 5 Denmark v Commission* [2007] ECR II-491, para 40.

[215] Section VIII(2) and (3) of the Practice Directions of the CFI of 14 March 2002 [2002] OJ L87/8; and Article 5(4), first subparagraph, of the Instructions to the Registrar of the CFI of 3 March 1994 [1994] OJ L78/32, as amended [2002] OJ L160/1.

[216] Case T-336/04 *TVDanmark and Kanal 5 Denmark v Commission* [2007] ECR II-491, para 43.

[217] ibid, para 44.

[218] Case T-266/02 *Deutsche Post v Commission* (order of 13 January 2005), para 23.

they are not opposed, or not opposed expressly and in detail.[219] Where, however, objections are raised to confidential treatment, it is necessary in respect of each relevant document or passage to balance the applicant's legitimate concern to prevent substantial damage to its business interests, and the interveners' equally legitimate concern to have the necessary information in order fully to assert their rights and state their case before the European Court.[220]

[219] ibid, paras 12, 14 and 15; Case T-289/03 *BUPA v Commission* [2005] ECR II-741, para 11; Case T-336/04 *TVDanmark and Kanal 5 Denmark v Commission* [2007] ECR II-491, paras 45–7; Case T-309/04 *TV 2/Danmark v Commission* (order of 1 March 2007), paras 17–19.

[220] Case T-30/89 *Hilti v Commission* [1990] ECR II-163, para 11; Case T-266/02 *Deutsche Post v Commission* (order of 13 January 2005), para 20; Case T-271/03 *Deutsche Telekom v Commission* [2006] ECR II-1747, para 10.

18

ENFORCEMENT IN THE NATIONAL COURTS

Main legislation, guidelines and other documents

Notice on cooperation between national courts and the Commission in the State aid field [1995] OJ C312/8

Study on the enforcement of State aid law at national level ('2006 National Enforcement Study')

Commission Notice – Towards an effective implementation of Commission decisions ordering Member States to recover unlawful and incompatible State aid ('Recovery Notice') [2007] OJ C272/4

A. Introduction

Role of the national courts. As discussed in Chapter 16 above, national courts and the Commission have complementary and separate roles in the application and enforcement of the State aid rules.[1] The complex economic analysis required to determine the compatibility of aid under Article 87(2) and (3) is a matter for the Commission. The Commission is also responsible for determining whether **18.01**

[1] Para 16.02 above; see also Case C-368/04 *Transalpine Ölleitung* [2006] ECR I-9957, para 37.

a State aid can be declared compatible on the basis of Article 86(2).[2] However, the national courts do have jurisdiction to apply the State aid rules in three situations. The first is the enforcement of the 'standstill clause' in the last sentence of Article 88(3). This prohibits the Member States from implementing aid until it has been approved by the Commission. The ECJ has held that this prohibition gives rise to directly effective rights which national courts must safeguard.[3] It is therefore the task of the national courts to provide effective remedies for the implementation of aid contrary to Article 88(3). This may include actions against competitors as well as against State authorities. Secondly, national courts have the power to enforce decisions of the Commission taken under Article 88(2).[4] Thirdly, national courts may directly apply the provisions of any block exemption adopted under Article 89.[5] These three types of proceedings are addressed in sections B to D below.

18.02 **Application and interpretation of Article 87(1).** While Article 87 is not itself directly effective, national courts may (and often must) apply and interpret Article 87(1). In particular, it is necessary to apply the concept of aid in order to determine whether a measure is indeed State aid which ought to have been notified pursuant to Article 88(3).[6]

18.03 **Preliminary references.** National courts may (and often do) refer a question to the ECJ for a preliminary ruling under Article 234. Many references in the State aid field have raised the interpretation of Article 87(1).[7] Such references may become less frequent with the development in the last decade of the Court's jurisprudence on the concept of aid. Nevertheless, the Court's recent judgment in *GIL Insurance* underscores the point that a national court should not too readily assume the answer to a complex question of interpretation of Article 87(1). In that case the Court declined to answer referred questions about the effect of a supposed State aid on competition and trade because it held that, contrary to the view of the national court, the tax measure in question was justified by the nature and general scheme of the system and therefore not aid in any event.[8] A less developed area,

[2] As discussed at para 3.69 above, while in other contexts Article 86(2) is directly effective and may thus be applied by the national courts, the requirement to notify a State aid even where Article 86(2) applies means that there is no scope for a national court to apply it in the State aid context.

[3] Case 120/73 *Lorenz v Germany* [1973] ECR 1471, para 8; Case C-368/04 *Transalpine Ölleitung* [2006] ECR I-9957, para 38.

[4] Case 77/72 *Capolongo v Maya* [1973] 611, para 6.

[5] ibid.

[6] Case 78/76 *Steinike & Weinlig v Germany* [1977] ECR 595, para 14; Case C-44/94 *Namur-Les Assurances v OND* [1994] ECR I-3829, para 16; Case C-143/99 *Adria-Wien Pipeline* [2001] ECR I-8365, para 29; Case C-368/04 *Transalpine Ölleitung* [2006] ECR I-9957, para 39.

[7] Including a number of seminal State aid cases such as Case C-379/98 *PreussenElektra v Schleswag* [2001] ECR I-2099, Case 53/00 *Ferring v ACOSS* [2001] ECR I-9067 and Case C-280/00 *Altmark* [2003] ECR I-7747.

[8] Case C-308/01 *GIL Insurance* [2004] ECR I-4777, paras 48–79, discussed at para 2.131 above.

which is increasingly the subject of references by national courts, is the scope of the national court's powers and duties in the enforcement of the State aid rules,[9] which is the subject of this chapter. A national court may also legitimately query the effect of a Commission decision.[10] In certain circumstances, the validity of a decision may also be questioned.[11] But a preliminary reference may not be used to challenge the validity of a Commission decision where the party concerned could have brought an application for annulment of the decision under Article 230 EC but failed to do so, or was unsuccessful.[12] Nor can national courts refer questions of compatibility of State aid with the common market, since a decision on that matter is not within the jurisdiction of the national courts.[13]

Clarification from Commission. The Commission's notice on cooperation between national courts and the Commission indicates that national courts may request legal or economic information from the Commission, particularly in relation to the characterization of a measure as State aid under Article 87(1) and the application of Article 88(3).[14] The Commission must respond as quickly as possible to such requests.[15] Any answer given by the Commission is, however, neither definitive nor binding on the requesting court, and does not prevent the national court from making a preliminary reference.[16] While this procedure could be a useful source of guidance for national courts, to date it appears rarely, if ever, to have been used.[17] **18.04**

[9] See eg Case C-368/04 *Transalpine Ölleitung* [2006] ECR I-9957.

[10] See eg the second question in Cases C-261-262/01 *Van Calster* [2003] ECR I-12249, addressed at paras 66–77.

[11] For a recent example see Case C-390/06 *Nuova Agricast* (judgment of 15 April 2008).

[12] See further para 18.30 below. Obviously this bar does not apply where the party concerned would not have had standing to bring an action for annulment: see eg Case T-141/03 *Sniace v Commission* [2005] ECR II-1197, para 40.

[13] Case C-256/97 *DMT* [1999] ECR I-3913, para 16; Order in Case C-297/01 *Sicilcassa* [2003] ECR I-7849, para 47; Case C-148/04 *Unicredito Italiano* [2005] ECR I-11137, para 43.

[14] Notice on cooperation between national courts and the Commission in the State aid field [1995] OJ C312/8, paras 9 and 29; see also Case C-39/94 *SFEI v La Poste* [1996] ECR I-3547, para 50. The Commission intends to replace the 1995 notice with an expanded and more user friendly version. It issued a draft for consultation in September 2008.

[15] *SFEI v La Poste*, ibid, para 50. In the draft replacement notice (see n 14 above), the Commission suggests that it will endeavour to supply information to national courts on request within a month, and to issue opinions requested by national courts (ranging from issues of interpretation of the State aid rules to methods of calculating benefit for the purpose of recovery or damage actions) within a four-month period. The latter period in particular may be thought to be somewhat unambitious.

[16] This is so as a matter of law, but is confirmed in the Commission's Notice on cooperation between national courts and the Commission [1995] OJ C312/8, para 30.

[17] Study on the enforcement of State aid law at national level ('2006 National Enforcement Study'), available on the DG Comp website at: <http://ec.europa.eu/comm/competition/state_aid/studies_reports/studies_reports.html>, p 43; hence the Commission's stated aim in the new draft notice (n 14 above) to 'make a fresh attempt at establishing closer co-operation with national courts by providing more practical and user-friendly support mechanisms'.

18.05 **2006 National Enforcement Study.** In April 2006 the Commission published the results of a study by external consultants, commissioned by DG Competition, on the enforcement of State aid law in the individual Member States.[18] That found that there had been a significant increase in the number of State aid cases brought in the national courts since a previous study conducted in 1999. However the great majority of cases initiated by private parties were those in which the litigant sought relief from a burden (mostly a tax) from which another party was exempted under the alleged aid scheme. Very few cases were direct actions against competitors. Moreover, procedures for the recovery of aid were often unclear. The authors recommended, *inter alia*, consideration of uniform standards and conditions for proceedings by competitors in respect of unlawful aid, and the adoption of guidelines regarding recovery of aid. The limited, albeit increasing, resort to national courts and in particular the fact that the national proceedings were not (in the Commission's view) generally aimed at curing the competitive distortions caused by illegal aid formed part of the impetus lying behind the Commission's desire to introduce an updated and improved notice on cooperation with national courts.[19] More generally, the relative lack of success of private actions in this area (as noted below, the study found no examples of successful damages actions or even of successful injunctions against the payment of aid) may indicate the continuing importance of vigorous enforcement by the Commission. Particular difficulties (or perhaps more accurately, disincentives to litigate) are faced by the competitor whose remedies lie, if at all, in the courts of another Member State.

B. Remedies for breach of Article 88(3)

1. Interpretation of Article 88(3)

18.06 **Standstill clause.** Article 88(3) provides that:

> The Commission shall be informed, in sufficient time to enable it to submit its comments, of any plans to grant or alter aid. If it considers that any such plan is not compatible with the common market having regard to Article 87, it shall without delay initiate the procedure provided for in paragraph 2. The Member State concerned shall not put its proposed measures into effect until this procedure has resulted in a final decision.

The last sentence of Article 88(3) is known as the 'standstill clause' or 'standstill obligation' and is the primary source of the national court's powers in the field of State aid. This provision is regarded as central to the proper functioning of the State aid procedure in Article 88. Its purpose is to give the Commission sufficient

[18] ibid.
[19] See n 14 above.

opportunity to review a plan to grant or alter aid, and to ensure that aid measures are not implemented unless and until that review has taken place and the measure is approved.[20] In applying Article 88(3), therefore, the national court does not decide on the compatibility of the aid. Rather its duty is to provide a remedy for the premature implementation of aid.[21]

Notified and unnotified aids. Article 88(3) will obviously be triggered where an aid has been implemented without any notification to the Commission, often because the Member State in question erroneously considers that the measure is not aid within Article 87(1). But the standstill obligation continues to apply during the Commission's investigation of the aid, and until its final (approval) decision.[22] Therefore Article 88(3) would also be breached if a Member State were to notify an aid measure, but then proceed to implement it before the Commission had reached a final decision approving that measure. **18.07**

Subsequent approval of aid. The powers of the national court under Article 88(3) are particularly important where an aid which has been implemented unlawfully, before a final decision is taken by the Commission, is ultimately approved as being compatible with the common market. In such a case the Commission has no jurisdiction to order recovery of any part of the aid.[23] But its approval decision does not have the effect of regularizing *ex post facto* the premature grant of aid, since if it did that would create an incentive not to wait for the Commission's approval before payment of an aid, and would deprive Article 88(3) of its effectiveness.[24] Even if an unlawful aid has been approved, therefore, the national court must provide a remedy for its premature and unlawful payment, to offset any competitive advantage gained by the undertaking by reason of the early payment.[25] **18.08**

---

[20] See Cases 91 and 127/83 *Heineken Brouwerijen* [1984] ECR 3435, paras 14 and 20; and Case C-301/87 *France v Commission ('Boussac')* [1990] ECR I-307, para 17. Note that the last sentence of Article 88(3) refers to the requirement for a final decision, rather than an approval decision. The scheme of Article 88 indicates, however, that the measure must be approved before implementation, and that assumption is endorsed by Article 3 of Regulation 659/99 ('Aid notifiable pursuant to Article 2(1) shall not be put into effect before the Commission has taken, or is deemed to have taken, a decision authorising such aid') and the case-law of the Court (see eg *Boussac*, opinion of AG Jacobs para 34; Case C-142/87 *Belgium v Commission ('Tubemeuse')* [1990] ECR I-959, opinion of AG Tesauro p 985; and Case C-174/02 *Streekgewest* [2005] ECR I-85, opinion of AG Geelhoed para 25).

[21] See Case C-354/90 *FNCEPA v Commission* [1991] ECR I-5505, para 14.

[22] Case C-39/94 *SFEI v La Poste* [1996] ECR I-3547, para 39.

[23] See para 16.89 above.

[24] Case C-354/90 *FNCEPA v Commission* [1991] ECR I-5505, para 16; Cases C-261-262/01 *Van Calster* [2003] ECR I-12249, para 63; Case C-368/04 *Transalpine Ölleitung* [2006] ECR I-9957, paras 41–2; Case C-199/06 *CELF* (judgment of 12 February 2008), para 40. That is the case even if the Commission states explicitly in its decision that its assessment relates to a period prior to the adoption of the decision: *Transalpine Ölleitung*, para 43.

[25] *FNCEPA*, ibid, opinion of AG Jacobs para 28; Case C-174/02 *Streekgewest* [2005] ECR I-85, opinion of AG Geelhoed paras 25–7. See further para 18.16 below.

18.09 **Prohibition of retroactive aid.** A further consequence of the standstill clause in Article 88(3) is that an aid measure may not be implemented on a retroactive basis in respect of any period before the Commission's approval decision. In *Van Calster* a Belgian aid scheme financed by parafiscal charges on slaughterhouses was established in 1987 without notification to the Commission. The Commission subsequently investigated the scheme and declared it incompatible with the common market. Several years later, a draft aid scheme replacing the 1987 scheme was notified to the Commission, which in 1996 declared it compatible with the common market. The Belgian authorities proceeded to implement the scheme in 1998. However, the 1998 legislation provided for the retroactive imposition of the parafiscal charges back to 1 January 1988—a period of eight years prior to the Commission's decision. The aim of the government was clearly to remedy the consequences of the failure of the original 1987 scheme. The Court held that this was incompatible with Article 88(3). 'If it were upheld, the Member States could immediately put a plan for State aid into effect without notifying it to the Commission and the consequences of a failure to notify could be avoided by abolishing the measure and reintroducing it simultaneously with retroactive effect.'[26]

18.10 **Remedies overview.** Where there has been a breach of Article 88(3), the national courts are required to protect the rights of persons concerned by providing permanent remedies for the unlawful implementation of aid.[27] These may include not only a declaration that the aid measure is invalid, but also an order for recovery of aid. In certain cases, other remedies from Member States such as reimbursement of charges financing the aid may be appropriate. Undertakings might seek damages, either from the Member State or from the beneficiaries of unlawful aid. Finally, interim relief in the form of suspension of aid is in principle available but difficult in practice to secure. These are discussed in the following sections.

2. Invalidity of national measures

18.11 **Primary consequence of breach.** The primary consequence of the grant of aid contrary to Article 88(3) is that the relevant aid measure is unlawful and invalid.[28] Moreover, since a Commission decision cannot regularize an unlawful aid

---

[26] Cases C-261-262/01 *Van Calster* [2003] ECR I-12249, para 60.

[27] As opposed to purely interim relief: see Case C-39/94 *SFEI v La Poste* [1996] ECR I-3547, para 67 and opinion of AG Jacobs para 71.

[28] See Case C-354/90 *FNCEPA* [1991] ECR I-5505, para 12; Case C-39/94 *SFEI v La Poste* [1996] ECR I-3547, para 40; Cases C-266/04 etc *Distribution Casino France* [2005] ECR I-9281, para 30; Case C-368/04 *Transalpine Ölleitung* [2006] ECR I-9957, para 40. Declarations of invalidity have twice been granted by the English courts, in *R v AG ex parte ICI* [1985] 1 CMLR 588 (Div Ct), [1987] 1 CMLR 72 (CA); and *R v Commissioners of Customs & Excise ex parte Lunn Poly* [1998] EuLR 438 (Div Ct), [1999] EuLR 653 (CA). For a discussion of English cases unsuccessfully seeking to build on *Lunn Poly* see K Bacon, 'State Aids in the English Courts: Definition and Other Problems' in Biondi, Eeckhout and Flynn (eds), *The Law of State Aid in the European Union* (Oxford University Press, 2004), 337–44.

measure, the national measure remains invalid even if the Commission subsequently finds the aid itself to be compatible with the common market.[29]

Invalidity of selective tax or charge. As noted above,[30] State aid cases often arise in the national courts where an undertaking seeks relief from a tax or other charge from which its competitor has been exempted. That issue arises particularly when the grant of aid occurs through the imposition of differential taxation, or where aid is financed by a parafiscal charge. However, Article 87(1) prohibits selective aids, not the selective imposition of charges. For this reason it was long unclear whether the invalidity of an unnotified aid also included its method of financing. The position has been clarified in a number of recent cases, which are discussed in detail in Chapter 2. The result of those cases is that there are now two situations where a tax or charge may itself fall within the standstill obligation in Article 88(3). The first is where a parafiscal or similar charge is an 'integral part' of an aid measure. That will be the case where the charge is designed specifically and exclusively to finance the aid, such that the revenue is hypothecated to the aid measure.[31] In such a case, the national court will be able to declare the charging provision invalid along with the aid measure. The second case is where the imposition of a tax or charge on one group of undertakings, but not on another, is the means by which aid is granted to the non-taxed group. In that case the aid measure is the tax itself,[32] and the tax itself is therefore unlawful under Article 88(3) unless notified and approved. Outside these two situations, an undertaking that has been taxed at a higher rate than its competitor will be able to challenge the lower rate of tax, but will not be able to impugn the validity of the higher rate. **18.12**

Effects of invalidity. In some cases, the successful annulment of the contested aid measure will provide an effective remedy for its unlawful implementation. That will be the case, for example, where an aid scheme has been enacted but no aid has yet been paid under the scheme, or (often more importantly) no charges have yet been levied to finance the scheme. More often, however, aid payments or related charges will already have occurred, and the claim to invalidity is the springboard for a claim to other remedies, such as the recovery of aid or reimbursement of charges. These are discussed in turn below. **18.13**

3. Recovery of aid

Normal consequence of breach of Article 88(3). Consistent with the Commission's practice of requiring repayment of unlawful aids that are found to be **18.14**

[29] Case C-39/94 *SFEI v La Poste* [1996] ECR I-3547, opinion of AG Jacobs, para 71. See further para 18.16 below for the remedies in such a case.

[30] See para 18.05 above.

[31] Cases C-261-262/01 *Van Calster* [2003] ECR I-12249, paras 44–9, and Case C-174/02 *Streekgewest* [2005] ECR I-85, paras 24–6.

[32] Case C-526/04 *Laboratoires Boiron* [2006] ECR I-7529, paras 30–40.

incompatible with the common market, the Court has held that in principle a finding that aid has been granted in breach of Article 88(3) should lead to its repayment under the procedural rules of domestic law.[33] The aim of the national court, as with the Commission, should be to restore the situation prior to the payment of the aid.[34]

18.15 **Defences to recovery.** By analogy with the principles applicable to recovery orders in the Commission's decision, and infringement proceedings in the Court, a Member State or aid beneficiary should be able to resist a recovery order in the national courts on the basis of absolute impossibility or principles of legal certainty. The Court has also held explicitly that the beneficiary of aid may rely on legitimate expectations in the national courts. In all cases, however, it will be necessary to show the existence of exceptional circumstances.[35] The mere fact of doubt as to the existence of aid (which will exist in many cases of non-notification which arise in the national courts) does not of itself justify non-repayment of the aid.

18.16 **Unnotified aid approved by the Commission.** The important difference between the powers of the national court and those of the Commission is that the Commission has no power to order recovery of an unnotified aid which it subsequently approves.[36] Nevertheless, its decision cannot retrospectively regularize the unlawful grant of aid.[37] It follows that where aid is granted before the Commission's approval the national court should, in principle, order recovery.[38] Community law does not, however, impose an obligation of full recovery in these circumstances. Where aid has been paid prematurely, but has ultimately been approved by the Commission, the 'undue advantage' to the aid recipient flows from the fact that it has received the aid earlier than it should have done pursuant to the Article 88(3). In monetary terms, it has benefited from the non-payment of interest which it would have paid on the amount in question had it had to borrow that amount pending the Commission's decision. It may also have benefited from an improvement in its competitive position as against other operators in the market while the unlawfulness lasted (ie in the period before approval of the aid).[39] The correct remedy is therefore to require the aid recipient to pay interest in respect of the period of unlawfulness and, potentially, compensation for damage caused

[33] Case C-39/94 *SFEI v La Poste* [1996] ECR I-3547, paras 68–70, and opinion of AG Jacobs at paras 70 and 72.

[34] Case C-390/98 *Banks v Coal Authority* [2001] ECR I-6117, para 75.

[35] See discussion at paras 16.106–16.117 above. For a specific example see opinion of AG Jacobs in Case C-39/94 *SFEI v La Poste* [1996] ECR I-3547, para 76, acknowledged in the judgment at para 70.

[36] See para 16.89 above.

[37] See para 18.08 above.

[38] Case C-199/06 *CELF* (judgment of 12 February 2008), paras 45–6; provided that this is possible under national procedural rules: Case C-368/04 *Transalpine Ölleitung* [2006] ECR I-9957, para 56.

[39] *CELF*, ibid, para 51.

by reason of the premature payment of the aid if such claims are available in national law.[40] The court could in principle also order the recovery of the unlawful aid itself, but this is likely to be pointless in most cases since the Member State would have a right simply to re-implement the aid, lawfully this time.[41]

Approval subsequently annulled by the Court. Where an unnotified aid has been approved by the Commission, but that decision has subsequently been annulled by the Court, the obligation of the national court to provide a remedy for the consequences of unlawfulness will extend not only to the period between implementation of the aid and approval, but also to the period between the approval decision and the annulment of that decision. The Court has confirmed that in those circumstances, where an application for annulment is brought, the recipient of the aid will not be able to rely on any legitimate expectation following the approval decision, and pending the definitive ruling by the European Court.[42] **18.17**

4. Reimbursement of charges

Basis of claims to reimbursement. Undertakings frequently rely upon the State aid rules to seek the reimbursement of taxes or charges.[43] Such claims may arise in several different situations, including varying types of parafiscal charges and differential taxation. In such cases, the issue of reimbursement is very closely linked to the question of the concept of aid, which is discussed in Chapter 2. Historically, undertakings have sought reimbursement on the basis of two quite different arguments. The first is that the tax or charge itself is invalid under the State aid rules. The second is that reimbursement should be offered as an alternative to recovery of aid from the beneficiary. The European Court's response to these arguments is set out in the following paragraphs. **18.18**

Reimbursement as necessary consequence of invalidity. The circumstances in which a parafiscal charge or a tax measure may itself be invalid are set out at para 18.12 above. It is now clear that where a tax or charge is itself invalid, either because it is integral to a fund that it finances, or because the tax is itself the aid measure, the national court may and indeed must order its reimbursement as the necessary consequence of invalidity.[44] **18.19**

---

[40] *CELF*, ibid, paras 52–3; and on the availability of damages claims see paras 18.23–18.24 below.

[41] See *CELF*, ibid, para 53.

[42] *CELF*, ibid, paras 65–9.

[43] See para 18.05 above.

[44] Cases C-261-262/01 *Van Calster* [2003] ECR I-12249, para 64 and opinion of AG Jacobs para 37; and Case C-526/04 *Laboratoires Boiron* [2006] ECR I-7529, paras 37–48. To the extent that the earlier cases C-437/97 *EKW* [2000] ECR I-1157, para 53 and C-36/99 *Idéal Tourisme* [2000] ECR I-6049, paras 26–9 suggest that reimbursement cannot be ordered by a national court as a remedy for the unlawful implementation of State aid, these must now be regarded as incorrect.

18.20 **Reimbursement as discretionary alternative to recovery.** The position is less clear where the tax is not itself invalid, but where the taxpayer seeks reimbursement simply as an alternative to recovery, relying on the discretion of the national court in the grant of appropriate remedies for a breach of Article 88(3). In such a case, the argument is that the distortion of competition arising from asymmetrical imposition of the tax may be remedied either by requiring repayment by the beneficiary, or by 'levelling up the playing field' by granting the same benefit to all comparable undertakings. Indeed, as the aid complained of in such cases is an exemption or lower rate for the beneficiary and a charge or higher rate for the complainant, the remedy sought may be by way of restitution of allegedly overpaid tax, or the benefit of a lower rate.[45] In several cases national courts have referred questions concerning the interpretation of Article 87(1), in the context of proceedings for reimbursement of a tax. The fact that the ECJ has proceeded to rule on the substantive questions has been taken to imply that reimbursement may be ordered by a national court pursuant to Article 88(3).[46] These cases must now, however, be considered in the light of the *Banks* line of cases. In *Banks* the question arose whether a competitor could obtain the reimbursement of charges in circumstances where repayment by the aid beneficiary was impossible. The Court ruled that businesses liable to pay an obligatory contribution cannot rely on the argument that the exemption enjoyed by other businesses constitutes State aid, in order to avoid payment of that contribution.[47] That has been confirmed in subsequent cases.[48] In particular, in the 2006 case of *Transalpine Ölleitung*, Advocate General Jacobs delivered an opinion arguing extensively against permitting national courts to remedy an aid by extending it to other undertakings.[49] The Court appeared to endorse this reasoning, ruling that while a national court might order recovery of unlawful aid from its recipients, or compensation for the damage caused by unlawful aid, it may not remedy an unlawful State aid by extending it to further recipients, thereby leading to an increase in the effects of

[45] This was one of the issues referred to the ECJ by the VAT Tribunal in the Case C-308/01 *GIL Insurance* [2004] ECR I-4777, but which the ECJ did not answer as it disagreed with the premise of the reference that the differential tax could constitute State aid.

[46] See in particular Cases C-53/00 *Ferring* [2001] ECR I-9067 and C-126/01 *GEMO* [2003] ECR I-13769. In both cases the Advocates General (Tizzano and Jacobs respectively) rejected objections from the French government that the claimants in the national proceedings were not entitled to reimbursement on the basis of Article 88(3), and that the Court therefore did not have jurisdiction to rule on the questions referred: see their opinions at paras 20–4 and 35–48 respectively. In both cases the Court did not explicitly rule on the issue, but the fact that it proceeded to answer the questions referred may imply that it too considered the objection to be unfounded.

[47] Case C-390/98 *Banks v Coal Authority* [2001] ECR I-6117, para 80.

[48] Cases C-430-431/99 *Sea-Land Service and Nedlloyd Lijnen* [2002] ECR I-5235, para 47; Cases C-266/04 etc *Distribution Casino France* [2005] ECR I-9481, para 42; Cases C-393/04 and C-41/05 *Air Liquide Industries Belgium* [2006] ECR I-5293, para 43; Case C-368/04 *Transalpine Ölleitung* [2006] ECR I-9957, para 51.

[49] *Transalpine Ölleitung*, ibid, opinion paras 61–89.

the aid instead of its elimination.[50] The result of this is effectively to exclude a reimbursement order, save in those cases where the tax is itself invalid.

5. Damages

Damages generally. As noted in the foregoing paragraph, the Court in *Transalpine Ölleitung* expressly referred to the possibility that a national court might order compensation for the damage caused by the unlawful grant of aid. The Commission's Notice on cooperation between national courts and the Commission also indicates that a national court may award damages to parties whose interests are harmed.[51] Damages actions might involve claims by a competitor or other third party against the State or an aid beneficiary. An aid beneficiary might also seek compensation from the State where aid is subsequently declared to be unlawful and is recovered. These situations are addressed in turn in the following paragraphs. **18.21**

Claims against the State. In several cases, the Court has acknowledged that competitors of an aid beneficiary might have a claim for damages against the Member State as a result of the unlawful grant of aid.[52] In principle, such a claim could arise independently of any obligation on the State to recover aid granted in breach of Article 88(3),[53] and a competitor may be able to prove loss or damage despite full recovery of the aid. A damages claim against the State is likely to be most useful, however, in cases such as *Banks* where recovery is impossible. A damages claim might also be brought by undertakings other than competitors who have suffered loss as a result of the unlawful aid. One situation where such a claim could arise is where a creditor of the aid beneficiary is harmed by the recovery of the aid. The interests of the creditor would not normally be sufficient to prevent recovery taking place.[54] Instead, it would have to rely on an action in damages for any loss it suffered. However, the 2006 National Enforcement Study did not find a single national decision in which private parties were awarded monetary damages in respect of a grant of illegal aid to a competitor. **18.22**

---

[50] *Transalpine Ölleitung*, ibid, judgment paras 49 and 56–7. See also Cases C-393/04 and C-41/05 *Air Liquide Industries Belgium* [2006] ECR I-5293, para 45. Similarly, the Court of Appeal in *R v Secretary of State for Trade and Industry ex parte BT3G and others* [2001] EWCA Civ 1448, [2001] EuLR 822 was unpersuaded by the applicants' contention that the way to remedy the State aid alleged to have been granted through a payment holiday accorded to two successful bidders in a new round of mobile telephony licences was to grant the same holiday to the other successful bidders (see para 110).

[51] [1995] OJ C312/8, para 10. The same suggestion is made in the draft replacement notice (see n 14 above).

[52] Case C-142/87 *Belgium v Commission ('Tubemeuse')* [1990] ECR I-959, opinion of AG Tesauro p. 985; Case C-39/94 *SFEI v La Poste* [1996] ECR I-3547, opinion of AG Jacobs para 77; Case C-390/98 *Banks v Coal Authority* [2001] ECR I-6117, para 80.

[53] *SFEI v La Poste*, ibid, opinion of AG Jacobs para 77.

[54] See paras 16.111 above.

18.23 **Claims against the beneficiary of aid.** The Article 88 procedure is directed at the Commission and the Member States, not the beneficiary of aid. For this reason, in *SFEI v La Poste*, Advocate General Jacobs thought that competitors should not have a remedy in damages against an aid recipient. He also thought that the remedies of recovery of the aid, and possibly damages against the Member State, were sufficient to provide effective redress for a breach of Article 88(3).[55] The Court agreed that *Community* law did not provide a basis for a recipient of aid to incur liability simply because he had failed to verify whether the aid was duly notified to the Commission. But it held that this did not prevent liability arising under *national* provisions of non-contractual liability. If, under national law, an undertaking is liable where it accepts unlawful assistance causing damage to other undertakings, then the same should apply in respect of aid paid in breach of Article 88(3).[56] More recently in *CELF* the Court has confirmed that a damages remedy might be appropriate in cases where a Member State has unlawfully paid aid without notification, but where the aid has subsequently been approved by the Commission.[57]

18.24 **Legal basis of claims against beneficiary.** The 2006 National Enforcement Study noted that the legal basis for an action against competitors was unclear in a number of Member States. This point was considered in slightly different circumstances (the alleged misuse of approved aid, rather than receipt of illegal aid) by the English High Court in *Betws Anthracite Ltd v DSK Anthrazit Ibbenburen*.[58] Betws, a British anthracite supplier, claimed damages against a recipient of State aid in Germany that had, according to a Commission decision addressed to Germany and taken under Article 4(c) of the ECSC Treaty, misused State aid by applying it to supplies of domestic anthracite which was not one of the approved uses of the aid. This allegedly caused the claimant loss by enabling the defendant to sell below cost into the British market. The High Court held that Betws had no cause of action against the defendant in Community law. Further, although no English law cause of action was pleaded, the judge indicated that he thought there was none. Similarly in Germany there is doubt that there is a national law action for competitors, and at least one judgment has held that there is no directly enforceable right in competitors, as Articles 87 and 88 are not intended for the protection of competitors.[59] In contrast, in some other Member States, there appears to be no difficulty in the concept of the beneficiary of illegal aid being held liable to compensate

[55] Case C-39/94 *SFEI v La Poste* [1996] ECR I-3547, opinion of AG Jacobs paras 82–3.

[56] ibid, judgment para 75.

[57] Case C-199/06 *CELF* (judgment of 12 February 2008), paras 53 and 55.

[58] [2003] EWHC 2403 (Comm), Morison J.

[59] See the chapter on Germany in part I of the 2006 National Enforcement Study, sections 2.1.2(a) and 2.1.4.

competitors on the basis of unfair competition laws (as seems to be the case for example in Italy[60] and France[61]).

Claims by the frustrated aid beneficiary. The paragraphs above consider claims by 'innocent' third parties who have suffered loss as a result of the unlawful grant of aid, or its recovery. In some cases, however, claims have been brought by aid beneficiaries themselves, as of a result a failure to obtain aid which has been declared unlawful. It has been suggested that an aid beneficiary might be able to claim damages against a Member State in relation to suspension or cancellation of an unlawful aid payment.[62] The better view, however, is that such a claim would be contrary to Community law, since it would entirely undermine the procedural rules of Article 88(3).[63] Furthermore, it would be questionable whether the aid beneficiary could in such a case show any loss, if the payment of which it had been deprived was unlawful in any event. For the same reason in the case of *Lener Ignace* the French courts rejected a claim in negligence brought by an undertaking for the failure of its consultant to submit an application for the payment of social security contributions by the relevant deadline.[64] The contributions had been found by the Commission to be State aid, and its decision had been confirmed by the ECJ.[65] Therefore since the aid scheme in question was unlawful, the undertaking had suffered no reparable loss. **18.25**

6. Procedure in the national courts

Principles of equivalence and effectiveness. Since there is no Community legislation or even guidance as to the procedural requirements for the enforcement of Article 88(3) by national courts, it is for each Member State to determine the **18.26**

60 See the Supreme Court case summarized in the chapter on Italy in part I of the 2006 National Enforcement Study at para 3.2.14.

61 See the chapter on France in part I of the 2006 National Enforcement Study, section 2.1 and para 3.4.6.

62 Case C-142/87 *Belgium v Commission ('Tubemeuse')* [1990] ECR I-959, opinion of AG Tesauro p 985. Such damages appear to have been awarded in a French case, *SA Fontanille*, summarised at para 3.6.2 of the section on France in part I of the 2006 National Enforcement Study, although the court there specified that the quantum of the award could not be the amount of aid payable under the illegal scheme, could not be an indemnity as that would run counter to the *effet utile* of the EC State aid rules and should be reduced by a quarter as the recipient should have exercised sufficient diligence to appreciate that the aid was illegal.

63 See Cases 106-120/87 *Asteris v Greece* [1988] ECR 5515, opinion of AG Slynn p 5530; and by analogy Decision 92/317/EEC *Portuguese telecommunications markets* [1992] OJ L171/54, section VII, where the Commission pointed out that a provision in a contract, allowing the State to indemnify an undertaking if the Commission were to order recovery of aid, would neutralize the Commission's decision requiring recovery and was therefore illegal under Article 87(1).

64 *Lener Ignace v Dominique Beauvois* [1994] 2 CMLR 419.

65 In Case 52/83 *Commission v France* [1983] ECR 3707.

relevant procedural rules for any of the types of claims discussed in the foregoing sections.[66] This is, however, subject to the two paramount requirements which apply to all Community law remedies in national courts: first, that the domestic rules are not less favourable than those governing rights which originate in domestic law (principle of equivalence); and secondly, the rules must not render impossible or excessively difficult in practice the exercise of rights conferred by the Community legal order (principle of effectiveness).[67] The Court has also held that the national courts, in this context, must take fully into consideration the interests of the Community.[68]

18.27 **Standing.** A particular problem that may arise in national proceedings is the standing of an undertaking to bring proceedings to enforce Article 88(3). A national court's procedural rules on standing are subject to the principle that they must not undermine the right to effective judicial protection when exercising the rights conferred by Community law.[69] It follows that, in determining whether national standing rules give effect to rights under Article 88(3), it is necessary to take account of the remedies recognized as a matter of Community law for breach of the standstill obligation.[70] Where, for example, the Court has held that an individual is entitled to reimbursement of a tax which is an integral part of an unlawful aid measure, the question of whether that individual has been affected by the distortion of competition arising from the aid measure is irrelevant to the assessment of his interest in bringing proceedings.[71] In such a case, therefore, Article 88(3) may be relied upon by an undertaking that is not a competitor to the aid beneficiary. In other cases, however, the interest of an undertaking as a competitor may be relevant.

18.28 **Interim relief.** A national court should in principle be able to grant interim relief in proceedings under Article 88(3), for example by ordering the freezing or return of aid which is alleged to be unlawful.[72] This may be appropriate pending trial of the action, or where the court has made a preliminary reference to the ECJ (or sought guidance from the Commission). In the legal systems of most Member States, the conditions for interim relief are similar to those which apply to the

[66] Case 120/73 *Lorenz* [1973] ECR 1471, para 9 (raising issue of own motion); Case C-368/04 *Transalpine Ölleitung* [2006] ECR I-9957, para 45 (remedies in general); Case C-526/04 *Laboratoires Boiron* [2006] ECR I-7529, paras 51 and 56 (burden of proof).

[67] *Transalpine Ölleitung*, ibid, para 45; *Laboratoires Boiron*, ibid, para 51.

[68] *Transalpine Ölleitung*, ibid, para 48.

[69] Case C-174/02 *Streekgewest* [2005] ECR I-85, para 18. See also the general principles of equivalence and effectiveness in para 18.26 above.

[70] *Streekgewest*, ibid, opinion of AG Geelhoed para 54.

[71] *Streekgewest*, ibid, judgment para 19.

[72] Notice on cooperation between national courts and the Commission [1995] OJ C312/8, para 10.

interim suspension by national courts of Community measures:[73] the applicant must show a *prima facie* case, urgency, and irreparable harm caused to it in the event that the aid is put into effect.[74] Where an undertaking is seeking to prevent aid being paid to a competitor, the last condition will usually be very difficult to satisfy.[75]

C. Enforcement of Commission decisions

Enforcement of recovery. Where a Commission decision finds that aid already paid is incompatible with the common market and requires recovery, responsibility for recovery then lies with the authorities of the Member State concerned, and in principle recovery must be effected according to national procedural rules.[76] Proceedings may then be brought in the national courts if the beneficiary resists recovery. Where that occurs, Article 14(3) of Regulation 659/1999 requires the Member State concerned to take all necessary steps which are available in its legal system, including provisional measures, 'without delay'. Recovery procedures vary significantly between Member States, and Community law does not prescribe which procedure the Member State should apply to execute a recovery decision.[77] As with the enforcement of Article 88(3), however, national procedural rules such as time limits may not be applied in such a way that recovery is rendered practically impossible or excessively difficult.[78] In addition, in its Recovery Notice, the Commission indicated that national authorities should select the procedure more **18.29**

[73] See paras 18.32–18.33 below.

[74] 2006 National Enforcement Study, p 47.

[75] It is perhaps for this reason that the 2006 National Enforcement Study states that it found no case in which a claimant had successfully applied for interim relief to stop the grant of illegal aid to a competitor (although the statement may be too sweeping: there seems to have been a successful application to prevent aid being disbursed pending notification to the Commission in the *Essent Kabelcom* case referred to in the chapter on the Netherlands at para 3.1.6). Proof of harm might be easier where an integral part of the aid measure is a tax or charge on the claimant which finances the aid (see paras 2.76–2.81 above). In such a case the claimant could rely not only on the benefit to his competitor but also on direct harm to himself. In a rather different context, the President of the Commercial Court of Brussels issued an order preventing the participation by an Italian company in a public procurement procedure on the basis that it was in receipt of illegal aid from the Italian authorities: see para 3.1.2 in the section on Belgium in part I of the 2006 National Enforcement Study.

[76] See para 16.92 above; and see generally the Commission's Notice – Towards an effective implementation of Commission decisions ordering Member States to recover unlawful and incompatible State aid ('Recovery Notice') [2007] OJ C272/4.

[77] Recovery Notice, paras 51–2.

[78] Case C-142/87 *Belgium v Commission ('Tubemeuse')* [1990] ECR I-959, para 61; Case C-480/98 *Spain v Commission* [2000] ECR I-8717, para 34; Case C-232/05 *Commission v France ('Scott Paper')* [2006] ECR I-70 (national rule under which administrative measure automatically suspended upon commencement of court proceedings should not have been applied as it prevented effective recovery); and see Recovery Notice, para 52.

likely to secure the immediate execution of the decision, and should use fast-track procedures where possible under national law.[79] The Court has also held that French provisions requiring the automatic suspension of a demand for repayment of aid, when challenged in the courts by the aid beneficiary, contravened the conditions of Article 14(3) and should not, therefore, have been applied.[80]

18.30 **Defences to recovery.** In proceedings for the enforcement of a recovery decision, an aid beneficiary will be able to advance the same defences as could be put forward in relation to recovery pursuant to Article 88(3).[81] It is the responsibility of the national court to assess those defences, including any difficulties pleaded by the Member State in respect of the implementation of the decision.[82] In proceedings for the enforcement of a Commission decision, however, the question may also arise as to the validity of that decision itself. In the important case of *TWD*, the Court held that the recipient of aid cannot, in an action brought in the national courts, call into question the validity of a Commission decision, if he could have challenged the decision in an application for annulment under Article 230 but the time limit for an annulment action has expired.[83]

18.31 **Compatibility decisions.** If the Commission has found aid to be compatible with the common market, it is open to a competitor to bring proceedings in the national courts contesting a subsequent decision of the authorities to grant specific aid pursuant to the Commission's decision.[84] Proceedings might also be brought by a frustrated applicant for aid under an approved scheme.[85] In such a case, again, if the claimant would have had standing to bring an application for annulment of the decision but has failed to do so, the *TWD* rule will operate to prevent him from impugning the decision in the national courts.

18.32 **Preliminary references and interim relief.** In the case of both recovery decisions and compatibility decisions, where a challenge to the validity of the decision itself is made and is not barred by *TWD*, the national court would have to refer the matter to the ECJ for a preliminary ruling under Article 234 EC as it has no power itself to declare the decision invalid.[86] In extreme cases, where the national court has serious doubts as to the validity of the decision, and where there is both urgency

---

79 Recovery Notice, para 52.

80 Case C-232/05 *Commission v France* [2006] ECR I-10071, paras 51–3; and see Recovery Notice, para 53.

81 See para 18.15 above.

82 Case T-354/99 *Kuwait Petroleum v Commission* [2006] ECR II-1475, para 69.

83 Case C-188/92 *TWD Textilwerke Deggendorf* [1994] ECR I-833, paras 17 and 18; confirmed in Cases C-346/03 and C-529/03 *Atzeni and others v Regione autonoma della Sardegna* [2006] ECR I-1875, para 31.

84 Case T-330/94 *Salt Union v Commission* [1996] ECR II-1475.

85 See eg the main proceedings in Case C-390/06 *Nuova Agricast* (judgment of 15 April 2008).

86 Case 314/85 *Foto Frost* [1987] ECR 4599.

and the likelihood of irreparable damage resulting from the decision, the court could grant interim relief suspending the national enforcement measures,[87] or provisionally disapplying the decision itself,[88] pending the ECJ's ruling on the reference.

Stay of proceedings. National proceedings relating to the enforcement of a Commission decision may arise in parallel with an application in the CFI for the annulment of the decision. In such a case, it would seem that, by analogy with the ECJ's *Masterfoods* case-law on the risk of parallel and conflicting decisions between the Commission and the national courts in the competition context, the national court should stay its proceedings pending final judgment on the action for annulment, unless it considers that a preliminary reference is warranted, unless it can satisfy itself that there is no risk of conflict (ie whatever the outcome in Luxembourg).[89] In a recovery case, the national court might also order a stay of the recovery order on the same principles as applicable to interim relief in a preliminary reference case, set out in the foregoing paragraph.[90] **18.33**

D. Application of block exemptions

Direct effect. The final area in which the national courts may be called on to apply the State aid rules is in connection with block exemptions. The State aid block exemption regulations are, like all Community Regulations, directly applicable in Member States, and can therefore be applied directly by the national courts. In the event of doubt as to their interpretation, a national court may always refer a question to the ECJ for a preliminary ruling under Article 234. **18.34**

[87] Cases C-143/88 and C-92/89 *Zuckerfabrik* [1991] ECR I-415.

[88] Case C-465/93 *Atlanta Fruchthandelsgesellschaft* [1995] ECR I-3761.

[89] Case C-344/98 *Masterfoods v HB Ice-Cream* [2000] ECR I-11369. cf judgment of the Irish High Court in *Belgium v Ryanair* [2006] IEHC 213, refusing a stay of recovery proceedings on the grounds that there was no risk of conflict of judgments within the meaning of *Masterfoods*.

[90] Such a stay was ordered by the English High Court in *Dept of Trade v British Aerospace* [1991] 1 CMLR 165. The decision in question was annulled in Case C-294/90 *BAe and Rover v Commission* [1992] ECR I-493. The *British Aerospace* case is the only English case on recovery orders. The 2006 National Enforcement Study, surveying the very different rules applicable in the various Member States and considering the delays to which they could lead, recommended the adoption of best practice guidelines (p 539). The Commission has subsequently adopted its Recovery Notice which addresses this issue.

INDEX